S0-ACI-879

RARE EARTHS: Forbidden Cures

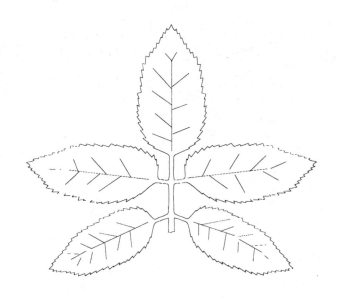

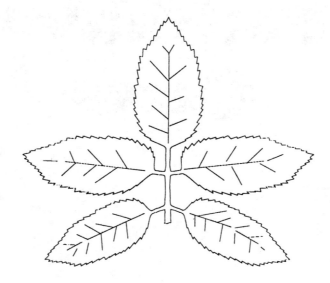

RARE EARTHS: Forbidden Cures

Joel D. Wallach, DVM, ND
and
Ma Lan, MD, MS

Donated by: Sally Price 10-11-96

"It works"

FRONT COVER: Electron photomicrograph of a selenium deficient liver mitochondria from a Cystic Fibrosis monkey. Magnified 126,000 times. Note the helical crystal structure (RNA/DNA) of the precipitated inner membrane of the mitochodria.

BACK COVER: The authors, Drs. Wallach and Ma Lan, pause on the "Great Wall" on their trek to northern China in search of forbidden cures.

The information in this book is intended to be medical instruction. The purpose of RARE EARTHS is to be educational and informative. It is assumed the user, as their own primary health care provider will consult with or refer themselves to an ND, DC or D.V.M. as they deem necessary!

Library of Congress Cataloging in Publications Data:
Wallach, J.D. and Lan, Ma

RARE EARTHS: The Forbidden Cures
     Bibliography:
     Includes index

1. Mineral Deficiency Diseases 2. Pica 3. Cannibalism 4. "Bad Seeds"
5. Holistic Health Care 6. Alternative Self Help 7. Nutrition

RARE EARTHS
First Edition, November 1994
Second Edition, May 1995
Third Printing, January 1996
Fourth Printing, February 1996
Fifth Printing, June 1996

Copyright © 1994 by Joel D. Wallach, Ma Lan and Double Happiness Publishing Co.
All Rights Reserved.

No part of this book may be copied or republished in any form without written consent of the authors and publishers.

Printed and Published by Double Happiness Publishing Co.
P.O. Box 1222 Bonita, CA 91908

Dedication

This book is dedicated to individual health freedom; freedom of choice in health care, the constitution of the United States and to the separation of medicine and state as with the separation of church and state.

"Strive to preserve your health, and in this you will the better succeed in proportion as you keep clear of the physicians."

-LEONARDO DA VINCI
1451

Acknowledgements

This book was put together at the urging of multitudes of individuals seeking optimal health and longevity through colloidal mineral supplementation. Literally thousands of references were employed in gathering materials for this book, so we have chosen to limit the number of references or the bibliography would have outweighed the text! We borrowed heavily from the Scientific American, Natural History, National Geographic, USA Today, New York Times, San Diego Union Tribune, Los Angeles Times, The Denver Post, the St. Louis Post Dispatch and literally hundreds of different local newspapers from across America to make RARE EARTHS: The Forbidden Cures, a timely, informative and very useful book. Many thousands of hours were spent in the medical library at UCSD in LaJolla, CA. and on airplanes gleaning details from newspapers and scientific literature. Actual news clippings and obituaries are used to illustrate "real life" human diseases or events that can be directly attributed to mineral deficiencies. The extraordinary help and technical advice of Vince Marasigan, Dr. Gerhart Schrauzer, Robert L. Snook, Ron L. Snook, Dr. Patricia Hastings, Wm. H. Moore, Esq., Margie Skinner, Eldore Hanni, Char Murphy, Eve Stahl, Jacque Dreher and Anthony Peñafuerte along with the staff of the Double Happiness Publishing Co. allowed us to have a joyous second "home delivery" (the first being, Let's Play Doctor in 1989).

Table of Contents

About the Authors

Joel D. Wallach, BS, DVM, ND

Dr. Wallach had been involved in biomedical research and clinical medicine for 30 years. He received his B.S. degree (Agriculture) from the University of Missouri with a major in animal husbandry (nutrition) and a minor in field crops and soils; a D.V.M. (veterinarian) from the University of Missouri; a three year post doctoral fellowship from The Center for the Biology of Natural Systems, Washington University; and an ND from the National College of Naturopathic Medicine, Portland, Oregon. He established and developed a unique family practice (used veterinary nutrition on human patients) in Portland, Oregon which he operated for 12 years.

Dr. Wallach's research has resulted in the publication of more than 70 peer review and refereed journal articles in the fields of nutrition and pharmaceutical research, major contributions to eight multi-author text and reference books including the Merck Manual and authorship of a definitive text/reference book on the subject of comparative medicine (W.B. Saunders Publishing Co., 1983).

Dr. Wallach's research in comparative medicine is based on more than 17,500 pathology cases from the University of Missouri, Iowa State University, The Center for the Biology of Natural Systems, Washington University, the St. Louis Zoological Gardens, the Chicago Zoological Gardens, The Yerkes Regional Primate Research Center, Emory University, the National College of Naturopathic Medicine, Portland, Oregon and the Harbin Medical University, Harbin, Hei Long Jiang, Peoples Republic of China. He was a member of NIH site visit teams for facilities using animal models for the study of human disease for four years and was a member of the 1968 NSF ad hoc committee that authored the 1968 Animal Welfare Act (humane housing and care of laboratory and captive exotic species); and a Consulting Professor of Medicine, Harbin Medical University, Harbin, Hei Long Jiang, Peoples Republic of China.

Dr. Wallach was the recipient of the 1988 Wooster Beach Gold Medal Award for a significant breakthrough in the basic understanding of the cause and pathophysiology of Cystic Fibrosis- the gold medal was awarded by the Association of Eclectic Physicians. He was nominated for a Nobel Prize in Medicine in 1991 by the Association of Eclectic Physicians for his notable and untiring work with deficiencies of the trace mineral selenium and its relationship to the congenital genesis of Cystic Fibrosis.

Dr. Wallach has appeared frequently on local and national network television (including a special with ABC's 20/20) regional and national talk radio programs as an expert on trace mineral and rare earth deficiency diseases. Dr. Wallach is also the host of his own talk show radio program (Let's Play Doctor) in Palm Springs, California every Saturday morning. Because of his free-wheeling style of humor and ability to zero in on the basic truth in health he is widely known as the "Rush Limbaugh" of alternative health.

Ma Lan, M.D, M.S.

Dr. Ma Lan was educated in the Peoples Republic of China. Dr. Ma Lan received her M.D. from Beijing Medical University, took her residency in Peoples Hospital, Beijing and was a staff surgeon at the Canton Air Force Hospitals for eight years; she received her M.S. (Master of Science) in transplant immunology from Zhong-Shan Medical University, Canton, Peoples Republic of China. As with all Chinese doctors, Dr. Ma Lan was trained in Traditional Chinese Medicine (i.e.- acupuncture, herbs, manipulation, massage and hydrotherapy) prior to entering the western-style medical school.

Dr. Ma Lan's research credits include being an exchange scholar at Harvard School of Medicine, Boston where she trained residents how to perform laser microsurgery; a research fellow in laser microsurgery at St. Joseph's Hospital, Houston; the Department of Orthopedic Microsurgery at the Medical College of Wisconsin, Milwaukee and the Department of Pharmacology at the University of California. Dr. Ma Lan has ten peer review publications to her credit in the fields of transplant immunology and microsurgery.

Lastly, Dr. Ma Lan was "sent to the countryside" for three years of hard labor during the "Cultural Revolution" of China, her crime was "being an educated person and potentially dangerous to the revolution;" during those hard years of forced labor she was able to quietly be a doctor during her rest periods for a small farming village in the north of China using only traditional Chinese Medicine. If all medical doctors were as devoted to their patients as Dr. Ma Lan is the world would be a wonderful place!

Introduction

This is a book by two physicians and research scientists whose background, training and experience qualify them uniquely to write for the public as well as the scientific literature to which they have contributed numerous articles and learned books.

This is also a book that is badly overdue and vital to the welfare of every American from newborn infants to those of us with grey hair and dentures, both of which we could have avoided had this information been made available 30 years ago.

In 1985, the National Research Council published its report on "Nutrition Education in U.S. Medical Schools". The council's committee on Nutrition Education in Medical School had carefully surveyed the state of the subject and concluded the "nutrition education programs in U.S. Medical Schools are largely inadequate to meet the present and future demands of the medical profession".

The committee reported that since the middle of this century, the science of nutrition has advanced far beyond the assumption that overt symptoms of deficiency are the only attributes of malnutrition and also reported that "amongst recent advances, nutrition research has elucidated the function, essentiality and interaction of several trace minerals, uncovered the intricate role of nutrients in the immune response, and demonstrated that dietary factors, although not the sole determinants, are among lifestyle variables that may significantly influence the outcome of chronic degenerative diseases such as atherosclerosis and cancer".

This is all a polite way of saying what many of us who have been involved since the 1950's and 1960's in the assessment of health care have long observed about the role of the allopathic medical profession with regard to nutrition.

Medical education since 1950 has inculcated in most of the M.D.'s in practice today, and active anti-nutritional bias.

The myth that eating of the four food group each day will ensure the average American an adequate dietary intake of all essential nutrients, while often repeated by physicians trained since 1960 until the present time, has been increasingly shown to be false and misleading in the extreme.

For decades, the American Cancer Society loudly proclaimed that nutrition had no role in either the prevention or treatment of cancer- about 10 years ago, the National Cancer Institute published its epochal report on Diet, Nutrition and Cancer, proclaiming the pivotal role of nutrients in cancer in both prevention and treatment.

Unfortunately, most of the M.D.'s in practice lacked sufficient training in nutrition to comprehend the report or implement it in their practices.

Thanks to the public media, television, newspapers and magazines, as well as several well-written books, most literate Americans are aware of the pivotal role of nutrition in health maintenance and disease prevention and treatment, as noted by the National Research Council in the preface to its report.

Many Americans have also had the unpleasant experience of discovering for themselves that most M.D.'s are less aware of these factors than are their secretaries and that, at present, and until sweeping changes are made in medical education, the average M.D. is not a reliable source of information and advice about nutrition and health.

The average American would do far better to consult a Veterinarian, since Veterinarians receive an excellent education in nutrition, far more extensive than that of M.D.'s.

In some measure, reading this book serves that purpose since one of its authors, Dr. Joel Wallach has the distinction of being both a well-trained Veterinarian, indeed, a veterinary pathologist and a physician, who is cross-trained in both animal and human pathology and disease- Dr. Wallach is a comparative Pathologist, trained to relate animal disease and nutrition and human disease and nutrition.

He is an ideal person to give us insight into some of the burning health care issues of today. Having been trained first as a veterinarian, he came to his training as a Naturopathic physician already possessed of considerable expertise in the role of nutrients in the prevention and treatment of diseases.

His stunning discovery of the pivotal role of a trace mineral, Selenium, in the etiology and prevention of Cystic Fibrosis while a research veterinary pathologist ultimately led him to become trained as a Naturopathic physician.

Dr. Wallach was nominated in 1991 for the Nobel Prize in medicine by the Association of the Eclectic Physicians, may yet receive the Nobel Prize for this accomplishment, but whether or not his nomination for that honor succeeds, he is certainly deserving of our rapt attention when he speaks and writes about trace mineral nutrition and health. His lucid insights into the prevention of degenerative disease and the attainment of health, defined as high level wellness, should receive the rapt attention of everyone who is interested in getting and staying healthy in a world and a society that is increasingly unhealthy to live in.

In my 30 plus years of practice as a Health Lawyer, engaged mainly in representing those courageous physicians and scientists who have attempted to refocus the medical profession's attention back to nutrition and natural healing and away from its exclusive preoccupation with the synthetic pharmaceuticals which are rapidly being demonstrated to cause more problems than they cure, I have been associated with Dr. Wallach as a friend, a consultant and a most lucid and knowledgeable expert witness for court cases on countless occasions and I emerge from each encounter with him in awe of his intellectual attainments and breadth of knowledge and insight into health and medicine.

We are facing, we are told by our politicians, a crisis in health care. Political solutions revolve around juggling insurance coverage and methods of payment for the cost of such care which, in the United States, has reached the epic sum of One Trillion Dollars this year.

The solution to our health care crisis will not be reached by political debate, mandatory health insurance, or throwing more money at the problem. The disastrous "War on Cancer" which has consumed Billions of Dollars and produced no cures and the "AIDS Crises" are eloquent testimony as to the futility of political solutions to health care problems.

Around a century ago, the government got involved in health care, and health and the National Budget have been on a collision course with disaster ever since that occurred. In the 1910 takeover of "scientific medicine," nutrition, as a part of health care, was relegated to the status of a red headed, cross-eyed orphan, while the glamour of high tech pharmaceuticals and genetic engineering have consumed much of the research budget with results that are becoming all too apparent now- the crisis in health care.

We are told that antibiotics are failing- that more and more bacteria are now antibiotic resistant- tuberculosis and poliomyelitis are back, other diseases claimed to have been conquered are returning in more virulent forms. To this must be added the increase in the rate of degenerative disease, coronary artery disease, cancer, crippling arthritis, diabetes and AIDS for none of which "scientific medicine" has found real answers.

There may be several causes for these failures but a very basic cause has been the ignoring of the pivotal role of nutrition in health and disease. Allopathic medicine has an active anti-nutritional bias - it has resisted acknowledging the role of nutritional deficiency as the etiology of hundreds of diseases for centuries.

The grudging admission that a few diseases could have a nutritional deficiency etiology has been won over the loud denials and angry denunciations of allopathic physicians; scurvy, beri-beri and pellagra are examples of nutritional deficiency diseases which were long held by allopathic medicine to be infectious and whose discoverers found incredible vilification for their elucidation of the nutritional deficiency etiology. More modern nutritionist, including Drs. Ma Lan and Wallach, have fared little better.

Since there is no glamour in the stock market and no large corporate profits to be won from the manufacture and sale of simple trace nutrients which are unpatentable, there is no incentive for funding this crucial area of research. But until the attention of both clinical medicine and medical research is redirected to this basic health problem, we will continue to face a crisis in health care.

Thanks to three quarters of a century of 'scientific agriculture' with the use of synthetic fertilizers, the soil of our farm lands has been leached of its trace mineral content and our food supply is often times lacking in these essential nutrients, which are not added back to the soil.

Drs. Ma Lan and Wallach have presented in this volume a very useful compilation of current information on trace minerals and trace mineral deficiencies in health and disease. They have done so in their usual fashion, in both an informative and an entertaining manner.

Their elucidation of the role of trace mineral deficiency in the etiology of violent behavior, while often times grisly, is provocative. The message is quite clear; until we as a society turn our attention away from high technology and begin to receive a basic diet containing all essential nutrients, we will continue to suffer epidemics of both chronic and acute diseases as well as social problems.

Until we take positive steps to provide our bodies with the basic building blocks of life, neither our bodies nor our minds will operate at efficient levels, and our health and our society will continue to deteriorate.

We cannot depend on our politicians and bureaucrats to do this for us - indeed, it is a result of governmental agricultural programs that our soil is now depleted of the essential trace minerals of which Drs. Ma Lan and Wallach write so entertainingly. We cannot depend on most of the medical profession to do this for us, they simply have not been trained to do so.

Health is and always will remain an individual responsibility and one which no amount of paternalistic government can provide. We can, at best, hope that governmental involvement in health care will lessen and this is, perhaps, a forlorn hope.

We must set about to learn for ourselves what nutrition is essential and how we as individuals can secure for ourselves and our families those nutrients which are so essential for health and life. "RARE EARTHS" is an enormous first step in that direction, and points the way towards the restoration and maintenance of our health and the realization of our genetic potential.

All life on earth evolved during the Precambrian era, in the mineral rich Precambrian sea, and all of the minerals which enriched that Precambrian sea were incorporated in the single cells which eventually became man, animals and plants.

Those minerals, in the amount occurring in that sea, are essential for life and for the proper growth, development and function of all life-plant and animal.

It has taken our civilization a brief three quarters of a century to undo what millions of years of evolution have provided, a place where men, animals and plants can thrive and lead a healthy symbiotic existence.

RARE EARTHS: Forbidden Cures, is about what we must do to restore the trace mineral balance to ourselves and to our environment if we expect to survive another three quarters of a century of government funded and directed scientific agriculture and health care, and reach our biological destiny and potential.

Seneca, two thousand years ago, taught us that those who ignore the lessons of history are doomed to relive them - we had better study the lessons of the past century about the minerals we have depleted from our soil, our food and our bodies- if we do not, we, as a species, may not be here to relive them during the coming century.

As Drs. Ma Lan and Wallach, in their dynamic way, teach us here, proper mineral nutrition is essential to life and even civilization. Look at Rwanda, Haiti, and Somalia and behold the future of America if we continue to ignore the vital message so lucidly set forth in this book.

RARE EARTHS: Forbidden Cures has led us to the water of knowledge- it's up to us to pick up the ladle and drink, and drink we must if the human race is to survive.

- WM. H MOORE, M.D., J.D.

Foreword

"RARE EARTHS" is long overdue. As an investigative reporter and the author of the best selling book, "Oxygen Therapies," for seven years I have incessantly traveled back and forth across America and the English speaking world educating large groups of people about the fact that when properly applied, oxygen therapies are amazingly effective in the treatment of diseases. I've been a guest on over 1,100 radio and television talk shows, and in-between I've interviewed thousands of people.

The REAL WORLD EVIDENCE I have collected during my travels leads me to an unshakable conclusion - I have observed the fact that Americans are hurting. America is sick, and Americans (and everyone else) are slowly dying and suffering from emotional problems as a result of RAMPANT, WIDESPREAD AND UNRECOGNIZED DEFICIENCIES of three substances. Oxygen, minerals and clean oxygenated water! These observations are not just concepts, but the absolute, the most basic elements necessary to life, health and to happiness.

You must have lots of oxygen at every moment. Try holding your breath if you don't believe me, you will soon get the picture! Hit yourself. You are solid. You are solid because you chewed your food, digested it and rendered it down to the basic elements it contained and then your life force turned them into your body. These elements (which are now your body and its various chemicals) are floating in an ancient internal sea. Your body is this ancient sea of 66% water, even your bones are 20% water. The oxygen must be fresh, unpolluted and abundant, the minerals must be available in the full spectrum of the essential variety, and they must be easily absorbed and utilized - they must in fact be plant derived colloidal minerals!

Two of the top experts on the subject of the absolutely essential bio-available plant derived colloidal minerals wrote this book you are now about to read. Drs. Ma Lan and Wallach have "connected the dots" by collecting all of the known information on the deficiency diseases caused by a lack of minerals, trace minerals and Rare Earths under this one cover and are presenting the information to you dynamically, humorously, and in the easy reading style for which they have become recognized since the first printing of their acclaimed previous work, "Let's Play Doctor!"

Ninety five percent of all chronic and degenerative diseases that afflict humans can be prevented and cured by giving back to the body the missing basic elements of life. Each of us must be responsible to keep ourselves healthy, and to cure ourselves when necessary and stop thinking (and hoping) that authority figures like doctors and our government will take care of it for us. They won't, they can't, and they don't want to learn how to do it.

In the past five years I have come to personally know Drs. Ma Lan and Wallach, since we often appear in the same venues around the world. I know them to be tireless teachers, researchers and investigators, crisscrossing America 300 days out of each year to make sure the timely updated message gets to you. Whether you have a simple disease such as the loss of the sense of smell or brittle finger nails, or a more serious disease such as arthritis, cancer, osteoporosis, hypertension, AIDS, depression or have a hyperactive child with Attention Deficit Disorder, or have a loved one who is prone to violence or destructive behaviors, you will benefit from "RARE EARTHS."

"RARE EARTHS" can save you an enormous amount of unnecessary misery, save you an enormous amount of money, and if it's wisdom is applied consistently and correctly, has every chance of adding many healthful years to your life. If you don't read this book and you don't apply the simple solutions for the many ailments and conditions it provides, their resolutions may remain a mystery to you and your doctors, and you will spend years of wasted energy and lots of money on ultimately useless medications without finding the true solutions you desire and need. I heartily recommend "RARE EARTHS" to you!

Ed McCabe, Investigative Medical Reporter
Author of the best seller - "Oxygen Therapies"

Preface

Before written history, it took 100,000 years to double the Earth's human populations; after the dawn of agriculture, (5,000 to 8,000 years ago) it took 700 years to double the population of human kind; today at the brink of the 21st century, it takes only 35 to 40 years to double our numbers! As a result of this avalanche of flesh, this pulsing crush of beings - the intercultural competition for our human bodily raw materials, the very basic stuff of life, optimal health and longevity has reached a cataclysmic pitch!

Great cults oftentimes called "way of life," religions or faiths by health leaders or "gurus" with hundreds, thousands or even millions of zealous "followers" and "believers" evangelize vegetarianism, macrobiotics, biofeedback, meditation, exercise, pure thought, yoga and free medical care for all (usually vote-buying politicians!); yet none of these practices have extended the human lifespan in America to more than 75.5 years- only 62% of our human genetic potential for longevity of 120 to 140 years.

The greatest scientific thinkers (usually legends in their own minds) frantically search, explore and grope for ways to "hang on" until some serendipitous "miracle discovery" (usually patentable!) occurs that will save the day.

Physicians (allopathic MD's) tell us " the way to health and longevity is in the eating of the four basic food groups," (an update on this primitive theme is the pyramid of nutrition that hails six food groups), reduce your fat intake and don't smoke. Those individuals with ultimate faith in the allopathic medical profession pay a great price to have themselves quick frozen in liquid nitrogen (Cryogenic Suspension) to extend their "shelf life" until a cure can be discovered for their terminal disease!!!

The "Immortalists," an anti-death cult believe that if they disregard death and all of its trappings (i.e.- cemetery plots, burial insurance, etc.) they will not die.

Unfortunately, the entire complement of the 90 essential nutrients required for optimal health and longevity historically found in our Earthly foods are no longer there - they are either totally absent or their availability is so highly variable that your chances of obtaining them from food alone is more of a gamble than a Las Vegas "crap-shoot"!!!

U.S Senate Document 264 (1936) and the 1992 Earth Summit Report (Rio) on mineral depletion rates of the world's farm and range soils point out graphically that our Earth's soils are anemic - the soil should contain 60 of them, there are few or none! Dozens of the sixty formerly abundant soil elements (selenium, arsenic, tin, aluminum, chromium, vanadium, molybdenum, nickel, etc.) were, just a short time ago, thought to be totally toxic with no possibility of essentiality by the allopathic medical profession and they made sure they were not in our food!!! When the four food groups fail us (and they always do), surgeons sell us bionic joint replacements and hawk organ transplants - this bionic parts service and flesh recycling has not pushed back the curtain of death for Americans further than the 75.5 year barrier. The 75.5 year average life span for Americans places us at 17th in longevity when we are compared with the other industrialized nations and this level of boastful "success" falls far short (as much as 50% short) of our human genetic potential for longevity of 120 to 140 years.

The two year long Biosphere II experiment in Arizona concocted by Roy Walford placed six inhabitants (including himself) in a self-contained, self-perpetuating unit, ("Biosphere II"- Earth being Biosphere I) to hedge against environmental disaster or perhaps as a prototype for establishing a pioneer colony on a far flung planet, is romantic but hardly practical for the masses of we poor Earth bound sods.

Walford erroneously believes (through faulty translation of animal data) that severely reduced caloric intake alone can extend human life spans by 30 to 40% (up to 120 to 140 years) - from the earliest reduced calorie/longevity experiments a critical review of the data was necessary to reveal the basic truth - that is, the level of minerals in all of the various low calorie diets (calories reduced by 30, 45, and 60%) regardless of their calorie level remained the same!!!

It is not the reduced calorie level that gave the rats their extended life spans by 30, 40 and 50%, but rather it is the increased concentration of mineral per calorie in the diet!!! Walford was so obsessed with the low calorie theme that he deliberately downplays the relative increase in mineral concentration. Upon their exit from Biosphere II, after their two years self-imposed minimal calorie intake, five of the six Biospherians (excluding Walford) wanted only pizza and junk food (a manifestation of pica)- they also complained that the normally sociable group had broken down into argumentative behavior over everything and over every minor decision!!! In addition, two of the Biospherians a short time after their scheduled exit from the dome illegally broke into steal records- criminal behavior!

We humans require the 90 essential nutrients in our diet daily in optimal levels to not only prevent debilitating developmental and degenerative diseases but also for normal sociability, for preventing criminal behavior (there are now 1,000,000 prisoners in American jails!) and to reach our genetic potential for longevity (the 120 to 140 year mark is ever within our grasp!). We had better "get our shit together" on Earth before we fly off to space stations and find ourselves having "gone a bridge too far" before we truly understand the basic mineral needs of our own emotions and flesh.

The blue chip drive in the 90's to patent genetically engineered crops ("Frankenstein Food"), enzymes, hormones, bacteria, animals and even humans (identical humans can now be cloned at the embryonic stage - the "Boys from Brazil" are here!!), health and even longevity is a heroic if not greedy effort by our entrepreneurial scientist; however, genetic potential without the basic raw materials to support the process of development and extended maintenance of the flesh is inherently faulty in its premise!!

Expecting genetically engineered flesh to develop, maintain itself, reach its genetic potential for longevity and perform without the basic stuff of life is to expect the Mercedes (famed for its German engineering that allows it to be driven for 300,000 miles before it needs a major overhaul or a new engine) to run from San Diego to L.A. (a distance of 150 miles) at 70 mph without any oil or coolant!!! Even the Mercedes engine, that German wonder of automotive engineering, will become a burned up mass of expensive metal before you could drive 50 miles!!

Allopathic M.D.'s knowing the basic needs of the internal combustion engine rabidly adhere to their Mercedes maintenance program every 1000 miles with the very best motor oil, grease and coolant, yet recommend vigorous exercise for their patients without insisting the patient also take in critically measured levels of the 90 essential nutrients required for human physical, emotional and mental maintenance and even life itself!!!

RARE EARTHS: The Forbidden Cures - will give you facts and proven truths and the knowledge, tools necessary and identify the elemental raw materials of life no longer found in our food; it identifies the raw materials necessary to turbocharge and empower yourself, your families and friends lives with power packed health, vitality and the ability to reach your genetic potential for longevity!!! RARE EARTHS is hard ball - it will shock you by revealing many facts and truths that are 180 degrees from what the allopathic medical community has led you to believe - it is reality that they (the allopaths) cannot keep you healthy or save you, only those of us who take personal responsibility for maintaining and enriching our physical bodies with as much zeal as we do our Mercedes or "Beamer" are going to make it!!! Your president (or his wife), governor, mayor, councilman, postman, physician or even your spouse can't do it for you (they can't even help themselves!!!) - only you, only you !!!

The good news is we do have "control groups" (for a comparison with ourselves) who consistently make it to the end point of the human genetic potential for longevity (120 to 140 years) healthfully with great vitality and without "high tech medicine" or the "skills" of allopathic M.D.'s. This control group has been identified as five ancient and highly diverse cultures with common denominators that include healthful disease free longevity and unlimited access to adequate levels of all 90 essential nutrients required by humans including access to unique natural sources of plant derived colloidal mineral- RARE EARTH!! If you access and plug into the plant derived RARE EARTHS used for thousands of years by certain tribes of Tibetans, Russian Georgians, Armenians, Azerbaijanies, Abkhazians, Hunzakuts, Vilcabambas or the Titicacas you can make it too!!!

- Dr. Joel D. Wallach and Dr. Ma Lan

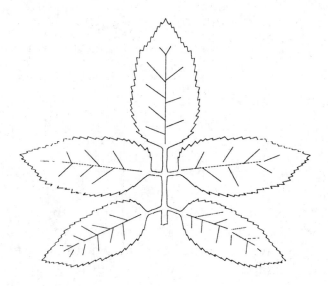

Chapter 1

GENESIS

"There is a grandeur in this view of life, with its several powers, having been originally breathed into a few forms or into one; and that, whilst this planet has gone cycling on according to the fixed law of gravity, from so simple a beginning endless forms most beautiful and most wonderful have been and are being evolved."

-Charles Darwin
The Origin of Species

It doesn't matter whether one is a creationist or a student of evolution - our immediate mutual problem is that the Earth, our planet is a limited finite resource for the raw materials that are the basis of all plant, animal and human life as we know it.

Living organisms procure their raw materials of essential elements for reproduction, development, growth and maintenance and for longevity from a thin blanket of matter and gas on or just above the Earth's crust. The relative amounts and kinds of elements in the Earth's surface and from occasional alien meteorites crashing into Earth have been identified and cataloged by actual chemical analysis; elements in the sun and other stars have been identified and cataloged by the technique of spectrometry.

The biblical account of the formation of Earth accepted by the Jewish and the kaleidoscope of Christian faiths is brief, however, the details need not be there for it to be true any more than the details are not necessary when grandma says, "I baked you a dozen cookies" - you know she selected and ground the whole wheat berries into flour, sifted the flour, added filtered water, the aluminum free baking powder, butter (yes butter, not margarine), honey, yeast, chocolate drops and walnuts, took spoons of the finished cookie dough, plopped them on a greased cookie sheet and then baked them into perfectly wonderful and chewy chocolate chip-walnut holiday cookies - although she never shared the details of her activities, we inherently knew she did!!

The biblical account of the Earths formation (Genesis) goes like this:

"In the beginning God created the heaven and earth. And the earth was without form, and void; and darkness was upon the face of the deep. And the spirit of God moved upon the face of the water. And God said, Let there be light; and there was light. And God saw the light, that it was good: and God divided the light from the darkness. And God called the light day, and the darkness He called night. And the evening and the morning were the first day. And God said, Let there be a firmament in the midst of the waters, and let it divide the waters from the waters. And God made the firmament and divided the waters which were under the firmament from the waters which were above the firmament; and it was so. And God called the firmament Heaven.

And the evening and the morning were the second day. And God said, Let the waters under the heaven be gathered together under one place, and let the dry land appear: and it was so. And God called the dry land Earth; and the gathering together of the waters called the seas: and God saw that it was good. And God said, Let the Earth bring forth grass, the herb yielding seed, and the fruit tree yielding fruit after his kind, whose seed is in itself, upon the Earth: and it was so."

Like grandma's cookies we don't need to know the details to appreciate the fact that the Earth or the steaming delicious chocolate chip cookies appeared miraculously before us to see, smell and savor!!

The only scientific chemical theory of the origin of the Earth and its elements was crystallized by E.M. Burbridge in 1957 - according to his theory, all of the Earths elements can be built up electron by electron from hydrogen gas; hydrogen atoms in space condense together by gravitational attraction into clouds of gas which ultimately condense into stars.

The Burbridge theory goes on to say - as the atoms of hydrogen are attracted to each other, the resultant gravitational energy is converted into heat which is retained in the interior of an embryonic star. As there would be no loss of heat from the interior of the young star except by radiation; the interior temperature of the star steadily rises as the star attains mass. When the stars internal temperature has risen to 5 to 10 million degrees Kelvin, thermonuclear reactions ignite resulting in a conversion of hydrogen (H) into helium (He). For massive stars, the conversion of the total hydrogen core into helium generates a huge quantity of energy and would require a million years; for smaller cooler stars, such as our sun, the H to He conversion might take as long as 6,000,000 years.

At temperatures of one trillion degrees Kelvin the helium molecules react exothermically to become ^{12}C (a form of carbon) initiating chain reactions resulting in the genesis of new minerals:

$$^{3}He \longrightarrow HEAT \longrightarrow {}^{12}C + {}^{7.3}MeV$$
$$^{12}C \longrightarrow {}^{4}He \longrightarrow {}^{16}O \longrightarrow {}^{4}He \longrightarrow$$
$$^{20}Ne \longrightarrow {}^{4}He \longrightarrow {}^{24}Mg$$
$$^{24}Mg \longrightarrow {}^{4}He \longrightarrow {}^{28}Si \longrightarrow {}^{4}He \longrightarrow$$
$$^{32}S \longrightarrow {}^{4}He \longrightarrow {}^{36}Ar$$
$$^{36}Ar \longrightarrow {}^{4}He \longrightarrow {}^{40}Ca$$

Because of the limits of the laws of energetics the thermonuclear formation of mineral nuclides stops here, although ^{44}Ca and ^{48}Ti could be generated. At this level of star formation few nuclides have individualized and the heavier minerals are still absent. At 2 x 1,000,000,000 degrees Kelvin free neutrons are formed by the combination of ^{21}Ne and $^{4}He \longrightarrow {}^{24}Mg + 1n$ (neutron). The ^{21}Ne is formed in the outer reaches of the star from:

$$^{20}Ne + 1H \longrightarrow {}^{21}Na \longrightarrow {}^{21}Ne + B+.$$

As all of the heavier minerals and elements are synthesized, neutrons are snagged slowly, i.e.- one every thousand years forming bismuth and the lighter radioactive elements.

Rapid neutron capture takes place at extremely high temperatures (5 x 10,000,000,000 degrees kelvin); at these high heat conditions mineral or crystal "growth" occurs rapidly and any given nucleus will capture 2 to 20 neutrons per second. This reaction follows a much different result from the slow neutron capture, as they capture additional neutrons before decay of the original ones occurs resulting in some very heavy elements such as

Californicum.

Energetically, the final result of heating any nuclei above 5 x 10,000,000 degrees Kelvin is the formation of ^{56}Fe, as this is the most stable nucleus. If the new star is small it converts much of its core to iron and becomes a " White Dwarf " which cools. The larger stars convert their cores to iron in seconds; the resulting change in density generates a catastrophic implosion of the core and an outer explosion known as a "Supernova."

"Supernovae" are very rare, actual astronomical observations indicate they occur about once every 300 years in each galaxy; however, they are extremely important in the genesis of the individual elements.

The Supernova explosion flings a large amount of new matter into space where the heavy elements condense in the clouds of gas constituting new stars or they may be attracted to and captured by the gravity of ancient stars. Trace levels of deuterium, lithium, beryllium and boron are due to the rapid consumption of the minerals by nuclear reactions. The relatively high levels of the alpha nuclei ^{16}O is a result of the great stability of the nuclei towards additional nuclear reactions. Eighty per cent of the Earth's crust consists of the four alpha - nuclides : ^{16}O, ^{24}Mg, ^{32}Si, and ^{40}Ca.

The quantative peak centered on ^{56}Fe is caused by maximum nuclear binding energy; the main nuclides comprising this peak are titanium, vanadium, chromium, manganese, iron, cobalt and nickel - all of which tend to be very common in the Earth's crust and molten core.

During slow neutron capture ^{90}Zr, ^{138}Ba and ^{208}Pb are formed. During rapid neutron-capture the life of radionuclides are very brief with N=50 (i.e. ^{80}Zn, ^{81}Ga, ^{82}Ge, ^{83}As,

and ^{84}Se), N=82 (i.e. ^{124}Mo, ^{125}Te, ^{126}Ru, ^{127}Rh, ^{128}Pd, ^{129}Ag, ^{130}Cd, ^{131}In, ^{132}Sm) and N=126 (i.e. ^{184}Ce and ^{194}Er). These nuclides decay and through loss of beta particles form ^{80}Se, ^{84}Kr, ^{124}Sn, ^{132}Xe and ^{184}W to ^{194}Pt.

Stable isotopes of Al, Cl, Cu, Ga, K, P, Pr, Ta and Y arose from slow neutron-capture, whereas those of Ag, Au, Br, I, Ir, Ho, Rh, Tb, Th, Tm, and U are formed by rapid neutron - capture.

Burbridge's theory of the origin of the stars and the Earth, to say the least, is complex, detailed and controversial; some researchers support his theory of the condensation of hot gases with the subsequent transmutation of one element to another; others favor an accretion of cold gases. The technique of radiodating puts the Earth's genesis or "birth" at 4 to 5 billion years ago. One billion years equals an aeon. Regardless of which basic theory is believed, biblical or "big bang," all must agree that the geochemical fractionation of the Earth's elements continues even today although at an almost imperceptible snail's pace and that the Earth is still not in geochemical equilibrium.

Radioactive dating is a powerful method of measuring relative geologic time. It has been employed in the estimate that the Earth is 4.5 to 5 billion years of age. Even with radioactive dating techniques the embryologic stages of terrestrial development, including the accumulation of the great iron core and the genesis of the relatively light and movable land masses, have remained obscure because of the numerous events (i.e. thermal and geochemical) that can reset the "radioactive clock."

As land masses float, migrate and relocate across the Earth's surface, the elements on the ocean floor sink and recycles into the hot interior of the mantle and core;

when land masses are forced into each other mountain ranges are born. Molten elements find their way through the continental faults, frequently breaking to the surface as lava. Over time, wind and water erosion wears off the mountains and results in mineral rich silt and sediments being swept into valleys, creeks, rivers and oceans where they eventually are returned to the Earth's mantle. Periodic floods historically enriched the soil of the flood plains and "bottom land" with life-giving mineral rich silt that accumulated for millions of years.

Geophysicists use a variety of tools and techniques to date the elements of the Earth and track it's continued development; these tools have strengths and weaknesses, but they have the same basic goal of recording the relative abundance of a radioactive isotope and the subsequent non-radioactive isotope, that it decays into. Each radioactive isotope eventually decays into a final stable product and by knowing the relative rate of decay for each isotope and assuming you start at zero, one can draw a conclusion of how long the decay final products have been accumulating in a rock. Investigators, who wish to date rocks preferentially examine isotopes of uranium as uranium decays into stable lead - leading to the name "the uranium-lead method" of dating. Zircon crystals are the common source of radiodating material. The useful zircon crystals are found in granitic rocks, metamorphic rocks, volcanic rocks and in silt or sediment resulting from erosion of those rocks. As zircon crystals resist heat and weathering by wind and water, they usually survive intact in rocks that have undergone multiple metamorphic episodes.

A concern with the uranium-lead radioactive dating is that rocks subjected to extreme heat can lose significant quantities of lead, thereby "resetting" the radioactive geologic clock. In 1956 George W. W. Wetherill, of the Carnegie Institute invented a process to minimize the dating flaws of the uranium-lead method. His technique counts on the fact that there are two radioactive isotopes of uranium-uranium 238 and uranium 235. Each of the two isotopes of uranium decays into its own stable form of lead-U238 becomes lead 206 and U235 becomes lead 207; therefore, investigators can estimate a rocks age from the relative amounts of two separate materials.

In undisturbed zircon crystals a comparison of the abundance of the two uranium-lead abundance ratios intersect a curve known as the Concordia curve; these intersect locations on the curve estimate the age of each crystal. Zircon crystals from Mount Nanyer (Australia) are estimated to be 4.1 to 4.2 billion years old. Zircon crystals from the Acasta gneiss (Canada) are thought to have crystallized 3.96 billion years ago. Of special interest is the fact that the Acasta gneiss is a small clump of metamorphic rocks southeast of Great Bear Lake in the Canadian Northwest Territories. It is estimated that the Acasta gneiss is the metamorphosed result of the oldest known intact solid rock on the Earth's surface.

The scary part of all this dating data is evidence that the total volume of continental crust in existence before 4 billion years was "minuscule". At the projected rate of Earth's population growth (12 billion by the year 2050), we will outstrip or outrace the Earth's ability to create and place additional silt (minerals) in our farm soil. Four billion years is too long to wait for the next batch of cookies!!!!

Additional studies of the relative abundance of isotopes of neodymium, strontium and lead in continental and oceanic crusts show that little more than trivial amounts of land mass crust existed before 4 billion years ago. 3.8 billion years ago the Earth's mantle separated into the lighter and heavier components, realigning the raw materials from which continents formed. Continental growth picked up speed and continued at a "rapid" pace until 2.5 billion years ago.

The Earth's more recent geological history (less than 1.3 billion years) is investigated by the "potassium-argon" method. Potassium 40, a rare radioisotope of potassium decays to a stable form of argon - argon 40, a heavy form of the inert gas argon which has a half life of 1.3 billion years. By determining the accumulation of argon 40 in potassium rich rocks an estimate of when the rock became solid can be proposed. This method is particularly useful for studies of the Earth's development (and decay) over the last 500 million years.

Three major segregations of the Earth's elements can easily be recognized; initially the primal Earth, heated by the radioactive decay process separated into three onion - like concentric layers:

We have limited indirect data on the Earth's core and mantle, which in fact make up most of the Earth's solid mass; the crust on the other hand has been intimately probed, analyzed, gouged and extracted.

The Earth's crust is cooled and solid, whereas the inner layers of the mantle and core are in various states of molten (magma) minerals which are on occasion ejaculated to the surface of the planet by volcanos. When the Earth's crust was initially cooling it separated into a series of minerals, crystallizing into igneous rocks in a definite order, the by-products being liquid water and gaseous nitrogen which formed the great oceans and seas and the nitrogen that makes up the majority of our atmosphere.

Origin of Some Essential Elements of Earth:

The igneous rocks continue to slowly

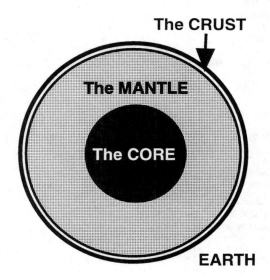

The CRUST

The MANTLE

The CORE

EARTH

Element	Origin
B	Spalletion in star atmostsphere
C	99% helium fusion; 1 % proton - capture
Ca	99 % alpha - capture; 4 % slow neutron capture
Cl	slow neutron capture
Co	high temperature nuclear fusion
Cu	slow neutron capture
Fe	high temperature nuclear fusion
H	primal (or Gods work)
I	rapid neutron capture
K	slow neutron capture
Mg	77 % alpha-capture; 23 % slow neutron capture

Table Continues on Next Page

Table 1-1

Composition of soils[1]

Element	Mean ppm dry soil (range)
Ag	0·1 (0·01–5)
Al	71000 (10000–300000)
As	6 (0·1–40)
B	10 (2–100)
Ba	500 (100–3000)
Be	6 (0·1–40)
Br	5 (1–10)
C	20000
Ca	13700 (7000–500000)
Cd	0·06 (0·01–0·7)
Ce	50
Cl	100
Co	8 (1–40)
Cr	100 (5–3000)
Cs	6 (0·3–25)
Cu	20 (2–100)
F	200 (30–300)
Fe	38000 (7000–550000)
Ga	30 (0·4–300)
Ge	1 (1–50)
Hf	6
Hg	0·03 (0·01–0·3)
I	5
K	14000 (400–30000)
La	30 (1–5000)
Li	30 (7–200)
Mg	5000 (600–6000)
Mn	850 (100–4000)
Mo	2 (0·2–5)
N	1000 (200–2500)
Na	6300 (750–7500)
Ni	40 (10–1000)
O	490000
P	650
Pb	10 (2–200)
Ra	8×10^{-7} ($3–20 \times 10^{-7}$)
Rb	100 (20–600)
S	700 (30–900)
Sb	(2–10?)
Sc	7 (10–25)
Se	0·2 (0·01–2)
Si	330000 (250000–350000)
Sn	10 (2–200)
Sr	300 (50–1000)
Th	5 (0·1–12)
Ti	5000 (1000–10000)
Tl	0·1
U	1 (0·9–9)
V	100 (20–500)
Y	50 (25–250)
Zn	50 (10–300)
Zr	300 (60–2000)

[1] The figures refer to oven-dried soils. Soils near mineral deposits have been omitted in computing ranges. Insufficient data are available for Ag, Be, Cd, Ce, Cs, Ge, Hf, Hg, La, Sb, Sn, Tl and U, and the values quoted for these elements may require revision.

Element	Origin
Mn	high temperature nuclear fusion
Mo	60 % slow/20 % fast rapid neutron capture; 20% proton capture
N	proton capture by 12 C
Na	slow neutron capture; proton capture
O	96-99 % alpha-capture; 0.04 % proton capture
P	slow neutron capture
S	95 % alpha capture; 5 % slow neutron capture
Se	85 % rapid/14 % slow neutron capture; 1 % proton capture
Si	92 % alpha capture; 8 % neutron capture
Zn	9.5 % slow/ 0.5 % rapid neutron capture

decompose or are slowly destroyed or dissolved by physical (heating or freezing), chemical (acid rain, soil ph, etc.) or biological processes (microorganisms, plant roots and lichens). The universal solvent, water, aided by various natural solutes, by microorganisms, higher plants, sand blasted by wind, frost splitting or the weight of glacial ice denude and "digest" all exposed rock surfaces into mineral rich "rock flour," dust and silt. These silts and mineral products of degradation (Table 1-1) are swept into the rivers (Table 1-2), then to the oceans and seas (Table 1-3) forming sediments on the floors of the rivers and oceans.

Subaquatic sediments are slowly compressed forming sedimentary rocks through a process known as diagenesis. Continen-

tal migration has elevated some of these sedimentary rocks forming large land masses. These sedimentary deposits are deeply buried and at great depths are subject to enormous heat and pressure producing metamorphic rocks. The resultant Biosphere I or Earth is almost a perfect sphere or globe, with 71 % of its surface covered by water (i.e. - oceans, seas, lakes, rivers and streams) which is a dilute solution of every mineral on Earth !!

The Earth's crust is thinnest and the mantle most accessible in the central Pacific region near Hawaii. The lava (originating from the Earth's mantle) from Hawaiian volcanoes cools and solidifies into dunite. Dunite is an igneous rock consisting primarily of the mineral olivine which is an impure magnesium silicate (which is why Hawaiian rain forests are so green and lush - the magnesium is part of the chlorophyll molecule).

The Earth's core is not accessible to our current technology and therefore direct scrutiny, but is believed to be primarily iron with two to three percent nickel. The primary geochemical consequences of these first events is that the Earth's crust is relatively depleted of iron and related elements (i.e. - Co, Cr, Ir, Mo, Ni, Os, Pd, Pt, Rb, Ru, and V) and probably in magnesium.

Chemical analysis of meteorites shows that they are iron contaminated with carbon, sulphur and phosphorous suggesting the high probability that such minerals are also contaminants of the Earth's iron core.

Olivine (Mg_2SiO_4) forms first and sinks to the bottom of the melt during the process of magmatic crystallization; four iron salts, forming the minerals pyrrhotite (FeS), magnetite (Fe_3O_4), chromite ($FeCrO_4$) and ilmenite ($FeTiO_2$) crystallize out second. Iron pyrrhotite is the most abundant of the four,

Table 1-2 Elementary composition of soil solutions and river waters in ppm [1]

Element	Soil solution [2] Median	Soil solution [2] Range	River water [3] Median	River water [3] Range
Ag			0·00013	0·00001–0·0035
Al			0·24	0·01–2·5
Ar			0·6	
As			0·0004	< 0·0004–0·23
Au			< 0·00006	
B		0·03–10	0·013	0·01–1
Ba			0·054	0·009–0·15
Be			0·001	0·0001–0·001
Br		< 0·001–0·01	0·021	0·005–140
C (HCO₃⁻)	4	2–7	11	6–19
Ca	32	1–60 (–1500)	15	4–120
Cd			0·08	
Cl	·10	7–50 (–8000)	7·8	5–35
Co			0·0009	< 0·006
Cr			0·00018	0·0001–0·08
Cs			0·0002	0·00005–0·0002
Cu		0·01–0·06	0·01	0·0006–0·4
F			0·09	
Fe		0·1–0·25 (–25)	0·67	0·01–1·4
Ga			< 0·001	
Hg			0·00008	
I		0·01	0·002	
K	3·5	1–11 (–400)	2·3	1·4–10
Li			0·0011	0·00007–0·04
Mg	25	0·7–100 (–2400)	4·1	1·5–6
Mn		0·02–2 (–800)	0·012	0·00002–0·13
Mo		< 0·001	0·000035	< 0·007
N (NO₃⁻)		2–800	0·23	0·01–0·8
Na	15	9–30 (–3500)	6·3	3–25
Ni			0·01	0·0002–0·02
P	0·005	0·001–30	0·005	0·001–0·3 (–12)
Pb			0·005	0·0006–0·12
Ra			3·9 × 10⁻¹⁰	
Rb			0·0015	< 0·008
Rn			1·7 × 10⁻¹⁵	
S	5	< 3–5000	3·7	0·9–30
Se		0·001–3	< 0·02	
Si		0·5–12	6·5	2–12
Sn			0·00004	
Sr		< 0·1	0·08	0·003–0·8
Th			0·00002	
Ti		≤ 0·07	0·0086	< 0·11
U			0·001	0·00002–0·05
V			0·001	< 0·007
Zn		0·1–0·3	0·01	0·0002–1
Zr			0·0026	0·00005–0·022

[1] Many elements vary in abundance in river water seasonally (e.g. Si) or even from day to day (e.g. Mn). Abnormal ranges are given in parentheses.
[2] Swaine (1955), Wiklander (1958), Vinogradov (1959), Fried and Shapiro (1961), Barber *et al.* (1963), Bowen and Cawse (1965).
[3] Livingstone (1963a), Durrum and Haffty (1963).

The elements in sea water[1]

Table 1-3

Element	Chemical form	ppm	Residence time (years × 1000)	Percentage retention
Ag	$AgCl_2^-$	0·0003	2100	0·4
Al		0·01	0·1	0·00001
Ar	Ar	0·6		140
As	AsO_4H^{2-}	0·003		0·15
Au	$AuCl_4^-$	0·000011	560	0·25
B	$B(OH)_3$	4·6		46
Ba	Ba^{++}	0·03	84	0·006
Be		0·0000006	0·15	0·00002
Bi		0·000017	45	0·01
Br	Br^-	65		2300
C	CO_3H^-, organic C	28		12
Ca	Ca^{2+}	400	8000	0·9
Cd	Cd^{2+}	0·00011	500	0·05
Ce		0·0004	6·1	0·0006
Cl	Cl^-	19000		13000
Co	Co^{2+}	0·00027	18	0·001
Cr		0·0005	0·35	0·00004
Cs	Cs^+	0·0005	40	0·04
Cu	Cu^{2+}	0·003	50	0·005
F	F	1·3		0·2
Fe	$Fe(OH)_3$	0·01	0·14	0·000016
Ga		0·00003	1·4	0·0002
Ge	$Ge(OH)_4$	0·00007	7	0·004
H	H_2O	108000		6850
He	He	0·0000069	20000	0·05
Hf		< 0·000008		< 0·00024
Hg	$HgCl_4^{2-}$	0·00003	42	0·03
I	I^-, IO_3^-?	0·06		1·1
In		≪0·02		
K	K^+	380	11000	1·6
Kr	Kr	0·0025		130
La		0·000012	0·44	0·0009
Li	Li^+	0·18	20000	0·75
Mg	Mg^{2+}	1350	45000	5·1
Mn	Mn^{2+}	0·002	1·4	0·0002
Mo	MoO_4^{2-}	0·01	500	0·6
N	Organic N, NO_3^-, NH_4^+	0·5	2·5	220
Na	Na^+	10500	260000	40
Nb		0·00001	0·3	0·00004
Ne	Ne	0·00014		2
Ni	Ni^{2+}	0·0054	18	0·005
O	OH_2, O_2, SO_4^{2-}	857000		164
P	PO_4H^{2-}	0·07		0·006
Pa		2×10^{-9}		0·13
Pb	Pb^{2+}	0·00003	2	0·000002
Ra		6×10^{-11}		0·006
Rb	Rb^+	0·12	270	0·12
Rn	Rn	6×10^{-16}		0·1
S	SO_4^{2-}	885		300
Sb		0·00033	350	0·15
Sc		< 0·000004	5·6	< 0·00002
Se		0·00009		0·16
Si	$Si(OH)_4$	3	8	0·001
Sn		0·003	100	0·1
Sr	Sr^{9+}	8·1	19000	1·9
Ta		< 0·0000025		< 0·0001
Th		0·00005	0·35	0·0005
Ti		0·001	0·16	0·00002
Tl	Tl^+	< 0·00001		< 0·002
U	$UO_2(CO_3)_3^{4-}$	0·003	500	0·1
V	$VO_5H_3^{2-}$	0·002	10	0·001
W	WO_4^{2-}	0·0001	1	0·006
Xe	Xe	0·000052		300
Y		0·0003	7·5	0·0008
Zn	Zn^{2+}	0·01	180	0·01
Zr		0·000022		0·000012

[1] Goldberg (1963), Goldberg (1965), Schutz and Turekian (1965).

as it carries down with it considerable phosphorus and the elements joined with insoluble sulfides (i. e. - cobalt, copper, nickel and zinc). The bulk of the magma solidifies next sequentially forming a series of rocks that contain lower amounts of iron and magnesium, but with elevated levels of potassium, silicon and sodium.

The first rocks to be identifiable are gabbros, second the diocites and lastly the granites, all of which are different collections of silicate minerals, of which feldspar constitutes 60 %. Feldspars are primarily aluminosilicates of calcium, potassium and sodium with numerous elemental contaminants. Quartz (SiO_2) is a very pure mineral crystal; smaller amounts of accessory minerals are formed next (i. e. - Ca_5{F OH } $(PO_4)_2$), chalcopyrite ($CuFeS_2$), fuorite (CaF_2), monazite ($CePO_4$), titonite ($CaTi${O,OH, F} SiO_4), xenotime (YPO_4) and zircon ($ZrSiO_4$).

The trace minerals and rare earths are deposited in cracks and fissures left in the cooling rocks already solidified resulting in rocks called pegmatites; these elements have ions that are either too large (i. e. - Au, Cs, Hg, Nb, Sb, Ta, Th and U) or too small (i. e. - B, Be and Li) to fit into the crystal lattice formed earlier. Many of these minerals are highly soluble in water and are therefore leached out to be recycled many times in a specific area. As rocks weather, all the rock conglomerate of minerals are leached out leaving residues of several resistant oxides ($Al2O_3$, FeO_2, SiO_2, TiO_2 and ZrO_2). All the elements readily dissolve in rain water and are eroded into streams, rivers and oceans where they are precipitated again by chemical or biological systems.

Clays constitute a large portion of the oceans sediments. The clays of the Atlantic Ocean consist largely of kaolinite in tropical latitudes and illite in temperate latitudes. Aluminum, iron and silica in aqueous solutions readily form tiny particles of colloidal proportions which usually precipitate out as inorganic "clay" found in sea beds and various types of soils.

Clay particles have a great affinity for potassium and less for sodium although these two ions are found in equal amounts in igneous rocks. They are easily leached out but potassium is selectively held by clay which results in the elevated sodium levels in sea and ocean water. In many tropical rain forests silica is leached faster than aluminum or iron, therefore the residual soils are mainly hydrous oxides of aluminum and iron.

Large quantities of silica (SiO_2) are precipitated out as "sand" from solution in the ocean by diatoms (plankton), dinoflagellates and protozoa which form their cell walls from silica. Manganese nodules (0.1-10 cm dia) are common in marine sediment. The oxides of iron and manganese may also be precipitated by bacteria in acid fresh water bogs.

Iron sulfide (FeS_2) is formed in anaerobic marine sediments by direct bacterial reduction of sulfate to sulfide or by bacteria which release hydrogen sulfide which precipitates with Fe, Co, Cu, Mo, Ni, Zn, etc. from solution in sea water. These conditions are found in the Black Sea and numerous Norwegian fjords. Calcium carbonate ($CaCO_2$) or limestone is precipitated in warm shallow waters by living organisms. So much carbon dioxide is removed from water by aquatic photosynthesis by algae that calcium carbonate often precipitates chemically; it is also secreted by red algae, corals and molluscs.

Strict biolithes (minerals or "stones" derived from living organisms) include peat, humus (including humic shale), and petroleum. They are initially formed by chemical reduction of dead plants and plankton by bacteria under anaerobic conditions. Algal limestones and diatomaceous silica usually are classed with the biolithes:

Diagenetic Changes

Residual oxides ——————————> sandstone
Clay ——————————————> shale
Iron sulphide ————————————> pyrite
Ca carbonate ————————> limestone or dolomite
Peat ——————————————> coal
Petroleum ——————————————> asphalt

Metamorphism

Sandstone ——————————————> Quartzite
Shale ——————————> Slate, Schist or Gnesis
Limestone ——————————————> Marble
Coal ——————————————> Graphite

"Soil," in its infinite number of forms, is the last part of the geological genesis puzzle - it is basically the product of climate and the effects of living organisms upon rocks; its physical nature and chemical composition (Table 1-1) is determined by the make up of the parent rock in a particular location and by the natural forces attacking them. As a rule of thumb regions with similar climates have like types of soils, but each type of soil has numerous variations related to the underlying rock, topography or vegetation.

Soil structure is comprised of three distinct layers:

A: Humus or decomposed plant material - this is the "organic" layer of the soil ("top soil"); usually the mineral elements are rapidly lost by the leaching affects of water, rain, irrigation, "mining" by plant growth (wild and cultivated) and acid rain.

B: Sand and accumulations of some of the mineral elements leached from layer A.

C: Subsoil, gravel or parent rock

Soil is a dynamic "living" environment, an ecosystem unto itself, the health of which we are all dependent upon for our own health and longevity - Frances Moore Lappe said it very well, " If you eat, you're involved in agriculture."

Coarse inorganic particles with a diameter greater than 0.0002 cm contribute from 5 to 90 % of the dry weight of most soil and may be separated into gravel, sand and silt depending upon particle size and character.

Colloidal inorganic particles have a diameter of less than 0.0002 cm; they can be separated by mass or size in a water column. Inorganic colloidal particles usually comprise less than 10 to 80 % of the dry weight of soils and are responsible for soils color, texture and ion-exchange properties.

The soil solution, or water held in soil capillaries which contains dissolved matter can be extracted by centrifugation and may comprise as much as 50 % of healthy soil by weight. The soil solution is important as a media for the propagation of microorganisms and as an efficient medium for the rapid growth of plant rootlets.

The soil atmosphere is comprised of various gases in equilibrium with the soil; it can be measured by use of a vacuum pump and may constitute up to 50 % of healthy soil by volume.

The actual organic matter in soil is very difficult to separate from the colloidal inorganic matter in the soil; it is usually found as 1 to 50 % of the dry weight of soil and rarely up to 90 %. Organic matter in the soil primarily originates from plant debris and dead microorganism (i.e.-bacteria and fungi).

The living organisms in the soil are of infinitely greater numbers and varieties than those species found on top of the soil. Soil organisms are for the most part unicellular, however, worms can be important in excavating minerals from subsoils and bring them to the Earth's upper layers in their manure or digestive "casts". Worms also carry plant debris from the surface of the Earth into the humus layer where micro - organisms feed upon them. Micro - organisms make up 0.1 to 0.2 % of soil by weight. Soil microorganisms, although small in percentage of total weight of the soil are indispensable for soil formation and for the regulation process of ph (acid balance), nitrogen fixing (fertilization) and oxidation potentials.

Fossils of 11 species of microorganisms including bacteria and blue-green algae have been identified in the 3.5 billion year old rocks of western Australia. It is thought that "life " began and failed many times before these "false starts" finally took hold, survived and finally flourished. These starts of "life" appear to have begun in ocean floor cracks called hydrothermal vents (underwater hot geysers) that contain little known ecosystems populated by unique heat tolerant organisms.

These "hot world" ecosystems of the sub oceanic geysers contain giant tube worms, blind shrimp and sulfur-consuming microbes that are the closest living relatives to the first recognizable living microorganisms on Earth. It is of interest to note that the only other surviving ancient life forms

that old are microorganisms living today in the dry land steam geysers like those found in Yellowstone's Octopus Springs.

The "hot world" theory for the beginning of life has many scientific supporters. "The hotter it is, the easier life is " says Everett Shock, a graduate from Washington University. One serious question remains - did the organisms of the first known life forms on Earth originate on the surface of the ocean and the surviving species drifted or migrated to the geysers for protection against "killer events" on the ocean's surface or did they originate as life forms in the cracks in the ocean floor?

Minerals are intimately involved in the theory of " life began in the ocean " or "warm pond" as Darwin thought. The multitude of minerals and elements in sea bed clay are thought to be the precursors of RNA (living strings of specialized amino acids that are able to replicate themselves). The theory goes on to postulate that the surface bubbles on the ocean (5 % of the oceans surface is bubbles at any single moment) is the laboratory where "life" began - it is a fact that the membrane of the bubble, that iridescent biochemical wonder lab that makes up the bubble wall concentrates minerals and organic chemicals essential to life such as Rare Earths, trace minerals, copper, zinc and phosphate salts. All ocean surface bubbles burst, and as they burst they ejaculate the mineral soup concentrate into the atmosphere that interfaces with the water's surface.

Ultraviolet light catalyzed energy synthesis is similar to higher plant photosynthesis and when it is available and in contact with the mineral soup concentrate from the burst bubbles "life" can ignite just as flint and steel provides the spark to ignite dry tender !!

Only two groups of organic molecules can spontaneously copy themselves, RNA (ribonucleic acid) and DNA (deoxyribonucleic acid). Like enzymes (proteins that do work) RNA and DNA (Table 1-4.) are long unbranched molecules made up of nucleotide subunits, and like amino acids can be organized easily from uncomplicated inorganic molecules.

The nucleotides have side chains known as "bases," but there are only four common ones and they are found in nature as two pairs, each with a strong electrochemical attraction for each other. As the "bases" in a chain of RNA attract their mirror counterpart from a solution, a complimentary sequence is built that can separate from the original "parent" RNA; when this new complementary molecule attracts its mirror sequence of "bases" an exact likeness of the original RNA chain is manufactured.

RNA is considered by many to be the first "living" molecule because it acts as a catalyst like an enzyme as well as replicating. RNA models point to a geometric structure that folds back on itself every three bases forming a series of "notches". Each notch has a negative charge on one side and a positive charge on the other - just the correct geometry to capture 20 or so free amino acids alternatively by the "head" or "tail" and become an amino acid complex known as a protein. The side chains of the amino acids projects into the areas between the bases.

A "condensing agent," a molecule that removes water, such as a polyphosphate (a complex of a mineral with the organic molecule) joins the amino acid; when the environmental conditions became dry the resultant product is a reproducible protein.

RNA alone could not produce life as we know it; however, evidence shows that RNA did come together with a dead-ended protein and intertwined together they became "life."

Whether or not this "life beginning" was an accident of chance or the gift of the loving hand of God molding the clay will probably be argued forever.

We have observed the paleontological path of life's beginnings; we have categorized and catalogued the "Age of Invertebrates;" the "Age of Fishes;"; the "Age of Reptiles;" the "Age of Mammals;" and the grand finale - the" Age of Man."

Life as we know it is not the "Age of Man;" it is not even the "Age of Insects" - it was "in the beginning," it is presently and it will always be until the sun explodes and dies the "Age of Bacteria."

Bacteria began the great trek 3.5 billion years ago, they have been ultimately successful - they endure a wide range of biochemical environments and cannot be "nuked" into extinction; they overshadow all other organisms in numbers and species variety. The numbers of Escherichia coli bacteria alone in the bowels of one human being surpass the numbers of all humans that have ever lived!!!

Fossilized sediments in 3.5 billion year old chert and lava formations show that our early sea water was not made up of minerals from erosion but rather from circulation of water through the hot water vents in the floor of the sea - the atmosphere was rich in carbon dioxide and contained little if any oxygen - life as we know it did not exist.

The early Earth organisms were anaerobic bacteria whose fossilized remains are permanently imprinted in chert and stomatolites (layered domed-shaped formations created by megacolonies of cyanobacteria). These anaerobic organisms

Table 1-4   ppm elements in dry nuclei, DNA and mitochondria from mammalian tissues [1,2]

Element	Isolating solution	Nuclei	Nuclear DNA	Mitochondria
Al	Aqueous	170 (1) D		
Ca	Non-aqueous	13500 (6) W		
Ca	Aqueous	210 (2) D, T		250–2800 (3) Sr, T, Ho
Cl	Aqueous			500 (1) Ho
Co	Aqueous	0·46 (1) S		
Cu	Aqueous	7 (2) D, T	10 (2) St	18 (1) T
Fe	Aqueous	140 (2) D, T	130 (1) St	230 (1) T
K	Non-aqueous	20400 (3) I		
K	Aqueous	8000 (4) I, T		1000–7400 (4) Ho, M, Sr, T
Mg	Non-aqueous	800 (6) W		
Mg	Aqueous	70–1100 (2) D, T		330–5000 (3) Ho, Sr, T
Mn	Aqueous	1–17 (3) D, L, T	5·2 (2) St	11 (1) T
N	Aqueous	128000 Sp	136000 Lo	110000 Sp
Na	Non-aqueous	6300 (3) I		
Na	Aqueous	830–2100 (4) I, T	370 (2) St	190–810 (4) Ho, M, Sr, T
P	Non-aqueous	25000 (6) W	82000 Lo	
P	Aqueous			3100 (1) Ho
S	Aqueous	1500 Sp		
Zn	Aqueous	3–140 (3) D, H, T	95 (1) St	39 (1) T

[1] References for Table 5.10:

D—Dounce and Beyer, 1948

H—Heath, 1949

Ho—Honda and Schwartz, 1956

I—Itoh and Schwartz, 1956

L—Lang et al., 1951

Lo—Long, 1961

M—Macfarlane and Spencer, 1953

S—Siebert, et al., 1951

Sp—Spector, 1956a

Sr—Spector, 1953

St—Stehlik and Altmann, 1963

T—Thiers and Vallee, 1957

W—Williamson and Gulick, 1944

[2] Figures in brackets are the number of analyses on which the quoted range or mean is based. Note the difference between the contents of Ca, K, Mg and Na when the isolating solution is aqueous or non-aqueous.

(cyanobacteria) flourished in the Earth's early carbon dioxide rich and zero oxygen atmosphere. Carbon atoms are found in two stable forms that differ only by a single neutron; because photosynthetic organisms exclusively use the lighter form of carbon, they leave a chemical trail that is easily identified.

Three billion years before the appearance of trilobites, life began as complex microbial communes. Some descendants of the carbon dioxide using organisms that first appeared on the newborn Earth are still flourishing - in the stinking anaerobic mud of swamps, the oxygen poor depths of the Black Sea, at the stoma of hydrothermal vents on the ocean floor and in our own human gut.

In the beginning, species of bacteria developed the ability to convert the energy from sunlight into the creation of "organic" (carbon based) molecules from carbon dioxide dissolved in sea water - thus photosynthesis appeared, and it was "ecologically liberating" - given enough time, life as we know it was inevitable and would in fact cover the surface of the Earth.

The greater numbers of photosynthetic bacteria principally use hydrogen sulfide and its related compounds for the electron source needed for photosynthesis. Cyanobacteria were able to use a universally available raw material (water). The cyanobacteria (blue-green scum in ponds, puddles and bird baths) became the greatest manufacturers of organic matter on Earth; and because they produce oxygen as a byproduct of photosynthesis, these microbes charted a new course for spaceship Earth, carving a new ecological niche in the bios for oxygen dependant (aerobic) metabolism used by species as diverse as bacteria to man.

The "oxygen revolution" didn't happen overnight, cyanobacteria only began releasing oxygen into the atmosphere 3.5 billion years ago, however, signs of aerobic life in the soil didn't appear until 2.1 billion years ago (1.4 billion years later!!) when atmospheric levels of oxygen increased from one percent of today's atmospheric oxygen levels to 10 percent of today's oxygen levels.

At the higher concentrations of atmospheric oxygen ozone (O_3) formed an onion-like protective shield on the outer layers of our atmosphere, protecting new life from the devastating lethal effects of ultraviolet radiation.

The now oxygen enriched atmosphere had limitless biological potential for diversity of life - new species were able to use oxygen for energy-yielding "respiration" where organic raw materials (i.e.-carbohydrates, fats, proteins and vitamins) could be fragmented into carbon dioxide and water. During the "oxygen revolution" more and more species of aerobic bacteria formed by mutations from the original species - the anaerobic bacterial species eventually were limited by a reduced habitat, although they still played a critical role in the ecosystem by recycling carbon.

The primitive bacterial organisms were "prokaryotic" - a basic cell surrounded by a cell membrane, however, they lacked a nucleus so their genetic material floated freely in the cytoplasmic soup. Eventually there came the "eukaryotic" cells, microorganisms whose genetic material was encased in a nuclear membrane.

Oxygen started the "eukaryotic cells on the path to ecological fulfillment, not because they developed respiration themselves, but because they phagocytized (engulfed) bacteria that did!! These aerobic bacteria ingested by the eukaryotic cell became the precursors of organelles called mitochondria (energy producing micro-organs in the cytoplasm of all modern day eukaryotic species including man).

In China, North America and Australia, fossilized evidence and recognizable biomolecules are found in ancient rocks dating back 1.9 to 1.7 billion years ago and prove that eukaryotic species became significant players in the Earth's marine environment (i.e.-seas and oceans).

The "oxygen revolution" exploded in a profusion of aerobic species in the Earth's terrestrial ecosystems, initially supporting eukaryotic protozoa and algae but not enough yet to support complex animals or plant species.

Animals and the evidence of their presence (i.e.-trails, tracks and fecolithes) do not appear in the fossil record until 600 million years ago. Just prior to the appearance of "animals," huge quantities of organic material (corpses of billions of tons of decomposing microorganisms) were buried in the sediment of shallow seas and oceans.

The high rate of organic carbon sediment accumulations occurred at the same time as great tectonic plate shifts took place; mountain ranges were formed and oceans and seas became deeper.

The fossil evidence shows that the "sulfur cycle" ran amuck at the same time resulting in a mass precipitation of pyrite in deep sea muck. The resultant atmosphere contained larger amounts of oxygen - enough at this point to support large complex animal species - the Phanerozoic Aeon was heralded in.

The first "animals" to be identified in fossils were the sea anemones and jellyfish, worms; at the beginning of the Cambrian period (545 million years ago) trilobites, molluscs, annelid worms and invertebrate members of the phylum, Chordata appeared.

Cyanobacteria, by producing oxygen as a waste product provided a new niche for aerobic organisms, in the Phanerozoic age, organisms became or created new environments for other species. The colonization of the "soil" of the new continents by complex plants provided food and environments for arthropods (insects) and vertebrates.

Organic compounds (i.e.-acids and enzymes)) synthesized by bacteria and other microbes began to digest wood and rock.

Insects set up symbiotic relationships with flowering plants (i.e.-bees, aphids and ants) while vertebrates developed systems for consuming fruits and seeds. In "God's Trombone", an American poem, James Weldon Johnson fills in between the lines on God's life creation moves after the creation of Earth :

Then God walked around, and God looked around on all that he had made. He looked at his sun, and he looked at his moon, and he looked at his little stars; He looked on his world with all its living things And God said: I'm lonely still. Then God sat down - on the side of a hill where he could think; by a deep wide river he sat down; with his head in his hands, God thought and thought, till he thought : I'll make me a man! Up from the bed of the river God scooped the clay: and by the bank of the river he kneeled him down; and there the great God almighty lit the sun and fixed it in the sky, flung the stars to the most far corner of the night, who rounded the earth in the middle of his hand; this Great God, like a mammy bending over her baby, kneeled down in the dirt toiling over a lump of clay till he shaped it in his own image; then into it he blew the breath of life and man became a living soul.

Amen! Amen!

Fig 1.1 Biological and Geological History of Earth.

Aeons before present

0 -   Present (20th century man)

          Seed plants, mammals and insects dominate .Abundant coal deposits and
          humic shale (mostly club mosses and tree ferns) First abundant fossil
          animals, many with calcareous tissues. All modern phyla present.

0.5 -   First fossil protozoa

1.0 -   Abundant calcareous fossil algae: North Africa

          Atmosphere changes from anoxygenic to oxygenic owing to photosynthesis

1.5 -   First fossil algae and fungi : Canada

2.0 -   First fossil sulphur bacteria : South Africa (anaerobic with O_2 by product)

2.5 -   First biogenetic limestones : South Africa

3.0 -   First rocks appear in the Earth's crust

3.5 -

4.0 -   Differentiation of Earth's crust, mantle and core; crust melted by
          radioactive heating

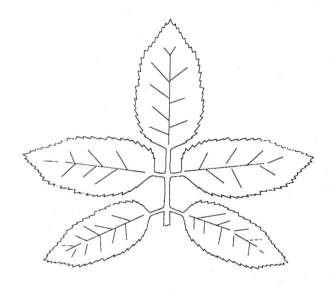

" Even its basic makeup defies logic. Salt is a blend of sodium and chlorine - the first a metal so unstable that it bursts into flame when exposed to water; the second a lethal gas. When we swallow the blend, it forms hydrochloric acid in our stomachs. Suicidal? No, an absolute necessity for life." -

- G. Young
National Geographic

Chapter 2

MINERALS: The Currency of Life

Minerals and mineral supplements to our meals are in fact a necessity of life. Since before recorded history man craved and consciously consumed minerals including the major minerals, trace minerals and Rare Earths in the form of clays, salts, animal tissue (bones and meat) or colloidal mineral rich plants.

The basic functions of life itself cannot be performed without minerals, either as a major part of the function or as a catalytic cofactor (i.e. - RNA, DNA, subcellular and digestive enzymes and the utilization of vitamins) - yet despite more than 10,000 years of human experience the allopathic medical profession would have us believe that all we modern humans need for optimal health and longevity is their stewardship, the four food groups, pharmaceuticals, radiation, surgery and organ transplants!!

Simply said, minerals are the currency of life. The medical profession ignores this truth to the point past the absurd - the most profound example we can think of is salt.

Physicians would have you believe that you need little or no salt (they must think we're dumber than cows for the first food item a good husbandryman puts out for his livestock is a salt block!!); however, the multibillion dollar a year snack food industry is well aware of your need and craving for salt and other minerals.

In July of 1993 thousands of people on the east coast of the United States were swooning and fainting and hundreds dying during a sweltering heat wave that soared above 110 F; the effects of the heat wave on the population were so dramatic that the body count was published in newspaper headlines as though they were fallen American soldiers in a far off place. No one it seemed knew what to do; the state medical examiner of Pennsylvania said "we don't know why so many have been affected by the heat - half of the dead and hospitalized had air conditioners." The cause was screaming at the medical profession but no one voiced or printed the appropriate public warning.

We knew the horrible toll was the result of a simple salt or sodium deficiency (your basic heat stroke that any boy scout could diagnose and recognize and remedy with water and salt); yes, a salt deficiency caused by the allopathic paranoia of salt.

The human tragedy of the heat wave of '93 was a direct result of the allopathic doctors who put their charges (their patients) on reduced or salt free diets for high blood pressure or heart disease. About a week after the carnage the state medical examiner's office again marveled from his pulpit, "the only common denominator we found in the dead and affected during the heat wave was that they all had heart disease or high blood pressure." Yes, as we predicted they had all been placed on low salt or no salt diets by their physicians and of interest was the fact that those reaching the emergency room and those who were successfully treated were treated with IV saline solution (salt water!!!).

The medical profession must think we are dumber than cows! What is the first thing that a livestock farmer, husbandryman or rancher puts out for their livestock - a salt block (and they have been doing it for thousands of years). And the animals get salt free choice in unlimited amounts and they don't get high blood pressure!!! Aristotle even noted (Historia Animalicem VIII) that "sheep are healthier when they are given salt."

Where it was rare, salt was traded ounce for ounce for gold, brides or slaves. Salt and salt rich clays were the first mineral food supplement consciously used by man, most probably since the dawn of time. The Roman statesman Cassiodorus was quite observant when he said, "Some seek not gold, but there lives not a man who does not need salt."

Rome's major highway was called the Via Salacia (salt road) - soldiers used it to carry salt up from the Tiber River where barges brought salt from the salt pans of Ostia. Soldiers worth their salt were paid a "salary" - the word salary is derived from salarium, money paid to soldiers to pay for their ration of salt. Salt coins and discs were reported in Cathay by Marco Polo. Salt discs in Ethiopia were "salted away" in the kings treasury. The production of salt as a food supplement for man and beast is as old as civilization itself. Salt was produced in shallow ponds of sea water through evaporation and by mining rock salt from large land locked deposits. The Hallstatt salt mine is one of the oldest commercial salt businesses on Earth - it is located 50 miles from Salzburg (Salt Town) salt has been mined from the Hallstatt mine since the early Iron Age. Salzberg (Salt Mountain) contains a salt deposit 2,000 feet wide 2,500 feet deep - today there are 25 miles of galleries created by the centuries of salt mining. The salt from the Hallstatt Mine was exported and traded to the Celtics.

Taxation of salt in China started in 2,200 B.C. under the administration of Kuan Teu. The Chi Kingdom (800 B.C.) became the richest kingdom in the world through salt tax and export revenues.

During the Wuti (Han Dynasty) special appointees were in charge of all salt taxes in China. In 700 B.C. the T'ang Dynasty controlled 18 salt lakes and 640 salt wells under a Board of Revenue.

Marco Polo observed the great importance of salt in China in 1200 A.D. He described cakes of salt that were officially stamped with the "Great Khan's" likeness and used as currency. In the 1700's A.D. the Chinese salt merchants under a government monopoly held the largest wealth of any commercial industrial group in China.

The rock salt mines of the Alps (Salzberg, Hallstatt and Durrenberg) played an essential role in the development of cultures in ancient prehistoric Europe. Tools found in the salt mines date back to the Bronze Age (1400 B.C.). Early communities sprang up around salt springs as humans followed and hunted wild herbivores that were drawn to the springs by their craving for salt and minerals. To obtain salt from these dilute springs, hunters kept wood fires continuously burning to boil away the water; these salt-boiling peoples are recorded as far back as the Neolithic Ages.

Whole forests were burned from Tyrol in the Alps, Moselle and Franche-Count, France; the Soale and Lueburg, Germany and Droitwich, England to support this salt industry! Before the Norman invasion of England, salt pans of Cheshire and Worchestershire (famous for its sauce) supplied England and Gaul, going south to the Thames River with the subsequent establishment of London.

From the 9th to the 14th centuries peat was soaked in sea water, dried, burnt and the minerals of the resultant ash were then extracted with sea water; many millions of tons of peat were harvested for this mineral/salt dietary supplement process for commercial trade. Mesopotamian towns specialized in the salt production industry and transported salt up the Tigris and Euprates Rivers. Jericho (8000 B.C.), near the Dead Sea and the salt mountain of Mo are the oldest known agricultural communities that participated in the salt trade.

An elaborate salt trade was developed by the merchants of Venice and by the 6th century the salt trade from the villages surrounding the city was its main business. By 1184 Venice controlled the export of Chioggia salt and by the 14th century was providing salt to Alexandria, Cyprus and the Balearic Islands.

The salted herring trade developed in the 1300's; the process of salting fish as a method of preservation was perfected by the Dutch and at its peak produced 3 billion salted herring annually using 123 million kg of salt per year.

In the beginning of the 20th century salt pork and salt herring provided the main source of animal protein for most of Scandinavia with a daily per person consumption of 100 gm or a quarter of a pound!!

Perhaps the most famous and romantic modern day part of the salt industry occurred in Africa. Twice each year great camel caravans carried salt slabs from the Taoudeni Salt Swamp in the Sahara to Timbuktu in Mali. Two thousand to 25,000 camels (only 25 % survived the journey) were used to carry over 300 tons of salt slabs more than 720 km.

Salt was also an important force in the African slave trade as captured children from warring tribes were sold into slavery in exchange for salt. In other parts of salt poor Africa humans developed the practice of drinking cattle blood or urine to obtain salt. The residents of the Sierra Leone coast gave all they possessed, including their wives and children in exchange for salt - because salt is an absolute requirement for life and because salt is not equally distributed on Earth and coveted by the have-nots, It is said by African tribesman, "He who has salt has war."

In France the salt tax was so strict that some 3,500 people were put to death before the revolution for not paying the salt tax. The French salt tax was only abolished in 1946!!!

The British imposed salt tax on India was despised by all of India. Ghandi (1924) published a monograph (Common Salt) in protest of the government monopoly. Ghandi pointed out that the grains and the green foods of India were very low in sodium and because of the vegetarian habit of the majority of tropical Indians they required a significant salt supplement to their diet. In 1930 Ghandi led 78 supporters on a 300 Km "Salt March" protest from Ahmedabad to the sea. He swam in the sea and picked up a crystal of salt at the beach and walked back to Ahmedabad, where he was promptly arrested and thrown into prison. Angered, 100,000 Indians revolted against the salt tax and were arrested after they too picked up untaxed salt. The British salt tax was finally repealed in 1946.

Death of soldiers from sodium loss historically occurred during military operations in tropical countries. Soldiers in the desert could lose 24 pints of water per day as sweat, which included a loss of 70 to 100 gm (a quarter of a pound) a day of sodium !!!

There was also the interesting fact that in the old criminal law of Holland, a particularly terrible and much feared punishment was to restrict criminals to a diet of bread and water without salt!!!

Salt is known as the universal and most widely used food supplement and condiment. So great is the human craving for salt, and the relish of it that we are led to consider that a love of it is one of the most dominating of our natural instincts and that salt itself is in fact necessary to the health and even the life of man.

Paracelsus first recommended tin to expel worms in the Middle Ages. Alchemists produced mosaic gold (aurum musivum) by alloying tin with mercury and then distilling this mixture with sulfur and ammonium chloride. The resultant gold-like color gave it its name. Tin was also used as a sweat inducer and a purgative for fevers, hysterical complaints (PMS) and venereal diseases.

Nicolas Monardes (1493-1588) a Spanish physician published Historia Medicinal. In the second volume is a scientific dialogue on the "virtues" of iron; however, iron was not generally accepted for medical use until the 1600's when Nickolas Le'mery found iron in animal tissue ash. In 1745 V. Menghini demonstrated the iron in tissue was found primarily in red blood cells. Dr. Willis' "Preparation of Steel" was iron filings and tartar roasted and given in wine as a syrup or pills. Dr. Thomas Sydenham (1682) recommended in all diseases involving anemia, bleeding (if the patient was strong enough) followed by a course of Dr. Willis' "Preparation of Steel."

In 1850 it was reported in a medical journal that a woman who had lost three premature pregnancies was given "iron scales from the smiths anvil, steeped in "hard" cider during her entire pregnancy. The woman's appetite increased, her digestion, health and spirits improved. She delivered a full term boy and who was so strong that he could walk by 9 months of age; at age five he was so tall and strong that he became known as the "iron baby."

Lead (the Extract of Saturn) or vegitomineral water was used medicinally for over 2,000 years. Externally lead was used as an astringent for wounds and internally as a purgative. Many argued against its use because of its toxic properties, but the supporters for the use of lead pointed to the fact that arsenic and mercury were also poisonous in large amounts but used medicinally in small amounts without ill effect. Thomas Gouland (d 1784) a French surgeon and counsellor to the king was a great proponent for the use of lead as a therapy.

"Environmental lead in building construction can cause learning disabilities, anemia and bone deformities, especially in children." The United States government spends multi-millions of our tax money in the form of grants to HUD projects to remove lead based paint and caulking from public housing projects to prevent children from eating the lead based materials (they eat the lead based material as a result of an affliction known as "pica", a symptomatic disease of mineral deficiencies - give the kids minerals and they will not eat the lead paint - it is better for the kids and its a lot cheaper!!!!

In 1884 manganese as permanganate of potash was used as an emetic (produced vomiting) and was so reported in the Medical Gazette by Alexander Ure. The therapeutic use of manganese was first reported in Macon, France where manganese miners were "uniformly cured" of scabies (mites) dermatitis of various forms. These reports by the miners lead to a general use of manganese for skin ointments to cure external skin diseases.

The French also found that oral manganese could be "superior" to iron in curing certain anemias. During the 1800's manganese was used very effectively in treating amenorrhea (deficiency of menstrual flow). In 1883 Franklin H. Martin (1857-1939) also demonstrated that manganese was valuable for treating menorrhagia (excessive bleeding during menstrual periods) and metorrhagia (bleeding at times other than menstrual periods).

Dr. Costa reported the use of bromide of nickel as a therapy for epilepsy and similar diseases. In 1884 a "controlled" study was made at the Jefferson Medical college Hospital, Philadelphia; it was reported that "nickel worked best in cases where attacks occurred regularly and at long intervals and when there was a hysterical or hypochondriacal feature to the case."

Adair Crawford (1748-1795), physician at St. Thomas Hospital investigated the therapeutic value of borytes (chlorinated barium) and determined that it was useful in certain cases of scrophulous (tuberculosis of the cervical lymph nodes), he also thought that it usually improved the appetite and general health. Barium was also reported to act as an evacuant, a deobstruent, and a toxic side effect noted included nausea and vertigo. Barium sulfate is used today as an opaque contrast medium for X-rays of the digestive tract (upper and lower G.I. series) to aid in the diagnosis of ulcers, cancer, diverticula and adhesions.

Walter Harris in 1689 published a book on infant diseases. In his book Harris emphasized the value of calcium for the treatment of infantile convulsions (many physicians of the day referred to these 'fits' as epilepsy). Rickets was known to be related to a calcium deficiency as early as 850 B.C. in the days of Homer!!!!

Jean Astruc (1684-1766), a professor at the College Royal de France, Paris recommended the treating of "rickets" with solutions of calcium and sodium phosphate but because the therapy was so cheap and lacked the mystery requiring a visit to the physician few other M.D.s supported the use of calcium for bone diseases of children!

Calcium chloride (muriate of lime) had

its supporters as a therapy for tuberculosis including French physician Antoine-Francois de Fourcray (1755-1809). John Thompson (1745-1846) was a skeptic and felt calcium might put tuberculosis in remission but doubted cures. Samuel Cooper (1780-1848) in the 6th edition of the Dictionary of Practical Surgery (1909) stated " I have seen the muriate of lime given in several cases of scrofula but without any beneficial effect on the disease."

In 1855, John Cleland, an anatomist at the University of Edinburgh used saccharated lime (calcium gluconate) as a tonic and antacid. In 1859 a family self-help handbook, Arts Revealed and Universal Guide, offered a single cure (calcium phosphate and cod liver oil) for "consumption, scrofula, general infantile atrophy, rickets, diarrhea and tuberculosis." Almroth Edward Wright (1861-1947), an Irish pathologist in 1891 defined the role of calcium in the clotting of blood, however, Nickolas Maurice Arthus (1862-1945) independently made the discovery and published his research a year earlier.

In 1854 James Young Simpson (1811-1870) a professor of obstetrics at the University of Edinburgh supported the use of oxalate of cerium to treat the morning sickness associated with early pregnancy. In 1860 Charles Lee, house physician to Blockley Hospital, Philadelphia reported the successful use of cerium for the control of vomiting associated with phthisis (pulmonary tuberculosis), pyrosis (severe heart burn), hysterical vomiting and atonic dyspepsia (lack of muscular tone of the gastrointestinal tract).

To the ancient Greeks and Romans, niter could be either carbonate of sodium or carbonate of potassium. To the alchemist and to Roger Bacon the term niter always meant nitrate of potash (potassium). In 1672 Peter Seignette (d 1716), a French apothecary created Rochelle Salt (named for his place of residence) by adding carbonate of soda to cream of tartar and carbonate of potash. Rochelle Salt is used even today as a saline cathartic - potassium sodium tartrate.

R.A. de Bonsdorf, University of Finland discovered the rodohydrargyrate of potassium (iodine of potassium and dentiodide of mercury in an aqueous solution); seven years later this "alloy" was regarded as a panacea by Wm. Channing of New York. Conditions that had universally improved following its use included "chronic bronchitis, whooping cough, pulmonary T.B., thrush, tonsillitis, pharyngitis, chronic gastroenteritis, colitis, gout, diabetes, dysmenorrhea, amenorrhea, vaginitis, cervicitis, herpes, psora, psoriasis, edema (dropsy), eye infections and scrofula."

Lithium was discovered in mineral water in 1817 by August Arfvedson in a Swedish Laboratory of Berzelius. Its use in mental illness dates back to 400 A.D. when Caelius Aurelianus prescribed lithium containing waters for mental illness.

In the 1840's it was reported that lithium salts combined with uric acid dissolved urate deposits. Lithium was then used to treat kidney stones, "gravel", gout, rheumatism as well as a plethora of physical and mental diseases.

Health spas picked up on the notoriety that lithium was getting and marketed themselves with exaggerated claims of the lithium in their hot mineral springs, even going to the extent of adding the word "lithia" to their names to woo the public. Because of public access to lithium salts in spas (i.e.- Russia, east and west Europe, U.S.A., Japan and South America) physicians looked for other arthritis therapies. The current medical use of lithium is limited to psychiatric patients, especially manic depression. We would like to see lithium added to the public water supply and eliminate fluoride!!!

The golden age of detailed and large scale research projects into the essentiality of various minerals in animal nutrition occurred between 1920 and 1978 - the curiosity for the pathophysiology of mineral deficiency diseases was dealt a mortal blow by the discovery of penicillin and totally killed in the ranks of allopaths by the drive to find patentable genetic techniques to treat all disease from farting to cancer. While the studies of nutrition have become the stepchild of 21st century science the unquenchable basic mineral needs of our human flesh cry out from the waiting rooms of physicians offices, hospital wards and mortuaries.

There are 75 metals listed in the periodic chart, all of which have been detected in human blood and other body fluids - we know that at least 60 of these metals (minerals) have physiological value for man. Organically not a single function in the human body can take place without at least one mineral or metal cofactor.

"On an inorganic chemical basis little distinction can be made between the metals. Both metals and non metals enter actively into chemical reactions. The difference reveals itself in the physical properties. By common agreement, those elements that possess high electrical conductivity and a lustrous appearance in the solid state are considered to be metals" according to Bruce A. Rogers, metallurgist and physicist.

Gold, silver and copper were probably the first metals (minerals) discovered in their native nugget form. It is likely that gold was first to be discovered, as it is the most widely distributed of all metals found in nature as nuggets. As gold is resistant to corrosion, the bright color of a gold nugget would attract the attention of an observant primitive human, and no doubt it would have peaked his curiosity when it wouldn't chip or break like other weapon and tool making rocks. However, gold, even untooled made a very special ornament. Because of its rarity and softness, native silver nuggets, like gold did not lend themselves to the making of tools or weapons. Copper was more abundant and could be fabricated much more successfully into tools and weapons. Even though copper corroded or oxidized very quickly, stream erosion or simple abrasion or scraping would reveal a brilliant metal surface. Once identified as a usable metal and some significance attributed to the discovery, the locality would be searched in some detail for more of the bright metal leading to discoveries of large chunks or veins too large to be carried off.

A workable sized chunk of copper would be smashed and hammered until it became the desired shape (i.e.- a blade , scraper or awl) and during the process of hammering it became harder. Copper hardens at ordinary ambient temperature and when it was shaped into a blade or spike it had numerous advantages over stone or flint (didn't break, stayed sharp with use, etc.). Somewhere along the way man made two historical and vital discoveries that changed his world forever: 1) metals could be extracted from mineral bearing rocks (smelting). 2) metals could be melted and "cast" into desired shapes in a mold. Which came first is an unanswerable question - like which came first the chicken or the egg. It seems logical, however, that smelting preceded casting. When early man built his security or cooking fire on copper containing rocks, the charcoal from the fire embers reduced the metal from the ore. After observing this phenomenon that produced pure copper several times, man was launched into the Copper Age. We know several details of man from this period through the discovery of the "Ice Man".

In 1992 a 5,000 year old "Ice Man" was found frozen and freeze dried in melting glacial ice in the Italian Alps. His possessions included grass insulated boots and coat, a long bow and arrows, bone and antler tools and last but not least a copper axe.

"Civilization" on a large scale had its beginnings in the large river valleys of China or Egypt around 6000 B.C. It is highly probable that the art of metallurgy flowered and flourished, like that of agriculture under the encouragement and funding of wealthy rulers. Advancements in metal and mineral technology were halted by the devastation of the "Great Flood" (approximately 4000 B.C.); but began again in earnest when the waters receded. Jewelry and weapons discovered during the excavations at Ur in Sumer (the southern portion of ancient Babylonia) revealed that the casting of copper, silver and gold and the smelting of copper from ore began around 3500 B.C. Very crude jewelry and hammered metal implements were found that dated more than 2000 years earlier!! A lead statue in the British Museum shows the Egyptians were mining and working lead with some degree of sophistication as early as 3400 B.C.

In the beginning, Metal Age man still relied a great deal on stone and bone tools and weapons because pure copper was too soft for serious use. In some areas copper ore was contaminated with other minerals; smelting this mixed ore produced a much harder stronger "alloy" that was easier to toughen and cast. If the contaminant was tin oxide (cassiterite) the resultant alloy was early "bronze."

At 2000 B.C. the metallurgists of Hissarlik (ancient Troy) perfected the art of bronze making and tooling. A delay in a universal Bronze Age occurred because tin ores do not occur as commonly as do those of copper. A large import trade for tin ore developed in Egypt because their copper ore was rather pure and free of tin contamination. There are snippets of information and clues that suggest iron was smelted from ore as early as 4000 B.C.; however, what is described as the Iron Age did not occur until 1400 B.C. An iron dagger found in the tomb of Tutankhamen dates back to 1350 B.C. and is thought to be the oldest surviving iron tool or implement crafted by man.

A letter written to Pharaoh Rameses II just after 1300 B.C. by the king of the Hittites document the first recorded reference to man-made iron. Steel was first produced in quantity in India five hundred years preceding the Christian Era.

Writers of the "classics" record the earliest accounts of the production of mercury from cinnabar (mercuric sulfide), but because it was liquid in its pure physical form they did not class mercury as a metal; by the 8th century A.D. mercury was universally recognized as a metal.

Pure arsenic and antimony produced from their sulfides by the Arab scholars and alchemists Abu-Musa-Jabor-Ibin-Haiyun (Geber 721-766 A.D.) were not recognized as metals because of a limited classification system. In the 8th century there were only seven known metals and each was tied by astrology and alchemy to the known planets:

Gold - sun - sol

Silver - moon - lunas
Iron - mars
Mercury - Mercury - (quick silver)
Lead - Saturn
Tin - Jupiter
Copper - Venus

The awareness of and the employment of metals for medicine, tools and weapons did not spread universally over the Earth. For example, when the Aztecs and Incas were "discovered" by the Spanish early in the 16th century the Spaniards reported "the savages to have almost no metallurgical skills; however, they did use native metals to tip their axes and knives which were made of gold which they regarded as a utility metal as we regard iron."

European pioneers exploring North America found that Indians did not have any interest in the mineral wealth of the continent for medicine or weapons - "they used native metals such as copper and gold, but they did not dig ore or smelt metal. It is incredible that only 200 years ago that so much of the world was ignorant of the importance of metals and minerals."

Today metals and minerals are classified in groups:

1) **common metals** - those produced in large quantities
2) **precious metals**
3) **light weight metals** - essential to transportation
4) **noble metals** - resistant to high temperature oxidation
5) **base metals** - are chemically reactive
6) **soft, low melting, rapidly oxidizing alkali metals**
7) **alkaline earth metals**
8) **rare earth metals**
9) **semimetals** - reduced electrical conductivity
10) **refractory metals** - have high melting points (jet engine construction)

In 1958 Parr pointed out that aluminum and magnesium and their alloys are in use in medicine and hospitals every day; the alloy varieties of brass and bronze have become so numerous that they include almost every known element. Zirconium, titanium and uranium are no longer unknown to the hospital technician or the man on the street.

The precious metals include coinage metals such as silver, gold, platinum, palladium and iridium which are used for jewelry as well as for medical devices and instruments. The first mint coin system was recorded in Lydia in Asia Minor, bordering on the Aegean sea around 700 B.C. An alloy of gold and silver (electrum) was stamped into coins for the specific purpose of trade for tin ore.

In 490 B.C. the Persian fleet remained a political and trade threat, even after the Athenians led by Alexander the Great had defeated the formerly omnipotent and all conquering Persian armies of Darius I (558-486 B.C.) at Marathon. Thermistocles (527-460), an up-and-coming Athenian politician and backer of sea power, proposed building a merchant and military fleet second to none which would require huge amounts of capital and resources of all types. This commitment to build the fleet resulted in the first use of silver minted as money. The silver was mined from a large vein in Laurium, near Athens.

The Laurium silver ore was contaminated with lead and was separated by a method known as "cupellation." The lead-silver mixture was heated to melting in a cupel (a shallow clay pot) and an air stream directed across the surface of the hot liquid metal. As lead oxidizes sooner than silver the resultant lead oxide could be skimmed from the surface of the liquid alloy, leaving a pure metallic silver. If there was any gold original alloy, cupellation produced the gold-silver alloy Electrum. A method for the separation of gold from silver became known about 300 B.C.

The silver mines at Laurium allowed Athens to mint a uniform silver coin and to assume a dominant role in trading with Greece as a whole and Asia Minor. Many Greek coins were minted by Greek cities carrying medical symbols and emblems. As early as 360 B.C. coins stamped at Epidaurus and Cas carried the head of Aesculapius, the god of medicine. Roman coins often displayed the bust of Salus, the Roman name for Hygieia - the daughter of Aesculapius.

Roman coins were minted from brass. Brass was an accidental copper and zinc alloy discovery. Brass was unknown before the Roman Empire. The Bactrians, Roman contemporaries, who live in the north of what is now Afghanistan minted copper-nickel coins with nickel at 20 %.

To avoid the use of paper money that was in general circulation by lepers from the leper colony of Culion Island, Phillipines, the Phillipine government in 1913 minted aluminum coins. The aluminum coins corroded after contact with antiseptics used by the lepers, requiring that latter issues be minted from nickel. It was the search for gold that led the Spanish to the conquests of the Americas. Columbus' goal was to find a western route to China and India which he thought he found when he initially landed in the Bahamas. The gold bejeweled natives told him more gold was to be found to the south. Harboring in Cuba and Haiti, he confiscated gold from the local natives who had collected the gold from local streams.

The Spanish under the leadership of Hernando Cortez (1485 -1547) conquered Moctezuma (1480-1520) after Moctezuma tried to bribe away Cortez with large gifts of gold. The priceless value of such large quantities of gold only fanned the flame of greed in the Spanish for more of the American gold. The brutality and massacres inflicted on the Aztecs was in vain; the gold resources of Mexico were far less then expected; Cortez had mistaken the centuries of accumulated wealth of the Aztecs and Incas for current production. Peru came under Spanish domination in 1531 and within a few years the west coast of South America was under complete Spanish rule. Gold and silver were mined by forced slave labor who were subjected to terrible hardships. The only comfort offered to the slaves was a local herb called coca (cocaine) which according to the Spanish "enabled men to go without food, water or sleep and to stay warm while others froze and to work for hours without rest."

Persian born, Sina, or Avicenna (980-1037) known to his contemporaries as the "prince of physicians", was a successful practitioner in the court of Baghdad. His high standing lends credibility to the story that he gave his high ranking patients pills coated with gold and silver foil, not only to make them more attractive and palatable but also "to add to their therapeutic efficiency." Avicenna is also credited with employing metallic gold as "a purifier of the blood."

From the beginning economic considerations played a significant role in the treatment of choice by physicians, their remedies and supplements for patients. Remedies containing rare herbs or minerals were expensive and were used only for those wealthy and able to pay, while prayers for the poor were paid for with modest offerings to the local temple. The common remedy of the priest/physician was the amulet. Amulets for the poorer segments of the community might be made of fish bones or linen bags, while gold and other minerals or metallic beads or discs were offered to the wealthy and their children. The exact choice was important as all minerals, metals, plants and animals were given magical powers (as in Ayruvadic medicine).

Since there were no pharmacies in Egypt prior to 1552 B.C. the choices of minerals for treatment were limited to antimony sulfide, copper acetate, copper sulfate, copper carbonate, sulfur, salt and sodium carbonate. Iron, lead, magnesia, lime, soda, nitre and vermilion were also employed, especially for the poor.

The Babylonians and Assyrians were ahead of the Egyptians in using medicinal minerals. White and black sulphur, sulfate of iron, arsenic, yellow sulfide of arsenic, arsenic trisulphide, black salt peter, antimony, iron oxide, magnetized iron ore, sulfide of iron, pyrites, copper dust, verdigris, mercury, alum, bituman (coal), naphtha, calcined lime, etc. Gold was used widely for supplements and therapies, however, not everyone believed that it did any good towards healing. According to an unidentified writer from the 1600's:

" The ancients put leaf gold into many compositions; but I know not for what end but to feed the eye; for its substance is too solid and compact to be dissolved by our heat, and brought into act; nor is it available that some make the virtues, or spirits of gold sympathizing to those of the heart, and therefore give leaf gold; for by the same facility it may destroy the heart. And it may be applied outwardly in greater quantity, and with more profit, with little or no inconvenience."

There is evidence that gold was used as a therapy by the Chinese as far back as 2,000 B.C. Pao Pu Tzu (253-333 A.D.) recorded that metals and minerals had an important role in the search for immortality!! According to Pao Pu Tzu in his Nei Pieu, the highest ranking " medicines of the immortals" was cinnabar (red mercuric sulfide). "Take three pounds of genuine cinnabar, and one pound of white honey, mix them. Dry the mixture in the sun, roast the dry mixture over a fire until it can be shaped into pills. Take ten pills the size of a hemp seed every morning. Inside of a year white hair will turn black, decayed teeth will grow again, and the body will become sleek and glistening. If an old man takes this medicine for a long period of time, he will develop into a young man. The one who takes it constantly will enjoy eternal life and will not die."

"Cinnabar and gold combinations were considered as medicines par excellence and were frequently used in combination with excellent results in the attainment of immortality. Preparations in which silver was the chief ingredient had only a limited degree of efficiency in producing immortality... cinnabar was also a favorite ingredient in life prolonging concoctions by virtue of its producing mercury, the living metal, when subjected to heat."

The British pharmacologist/historian, C.J.S. Thompson found it "somewhat curious that while the alchemists of the west were always in doubt as to what constituted the true philosopher's stone, the Chinese seemingly had no doubts as to its identity. Cinnabar was regarded by the early Chinese alchemist as the wonderful body which was supposed to have the mysterious power of converting other metals into gold, and when used as a medicine would prolong life for an indefinite period. "

The Chinese prized mercury as an elixir, while East Indian physicians (800 B.C.-1000 A.D.) used it for skin diseases including smallpox and syphilis. Other minerals in the Hindu materia medica included gold, silver, copper, tin, lead, zinc, arsenic, iron, borax and aluminum.

The Greek physician Hippocrates (460-377 B.C.) obtained most of his drugs from the plant and animal kingdoms, but he is credited with using alum, copper, lead and maybe cinnabar. The Roman historian Pliny, The Elder (23-79 A.D.), who was killed early in life by the toxic gases from the eruption of Mount Vesuvius ("he was suffocated by the gasses when he approached too near"), before he died he devoted 13 books of his Natural History to medicine - he recorded many curiosities about plants and drugs (metals), highlights of Roman medicine, and its authors many slaps at physicians (for which we love him dearly). Most of the minerals used in Roman medical circles were known to Pliny, including iron, lead, nitrum, salt, gold, tin, silver, realgar (arsenic sulfide), copper and misy (a combination of the sulfates of copper and iron).

Through the end of the 1400's the alchemists did not make any further contributions of a substantial nature to the advancement and practice of medicine but they engendered an "erratic genius" who pioneered in the fields of pharmacology and pharmacotherapy. He was none other than Theophastus Bombastus von Hohenheim,

or Paracelsus (1493 - 1541) - he was hailed as "the most original medical thinker of the 16th century." He was a prolific writer; before the age of 25 he raised eyebrows with the alchemist by writing " Alchemy is to make neither gold nor silver, its use is to make the supreme essences and to direct them against diseases." Paracelsus arrived at these conclusions after a great deal of experience with minerals, metals, metallurgy and alchemy. Between the ages of nine and 16 years of age Paracelsus enrolled in both the Bergschule at Villach and a nearby Benedictine school at St. Andrew's Monastary. These schools were located in the mining areas of Europe.

In 1510 Paracelsus enrolled in the University of Basel. He was profoundly aware and complained that the university was giving him only boring reiterations of ancient formulas. At age 22 he worked in the silver mines and laboratories in the Tyrol about 30 Km from Innsbruk. Paracelsus' experience in the mines taught him the risks and occupational diseases of the miners. His work with chemists and alchemists revealed the futility of "gold-cooking", and he recognized that the alloys and solutions in their crucibles, retorts and phials could be converted to the making of medicines - in fact "that all minerals subjected to analysis might yield curative and life-giving secret." These combined experiences allowed Paracelsus to "enter into the inner most recesses of nature" and to understand the basics of metallurgy with such skill and acumen as to cure disease. Paracelsus' research into minerals and disease led him to the discovery of the medical value of chloride, sulfate of mercury, flowers of sulfur and antimony.

Topical zinc ointments used today were developed by Paracelsus as a young man.

In his medical practice he also used iron, lead, copper, potassium and arsenic. He formulated the theory that "the healthy human body is a particular combination of medical substances (i.e. -vitamins, minerals, amino acids and essential fatty acids), with illness resulting from a disturbance of this combination (i.e. -deficiency diseases!)". Consequently, illness could be cured only through the employment of chemical or mineral medicines. It was because of this insight, that he broke away from the teachings of Galen and Avicenna, the recognized medical authorities, putting himself into conflict with the medical establishment (and for this we dearly love him!!).

Experiments with antimony (emetic tartar) were pursued during the 19th century but were inconclusive. Today in the U.S. the use of antimony is strictly controlled, but in tropical countries it is used commonly as an antiparasitic agent.

Antimony sulfide was known in ancient times but was not initially regarded as a metal. As late as 1677 in the London Pharmacopeia, there was a differentiation between true metals (i.e.- gold, silver, copper, tin, lead and iron) and metallis affinia (i.e.- cinnabar, mercury { argentum vivum } and antimonium). Antimony is thought to have been discovered by Basil Valentine (1393) (some believe this was a fictitious name for Paracelsus), a 15th century Benedictine Monk who lived in what is now Germany. It is said that he tried small amounts of antimony supplements on hogs, which fattened and showed unprecedented health and vigor. He was said to be so encouraged by the initial results of his pig experiments that he dispensed his new mineral to his fellow monks with "disastrous" results. What had been good for the pigs was bad for the monks, which caused Valentine to name his new metal anti-moine (anti-monk).

Paracelsus popularized the internal use of mercury in the form of calomel (mercurous chloride); the external use of mercury as frictions, fumigations and plasters for the cure of lues venerea (syphilis) dates from 1497. The famous Italian surgeon and anatomist Berengario da Carpi (1470-1530) of Bologna accumulated an immense fortune by inventing and prescribing frictions with mercurial ointments for syphilis. A colleague of da Carpi, Giovanni de Vigo (1460-1520), born in Rapallo near Genoa and physician to Pope Julius II, was a staunch advocate of fumigations involving cinnabar and starax (tree resin), he also adapted the internal use of the red precipitate (cinnabar) for syphilis and plague. According to Gabriele Fallopio (1523-1562), an Italian professor of anatomy ("Fallopian tubes"), shepherds gave liquid mercury (quick silver) to their sheep to kill worms and Antonio musa Brassatola (1500-1555) of Ferrara gave quick silver to children to kill worms. There is one account of a woman drinking one full pound of quick silver who suffered no noticeable ill effects!!!

Thomas Dover (1660-1742), famous for his Dover's powder (opium and ipecac), believed mercury to be of great value for diseases of the stomach and a variety of other diseases. "To take one ounce of quick silver every morning was the most beneficial thing in the world." In 1731 and 1732 it was "fashionable in London and Edinburgh to take one ounce of quick silver every morning for several weeks."

In 1735 there was an outbreak in New England of what was known as ulcerated or malignant sore throat (diphtheria). William Douglas (1692-1752), the only physician in Boston of his day with an M.D. degree, produced a successful form of treatment involving the use of dulcified (sugared) mercury and camphor.

In the early 1750's Edward Augustus Holyoke (1728-1829) of Salem, Ma. prescribed mercury for pleurisies and peripneumonias. In 1770 and 1771 when diphtheria (throat distemper) and scarlet fever with severe sore throat (strep throat) plagued New York City, Samuel Bard (1742-1821), professor of medicine at King's College, New York used mercury in children "without ill effect and to the manifest advantage of my patient; relieving the difficulty of breathing, and promoting the casting off the sloughs, beyond any other medicine." The internal use of calomel was accompanied by gastrointestinal symptoms so drastic that in the 19th century, not only chloride of mercury but also the other forms fell into general disfavor.

In the 20th century mercury poisoning from mercury amalgam dental fillings, industrial wastes and agricultural chemicals has been incriminated as the cause of multiple sclerosis (MS), Lou Gehrigs Disease (ALS) and Parkinson's Disease in adults and cerebral palsy and other neurological congenital defects in the developing fetus.

The Noble metals are easily distinguished by their property of not oxidizing but remaining bright when heated in air, therefore their natural use for jewelry and as "precious" metals." Royal "Touching" to cure the "Kings Evil (Morbus regius)" or scrufula (tuberculosis of the cervical lymph nodes) began in the 11th century and was continued in France until the1600's.

In 1492, Henry VIII created an elaborate ritual that involved the "gold angel" (a special coin minted in 1495) to be used as a "touchpiece." The Stuarts favored touchpieces of gold and silver that were hung around the necks of sufferers. "To be eligible for royal touching, patients were examined by physicians who certified that the complaint was in fact scrofula (T.B. of the neck lymph nodes). After being touched the patient received a gold piece - and it was generally believed that he would be free from subsequent attacks provided he kept his touchpiece." Royal touching in England ended in 1714 with the death of Queen Anne. From the time of Edward II (1284-1327) to that of Mary Tudor (1516-1558), English royalty made a Good Friday offering of gold and silver; the metal was converted into "cramp rings" that were worn to cure epilepsy, rheumatism and several muscular pains.

Gold was first used medicinally in America in 1811 when New York hospitals used it for the treatment of syphilis and "other lymphatic afflictions." In ancient times silver was associated with the moon which was believed to control the head and emotions (moon struck, lunacy, etc.); this relationship was firmly entrenched by the chemical doctors of the 16th century. Tincture of the moon (Tinctura luna) was long a popular remedy for epilepsy, melancholia and mania. Angelus Sala (1637) employed silver nitrate (lunar caustic) as a purgative and in brain and uterine illnesses. Robert Boyle concocted pilulae lunara by creating a mixture of silver nitrate and nitre, dried and formed with bread crusts into pills the size of small peas as a laxative. In 1826 John Higginbottom (1788-1876) of Nottingham, England published a monograph on the use of lunar caustic for the cure of wounds and ulcers caused by needles, hooks, bayonets, saws and for bites of leeches, rabid animals, insect stings and for "small punctures occurring during anatomical dissection and autopsy." He also removed tumors and cauterized the surgical wound with silver nitrate. In a December 1827 letter to the editor of The American Medical Recorder Dr. James Breen reported a successful treatment of severe inflammation of the eye with silver nitrate. In 1884 Carl Sigmund Crede (1819-1892), a German professor of obstetrics instituted the practice of preventing infantile (gonorrheal) conjunctivitis (ophthalmia neonatorium) with a single prophylactic drop of 2 % silver nitrate in each eye of all infants at the moment of birth.

Higginbottom also described methods of silver nitrate treatment for erysipelas, phelgmonous erysipelas, inflammation of the absorbents, phelgmonous inflammation, small irritable ulcers with varicose veins, senile gangrene (diabetic gangrene) and burns and scalds. The latter is of interest because it was not until 1965 that Carl A. Moyer of the Hartford Burn Unit (Washington University School of Medicine, St. Louis, Mo.) " introduced" silver nitrate treatment for burns by employing a 1/2 % silver nitrate solution frequently did the process reach general use.

Elisha Perkins (1741-1799) Died of yellow fever) was 18 when he began practicing medicine in Plainfield, Ct in 1759. He was a respected country physician for 40 years (known for riding horseback up to 40 miles for single house calls). He was elected to the chairmanship of his state medical association.

In 1796 Perkins invented and patented the "Tractors" - two dissimilar metallic rods with a "secret" alloy composition (one was an alloy of gold, copper and zinc and the other was silver, platinum and iron). These "Tractors" were alleged to relieve numerous painful ailments by a mere stroking of the affected areas of the body. In obtaining his patent, Perkins touched off a firestorm of controversy around the world. At home Perkins was praised by university professors, practicing physicians and even the Chief Justice of the United States, but he was expelled by his colleagues from his state medical society. The Royal Physicians of Denmark confirmed his observations and further attested to the value of the "Tractors" and their use and coined the term "Perkinism" for the procedure. Perkins believed his Tractors to be effective for relieving misery in practically all painful conditions, however, he proclaimed them especially effective for gout, pleurisy, crippling rheumatism, "inflammatory tumors (abscesses)" and in calming and sedating violent cases of insanity. He also believed his Tractor treatment, with antiseptics, could cure yellow fever effectively; when the New York yellow fever epidemic of 1799 was at its peak Perkins went there to demonstrate his Tractor therapy - he died of yellow fever in two weeks after arriving in New York.

In 1771 the Swiss physician Franz Anton Mesmer (1753 - 1815) conceived the principals of magnetism in the human hand. In 1792 Luigi Galvani (1737 - 1798) of Bologna introduced the concept of therapies based on animal electricity.

Bismuth is commonly found as a contaminant of lead ore. Le'mery in the 1600's called it, "a compound made in England from the gross and impure tin found in English mines." The medical lexicographer John Quincy (d 1722) thought that "bismuth was composed of tin, tartar and arsenic, made in the north of Germany." It is this tight association with tin, lead and arsenic and other metals that has led to confusion about bismuths use in medicine. As current as 1818 the French toxicologist Mathieu-Joseph-Bonaventure Orfila (1787-1853) was warning of the dangers of arsenic poisoning from the internal administration of bismuth.

Georg Agricola (1490-1555), the German patriarch of mineralogy, called bismuth by its name in 1546 but it may have been isolated and identified as early as 1470. Agricola thought of bismuth as a form of lead; some alchemists of his time thought bismuth gradually transmutated to silver over time.

Alexander Marcet (1770-1822) of Guy's Hospital, London, had delivered a paper which, when published in 1805, had brought the oxide of bismuth ("magistrey of bismuth") to the general use of the medical profession. At that time it was chiefly used by the general public in cosmetics to whiten the complexion. Marcet and other physicians used it to treat dispepsia and ulcers - "In pyrosis (burning sensation in the stomach), cardialgia (heartburn) and other local afflictions of the stomach, the oxide of bismuth seems well calculated to afford relief."

The French physician Armond Trousseau (1801-1867) stated," when an individual in good health takes sub-nitrate of bismuth, the only phenomenon to be noticed is constipation, but the nervous functions, the animal heat, the movements of the heart, the urinary and cutaneous secretions are not influenced in an appreciable manner."

In 1868 Adolf Kussmaul used bismuth to treat gastric ulcers. Bismuth is still in general use today as an OTC (over the counter "drug") to soothe the irritated gastrointestinal tract, diarrhea and dispepsia as the tasty pink Pepto Bismol!! Bismuth in combination with tetracycline is claimed to be a cure for peptic ulcers caused by the bacteria *Helicobacter pylori* by the National Institutes of Health in 1994!!

Aqua Toffana, an aqueous solution of arsenic, was named after Toffa, a woman prisoner executed with arsenic in Naples in 1709. Arsenic was commonly used as a treatment for syphilis in the 1500's. Thomas Fowler of Staffordshire, England has been honored as the only author who has systematically treated and recorded the virtues of arsenic " Medical Reports on the Effects of Arsenic in the care of Argues, Remittent Fever and Periodic Headaches."

Benjamin Rush, M.D., a signer of the Declaration of Independence and this nation's first Surgeon General is famous for his statement:

"The Constitution of this Republic should make special provisions for Medical Freedom as well as Religious Freedom. To restrict the art of healing to one class of men and deny equal privileges to others will constitute the Bastille of medical science. All such laws are un-American and despotic."

Rush became aware of arsenicals in 1789. One of his students, Nathaniel Potter on returning to Philadelphia in 1792 told Dr. Rush of the wonders of arsenic as used in England. They used arsenic on herpetic eruptions with "good results after they had resisted the usual remedies." Rush also used arsenic to treat cancer.

Early in the 19th and late 18th centuries, physicians generally opposed the use of arsenic "because it was a poison." A most famous answer to these skeptics was put forth by Wm. Withering, " Poisons in small doses are the best medicines; and the best

medicine in too large doses are poisonous."
- appeared in A Botanical Arrangement of
all Vegetables Naturally Grown in Great
Britain According to the System of the Great
Linnaeus (1766).

Research in the medical uses of arsenic
remained very active until 1945 when penicillin came into general medical use and was
thought to be a superior treatment for syphilis with fewer side effects. Arsenic is still used
today for the systemic treatment of sleeping
sickness (Trypanosomiasis) and amoebic
diseases. It is now generally accepted that
arsenic is in fact in trace levels an essential
element for optimal health and longevity.

Erasmus Ebener (1509) of Nerenberg is
credited as the first to recognize metallic
zinc. Paracelsus named the new mineral
zinken:

> "There is another metal, zinc,
> which is in general unknown. It is a
> distinct metal of a different origin,
> though adulterated with many other
> metals. It can be melted, for it con-
> sists of three fluid principles, but it
> is not malleable. In its color it is un-
> like all others, and it does not grow
> in the same manner; but with its
> ultima materia I am as yet unac-
> quainted, for it is almost as strange
> in its properties as argentum vivum
> (quicksilver)."

In 1869 zinc was recognized as an essential nutrient for plants and animals, prior
to this time there were great debates as to
what zinc was:

> "Albertus Magnus held that it
> was combined with iron; Paracelsus
> leaned to the idea that it was copper
> in an altered form; Kunchel fancied

it was 'congealed mercury';
Schlutter thought it was tin rendered
fragile by combination with sulfur;
Le'mery supposed it was a form of
bismuth; Stahl held that brass was
a combination of copper with an
'Earth' (zinc) and phlogiston (fire);
Libavius (1597) described zinc as a
'peculiar' kind of tin!!!"

Joseph Lister (1827-1912) developed his
concept of antisepsis first trying zinc chloride but later turned to carbolic acid. Dr.
Campbell Morgan (1813-1876) surgeon to
the Middlesex Hospital, London used zinc
chloride after cancer surgery and amputa-
tions and reported, " in many cases wounds
have healed in 24 hours, without the least
fullness or swelling, and leaving a scar line
which after a short time could hardly be
seen or felt."

A severe drought was upon England
during the summer of 1618, Henry Wicker
of Epsom, a large village 17 miles south of
London, searched far and wide for a source
of water for his cattle. He found a small hole
filled with "bitter" water, he enlarged the
hole but the cattle refused to drink the foul
water. Before long this magnesium rich
spring was found to produce water that was
beneficial for external and internal medical use. For the next 10 years only the local
people used this healing spring; about that
time Lord Dudley North "under a melan-
choly disposition (constipation, depression), drank the mineral waters as a medicine and noted it to be a very effective purgative." "Epsom Water" was rapidly accepted as an internal remedy and purifier
of the blood. During the reign of Charles II
Epsom became a fashionable play ground
for the rich - so much so, that in 1690, the
Lord of the manor built a 70 foot long ball-

room. In 1695 a botanical histologist Nehemiah Grew (1641-1712) finally isolated magnesium sulfate from the Epsom water. By 1700 Epsom was averaging 2,000 daily visitors. Magnesium carbonate (magnesia alba) was admitted to the London Pharmacopoeia in 1787. In 1808 magnesium as the pure metal was isolated by the famous English chemist Humphry Davy (1788-1829). Davy also experimented with barium oxide, strontium oxide and calcium oxide (lime). Initially Davy called magnesium - magnium because " Magnesium has already been applied to metallic manganese."

In 1905 and 1906 Samuel James Meltzer (1851-1920) and his associate John Auer (1875-1948) at the Rockerfeller Institute researched the effects of magnesium salts on tetanus. They also demonstrated the anesthetic values of magnesium. In 1925 Edmond Meyer Lazard introduced IV injections of magnesium sulfate in eclampsia (convulsions of pregnancy). Veterinarians routinely use magnesium sulfate with chloral hydrate (Micky Finns') as a short acting anesthetic to geld horses.

Despite the endless historical support for minerals as essential nutrients and safe efficient therapies for human disease the allopathic medical profession relentlessly kept turning toward the more dramatic "therapies."

A classic example of the philosophy of the allopath in the face of a disease that can be relieved or cured by nutrition is the medical abuse of President George Washington who was suffering from influenza (dehydration and diarrhea) - chicken soup, some herbs (Echinacia, Goldenseal) and bismuth would have been a safe and effective approach for the Father of our Country, however, as you will see the descrip-

tion of the final agony of George Washington as he lay dying from his allopathic physicians attentions (Eclectic Gleaner, 1858) you are better off with a grandmothers approach than suffer the best medicine from the best physicians of the medical profession:

"Think of a man being, within the brief span of a little more than twelve hours, deprived of 80 or 90 ounces of blood (six pints); afterward swallowing two moderate American doses of calomel (mercury) and five or six grains of emetic tartar (antimony); vapors of water and vinegar frequently inhaled; blisters applied to his extremities (mercury); a cataplasm of bran and vinegar applied to his throat, upon which a blister had already been affixed, is it surprising that when thus treated the afflicted general, after various ineffectual struggles for utterance at length articulated a desire that he might be allowed to die without interruption?"

> "Those who now advocate eating natural foods as the only source of vitamins and minerals live in a dream world of yesterday. What was yesterdays law is todays folly. It really doesn't matter how well you balance your meals, or if you're a meat-eater, vegetarian, or a raw-foodist, you still run the risk of malnutrition if you try to get all your vitamins and minerals exclusively from the foods you eat."
>
> - Paavo Airola, PhD
> *The Airola Diet and Cook Book*

Chapter 3

OUR EARTH IS ANEMIC:
The Argument for Expensive Urine!

Our Earth is anemic!!!! A potentially apocalyptic mixture of mining, deforestation, farming, irrigation and acid rain has shifted, eroded or leached our life giving and life-sustaining raw materials from our formerly mineral rich land. Unfortunately we were given a finite amount of raw materials in the Earth's crust and without regular and large numbers of mineral rich meteors or volcanic eruptions (i.e.- Mt. St. Helens, eastern Washington; Mt. Pinatubo, Philippines, etc.) we are forced to make do with what we have. There are those who would remineralize mountain ranges, forests, farms and yes, whole continents to get minerals into our crops and therefore into our human food chain; but put into economic perspective these dreams are not sustainable. To remineralize the Earth is technically possible but as a realistic project would be an economic impossibility.

To remineralize the Earth for one growing season we would have to grind up the equivalent of Mauna Loa, the colossal Hawaiian mountain, each year and redistribute the resultant rock dust several times each year to coincide with soil preparation and planting. To comprehend the enormity of this task one has to appreciate that Mauna Loa is the most massive mountain in the world and is also the largest volcano; Mauna Loa rises 13,677 feet above the surface of the Pacific Ocean - an additional 17,000 feet drops from the water's surface to the ocean floor making it technically taller (almost 1 mile taller!) than Mt. Everest. Mauna Loa's total mass is 100 times larger than that of Mt. St. Helens in Washington state and the lava that forms the massive dome could cover the land masses of the Earth with four feet of additional mineral dust. As a result of such a Herculean effort your hamburger would reach the eye-popping price of $275 per pound and corn $35 per ear - how would that be for sticker shock!!

When Charles Darwin sailed the Beagle to the east coast of South America in 1833, he recorded a fine, red dust accumulating on his ship each day and correctly deduced that the dust originated in west Africa. This African dust in its westerly flight travels all the way to the Amazon and the rainforests where it is essential to replenishing the rain leached mineral poor soils of the rainforests annually! Man has always realized the enormity of the great and tireless power of the Earth's winds, but their importance to the biological vitality of the Earth and the mineral value of our food is far beyond what we have ever dreamed. There are many wind currents , east to west, that transport great loads of mineral dust across predictable routes, "linking ecosystems hundreds and even thousands of miles apart." Billions of tons of mineral rich dust from the deserts of Asia and Africa annually fertilize oceans and rainforests halfway around the world.

Michael Garstang, professor of meteorology at the University of Virginia in Charlottesville says, "During the violent Amazonian rainstorms, the particulates that originate in African deserts are literally sucked out of the sky." Garstang and his colleagues calculate that 13,000,000 tons of African and Asian mineral rich dust enter the Amazonian soils each season to enrich the rain leached and depleted tropical soils!!! The wind-borne African dust adds essential and critical minerals to help maintain the rainforests productivity. "While the Amazon Basin teems with life the soil itself lacks reserves of nutrients, especially phosphates, which spur plant growth. The historical record shows that the Amazon rainforest has periodically shrunk to a fraction of its present size, then bounded back

again, and the researchers now believe that it expands and contracts as the amount of nourishing African dust waxes and wanes with mirror changes in the Saharan desert."

The principle minerals found in the coarse inorganic fraction of soil are directly related to those minerals present in the local parent rock. Minerals that are resistant to weathering (i.e.- quartz) are especially abundant in soils while minerals that weather quickly are rare or are absent. It is therefore possible to calculate the relative age or maturity of a soil covering igneous rocks from its content of primary minerals (i.e.- feldspar, mica, amphiboles and pyroxenes); these relatively soluble minerals are common in young soil and less abundant in mature soils and absent from senescent soils. Soils covering sandstone often contain 90 to 99 % quartz; those soils overlying limestone are made up of as much as 80 % calcium carbonate.

It is obvious that minerals are not equally distributed in soils. The scary part is that fields where our food crops are grown do not contain a uniform blanket of minerals, if they contain any nutritional minerals at all, they occur in veins much like the chocolate swirls found in chocolate ripple ice cream - at best depending solely on getting minerals from food grown in soil is a very risky crap shoot!!

Trace elements are defined as those elements present in soils in amounts of less than 0.1 % by weight. Sixty percent of all trace minerals are found in the coarse inorganic fraction of the soil including Ba, Be, Co, Cr, Cu, Ga, La, Li, Mn, Mo, Ni, Pb, Rb, Se, Sr, V, Y and Zr.

Rare Earths refers to any of a large series of very similar oxides of metals obtained from widely distributed but relatively scarce minerals. The Rare Earth metals are often divided into three groups, according to the method of separating them:

1) **the cerium metals** (lanthanum, cerium, praseodymium, neodymium, illinium, samarium).

2) **the terbium metals** (europium, gadolinium, terbium).

3) **the yttrium or ytterbium metals** (dysprosium, holmium, erbium, thulium, yttrium, ytterbium, lutecium).

The atomic numbers of these Rare Earth metals (with exception of yttrium, considered by some not to be a true Rare Earth metal) are consecutive (from 57 to 71). Beryllium, hafnium, scandium, thorium and zirconium are also included as Rare Earths by some geochemists. Rare Earths added to laboratory animals diets as a supplement to the well recognized major and trace minerals have doubled the expected life span of the species. Human nutrition pundits recognize new nutrients as valuable for humans anywhere from 50 to 1000 years after they are recognized in animal nutrition. These Rare Earths, known to be so vital to animal health and longevity (and most probably our human health and longevity) are no longer found in our food supply in any consistent or significant amounts - the only warranty to adequate Rare Earth intake for us humans is daily supplementation!!

Basic soils tend to be rich in minerals whose ionic radius is close to that of magnesium, i.e.- Co, Cr, Cu, Fe, Mg, Ni, Se, Ti, V and Zn. Acidic soils containing feldspar that have ionic radius' close to silica, calcium or potassium, i.e. - Al, Ba, Ca, Cs, Hf, K, La, Na, Nb, Pb, Rb, Sr, Ta, Tl, Y and Zr, Limestones are rich in elements which form insoluble carbonates, i.e.- Ba, Ca, Mg, Mn, Pb and Sr.

Colloidal inorganic particles are referred to as clay; clay minerals are primarily aluminosilicates, many of which swell in water and act as ion exchangers. The hydrous (water) oxides of aluminum, iron and manganese are responsible for the natural colors of most clays, i.e.- blue, gray, red, orange, black; they also function as scavengers for phosphate and some trace minerals and Rare Earths:

Formulae of Common Clay Types			
Clay	**Formula**	**Source**	**Occurrence**
Muscovite	$K_2Al_2Si_6Al_4O_{20}(OH)_4$	Micas	Many soil types
Biotite	$K_2A_{12}Si_6(Mg_4Fe_2)O_{20}(OH)_4$	Micas	Many soil types
Vermiculite	$K_{1.1}Al_{2.3}Si_{5.7}Al_{0.5}Fe_{07}Mg_{4.8}O_{20}(OH)_4$	Micas	Many soil types
Montmorillonite	$K_{0.8}Al_{0.3}Si_{7.7}Al_{2.6}Fe_{0.9}Mg_{0.5}O_{20}(OH)_4$	Mica	Many soil types
Chlorite	$Fe_2Mg_8(OH)_{12}Si_6Al_4O_{20}(OH)_4$	Serpentine	Podzols, Deserts
Attapulgite	$Mg_5Si_8O_{20}(OH)_2(H2O)_8$	Basalt	Deserts
Halloysite	$Si_4Al_4O_{10}(OH)_8(H2O)_4$	Granite	Podzols, Tropical
Kaolinite	$Si_4Al_4O_{10}(OH)_8$	Granite	Podzols, Tropical

A good representative of a local or regional soil solution is river water (Table 1-2), which usually reflects the average composition of the soil solutions in water sheds they drain. In regions of high rainfall, soil elements are almost all leached from the soil (i.e.-rainforests and wet temperate zones); in acid soil, mineral elements concentrate in the surface layers, especially where saline (salt) water is drawn to the surface from subsoil by capillary action - this leads to the formation of crusts of sodium chloride ("salting"). The solubility of crystalline silica in distilled water is 6 ppm; silica ground to a particulate diameter of 0.0004 has a solubility of 30 ppm.

In well drained soils, the "soil atmosphere" is almost exactly equivalent to the atmosphere. In poorly drained soils the oxygen content declines and the carbon dioxide levels increase to 5-10 % by volume. In permafrost soils there is no free oxygen and the soil atmosphere consists of 80 % nitrogen and inert gases and 20 % carbon dioxide by volume.

The conversion of oxygen to carbon dioxide is caused by the microorganisms that decompose organic matter. There are basically two types of soil organisms - those that require oxygen (aerobic) and those that do not like oxygen and thrive best in reduced or zero oxygen levels (anaerobic). At less than 100 ppm oxygen the soil becomes anaerobic.

In addition to the large number of microscopic organic molecules, many of which dissolve in the soil solution, soils contain insoluble, polymeric organic matter known as humus. Humus is in dynamic equilibrium, being oxidized by some organisms and being formed from organic debris by others. Its structure and composition is not completely understood, but it is heterogeneous and contains 55 % carbon, 0.6 - 5.4 % non-basic nitrogen and small amounts of sulfur.

Humus particles are of colloidal dimensions and bind so strongly to particles of clay and hydrous oxides that it is difficult to separate them intact. The small organic particles in the soil include a great variety of acidic compounds. They are products of partial decomposition of organic polymers by bacteria and fungi and include the common amino acids, acetic acid, butyric acid, citric acid, formic acid, 2- keto gluconic acid, malic acid, oxalic acid, tartaric acid and a variety of lichen acids. These acids lower the ph (acidify) of the soil solution which increases the rate of dissolution of primary minerals and to chelate and thus make more soluble many inorganic elements including Al, Cu, Fe, Ni, P and Zn.

Resident organisms living in the soil are divided into three groups, i.e.- producers, predators and decomposers. Producers include algae and bryophytes which live on the exposed surface of the soil; and green vascular plants that have roots that penetrate from 0.1 to 50 meters or more into the Earth's crust. The green plants "fix" carbon dioxide from the air while the roots take up inorganic ions (minerals) from the soil solution and convert them to highly available plant colloidal minerals. Closed plants take up or "mine" 0.01 kg (10 mg) of minerals per square meter per year or approximately 48.4 grams per acre per year. Unless the entire plant is returned to the soil each year (as in leaf mulch or a tree falling and decomposing in the forest) the plant essentially "mines" the minerals from the soil (as in harvesting crops) to be carried off and used somewhere else, thus depleting the soil's native reserves of minerals.

The predators living in the soil include

armies of tiny arthropods, mites and springtails and lesser numbers of larger animals such as earth worms and grubs. They derive their nutrition from partially digested inorganic material, by further digesting the "soil" they release more elements from the organic mix which makes them more available for plants.

The decomposers are microorganisms which make up only a small fraction by weight of soil yet they are essential to soil health. Their metabolic processes are geared to aerobic decomposition of organic matter, however, they can and do oxidize or reduce a large number of inorganic soil constituents. Ancient exhausted soils (i.e.- oxisols and altisols), contain very little organic matter and are poor in minerals and plant nutrients; they are mainly either kailinite derived from granite and/or acidic rocks, or out of the hydrous oxides of gibbsite or goethite which are derived from basalt and/or basic rocks.

Soil conditioners such as animal manure, green manure (cover crops such as clover, beans, etc.), compost, humic shale, mulch and sphagnum moss increase the soil organic matter which feeds the soil organisms, increases the percentage of soil atmosphere and the water holding capacity which in turn increases the yield in tons and bushels per acre yet does little or nothing to increase the mineral content of the crops.

Rotating crops and "resting" the field every seventh year will increase the nitrogen levels of the soil and thus increases the yields in tons and bushels but does not appreciably increase the mineral content of the food grown on the fields. In the frozen tundra, the rates of weathering and of production of organic matter are very slow, and the soils (entisols) contain many primary minerals; they also contain high levels of organic matter since this is decomposed very slowly, especially in bogs:

"Ahu, from time immemorial the bogs have been worthless except for the snipe and the hare - and paddies like myself who work them for a winter's warmth."

On the surface, bogs are like a miniature forest of sphagnum mosses, heath and sedges; farmers have historically cut blocks of the black gelatinous peat from the depths and dried them to insulate their homes and fuel their fires. Found on all continents except Antarctica, bogs are predominantly found in the northern latitudes where withdrawing glaciers created depressed wetlands with little or no drainage. Bogs that are perpetually fed by springs are called "fens".

Wetlands, in their deep layers contain high levels of humic acids. In their unique anaerobic environment the extraordinarily well preserved remains of more than 2,000 humans have been found - most of them dating back 2,300 to 8,000 years ago. Waterlogged plants in the anaerobic environment of the bog are slow to decompose. Dead plant material accumulates and becomes "peat" - the precursor of coal. The sphagnum mosses actually produce large amounts of substances with "antibiotic" characteristics and create an acid environment. In many parts of New England and Wisconsin glaciers created "kettle" holes which filled in with peat vegetation.

A cross section of plants typically found in a peat bog and what they contribute to the bog ecosystem include:

Leather leaf - photosynthesis
Rosemary - photosynthesis
Orchids - are symbiotic with acid adapted fungi which release plant

nutrients from the peat.

Pitcher plant - catches insects for nitrogen (amino acid) source
Sundew - catches insects for nitrogen (amino acid) source
tea - folk & Indian medicine and food
Cranberry - folk & Indian medicine and food
False Soloman's seal - folk remedy for arthritis

Sphagnum moss is universally valued for agriculture and horticulture as a soil conditioner and a source of humic acids. Indians used the dried moss for baby diapers; in WW1 surgical dressings were made from the dried moss. Germany, Belgium, the Netherlands and Denmark have consumed nearly all of their native supply of commercially harvestable peat bogs. Generally, peat is low in minerals as the acid environment leaches the minerals from the surface layers into the deeper layers as they flow away from the bog with the exiting springs.

In coniferous forests the dead organic materials shed by the trees covers the soil where it is decomposed by fungi. The decomposition products include many organic acids which leach iron and aluminum out of the soils upper layers forming podzol or spodosol in the lower layers.

In deciduous forests the dead organic leaf litter on the forest floor is mixed with the surface layers of soil by earth worms, which are more numerous in deciduous forests than in the acid coniferous soils. The resulting soils are known as brown forest soils (inceptisols) which have a high content of clay and humus.

In grasslands the dead organic matter consists mainly of grass roots, which are intimately mixed with the soil. The rainfall is frequently too low to cause a leaching of the minerals, so the resulting virgin prairie soils tend to be rich in plant organic nutrients; they are known as chernozems or mollisols, and have a high content of clay and humus. In deserts and acid regions the covering vegetation of herbs, cactus and woody shrubs does not cover the soil surface and does not return much organic matter to the soil. The low rainfall results in little or no leaching; the rate of clay formation in the desert soil is very low. Soluble inorganic soil constituents tend to accumulate in closed natural basins or salt lakes (The Great Salt Lake or The Salten Sea). These desert soils are known as serozems or aridisols.

Plants and animals that accumulate and concentrate unusual amounts of minerals are known as accumulator organisms (Table 3-1).

As far as supplements go, vitamins have historically "gotten the glory" and minerals were mere stepchildren in the "multiple vitamin" - everyone asks, "Dear, did you take your vitamins today?" Of course they mean, "Dear, did you take your multiple vitamins and minerals today?" As a result of minerals being found historically free in nature or bone meal and thus accessible to most everyone, the medical community rarely looks at minerals as something to prescribe or recommend.

Minerals, however are in fact required by any and all body functions from the basic subcellular molecular biological "metallic fingers" of RNA and DNA to electrochemical, catalytic, structural, reproduction, maintenance, repair and a plethora of miscellaneous functions.

As important as minerals are to human flesh and the very existence of man, human-kind has placed more value on ma-

Table 3-1 .Known Accumulator Organisms

Al	Club mosses or lycophytes	Fe	Bacteria, plankton and horse tails
As	Brown algae & coelenterates	I	Diatoms, brown algae, sponges,
B	Brown algae & sponges		coelenterates and marine annelids
Br	Brown algae, sponges, coelenterates and molluscs	Mn	Ferns and marine crustaceans
		Na	Soft ceolenterates
Ca	Protozoa, sponges, coelenterates, echi noderms, molluscs and vertebrates	Si	Horse tails, diatoms, protozoa and sponges
Cl	Soft coelenterates	V	Ascidians
Cu	Annelids, orthropods and molluscs	Y	Ferns
F	Vertebrates	Zn	Coelenterates

chines, futures, stocks and bonds, hospitals, space travel, light weight metals for jet planes, fat free diets and bans on smoking than on our metabolic need for minerals themselves.

The scary part is we have had official warnings since 1936 (58 years ago)!!!U.S. Senate Document # 264, published by the 2nd session of the 74th Congress (1936) stated:

"Do you know that most of us today are suffering from certain dangerous diet deficiencies which cannot be remedied until the depleted soils from which our foods come are brought into proper mineral balance ? "

"The alarming fact is that foods - fruits and vegetables and grains, now being raised on millions of acres of land that no longer contains enough of certain needed minerals, are starving us - no matter how much of them we eat! "

"You'd think, wouldn't you, that a carrot is a carrot - that one is about as good as another as far as nourishment is concerned? But it isn't; one carrot may look and taste like another and yet be lacking in the particular mineral element which our system requires and which carrots are supposed to contain."

"Laboratory tests prove that the fruits, the vegetables, the grains, the eggs, and even the milk and the meats of today are not what they were a few generations ago (which doubtless explains why our forefathers thrived on a selection of foods that would starve us!)."

"No man of today can eat enough fruits and vegetables to supply his stomach with the mineral salts he requires for perfect health, because his stomach isn't big enough to hold them!"

"It is bad news to learn from our leading authorities that 99 % of the American people are deficient in these minerals, and that a marked deficiency in any one of the more important minerals actually results in disease. Any upset of the balance, any considerable lack of one or another element, however microscopic the body requirement might be, and we sicken, suffer, and shorten our lives."

"Lacking vitamins, the system can make some use of minerals, but lacking minerals, vitamins are useless."

There are those who would say that the statements in U.S. Senate Document # 264 are out of date and not relevant to today as we have better analytical tools to find nutrients in the soil we couldn't find 58 years ago. Yes, we have better and more accurate tools with which to measure minerals in our farm and range soils today; however, the mineral content continues to deteriorate at an ever accelerating pace as a result of farming, grazing, irrigating and acid rain. This means that if we depend solely upon our food for our daily share of minerals for our bodies requirements, we have less of a chance of accomplishing it than winning the $100,000,000 lottery or a Las Vegas "Crap Shoot."

In June of 1992, an Earth Summit Report was issued in Rio that documented the decline in numbers of various rare and endangered species, enlarging holes in the ozone layer, disappearence of tropical rain forests and indigenous peoples - yet the most important and immediate crisis facing the human race was glossed over and relegated to the rear pages of the voluminous report - the decline of nutritional minerals in farm and range soils by continent over the last hundred years.

The findings of the Earth Summit Report are staggering in face of the percentages of decline of mineral values over the last hundred years and they in fact give numerical weight to what was reported in U.S. Senate Document # 264 - 58 years earlier!! The results of the Earth Summit Report on the decline of mineral values in our farm and range soils show that North America (United States, Canada and Mexico) is far more affected than all other continents:

	Minerals
Continent	% Depleted over 100 years
Africa	74 %
Asia	76 %
Australia	55 %
Europe	72 %
North America	85 %
South America	76 %

How could American soils become so anemic ? Don't we fertilize ? What about organically grown food ? To understand our planets plight we have to understand soil, water and our human agricultural history, for man with all his progress makes the same mistake over and over and over again!!!

"How readily we manipulate our soil. We rearrange and restructure it. We pump it full of chemicals, we flood it, we drain it. On its health the fate of empires has rested. Yet we avoid it. In our cities, rivers of concrete keep us from its touch. Naked it tends to offend the eye. But a close look reveals that the soil is an essential bridge between the rock below and the life above. It is dynamic and vital, and far too easily - and frequently abused."

- Boyd Gibbons
National Geographic

In the 4,000 years between the formation of the first nation-states and the early

Christian era, the Earth's human population increased from approximately 87 million to 225 million. Eighty percent of these peoples lived under the cruel military heel of the Romans, Chinese Han or the Indian Grupa Empires. The populations of the core areas (the seats of government and enterprise) closely associated with the great river valleys did not rise without population curbs during their 4,000 years of development. There was a finite limit to how many humans and animals could be supported and crowded into the fertile flood plains (high mineral silt) of Egypt, Mesopotamia, India and China.

Outside these core areas of growth and development, populations continued to increase as larger empires and additional secondary and tertiary empires arose; however, one by one the original core areas eventually reached the upper limits of what populations they could support. Our most reliable information on ancient population dynamics comes from ancient Chinese population figures that accurately span more than 2,000 years. Authoritative census data shows that for the period A.D. 2 to A.D. 742 China's total average population hovered at 50 million with peaks of 58 million and lows of 48 million.

"Century after century the standard of living in China. Northern India, Mesopotamia, and Egypt hovered slightly above or below what might be called the threshold of pauperization. When population density in a particular region climbed too high, standards of living dipped below the subsistence threshold. This led to wars, famines, and population decline; With lower densities, the standard of living would rise more to a point slightly above the long-term average."

China's population growth rate hovered at nearly zero for almost 2,000 years. After 1450, however, the bounty of food in terms of tons produced by the introduction of new varieties of rice, sweet potatoes and American Indian corn allowed the Chinese population to increase again.

Modern population experts are amazed by the "stationary" characteristic of the human populations of dynastic cultures. Kings, emperors, pharaohs and their courts appeared and disappeared every ten years or so. Dynasties rose and fell; however, the plight of the coolie, ryots, and fellahin went on endlessly, just a tad above the subsistence level. The old empires were "warrens" packed with illiterate peasants laboring from before dawn to after dark to produce only a marginal high carbohydrate low protein vegetarian diet, hardly better off than their livestock. It is interesting (and worrisome) to note that these near starving totalitarian states survived for thousands of years longer than any other form of government known to date which illustrates the fact that there is no warranty in "progressive" human cultures that ensure material or moral gain!

Each ancient culture developed their unique fabric of social life. Yet for all their dissimilarities, China, India, Mesopotamia and Egypt shared almost identical forms of political economy. They each had a centralized class of bureaucrats and lineage for despotic lords claiming mandates from heaven or that they were themselves gods. Governments provided communication by building and maintaining roads and canals to link rivers to far flung villages. The "state was stronger than society." The government's right to collect taxes, take materials and conscript humans for beasts of burden was without limit.

Censuses were carried out village by

village to estimate availability of labor and taxable population bases; governments sent forth great armies to construct huge state projects such as tombs, pyramids, defensive barriers and palaces of gargantuan proportion and design. In Egypt alone 100,000 people were required to carry out the projects of the Old Kingdom; a conscripted labor force of 84,000 was raised to work for 80 days each year for 20 years to build the Great Pyramid of Cheops.

China used a million men at each season to build the Great Wall; a second million labored to build the Grand Canal - over 2,000,000 per month were put to labor in the construction of the Sui Dynasty's Eastern capital and imperial palace during the reign of Emperor Yang (A.D. 604-617).

The ancient empires shared another feature - each was a "hydrolic society." They developed in arid or semiarid plains and valleys fed and more importantly periodically flooded by great rivers that originated in high rocky snow covered mountains or rain forests. By means of dams, canals, flood control, and drainage projects, governments delivered water and mineralized silt to the peasants fields. Applied in steady and unlimited amounts relatively high ´ yields of highly mineralized grain per acre were possible as long as the primary river flooded annually! The larger the river, the larger the food production potential of the area through which it flowed (i.e.- Nile, Yangtze, Ganges, Themes, Danube, Mississippi, Missouri, Ohio, etc.). However, the larger the river - the greater were the problems in harnessing its potential. The dynastic governments and empires constructed huge networks of ponds and canals, ditches, dams, levees and drainage ditches in attempts to regulate and control flow of water and silt.

The scale of the hydrolic projects required literally changing the face of the Earth - leveling mountains, modifying river banks, digging and directing new river beds to change the course of the river. The herculean task of conscripting labor, overseeing construction, feeding and housing the armies of humans required for such tasks could only be carried out by the state working to a single master plan.

The unique capacity of hydrolic states to recover regardless of regular dynastic collapse, civil war and invasions by hordes of barbarians is a characteristic of the symbiosis between their political structures and their ecological adaptation.

The enormous size and endless lists of complex new rules and laws passed by the emperor gave lords and high ranking state officers and the lesser bureaucrats an environment in which they could quench their own greed at the expense of their constituents (kind of sounds like the American government doesn't it!!!). Even if the supreme ruler was just and benificent the bureaucracy fattened themselves at the expense of the general population.

Corruption grew geometrically with the number of years the dynasty or empire stayed in power. Public works projects became neglected, dikes sprung leaks, canals became choked with undistributed silt and agricultural production declined. Incompetence in maintenance, human error and natural catastrophes added to the political erosion - a reigning dynasty or empire could no longer support the vast armies required to protect their borders and maintain internal order.

Ripped by internal strife the empire became vulnerable to the barbarian hordes from outside the walls, to the expansionist dreams of their, now stronger neighbors and their own disenchanted peasant masses - the dynasty or empire then collapsed. Famine, poverty, plagues, mass burials or cremation, rotting corpses, mass suicides, cannibalism, anarchy, hundreds of thousands of refugees set out to find new prosperity and safety, civil war, riots and wide spread looting were common, roving gangs and deserters from the armies prayed on the populace as well as looted public and royal tombs (Somalia, Rwanda, Haiti, Bosnia-Serbia, Easter Island, etc.).

Regardless of who came to power and ran the new state, if they wanted to enjoy the benefits of winning the war and taking over the territory, their first task would have to be repairing the dikes, dredging the silt and reed choked canals, reconstructing crumbled levees and breathing new life into the basic hydrolic form of agriculture. This cycle was repeated over and over- water and silt were so basic and so important to life itself that drawings on the mace head of the Scorpian King illustrates in 3100 B.C. the ruler at a ground breaking ceremony for a new irrigation canal!

The New World had its hydrolic societies too, including the pre-Columbian mesoamerican cultures of the coasts and highlands of Peru who built complex terrace and aqueduct irrigation systems as well as by the Teotihuacan and the Aztecs' cannibal societies of the Valley of Mexico. These hydrolic societies cultivated maize, potatoes and blue-green algaes as carbohydrate sources - their soils lacked the minerals required to raise livestock and maintain human health so they developed complex ritualistic cannibal societies to justify the wholesale consumption of human flesh and bones as their main protein and mineral source.

The settling of the Americas by Europeans introduced dry land farming that relied on rain and snow as water sources for agriculture - land was free for the taking all one had to do was clear the forests or plow the prairies. Unfortunately, without the annual flooding and supply of silt supplied in the great flood plains of the hydrolic societies and smaller river bottoms the land "played out" in five to ten years forcing the small farm family to pack up and move west to new still "virgin" or untilled soils.

The first signs that the soil was "played out" did not appear as obvious changes in the crops, but rather in the humans and livestock relying on the land as a food source. The newborn infants, calves, lambs and pigs were underweight, weak and died, the women, cows, ewes and sows became infertile, pneumonia and flu killed people and animals of all ages during the winter, adult humans and animals died of new unheard of diseases many years before their expected time for death. To escape these terrible places of death and despair people unceremoniously packed up and left.

Those who could not or would not leave their exhausted homesteads finally observed declines in production, followed by outright crop failure, erosion and dust bowl formation. This scenario occurred over and over on small individual farms of America finally culminating in a total ecological collapse that produced the great dust bowls of Oklahoma, Texas, Nebraska, Iowa and Kansas in the 1930's.

The problem of the soil "playing out" was not a mystery but an accepted part of the process of life and death in dry land farming plains communities. There were numerous ways in which to slow the process including the biblical method of letting the land rest every seventh year, the application of animal manure to replace used up organic matter, green manure (plant debris or ground cover crops grown to specifically protect against wind erosion, hold moisture and add nitrogen to the soil), composting plant and animal wastes to add to the humus of the soil and the application of guano (large quantities of nitrogen rich droppings from shore birds) and lastly the commercial fertilizers. These procedures and applications only slowed or delayed the process of crop failure while initially keeping tonnage and bushel production up.

While nearly all farmers understand the necessity to maintain the optimal level of organic material and humus in their fields to sustain tonnage production, very few realize the slow insidious leaching and depletion of the life giving minerals (mining) from their land - after all we pay them for tons and bushels not for an analysis of minimal levels of various minerals in each carrot, potato, broccoli or bushel of wheat or rice! This belief is summed up in a statement by a professor of soils from Iowa State College of Agriculture Henry Cantwell Wallace (George Washington Carver's favorite teacher and editor of the Wallace's Farmer), "Nations endure only as long as their topsoil." The statement should relay the message that " Nations endure only as long as nutritional minerals are available in their top soils!"

An interesting side note is that George Washington Carver would take Wallace's grandson for walks in the woods and fields to talk about plants — that boy later became the Secretary of Agriculture and then went on to become the Vice President of the United States two years before Carvers death.

George Washington Carver was born a slave just before the outbreak of the Civil War - Carver grew up on bottom land near Diamond Grove, Missouri in the foothills of the Ozark Mountains in southwestern Missouri and knew the value of silt and river muck. He realized that mono cropping or growing a single crop over and over, season after season sped up the loss of fertility and thus production.

In the post Civil War South, that "ol' debbil cotton" was the primary cash crop; as a mono crop it quickly mined the soil of mineral nutrition and production fell precipitously adding to the misery of the war drained South. In an experimental plot, Carver observed that the production of the land could be increased many fold over commercial fertilizers by folding into the soil dropped leaves from the forests, rich muck from the swamps (silt) and simple barn yard manure.

Carver also learned that increasing the nitrogen in the soil by rotating crops actually enhanced production in terms of tons and bushels. By finding numerous uses for the peanut (everything from lubricating oils for machinery to peanut butter) Carver was able to quickly encourage crop rotation as a general farm practice and thus brought back the agricultural industry of the Old South for both food and cash crops.

Dealing with silt, muck and manure is a messy smelly business at best so it was not too difficult for the fertilizer industry to woo the farmers and ranchers into using convenient liquid or pelleted chemical fertilizers containing N P K. The letters N P K represent nitrogen, phosphorous and potassium - primary nutrients required by crops to give the farmer a maximum yield per acre of land in terms of tons and bushels.

Percentages of the three nutrients, N P K, in fertilizers will vary with the type of crop but the basic fertilizer since the turn

Global Food Shortage Looms, Experts Say

By DONNA K. H. WALTERS
TIMES STAFF WRITER

Unless more attention—and money—are focused on agricultural research and conservation, the tragic famine in Somalia will seem "infinitesimal" compared with the massive food shortage the world will face by the end of the decade, leading agricultural researchers warned Friday at a symposium in Washington on food, poverty and the environment.

Even as a United Nations-led network of research centers begins work with relief agencies on the difficult process of restoring Somalia's devastated agricultural system, other scientists in the network are focusing on farming techniques and crops designed to safeguard and enhance the world's vulnerable food supplies.

At the symposium, which drew agriculture experts from around the world, announcements of progress in farming techniques and crop breeding were the hopeful spots amid dire predictions that by the year 2000, the annual shortfall in food needed to feed the world's hungry could climb to 90 million tons—eight times the shortage that exists in sub-Saharan Africa today.

"In eight years, sub-Saharan Africa will have a shortfall of 50 million tons, and there's no way they can afford to import that much food," said Per Pinstrup-Andersen, director general of the International Food Policy Research Institute, which sponsored the symposium.

Dramatic improvements in crop yields will be needed in the next 20 years to stave off disastrous starvation, Pinstrup-Andersen said. A

> **'In eight years, sub-Saharan Africa will have a shortfall of 50 million tons.'**
>
> **PER PINSTRUP-ANDERSEN**
> *Agricultural researcher*

40% increase in production per acre is possible, he said, but not if the worldwide network of agricultural research centers continues to be starved for funds.

Annual international assistance to developing countries for agricultural programs fell to $10 billion from $12 billion during the 1980s, and individual governments' support for their own research and conservation programs has fallen even more sharply.

Key advances in production of rice, the staple food for 1.5 billion people in developing countries, were announced by Gustavo Nores, director general of the International Center for Tropical Agriculture in Cali, Colombia.

Nores said the center has developed a "rice-pasture" farming technique for use on savannas that could ease encroachment into Amazon rain forests. The system uses a new rice that can be grown on grassland used for cattle grazing.

In addition, a team of scientists from the Colombian center and Purdue University has made what could be a significant breakthrough in conquering rice blast, a disease that has long frustrated researchers, Nores said.

Such advances often rely on stores of seeds and plant materials in "seed banks" throughout the world. Many of those stores are increasingly endangered, the symposium was told.

The situation is grave at the Vavilov Institute in St. Petersburg, Russia, the grandfather of all seed banks and once the most important collection of plant materials in the world. Seed collections throughout Eastern Europe are also in dire straits, said Geoffrey Hawtin, director general of the International Board of Plant Genetic Resources.

"These governments are so strapped for cash, they're talking about staff cuts of 20% to 70%," Hawtin said.

Rwandan exodus

By Reid G. Miller, AP

FLEEING BLOODBATH: Thousands of Rwandans cross the border into Tanzania, seeking refuge from the carnage in their homeland; tribal warfare has taken at least 100,000 lives. An estimated 250,000 people have fled, and relief workers fear they are just the first wave. **(U.S. military help sought, 4A)**

220,000 fleeing Rwandans fed

REUTERS

NGARA, Tanzania — Aid agencies distributed food to 220,000 Rwandan refugees in Tanzania yesterday and an aid worker said as many as 700 corpses were floating down the border river every 24 hours.

Officials said enough food was handed out from the International Committee of the Red Cross (ICRC) for 220,000 refugees who came into northwest Tanzania within 24 hours from last Thursday.

The United Nations estimates the number of refugees who arrived through the Rusomo bridge border-crossing point at more than 250,000, but says most were in good health and were members of Rwanda's majority Hutu tribe.

Bloated corpses have been floating down the rain-swollen Kagera River from the Rwandan interior for more than a week.

Some refugees say the bodies are those of members of Rwanda's Tutsi minority killed by extremist Hutu militiamen.

International aid agencies are building what is expected to be the largest refugee camp in the world, 11 miles west of the border, for the thousands who fled after Rwandan troops abandoned the border crossing and before rebels captured it.

Also yesterday, an ICRC spokesman said 18 people were killed when at least two mortar bombs exploded late Sunday near the Saint Famille church complex in the Rwandan capital of Kigali.

U.N. peacekeepers did not know the source of the fire, which came during one of the heaviest days of shelling of the city since civil war broke out.

In other developments:

■ The rebel Rwandan Patriotic Front said it will not take part in any U.N. efforts to resolve the Rwanda crisis until the U.N. special representative has left the country. The statement said U.N. special envoy Jacques-Roger Booh-Booh of Cameroon has "behaved in a very partisan manner."

■ The White House said it is sending two envoys to countries bordering Rwanda in an effort to get talks started to end the fighting. The United States also pledged $15 million toward a U.N. emergency relief fund.

■ The U.S. ambassador to the United Nations, Madeleine Albright, said Washington will call for an international arms embargo against Rwanda, but she ruled out sending any U.S. forces to the area.

■ Kofi Annan, the U.N. under-secretary-general in charge of peacekeeping, told a U.S. Senate subcommittee he doubted the Organization of African Unity was capable of mounting a peacekeeping operation in Rwanda.

Planet at biological limit? Troubling evidence cited

The Associated Press

Slowed growth in world food supplies provides real evidence that the planet's biological limits may have been reached, an environmental group says.

Among the signs: a three-month doubling of world rice prices, millions of acres of rangeland chewed down to uselessness, spreading water shortages and an $80,000 tuna.

"As a result of our population size, consumption patterns, and technology choices, we have surpassed the planet's carrying capacity," Worldwatch said in its 11th annual "State of the World" report on global environmental and social conditions.

The growing pressure on world food resources points to hungry times ahead as Third World populations continue to explode, said the report, released Saturday.

For more than two decades, scientists have been saying that the world can produce enough food to feed all its inhabitants, that hunger problems can be solved by increasing yields and improving distribution.

But this new report says family planners, not farmers or scientists, hold the key to future food supplies.

Lester Brown, Worldwatch president, said in an interview that his staff of economists and social scientists has been noticing the trend for a few years now, but the critical picture only came into focus with this year's research and analysis. Worldwatch, whose report is being published in 27 languages, is a private, non-profit research group.

Without radical scientific breakthroughs, large increases in crop yields that have allowed production to keep up with 40 years of rising consumption will probably not be possible, Brown said.

"Human demands are approaching the limits of oceanic fisheries to supply fish, of rangelands to support livestock and, in many countries, of the hydrological cycle to produce fresh water," Brown said in the report.

The study notes that from 1950 to 1984, world grain production grew 260 percent, raising per-capita production by 40 percent. Over the same period, the world's waterways yielded so much fish that the seafood catch per person doubled.

"But in recent years, these trends in food output per person have been reversed with unanticipated abruptness," the report said.

It points to several trends:

● Fish harvests from the world's oceans have leveled off at about 100 million tons a year, which may not be exceeded. Brown noted that seafood prices are rising rapidly, and a bluefin tuna can now bring as much as $80,000, or more than $100 a pound.

● Water bodies are increasingly polluted and fresh water shortages are occurring in the United States, Mexico, China, India and the Mideast.

● Grain production has slowed dramatically in the last few years, with per-capita output of rice, corn and wheat falling 11 percent since 1984. Worldwide stocks of rice are at 20-year lows, and the price on the Chicago Board Trade has doubled since Aug. 30.

● Fertilizer use has dropped 12 percent since 1989, evidence that maximum yields may have been reached for many crops.

● Cropland has increased only 2 percent over the last decade worldwide, with topsoil disappearing and some areas such as China rapidly losing farmland to industrialization.

● Overgrazing, deforestation and agricultural mismanagement have ruined 5 million acres since 1945.

While some of the limits may be good news for agriculture and the fishing industries, which can expect higher prices, they are bad news for millions of people.

U.S. Fishing Fleet Trawling Coastal Water Without Fish

By TIMOTHY EGAN
Special to The New York Times

SEATTLE, March 6 — For the volunteers who count fish returning from the sea to fresh water, this has been the loneliest year ever. The surging Pacific salmon and steelhead are gone; what the fish counters at the Puget Sound ship locks see when they stare at the glass wall separating them from the water is nothing but a reflection of their own faces.

Across the country, in Gloucester and New Bedford, Mass., the story is the same. After 350 years, the oldest American fishing area is largely barren of the great swarms of haddock, cod and flounder that sustained more than 10 generations of New Englanders and became millions of fish sticks.

The Atlantic fishermen have asked that the Government treat them like earthquake disaster victims. Last week, they honked their boat horns in Boston Harbor to draw attention to their plight. To some, it was a funeral dirge.

Echoes of a Sad Song

From Chesapeake Bay, where oystermen are fading like fog in the afternoon sun, to the Gulf of Mexico, where grouper and red snapper are mostly a memory, people who pull fish from the sea for a living are singing the same sad song.

Government officials say most of the major commercial fishing areas in this country outside Alaska are in trouble, and worldwide, 13 of the 17 principal fishing zones are depleted or in steep decline.

As for salmon in the Pacific Northwest, and three main commercial species in New England, the decline is catastrophic — threatening to wipe out not only whole industries but also cultures and communities that are fused to the cycles of tide and sea currents.

A Year Without Salmon

For the first time, there may be no ocean salmon fishing on the West Coast this year, a situation roughly akin to Georgia not producing any peaches.

Fishing communities in Massachusetts are in such bad shape that Gov. William F. Weld last week requested emergency financial aid from the Federal Government. Thousands of fishermen are in "immediate danger" of losing their homes and boats this spring, Mr. Weld said.

But aside from devotees of wild fish, consumers may not notice a shortage of fish at the supermarket. In recent years, farm fish raised in pens in Norway or South America have flooded the market, driving down the price of fish.

In some cases, the lowered prices have led fishermen to harvest more ocean fish in compensation. About 40 percent of the

Continued on Page A10, Column 1

Declining Fish Catches

The Magnuson Act, passed in 1976, regulates fishing in United States waters. Commercial catches since the act:

Chinook salmon on the West Coast, not including Alaska.

5.00 million fish
3.75
2.50
1.25
0

'76 '80 '85 '90'92

The primary commercial species, or "groundfish" — mostly cod, haddock and founder:

200 thousand tons of fish
150
100
50
0

'76 '80 '85 '90'92

Source: National Marine Fisheries Service

The New York Times

of the century has been N P K. It only takes 5 to 10 years for agriculture to "mine" the minerals from the soil by cropping. Irrigation while providing water for increased production in terms of tons and bushels actually speeds up the leaching of nutritional minerals from the land and the rate of mineral "mining" by the rapidly growing crops. This has gone on for over 100 years and now we are "paying the piper" in spades in the form of increased rates of degenerative diseases.

Our Earth is anemic! In short this means we can no longer get the 60 nutritional minerals we need from our food and if we are to sustain ourselves and our children physically and mentally we must very consciously supplement our daily intake of food with the 60 nutritional minerals just as we consciously make sure our Mercedes has the finest motor oil in it!

It is projected that by the year 2100 there will be more than 12 billion people on this Earth - there is no way that our farm soils can sustain the nutritional value of our soils, our food or ourselves. Genetic engineering, better varieties of wheat, rice and corn and perhaps even better fertilizer will produce more tons and bushels of crops that are tastier and have longer shelf life ("Frankenfoods") - but they will not sustain us, they will not prevent birth defects, they will not nurture our babies and they will not forestall learning deficits or antisocial or criminal behavior.

"A food craving is like love at first sight. It's instantly recognizable, but veiled in mystery. Whether you crave a granola bar or a burger, substitutes will leave you wanting; a bowl of granola is not a granola bar, and a meatball is not a burger. Cravings demand the real thing. Unlike hunger, cravings - if unindulged - will persist on a full stomach. All I know was I wanted it, lusted for it, I had to have it."

-Joan Goldberg
American Health

Chapter 4

PICA & CRIBBING (Cravings & Binges)

Obesity and overweight problems are synonymous with Americans. Nibble, nibble, nibble all the way home. "Pica" is a seeking, a craving with licking and chewing behavior that has its genesis in mineral deficiencies - interestingly enough neither vitamin deficiency, protein deficiency or calorie deficiency initiates this "pica" behavior, nor will supplementing vitamins or eating sugar, carbohydrate, fat or protein quench it!!!

Since American soils are critically deficient and depleted in minerals it is no surprise that pica, cribbing and cravings dominate the American scene. America is minerally deficient - dieters, athletes, vegetarians, meat eaters, embryos, children, teenagers, young adults and seniors.

The snack food and fast food industries are aware of this relationship between pica, cribbing, cravings, sugar binges and salt hunger and they use it to their advantage by liberally salting or sweetening their products. Unfortunately for us our bodies temporarily translates sugar and salt consumption as a fulfillment of the craving for nutritional minerals (i.e.- if we lack iron, salt or sugar will temporarily satisfy our pica behavior initiated by the iron deficiency).

Historically, the consumption of salt to satisfy a pica behavior was of value because salt was not processed and did often times contain trace minerals and Rare Earths. Today, salt consumption, although contrary to popular belief, is not in and of itself harmful; it does present the problem of allowing our bodies to think we are getting minerals (the equivalent of the "empty calorie diets", i.e.- processed food calories without vitamins).

Farmers and husbandryman use the salt hunger of animals to ensure the consumption of trace minerals by incorporating trace minerals in salt blocks containing 85% salt - anything less than 85% sodium chloride in a salt block will be ignored by the animals even if they have major mineral deficiencies!!

"Cribbing" is a name given to a particular form of pica in domestic animals. A good husbandryman knows when a horse (Fig. 4-1) or cow "cribs" (chews or gnaws on a wooden feed box, fence, hitching post or barn door), the animal really has a craving for minerals. Such mineral starved animals will at first eat large amounts of supplemental minerals until they are satisfied, then they will automatically reduce their level of consumption to a maintenance level.

"Salt appetite" is very striking in both pregnant animals and humans. Bizarre cravings are legendary in the pregnant human. From antiquity, the description of cravings or "pica" in humans relates its major incidence to pregnant women. The Hawaiian King Kamehameha's mother, Queen Kekuiapoiwa had cravings for eyeballs, although she specifically wanted chiefs eyes, she was given the eyes of sharks to eat.

We have seen a hundred pregnant sheep in Montana lined up along an embankment eating clay (this is a form of pica known as "geophagia" or earth eating geophagia is very common in minerally deficient pregnant humans).

Pica, or perverted appetite or irresistible cravings with the eating of bizarre or unsuitable nonfood substances (or fattening non-foods) has been a curiosity for philosophers, doctors and priests for thousands of years. Pica as a symptom of mineral deficiencies is universal in the world and has been reported in animals and humans of all age groups. In modern times the easy availability of candy, sugared - high calorie snacks, soft drinks and junk foods has led to obesity when people feel the deep cravings of pica.

A doctoral thesis on pica by Agustus Fridericus Mergiletus (1701) begins with the definition of pica: " The malady pica is called "kitta" in Greek. Its derivation comes from the name of the common magpie because the bird ("pica" is the Latin name for "magpie") itself is believed to suffer from some malady ... because it flits from tree to tree constantly seeking food or because it enjoys all sorts of foods."

A catalogue of bizarre instances of pica is found in Mergiletus' thesis. In men, he recorded one individual who ate leather, wood, nestlings and live mice (sounds like an initiation into a fraternity); a second consumed woolen garments, leather, a live cat, and some mice; a third ate cats' tails and decomposed human bodies with maggots!!

In Mergiletus' female subjects he recorded women who ate human flesh including one particularly horrible lady -"she lured children with sweets, killed them and pickled them for her daily fare (sounds like a female version of Jeffrey Dahmer). The murders were only discovered when the woman's cat stole the pickled hand of a child and carried it over to the neighbors house."

The most common description of pica by Mergiletus were of women's desire for mud and mortar scrapped from walls (just like modern children who eat caulking and lead paint - we have often said that children who eat lead paint (Fig. 4-2) are screaming for minerals for their mineral starved bodies - give them minerals and they won't eat lead paint); girls who ate their own hair; girls who ate cotton, thread from their own clothes, raw grain and lizards.

Mergiletus also described pica in animals including cats that ate wood ash and pregnant hunting dogs that ate unusual objects.

Cooper (1957) in her classic report on

Fig. 4-1 Hitching rail chewed by mineral deficient horses ("pica" or "cribbing").

Fig. 4-2 Lead paint chips in stomach contents of a dead baboon
that chewed zoo cage bars.

pica refers to several ancient and medieval writers who emphasized the occurrence of pica in pregnant women, i.e. - Aetios noted pregnant women to crave various and odd foods, some salty and some acid; some, he said "crave for sand, oyster shells and wood ashes." Aetios recommended a diet including "fruits, green vegetables, pigs feet, fresh fish and old tawny fragrant wine."

Boezo (1638) noted that pica occurred most often in pregnant women. Boezo saw pica as a physiological problem, and is the first to mention iron preparations as a treatment for pica - he suggested "one and one half scruples of iron dross taken for many days as wonderfully beneficial for men and women." Boezo also noted "the case of a virgin who was accustomed to devour salt in great quantities from which chronic behavior she developed diarrhea and wasting (Addison's Disease ?)."

Christiani of Frankfurt (1691) reported a woman who ate 1400 salt herrings during her pregnancy. LeConte (1846) suggested that animals eating earth do so because of "want of inorganic elements."

In modern times, the substances frequently reported as eaten as a result of pica behavior in humans includes paper, metallic gum wrappers, ice, dirt, coal, clay, chalk, starch, baking powder, pebbles, wood, plaster, paint, chimney soot, hair, human and animal feces (kitty litter box!) and cloth. Because of social constraints on our public behavior most people under public scrutiny who display pica eat sugar, snack food or soft drinks when they crave minerals - many smoke, drink alcohol or use street (or prescription) drugs in an attempt to satisfy a nagging underlying craving.

Ice eating (pagophagia) is also common, especially for iron deficient children and adults.

Worms have been reported as a cause of pica - Ankylostomiasis, ascariasis, oxyuriasis and others have been blamed. Parasites of course can cause anemia and malnutrition by direct blood sucking from the host or by competing for food in the gut. The resulting anemia is in fact perceived by the body as an iron deficiency resulting in pica.

Pica is more frequently seen in the poor and the obese; however, David Livingston observed that "both slaves and the gentry developed pica" in Africa. In Africa pica, is viewed by tribal peoples as a magical superstitious behavior.

Henrock (1831) attributed pica to "paucity of good blood and lack of proper nutrition." Waller (1874) reported that David Livingston observed many cases of clay and earth eating (geophagia), a frequent form of pica in pregnant women.

Orr and Gilka (1931) and de Castro (1952) recognized that "edible Earths might be rich in sodium, iron and calcium." Gelford (1945) reported that pica was common in Kenya amongst African tribes (Kikuyu) living mainly on a vegetarian diet; but absent in those people eating diets rich in animal flesh, blood and bones (Massai).

Richter (1955) reported Kirkam and Birch's Analysis of 20 samples of edible clay from Africa:

Clay Minerals	Per cent
Silica	47.76
Aluminum oxide	22.03
Sodium oxide	4.87
Potassium oxide	2.88
Iron oxide	4.98
Manganese oxide	0.32
Calcium oxide	2.97
Magnesium oxide	1.08
Phosphorous pentoxide	0.13

Dickens and Ford reported that 25% of all children ate earth. Cooper (1957) reported a 21% rate of pica in American children referred to the Mother's Advisory Service in Baltimore.

Lanzkowsky (1959) reported that 12 children with pica had hemoglobin that ranged from 3 g% to 10.9 g% with a mean of 7.89% +/- 2.64. The institution of iron (i.m. - iron dextran) "resulted in a cure for pica in one to two weeks." Again, if children have sufficient nutritional minerals they will not eat lead paint.

McDonald and Marshall (1964) reported on 25 children who ate sand. They divided the group in half; they gave one group iron and the other group saline (salt solution). After three to four months 11 of the 13 children given iron had lost their pica behavior compared with only 3 of the 12 given saline.

Reynolds et al (1968) reported that 38 people with anemia exhibited pagophagia (ice eating) as the most common form of pica; twenty two of 25 had their symptoms of pica disappear after correcting the iron depletion.

Woods and Weisinger (1970) reproduced pagophagia experimentally in rats by withdrawing blood. The pagophagia in the anemic rats was cured when the anemia was cured. It is of interest to note that pica or cribbing behaviors are not produced by vitamin deficiencies!!!

Two thirds of the 153 pregnant women studied by Taggart (1961) developed cravings. The most common craving was for fruit, pickles, blood pudding, licorice, potato chips, cheese and kippers. A craving for sweets, vegetables, nuts and sweet pickles came in second place.

Phosphate appetite was described by LeVaillant (1796) as the anxious search by cattle in phosphate deficient South African pastures for discarded dog bones (osteophagia); they also chewed on wood (pica) and each others horns. Bone chewing (osteophagia, a form of pica) has been reported in many wild species of herbivores including reindeer, caribou, red deer, camels, giraffe, elephant and wildebeest. We have seen elephant eating limestone roadbeds and large termite heaps as ready and available mineral supplements. A search for calcium rich edible clays and soils and territorial disputes over limited supplies led to wars in tribal Africa.

It was demonstrated that calcium deficient weanling rats will consume large amounts of a lead acetate solution (even though they taste bad) when compared with calcium fed controls. The Oriental diet is extremely low in calcium leading them to habitually and preferentially eat bones (when Dr. Ma Lan and I were courting she ate the bones and gave me the fillets) partially leached of calcium with vinegar.

There is no evidence of a specific pica behavior for a magnesium supplement when laboratory animals are fed a magnesium deficient diet. Magnesium deficient animals will crave and eat common salt. Magnesium tastes bad enough that animals will die of magnesium deficiency initiated seizures rather than consume a pure magnesium supplement. It has been suggested that recovery from a magnesium deficiency can be a very unpleasant process, enough so that the bad taste of magnesium supplements normally required for recovery exceeds the unpleasant features of the deficiency!!

A natural potassium deficiency is highly unlikely as all grains, fruits and vegetables tend to be rich in potassium - a potassium deficiency can be common in those individuals taking diuretics for high blood pressure or weight loss.

Potassium deficient rats are hyper alert and lick everything including their metal cage, lab equipment, each other and urine puddles. It is of interest to note that even with a severe potassium deficiency laboratory rats have a strong craving for sodium chloride (salt)!!!.

Chromium and vanadium deficiencies are manifested by thirst for liquid (soft drinks being the usual first choice and water the last) and hunger for carbohydrates (i.e.- soft drinks, coffee and tea with added sugar, alcohol, pasta, desserts, bread, etc,). The "munchies", cravings for alcohol and candy cravings (especially chocolate) are sure signs of a chromium and vanadium deficiency.

The preteen and teen age infatuation with snack foods, drugs, smoking and alcohol appear to be the result of pica - because they are so minerally deficient they are seeking something, anything, to put in their mouth that will satisfy an irresistable craving for minerals.

God help us, through massive Hollywood film, television, newspaper and magazine advertising our culture guides our children to snack food, drugs, alcohol and smoking rather than mineral supplements just as surely as the Pied Piper hypnotized the rats to follow him with his pipe music!!!

"I ate his liver with fava beans and a good Chianti"

-Dr. Hannibal Lechter
Silence of the Lambs

Chapter 5

"DIVINE HUNGER"
(Cannibalism, vampires & werewolves)

The anthropological debate over cannibalism has raged over three theories of origin: 1) The satisfaction of certain psychosexual needs; 2) utilitarian adaption - humans adapt to extreme famine by eating other humans; 3) a cultural logic of the cycle of life, death and reproduction (usually endocannibilism or "mortuary" cannibalism).

Statistically cannibalism can be tied to hunger, but hunger for calories and protein alone cannot be tied to cannibalism, so we will add a fourth category of cannibalism; 4) the ultimate extension of pica (bizarre cravings and behavior resulting from extreme mineral deficiencies).

The 1973 movie Soylent Green starring Charleton Heston as a police investigator, portrayed a "benevolent" government in the year 2022, that had to deal with mind boggling over population - 40 million people in New York City alone and a depleted food supply. On Wednesdays the boring New York soup lines gave out rations of Soylent Green, said to be soy meal fortified with algae from the sea. In actuality, people who couldn't handle the stress any more were being "humanely" terminated and their

corpses butchered, processed and converted into Soylent Green!!

Food riots resulted in people being scooped up by huge front end loaders and then to be terminated and ground up into Soylent Green. Beef was only for the ultra rich and the high government officials; eating and the search for nutritional minerals became an obsession (pica) without end.

Cannibalism undoubtedly occurred before written history; sometimes opportunistically for outright survival reasons; sometimes as an extension of extreme pica; and sometimes as a ritualized method of recycling protein, minerals and Rare Earths necessary for life and reproduction in an otherwise depleted and hostile ecosystem.

Shipwrecked sailors in the 1700's first ate the bodies of their drowned comrades; then when the original corpses were consumed, they murdered and ate the weaker members of their party (i.e.- wounded, children, women, old people, etc.) for food. The Vietnamese boat people survived weeks and months at sea by eating their dead comrades and relatives.

In 1847 the Donner party survived a terrible winter in the Sierra Nevada's by eating members of their own expedition. The Donner party legend is really a story of James and Margaret Reed, a well-to-do farmer from James Town, Illinois who built a larger than average wagon to haul their worldly goods and their children from Illinois to California.

They started on the 2,000 mile trip in April of 1846 armed with a copy of Lanceford Hastings' book, *Emigrants Guide Book* and a lot of dreams. In July of 1846 the original train split, with one half going the northern "Oregon Trail" route which was longer but well known. The other half of the original train hoping to save a month by going the southern route through Truckee Pass described in Hastings' book.

In September of 1846, the Donner party found out the southern trail was only a foot path for well seasoned mountain men not for heavily laden wagons, women and children.

The wagons returned east for several days travel to Truckee Flats in November of 1846 where there was fresh water and plenty of timber to build temporary cabins to "hole up in and ride out the winter."

One man, Charles Stanton, volunteered to go ahead and return with supplies. Shortly after Stanton left, James Reed was attacked by a teamster in a disagreement over snarled teams; Reed defended himself and killed the teamster with his knife - he was banned from the train as punishment, so he went over the mountains to California to get help for the now snow bound wagon train, leaving behind his wife and children.

Stanton's rescue party returned first with what food they could carry on their backs but were trapped by what amounted to a 22 foot accumulation of snow. People were now boiling and eating buffalo skin blankets, their dogs and shoes.

Several men and their Indian guides Louise and Salvador set out west again to get more help and food - this time they were trapped themselves by deep snow drifts and after their food ran out the desperate rescuers summarily shot and ate their Indian guides - the cannibalism had started.

On Christmas day Mrs. Reed fed everything she could find to her children, including a few beans and an old cow skin as a special holiday meal. Cannibalism was rife in the rest of the expedition with the stronger individuals carving up and eating the dead - later there would be questions about whether or not all of those that had been eaten had died of natural causes.

Early in January 1847 about a dozen of the stronger men and women headed west in an attempt to cross over the mountains but were trapped by the 22 foot snow. They dug a "well" out of the snow and huddled in it for three weeks eating their dead.

In February 1847 another rescue party led by James Reed (he had been conscripted and forced to fight in the Mexican American War) brought supplies to the "well" survivors which included his wife, and then he pushed on to Truckee Flats where his children had been left with a trusted neighbor. Out of the original 86 in the Donner Party 47 survived - the Truckee Pass was renamed Donner Pass in remembrance of the six month ordeal.

During the winter of 1874 five prospectors hired Alfred Packer (the Colorado Cannibal) to guide them through the Colorado San Juan Mountains to dig for gold and silver. When Packer returned to his town of Lake City, Colorado six weeks after a heavy snow fall without the five prospectors the authorities were suspicious (especially since he was fatter than when he had left, he was throwing around a lot of money and he was more interested in drinking than eating).

A traveling free lance artist named John Randolph found the Packer expeditions campsite and drew the grisly scene for Harper's Weekly. Randolph had found the mutilated bodies of Shannon Bell, Isreal Swan, James Humphrey, George Noon, and Frank Miller - all had been hacked to death by axe blows to the head and their arms and legs filleted!!!

Packer fled before he could be arrested, but was finally captured nine years later. Packer was convicted of murder and sentenced to death, but on appeal was awarded a new trial on a legal technicality. He was found guilty in his second trial and sentenced to 40 years of hard labor. In 1900 a Denver Newspaper reporter raised doubts about Packers guilt and he was paroled in 1901. Packer died quietly "of natural causes" in 1907.

In October of 1972 a small charter plane carrying a private Christian Brothers schools rugby team from Uruguay to a match in Chili crashed at 11,500 feet in the Andes; the passenger list included players, coaches and relatives - 45 in all. Twelve were killed on impact, four died of their injuries within the next 24 hours - 29 lived through the first 24 hours

Initially, for the first ten days, the daily fare for the survivors was limited to one square of chocolate, a teaspoon of jam, a thimble full of toothpaste and a deodorant capful of wine.

After ten days they learned from a battery transistor radio that the search for survivors had been abandoned. They voted to eat the corpses of the dead in hopes of surviving until spring. The young cannibals ate blood clots from the hearts and strips of raw liver daily as a source of vitamins and minerals, body fat was eaten for calories and muscle was eaten for protein.

A week after the group was reduced to cannibalism an avalanche of snow smothered eight more of the hapless athletes - one of the boys exclaimed, "after that, there was more in the larder."

Two of the stronger boys were fed extra amounts of the grisly food to give them strength for an attempt to go for help. After a few false starts they actually made it to Chile and brought back help.

The survivors were down to eating the brains and the fingers of the dead when rescued on December 22 of 1972 -the rescue was heralded as the "Christmas Miracle." The ordeal lasted for 72 days - 16 survived.

Unlike the specter of cannibalism for survival, the issue of cannibalism as a cultural mode of recycling meager supplies of protein and essential vitamins and minerals is of importance when viewed as a supplement recycling program - the ultimate in conservation!

Cannibal cultures are usually found in hot equatorial environments where essential mineral elements are leached from the soil by high rainfalls and/or irrigation type agriculture.

The habit of cannibalism, including the consumption of ground up human bones added to alcoholic drinks and other foods appears to be a ritualized attempt to recycle essential minerals - this form of cannibalism is typified by the "mortuary" cannibalism of the Papua New Guinea who cook and eat their dead friends and relatives rather than burying or cremating them.

"Mortuary" cannibalism, the consuming of ones own dead as a replacement for the burial ceremony, "passes on the scarce elements of life" so they will not be lost to the family. The Hua tribe of the New Guinea highlands have survived on slash and burn agriculture for over 350 years; the sweet potato being the primary food crop.

The Hua have large pig herds which are consumed during weddings and annual ceremonies and then only the men are allowed to eat the pork. Because of the general lack of protein and minerals the tribes population is small and kwashiorkor (swollen fluid filled bellies from protein and mineral deficiencies) is common. The Hua translate the swollen bellies of Kwashiorkor in men as "men being pregnant!!"

The Hua believe that the life force or "Nu" or "Chi" is not a renewable resource and must be recycled - balding, a sign of loss of "Nu" is occurring in younger and younger men and women with each succeeding generation as they become more and more depleted of minerals. Hua women even breast feed baby pigs for male consumption during feasts and rituals, further depleting their own personal mineral reserves. It is these beliefs and practices and the never ending cravings for salt and minerals that explain the mortuary cannibalism practiced by the Hua women.

When a man dies amongst the Hua, men carry his body inside his mother's or wife's house and lay the corpse on the ground. The female relatives crowd around the corpse and have a ritualized wailing display of grief. After four or five days the male relatives remove the corpse and place it on a high platform so the juices and minerals of the decomposing body will fertilize the family garden; however, the women, unable to control their grief (or pica) pull the body off of the platform and butcher the body, carrying portions of the corpse inside men's houses where ordinarily no females are allowed - the women hide for several days while they divide, consume and digest the mans flesh. A year after the mortuary cannibalism of a male relative the bones are pulverized and spread in the garden to nourish the soil.

Evidence for cannibalism dates back to Pekin man, Neanderthal and Cro-magnon man. Excavated skeletons revealed skulls that had been ritualistically opened and the brains scooped out for consumption. The Greek historians Herodotus and Strabo recorded cannibalism by the Scythians, Massogetae and the Issedones characterized by the killing and eating of their disabled elders. Cannibalism was also reported in Europe and Ireland in the Middle Ages:

"Fee Fi Fo Fum, I smell the blood of an Englishman; be he live or be he dead I'll grind his bones to make my bread"

- The Giant
Jack and the Bean Stalk

Marco Polo reported Chinese and Tibetan cannibalism. Although isolated incidents of survival, murder or political cannibalism have been reported in every culture of the world, the highest levels of organized and ritualized cannibalism almost always occur in minerally depleted tropical areas of the globe.

Australian and African tribesman also practice "mortuary" cannibalism. Indian tribes of the northwestern and northeastern parts of the Americas ate human flesh as part of a sacrifice to their gods of fertility and war. Ugandans held great cannibal feasts to honor their battle dead and show disdain for their dead enemies.

In parts of Africa, South America and

cannibal Melanesia (the Fangs of Gaboon who are legendary for filing off their teeth to mimic the large canine teeth of large carnivores), the victors ate the corpses of an enemy as a show of contempt - in many cases limbs and genitals were hacked off from the still living victims, roasted and eaten before their eyes as an added torture.

Nineteenth century Fiji is famous for its accounts of cannibalism by Christian missionaries. In 1838 the Rev. David Cargill of the Methodist Society sent a letter to London:

"When about to offer a human sacrifice the victim is selected from among the inhabitants of a distant territory or is provided by negotiation from a tribe which is not related to the persons about to sacrifice. The victim is kept for some time, and is supplied with an abundance of food, that he may become fat. When about to become immolated, he is made to sit on the ground with his feet under his thighs and his hands placed before him. He is then bound so that he cannot move a limb or a joint. In this posture he is placed on stones heated for the occasion (and some of them are red hot), and then covered with leaves and earth to be roasted alive. When cooled, he is taken out of the oven and his face and other parts are painted black, that he may resemble a living man ornamented for a feast or for war; he is carried to the temple of the gods and, being still restrained in a sitting posture, is offered as a propitistory sacrifice. These ceremonies being concluded, the body is carried beyond the precincts of the conse-crated ground, cut into quarters, and distributed among the people; and they who were the cruel sacrificers of its life are also the beastly devourers of its flesh..."

Fijian chiefs did not regard human victims to be "in the shape of food", however, since cannibalism was an intimate part of their culture the practice was given royal consent. Cannibalism became part of their culture because of limited food supplies on the islands.

The Orokaiva Polynesians state that their justification for eating humans was to "satisfy their deep craving (pica) for good food". All prisoners captured in intertribal wars and raids were consumed; so regular were these events that human corpses were handled like carcasses of animals killed in a hunt; bodies of adults were tied hand and foot to shoulder poles and children were slung over the warriors shoulder like a dead turkey or rabbit. An account by a Cook Island Polynesian missionary of a New Caledonian war in 1879 is as follows:

"I followed and watched the battle and saw women taking part in it. They did so in order to carry off the dead. When people were killed, the men tossed the bodies back and the women fetched and carried them. They chopped the bodies up and divided them ....when the battle was over, they all returned home together, the women in front and the men behind. The women-folk carried the flesh on their backs; the coconut-leaf baskets were full up and the blood oozed over their backs and trickled down their legs. It was a horrible sight to behold.

When they reached their homes the earth ovens were lit at each house and they (cooked) and they ate the slain. Great was their delight, for they were eating well that day. This was the nature of the food. The fat was yellow and the flesh was dark. It was difficult to separate the flesh from the fat. It was rather like the flesh of sheep.

I looked particularly at our households share; the flesh was dark like sea cucumber, the fat was yellow like beef fat, and it smelled like cooked birds, like pigeon or chicken. The share of the chief was the right hand and the right foot. Part of the chiefs portion was brought for me, as for the priest, but I returned it. The people were unable to eat it all; the legs and the arms only were consumed, the body itself was left, that was the way of cannibalism in New Caledonia."

Changes in taste of human flesh (variety) were afforded by the crews of hapless vessels sunken in storms or by those who unwittingly stopped at the cannibal island for food and water.

For the Aztec, human sacrifice and cannibalism was an essential part of their culture - it was a ritual slaughter in a state sponsored program (Soylent Green):

"A regular supply of victims for the priests was necessary for ensuring the beneficial motion of the sun and the fertility of the crops and men. The procedures of sacrifice were elaborated constantly. Each had a deep symbolism. Following the ritual removal of the heart from the still living victim by the High Priest (the breast of the victim having been opened with a knife of obsidean), the heart was held up to the sun that each might give strength to the other. The body was thrown down a flight of a 100 or more stone steps (probably a method of tenderizing the tough stringy slaves and warriors) where it was cut up and eaten by the warriors, their families and their close associates."

Toxcatl, the great Aztec feast, involved sacrificing a carefully selected victim who was groomed for the year before hand as something between a king and a god. For the three weeks of April preceding the ceremony he was attended to day and night by four beautiful young maidens. They were the embodiment of the goddess of flowers, the goddess of young corn, the goddess of our mother among - the - water and the goddess of salt. "They were beautiful, ardent and dedicated and he lived a life of supreme voluptuousness. On the day, he said farewell to the four goddesses on a hilltop near the great lake. He walked on alone to the temple where the priests awaited, and as his shadow crossed the threshold the priests seized him and the High Priest sacrificed him. Immediately, when his heart ceased to palpitate his successor was announced and the ritual recommenced."

To justify the scale and methodical cannibalism of the Aztec's the perspective has to be placed on mineral hunger (pica) since calories from maize and fresh water lake algae were plentiful. Cannibalism was an extreme societal evolution for the Aztec culture; under conditions of total environmental collapse, very high population pressure, the dependence on maize agriculture, almost total depletion of wild game, the inability to maintain domestic animals (minerally depleted soil in the Valley of Mexico) led to endo and exo cannibalism.

Increased agricultural production in the form of tons and bushels was possible and in fact a constant project of the Aztec nobels, but to satisfy the craving for minerals required meat and bone!!! Cannibalism was the logical solution in the eyes of the Aztec.

Michael Horner, an expert on the demographics of central Mexico records that during the Spanish conquest (1450's) one per cent of the total Aztec population or 250,000 humans were killed and eaten annually!!! Cortez' noted that one of his men leading a punitive expedition against the Aztec came across "loads of maize and roasted children which they (Aztec warriors) had brought as provisions and which they left behind them when they discovered the Spanish coming"

The human flesh eaten after the sacrifice was not part of the ritual itself but looked upon as "leftovers" of the gods and was returned to the original captor as a reward for having satisfied the deity. Such rewards of human flesh were necessary because the Aztec warriors were recruited from the starving masses of commoners who rarely ate meat of any kind - they obtained their primary calorie source from maize, beans and a "floating substance" (algae).

Famine for the out of control Aztec population was commonplace and the commoners faced severe annual food shortages. An extreme famine in 1450 forced the Aztec nobles to empty the grain stores accumulated over a decade to prevent rebellion amongst the masses.

Aztecs kept prisoners in wooden cages for extended periods of time to fatten prior to being killed and eaten and to conserve a perishable asset as they did not have refrigeration or other methods of preservation of meat.

After capturing three of the enemy, the basic warrior was promoted to " master of the youths"; they were also allowed to host a cannibal fiesta for blood relatives - thus they were rewarded in human flesh in an economy totally without other forms of meat.

The Aztec nobles were able to recruit warriors from the general commoner population by promising "meat rewards" to successful individuals - the nobles were able to pump up and create an "invincible war machine" with the promise of meat - human meat!!! The underlying genesis of the much acclaimed Aztec war machine was the total ecological collapse of the Valley of Mexico with the resultant depletion of soil minerals.

The Spanish were told, that at the dedication of the pyramid of Tenochtitlan four queues of captives streamed out like spokes for two miles each. These prisoners were killed by "teams of priests" who worked 24 hours a day for four days - given two minutes per killing the historian Sherburne Cook projected the number killed at that "super Bowl" of sacrifices at 14,100. To confirm such numbers one only has to go to the writings of Bernal Diaz and Andres de Tapia who recorded that in the plaza of the Aztec city of Xocotlan "there were piles of human skulls so regularly arranged that one could count them, and I estimated them at more than 100,000 of them."

When Tapia entered the city of Tenochtitlan and observed the great skull rack in the center plaza he wrote:

"The poles were separated from each other by a little less than a vara (approximately a yard), and were crowded with cross sticks from top to bottom, and on each cross stick there were five skulls impaled through the temples: and the writer and a certain Gonzalo de Umbria, counted the cross sticks and multiplying by five heads per cross stick from pole to pole, as I said, we found that there were 136,000 heads."

Descriptions of individual sacrifices by the Aztecs are found in great detail in the Spanish record. The walls, killing alters and the floors on top of the pyramids were black with encrusted blood from the daily parade of victims - the temples stank of death and dried blood and blood gorged bluebottle flies were there buzzing in hordes.

The great number of captives and slaves did not go willingly up the 114 steps to the tops of the pyramids to be killed - most fought, many fainted but all were eventually dragged up the steps by their hair. After having their chest cut open and their hearts literally torn from their breast, blood was collected by the priest and given to the captor, the body was then thrown down the steps of the pyramid to a tiny walled square below. Old men called Quaquacuiltin, laid hold of the now lifeless and broken body and carried it to their individual temple were they dismembered it and divided the meat in order to roast and eat them:

"and things being so, they (the captives) were made to arrive at the top (of the pyramid), before (the sanctuary of) Utizilopochtli. Thereupon one at a time they stretched them into the hands of six offering priests; they stretched them out upon their backs; they cut open their breasts with a wide bladed flint knife. And they named the hearts of the captives "precious eagle-cactus fruit". They raised them in dedication to the sun, Xippilli, Quauhtleuanitl. They offered to him; they nourished him. And when the heart had become an offering ... these captives who had died they called eagle men. Afterwards they rolled them over; they bounced them down. They came breaking to pieces (a method of tenderization); they came head over heels; they each came head first, they came turning over and over. Thus they reached the terrace at the base of the pyramid ...They took them to their calpulco, where the taker of the captive had made his undertaking, had said his say, had made his vow. From there they removed him in order to take him to the house of the captor, in order to eat him."

Like most legends, the vampire and werewolf legends have a basis in fact - imagine mineral starved gentry with absolute power over life and death of their subjects - imagine a Jeffrey Dahmer as a 15th century king with absolute power and you have Dracula, the Prince of Darkness !!!! Romania was ruled by prince Dracula (1431); Europe spanned from the Atlantic Ocean to the Baltic and all of the nation states were joined together by dynastic bonds of vassalage and feudal honor. Dracula was born in Transylvania a place that was inhabited by Daco Romans since AD 101 and AD 105. The Dacians were conquered by the Romans as the eastern most frontier of the

Roman Empire thus the name Romania. The home of Dracula is located north of the Carpathian Mountains and named Trans-silva by early Roman travelers - translated from Latin it means - densely forested.

Because of the location of the Ottoman Turks to the southeast and the Tartar's Golden Horde to the northeast Romania was a political, cultural and religious flashpoint. Turkish invaders burnt villages and fields, killed large numbers of the Romanian population and brought long smouldering death after the wars in the form of syphilis, tuberculosis, leprosy, and small pox. Natural catastrophes added to the miseries of the Transylvanians in the form of floods, poor harvests, earthquakes and clouds of locusts that flew into their fields from the east. A deep belief in the forces of evil and black magic, burning of witches and other superstitions were common in those times.

Young Vlad Dracul was born and grew up as the prince of darkness in those terrible times. Vlad's great grandfather was Mircea the Great, known widely in his own time as a great negotiator and possessor of excellent diplomatic talents. His seat of power was Wallachia, the region bordering Transylvania.

To avoid capitulating to the Turks, Mircea the Great signed a treaty with Sigismund of Luxembourg in 1395. After the alliance was formed Mircea joined Sigismund in a Christian Crusade against the Ottoman Turks. Mirceas grandson Vlad was sent as an apprentice to the court of Sigismund where he was inducted into the Order of the Dragon, which granted young Vlad the grace of the Prince. Vlads duties were to protect Catholicism, fight the Turks, protect widows and children and protect the German king.

In February 1431 Vlad was made a knight of the Order of the Dragon. Required of the new knight was the wearing of two capes-one green-symbolic of the dragons color to be worn over red garments to symbolize the blood of martyrs, the second cape was black (adopted by Bram Stoker's "Count Dracula").

When prince Vlad returned to Transylvania, he was called "Dracul" by the nobles of Wallachia as they recognized his newly acquired honor as a Draconist. The name "Dracula" used by Bram Stoker was the name given to Vlads son, as the suffix "a" means "son of" in Romanian - Dracula then was born, and his infamous crimes made the name Dracula synonymous with evil.

Vlad had the official title of Prince of Wallachia, however, his older half-brother Alexandru Aldea grabbed the throne. Young Vlad Dracul was appointed military governor with the responsibility of guarding Transylvania's borders.

Vlad Dracul's base of power was in the great fortress of Sighisoara. While stationed there Vlad fathered three sons the second of which was named Vlad Dracul, born in December 1431 he became infamous as Prince Dracula or Vlad The Impaler!!!

In 1434 Sigismund ordered young Vlad to take over the court in Wallachia because Alexandru had become "too chummy" with the Turks. The Young Dracula was of the age to apprentice knighthood and as such was taught swimming, fencing, jousting, archery, court etiquette, and horsemanship befitting a knight. He learned political science - very simple in his day - "better to be feared than loved."

Young Dracula had a "morbid" obsession with the hangings and torture of criminals. He learned many methods of torture including rectal impalement as a young military officer. After many adventures Vlad Dracula by now aged 25 seized his throne (1456) in Wallachia after his fathers death.

Dracula very quickly became known throughout Europe as the living embodiment of evil. One notable event occurred when some Italian ambassadors came to Dracula's court and as their custom demanded kept their skull caps on; when Dracula asked what was the meaning, they answered, "This is our custom. We are not obliged to take our skull caps off under any circumstances, even an audience with the sultan or the Holy Roman Emperor." Dracula then responded by saying," In all fairness, I want to strengthen and recognize your customs." Then in a methodical manner the Prince of Darkness had his attendants nail the skullcaps on the heads of the envoys!

Dracula punished who he considered to be the parasites of society, one such event is so well known it was translated into German, Russian and Romanian:

"Having asked the old, the ill, the lame, the poor, the blind, and the vagabonds to a large dining hall in Tirgoviste, Dracula ordered that a feast be prepared for them. On the appointed day, Tirgoviste groaned under the heavy weight of the large number of beggars who had come.

The prince's servants passed out a batch of clothes to each one, then they led the beggars to a large mansion where tables had been set. The beggars marveled at the prince's generosity, and they spoke among themselves, "Truly it is a prince's kind of grace." Then they started eating. And what do you think they saw before them: a meal such as one would find on the prince's own table, wines and all the best things to eat which weigh you down. The beggars had a feast that became legendary. They ate and drank greedily. Most of them became dead drunk. As they became unable to communicate with one another, and became incoherent, they were suddenly faced with fire and smoke on all sides. The prince had ordered his servants to set the house on fire.

They rushed to the doors to get out, but the doors were locked. The fire progressed. The blaze rose high like inflamed dragons. Shouts, shrieks, and moans arose from the lips of all the poor enclosed there. But why should a fire be moved by the entreaties of men? They fell upon each other. They embraced each other. They sought help, but there was no human ear left to listen to them. They began to twist in the torments of the fire that was destroying them. The fire stifled some, the embers reduced others to ashes, the flames grilled most of them. When the fire naturally abated there was no trace of any living soul."

Individual cruelty was a hallmark of Dracula's reign:

"If any wife had an affair outside of marriage, Dracula ordered her sexual organs cut (out). She was then skinned alive and exposed in her skinless flesh in the public square, her skin hanging separately from a pole or placed on a table in the middle of the marketplace. The same punishment was applied to maidens who did not keep their virginity, and also to unchaste widows. For lessor offenses, Dracula was known to have the nipple of a women's breast cut off. He also had a red-hot iron stake shoved into a women's vagina, making the instrument penetrate her entrails and emerge from her mouth. He then had the women tied to a stake naked and left her exposed there until the flesh fell from the body, and the bones detached themselves from their sockets."

Prince Dracula, because of his total power without bridle, was the "greatest" psychopath history has ever recorded. Along the road to his palace, Dracula had installed a "forest" of hundreds of stakes the diameter of broom sticks - some ends were rounded and greased, some were sharpened to a point. Each of these stakes were used to impale an individual through the rectum - sharpened stakes for ones he wanted to die quickly and the rounded ones for those destined for a slow miserable death. These events were always timed to coincide with the visit of a head of state from another province or country "to make a lasting impression" of Dracula's power and resolve to keep it (again Bram Stoker used the impalement through the heart with a wooden stake as the only method of dispatching a vampire).

The dead were "chopped up as meat, their blood drunk from goblets and their limbs, hearts and livers cooked in every fashion for Dracula and his court." The total number of his victims exceeded 100,000 which amounted to 20% of Wallachia's total population!!! The fear of impalement was so great during Dracula's reign that the rate of idleness, theft and more serious crimes fell to zero!!!!

Thus the legend of the "vampire" Count Dracula was born out of the true recorded history of a serial killer who drank the blood and ate the flesh of his victims to satisfy his bizarre cravings for minerals (pica) he couldn't get any other way.

Gilles de Laval, Baron de Rais, Marshall of France and the champion of the Maid of Orleans was the wealthiest and most powerful man in Europe. His personal bodyguard of 200 war hardened knights who had fought along side of him in the army of Joan of Arc in the defeat of the English - Gilles lived at a lavish level that exceeded even that of Charles VII the king of France.

In September 1440, 47 charges were brought against Gilles during the French Inquisition as a heretic. In fact after many years of indulging in rich French pastries, huge quantities of wine and other delicacies Gilles had developed pica and began a life as a depraved pedophile, murderer, serial killer and vampire!!!

First Gilles became an alchemist dabbling in the search for "the philosopher's stone," which he believed would transmute lead and mercury into gold and find cures for his bizarre cravings; he then began to sacrifice children and maidens, delved into sexual sadism, drank their blood and prayed to "dark gods and demons."

Gilles was brought before the Bishop of Nantes and the Inquisitor General of France - there were six court hearings and 110 witnesses charging de Rais with the murders of 800 children!!!

Charge number 15 against Gilles pretty much summed it up:

"According to the lamentable outcries, tears and wailings and denunciations coming from many people of both sexes, crying out and complaining of the loss and death of children, the aforesaid Gilles de Rais has taken innocent boys and girls, and inhumanely butchered, killed, dismembered, burned and otherwise tortured them, and the said Gilles has immolated the bodies of the said innocents to the devils, invoked and sacrificed to evil spirits, and has foully committed the sin of sodomy with young boys and in other ways lusted against nature after young girls... while the innocent boys and girls were alive, or sometimes dead, or sometimes even during their death throes."

After being found guilty, Gilles was executed by garotte (slow strangulation by means of a cord that was tightened around the neck by twisting a stick).

The most infamous of all of the ancient female vampires was the Countess Erzsebet Bathory of Hungary. Her hapless teen age female victims were recruited as servants for the Castle Csejthe. After one of her intended victims fled the castle and notified the town officials of the castles horrors, the castle was raided by the local constables in the year 1610 and the countess tried and found guilty of murdering and consuming the blood of 650 teen-age virgins.

The countess bled her victims to death through numerous punctures inflicted in their necks - their blood was collected in tubs for drinking and for bathing in. In addition to her ceaseless craving for blood to drink she also believed the blood of virgins would give her immortality. The punishment meted out to the vampire countess was that she be sealed in and walled up

never to hear a human voice or see another human - she died of "natural causes" 30 years later in 1640.

North America had its share of ancient vampires and werewolves too. "Cannibal monsters" are the werewolves of the North American Indian cultures:

1) **The Windingo** - from the Algonkian Indians of the northeastern regions of North America.

2) **The Wechuge** - from the deep forest Athopaskan Beaver Indians of the northwest of North America.

3) **The Man Eater** - from the Kwakiutt Indians from the northwest coast of North America.

In the early 1600's the "Windingo psychosis" or cannibalistic madness was recorded amongst the Algonkian Indians (the northern neighbors of the Iroquois). The earliest reports by Europeans were found in 1635 in the personal logs of the Spanish priests known as "Jesuit Relations." LeJeune's Relation describes cannibalism following a two year famine:

"In 1660-1661, several Cree deputies of the Jesuits were described as being seized with an unknown ailment that combined lunacy, hypochondria and frenzy, which affects their imagination and causes them a more than canine hunger (werewolves). This makes them so ravenous for human flesh that they pounce upon women, children and even upon men, like veritable werewolves and devours them voraciously, without being able to appease or glut their appetite (pica) - ever seeking fresh prey, and as more greedily, the more they eat. This ailment attacked our deputies and (the Jesuits report) ...as death is the only remedy among these simple people for checking such acts of murder, they were slain in order to stay the course of their madness."

Modern serial killers are the vampires and werewolves of our time; usually easier to catch than the ancient ones because of high tech police methods they are none the less formidable. Like the ancient vampires and werewolves, their modern counterparts have flagrant histories of nutritionally deficient diets and awful eating habits which of course lead to sociopathic behavior. Modern serial killers are appearing almost at the rate of one each week which can be attributed to the now precipitous decline and depletion of minerals in our soil and thus our food supply.

Of interest are the common behavioral threads that connect "vampires," "werewolves" and serial killers and which are recognizable at an early age - ancient and modern:

1) Ritualistic behavior (often written off as "Satan worship").
2) They "look sane" to the casual observer.
3) Explosive rage and temper over little things.
4) Seeks help for bizarre cravings (pica), bed wetting, nightmares and "emotional problems."
5) Confabulations (makes up stories when they can't remember the truth)
6) Suicide attempts.
7) History of assault (usually sexual in nature).

8) History of smoking, alcohol and or drug abuse (pica).
9) History of difficult pregnancy (fetal alcohol syndrome or maternal nutritional deficiencies during pregnancy).
10) History of extraordinary cruelty to animals.
11) Fascination with fire and arson and pain inflicted by fire.
12) Overt biochemical or nutritional deficiencies (these are ones even an M.D. will recognize, i.e.- loss of the sense of smell and taste or zinc deficiency).

The first of the modern vampires (serial killers) was Jack the Ripper. For a mere three months in 1888, from the end of August to the beginning of November, Whitechapel in the east of London was stalked and terrorized by a serial killer. The five murder victims were all prostitutes, each attacked from behind, their throats slashed and in four of the five killings the bodies were mutilated, dissected and cannibalized.

There had been serial cannibals (Table 5-1) in the 17th and 18th centuries but "Jack" was the first to toy with the police through the news media. "Jack" was never officially caught and identified, however, several suspects were accused:

1) John Druitt Montague, a disbarred lawyer who drowned himself exactly when the Whitechapel murders ceased.

2) George Chapman (triple wife killer)- Frederick Abberline, a chief investigator in the "Ripper" murder cases stated on the arrest of Chapman,: "You've got Jack the Ripper at last."

3) HRH Prince Albert Victor, Duke of Clarence (grandson of Queen Victoria).

Given the level of anticrime technology at the time of the "Ripper" killings it is not surprising that no one was brought to trial or convicted. A certain James Maybrick, however, left a diary that all but convicts him posthumously as the real "Jack the Ripper."

Maybrick was born on October 24, 1838, his grandfather was in fact the parish clerk. At age 14 years James' younger brother Michael, a gifted musical composer, joined the Carl Ross Opera Company and played in the concert halls of Britain and the United States. Michael wrote many popular songs and became part of the "pop" musical generation of the Victorian days - of interest is one of his songs entitled "We All Love Jack." In 1848 another younger brother of James died mysteriously (retrospectively probably "Jacks" first killing at age 10).

In 1874 when Maybrick was 36 he shuttled back and forth between Liverpool in Britain and Norfolk in the U.S. as a cotton broker. In 1877 Maybrick caught malaria, his initial prescription of quinine failed and he was given arsenic and strychnine. Maybrick complained of numbness in his limbs and constantly rubbed the backs of his hands, his arsenic consumption increased (pica) even after his malaria disappeared.

Maybrick met the beautiful 18 year old red head, Florence (Florie) Chandler while on one of his trans Atlantic shuttles and at age 41 he married this beautiful girl.

By 1882 Maybrick was consuming arsenic almost hourly, taking it in tea, grits and broth. He would add seven or so drops of a liquid arsenic solution to his food and drink five or more times a day (equivalent of 1/3 grains of arsenic a day!). It was fashionable in those days to consume arsenic and strychnine as an aphrodisiac.

A toxicologist of the day stated, "When once they start the habit of arsenic eating they remain slaves for life... Once they enter on the downward path, there is no looking back, as it is asserted by toxicologists that if they are ever prevented (from) obtaining their daily dose they may say, with truth, 'the pains of Hell got hold of me' and they experience all the dreadful horrors of slow arsenic poisoning."

In 1887 Florie suspected James had a mistress in Liverpool (thought to be one Sarah Ann Robertson). While James was away on one of his frequent business trips Florie began having affairs with Alfred Brierley, a fellow cotton broker of Maybrick. Accidently Maybrick spotted Brierley and Florie together on the fashionable shopping street called Whitechapel St. in Liverpool.

After catching the lovers together his references to Florie in his diary changed from "his darling Bunny" to the "bitch" or the "whore." He refers to himself as "Sir Jim" or "Sir Jack" (a common nick name during Victorian times for John or James):

> "I took refreshment at the Poste House, it was there I finally decided London it shall be. And why not, is it not an ideal location? Indeed do I not frequently visit the Capital and indeed do I not have legitimate reason for doing so. All who sell their dirty wares shall pay, of that I have no doubt. But shall I pay? I think not. I am too clever for that.... The bitch and her whoring master will rue the day I first saw them together."

Maybrick committed his second killing

as a trial run for the "Ripper" murders. He killed a prostitute in Manchester which he recorded in his diary, "I said Whitechapel it will be and Whitechapel it shall... Whitechapel, Liverpool/Whitechapel, London, Ha Ha. No one could possibly place it together. And indeed for there is no reason for anyone to do so. Tomorrow I travel to Manchester. Will take some of my medicine (arsenic) and think hard on the matter....I will force myself not to think of the children..... Time is passing much too slowly. I still have to work up the courage to begin my campaign. I have thought long and hard over the matter and still I cannot come to a decision to when I should begin. Opportunity is there, of that fact I am certain... my medicine (arsenic) is doing me good, in fact I am sure I can take more than any other person alive. My dear God my mind is in a fog. (The next days log) The whore is now with her maker and he is welcome to her. There was no pleasure as I squeezed. I felt nothing. Do not know if I have the courage to go back to my original idea. Manchester was cold and damp very much like this hell hole. Next time I will throw acid over them."

When Maybrick began the "Ripper "killings there were 80,000 prostitutes in London and 1200 in the Whitechapel area alone:

Polly Nichols was last seen alive by her friends at 2:30 a.m. criss crossing Whitechapel Road looking for a client. It was here she ran into Maybrick and by 3:40 a.m. Polly was dead.

Maybrick held Polly against a stable corral gate by the jaw with his left hand and summarily strangled her, as she dropped lifeless to the ground he used his shiny new butcher knife to cut her throat to the vertebrae (he tried unsuccessfully to decapitate her):

Table 5-1	The Five Whitechapel "Jack the Ripper" Victims			
Name of Victim	Date 1888	Time	Location of Killing	Mutilations Discovered
Mary Ann "Polly" Nichols	Friday, August 31	3:45 AM	Buck's Row	Disembowelled
Annie Chapman	Saturday, September 6	6:00 AM	29 Hanbury St.	Uterus Removed
Elizabeth Stride	Sunday, September 30	1:00 AM	Duffield's	No Mutilation
Catherine Eddowes	Sunday, September 30	1:45 AM	Mitre Square	Uterus and Left Kidney missing Flap cut on each cheek
Mary Jane Kelly	Friday November 9	10:45 AM	Miller's Court	Gross Mutilation Heart Missing

"I have shown all that I mean business, the pleasure was far better than I imagined. The whore was only too willing to do her business. I recall all and it thrills me. There was no scream when I cut. I was more than vexed when the head would not come off. I believe I will need more strength next time. I struck deep into her. I regret I never had the cane, it would have been a delight to have rammed it hard into her. The bitch opened like a ripe peach. I have decided next time I will rip all out. My medicine (arsenic) will give me strength and the thought of the whore and her whoring master will spur me on no end."

Annie Chapman, Maybricks second "Ripper" victim connected with Maybrick about 5:30 a.m. on September 8, 1888 - the agreement for sex was actually struck in front of a witness then they left together to find a secluded spot in the small back yard at 29 Hanbury St. where 17 sleeping workers had not yet awakened.

Maybrick strangled Annie then attempted to cut her head off with no success; he then cut open her abdomen and draped her intestines over her left shoulder, removed her uterus and part of her abdominal wall. He entered into his diary just before his second murder:

"The gentle man with gentle thoughts will strike again soon: I have never felt better, in fact, I am taking more than ever (arsenic) and I can feel the strength building up within me. The head will come off next time, also the whores hands. Shall I leave them in various places about Whitechapel? Hunt the head and the hands instead of the thimble. ha ha. Maybe I will take some part away with me to see if it does taste like fresh fried bacon."

Maybricks third "Ripper" victim was Elizabeth "Long Liz" Stride, who was last seen alive with a "well dressed client" at 12:30 a.m. on September 30, 1888 by constable Wm. Smith. Sometime between 12:30 a.m. and and 1:00 a.m. Maybrick drug "Long Liz" into the enclosed courtyard at Duffield's yard by her neck scarf, strangled her then he cut her lifeless throat and neck in a futile attempt to cut her head off. The abrupt appearance of a costume jewelry salesman into the courtyard prevented Maybrick from further mutilating "Long Liz's" body - the mans horse "shyed at the sight of the heap ("Long Liz's" body)" in the court yard causing him to poke at it with his buggy whip while Maybrick stood paralyzed with fear just a few feet away in the shadows:

"To my astonishment I cannot believe I have not been caught. My heart felt as if it had left my body. Within my fright I imagined my heart bounding along the street with I in desperation following it. I would have dearly loved to have cut the head of the damned horse off and stuffed it as far as it would go down the whore's throat. I had no time to rip the bitch wide, I curse my bad luck. I believe the thrill of being caught thrilled me more than cutting the whore herself. As I write I find it impossible to believe he did not see me, in my estimation I was less than a few feet from him. The fool panicked, it is what saved me. My satisfaction was far from complete, damn the bastard, I cursed him and cursed him, but I was clever, they could not out do me. No one ever will."

Maybrick walked fast away from the murder scene of "Long Liz" and ran into Catherine Eddowes at about 1:35 a.m. in Mitre Square - still on the 30th of September 1888. Maybrick pushed her to the ground and strangled her then he attempted to cut her head off without success - frustrated he slashed and mutilated her face, cut off her eyelids, lower jaw and upper lips!!! Parts of Eddowes nose and ears were sliced off. Maybrick carved an inverted V under each eye (no one noted that together they formed the M for Maybrick). Maybrick next devoted his attention to his victims abdomen which he cut open, removed her intestines which he piled by her side and then he removed her uterus and left kidney and took them with him. His diary entry reads:

"One whore no good, decided Sir Jim strike another. I showed no fright and indeed no light, damn it the tin box was empty... Sweet sugar and tea could have paid me small fee. But instead I did flee and by the way showed my glee by eating cold kidney (Catherine Eddowes left kidney!!!) for supper."

On October 1, 1888 the London Daily News published what was to become the most "infamous" letter in the history of all crime - for without the letter (dated September 25, 1888) which was written in red ink, the Whitechapel "Ripper" murders would just have been listed with other murders of prostitutes in a dusty police unsolved file:

"Dear Boss,
I keep on hearing the police have caught me but they won't fix me just yet. I have laughed when they look so clever and talked about being on the right track. That joke about Leather Apron gave me real fits. I am down on whores and I shant quit ripping them till I do get buckled. Grand work the last job was. I gave the lady no time to squeal. How can they catch me now. I love my work and want to start again. You will soon hear of me with my funny little games. I saved some of the proper red stuff in a ginger beer bottle over the last job to write with but it went thick like glue and I can't use it. Red ink is fit enough I hope ha ha. The next job I do I shall clip the ladies ears off and send to the police officers just for jolly wouldn't you. Keep this letter back til I do a bit more work, then give it out straight. My knife's so nice and sharp I want to get to work right away if I get a chance.

Good luck.
Yours truly
Jack the Ripper

Don't mind the trade name. Wasn't good enough to post this before I got all the red ink off my hands, curse it No luck yet. They say I'm a doctor now. ha ha."

Maybrick turned 50 years old on October 24, 1888 and wrote in his diary:

"I was forced to stop myself from indulging in my pleasure (killing prostitutes) by taking the largest dose (arsenic) I have ever done. The pain that night has burnt into my mind. I vaguely recall putting a handkerchief in my mouth to stop my cries. I believe I vomited several times. The pain was intolerable, as I think I shudder. No more.

I am convinced God placed me here to kill all whores, for he must have done so, am I still not here. Nothing will stop me now. The more I take ((arsenic) the more stronger I become. Michael (Maybrick's brother) was under the impression that once I finished my business I was to return to Liverpool that very day. And indeed I did one day later. ha ha...."

Maybrick's last "Ripper" victim was a dead ringer for his wife Florie. Mary Jane Kelly was 25 years old, had red hair like Florie and was different from the other prostitute victims in that she was slim and pretty.

Kelly was last known to be alive in the early morning hours of November 9,1888 because she disturbed her neighbors by singing a victorian ballad (Only A Violet I Plucked From My Mothers Grave) in a loud voice.

A witness saw Kelly take a client (Maybrick) to her 12 foot square room in a Miller's Court after 2:00 a.m. At 4:00 Kelly's neighbors heard a women scream "murder" but they did nothing as such screams were common in their rough neighborhood. Kelly's client was heard leaving her room at 5:45 a.m.

At 10:45 a.m. Kelly's landlord called to collect the rent. When she didn't answer his knock he looked in her window and saw her horribly mutilated body.

The coroners report of the murder scene decribed poor Kelly's body:

"The whole surface of the abdomen and thighs was removed and the abdominal cavity emptied of its viscera. The breasts were cut off, the arms mutilated by several jagged wounds and the face hacked beyond recognition of the features. The tissues of the neck were severed all round to the bone.

The viscera were found in various parts viz; the uterus and kidneys with one breast under the head, the other breast by the right foot, the liver between the feet, the intestines by the right side and the spleen by the left side of the body. The flaps removed from the abdomen and thighs were on a table"

A supplementary report from the coroner's autopsy read: "The pericardium was opened and the heart absent." This fact was never made public but was clearly noted in Maybricks diary.

Maybrick's diary account of the murder and mutilation included:

"I left nothing of the bitch, nothing. I placed it all over the room, time was on my hands, like the other whore I cut off the bitches nose all of it this time. I left nothing of her face to remember her by... I thought it was a joke when I cut her breasts off, kissed them for awhile. The taste of blood was sweet (pica), the pleasure was overwhelming, will have to do it again. It thrilled me so. Left them on the table with some other stuff. Thought they belonged there. They wanted a slaughterman so I stripped what I could, laughed while I was doing so. Like the other bitches she ripped like a ripe peach."

Maybrick became seriously ill in April 26, 1889 and his doctor was summoned because of headaches (hypoglycemia or diabetes resulting from chromium and vanadium deficiencies), numbness (B_{12} deficiency) of his legs and leg cramps (calcium deficiency) so bad "they were like iron bars." Maybrick told his doctor he was taking arsenic and strychnine to "abate his cravings." His doctor recommended,"meat once a day and beef tea thickened with Du Barry's Revalenta which was a Victorian "cure all" for "indigestion, flatulency, dyspepsia, phlegm,constipation, all nervous, bilious and liver complaints, dysentery, diarrhea, acidity, palpitation, heartburn, hemorrhoids, headaches, debility, despondency, cramps, spasms, nausea, sinking fits, coughs, asthma and bronchitis, consumption and also children's complaints."

Now Maybrick was buying arsenic at the bulk in 300 grain quantities. His pica and unabated cravings for minerals had finally gotten so bad, that in an effort to quench them he overdosed himself and died in his own bed after an agonizing week of subacute arsenic poisoning at 4:00 a.m. on May 11, 1889.

The ironic part of the "Ripper" case is "Jack's" wife was wrongly convicted of his murder as it was said she wanted his insurance money!!! Even though the legal system was unaware that she was the wife of "Jack the Ripper,"Flories seven day murder trial was the court case of the century; she was supposed to have soaked fly paper in vinegar to extract arsenic with which to kill her husband - the sensational trial created "Maybrickmania" in the London tabloids. The jury took just 35 minutes to deliberate and find her guilty, the magistrate condemned her to death by hanging.

The scaffold was in fact being constructed just outside of Florie Maybrick's cell when she was given an 11th hour reprieve - the Home Secretary, Henry Mathews commuted her sentence to life in penal servitude - had unsuccessfully tried to capture and try "Jack the Ripper" (Florie's husband) a year earlier!!!

Since the "Jack the Ripper" killings it seems there appears a new serial killer (Table 5-2) each week (the soils are depleted of minerals so the rate of pica and depraved attempts to quench the cravings with human blood and flesh increase at a geometric rate!!).

FBI files contain no less than 5,000 unsolved serial killer victims a year in the United States alone!! Most of these cases are simply written off as victims of "Satanic Cults" because their blood, hearts, livers and other organs are missing (consumed in vampire and cannibalistic rites)!!! If we do not get minerals into these mineral starved generations they will consume us in a primal effort to obtain minerals themselves - counselors, gun laws, more jails or more police on the streets will not save us as an army of people obsessed with cravings that they don't understand and they believe can only be quenched with human blood and flesh would rise up, riot and create a bloody anarchy (i.e.- Somalia, Rwanda, etc.)!!!!

The serial killer most likely to be voted a modern day "werewolf" would be Andrei Chikatilo, the Russian known as the "Red

Ripper." To make a long 12 year horror story short he circulated through three killing fields in and around Rostov for 12 years - all of his victims were young girls and boys or young women.

Chikatilo methodically stalked his 52 victims and killed them with one of his many knives - he took parts of them including nipples, uterus and genitals, but expressed a particular fondness for " the chewy pink uterus (pica)" which gave him considerable satisfaction as he chewed them raw.

Andrei Chikatilo, first a teacher in a boys school (he was forced to resign when he was caught sexually abusing the boys), then a parts buyer for a state run factory and a raw materials locator, was found guilty of 52 mutilation murders and cannibalism and sentenced to death which was carried out by a Russian firing squad in 1994 after Russian President Yeltson denied a plea for clemency to Chikatilo.

Edward Geins is of particular interest as he was the real life inspiration for the "Buffalo Bill" serial killer in the 1991 movie, Silence of the Lambs. Geins farmed a "played out" subsistence farm in Plainfield, Wisconsin. He started his werewolf practices by robbing bodies from graves to study human female anatomy!!!

Geins skinned the corpses and either wore the skin himself like a shawl until it putrefied or he dried it as lamp shades; in some instances he dried the skins over the dress maker's dummy as was portrayed in silence of the lambs.

In 1954 Geins killed for the first time. The last killing of Geins was in 1957 when suspicious police raided his farm they found the headless and butchered body of Bernice Worden hanging by its feet from the barn rafters. A search of the house revealed parts of humans everywhere and a refrigerator full of human flesh and organs cut up into meal sized portions.

Geins' primary food source was grown on his played out farm - his minerally depleted food supply resulted in severe mineral deficiencies in him which probably produced his bizarre cravings (pica) for human flesh.

Waneta Hoyt is accused of killing each of her five infant children by smothering them with a pillow over a six year period - they were initially diagnosed as SIDS victims (Sudden Infant Death Syndrome), but a good pathologist proved all five were suffocated with a pillow.

Hoyt has diabetes (chromium and vanadium deficiency) and in her written confession she stated," I knew something was wrong with me. I feel I'm a good person, but something was wrong with me."

Something was wrong with Hoyt just as it is with literally millions of other Americans - her behavior and judgment were changed from that of a "good Christian farm wife" to that of a sociopath serial killer as a result of mineral deficiencies.

In ancient times "vampires" were dispatched with wooden stakes through the heart; "werewolves" were destroyed with silver bullets or silver spear heads - will jails, more police, social workers, Prosac and psychiatrists be effective against these legendary monsters today? We think not. If we do not remineralize our younger generation we will be consumed by them!!!!!!

"Evil is unspectacular and always human, and shares our bed and eats at our own table."
                    - Herman Melville

Discovery of body in Britain leads to 6 others; police continue search

Associated Press

Gloucester, England
No one remembers seeing Heather West since the summer of 1987, when she was 16 years old.

Police didn't start looking for her in earnest until last month. They found her body on Feb. 26, buried in the back yard of her home.

Since then they have found six more bodies on the property — two others buried in the yard and four under the basement — and they still are looking.

It looms as Britain's worst case of serial murder in more than a decade. Police said the search may spread to other parts of Gloucestershire, and they don't know how many victims they may find.

"We've no idea," police spokeswoman Hillary Allison said Monday. "We're just going to continue digging and searching until we find anything else."

Heather's father, Frederick West, 52, was charged last week with killing her and two other women — one of them a pregnant lodger, 18-year-old Shirley Ann Robinson, and the other an unidentified woman in her 20s. Three other victims also were women, but the sex of the seventh, unearthed yesterday in the basement, has not been determined.

Police have not said how the victims died.

Gloucester Chief Inspector Colin Handy said there had been rumors and local gossip for years about the shabby, end-of-row house at 25 Cromwell St.

No one investigated until a local constable decided to take a harder look, Handy said. He refused to give details and would not identify the officer.

Police used a radar device developed to detect buried land mines in the search. "It told us to dig in three places [outside]. We found three bodies," Handy said.

The search moved to the basement during the weekend, and the four other bodies were found.

Handy said once police have finished searching the three-story Victorian house, including demolishing an addition built by West, they will search other sites around Gloucester, 85 miles northwest of London.

National circulation newspaper the Daily Telegraph said police have opened missing persons files dating back to the 1960s in their hunt for possible victims.

Police also are looking for West's first wife, Catherine, and their daughter, Charmaine. Another daughter, Anna, has been located.

Catherine West's relatives said they have not seen her nor Charmaine for years, police said.

The Wests split up some time before 1972, when West married his second wife, Rosemary.

LOS ANGELES TIMES

WEDNESDAY, FEBRUARY 16, 1994

RUSSIA

Killer Executed in Deaths of 52

Russia has executed serial killer Andrei Chikatilo, convicted of 52 murders in three former Soviet republics during a 12-year rampage, the Interfax news agency said in Moscow. Chikatilo, known as the "Rostov Ripper," was shot in the southern region of Rostov-on-Don after President Boris N. Yeltsin rejected an appeal for clemency, the agency said. The former teacher was found guilty of raping and murdering 21 boys, 14 girls and 17 older women in Russia, Ukraine and Uzbekistan starting in 1978. He was arrested in 1990.

Italian farmer denies killing 8 couples

ASSOCIATED PRESS

FLORENCE, Italy — A 68-year-old farmer wept and proclaimed his innocence at the start of his trial yesterday on charges of murdering eight young couples.

The trial began 26 years after the first victims were fatally shot by an assailant dubbed the "Monster of Florence." The killings continued in and around the city until 1985.

The 16 victims, who included a German couple and two French tourists, all were shot with the same .22-caliber Beretta pistol in or near their cars.

"Why don't they believe me?" Pietro Pacciani asked reporters. "They want to try someone who is not involved. I'm a scapegoat."

Wearing an old blue raincoat, he wept throughout the hearing. The lawyers and judge discussed technical matters and the trial was adjourned until tomorrow.

Pacciani, who lived in a small town near Florence, was formally placed under investigation in 1991.

"At least we've finally arrived at a trial," said Renzo Rontini, father of Pia Rontini, slain in 1984.

S. African held in serial killings

REUTERS

CAPE TOWN — A scar-faced male bodybuilder appears in court today as the prime suspect in a hunt for South Africa's worst serial killer — the "Station Strangler."

The 29-year-old teacher with a history of mental illness faces a charge of killing the latest of 22 victims strangled in an eight-year rampage that horrified Cape Town.

The suspect, identified by a deep scar on his right cheek, was arrested last week in a huge hunt for "the Station Strangler" who lured 21 boys and a man away from railway platforms, raped and strangled them, and dumped the bodies in his own personal graveyard.

The man worked as a primary school teacher in the mixed-race community of Mitchells Plain, home of some of the Strangler's young victims, boys between 9 and 15.

A psychological profile compiled to aid police shows a remarkable resemblance to the suspect.

The profile described the Strangler as intelligent, a neat dresser and working in a job such as a policeman, priest or teacher. It also said he was likely to be a single, bilingual mixed-race man.

Drifter Jailed in N. Carolina Is Charged in 10 Murders

CHARLOTTE, N.C.—A man police say strangled neighbors and women he worked with during a killing spree that lasted nearly two years was charged Sunday with 10 counts of murder.

Henry Louis Wallace, 28, was arrested Feb. 4 after a theft at a shopping mall but was released. He was arrested again Saturday, and police said four of the 10 murders were reported between his release and Saturday's arrest.

Police said Wallace was a drifter who settled in Charlotte three years ago. He had no permanent address and worked in various restaurants, Deputy Police Chief L.R. Snider said.

Most of the victims lived in the same section of east Charlotte as Wallace.

Police didn't offer details as to how they identified Wallace as a suspect.

—Associated Press

Star Tribune

Wednesday
March 9/1994

Before dying from AIDS, suspect admits 21 slayings in Illinois, Indiana

Associated Press

Naperville, Ill.
A suspected serial killer who died of complications from AIDS on death row confessed to killing 21 young men he lured with drugs, alcohol and money, his attorney said Tuesday.

The disclosure provided some answers to a decade of questions about Larry Eyler, who died Sunday. Authorities had considered him the prime suspect in the murders in Illinois and Indiana in the early 1980s. He was convicted in only two killings.

"The reason I'm here is so that the families know, he did confess to the murders of your sons," attorney Kathleen Zellner said at a news conference attended by families of Eyler's alleged victims. "He told me that, and I hope that can bring you some peace of mind." Zellner, who had handled Eyler's appeals, said that he described the killings to her over the past three years, and that she persuaded him to let her release his confession after his death.

She released a list of 21 killings to which she said Eyler had confessed, along with the places and dates where the victims were found between 1982 and 1984. Zellner's list gave no names for seven of the victims; 11 were found in Indiana, nine in Illinois and one body has never been found, she said. She also released a handwritten 1990 letter from Eyler to former Illinois Gov. James Thompson offering to confess to the killings. Zellner said the letter was never mailed.

Zellner said an accomplice helped Eyler commit four of the killings. She did not name the alleged accomplice but said she knew the person's identity and urged others who may have been targeted as victims or helped in moving evidence to come forward. Eyler lured his victims with offers of liquor, drugs and money, Zellner said, then drove them to remote areas where they were handcuffed, gagged and blindfolded and had their feet bound. Not all of Eyler's victims were gay, Zellner said, and Eyler never had sex during the abductions.

Law enforcement authorities said Zellner's disclosure wasn't surprising, because Eyler had long been the prime suspect in many of the killings.

"The victims' families got more out of this than law enforcement did," said Andy Knott, spokesman for the Cook County state's attorney's office in Chicago. Knott also said the confession alone doesn't prove that Eyler was the serial killer.

Confessions of alleged serial killer

On Tuesday, Larry Eyler's attorney detailed his confessions of 21 murders; he allegedly committed 17 alone and four with an accomplice. Eyler died Sunday at Pontiac Correctional Center, where he was on Death Row for the 1984 murder of 15-year-old Daniel Bridges of Uptown.

Eyler's alleged victims

Locations and dates of murders; in chronological order.

1 Steven Crockett, age 19*
Kankakee
Oct. 23, 1982

2 John R. Johnson, age 25
Lake County, Ind.
Dec. 25, 1982

3 John L. Roach, age 21
Putnam County, Ind.
Dec. 28, 1982

4 Steven Agan, age 23*
Newport, Ind.
Dec. 28, 1982

5 Edgar Underkoffer, age 27
Danville, Ill.
March 4, 1983

6 Gustavo Herrara, age 28
Lake County, Ill.
April 8, 1983

7 Ervin Dwayne Gibson, age 16
Lake County, Ill.
April 15, 1983

8 Jimmy T. Roberts, age 18
Cook County
May 9, 1983

9 Daniel Scott McNieve, age 21
Indianapolis/Belleville, Ind.
May 9, 1983

10 Unidentified male
Ford County, Ill.
July 2, 1983

11 Ralph Calise, age 28
Lake County, Ill.
Aug. 31, 1983

12 Unidentified male
Rensselaer, Ind.
Oct. 15, 1983

13 Michael Bauer, age 22
Newton County, Ind.
Oct. 19, 1983

14 John Bartlett, age 19
Newton County, Ind.
Oct. 19, 1983

15 Unidentified male
Newton County, Ind.
Oct. 19, 1983

16 Unidentified male*
Newton County, Ind.
Oct. 19, 1983

17 Unidentified male
Effingham, Ill.
Dec. 5, 1983

18 David M. Block, age 22
Lake County, Ill.
May 7, 1984

19 Unidentified male*
Eyler's Chicago apartment
June 1984

20 Richard Wayne, age 21
Indianapolis/Belleville, Ind.
Dec. 7, 1984

21 Unidentified male
Indianapolis/Belleville, Ind.
Dec. 7, 1984

*Victims allegedly murdered by Eyler and an accomplice.

Source: Kathleen Zellner, Larry Eyler's attorney

Chicago Tribune

Table 5-2 . Notorious serial killers (Vampires, Werewolves and cannibals)

Name	Date	Cannibalism/ Mutilation	Location	No. of Victims
Angel Makers	1914-29	Unknown	Budapest, Hungary	300
Vampire Rapist	1968	Yes	Calgary, Canada	4
Moors Murders	1965	No	Manchester, England	5
Joseph Briggen	1902	Yes	Sacramento, California	13
Jerry Brudos	1968	Yes	Portland, Oregon	7
Theodore "Ted" Bundy	1972	Yes	WA,Ut, CO	19 -50
Butcher of Kingsbury Run	1935 -1939	Yes	OH, PA	12
Vampire of Sacramento	1978	Yes	Sacramento, California	6
Red Ripper	1978 - 90	Yes	USSR	52
Carroll E. Cole	1971 - 79	Yes	CA, NV,TX, WY, OK	35
Norman J. Collins	1967 - 69	Yes	Collins, Michigan	7
Adolfo Constanza	1987	Yes	Metamoros	15
Juan V. Corona	1971	Yes	Yuba Co., California	25
Jeffrey L. Dahmer	1991 - 92	Yes	WI, IL	17
Karl Denke	1924	Yes	Poland, Germany	30
Boston Strangler	1962 - 64	Yes	Boston	13
Herman Drenth	1920 - 31	Yes	West Virginia	55
Metal Fang	1980 - 89	Yes	Kazakhstan, USSR	7
Albert Fish	1917 - 28	Yes	Washington, D.C.	12
John W. Gacy	1978 - 80	Yes	Illinois	33
Edward Gein	1954 - 57	Yes	Plainfield, WI	2 - 25
Berlin Butcher	1917 - 21	Yes	Berlin	50
Butcher of Hanover	1919 - 24	Yes	Hanover	27
Teet Haerm,M.D.	1984 - 86	Yes	Stockholm, Copenhagen	8
Jack the Ripper	1888	Yes	London	5 (+2)
Randy Kraft	1972 - 83	Yes	MI, OR, OH, WA, NY	67

Table 5-2 . Notorious serial killers (Vampires, Werewolves and cannibals   (Continuation)

Name	Date	Cannibalism/ Mutilation	Location	No. of Victims
Vampire of Dusseldorf	1929 - 30	Yes	Dusseldorf	9
Henri Landru	1917 - 19	Yes	Gambais, France	300
Monster of the Andes	1970 - 80	Yes	Ecuador, Peru, Columbia	300
Henry Lee	1960 - 83	Yes	U.S.A.	310
Lucas Sydney	1961 - 62	Yes	Sydney, Australia	4
Gennadiy Mikasevich	1971 - 85	Unknown	Soloniki, Russia	36
Monster of Florence	1968 - 86	Yes	Florence, Italy	32
Alfred Packer	1874	Yes	Colorado	5
Elifasi Msomi	1953 - 55	Yes	Natal, So. Africa	15
Hermann Mudgett,MD	1891 - 95	Yes	Chicago	200
Dennis Nilsen	1978 - 83	Yea	London	16
Marcel Petiot, M.D.	1928 - 44	Yea	Villeneuve, France	63
Jesse Pomeroy	1874 - 76	Yes	Boston	29
Lucian Staniak	1964 - 67	Yes	Poland	20
Holocaust Man	1973 - 79	Arsonist	England	25
Yorkshire Ripper	1976 - 81	Yes	Yorkshire	13
Green River Killer	1982 - 84	Yes	Washington	47
Frank Potts	1994	Yes	NY, PA, AI, KY, GA, FL	15
Henry L. Wallace	1994	Unknown	North Carolina	10
Danny Rolling	1989	Yes	Gainsville, FL	5
Joel Rifkin	1993	Yes	Long Island, NY	17
Waneta Hoyt	1965 - 71	No	Newark, NY	5
Station Strangler	1986 - 1994	Yes	Cape Town, South Africa	22
Larry Eyler	1984 - 94	Yes	Indiana	17
I-70/1-35 Killer	1991 - 94	Unknown	MO, IN, TX	5

" He had in his hand a heavy cane, with which he was trifling; but he answered never a word , and seemed to listen with an ill-contained impatience. And then all of a sudden he broke out in a great flame of anger, stamping with his foot, brandishing the cane, and carrying on (as the maid described it) like a mad man. The old gentleman took a step back, with the air of one very much surprised and a trifle hurt; and at that Mr. Hyde broke out of all bounds and clubbed him to the earth. And the next moment, with ape - like fury, he was trampling his victim under foot, and hailing down a storm of blows, under which the bones were audibly shattered and the body jumped upon the roadway."

- Robert Louis Stevenson
  The strange case of Dr. Jekyll and Mr. Hyde, 1886

Chapter 6

"THE BAD SEEDS":

The Jekyll and Hyde Syndrome

The "Dr. Jekyll and Mr. Hyde" Syndrome is very descriptive of children, teens or adults who at one moment turn from being "little angels" and the "salts of the earth" to little monsters, sociopathic rebellious teens (many of whom in their rage assault or kill friends, siblings and parents) and abusive adults who hurt or kill their spouse or children. The sad part is most of these people, often times labeled "bad seeds," don't need counselors or psychiatrists - they need nutritional advice - especially advice about mineral requirements and no sugar diets (the See Food Diet). Unfortunately many of the individuals will wind up in jail or hurt or even kill someone before anyone pays attention - American jails are full of such wasted mineral deficient souls. What kind of society are we that approves of

metamphetamines, tranquilizers and uppers but not mineral supplements? The "Mr. Hyde" side of a child may be cute or frustrating depending upon your mood, however the "Mr. Hyde " side of a teenager or adult of any age with a hammer in their hand is pretty scary.

Each year 1,000 to 1,500 American children under the age of 18 are arrested for murder or manslaughter following their explosive rages. Most are apparently senseless acts unrelated to drugs or gang warfare, the violence and the killing far outweighing the stated cause of the attack, i.e. "I shot my mother and father because they made me do my homework instead of letting me go to the mall with my friends!" The Menendez brothers (35 years old) who murdered their parents in cold blood for alleged

City's killing pace: 1 murder every 10 hours

By John W. Fountain
TRIBUNE STAFF WRITER

Murder in Chicago continues at a record pace, with 291 people killed so far this year, a rate of one homicide every 10 hours, police records showed Thursday.

The nearly 300 homicides also represent a more than 20 percent increase over the 241 people killed during the same period last year and reflects a surge in gang violence, police and analysts said.

Last year, 247 people were killed from January through the end of April.

"It's getting worse, clearly, and the gang-related aspect is going up," said Dr. Carl Bell, a psychiatrist and the president of the Community Mental Health Council.

Bell, who has studied urban violence for about 20 years, said most homicides historically have resulted from "interpersonal altercations" where victims are family or friends of the offenders. Surges in gang-related homicides have contributed in previous years to the murder tolls, but historically have been outpaced by other types of homicide, experts said.

Of the 220 people murdered by the end of March, only 30 have been classified as gang-related, police said. The 291st person, 60-year-old Paul Mike, was shot during an attempted robbery Wednesday night near his home in the 2000 block of West 80th Street, police said.

Still, the recent escalation of shootings among street gangs has left victims caught in the crossfire and contributed to the rising fear of residents. It is an escalating drug war among several gangs feuding internally over control of territories that has led to an increase in shootings, police and observers

Deadliest start to a Chicago year

Through 5 a.m. Thursday, 291 people had been slain in Chicago, setting a record for the most murderous first four months of the year. Fifty more people have been killed than at the same time last year.

Murder victims

Number of people killed in Chicago; January through April

1994: 291*

1986   '88   '90   '92   '94

*Through 5 a.m. April 28

Violent deaths in 1994

Seventy-one percent of victims were shot to death. **Total: 291**

209 gunfire deaths

82 deaths not by gunfire

Source: Chicago Police Department

Chicago Tribune/David Jahntz

agreed.

Jamone Ross, 10, became a casualty of that war Sunday when he was shot while sitting on his bicycle in his South Side neighborhood. Another 10-year-old, Rodney Collins, was shot March 29 when caught in the crossfire while riding his bi-

SEE MURDER, PAGE 20

abuses going back to when they were kids are perfect examples of such sociopathic individuals.

Twenty five per cent of Americans are under the age of 18 and approximately 11 percent of all people arrested for murder and manslaughter are under 18 -16,326 murders were reported in 1988, of those 1,765 were commited by juveniles. Eighty five percent of all juvenile killers are 15, 16 or 17 years old; less than one percent are under 15 years old. In 1988, 0.6 % or three of the 1,765 killings were commited by children under nine years of age.

Arrest figures or even court records do not reflect the true numbers of "bad seeds" who perpetrate assaults, commit murder or manslaughter as most states look at children under seven as "incapable of criminal conduct"; however, a glimpse of reality of the minerally deficient child can be seen in the 1957 movie "The Bad Seed." Patti McCormick played Rhoda (the "Bad Seed"), a well-to-do student in a private school, yet a classic sociopathic little girl (she was very fond of candy, chocolate and ice cream), who at age 10 first killed her aging baby sitter by pushing her down the icy steps to speed up her promise - she had promised Rhoda a glass globe with a little house and snow inside when she died.

Rhodas second killing was a little boy in her class who won a first prize medal in an English composition contest - Rhoda coveted the medal and when he refused to turn his hard won medal over to her she beat him with her metal shoe cleats and then she drowned the little boy at a school picnic. Lastly, Rhoda killed the gardener by setting his straw bed on fire when he suspected her of killing the little boy and teased her about it.

Rhoda was plotting to kill her aging aunt to get the parakeet she was promised when her aunt died; her mother figured out her sociopathic behavior and gave little Rhoda sleeping pills (exchanged for her daily vitamins) to put an end to her murderous ways, but Rhoda survived. In the end Rhoda was killed by lightning as she fished in the pond to get the little boy's composition medal thrown there by her mother.

A 1993 remake of the Bad Seed starring McCaully Culkin who plays Henry is called "One Good Son"; this movie has all of the known updated behaviors of sociopathic kids who create mayhem and kill. Henry, the oldest of three children from an upper middle class family, kills his infant brother by drowning him in the bath tub because he wants his yellow bath duck back that had been handed down to the infant; Henry kills dogs, causes a huge highway pile up by throwing a dummy onto a highway, attempts to murder his younger sister by slinging her out onto the thin ice of a partially frozen skating pond; and lastly tries to kill his mother by pushing her over a cliff after she finds out that Henry killed his baby brother and suggested he need psychiatric help.

Henry is foiled in the attempt on his mother's life by a cousin who recognizes Henry for what he is and in the end given the choice of saving her own sociopathic son Henry or her nephew from dropping off of the cliff she chose to let her sociopathic son die.

Henry's mother let him die in the movie because she had no hope he could be helped and knew he would be placed in a facility for the criminally insane or jail - what a waste. In reality all Rhoda or Henry needed was a sugar free diet and regular supplementation with the 90 required nutrients each day including chromium, vanadium and lithium!!!

Between 1973 and 1979 a British teen ager (started his serial arson murders at age 13) set residence fires with the express purpose of killing - he was to become known as "Holocaust Man." His 25 victims included two infants, an elderly woman of 82, a 72 year old recluse and several epileptics; in one fire alone he burned to death 11 old men in a nursing home.

"Holocaust Man" was in fact Peter Dinsdale (alias, Bruce Lee), an epileptic who was born with an atrophic (withered) right arm - his mother was a prostitute who no doubt drank alcohol and did drugs during her pregnancy. Of his relationship with his mother he said," Ever since I can remember it has been, do this,do that, where are you going? Go to bed, I've got a man friend coming: I don't want him to know I've got a kid, especially a crippled one. Do this. Do that. I just got sick."

David Brewer, 34, was a pigeon breeder who "clipped" Bruce Lee's ear when he was caught disturbing Brewer's pigeon loft. In taking revenge Lee twisted the head off of each and every pigeon in the loft!!

Lee then found Brewer asleep in a drunken stuper; he poured paraffin over him and set him on fire - Brewer remained in a coma for seven days before he died.

In his confession Lee finished his statement by saying," I'm only happy when I see houses burning and people roasting. The screams make me feel very powerful."

American children under the age of 18 account for 17% of all reported arrests and 33.3 % of arrests for serious crimes (i.e.- burglery, larceny, theft, motor vehicle theft and arson); and 16 to 17 % of the arrests for all major violent crimes combined (i.e.- murder, rape, robbery and aggravated assault).

Children under the age of 15 years account for about 5 % of all reported arrests, 13 to 14 % of arrests for serious property crimes and 5 % of arrests for all major violent crimes combined; children under 10 regularly account for 1 % of the annual arrests for major crimes and about 0.5 % of all arrests.

Like age, gender is related to rates of participation in homicide. Juvenile murders and manslaughter like all crime are more likely to be commited by males. Female juveniles are statistically unlikely to kill, however, some of the most dreadful teenage killers are girls!!!

Putting together the appearence of the male hormone testosterone during puberty between 14 and 18, mineral deficiencies (especially copper, chromium, vanadium and lithium) and high sugar intakes (i.e.-apple juice, grape juice, sugar drinks, colas, ice cream, candy, boxed cereals, pastries of all kinds, etc.), it is not surprising that our jails are full and death row is populated by hundreds of teens waiting to be executed for murder!!! Testosterone surges, high sugar intake and mineral deficiencies are as explosive a mixture as matches, nitroglycerine and gun powder combined!!!!

Race and ethnic background are consistently important variables in child committed homicide. Black children are over represented among juveniles arrested for murder and manslaughter - 18 % of all Americans under the age of 18 are black, yet in 1988 over 57 % of all teen killers were black!!! Hispanics comprise only 8 % of the American population yet 25 % of all homicides are committed by Hispanics under the age of 18!!! Add to the testosterone surge, high sugar intake and mineral deficiencies

One man, more than 100 fires: Seattle area's wave of terror

By Lori Sharn
and Deeann Glamser
USA TODAY

EVERETT, Wash. — Meet Paul Keller: 28-year-old former advertising salesman, church choir member — and one of the most prolific arsonists ever to strike the USA.

For six months in 1992 and 1993, he terrorized the Seattle area, setting more than 100 fires that cost at least three lives and an astounding $35 million in damage.

Keller's one-man crime wave is just a small part of the persistent and frightening arson problem plaguing the USA.

Churches in Florida; Amish barns in Pennsylvania; government buildings in Montana — all are recent targets of serial arsonists.

And while no one knows what percentage of fires are set by serial arsonists, there may be 250 serial arsonists at large in the USA, says Dave Icove, formerly with the FBI's National Center for the Analysis of Violent Crime.

Some of them may be like Paul Keller — confused and contradictory, a mass arsonist who says he doesn't know why he set the fires and sometimes forgot about them until turning on the evening news.

Still, like many arsonists, he sometimes stayed to watch his handiwork.

"Mainly what I noticed was how incredibly fast they took off," Keller said in a jailhouse interview. "They burned so fast. It blew me away.

"It wasn't exciting — it upset my stomach."

Investigators say Keller was uniquely armed to spread chaos and fear, with an incredible knowledge of both local geography and firefighting.

Keller — twice rejected as a volunteer firefighter and possibly angry about it — knew every station in the area and avoided police suspicion in part because of his neat appearance and costly wardrobe.

"They don't make serial ar-

By Jim Leo, Everett Herald via AP

IN EVERETT, WASH.: A fire in 1992 at North Cascades Building Materials was attributed to serial arsonist Paul Keller.

sonists like Keller," says Alcohol, Tobacco and Firearms agent Dane Whetsel. "Here is a man who has spent his whole life preparing for this event."

Keller, who admits his crimes — including a retirement home fire that killed three women — says he never meant to hurt anyone. "I am not a bad guy," he says.

After midnight, a cry of 'Call 911'

The arson wave began Aug. 6, 1992. Keller said he had been drinking for several hours when he drove into a cul-de-sac where three houses were under construction.

Using a pocket lighter, he lit the tar paper. The houses burned to the ground.

Three days later, two churches were set ablaze in one night. By September, the arsonist was torching homes while people slept inside.

On many nights, he manipulated firefighters, setting one fire, waiting until the trucks left — then lighting another near the now-empty station.

Firefighters went on a massive public education sweep: They knocked on doors and handed out fliers. Residents moved firewood away from houses, got rid of debris, even locked up plastic lawn chairs.

The Metcalf family in suburban Lynnwood was concerned about the arsons, but not wor-

ried. The family went to sleep on an October night with the garage door locked in place, but open about a foot for their miniature poodle, Taffy.

Rod Metcalf, 40, a contractor, awoke shortly after midnight. Heavy smoke was pouring from the garage.

"Call 911," Rod yelled to his wife, Terry. He ran screaming down the hall, knocking on doors to awaken his seven children, ages 4 to 17.

It was the first of 7 fires that night, all within Snohomish County Fire District No. 1.

As attacks intensify, clues begin to surface

Two months later, Frankie and Bill Geddes were getting ready for bed when they heard a "whoosh" sound. The Geddes, both 77, lived above the boat storage warehouse at their Marysville, Wash., marina. Bill Geddes dashed downstairs and saw a ball of flame rolling across the boats.

"We just got out with our lives," says Geddes. "Five more minutes and we'd have been cremated."

As Keller became more brazen, a special task force began noticing some clues:

▶ The fires mostly were set waist- or chest-high — as opposed to near or on the ground — and never during foul weather. Apparently, the arsonist didn't like to get dirty.

By Robert Sorbo, AP

KELLER: Doesn't know why he set fires; sometimes forgot about them until seeing TV news.

▶ One witness was adamant about seeing a black Ford Taurus leaving a fire. Later, another witness saw a light blue or silver American car with temporary plates.

"It . . . led us to think he was probably a traveling salesman," says Lt. Randall Litchfield of the Seattle Fire Department. "Both were plain-Jane fleet-type cars."

▶ Keller also was leaving records that later would tie him to fire scenes. He purchased gas with a credit card about 90 miles east of Seattle, where four fires were set, and used his cellular phone constantly.

"It left a footprint wherever he would go," Litchfield says.

The task force was getting close, but didn't know it yet.

Arson

The USA has one of the worst fire fatality rates in the industrialized world, and among the leading causes is arson — a killer blamed for more than 600 deaths a year. Underreported and hard to solve, arson soon may be the nation's leading cause of fire deaths, a crime against people, not just property.

By Lori Sharn
USA TODAY

Earlier this week, police claim Julius Kuntu got mad at his landlord and torched the Chicago apartment building where he used to live.

Seven people died, including four children; Kuntu has been charged with murder.

Far from being an isolated example of revenge, experts say the Chicago blaze is part of their growing concern over arson, which is on track to become the USA's top fire killer.

Not only does arson cause about $2 billion a year in damage, but if current trends continue, it will surpass careless smoking to become the leading cause of fire deaths by the end of the decade, says fire protection consultant Phil Schaenman of TriData Corp. Right now arson is linked to about 19% of fire deaths — the second leading cause.

Some experts also believe arson is being used with increasing frequency by gangs and others as a tool of fear, retaliation and murder.

Three weeks ago in St. Paul, Minn., an arsonist killed five children. Police are investigating whether their older brother, a murder witness, was the target of a gang menber.

In Prince Georges County, Md., last year, teen-agers threw a gasoline-filled beer bottle into the apartment of a shooting witness. She escaped, but the fire killed a 1-year-old girl.

"If you burn down an apartment building, everyone knows you're to be feared," says Jim Estepp, Prince Georges County fire chief.

A study of arsons in Los Angeles, Chicago, Philadelphia, Kansas City, Mo., and New Haven, Conn., shows this profile: 21% are drug-related, with re-

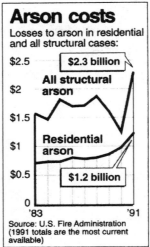

Arson costs

Losses to arson in residential and all structural cases:

$2.3 billion

All structural arson

Residential arson

$1.2 billion

'83   '91

Source: U.S. Fire Administration (1991 totals are the most current available)

By Elys A. McLean, USA TODAY

venge as the motive 14% of the time, and gang members were involved 12% of the time.

A quarter of drug-related arsons were at occupied dwellings, implying "intent to murder," the study says.

"We did not anticipate anywhere near that number," says James Brown, explosives division chief of the Bureau of Alcohol, Tobacco and Firearms. "We've got a lot of problems out there related to narcotics."

In big cities and urban areas, incendiary or suspicious blazes are the leading cause of fire deaths — responsible for a third of fatalities. Nationwide, the number of fire deaths linked to causes other than arson is falling, but deaths linked to incendiary or suspicious fires is holding fairly steady.

The FBI says 15% of arson cases are cleared by arrest or other means. But the National Fire Protection Association estimates only about 2% of "set fires" lead to convictions.

Experts believe many arson fires are never identified as

Portrait of a serial arsonist

Interviews with 83 convicted serial arsonists show they set an average of 31.5 fires each, starting at an average age of 15. Also, 94% are male, 82% white and 66% single and their average education level is 10th grade. Other findings from the interviews, completed in 1992:

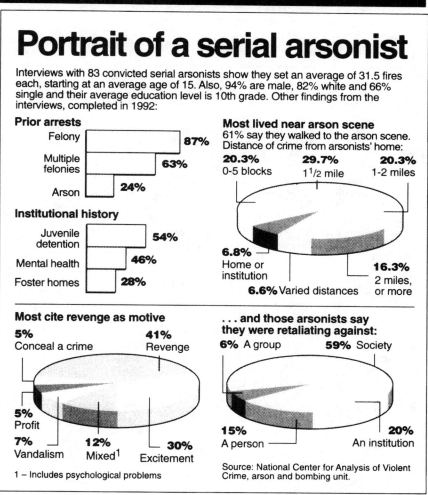

Prior arrests

Felony **87%**

Multiple felonies **63%**

Arson **24%**

Institutional history

Juvenile detention **54%**

Mental health **46%**

Foster homes **28%**

Most lived near arson scene

61% say they walked to the arson scene. Distance of crime from arsonists' home:

20.3% 0-5 blocks

29.7% 1½ mile

20.3% 1-2 miles

6.8% Home or institution

16.3% 2 miles, or more

6.6% Varied distances

Most cite revenge as motive

5% Conceal a crime

41% Revenge

5% Profit

7% Vandalism

12% Mixed[1]

30% Excitement

1 – Includes psychological problems

. . . and those arsonists say they were retaliating against:

6% A group

59% Society

15% A person

20% An institution

Source: National Center for Analysis of Violent Crime, arson and bombing unit.

By Nick Galifianakis, USA TODAY

Los Angeles Times

TUESDAY, NOVEMBER 8, 1994

LOS ANGELES TIMES

Boy, 14, Sentenced to 9 Years in Prison for Killing Child

From Times Wire Services

BATH, N.Y.—Heeding a heart-broken father's plea, a judge sentenced a 14-year-old boy Monday to nine years to life in prison—the maximum possible—for luring a 4-year-old boy into the woods and crushing his skull with a rock.

The killer, Eric Smith, cast his eyes downward but showed no emotion.

Eric, 13 at the time of the slaying, was tried on the murder charge as an adult. He had confessed in 1993 to leading Derrick Robie on a supposed shortcut to a day camp they attended in the western New York village of Savona. In an overgrown lot, Eric choked the boy and bashed his head with a 26-pound rock. He then sodomized the body with a stick.

"When Derrick came into this world I cried and when Derrick left this world I cried," Dale Robie, his voice trembling, said in asking the court for the maximum sentence. "I have felt the whole realm of loving and losing."

"I pray that this person will never have the opportunity to take the life of another child," Robie told the court.

The defense had argued unsuccessfully that Eric suffers from "intermittent explosive disorder," characterized by uncontrollable violent impulses.

His lawyer, Kevin Bradley, Monday described his young client as "a sick boy in need of treatment." Eric will serve at least the first part of his sentence at a lockup for juveniles; he could be transferred to prison at 18.

Eric could be free by age 22 and "back among us at some point in his 20s," prosecutor John Tunney said.

Residents of the rural community at first believed that a stranger was responsible for the murder until a relative of Eric Smith found inconsistencies in his recollection of events and brought him to the attention of investigators.

Under state law, a child as young as 13 can be tried as an adult for murder but faces a more lenient sentence. An adult convicted of murder can get 25 years to life.

USA TODAY · FRIDAY, MAY 27, 1994

FAMILY SLAYINGS: High school honor student Clay Shrout, 17, shot his parents and two sisters, calmly went to trigonometry class, briefly brandished a weapon and announced, "I've had a really bad day, I just killed my family," authorities in Union, Ky., said. He's charged with murder, kidnapping, menacing and disorderly conduct. Police identified the victims as Walter Harvey Shrout, 43; his wife, Becky Shrout, 44, and daughters Kristen Shrout, 14; and Lauren, 12.

AP

SHROUT: 'I've had a bad day.'

THE WASHINGTON POST

FRIDAY, MAY 27, 1994

Kentucky Honor Student Held In Slaying of His Family

UNION, Ky.—A high school honors student killed his parents and two sisters yesterday morning, calmly went to trigonometry class, showed the teacher and classmates his gun and surrendered, saying, "I've had a bad day," authorities said.

Clay Shrout, 17, described by one neighbor as "really weird" and always dressed in black, was being held in the Kenton County Jail, charged with four counts of murder.

Police identified the victims as Walter Harvey Shrout, 43; his wife, Becky Shrout, age unknown; and daughters Kristen, 14; and Lauren, 12.

Police arrested Shrout at Ryle High School in this rural, affluent suburb of Cincinnati after he surrendered to Assistant Principal Stephen Sorrell.

THE NATION'S NEWSPAPER

50 CENTS

NO. 1 IN THE USA . . . FIRST IN DAILY READERS

YOU CAN BUY YOUR HOME AWAY FROM HOME

YOU DON'T HAVE TO BE A MILLIONAIRE TO AFFORD A 2ND PLACE, 1B

'FRANKENSTEIN' A ★★½ GOTHIC BODICE-RIPPER

▶ MOVIE REVIEWS, 4D

WEEKEND EDITION

By Peter M. Fredin

BEAVER CREEK, COLO.: Time-share paradise, **1B**

10 Frantic Days

Oct. 25: 'He's got my kids.' Susan Smith says carjacker took Michael, 3, and Alex, 14 months.

Oct. 26: The FBI joins in nationwide search.

Sight and Sound Studio

Halloween: Yellow ribbons appear in town.

Nov. 2: 'Whoever has my children please, please bring them back.' Police search her home.

Nov. 3: People gasp at news of murder charges.

Police: Mom killed kids

Missing car, two bodies pulled from lake

By Gary Fields
and Robert Davis
USA TODAY

Police Say Baby Slain by Mother, Thrown to Dogs

By LISA O'NEILL
SPECIAL TO THE TIMES

A 19-year-old woman was arrested in Pomona on suspicion of killing her newborn son and throwing his body into the back yard of a neighbor's home where pit bulls were kept, police said Wednesday

Araceli Banda Garcia, who has two other children, was being held without bail at Sybil Brand Institute on suspicion of murder after her arrest Tuesday night, said Lt. Ron Frazier of the Pomona Police Department.

"We believe that the suspect intentionally murdered the infant and have evidence to support a homicide charge," Frazier said.

The mutilated body of the baby boy, whose arm was missing and whose testicles had been severed, was found Friday afternoon in the yard of a house in the 500 block of Orange Grove Avenue.

Police initially believed that one or both of the pit bulls mauled the nine-pound

Please see BABY, B8

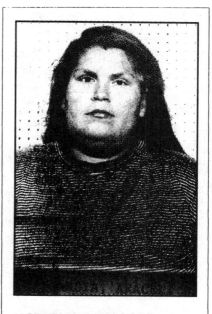

MOTHER ARRESTED: Araceli Banda Garcia, the mother of a newborn baby apparently discarded in a Pomona yard, was arrested and booked for investigation of murder, police said. Police now do not believe that the pit bulls killed the baby. **B1**

the peer group pressures not to "lose face" or to "be macho" you have an explosive mixture equal to matches, nitroglycerine, gun powder and jet fuel!!!! You just know what is going to happen.

Economic background is supposed to have a great deal to do with the crime rate, the poorer the family the more likely the children will get into trouble - on the surface this is correct, but it is the high starch, high sugar diets and the low mineral (i.e.-copper, chromium, vanadium and lithium) food intake of the poor that are the true bottom line causes. As the medical profession still doesn't believe in a disease as real and simple as low blood sugar, it is easy to see why social workers, medical doctors and psychiatrists have missed this one by a country mile!!!!

Jennifer Capriati (tennis) and Tonya Harding (figure skating) are two examples of people with money and bright futures who "fell apart" during the peak of their careers because of mineral deficiencies. Tonya Harding, a true sociopath was pictured many times on the news eating junk food and drinking 32 ounce colas. Capriati turned to drugs to satisfy her pica cravings. Capriati had been the darling of the tennis world at age 13; at 16 she became surly and non-communicative, she suffered tendonitis and bone spurs; at 17 she was a drug abusing runaway!!

The common denominator of both of these well to-do child athletes is mineral deficiencies (i.e.-copper, calcium, chromium, vanadium and lithium) - remember, we lose all minerals when we sweat and if we don't replace them we develop deficiencies. Then there are those who would blame being a "Bad Seed" on genetics.

A recent editorial in Time magazine by Dennis Overbye sums up this issue:

"Some of us it seems were born to be bad. Scientists say they are on the verge of pinning down genetic and biochemical abnormalities that predispose their bearers to violence. An article in the journal science last summer carried the headline EVIDENCE FOUND FOR A POSSIBLE "AGGRESSION" GENE. Waiting in the wings are child-testing programs, drug manufacturers, insurance companies, civil rights advocates, defense attorneys and anxious citizens for whom the violent criminal has replaced the beady eyed communist as the bogeyman. Crime thus joins homosexuality, smoking, divorce, schizophrenia, alcoholism, shyness, political liberalism, intelligence, religiosity, cancer and blue eyes among the many aspects of human life for which it is claimed that biology (genetics) is destiny. Physicist have been pilloried for years for this kind of reductionism, but in biology it makes everybody happy: the scientists and pharmaceutical companies expand their domain; politicians have "progress" to point to; the smokers, divorcees and serial killers get to blame their problem on biology (genetics), and we get the satisfaction of knowing they are sick - not like us at all."

A great study was done by Dr. Gerhard Schrauzer, professor and head of the department of chemistry at the University of California, San Diego relating the violent crime and hard drug use rate of Texas counties to the lithium level in the counties drinking water:

"Using data for 27 Texas counties from 1978-1987, it is shown that the incidence rates of suicide, homicide, and rape are significantly higher in counties whose drinking water supplies contain little or no lithium than in counties with water lithium levels ranging from 70 - 170 ug/L; the differences remain statistically significant ($p<0.01$) after corrections for population density. The corresponding associations with the incidence rates of robbery, burglary, and theft were statistically significant with $p< 0.05$. These results suggest that lithium has moderating effects on suicidal and violent criminal behavior at levels that may be encountered in municipal water supplies. Comparisons of drinking water lithium levels in the respective Texas counties, with the incidence of arrests for possession of opium, cocaine and their derivatives (morphine, heroin, and codeine) from 1981 to 1986 also produced statistically significant inverse associations.."

We would like to see lithium placed in our community drinking water to help control crime instead of fluoride which has produced cancer in laboratory animals!!!

To be sure, some few juvenile killers are literally "born to be bad," true hopeless psychotics because their mothers consumed drugs or alcohol (Table 6-1) during pregnancy and/or were deficient in one or more of the essential nutrients; however, most are not, and although most "Bad Seeds" wind up with one psychological diagnostic label or another most have mild behavior and/or learning disabilities brought on by the fetal drug or alcohol syndrome or preconception, natal or postnatal mineral deficiencies aggravated by high sugar diets (it is also known that certain food allergies, especially dairy can initiate explosive sociopathic behavior).

Even though most juveniles who in an explosive "Mr. Hyde" rage create mayhem or kill are not permanently or seriously disturbed, it is no surprise that most if not all demonstrate some obviously deviant behavior for some time prior to their assault or killing - most frequently antisocial behavior, drug abuse, fire setting, cruelty to animals, truancy, running away from home, bed wetting and pants wetting (long after toilet training), night terrors (night mares) and problems with getting along with age peers. For more than 30 years, clinicians and researchers of "child killers" have been intrigued with the correlation between enuresis (bed wetting) and juvenile killers. In 1961 an article entitled, "Enuresis in Murderous Aggressive Children and Adolescents", thus Dr. Joseph Michaels set the theoretical stage for the professional interest in the relationship.

Persistently enuretic individuals, Dr. Michaels suggested, "Can not hold their tensions, are impatient, and are impelled to act. They feel the urgency of the moment psychologically, as at an earlier date they could not hold their urine."

Our good friend Dr. Lendon Smith, the famous pediatrician and nutrition expert puts it another way:" Blood sugar is the fuel by which the brain derives it's energy;

Table 6-1

Physical defects associated with fetal alcohol syndrome

Abnormality	No. Affected / No. Observed (%)	
Growth and performance:		
Prenatal growth deficiency*	38/39	(97)
Postnatal growth deficiency*	37/38	(97)
Microcephaly*	38/41	(93)
Developmental delay or mental deficiency*	31/35	(89)
Fine motor dysfunction	28/35	(80)
Craniofacial:		
Short palpebral fissures	35/38	(92)
Midfacial hypoplasia	26/40	(65)
Epicanthic folds	20/41	(49)
Limb:		
Abnormal palmar creases	20/41	(49)
Joint anomalies (mostly minor)	17/41	(41)
Other:		
Cardiac defect (mostly septal defects)	20/41	(49)
External genital anomalies (minor)	19/41	(32)
Hemangiomas (mostly small, raised,		
strawberry angiomas)	12/41	(29)
Ear anomalies (minor)	9/41	(22)

*Data taken from 41 patients, including 11 whose cases were previously reported.
[2]2 S.D. or more below the normal for age; equivalent to below the 2.5 percentile.

whether awake or asleep the brain functions at a social level when it has plenty of fuel - when the blood sugar drops below the critical level, as in hypoglycemia, the brain ceases to function at a social level and will react violently to confrontative situations (night mares) and will not honor calls from the bladder (bed wetting).The spinal cord says to the brain," hey our bladders full, get up and go to the toilet!" - when the brain has sufficient levels of fuel it responds by saying, "hold on lets get up and go to the bathroom"; if the blood sugar is low during sleep (hypoglycemia) the brain will ignore the spinal cords request to deal with a full bladder, the spinal cord says,"To hell with this" and allows the bladder to contract and urinate in bed or in the pants during waking hours (The Exorcist).

While you are awake the brain low in fuel is very irritable, explosively reactive and can be very vicious because there are no longer any civilized social restraints which translates into Dr. Jekyll and Mr.Hyde explosive behavior, violence and today more frequently homicide."Our combined experience tells us that Dr. Smith is on the right track. It is a sad fact that Science Diet dog food has 40 minerals in it, Purina rat pellets have 28 minerals and not one human infant formula has more than 12 minerals (chromium, vanadium and lithium are totally absent) - a dog's life may not be so bad.

Major-General Sir Robert McCarrison was the personal physician to British King George V. He was sent on a four year mission to the Gilgit Agency of Hunza in what is now eastern Pakistan - to learn the reasons for the legendary health and longevity of the Hunza people. Part of his efforts included feeding experiments of more than 1,200 laboratory rats:

"Rats that ate the diets of Pathans and Sikhs increased their body weight much faster and were much healthier than those ingesting the daily fares of neighboring peoples such as the Kanarese or the Bengalis. Even more extraordinary, when his rats were fed the same diet as that of the Hunzas, a diet limited to locally produced grain, vegetables, fruits, and unpasteurized goats milk and butter, the rodents appeared to McCarrison to be the healthiest ever raised in his laboratory. They grew rapidly, never seemed to be ill, mated with endless enthusiasm, and had healthy birth defect-free offspring.

Autopsies showed nothing whatsoever wrong with their organs. Throughout their life times these rats were gentle affectionate, and playful. Other rats contracted precisely the disease of the people whose diets they were fed, and even seemed to adopt certain of the human's nastier behavioral characteristics.

Illnesses revealed at autopsy in rats fed the British diet filled a whole page for each rat. All parts of the rats' bodies - skin, hair, blood, ovaries, and womb - and all their systems - respiratory, urinary, digestive, nervous, and cardiovascular - were afflicted. Many of the rats, snarling and vicious ("Bad Seeds"), had to be kept apart if they were not to tear each other to bits!!!!"

We must point out that the highly mineralized Hunza have no jails or criminals or drug related problems of any kind. Disputes are usually over water rights or on rare occasion over a woman. Differences are settled quickly by the tribal elders and the worst punishment ever meted out is that of banishment from the Hunza Valley - what a difference minerals make!!!

Each of us can test ourselves or test loved ones (Fig. 6-1) who have problems: Have them draw their favorite animal before breakfast; then serve them a high sugar breakfast (i.e.- Apple juice, grape juice, boxed high sugar cereal, Pop Tart, muffin with honey, etc.); have them repeat their drawing at 30, 60, 90 and 120 minutes and see what happens - if the drawings are essentially similar there probably is little relationship between the diet and the individuals behavior and manners (or lack of them); however, if the character of the drawings changes significantly then you know exactly what to do.

Another useful tool for identifying a "Bad Seed") is coloring books - go back and look at the consistency of neatness and staying within the lines (Fig. 6-2), if it varies widely you have identified the problem. We recently went to a fast food restaurant in Grand Rapids, Michigan where the management was displaying colored drawings by children to raise money for some charity -about 25 % of the drawings were scribbled, wild and sinisterly colored with very dark colors - they were the renderings of obviously sugared out kids who were minerally deficient !!!

A serious look at the "Bad Seeds", mass murderers and serial killers reveals that as a group, they show startling evidence of their problems (Fig. 6-3) as early as six or seven years of age (very often becoming arsonists, animal killers or even perpetrate

their first human murder at this time).

Perhaps the most recent horror story was the two 10-year-olds (Robert Thompson and Jon Venables) who kidnapped and murdered two year old James Bulger. They were video taped in a Liverpool shopping mall bold as you please by an unmanned security camera dragging their victim screaming and kicking past no less than 32 witnesses on a 2.5-mile forced march to a railway yard in their own neighborhood where they finally bashed in his skull with bricks, stones and a 20 pound metal rod and then killed the child just to see someone die. After 18 days of court proceedings in the industrial town of Preston, England Crown Court Judge described the conduct of the two "Bad Seeds" as "cunning and very wicked." To Sgt. Phil Roberts of the Liverpool police, "it was a case of a couple of bad seeds, of inherent evil."

A three year old killed her 18 month old cousin in an apparent "vengeance killing" by drowning him in a bucket of mop water. The courts argue whether or not a child of three can in fact be charged with murder (remember Rhoda from the bad seed).

Parental child abuse and spousal abuse cases are rampant in America; the numbers and viciousness of the neglect and physical attacks are escalating wildly. Shelters for battered children and spouses are springing up everywhere. Serial killers, cult murders, mutilation and torture are common place headlines to the point that very little stuns us any more.

The president of the United States and our congressmen condemn the television and the film industry for explicit and suggestive violence that they feel is the root cause of our "Bad Seeds." Their view of cause and effect is watch violence and copy

Fig. 6-1

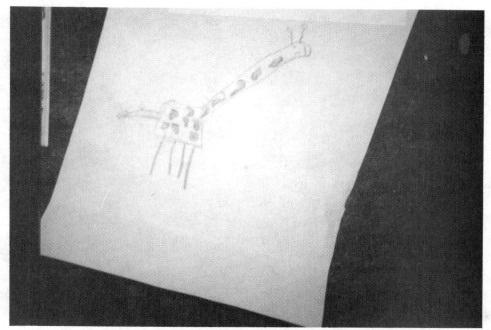

A. Six year olds drawing of a giraffe before high sugar breakfast.

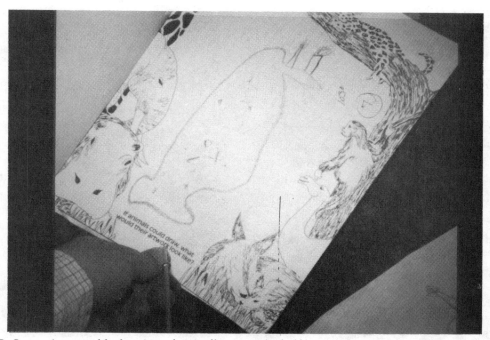

B. Same six year olds drawing of a giraffe one and a half hours after a high sugar breakfast.

Simple method for diagnosing ADD and ADHD associated with high sugar low Cr, V and Li diets.

Fig. 6-2

Before low sugar diets and Cr, Va and Li supplementation

Six weeks after starting low sugar diet and supplementation with Cr, V and Li.

Fig. 6-3

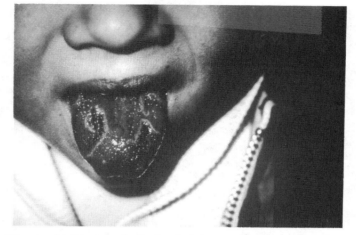

"Geographic" tongue indicates deficiency of B vitamins and Zn.

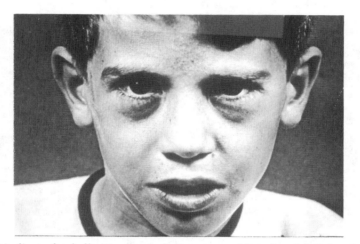

"Allergic shiners" indicate food allergies (including sugar problems) and deficiencies of Cr, V and Li.

"Allergic shiners" and depression are common early signs of teenage troubles and the "Bad Seed" syndrome.

Toddler's murder perplexes Britons

By William E. Schmidt
The New York Times

PRESTON, England — A day after a jury found two 11-year-old boys guilty of the abduction and murder of a Liverpool toddler, the police, politicians and psychiatrists across Britain were pondering questions the trial didn't answer: How is it that two otherwise normal children could commit such a barbaric crime?

At the end of 18 days of hearings in this industrial town 25 miles northeast of Liverpool, even Crown Court Judge Michael Moreland wondered aloud at what went so terribly wrong, describing the conduct of Robert Thompson and Jon Venables — both 10 years old at the time of the slaying in February — as "cunning and very wicked." He even suggested that violent videos may have been influential.

For Britain, the sheer horror of the crime, reinforced by grainy photographs from store security cameras that chillingly captured the boys' abduction of 2-year-old James Bulger, has continued to tug at the nation's conscience, stirring a mixture of revulsion, horror and fury, and raising larger questions

Nation left wondering cause of boys' cruelty

SPECIAL REPORT

about society's failure to protect and nurture its children.

Last February, people were haunted by the thought that what happened to young James could happen to their own children; now they look at the two killers and wonder if they could be their children, too. In a way, this search to understand is part of a healing process, what The Independent, a British newspaper, yesterday called "a remedy for our collective trauma."

What makes the Bulger case so remarkable, most agree, is the fact the crime was not a single act of impulsive behavior but a sustained ordeal that took place over a period of nearly three hours, from the time the two boys lured little James from his mother's side at a Liverpool shopping mall, bul-

lied him on a 2.5-mile forced march across town to their own neighborhood, and finally bashed in his skull with bricks, stones and a 20-pound metal rod along a lonely stretch of railroad track.

The jury agreed with prosecutors that the two boys were capable of knowing right from wrong. But so far, there seems to be little agreement on why the boys committed the crime.

To Sgt. Phil Roberts of the Liverpool police, it was a case of a couple of bad seeds, of inherent evil.

"I believe human nature spurts out freaks," he said. "These two were freaks who just found each other." One of them, Robert, was worse than the other, he said, but together a deadly combination.

Others see the crime as a symptom of a culture that enshrines violence. Already members of Parliament are picking up on Moreland's offhand remark about films on videotape — unsupported by any evidence introduced during the trial — and are proposing an official inquiry into the effects of vio-

Please see **MURDER** on 8A

Can a 3-Year-Old Murder? Is a Court The Place to Decide?

* * *

Girl, Now 12, Says She Killed Her Cousin; Police, Trying To Help, Charge a Felony

By WENDY BOUNDS
Staff Reporter of THE WALL STREET JOURNAL

CINCINNATI — Last Friday afternoon, a 12-year-old girl entered the police station here and confessed to drowning her infant cousin in a bucket nearly a decade ago — a death previously ruled accidental. The cops were confounded.

Locking up the girl seemed ludicrous. She was cooperative and hardly menacing, with her foster mother and a social worker by her side. Police took the child's statement and then let her go, dropping her off in a squad car. Says Sgt. Bob Disbennett: "There's no way you can prosecute someone who was a three-year-old when they committed a crime."

Hamilton County prosecutors saw it differently. When they heard of the case, they began looking for a way to get her whatever help the state might provide a child with a troubled past. Their solution was to have the police arrest her. Charge: murder, first-degree felony.

And so the next day, the little girl with the initials J.M. quietly returned to the police station where she turned herself in again for a crime she says she committed but kept secret for more than nine years.

Rights and Responsibilities

This time J.M. was given the right to remain silent. Then she was given a ride to the Juvenile Detention Center, where she spent the night in custody, alone. J.M. was sent home on Sunday and returned to the detention center on Monday morning for a hearing; she had no lawyer until that morning. Sgt. Disbennett says the sixth-grader "didn't ask for one."

People involved in the case are wondering whether a three-year-old could have a motive for murder, even an unconscious one, and whether she could really remember such an act. They are wondering why a foster parent would take a case like this to the police, and why a legal system seeking a compassionate response could end up reading a little girl her rights and bouncing her from the station house to a detention center to a court hearing.

"At the time the kid was charged, we just wanted a vehicle to get her into the system so she could get help," says state prosecutor Steve Martin. "This was something the system was not prepared to deal with. There seemed to be no other way when it was a Friday, and the courts had closed and this child just confessed to murder.

"We're not trying to lock her up," Mr. Martin says, "but if she's been carrying this around eight or nine years, we need to make sure she gets help."

"It's ridiculous," says Terry Weber, the girl's court-appointed attorney. "This should be over by now."

The case is in limbo at the moment; a hearing has been postponed until March 10 so that J.M. can undergo court-ordered psychiatric evaluation. Today the defense will move to dismiss the charge.

"This is a significant trauma to her," says Mr. Weber, who first met his unsmiling, hesitant client on Monday as she dodged television crews. "It doesn't matter whether or not she did it — I don't think we'll ever know. It should have ended on Monday."

The case actually revolves around two deaths in the same dysfunctional family, and how they may be linked in the clouded memory of a girl, sexually molested and in and out of foster care and therapy for most of her life.

Born in 1981, J.M. never knew her

Please Turn to Page A6, Column 1

violence (monkey see - monkey do) by susceptible young minds— nothing is further from the truth!!!

Our jails and mental hospitals are filled with "Bad Seeds," these sociopathic souls are people, who in their mineral deficient states have no human feelings of compassion or respect of life - no conscience!!!! Sociopaths who gain the most notoriety are the mass murderers, serial killers and cannibals who technically differ from psychotics who do antisocial acts at the bidding of a third party, usually voices - God, Satan, neighbors dog, etc. (i.e.- "Son of Sam") - by contrast sociopaths appear normal to the casual observer except for the lack of emotional attachments to other humans.

Another interesting observation is that the cultures that are note worthy for good physical health and longevity are also note worthy for not having jails and prisons overflowing with hoards of sociopaths and psychotics. Is it because they meditate, do yoga, or because they are vegetarians? The truth is so simple it eludes clever first world societies who have given up their individual control and responsibility for their health to the medical and scientific community who have promised to save them with high technology.

The increase in the numbers and violent behavior of American sociopaths and psychotics shows a direct connection with the rapidly declining mineral content of our soils and foods. Exhaustion of our minerally "played out" land and the resultant mineral deficient high sugar foods are unable to support us mentally or physically are now producing hordes of "Bad Seeds."

The most recent example of a total society destroyed by "Bad Seeds" unearthed by archaeologists is that of Easter Island, long famous for the armies of mysterious stone figures facing out to sea as if looking or pleading for visitors to come save them or to ward off unwanted attackers. It appears that this Island society of 10,000 people self destructed after it totally deforested the island and through neglect allowed a precipitous erosion of the top soil and farm land down to bed rock. As the trees disappeared people reverted to the use of human and animal dung for fuel instead of using the manure to rehabilitate the soil.

Easter Island was first inhabited in 500 A.D. and was in total environmental collapse by 1500 A.D. Evidence of all out warfare appears on Easter Island about 1200 A.D. with anarchy and marauding bands of mineral starved teenagers ("Bad Seeds"). Cannibalism between warring clans (street gangs) delivered the final blow to the Easter Island culture.

Throughout history it took 1,000 to 2,000 years to deplete the land in various countries to the point of total cultural collapse. In the United States intensive farming and the drive to feed the world has accelerated the depletion process which under our system of agriculture has taken only 250 years!!!

Early warnings of this mineral depletion of our soil and subsequent affect on our children are all around us, i.e.- they called him the "Iron Man", standing five foot ten inches and weighing in at a beefy 240 pounds, Craig Price pleaded guilty to mass murder. He told a Rhode Island judge that he broke into two suburban homes during the summer of 1987 and murdered four neighbors (two adult women and two little girls ages eight and ten. The victims were beaten and stabbed- one woman was stabbed 58 times when Craig was in a Mr. Hyde rage).

After hearing Craig Price's plea, the judge sentenced him to the stiffest sentence allowed under Rhode Island law - five years and 17 days!!

Craig Price, already on probation for assault and burglary, committed one of the murders when he was 13 and the other three murders just weeks later when he was 14! Craig was just 17 days shy of his 16th birthday when he confessed to all four murders, he was to do his time in the Rhode Island Training School and again be a free "man" on October 1994. After Craig was sentenced, he told a gang of his high school "brothers" ,"when I get out of here I'm going to smoke a bomber!! As the van pulled away to the training school Craig waved a victory sign and yelled, "Later Dudes."

Not one of his friends or neighbors could or would have predicted that Craig Chandler Price would be a serial killer. Before his arrest, Price was a popular high school football star, nicknamed "Ironman" because of his size - five foot ten inches tall and 240 pounds. "He was the boy next door," says Warwick, Rhode Island mayor Lincoln Chaffe. "On one level, he's a very normal guy. In his private life, he's stalking, planning, killing," says police Captain Kevin Collins.

Price in fact had hid his violent side - he still does. Price has refused therapy, knowing it could get him confined to a mental hospital for life.

On October 11,1994 Price will walk out of the training school and go free on his 21st birthday. "He's a serial killer who was temporarily stopped by his incarceration," says Captain Collins, who witnessed Price's grisly confession. "He just loves to kill.

There's no doubt that he's going to kill again." To understand just how dangerous Price is, when it was announced that he was going to be released his parents packed up and left town.

"There's no way to protect society on his release," says Collins, "people ask me what they should do if he moves to their neighborhood. I tell them to move!"

"The juvenile justice system was developed decades ago for a different type of criminal - when delinquency meant stealing hubcaps," says Claire Johnson, at the Institute for Law and Justice.

"Something just snapped inside, or maybe he just had a mean streak." That is how the local police chief of a small Texas town saw 16 year old Timothy Dwaine Brown. Timothy, who had been expelled from high school for threatening another student with a switch blade knife, beat his 11 year old brother to death with a baseball bat and then shot and killed his grandmother and stepfather with his deer rifle.

Timothy's parents had refused to let him see or call his girl friend - when his younger brother caught him on the phone with the girl and tattled, Timothy became enraged and became a "Mr. Hyde."

Each year, 1,000 to 1,500 American kids under the age of 18 kill friends or relatives. A few of the killings are out of greed, lust or revenge, but the overwhelming majority are murders involving impulsive rage and an exaggerated response to perceived provocation by the victim or still in many cases totally senseless.

Americans under the age of 18 make up 25 % of the total population and they are responsible for 11 % of the killings - about half of the adult rate. Although kids who kill are not mentally retarded, "a dispropor-

Violent crime up, China reports

BEIJING – Violent crime is on the rise in China, and Chinese are feeling increasingly unsafe, the nation's top prosecutor told the legislature yesterday. The annual report by Procurator General Zhang Siqing and a companion report by China's top judge, Ren Jianxing, provided few details. The reports said 574,176 people were charged with criminal offenses last year, 451,920 of whom were tried and sentenced. Neither report gave percentage increases or comparative figures for the previous year. They were five-year reviews and did not provide 1992 figures. China never has divulged many details about crime, but an official newspaper report in December quoted Ren as telling a meeting of judicial officials that violent crime was up 17.5 percent in the first 10 months of 1993. (AP)

MUTILATION TRIAL: Lawyers for two teen-agers charged in the sexual mutilation-murder of three 8-year-old boys near West Memphis, Ark., last May say the conviction Friday of a co-defendant could make it difficult to pick an impartial jury. Charles Jason Baldwin, 16, of Marion, and Damien Wayne Echols, 19, of West Memphis go on trial Feb. 22 in Jonesboro. Jessie Misskelley Jr., 18, was sentenced Friday to life in prison after a jury in Corning convicted him of murder in the three slayings.

Teen-Ager Is Guilty In Slaying of 3 Boys In an Arkansas City

CORNING, Ark., Feb. 4 (AP) — A teen-ager was convicted today in the slayings of three 8-year-old boys from West Memphis, Ark. He was spared the death penalty by a jury that rejected the most serious charge, capital murder.

The teen-ager, Jessie Lloyd Misskelley Jr., 18, was found guilty of first-degree murder in the death of a boy whom he had admitted chasing down. He was convicted of second-degree murder in the deaths of the other two boys.

Late this afternoon, Judge David Burnett of Circuit Court sentenced Mr. Misskelley to life and 40-year sentences to run consecutively, virtually insuring that he will spend all his life in prison. The first-degree murder conviction carried a maximum penalty of life in prison. The second-degree murders carried a maximum penalty of 20 years each.

Two other defendants are to be tried later.

The victims, Steve Branch, Chris Byers and Michael Moore, all second-graders, disappeared from their West Memphis neighborhood on May 5. Their bodies, nude, battered and hogtied, were found the next day.

Mr. Misskelley told the police in two tape-recorded interviews that he had watched as his two friends beat the boys, raped two of them and castrated one. The prosecution said the slayings might have been part of a Satanic ritual.

The case was tried in Clay County Circuit Court in this Northeast Arkansas town about 100 miles from West Memphis after Mr. Misskelley's court-appointed lawyer requested a change of venue.

The two other defendants are Damien Echols, 19, and Charles Jason Baldwin, 16.

S.F. losing battle on juvenile crimes

Friday, February 11, 1994

SAN FRANCISCO EXAMINER

Civil grand jury says The City should focus on core of serious repeat offenders

By Larry D. Hatfield
OF THE EXAMINER STAFF

Though half of all San Francisco crimes are committed by people under 18, The City is failing to adequately fight increasing juvenile crime because too many agencies are involved with competing, poorly coordinated and often contradictory programs, the civil grand jury said Thursday.

Throwing still more money and manpower at the problems is not the answer, the grand jury said in a 17-page report.

Instead, a better-coordinated system should focus on the hard core of serious repeat offenders — fewer than 300 juveniles who commit as much as 80 percent of serious juvenile crimes — and develop early detection and intervention programs for high-risk youths and their families.

Noting that The City already spends $43 million on its juvenile justice efforts without stemming the tide of youth crimes, the grand jury said, "The central problem is that a divisive and fractionated delivery system . . . is preventing our most troubled families and their children from receiving the health, education, social and police services they desperately need.

"Moving from an institutionalized system such as reform schools to a more community-based system such as group homes has had little impact on rehabilitation or prevention," the grand jury report continued. "A lack of coordination in the services offered has generally

[See GRAND JURY, A-14]

S.F. JUVENILE CRIME

The civil grand jury's report on the state of the juvenile justice system in San Francisco offered a chilling snapshot of crime committed by children. Among the findings:

▶ **OF 48,000** youths under 18 in The City, 3,600 — or 7.5 percent — were cited or arrested during the 12 months ending July 1993.

▶ **HALF OF ALL** crimes committed in San Francisco and one in five murders are committed by someone under 18. Although the homicide rate dropped 50 percent between 1991 and 1993, it was three times greater in 1991 than it was in 1988.

▶ **ARRESTS FOR** gun possession rose 47 percent between 1992 and 1993; robberies increased 137 percent from 1988 to 1993.

▶ **NEARLY HALF** of all juvenile crimes are violent.

▶ **HALF OF** the serious crimes committed by juveniles occur on Muni.

▶ **THREE OUT OF FOUR** young offenders are habitually truant from school.

▶ **THE MAJORITY** of crimes against the elderly are committed by juveniles.

TUESDAY, FEBRUARY 1, 1994

Teen-agers' drug use is on the upswing

By Mike Snider
USA TODAY

After more than a decade of decline, drug use among teen-agers now appears to be on the rise, a new study shows.

The latest survey of students in the eighth, 10th and 12th grades suggests that more are experimenting with marijuana, stimulants and LSD. Cigarette smoking also is increasing among all grades.

Overall, fewer students disapprove of drugs or consider them risky. More students also say they know how to get drugs if they want them.

To keep tabs on use of drugs among the USA's youth, University of Michigan researchers have surveyed students each year since 1975 for the National Institute on Drug Abuse. Last year, about 40,000 students in more than 400 schools were surveyed.

Their most recent responses should be heeded as "an early warning signal that this problem is not behind us," says researcher Lloyd Johnston.

Other survey findings:

▶ **Drugs.** About one-third of 12th-graders have used an illicit drug sometime in their lives.

▶ **Alcohol.** Drinking rates remained stable. Among 12th-graders, 63% have been drunk at least once and 29% have had five or more drinks in a row in the past month.

▶ **Cigarettes.** Half-a-pack-daily smokers range from 4% in eighth grade to 11% in 12th

Inhalants are a growing risk

Some of the most popular drugs among teen-agers — inhalants — may be found in the supermarket.

The number who sniff glues, solvents, gases, fingernail polish and aerosols may be headed toward an all-time high.

Only once since 1975, when a national high school drug-use survey began, has inhalant use been higher. In 1986, 20% of 12th-graders said they'd used an inhalant at some time. Last year, 19% of eighth-graders had.

Adults may overlook inhalants and kids "don't realize how dangerous" these products are, says Mathea Falco, president of Drug Strategies, a Washington, D.C.-based group monitoring anti-drug efforts. "They can be instantly lethal," she says, adding that a Maryland teen died last fall after she inhaled propane gas from an outdoor grill.

grade.

Drug czar Lee P. Brown says Clinton administration officials and advisers will soon discuss law enforcement, preventive and treatment programs to prevent "a new cycle of drug use and dependency."

LOS ANGELES TIMES

FRIDAY, MARCH 4, 1994

SAN FERNANDO VALLEY

No Drugs Found in Body of Youth After Fatal Rampage

Troubled teen-ager Christopher Golly was not under the influence of drugs or alcohol when he shot his father to death and then ambushed Los Angeles police with a military-style rifle, killing rookie Officer Christy Lynne Hamilton, the county's top medical examiner said Thursday.

Golly killed his father, called police to his Northridge home by calling 911 to report the slaying, and then opened fire on them before ultimately killing himself early Feb. 22.

After Golly's suicide, there was widespread speculation among friends and classmates that the youth's rampage was the result of his use of methamphetamine, a drug that can cause users to become violent and temperamental.

But Los Angeles County's chief medical examiner-coroner, Dr. Lakshmanan Sathyavagiswaran, said blood tests indicated that the 17-year-old had no alcohol or drugs of any kind in his system—not even residual levels—on the day of the shootings.

Illicit Drug Use Rises Among U.S. Teenagers

Survey Shows Reversal of Trend

By Pierre Thomas
Washington Post Staff Writer

Illicit drug use among American teenagers has increased in the last two years, reversing a trend of generally declining use that began in the late 1970s and the early 1980s, according to a long-term study by the University of Michigan's Institute for Social Research.

More teenagers are using marijuana, LSD, inhalants and stimulants, the survey of 51,000 students found. The report, conducted for the National Institute on Drug Abuse, also revealed a rise in cigarette use, but found that cocaine use, both in powder and crack form, held steady at low levels and alcohol use generally declined.

"These are disturbing findings," said Lloyd Johnston, a researcher on the survey, but he noted that the numbers still are below the levels of the 1970s. "It's an early warning to all sectors of society that the improvements of the last decade can't be taken for granted. Each generation of American youth is naive about drugs and has to learn the same hard lessons."

Some specialists say that surveys about drugs, particularly those involving young people, may be skewed because of the reluctance of some participants to tell the truth about illegal activity and the desire among others to brag. However, the University of Michigan

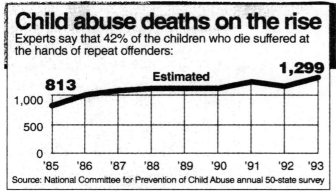

Child abuse deaths on the rise

Experts say that 42% of the children who die suffered at the hands of repeat offenders:

Source: National Committee for Prevention of Child Abuse annual 50-state survey

Illustration and graphic by Sam Ward, USA TODAY

Lifestyles fuel crisis in health care

By Nanci Hellmich
USA TODAY

Many of us could do our part to help solve the national health-care crisis if we led healthier lives.

A study released Monday by the American Medical Association shows at least $1 out of every $4 Americans spend on health care each year goes to treat conditions that result from alcohol abuse, drug use, smoking, street and domestic violence and other potentially changeable behaviors.

Of the nation's $546 billion health-care bill in 1988, more than $171 billion went toward treatment for these types of problems, says Dr. Daniel Johnson Jr., an AMA officer.

"Every person can make a difference ... by adapting a healthier lifestyle — getting proper exercise and nutrition, not using tobacco, not abusing alcohol and fastening our seat belts," he says.

The insurance system discourages patients from making cost-cutting decisions and insulates them from the true price of health care, he says.

Other costly factors: Not using smoke detectors, failure to get checkups that could uncover treatable conditions, engaging in dangerous recreational activities and having unprotected sex.

tionate number" have learning difficulties and have large numbers of behavioral and academic problems before they kill.

In a study by Dr. Dorothy Lewis on 14 kids on death row for murder only one was listed as mentally retarded and two had normal IQ , 10 had reading levels at their age for grade level and three never learned how to read until they were on death row. In addition, many other studies on juvenile killers show no neurological disfunction; many had alcoholic parents (fetal alcohol syndrome) or were themselves alcoholics (pica). A great deal of learned literature has been devoted to the "triad of enuresis, fire setting and cruelty to animals' - a collection of behaviors recorded in children who will later become violent teens and adults.

In one study of 72 kids who killed, Dr. Dewey Cornell discovered that 23 killed strangers, 34 killed aquaintences or friends and 15 killed family members. Kids kill in very inhumane ways with ropes, clubs, knives, cleavers, bare hands, bricks and 33 per 100 killings by kids are perpetrated with guns.

Guns used in juvenile killings are used in lower percentages in the younger age groups and increase in percentage with increasing age of the killer. Also, according to the FBI files the rate of murder by juveniles while involved in other crimes is related to age (hormones are again involved here).

Robbery, theft by force or the threat of force is the theft crime most likely to result in a killing and again the rate is directly related to age. When the thief was 12 to 13 fewer than two robberies out of a 1,000 resulted in a homicide; at age 14 the rate is 2.8 killings per 1,000 robberies; at age 15 the rate was 4 killings per 1,000 robberies; by 16 to 17 the rate was 6 killings per 1000 robberies; and by 19 the rate of murder was 14 killings per 1,000 robberies!!!

At 3:30 a.m. on june 25, 1988, the day he was to deliver his class valedictorian speech at his high school graduation in Niagra Falls, N.Y. 17 year old William Shrubsall beat his mother to death with a baseball bat. First in his high school class all four years out of 250 students, William had been accepted to one of Americas top universities with a full scholarship.

On the night of February 18, 1988, 16 year old David Brown invited a friend to go with him in the family van from Minnesota to Florida; when she asked what his parents would think, he told her," They won't be around to oppose it." That very night David used an axe to kill his mother, father, brother and sister!!!

Wesley Underwood, a 15 year old Texas boy, shot his mother three times in the back after they argued about whether or not he had hidden her knitting needles. Wesley was drinking wiskey and sniffing gasoline (pica) just before the murder.

A 15 year old Colorado boy and his 14 year old friend were charged with robbing, beating and stabbing to death the 15 year olds mother. The boy publically got along with his mother but was known to be an explosively aggressive bully. A friend of the boys said the killing was motivated by "boredom, all we want is somewhere to go."

A 15 year old girl from the suburbs of New York stabbed her mother to death after the mother made a comment about the girls poor grades.

Ginger Turnmire was 15 years old when she shot and killed her mother and father on April 26, 1986 - they were returning from a church picnic in rural Tennesse. After the murders, Ginger drove to the local mall where she bragged to her friends about what she had done.

At Ginger's pre trial hearing she chewed gum and winked at her friends. Prior to the killings Ginger was being treated for severe behavioral problems, had previously attempted suicide, was suspended from school for disruptive behavior and was addicted to drugs.

John Justice was 17 years old, a high school honor student in a suburban Buffalo school - on September 16, 1985 he killed his mother, brother and father by stabbing - he then killed his neighbor when he tried to commit suicide by ramming their car with his (after cutting his own wrists with a razor blade). When the police arrived to deal with the car accident, John told the police, "check #308 Mang, I killed them all." The killings were precipitated by the parents refusal to agree to pay for his college tuition!

On New Years Day 1987, in Washington State, 16 year old Sean Stevenson shot and killed both his parents and then raped and killed his 18 year old sister. The murders followed an argument over whether Sean could go to a party.

On September 8, 1984 in a suburb of Rochester, New York, 15 year old Patrick DeGelleke set his adoptive parent's home on fire. His mother died in the fire and his father died 11 days later from injuries of the fire. For several years before the killings Patrick had been in counseling for "emotional problems." At school he could not concentrate and day dreamt and stared into space a lot; generally quiet at home he would sometimes "erupt into violent uncontrollable temper tantrums." Patrick had a

history of skipping school and petty theft, when his parents petitioned the court to institutionalize him he went into a rage and set the fire.

On April 2, 1984, 14 year old Michael Smalley kidnapped a five year old girl in Ohio and slashed her throat. The girl's body was found in the attic of the families rented home. Michael was convicted of kidnaping and murder and sentenced to one year in the facility operated by the Department of Youth Services. Three and a half years latter Michael, now aged 17 years shot and killed his 15 year old sister on September 20, 1987. He was found guilty and sentenced to life in prison.

In 1987 Nicholas Elliott's mother enrolled him in a private Christian academy so that he would "overcome his shyness and learning problems." Nicholas, one of 22 black students in a school population of 500 white students was picked on and racially taunted by the white students.

On December 16, 1988, 16 year old Nicholas arrived at school with a semi-automatic handgun and 200 rounds of ammunition. He entered his class room in Virginia Beach, Virginia and started shooting, killing one teacher and seriously wounding another. Nicholas was an "isolated pressure cooker who exploded in (a Mr. Hyde) rage when tormented."

In April of 1985, nine year old Britt Kellum argued with his 11 year old brother before killing him with a 16 gauge shotgun. Britt's mother was found guilty of neglect, and custody of Britt and his two surviving brothers was awarded to their father. After four years of psychotherapy, Britt was charged with shooting his six year old brother to death. Britt who couldn't be tried as an adult was ordered "locked up pending further proceedings." If he was charged with murder his maximum sentence would be until he was 21 years old.

On March 6, 1989, Jessica Carr, a seven year old first grader from Pennsylvania was shot and killed while riding on the back of a snowmobile. The killing shot (dead center through the upper spine) was fired by a nine year old boy who said he was just,"playing hunter" with his dads .35 caliber hunting rifle fitted with a scope. The boy, an honor student and cub scout went to his parents bedroom, found the key to the gun cabinet and removed and loaded the rifle. After killing the girl with the shot through the back, he removed the empty cartridge from the rifle's chamber and hid it, then he replaced the gun in the cabinet, locked the cabinet and replaced the key in its hiding place.

The boy claimed he accidently fired the gun, but because the girl was hit "dead center" law enforcement forensic experts testified the shooting was a deliberate act in retaliation to the girls bragging that she was better than the boy at Nintendo!!! A ballistics expert also testified that that particular rifle could not be fired accidently unless struck by a stout blow directly to the hammer causing it to strike the firing pin.

Because of the overwhelming evidence and citing the boys stability, academic achievement, and the deliberate act of the murder the judge ordered the boy to stand trial as an adult - he will be the youngest person in America to be tried for murder in the 20th century.

Dr. Kay Tooley in her paper, The Small Assassins: Clinical Notes on a Subgroup of Murderous Children," she describes two six year olds who repeatedly try to kill their siblings. "Mary" set fire to her younger brother and tried to pour liquid bleach down the throat of her baby half-sister; "Jay" set fire to his sisters dress and later tried to drown her by holding her face under water at a swimming pool - classic "Bad Seeds." Mayo Clinics Dr. William Easson reported an eight year old who like Dr. Tooley's "small assassins" made numerous attempts at "murderous assaults" on a younger brother - he first choked him with his hands until the younger brother was "blue in the face;" next he tried to strangle the same brother with a belt; finally he was caught trying to drown his brother in a bath tub!!!

Doctors Theodore Pettiman and Leonard Davidman described nine "homicidal school age (6 - 11) children, seven of whom either had killed or tried to kill one or more of their siblings. Seven of these children had been under treatment for depression and three were classed as "borderline psychotics."

When these "Bad Seeds" grow up to be adults in addition to joining a high risk crime pattern group including assault and murder some of these kids will become quiet serial killers or explode and become mass murderers!!

Adult mass murderers have identical sociopathic backgrounds and histories of "explosive rages" - they have histories of fire setting, cruelty to animals and other children, bed-wetting, pants-wetting and nightmares. All of the early warning signs of the mass murderer are classic symptoms of chromium and vanadium deficiency (hypoglycemia), copper deficiency or a lithium deficiency aggravated by a high sugar diet.

Almost all mass murderers have a history of depression (hypoglycemia - chromium and vanadium deficiency and/ or a copper or lithium deficiency), spouse abuse, child abuse (lithium deficiency) and pica behavior of some kind (smoking, alcohol, drugs, addictions to candy, chocolate and soft drinks, etc).

"Mass" murderer is a descriptive term for a single killer who kills many victims in a short period of time. In 1977, Fred Cowan, a Nazi sympathizer took pistols and rifles to his work place where he killed four Jewish and black employees and a black passerby before killing himself. In December of 1989 a man wearing a camouflage uniform entered a classroom in Montreal and killed 14 women and wounded 12 before killing himself.

With "Spree Murderers", multiple killings take place over hours or days. In August 1987, Michael Ryan, carrying a Kalashnikov automatic rifle stalked the normally quiet English town of Hungerford leaving 17 dead (including his mother) and 14 wounded before killing himself.

The Killeen, Texas Luby's Cafeteria on U.S. Highway 190 was very busy during the week day lunch hour, especially on Wednesday October 16, 1991 - a long line of hungry customers filed through the serving line and many others were already seated and chatting and eating their meals. "A pleasant murmur of voices, punctuated by the clatter of silverware, enveloped the dining room." This particular cafeteria was normally frequented by senior citizens, but that days patrons included a mix of businessmen and professionals of all age groups, secretaries, service trade workers, store clerks, military personnel and school administrators and teachers.

At 12:40 p.m. a 1987 blue Ford Ranger lurched into the parking lot, turned around at the front of the building and screamed towards the large plate glass window to the right of the front door. To witnesses in the parking lot the driver appeared to have been "stricken ill" or looked as if "the truck was out of control."

Shattering the plate glass, the pickup jumped through the front of the building and rammed into several tables and their occupants before coming to a stop. Those who could were running away from the wreckage. Some were pinned under the truck and shattered tables. The driver, wearing sun glasses and waving a hand gun jumped from the truck shouting "this is what Belton did to me!"

The truck's driver aimed his pistol at a patron trying to pull himself out of the wreckage and killed him; he then turned and randomly yet with cool composure began to shoot the stunned diners. He attempted to kill every man, woman and child.

A public works employee called the police after pulling into the Luby's parking lot for lunch. The small town of Killeen in central Texas is known to millions of Americans because of its location near Fort Hood, the U.S. Army's largest military land installation.

To those hiding behind overturned tables, the killer's shouts were those of a "mad man" - he walked forward and killed "at leisure" pausing only to reload a new clip. One of his first victims was Olgica Taylor, who was having lunch with her daughter and four year-old granddaughter. The killer shot Mrs. Taylor twice and then aimed at the daughter - hesitating he said, " you get that baby and get out of here! Run and hide outside and tell everybody Bell County was bad!" His shots killed one for one and were just about three seconds apart.

Among those killed were an Army Lt. Colonial, a veterinarian and most of the county school administrators - from the victims body count the killer was obviously concentrating on killing women. Forty six people were shot, 23 killed (15 women and 8 men).

Within one minute of the first call the Killeen police arrived; as they entered the debris cluttered cafeteria they spotted the gunman - the killer shot at the police officers who then fired back. In trading shots four police bullets struck the killer- the mortally wounded mass murderer put his own gun to his head and killed himself.

The killer was identified as 35 year old George Hennard of Belton, Texas - a small town only 15 miles from Killeen. He had been permanently banned from his merchant marine status after being caught with drugs aboard ship. Hennard's neighbors described him as "sullen, rude and frequently terrifying." Hennard's shipmates called him a "loner who found trouble wherever he turned, a man who constantly paced back and forth and a man with a volatile temper that could be ignited over nothing."

The Hennard mass killing was almost a repeat of the August 1966 Austin, Texas mass killing by Charles Whittman from the 230 foot high bell tower on the Texas University Campus - he fired down on people on the ground for several hours before he was killed by police. The toll in Austin, only 50 miles south of Killeen, had been 16 dead and 32 wounded (this is an example of a county with a lithium deficient water supply!).

On July 18, 1984 James Oliver Huberty, 41 years old, killed 21 people and wounded 4 at a McDonald's restaurant in San Ysidro, California using automatic rifles and pistols - he killed men, women and children as they arrived by car and bikes for Big Macs and fries. He was finally killed by a shot through the heart by a police sharpshooter.

As a child Huberty had to wear leg braces to correct severe leg deformities (calcium and magnesium deficiencies). Huberty, according to his wife would go into violent rages over the least provocation and was on police blotters as having been abussive to his wife and kids.

One year before the McDonald's killings Huberty was laid off, lost his house and car to the bank. Money pressures had built up to the "melt down" levels just before the rampage. It is not a great surprise that Huberty had been in McDonald's earlier that day for a large Coke (no chromium, no vanadium, no lithium, no copper, too much sugar - no wonder!!!!!!).

Chou Muy Aing, a 17 year old Cambodian refugee, got off of the Portland, Oregon school bus on December 14,1987 and picked up her two young cousins (seven and six) from their baby sitter at 3:40 p.m. and headed for home. After a short walk they arrived home at 4:00 p.m., the Aing children plugged in the Christmas tree lights and turned on the T.V. Then the attacker appeared from behind the couch and buried a meat clever in each of the three childrens heads and then stabbed each numerous times with a large butcher knife obtained from the kitchen.

The horribly hacked bodies were discovered by an aunt - when police arrived at the Aing home their bodies were still warm.

Detectives found out that the Aing children's 17 year old cousin Narin Aing was staying at an American friend's house because of family disagreements. Narin worked part time to pay room and board, Narin was a very good student. As the detectives questioned him he began to relate details of the crime scene that only the killer could know - he was in his uncle's house eating rice without permission when his victims surprised him - he confessed to the murders.

On October 18, 1988 Narin was found on the floor of his cell dying of a suicidal overdose of drugs. Narin's favorite past time prior to the killings was to stop after school and drink colas with his friends; he was being treated for depression (chromium, vanadium, copper and lithium supplements and a sugar free diet would have prevented Aings problems).

Our nations 750,000 postal workers live on coffee and doughnuts, most smoke and very few supplement with vitamins or minerals so its no surprise that they are a collection of "time bombs" waiting to go off.

On November 14, 1991 in the 1,000 employee Royal Oak Post Office (a suburb of Detroit) a mass killing took place. At 8:50 a.m. a man pulled a sawed off shotgun out from under his coat and started firing. He shot three employees on the loading dock, as he walked inside he shot three more leaving four dead and six wounded, then after emptying his rifle he shot himself dead. The shooter was identified as 31 year old Thomas McIlvane. Fellow workers described McIlvane as a "crazy walking time bomb" - as a marine he had driven a tank over the car belonging to another marine who had argued with him.

On October 10, 1991 a fired postal employee shot and killed his former postal supervisor and her boyfriend in Wayne, New Jersey - he then went to the Ridgewood Post Office and killed two mail handlers

after a 4 and one half hour stand off, he surrendered.

On August 10, 1989 postal worker John Merlin Taylor of Escondido, California shot his wife dead in their home - he then drove to his postal branch in Orange Glenn where he killed two fellow workers, injured a third then killed himself.

On December 14, 1988 a postal worker in New Orleans wounded three postal workers and held his girlfriend hostage for more than 13 hours before surrendering.

The bloodiest massacre in postal history was recorded in August 20, 1986 in Edmond, Oklahoma when Patrick Henry Sherill, a part time postal worker killed 14 fellow workers before killing himself.

Although work pressure and the demands of the postal system have been given as the reason for these violent outbursts the truth is their eating habits (or lack of them) and failure to supplement with vitamins and minerals almost promise violent tempers and murderous outbursts. What they really need are sugar-free diets and supplements with chromium, vanadium, copper and lithium.

Probably the most notorious postal worker turned killer was David Berkowitz ("Son of Sam") classed as a psychotic killer because of his claims that "voices" from a third party (in Berkowitz's case his neighbor's dog!) instructed him to kill. His killing began in 1976 on July 29 he shot and killed Donna Lauria and wounded her friend with a .44 magnum he carried in a brown paper bag as they sat in a car talking.

On October 23, 1976 Carl Denaro and Rosemary Keenan were wounded in their car as they "necked" outside a bar in Queens, N.Y.; on November 27, 1976

FLORIDA TODAY, Friday, May 7, 1993

2 die in post office shootings

New York Times

LOS ANGELES — Two people were killed and four others wounded in separate shootings Thursday at post offices in California and Michigan. Disgruntled postal employees were blamed in both cases.

In Dana Point, Calif., 50 miles southeast of downtown Los Angeles, a postal worker who had been dismissed several months ago walked into a small post office and opened fire, killing a letter carrier, wounding a clerk and sending customers fleeing into the street, officials said.

The gunman was being sought by the police after fleeing in a blue pickup truck with a kayak on the roof.

Shortly afterward, a woman thought to be the gunman's mother was found dead in a house in nearby Corona del Mar. Just a few hours earlier in Dearborn, Mich., a postal worker who had been passed over for a job promotion shot three people, killing one, in a post office garage. He later was found dead of an apparently self-inflicted gunshot wound.

The shootings revived questions about security at post offices and about employment conditions in the Postal Service. There have been a series of shootings in post offices in recent years involving postal workers.

The worst of these came Aug. 20, 1986, in Edmond, Okla., where a part-time letter carrier killed 14 people before taking his own life.

In Washington on Thursday, the postmaster general, Marvin Runyon, issued a statement say-

AP

FBI SWAT team members prepare to move into the Dearborn, Mich., post office Thursday to search for the gunman who fired several shots, killing one person and wounding two others.

ing the Postal Service would offer counseling to employees at both post offices.

There is enough concern within the Postal Service about shootings that the service has set up a task force to address the issue, said Roy Betts, spokesman for the Postal Service.

In the California shooting, authorities identified the gunman as Mark Richard Hilbun, 39, a postal employee who was dismissed several months ago.

In the Dearborn shooting, the police identified the gunman as Larry Jason, 45.

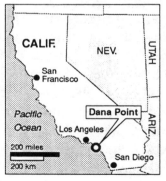

FLORIDA TODAY—AP

Donna De Massi and Joanne Lomino were shot and wounded while sitting on steps outside a house in Queens. All were killed or wounded with the same .44 caliber Bulldog causing Berkowitz to be initially called the ".44 killer."

On January 30, 1977 John Diel and Christine Freund were shot in their car in Queens - Christine was killed.

March 8,1977 17 year old Virginia Vaskerickian was shot and killed and on April 14. Valentina Suriani and Alexander Esau were shot and killed in their car in the Bronx.

Letters from the ".44" killer started arriving - the first found in a victims car addressed to the New York police depeartment stated:

"Dear Captain Joseph Barelli,
I am deeply hurt by your calling me a woman-hater, I am not. But I am a monster."

A letter adressed to columnist Jimmy Breslin of The New York Daily News:

"Dear Mr. Breslin,

Not knowing what the future holds I shall say farewell and I will see you at the next job? Or should I say you will see my handiwork at the next job? Remember Ms. Lauria. In their blood and from the gutter, "Sam's Creation .44."

Now the Daily News called Berkowitz the "Son of Sam." Not since "Jack the Ripper" had a series of killings in a large city had such an affect of mass hysteria as did Berkowitz's handiwork. On June 26,1977 Salvatore Lupo and Judith Plarido were wounded while they sat in their car.

On July 31, 1977 Stacy Moskowitz was shot to death and Robert Violante was blinded by a shot to the head as they sat talking.

Berkowitz's mistake came when he parked in front of a fire hydrant on the night of his last killing and the car was ticketed. A witness saw him throw away the ticket. When police found Berkowitz's car it had a loaded .44 Bulldog on the front seat! When the police caught Berkowitz they asked him who he was and he replied, "I am Sam."

Berkowitz was a 24 year old postal worker and a part-time auxillary policeman. He was diagnosed as paranoid as a child (too much Kool Aid and apple juice and not enough minerals). He began to hear voices in 1974 - "The Voices" were telling him to kill. The walls of his apartment were covered with scribbled messages - "Kill for My Master."

The genesis of the term, "Sam's Creation" came from Berkowitz's neighbor Sam Carrs black Laborador dog that barked all night and kept Berkowitz awake. Berkowitz wrote letters to Carr to no avail and on April 1977 he shot the dog. Berkowitz also wrote anonymous letters to police complaining about people bothering him (just like Andrei Chickatilo the "Red Ripper" did just before he started his killings!!)

Berkowitz was sentenced to 365 years in Attica State Prison.

The most infamous of the modern day "Bad Seeds" has to be Jefferey Dahmer. In his first year of elementary school he began torturing small animals- a baby brother was born (his mother suffered deep depression during her second pregnancy and had depression and anxiety problems during her first trimester with Jeffrey). Dahmer's mother also took prescription medication for her anxiety and depression at the time when his brain was developing; it is well documented that the drugs can cause similar brain impairment as fetal alcohol syndrome!!!

At age six, Dahmer felt neglected because of the appearance of his baby brother and developed a hatred for him according to notes on his first report card!!

Dahmer began to collect large and colorful insects such as beetles, butterflies and dragonflies then graduated to mammalian road kills during his elementary school years. In a toolshed he named "The Hut" Dahmer kept hundreds of jars of dismembered and pickled parts of the road kills-after awhile he began experiments on dissolving their bodies with acid.

When Dahmer reached the age of 14 neighbor's dogs began to disappear - he had graduated from weird anatomist to killer! Dogs showed up decapitated and their headless bodies nailed to a tree, the heads impaled on sticks like a totem -"he loved skulls" said a former schoolmate.

In high school Dahmer became addicted to alcohol (pica). John Backderf, a high school classmate of Dahmers stated," I was always a little wary of him. I was never quite sure what he was going to do. He had this kind of creepy strength about him - an element of danger to him."

Dahmer would actually take cans of beer to school in his army field jacket and drink them between classes - he was a full blown alcoholic by the time he was 13 (pica). At age 18 in his senior year, Dahmer was tracing human bodies on the floor of the school with chalk.

Dahmer would do outrageous imitations of debilitated people which his classmates called "doing a Dahmer." Dahmer's favorite was his faked epileptic siezures - his informal cheering section once paid him $30 to "do a Dahmer" in an exclusive mall.

Dahmer's parents split up and divorced at the time of his high school graduation leaving him alone in a house with an empty refrigerator. Now age 18 Dahmer set out "trolling" in his car on Cleveland-Massillon Road in Bath, Ohio - he was looking for "anything." Here is where he came across a 19 year old hitchhiker named Steven Hicks. Dahmer stopped and gave Hicks a ride and then invited him home for a few drinks. It was June 25, 1978.

After a few beers and homosexual sex, Hicks decided to leave, Dahmer exploded into a "Mr. Hyde" rage and beat him to death with a barbell.

Dahmer dismembered Hick's body and placed the pieces in plastic garbage bags; he then placed the bagged body into the car trunk and drove off to dispose of the body.

Dahmer was pulled over by the police for driving like a drunk but passed the sobriety test so he was allowed to drive off without the car being closely examined!!! He was so frightened that he turned around and went home with the body and placed it in the crawl space of the house - after a few hot June days the flesh began to decompose and smell; this was temporarily solved by burying the flesh filled bags in a shallow grave in his back yard.

After a few weeks Dahmer decided to dig Hick's remains up and cut all of the muscle from the skeleton - he placed the filleted flesh in jars of acid and dissolved the meat into sludge which he flushed down a back yard drain; he then used a sledge-hammer to pound the bones of the limbs,

'Compulsions' encourage Dahmer dementia

By Debbie Howlett
USA TODAY

DAHMER: Serving 999 years for murders of 17 young men

Milwaukee serial killer Jeffrey Dahmer tells *Inside Edition*, in a wide-ranging interview, that sometimes "I still do have those old compulsions."

Dahmer, serving 999 years in a Wisconsin prison for the grisly murders of 17 young men, says he killed not out of anger or hate, "but because I wanted to keep them with me. . . . At the time, it was almost addictive; it was almost a surge of energy I would feel."

The tabloid TV show's first of three segments airs tonight.

Dahmer was arrested in July 1991 when a man in handcuffs led police to the apartment where Dahmer kept body parts in a vat of acid. In the interview he says:

▶ After the first murders, "I was branching out, that's when the cannibalism started, eating the heart and the heart muscle. It was a way of making me feel that they were part of me. At first, it was just curiosity."

▶ "I tried to keep the person alive by inducing a zombie-like state by injecting first a diluted acid solution into the brain or hot water. It never did completely work."

▶ "A compulsive obsession with doing what I was doing overpowered any feelings of repulsion. . . .I was dead-set on going with this compulsion. It was the only thing that gave me satisfaction in life."

spine and skull into small pieces which he threw off of a bluff into a dense woods to be eaten by calcium seeking rodents and birds!!!

Over the next 13 years, Dahmer went to Ohio State University briefly but left to join the army as he spent more time drinking than studying. In the military, Dahmer washed out of the military police academy and went to Fort Sam Houston, Texas to become a medic!!! The army paid for Dahmer to learn about drugs, pain killers, sedatives, drugs that paralyze the nervous system, and invasive medical procedures including the fine points of human anatomy.

After two years and two months, Dahmer was discharged from the army as a hopeless alcoholic. He spent six months in Miami, then moved to Milwaukee to live with his grandmother. He got a job drawing blood for the blood bank, it was now 1982.

Between 1985 and 1991 when he was captured, Dahmer killed 16 more young men and boys by drugging them, strangling them, having oral sex with the the dead bodies then dismembering them. He kept the skulls after cooking the meat off of them, he painted them and placed them around the apartment as trophies. The major portions of the bodies he converted to sludge in acid baths and flushed them down the drain. Dahmer began to eat the heart muscle and then the limb muscle "just to see what it was like," but after awhile he became addicted to human flesh (pica).

Decomposing flesh smelled so bad in Dahmer's apartment that neighbors complained to the police, however, Dahmer was able to convince them that he knew nothing of the cause.

Dahmer was finally caught when one of his intended victims escaped naked and in handcuffs and brought the police back to the apartment.

"A compulsive obsession with what I was doing overpowered any feelings of repulsion... I was dead set on going with this compulsion. It was the only thing that gave me satisfaction in life."

- Jeffrey Dahmer
Inside Edition

"The difference between the child prodigy (i.e.-music, art, math, physics, athletics, etc.) and the high school dropout is not genetics or income level of the parents, but rather the nutritional (and especially the mineral intake) compentancy of the child during pre and postnatal development"

- Joel D. Wallach, BS, DVM, ND
RARE EARTHS: Forbidden Cures, 1994

Chapter 7

GENETIC POTENTIAL:

The Outer Limits.

Pasteur brought about a revolution in medicine by associating bacteria or "germs" with disease - his work carried through to the late 1930's when penicillin was discovered. During that nearly two hundred year period it was thought that most disease including cancer and mental disease was caused by bacterial germs - the "discovery of the century." Everything in medicine was geared towards this bacterial theory; culture techniques, vaccines, antibiotic after antibiotic appeared to save us from bacterial disease.

After World War II viruses became important; techniques in identification and propagation (cell cultures) were developed and every effort was made to attribute every disease from cancer to mental disease to viral cause. The electron microscope, monkeys for vaccine production were the tools of the day - "virus technology was the discovery of the century."

The development of genetic mapping techniques has become the "discovery of the century"- today everyone knows that genetic defects cause everything from body odor to cancer and mental disease. Sound familiar?

Unfortunately the appeearence of every new scientific tool brings with it the great scientific con - grant getting. With fever pitch support from the scammed public, how can congress refuse us the information and tools for better health?

The truth is "genetic defects" are no more the root cause of all disease than is it a fact that all rivers run up stream. The terrible parallel between the medical fever over bacteria, viruses and genetic engineering is that preceding the "discovery of the century" was the development of a laboratory technique, i.e.- bacterial culturing, light microscope; viral culturing, cell cultures, electron microscope; genetic mapping, amniocentesis, test tube babies (actually veterinarians had been freezing semen and fertilizing and implanting eggs, "test tube babies" for 50 years before medical doctors ever dreamt of it) and the ultimate - "genetic engineering."

In both the "viral answer" and the "genetic answer" huge sums of money were drawn out of government coffers and private pharmaceutical firms for research and development, patents, stock options, and public offerings on the stock exchange flow freely - unfortunately none of these "answers" have yet won the war on cancer or any "genetic" disease.

The human does have a genetic potential for physical and emotional perfection and an upper genetic limit for height and longevity as does a flamingo, an angel fish, a cat, a dog and an elephant. The human genetic potential includes a disease free life with a programmed potential for longevity of 120 to 140 years. Attaining your genetic potential (the upper limits of what we can have out of life) for physical and emotional perfection and optimal longevity begins before the beginning!!

PRECONCEPTION:

Contrary to popular belief, our biological responsabilities as parents begin before conception! Preconception nurturing of your body (male and female, however, the major responsibility is weighed toward the woman, as embryonic success is dependent 100 % on the females nutrition) is essential to success and is a must if you are sexually active for a variety of reasons.

First of all, the beginning of a new life in animals and man is referred to as an embryo (Fig. 7-1) until complete developement occurs (90 days in the human), at which time the embryo becomes a fetus. The progression from a fertilized egg to embryo to fetus occurs in the first trimester (first one third of pregnancy) in all mammalian species with the exception of the marsupials. In marsupials, the baby is "born" as an embryo and finishes development in the mothers "pouch."

During the 90 days of embryonic development in man, all body tissues, organs and systems are formed, connected and jump started, leaving only the increase in size from a mouse-like human at 90 days of gestational age to the 6 to 10 pound human fetus at term (birth).

The complexity of the events leading to the neural streak on the embryonic disc becoming parallel neural ridges, which quickly rise from the disc and meet forming the neural tube which is destined to become the brain and spinal cord (including the 12 cranial nerves,i.e.-retina of the eye, the auditory nerves, glossal nerves of the tongue and the great vagus nerves that originate in the brain and innervate the organs of the chest and abdominal cavity); the segmental development of the muscular system and peripheral nerves; the wonder of the formation of the four chambered heart that is intimately integrated with the entire vascular system made up of miles of arteries, veins and capillaries; the ventral enfolding of the embryonic disc that becomes the thoracic and abdominal cavities complete with heart, lungs, liver, pancreas, stomach, gut, genito-urinary tract for reproduction and controlling wastes from the blood; and the endocrine system that provides the push/pull controls over the bodies development, physiological cycles, sexual and metabolic control and maintenance; and lastly the DNA, RNA and tens of thousands of subcellular enzyme cycles, pathways and systems that control emotions, sexual drive (and preferences), eye color, height potential and life itself are some of the "miracles" of life that ignite during this period.

The nutritional requirements of the egg,

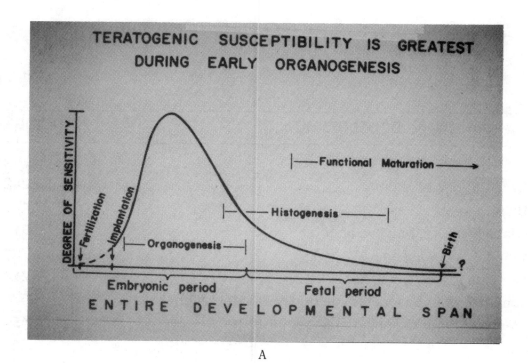

TERATOGENIC SUSCEPTIBILITY IS GREATEST DURING EARLY ORGANOGENESIS

DEGREE OF SENSITIVITY

Fertilization

Implantation

Organogenesis

Histogenesis

Functional Maturation

Birth

?

Embryonic period

Fetal period

ENTIRE DEVELOPMENTAL SPAN

A

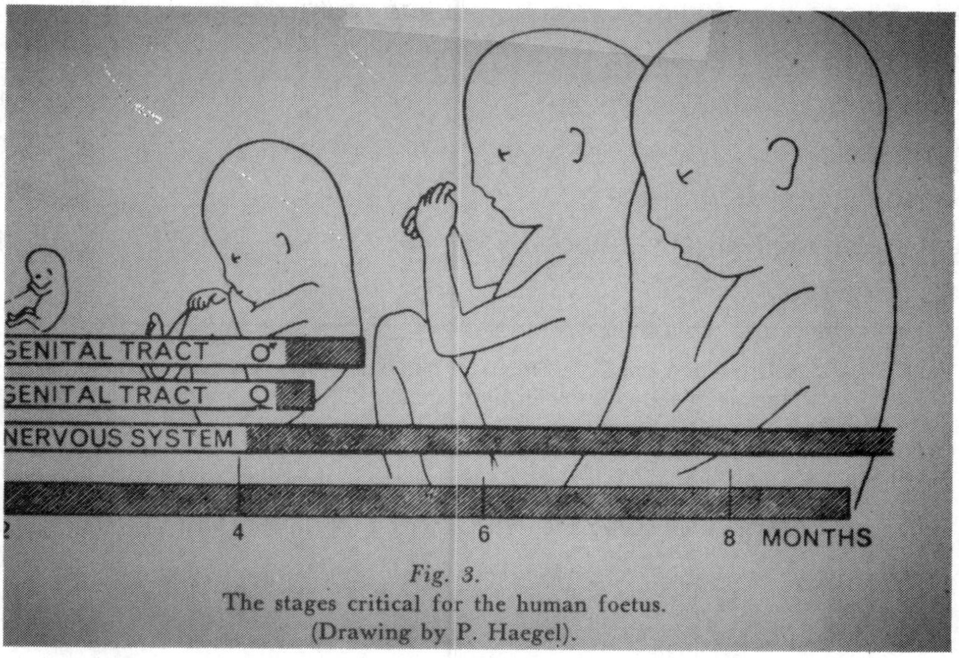

GENITAL TRACT ♂

GENITAL TRACT ♀

NERVOUS SYSTEM

2   4   6   8 MONTHS

Fig. 3.
The stages critical for the human foetus.
(Drawing by P. Haegel).

B

Fig. 7-1 Greatest risk for developmental defects in the human embryo
is in the first trimester of pregnancy.

BIRTH DEFECT	INCIDENCE
Cleft lip and/or cleft palate	2242
Clubfoot	1482
Polydactyly (more than five fingers)	817
Congenital heart disease	734
Spina bifida (defective spine)	712
Epispadinas or hypospadias (deformity of external genitalia)	572
Syndactyly (abnormal union of fingers)	451
Mongolism	423
Bone and joint deformities	386
Hydrocephalus (excess fluid about brain)	254
Omphalocele and eventration (navel hernia and protrusion of bowels)	229
Head and trunk deformities	225
Imperforate anus	188
Ear deformities	185
Tracheoesophageal deformities	144
Atresia of intestines (bowel obstruction)	115
Skin (birthmarks)	104

*Modified from Silberg, S. L., Marienfeld, C. J., Wright H., and others: Surveillance of congenital anomalies in Missouri; 1953-1964: a preliminary report, Arch. Environ. Health 12:641-644, 1966.

Table 7-1 Major congenital malformations reported among 1,135,156 live births in Missouri, 1953-1964.

Infant deaths in the USA

U.S. infant mortality dropped slightly between 1990 and 1991, from 9.1 to 8.9 deaths per 1,000 births. By state (story, 1D):

	1991	1990
Ala.	11.2	12.2
Alaska	9.0	10.1
Ariz.	8.7	8.9
Ark.	10.4	10.0
Calif.	7.8	7.6
Colo.	8.3	8.4
Conn.	-- 1	7.9
Del.	12.7	9.4
D.C.	16.2	18.6
Fla.	8.9	9.7
Ga.	12.4	11.0
Hawaii	6.5	7.3
Idaho	8.7	9.0
Ill.	-- 1	10.9
Ind.	9.0	9.9
Iowa	7.7	8.7
Kan.	9.4	7.7
Ky.	8.2	8.6
La.	9.6	10.6
Maine	-- 1	6.7
Md.	8.1	9.2
Mass.	6.8	7.6
Mich.	9.9	10.5
Minn.	7.2	7.3
Miss.	11.3	12.2
Mo.	10.2	8.6
Mont.	7.6	9.5
Neb.	7.4	7.8
Nev.	-- 1	8.5
N.H.	6.5	7.0
N.J.	-- 1	9.0
N.M.	8.5	8.8
N.Y.	-- 1	9.9
N.C.	11.0	11.0
N.D.	9.0	7.6
Ohio	9.5	9.5
Okla.	9.9	9.8
Ore.	7.6	7.5
Pa.	9.4	9.6
R.I.	7.8	7.0
S.C.	10.6	11.5
S.D.	9.0	9.8
Tenn.	9.7	10.4
Texas	7.7	7.8
Utah	6.0	7.3
Vt.	6.1	6.4
Va.	9.7	10.2
Wash.	7.4	7.9
W.Va.	9.0	9.5
Wis.	8.1	8.3
Wyo.	7.2	8.0

1 - not yet available
Source: National Center for Health Statistics

FLORIDA TODAY, Monday, November 29, 1993

9-week-old gets transplant at Shands

Associated Press

GAINESVILLE — Nine-week-old Gary Weems was "doing very well" Sunday after becoming the youngest patient ever to receive a heart transplant in Florida, officials at Shands Hospital said.

The youngster from Pensacola was operated on Saturday, and on Sunday he passed the halfway mark in what surgeons say is the most critical time period, the first 48 hours after getting the new heart.

"He is still in critical but stable condition," said hospital spokeswoman Kimberly Jordan. "That is typical for a heart-transplant patient at this stage. He's actually doing very, very well."

Gary was stable throughout the five-hour operation, performed by University of Florida surgeons, nurses and medical technicians, said Dr. Daniel Knauf, associate professor of thoracic and cardiovascular surgery at UF's College of Medicine.

"The first 24 to 48 hours are the most critical," said Dr. Eudice Fontenot, assistant professor of cardiology at UF.

Gary, son of Charles and Gari Weems of Pensacola, had idiopathic cardiomyopathy, a weakening of the heart muscle due to unknown causes. He was on a waiting list for a donor heart for four weeks.

"When Gary first arrived here more than one month ago, he was extremely ill," said Dr. Michael Greene, assistant professor of thoracic and cardiovascular surgery. "Fortunately, our cardiologists and intensive care nurses and physicians were able to stabilize and sustain him until a heart became available."

Shands released no information on the donor.

The UF-Shands neonatal-infant heart-transplant unit was established this past May, and there are now 46 institutions in the United States approved to do heart transplants for infants under 1 year of age and 43 for neonatal transplants, involving infants less than a month old.

The first successful newborn heart transplant was done at the Loma Linda University Medical Center in California in November 1985. The child lived until 1992.

The Shands program is dedicated to

CRAWFORD

Jennifer Crawford, daughter of Florida Agricultural Commissioner Bob Crawford. Jennifer was born in April 1980 with a heart defect, and died the following January.

Crawford, then president of the Florida Senate, has since worked to raise money for the infant heart program at UF-Shands.

"I can tell you from first-hand experience that there's probably nothing more of a nightmare to a parent than to realize their child needs extraordinary medical care, especially cardiac care," Crawford said through Shands.

THE DAY, THURSDAY, JULY 29, 1993 **A5**

Surgery saves one Siamese twin but doctors say other will die

By BILL ESTEP
Knight-Ridder Newspapers

Lexington, Ky. — The 2-month-old girl doctors hoped to save with a surgical separation from her twin sister has a very good chance for recovery, her doctors said Wednesday.

But today or Friday, or the next day, maybe, as her parents hold her as much as possible, the other twin will die because she has no kidney.

The decision to separate conjoined twins Brittany and Tiffany Lewis — knowing Tiffany would die as a result — was gut-wrenching for their parents, Kenneth and Angela Lewis of Corbin. But it was the best option because leaving the girls joined would have placed both of them at risk, doctors said.

"Nobody likes the cards they were dealt," Dr. Andrew Pulito said of the Lewises, "but I think they're trying to play the hand they were given the best they can."

Pulito, who helped lead the complex surgery to separate the girls, said Tiffany was not an acceptable candidate for a kidney transplant because she has several other serious medical problems.

Her parents, aided by doctors at the University of Kentucky Medical Center, decided against using life-support systems to keep Tiffany alive.

sperm, the chromosomes in the egg and sperm, the genes on the chromosomes are exquisitly critical before conception, during the embryonic period (Table 7-1), during the fetal period and during life outside of the uterus until we die!! Chromosomes and genes are critical in their second by second requirement for minerals, trace minerals, Rare Earths, vitamins, amino acids and essential fatty acids.

Because of the failure of the American (and the rest of the world, too) food supply to meet these hypercritical needs for nourishment of the chromosome, gene, sperm and egg 15 % of Americans are infertile generating a whole new specialty of fertility doctors praying financially on hopeful parents to be; the sperm count of men has dropped by 50% in the last 100 years, and 10 % percent of our babies are born with emotional (i.e.- learning disabilities, homosexuality, antisocial behavior, hyperactivity, etc.) and or chromosomal and or physical neural tube defects (i.e.-Down's Syndrome, spina bifida, anencephally, hydrocephalus, cerebral palsy,etc.) necessitating whole new medical specialties in pediatric disability problems. Additionally millions of people are born each year with totally unnecessary physical defects (i.e.- cleft palate (Fig. 7-2), cleft lip, heart defects, hiatal hernias, umbilical hernias (Fig. 7-3), extra and webbed digits,etc.), many of which are thought to be genetic defects (Down's Syndrome(Fig. 7-4), muscular dystrophy, cystic fibrosis(Fig. 7-1), diabetes, etc.) by the allopathic medical profession.

Injury to the chromosomes and genes of the human egg and sperm can be caused by radiation (very little of this happens because everyone is very aware not to expose their eggs and sperm to x-rays), toxic chemicals, prescription drugs, alcohol and micronutrient malnutrition, either overt malnutrition (i.e.- deficiencies of minerals, vitamins, amino acids and essential fatty acids) or the malnutrition of maldigestion and/or absorption.

Injuries or birth defects (i.e.-physical, emotional, biochemical and behavioral) that occur to the embryo and fetus and show up at birth regardless of cause are not genetic and are in fact preventable.

Let's take for example Down's Syndrome; for all its characteristic exterior features of domed forehead, medial canthal eye folds, lowered IQ and high risk for certain heart defects, it is the "trisomy" or the extra chromosome 21 that is the basis for Down's Syndrome.

Even as you read this chapter, the allopathic medical doctor believes that the "trisomy" of Down's Syndrome is a genetic or chromosomal defect that only manifests itself primarily in women over the age of 35. Statistically the "over 35" rule of thumb was true when women had eight to ten children (the poor woman would be depleted of minerals by the time she was over 35 so the last two or three embryos were at higher risk for trisomy).

Today, the teenage mother is no longer a rare phenomenon, they are having babies at an ever increasing rate and they have a higher risk of having babies with birth defects including Down's Syndrome than does the mother over 35. They and their babies are at higher risk because of teenagers poor dietary habits plus the fact that teen mothers are still children themselves requiring huge amounts of micronutrients to deal with puberty - they in fact compete with their own embryos for limited or non existent vitamins and minerals.

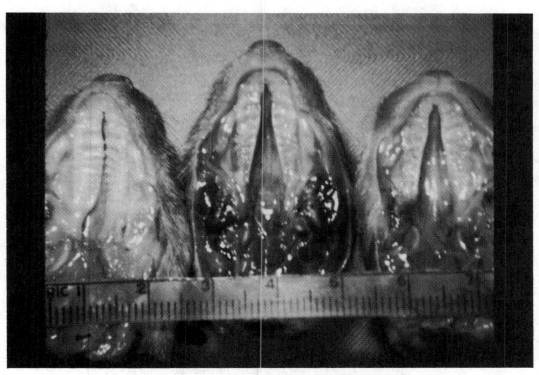

Fig. 7-2 Cleft palates in a small liter of newborn arctic foxes.

Fig. 7-3

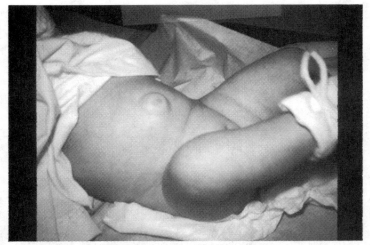

A - Simple Omphalocele (navel hernia)

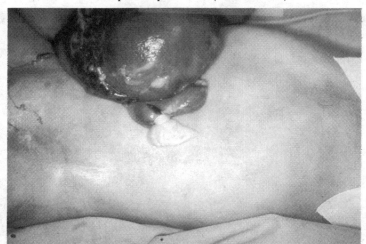

B - Eventration (hernia of stomach)

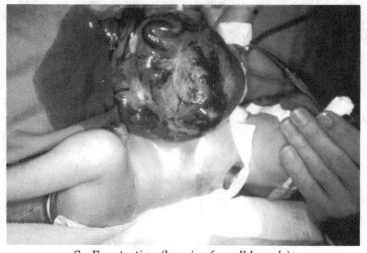

C - Eventration (hernia of small bowels)

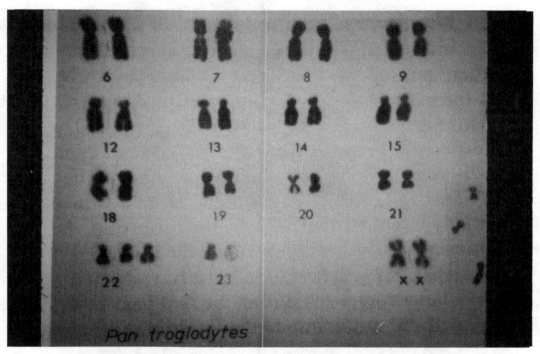

Fig. 7-4 Down's Syndrome (Trisomy 22) in the chromosomes of an infant chimp.

A) Muscular dystrophy in a ostrich chick

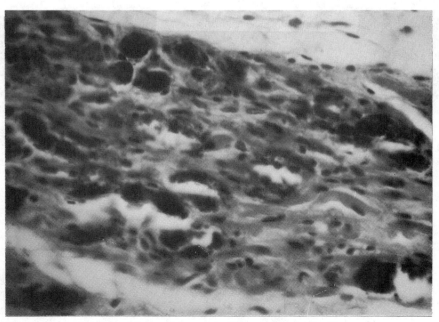

B) Microscopic view of damaged muscle fibers and calcification.
Fig. 7-5

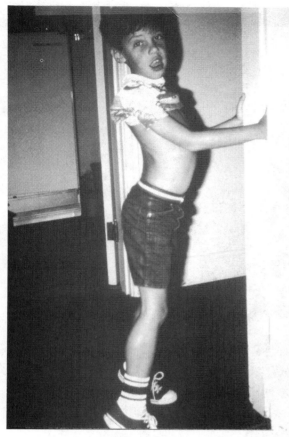

C

Muscular dystrophy in a boy (note enlarged calves).

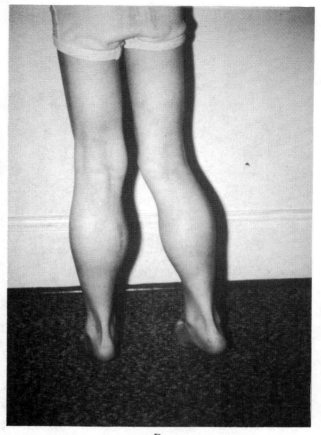

D

Muscular dystrophy in a boy (note enlarged calves).

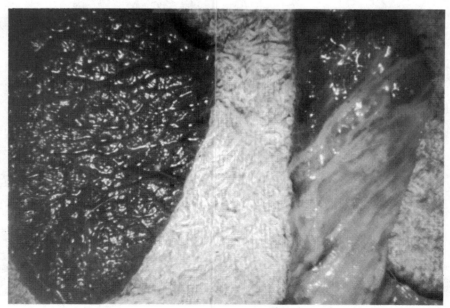

Fig. 7-5 (continued)

E

Normal muscle (left) and MD muscle (right)

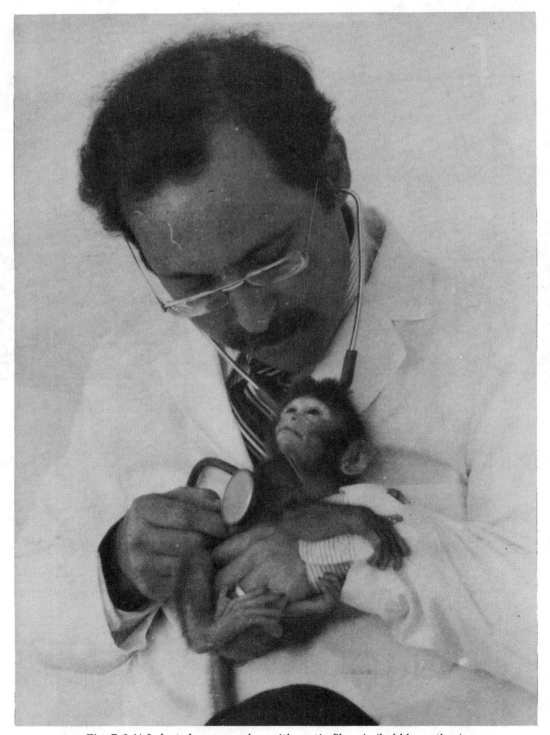

Fig. 7-6 A) Infant rhesus monkey with cystic fibrosis (held by author).

News Copy From
EMORY UNIVERSITY

Information Services
Emory University
Atlanta, Georgia 30322

John Rozier, Director
(Code 404) 329-6216

RELEASE DATE: Sunday AM's - March 5, 1978   March 3, 1978

SUBJECT: **First Case of Cystic Fibrosis
            Discovered in Nonhuman**

Scientists at the Yerkes Regional Primate Research Center of
Emory University have discovered cystic fibrosis in a young rhesus
monkey at autopsy--the first nonhuman case of this disease known
to medical science.

"This appears to be the first animal model of cystic fibrosis,
and we're excited about its implications," said Drs. Joel Wallach
and Harold McClure, veterinary pathologists at the Yerkes Center.

Since cystic fibrosis is thought to be a genetic disease, there
is a possibility that the parents or relatives of the affected
monkey can have additional offspring with cystic fibrosis.

An animal model of cystic fibrosis will permit investigators
to learn a great deal about the basic causes of the disease and how
it might be treated, the Yerkes scientists explained. At present,
the basic defect of the disease is not known.

Cystic fibrosis is a disease of children, adolescents, and
young adults which is characterized by abnormal mucus secretions
and fibrous scarring in various organs such as the pancreas, liver,
lungs, and reproductive and digestive systems. Many of its victims
die in early life of complications such as malabsorption and
pneumonia.

More than 25,000 white people in the United States have the
disease, but a much larger number--five percent of the white popu-
lation--are thought to be carriers of the recessive gene of cystic

-more-

A private, gift-supported institution with 7,500 students and 38,500 alumni, Emory University has served the South and the nation since 1836 as a center
of teaching, research and community activity. College, Graduate School, Schools of Medicine, Law, Theology, Dentistry, Nursing, Business Administration.

fibrosis. It is rarely seen in the black population or in people
of Asiatic origin.

The discovery came as Dr. Wallach, assistant veterinary pathologist at the Yerkes Center, was performing a routine autopsy on
a six-month old male rhesus monkey that had died of unknown causes.
He noticed pancreatic disease and bronchial mucus production;
evaluation of the tissue later under the microscope revealed "a
classic textbook case" of cystic fibrosis as pictured in human
medical literature, the Yerkes scientist said.

Studies of tissue from other organs confirmed that the monkey
was indeed a victim of cystic fibrosis, Dr. Wallach said. Dr.
Wallach's diagnosis was confirmed by Dr. Victor Nassar, an Emory
pediatric pathologist at Atlanta's Grady Memorial Hospital and by
Dr. John Easterly, pathologist at the Chicago Lying-In Hospital,
who is a national authority on cystic fibrosis.

A report on the discovery was made yesterday (Saturday, March
4, 1978) at a Primate Pathology Workshop held in Atlanta. Drs.
Wallach and McClure gave the presentation at Emory's Glenn Memorial
Building near Grady Hospital.

They said the affected animal was bred in a colony of rhesus
monkeys supported by the National Aeronautics and Space Administration for studies pertaining to the U.S. space program.

"We have here a classic example of serendipity," said Drs.
Wallach and McClure. "These animals were being studied for the
space program but are now also providing us clues in a different
area altogether."

-more-

Dr. Nelly Golarz de Bourne, histologist at the Yerkes Center, is conducting NASA studies on the monkey colony in collaboration with Dr. Geoffrey H. Bourne, Yerkes Center director. Their records go back at least 10 years, and include information pertaining to breeding and diseases of the animals.

"We can now go back and look at slides of animals that died to see whether any of them might have had any of the more subtle changes of cystic fibrosis," Dr. McClure explained.

"This discovery has made us aware that these animals can have the disease, so we can make an all-out search for new cases, both in the past and future. If we can breed a supply of animals with cystic fibrosis, using the parents, siblings, or other relatives of the one that had the disease, this will be a great boon to researchers."

Up to now, research efforts toward understanding and curing cystic fibrosis have been severely hampered by lack of an animal model.

"We are very fortunate that the rhesus monkey is the animal model that was found by Dr. Wallach, because more is known about this animal than about any other nonhuman primate," Dr. McClure said. "They are also available for research in fairly large quantities."

Dr. James A. Peters, medical director of the Cystic Fibrosis Foundation, which has its headquarters in Atlanta, commented: "We eagerly await the results of Dr. Wallach's studies because of the importance of an animal model to both basic and clinical research on cystic fibrosis."
He noted that Dr. Wallach will participate in a May 25-26 workshop in Bethesda, Md., on the animal model for the study of cystic fibrosis which will be jointly sponsored by the U.S. National Institute of Arthritis, Metabolism, and Digestive Disease and the Cystic Fibrosis Foundation.

From: Tom Sellers, Science Ed.

Fig. 7-6 C)

Lancet article, November 1985 supporting authors work
(congenital selenium deficiency as cause of cystic fibrosis).

1238   THE LANCET, NOVEMBER 30, 1985

PHYSICAL ACTIVITY PATTERN OF RURAL SOUTH INDIAN WOMEN

Activity	Average time (min/day)		
	Pregnant (n=31)	Lactating (n=31)	NPNL (n=53)
Personal	969	918	678
Domestic	294	198	307
Child care	23	172	35
Social	55	62	195
Field work	51	77	161
Animal care	32	13	37
Travel	2	..	19
Leisure	7	..	8
Other occupation	7	..	..
Business	..	..	..

NPNL = non-pregnant, non-lactating (age 20–29).

and 2010 (NPNL) kcal. This suggests that changes in activity pattern alone could account for a reduction in energy expenditure of about 16% between non-pregnant and pregnant states in these women. The predictions of daily energy expenditure are supported by our estimates of energy intake in the same women, also by 24 h recall, which were 1606±83 (pregnant) and 1997±88 (NPNL) kcal (mean±SEM).

Durnin et al speculate that the scope for changes in physical activity may vary from one population to another. We believe that in rural south India, where the normal level of physical activity is high, significant changes in activity occur in pregnancy and lactation. These may occur to such an extent that the energy intake and energy expenditure of pregnant women may be 15–20% below that of non-pregnant non-lactating women.

Department of Human Nutrition,
London School of Hygiene
    and Tropical Medicine,   G. McNEILL
London WC1E 7HT   P. R. PAYNE

1. Lawrence M, Lamb MH, Lawrence F, Whitehead RG. Maintenance energy cost of pregnancy in rural Gambian women, and influence of dietary status. Lancet 1984; ii: 363–65.
2. Roberts SB, Paul AA, Cole TJ, Whitehead RG. Seasonal changes in activity, birth weight, and lactational performance in rural Gambian women. Trans Roy Soc Trop Med Hyg 1982; 76: 668–78.
3. Houdek Jimenez M, Newton N. Activity and work during pregnancy and the post partum period: A cross-cultural study of 202 societies. Am J Obstet Gynecol 1979; 135: 171–76.
4. World Health Organisation. Energy and protein requirements. WHO Tech Rep Ser 1985 (in press).

SELENIUM DEFICIENCY, CYSTIC FIBROSIS, AND PANCREATIC CANCER

SIR,—In 1979 Wallach[1] advanced his environmental selenium deficiency theory of cystic fibrosis (CF), based on observations in a primate, questionnaires to 120 families with at least one affected child, and an understanding of the complex interactions between nutritional factors that promote or retard lipid peroxidation.[2] He concluded that CF could be "an acquired environmental disease that can be produced by a deficiency of selenium, zinc, and riboflavin and exacerbated by diets also low in vitamin E and rich in polyunsaturated fatty acids". This unorthodox view was dismissed[3] and concern was expressed about the recommendation of supplementary doses of selenium, since there was "lack of any evidence as to selenium deficiency" in CF children[4] (indeed, the implication was that selenium supplements with 25 µg selenium yeast daily had contributed to the deaths of two children). Dr Stead and colleagues (Oct 19, p 862) now provide clear evidence of selenium, with or without vitamin E, deficiency in young adults with the disease and raise the spectre of cancer (pancreatic and extrapancreatic) if the deficiencies are uncorrected.

The dilemma would be resolved if, instead of focusing on antioxidants alone, attention was also directed towards factors that increase the demand on tissue antioxidant stores—for example, increased production of oxygen and other chemical radicals via cytochromes P450. Our studies in patients with chronic pancreatitis illustrate this principle[5,6] and strongly suggest that this disease is a casualty of heightened, but unmitigated, "oxidative detoxification reactions". A modified concept in CF, with inappropriately high cytochrome P450 activities as the basic genetic defect—but which could be compounded by environmental factors—provides a framework within which published observations can be rationalised.[7]

(1) In patients with CF, as in chronic pancreatitis, theophylline clearance is raised,[5,8] indicating increased activities of hydrocarbon-inducible forms of cytochromes P450. The overlap between inherited and acquired exocrine pancreatic disease is further evidenced in the report of a family in which two members had CF and three had calcifying chronic pancreatitis.[9]

(2) Lesions resembling CF macroscopically and/or microscopically (tubular complexes) can be produced in animals by injecting carbon tetrachloride,[10] implanting benzo(a)pyrene,[11] or rendering the animals deficient in selenium.[1] These dissimilar methods share the ability to drive the mono-oxygenase/antioxidant axis in the direction of lipid peroxidation—by generating reactive drug intermediates, inducing cytochromes P450 and thereby increasing production of oxygen radicals, or depleting radical quenchers, respectively.

(3) Tissues affected in CF are just those which retain cytochromes P450 activities after birth.[12]

(4) Mucus secretion, so characteristic a feature in CF, subserves a role in antioxidant protection.[13]

(5) The reported increases in lactoferrin and lysosomal enzymes in serum and lipofuscin in tissues of CF patients are explicable—the first retards lipid peroxidation, the second reflects the vulnerability of lysosomes to oxygen radicals, and the third is a manifestation of excessive lipid peroxidation.

(6) Inducibility of some forms of cytochrome P450 is genetically determined; the placenta is generously endowed with mono-oxygenases; some environmental pollutants linger within the body long enough to cause placental enzyme induction in subsequent conceptions;[14] and prenatal induction of the mono-oxygenases can persist into adulthood. All these facts—and many others—allow the flexibility that is needed for any concept in the context of CF.[7]

To return to the question of antioxidant supplementation in CF, our evolving concepts suggest the need to titrate dosage to demand: this can be achieved only if all three components of the axis are considered (ie, inducers, promoters of induction, and antioxidants). The corollary is that "normal" serum levels of antioxidants are no guarantee that tissue levels are optimum in the face of chronically increased demand.

University Department of Gastroenterology,
Manchester Royal Infirmary,
Manchester M13 9WL   JOAN M. BRAGANZA

1. Wallach JD, Germaise B. Cystic fibrosis: a perinatal manifestation of selenium deficiency. In: Hemphill DD, ed. Trace substances in environmental health. Columbia: University of Missouri Press, 1979: 469–76.
2. Diplock AT. Metabolic and functional defects in selenium deficiency. Phil Trans R Soc Lond 1981; 294: 105–17.
3. Hubbard VS, Barbero G, Chase HP. Selenium and cystic fibrosis. J Pediatr 1980; 96: 421–22.
4. Snodgrass W, Rumack BH, Sullivan JB. Selenium: childhood poisoning and cystic fibrosis. Clin Toxicol 1981; 18: 211–20.
5. Braganza JM, Acheson DWK. Comparative radiological and morphological study of human pancreas. Gut 1985; 26: 1095–96.
6. Braganza JM. The pancreas. In: Pounder R, ed. Recent advances in gastroenterology: Vol VI. Edinburgh: Churchill Livingstone, 1985.
7. Braganza JM. Cystic fibrosis: a casualty of "detoxification"? Med Hypoth (in press).
8. Isles M, Spino M, Tabachnik E, Levison H, Thiesson J, MacLeod S. Theophylline disposition in cystic fibrosis. Am Rev Resp Dis 1983; 127: 417–21.
9. Paris J, Farriaux JP, Gerard A, Maryeille Ph. Etude des pancréatopathies observées dans les 3 générations d'une même famille. Lille Méd 1969; 14: 588–93.
10. Veghelyi PV, Kemeny TT, Pozsonyi J, Sos J. Toxic lesions of the pancreas. Am J Dis Child 1950; 80: 390–403.
11. Bockman DE, Black O, Webster PD. Dedifferentiation of liver and pancreas induced by chemical carcinogens. Gastroenterology 1979; 76: 104.
12. Baron J, Kawabata T, Redick J, et al. Localisation of carcinogen-metabolising enzymes in human and animal tissues. In: Rydstrom J, Montelius J, Bengtsso M, eds. Extrahepatic drug metabolism and chemical carcinogenesis. New York: Elsevier 1983: 73–88.
13. Cross CE, Halliwell B, Allen A. Antioxidant protection: a function of tracheobronchial and gastrointestinal mucus. Lancet 1984; i: 1328–30.
14. Wong TK, Evenson RD, Hsu ST. Potent induction of human placental mono-oxygenase activity by previous dietary exposure to polychlorinated biphenyls and their thermal degradation products. Lancet 1985; i: 721–24.

How can the "classic delayed genetic disease" such as Down's Syndrome appear at incredible rates in our child/mothers? It is true that Down's Syndrome is congenital (i.e.-born with the defect). It is true that there is a chromosomal defect (i.e.- trisomy 21); however, it is not true that Down's Syndrome is genetic!! Down's Syndrome is in fact the result of a preconception zinc deficiency which produces a chromosomal/DNA injury or defect similar in nature to the changes created by radiation (again it is interesting to point out that radiation despite all its horrible potential for chromosomal/DNA injury, causes less than one percent of all birth defects because we are all hyper aware of the dangers and avoid it!!).

Nutritional studies in animals and cell cultures have demonstrated that Trisomy or Down's Syndrome can be created at will in the laboratory by preconception zinc deficiencies during the formation and development of the sperm and the egg - these facts underscore the critical nutritional needs for sexually active men and women. It only takes $40 worth of supplements a month before and during pregnancy to prevent Down's Syndrome and in addition to the human tragedy it costs us a million dollars to care for each Down's Syndrome patient over their life time.

It has been clearly demonstrated in the laboratory animal, pet animal and agriculture that 98 % of all birth defects are not "genetic" in nature, but in fact are nutritional deficiencies of the egg, embryo and fetus and can be prevented by preconception nutrition. Working with these facts instead of denying them, the animal industry has all but eliminated tragic and expensive birth defects (there are no insurance plans private or government that would cover the economic loss of a birth defect in livestock) by supplying high quality preconception and gestational nutrition to breeding animals(Fig. 7-7).

A few pennies a day per animal worth of essential vitamins and minerals has virtually eliminated hydrocephalus, cerebral palsy, spina bifida, Down's Syndrome, heart defects, cleft lip, cleft palate, muscular dystrophy, cystic fibrosis, hernias, limb and digit defects from their breeding colonies.

To understand how the developing embryo are so dependent upon a proper and adequate supply of vitamins, minerals, amino acids and fatty acids, we have to appreciate that embryonic tissues develop faster physically and biochemically than the most aggressive cancer cells, this rate of growth and development requires dizzying amounts of essential nutrients to complete certain biochemical and tissue maneuvers on time - the train only passes by once, if it is missed there is no going back and the child will be born with one or more biochemical, physical, mental or emotional defects.

Genetic engineers refer to the essential mineral cofactors as "metal fingers" which are required to activate genes!!! In the absence of the appropriate "metal finger" DNA and genes are powerless!!!!

The awesome zinc requirements ("metal fingers") alone of the embryo for DNA, RNA replication and as a cofactor for enzyme activity is reflected in the fact that just about every physical defect discribed in man can be produced by an embryonic zinc deficiency; for example spina bifida is a well known embryonic result of a folic acid deficiency, yet folic acid supplementation only prevents 50 % of this defect - the other 50%

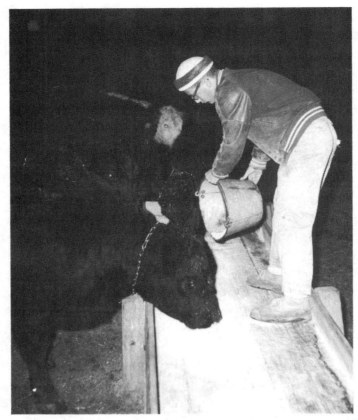

Fig. 7-7 A) Preconception nutrition to prevent birth defects starts at 4:30 a.m. Wallach as teenager feeds breeding cows vitamin, mineral and trace mineral enriched pellets.

B) The results of preconception nutrition is 100 healthy calves for 100 cows.

Fig. 7-7 C In a herd of 100 cows the bull (herd sire) is 50% of the herd-preconception nutrition for the herd sire assures maximum fertility. Wallach admires ideal form of young shorthorn bull.

is preventable by zinc supplementation!!

The animal industry has been able to eliminate 98% of all birth defects, not by bringing in new gene pools, "genetic engineering" and selective breeding programs as is generally believed (in fact the animal industry uses "in breeding," i.e.- mating father/daughter, mother/son, brother/sister to concentrate desirable traits rather than breed out birth defects).

The animal industry has eliminated birth defects in animals, not out of altruistic reasons, but rather to enhance profitability!! If a cow has a calf with a birth defect the cost of feeding and maintaining the cow that year is a financial loss as well as the loss of profits from the projected sale of the calf. There are no insurance companies private or government (i.e.- no major medical, no hospitalization, no medicare, no Blue Cross/Blue Shield) to cover the losses, therefore the farmer, the husbandryman and the rancher must bear the financial burden alone. To reduce his risk of financial loss the animal husbandryman has learned that it is simply cheaper to reduce his risk of financial loss from birth defects by supplementing with vitamins, minerals, amino acids and essential fatty acids in the form of preconception nutrition.

The clinical realities are that few nutritional deficiencies occur in the pure state; in other words if you can see one deficiency the odds are there are really hundreds of them!!! This is why hundreds of thousands of American children are born each year with catastrophic, tragic, family rending birth defects and multiple birth defects - not as the result of a "bad throw of the dice" genetic tragedy, but rather from the "prenatal vitamin" allopathic attitude which says, "I will take vitamins and minerals only after my doctor tells me I'm pregnant," and then in many cases only if a government program pays for it!!

Many women who have had multiple pregnancies "know the ropes" of pregnancy and the OB/GYN process so they often wait three or four months into their pregnancy before seeking obstetrical help from midwives, naturopathic physicians (or in the case of Oregon, chiropractors can deliver babies, too) and nutritional programs to "save money." Remember, the embryo has become a fully formed human at 90 days of gestational age (the brain spinal cord and heart form in the first 28 days of pregnancy) and all of the "prenatal" vitamins and minerals taken after that critical period will not correct any already created birth defects. It's kind of like Humpty Dumpty where "all of the kings horses and all of the kings men couldn't put Humpty Dumpty back together again."

Frequently, identical twins fail to completely separate and are joined somewhere along their midline (i.e.- head to head; chest to chest; abdomen to abdomen; pelvis to pelvis, etc.). This tragic congenital defect of incomplete division of the embryo is 100 percent preventable for $50.00 worth of preconception vitamins and minerals per month for three months prior to conception and each month during pregnancy.

A failure to follow the basic preconception nutrition philosophy has a high risk of being very costly in terms of unnecessary human misery as well as dollar cost.

Twin girls, Angela and Amy Lakeberg were born in Indiana June 29, 1993 - they were joined at the chest and shared a single severely defective heart and a single liver. Following separation the one twin (Amy) was sacrificed in order to save one (Angela).

Table 7-2
Deaths from congenital malformations in American newborns compared with deaths from diarrhea and enteritis.

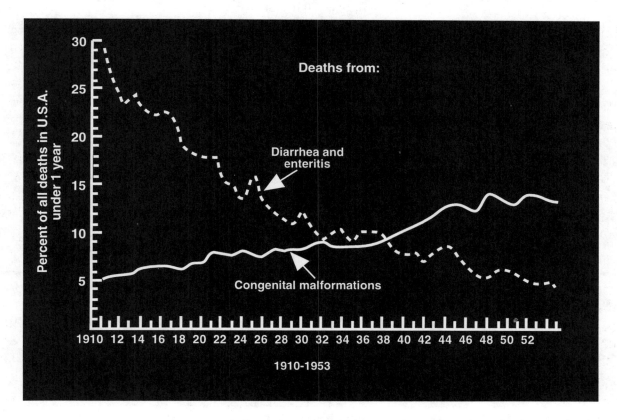

2-Headed Baby Legacy Of Chernobyl Accident

© 1993, Reuters News Service

KISHINYOV, Moldova — Doctors Monday said the 1986 Chernobyl nuclear disaster probably was responsible for the birth of a two-headed baby last week in the former Soviet republic of Moldova.

Doctors at the Moldova Republic Maternity Hospital in Kishinyov told Reuters the girl was born in the town of Taraclia Aug. 18 with two heads, two hearts, two sets of lungs and two spinal cords, although she had only one set of limbs.

The mother, who underwent a Caesarean operation to give birth, was not identified. She previously produced three normal children.

Her doctors said it was Moldova's worst mutation linked to the radiation effects of the power plant explosion at Chernobyl in the neighboring Republic of Ukraine.

"This is the first baby I know of born with two heads in my 20 years of work," Dr. Petru Stratulat, deputy chief surgeon at the hospital, told Reuters. "Probably it is one of the consequences of Chernobyl."

Since Chernobyl the number of malformed babies had increased by 30 percent to about 1,500 a year, despite a fall in the birthrate, he said.

"The chances of this baby's survival are practically nil," he said.

THE DENVER POST

Voice of the Rocky Mountain Empire

Final Edition /
35 cents in Designated Ar

lay, July 23, 1993   THE DENVER POST

A TINY DOUBLE HEADER

A two-headed red-eared turtle that hatched last week at Kliebert's Turtle & Alligator Farm in Hammond, La., is held in the palm of a Kliebert's worker Wednesday. Veterinarians report that the oddity, caused when cells do not divide normally, can occur in every species.

Associated Press / Randy Bergeron

Low-birth-weight babies on increase

ATLANTA — Federal health researchers yesterday reported a disturbing rise in the number of American children born with low birth weight, a health condition that ranks as a leading cause of death among infants.

The U.S. Centers for Disease Control and Prevention said the latest figures show that the number of low-birth-weight infants rose 6.6 percent to 66.4 per 1,000 live births between 1981 and 1991 after declining in the 1970s.

Officials said they were most concerned about an 18.1 percent jump in the number of children with the condition who were born prematurely. The rise in that category was most pronounced among blacks, who accounted for 21.6 percent of the total.

Reuters

ST. LOUIS POST-DISPATCH

SATURDAY, JULY 17, 1993

'Baby Jesse' Dies; Got 2 New Hearts

© 1993, Los Angeles Times

LOS ANGELES — Jesse Dean Sepulveda, who gained fame as "Baby Jesse" when he underwent a heart transplant 16 days after his birth, died Friday, just one month after a second transplant that doctors hoped would save his life. He was 7.

The boy died at Loma Linda University Medical Center in Riverside, Calif., 60 miles east of Los Angeles, hospital spokesman Dick Schaefer said.

Only last Monday, the hospital had reported that Jesse was being treated for rejection of the second new heart, which had received June 16.

Suffering from fatal hypoplastic left-heart syndrome, Baby Jesse became a nationally known household name June 10, 1986, when the 16-day-old infant successfully received the transplanted heart of a brain-dead baby from Michigan

ST. LOUIS POST-DISPATCH

THURSDAY, APRIL 14, 1994

Friends Rally Around Family Whose Son Needs Transplant

By Carolyn Bower
Of the Post-Dispatch Staff

Christopher Oldson turns 1 on Saturday, and friends of his family are raising money to save his life.

Christopher needs a liver and bowel transplant soon to survive. But the family must come up with a $200,000 deposit before Christopher can get the operation at the University of Nebraska Medical Center in Omaha.

Christopher is the son of Kathy and Russell Oldson. Russell Oldson is director of terminal development at TLC Lines Inc., a trucking company in St. Clair, Mo. On Wednesday the company collected $2,385 from employees and business associates, bringing the total raised for Christopher to $3,685.

On May 14 the company will hold a rummage sale at Interstate 44 and the first exit to St. Clair.

Russell Oldson joined TLC Lines about two months after Christopher was born in Dallas. Christopher was two months premature. Four days after Christopher's birth doctors diagnosed an inflammation of the intestines. He developed an infection. Doctors removed 80 percent of his intestines. He also developed bacterial meningitis and hydrocephalus. So far, medical bills exceed $800,000.

Two weeks after Christopher's birth, Russell Oldson lost his job. After the end of this month, the family will no longer have insurance. Christopher and his mother remain in a suburb of Dallas.

Oldson's co-workers have set up A trust fund for Christopher.

After eleven months and nineteen days the surviving Lakeberg twin, Angela, died - the medical cost alone for the attempt to fix what could have been prevented for $40 was over $1 million dollars to tax payers ($600,000 extracted from the taxpayers of Indiana alone).

We must insist that our health dollars be spent more wisely, the Lakebergs were on food stamps which they traded for drugs, the incomplete seperation of the twins was detected in early pregnancy by ultrasound and yet the medical community was so ready to take our money.

Veterinarians have eliminated most birth defects in the animal industry by employing two simple husbandry techniques:

1) Create biochemically complete animal rations in the form of pellets or a "meat loaf" so that every mouthful contains all essential nutrients every meal, every day - no buffet style eating where the animal could pick out its favorite part of the meal. This was a monumental task when you come to think of it because many animals have multiple births or litters which magnifies the pregnancies requirements for minerals and vitamins many fold because of the inter-embryonic competition for limited critical resources and very brief pregnancies!!! Before the problem of competition between embryos for limited nutrition supplies was solved, there might be as many as three to five "runts" (low birth weight babies) in a litter of eight and a similar rate of a variety of birth defects would occur.

2) The health provider (the veterinarian in this case) was made responsible for preventable losses such as birth defects and other financially devastating outcomes of pregnancy and they were taken off of a fee for service system. Veterinarians were placed on salaries and "contract herd health" ranching programs which made them responsable for herd health and production at a set fee (in affect, HMOs). Thus as a veterinarian you only get a contract next year if the rancher makes money this year.

The herd health system forced the veterinarian to seek out and put into effect economical and effective nutritional programs that would prevent catastrophic economic outcomes of pregnancy such as muscular dystrophy (muscle is meat)!!!!

For every 100 cows, the farmer and rancher feeds they demand a hundred pregnancies without complication,they demand a hundred healthy calves, delivered without the need for a ceasarian and they demand that each of those hundred calves reaches market weight or reproductive age without health complications - and they get it. Should our women and children get less health care than a cow?

There are literally dozens of human "genetic" diseases that can be prevented and in the early stages reversed or "cured" with minerals. Three very good examples of "genetic" diseases that can be prevented are cystic fibrosis, muscular dystrophy and Kawasaki Disease.

Cystic fibrosis (CF) is an important, potentially fatal disease of animals and humans, which was originally thought to be transmitted by a simple Mendalian genetic defect limited to white populations of central European origin; today CF has been diagnosed in virtually all peoples of the Earth including Blacks, Asians, American Indians, etc.

In the 80's, a concerted effort to identify "the CF gene" has led to three claims of the gene's discovery. After close scrutiny, the earlier two claims have been discounted by the general scientific community, because the studies were based on linked DNA markers whose exact relations to CF was not certain; the third claim (September 8, 1989, Science) is of particular interest because the authors estimate only a 46% accuracy in identifying CF in patients from families without a previous history of CF and a 68% accuracy in identifying CF patients in families with a privious history of CF. The authors go on to state "it is probable that this condition (CF) is also determined by other genetic or non-genetic factors" and that "the basic biochemical defect of CF has yet to be defined."

Cystic fibrosis is the "crime of the century," second only to diabetes (and that is only because diabetes affects millions and CF "only affects thousands each year") in that it is preventable, 100% curable in the early stages and can be far better managed in chronic cases than it is currently being managed by orthodox medicine.

Classically, the diagnosis of CF is made by employing any two of four recognized criteria (Table 7-3), but most clinicians are reluctant to make a diagnosis of CF without a positive sweat test.

The sweat test has been elevated by medical dogma to "the diagnostic test" for CF, yet there are no less than 17 known diseases and syndromes that also give a positive sweat test (Table 7-4), leading at least one group of investigators from the Cleveland Rainbow Childrens Hospital to refer to "CF as a syndrome (collection of diseases) rather than a disease."

Initially described in 1933, CF was originally thought to be the result of avitaminosis A (a vitamin A deficiency), because of specific vitamin A deficiency changes found in a subgroup of young patients diagnosed clinically with celiac disease.

In 1938, the term "cystic fibrosis" was coined because of a cellular atrophy in the

Table 7-3 . Four Critera for Clinical Diagnosis of CF
Exocrine pancreatic insufficiency Bronchiectasis Positive sweat test Family history of CF

Table 7-4 . Diseases and Syndromes that Reported Positive Sweat Test
Adrenal insufficiency Ectodermal dysplasia Nephrogenic diabetes insipidus Glucose-6-phosphate deficiency Pupillatonia/autonomic dysfunction Allergies Calcifying pancreatitis Anorexia nervosa Cystic fibrosis Focal hepatic cirrhosis Defect in prostaglandin metabolism Hypothyrodism Fucosidosis Mucopolysaccharidosis Malnutrition Kwashiorkor Diabetes

pancreas that reminded the pathologist of "cysts" when viewed under the microscope.

In 1952, the fact that congenital CF occurred in a significant number of CF patients was established.

The genetic theory of CF transmission was suggested by the congenital nature of CF, as described in two previously published papers. The first, a publication that appeared in 1913, was a case report of two children from a family of five who were born to a couple who were first cousins. One child died at the age of 11 months from dehydration and diarrhea (no autopsy was performed); the second was an eight year old child who had diarrhea at the time of the articles appearance - the author theorized that the clinical problem was "an inborn error of fat metabolism" and "probably the result of a simple Mendelian gene defect." This "from the hip" theory was enough to make the allopathic doctors believe that CF was genetic!!

The second paper of interest to the proponents of the genetic theory of CF transmission was an epidemiological study of 232 Australian families, in which 24.3% were diagnosed with CF. Six sets of twins, three identical and three fraternal, failed to shed clear light on the proposed genetic transmission.

It was well established by 1975 that the rate and severity of the pancreatic, liver, heart, lung and intestinal changes in CF, as well as the appearance of the positive sweat test were age and time related (Table 7-5).

In 1978, the first universally accepted diagnosis of nonhuman CF was made (Wallach) from the pancreas and liver of an infant rhesus monkey. The original CF monkey and two unrelated age peers (diagnosed with pancreatic and liver biopsy) were created iatrogenically (accident) by a selenium deficient diet fed to a normal breeding group of monkeys at the Yerke's Regional Primate Research Center destined for NASA space programs.

The diagnosis in the rhesus monkeys was confirmed by pediatric pathologists, considered to be experts on CF, from Grady Memorial Hospital, Emory University, Atlanta, GA; Department of Pathology, Johns Hopkins School of Medicine, Baltimore , MD; Department of Pathology, Chicago-Lying-In Hospital, School of Medicine, University of Chicago.

There was great excitement by everyone, including representatives of the CF Foundation until they learned that the CF in the monkeys could be reproduced with a selenium deficient diet. When the proposal was put forth that the pathognomonic (unique identifying changes) pancreatic lesions of CF, as well as the liver and heart changes of CF were in fact the result of a prenatal selenium deficiency, everyone came unglued - CF was a "genetic" disease and that was that!

The original proposal that CF could be caused by a prenatal selenium deficiency was based on a computer literature search of veterinary journals for tissue changes of pure selenium deficiency in a variety of laboratory species and personal observations of the pancreas, liver, heart, etc. of the selenium deficient monkeys.

In 1958, important nutrition papers were published presenting the rat and mouse as models for the essentiality of selenium in nutrition. In 1972, the chick model for selenium deficiency was introduced. In the case of the chicks, congenital selenium deficiency produced the most

creas. When these CF chicks were given selenium in the first 30 days after hatching the CF disease was totally reversible!!

Wondrous results have been observed and reported in CF patients faithfully supplementing with the 90 essential nutrients including colloidal selenium.

A review of over 350 published autopsy reports of CF patients revealed 79 reports of a unique cardiomyopathy identical with the cardiomyopathy of Chinese children in Keshan Province of the Peoples Republic of China. The cardiomyopathy in China was identified with and related to a selenium deficiency of the soil in Keshan Province by the WHO.

A review of 1,750 cases of Keshan Disease (KSD) in China revealed CF changes in 595 or 35% - for a "genetic" disease of white middle Europeans CF sure jumps around!!

Large scale, double-blind supplementation studies confirmed the original theory of a selenium deficiency cause for KSD.

From 1974 to 1977, preschool and school-age children were divided into two groups. Group one was made up of 36,603 children whose diets were supplemented with 1 mg sodium selenite orally three times per week; group two was a control group of 9,430 children given a sugar tablet placebo. At the end of a three year study, the rate of KSD in the selenium supplemented group dropped from 13/1,000 children to 1/1,000 children; the rate of KSD in the control group remained at 13/1,000. Continued long term studies, eventually involving over 500,000 participants, confirmed that supplemental selenium was specific for the prevention of KSD!!

Muscular dystrophy (MD) is another crime against the American people by the "orthodox" medical doctors for reasons of money - if the total truth was shared with the public, muscular dystrophy would be totally preventable but a whole medical specialty would be wiped out!!! As crazy as this seems, look at the veterinary industry where muscle is "king" (i.e.- pork chops, beef steak, lamb chops, roasts, ground red meat, chicken, turkey, etc.); muscular dystrophy (white muscle disease, stiff lamb

Table 7-5 . Age and Time as Factors in the Severity of Changes in CF				
Tissues	Newborn	2-3	6-12	Adult
Pancreas	75%	++	+++	85%
Liver	34%	26.8%	29.5%	29.5%
Lung	0%	50%	85%	100%
Heart	0%	+	++	+++
Intestine	75%	++	+++	100%
sweat test (+)	25%	85%	85%	85%

disease, mulberry heart disease in pigs, etc.) has been wiped out in the veterinary industry by simple selenium supplementation to pregnant animals and rapidly growing prepubic animals.

In addition to the overt selenium deficiencies in the American diet, the loss of intestinal villi associated with celiac disease (wheat gluten or cows milk albumin sensitivity) frequently results in an inability to absorb selenium even if it is in the diet. The best assurance of adequate selenium for a fetus is to supplement with chelated selenium (selenomethionine) or plant derived colloidal selenium.

Prevention is the name of the game with MD; the selenium levels in the diets and supplements of preconception women is important to the maintenance of pregnancy as well as the prevention of MD in all of its forms (i.e.- Duchenne {legs and back}, Erb {scapulohumeral}, Leyden-Moebius {pelvifemoral}, Landouzy-Dejerine {facioscapulo-humeral}, Becker's {benign juvenile}, and Gowers {hands and feet}), which are in reality artificial classifications of MD by groups of muscles initially affected by chance at diagnosis.

Keshan Disease (cardiomyopathy or heart muscular dystrophy {"mulberry heart disease"}) which is also caused by a selenium deficiency (Fig. 7-8) should be added to the list of muscular dystrophies.

Kawasaki Disease is a disease that has two parts. The human infant born with Kawasaki is born with a congenital coronary artery aneurysm (a separation of the middle and inner layers of the artery or a ballooning of a weakened artery) which is in fact a congenital copper deficiency, copper being required to manufacture and maintain elastic fibers in arteries as well as other tissues. The second part of Kawasaki disease is a Streptococcal invasion of the aneurysm site - Streptococcal infection will set up in the damaged artery wall following a leakage of bacteria into the blood following a Strep-throat infection or dental work.

Kawasaki Disease is totally preventable with preconception supplementation of copper (especially colloidal copper).

More difficult to understand than the physical birth defects are the biochemical behavioral, learning and emotional defects that are preventable with preconception nutrition. The principals for preventing the "Bad Seeds," children with emotional and learning defects are the same as those for preventing the physical birth defects. Children without a conscience (sociopaths), violent behavior, dyslexia, retardation, fetal alcohol or drug syndrome, ADD and homosexuality are all preventable for a few pennies per pregnancy but expensive and difficult to deal with after the fact.

Homosexuality was long thought to be an emotional/environmental aberration created in the child by improper role models and improper parenting; then homosexuality was related to a "choice of sexual preference." There is now a kaleidoscope of sexual behaviors, choices and displays; however, none of the members of this ever growing subculture can refute the fact that there are only two sexes - male and female.

A series of preventable embryologic events frequently result in physical and/or emotional and behavioral aberrations. These congenital defects can result in individuals who are neither male nor female or who could be both male and female at once, forming five commonly accepted classifications. Less understood is the increasing frequency of "gay" individuals who are physi-

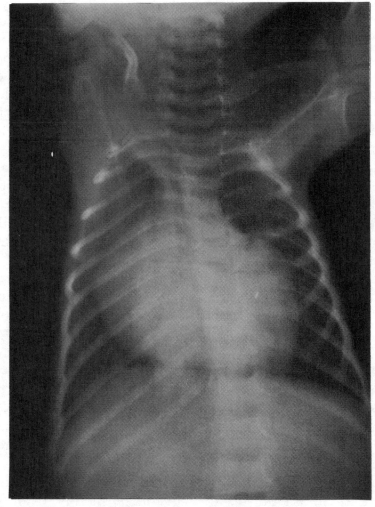

Fig. 7-8 Selenium deficiency cardiomyopathy in an infant rhesus monkey
(note massive heart enlargement) with cystic fibrosis.

TUESDAY, APRIL 19, 1994

ST. LOUIS POST-DISPATCH

James Carlyle Thompson, 21; Student At University Of Kansas

James Carlyle Thompson, 21, of Kirkwood died Saturday (April 16, 1994) in Lawrence, Kan., after collapsing at a fraternity soccer tournament.

The Douglas County coroner, Dr. Carol Moddrell, said Mr. Thompson died of a heart attack caused by the lasting effects of Kawasaki, a rare blood disease he suffered as a youth.

After Mr. Thompson collapsed on a soccer field at half time, fellow students tried to revive him. He died at Lawrence Memorial Hospital.

Mr. Thompson was a senior in architectural engineering at the University of Kansas. He was a Summerfield scholar, which is based on scholastic merit.

Mr. Thompson composed music, and he played the piano at the Beta Theta Pi fraternity house. In 1992, he served as musical director of the Rock Chock Review, a campuswide musical comedy show.

He attended high school in Hutchinson, Kan., where he was class valedictorian. His parents, James Carlyle "Pat" Thompson II and Margo Lyman Thompson, moved their family to Kirkwood in 1989.

A memorial service was held Monday in Lawrence. Burial will be private at the Bellerive Heritage Gardens in Creve Coeur.

In addition to his parents, Mr. Thompson is survived by two brothers, John Thompson of Kansas City and Brett Thompson of Kirkwood; and grandparents James C. Thompson and Audrey Thompson of Mission, Texas.

Memorial contributions may be made to the Burton and Doris Lyman Foundation Inc., 1 Financial Square, Bank of Kansas, Hutchinson, Kan. 63503 or to the Alpha Nu Chapter of Beta Theta Pi, 1425 Tennessee, Lawrence, Kan. 66044.

Researchers Say 2 Bacteria Cause a Children's Ailment

By LAWRENCE K. ALTMAN

A team of scientists says it has discovered the cause of Kawasaki syndrome, an ailment that often leads to heart disease in children. But experts on the disease said the claim might be overstated.

The findings, by scientists collaborating in Boston, Denver and Minneapolis, were made on 16 patients but have not been confirmed. Their report is being published tomorrow in The Lancet, a British medical journal.

The report attributes the cause of Kawasaki syndrome to toxins produced by two strains of widely prevalent bacteria: a novel strain of staphylococcus and a streptococcus.

Some confusion surrounded the report, however, because while the researchers explicitly claimed in a news release that they had found the cause, they were considerably more cautious in their scientific paper for The Lancet.

If the team of scientists headed by Dr. Donald Y. M. Leung of the National Jewish Center for Immunology and Respiratory Medicine in Denver is correct, Kawasaki syndrome will turn out to be similar to toxic shock syndrome, which is caused by another toxin produced by staph and strep bacteria.

Causes Childhood Heart Disease

Kawasaki syndrome generally strikes children under the age of 5, most commonly under age 2. Experts estimate there are 5,000 cases a year in the United States and many more elsewhere.

Kawasaki syndrome typically produces a spiking fever that lasts several days. A rash can appear anywhere on the body but tends to peel around the fingers and toes. It also produces a "strawberry tongue" that makes the tongue rough and swollen lymph nodes.

Such problems generally go away on their own after about two weeks. But the syndrome can produce a devastating and painless complication — aneurysms of the coronary arteries that nourish the heart. In rare cases, the aneurysms lead to a heart attack. Kawasaki syndrome has replaced rheumatic fever as the leading cause of acquired heart disease in children, some studies have found.

Injections of gamma globulin into a vein can reduce the risk of aneurysms. But because there is no diagnostic blood test for Kawasaki syndrome, doctors can diagnose it only by asking questions, examining a patient and, if indicated, taking an ultrasound of the heart. Some cases go undetected until heart damage appears.

The researchers said their next goal was to develop a test to help diagnose the syndrome.

The new study did not attempt to determine where the bacteria live in the environment or how people acquire them.

"That is what we are working on quite hard now," said Dr. H. Cody Meissner, an author of the report and the chief of the pediatric infectious disease program at the Floating Hospital, a unit of the New England Medical Center.

The disease is named after Dr. To-misaku Kawasaki, a pediatrician in Tokyo who first described it in 1967. The first confirmed case in the United States was diagnosed in Hawaii in 1971 by Dr. Marian Melish of the University of Hawaii.

From the start, many researchers have sought the cause of the syndrome. Some, like Dr. Yeung, have reported that it is a retrovirus. Others have pointed to various bacteria, and dust mites have also come under suspicion. But the cause has remained elusive.

In the new study, the researchers at the Floating Hospital found toxins produced by staph or strep bacteria in 13 of 16 children with Kawasaki syndrome and in 1 of 15 children in a control group. Toxins produced by staph were isolated from 11 of the 13 positive cases; strep toxins were found in the other two cases.

The researchers said the toxins acted as so-called superantigens, which activate a number of components of the immune system, provoking an extensive and dangerous immune response. Ordinarily, immune cells are programmed to respond to a specific antigen.

In their paper in The Lancet, the scientists employed cautious language, saying the findings "may provide im-

An answer on Kawasaki syndrome still leaves questions.

portant new insight into the potential infectious" cause of the syndrome.

But a news release from the New England Medical Center quoted Dr. Meissner as saying, "The discovery of a bacterial agent as the cause of this disease represents a major step forward in providing new insight into this acute illness of early childhood."

Optimism and Caution

Dr. Meissner said in an interview that he "would not want to stake my life on this being the cause, but if I were a betting person, I would sure bet that this is going to be the case." He said his team had also produced compelling evidence for a biological mechanism by which the bacteria could cause the disease.

But in a separate interview, Dr. Leung said, "We should be more cautious about that. We want independent confirmation."

Dr. Melish said her team at the University of Hawaii had failed to find evidence to support a similar theory in two studies since 1981 involving 90 patients. A multicenter study is now under way, she said.

Dr. Stanford T. Shulman, the chief expert on pediatric infectious disease at Children's Memorial Hospital in Chicago, said the claim for discovering the cause of Kawasaki syndrome was "an overstatement." But he added, "It is an intriguing association that needs further study."

cally normal males or females.

In firstly talking about congenital defects," intersex" is the medical term used to describe the term hermaphrodite. A female hermaphrodite might possess one testicle and one ovary, a male pseudo hermaphrodite could have testes and some recognizable female genitalia but lack ovaries, and a female pseudo hermaphrodite may have ovaries and some noticeable features of male genitalia but no testicles.

The high profile sexual conversion of "Christine Jorgenson" opened the subject of intersexuals to the general public. At the 1972 Olympic Games, held in Munich, Germany all female athletes were subjected to a chromosome test. A hair from their head was used to determine their genetic sex -"female" athletes with the male chromosome pattern were disqualified. Two famous Russian "sisters" (Tamara Press, the world champion shotputter and Irina Press the world champion Pentathlon athlete) retired from world competition when the chromosome test was made an Olympic requirement.

John Money of John Hopkins University, a specialist in the field of congenital sexual organ defects (defects that are found at birth and related to mineral or vitamin deficiencies of the embryo) states that "intersexuals can constitute as many as four percent of all births."

Very few intersexuals maintain their faulty dichotomy of sex and most are identified at birth and placed in programs of hormonal and surgical corrections to enable them to blend into the heterosexual society as normal males and females. The goals of these programs are clearly nonjudgemental and humanitarian and are to be applauded. However, the social and sur-

gical problems of intersexuals could be totally avoided by proper preconception nutrition of the embryo.

The term "hermaphrodite" is a connection of the Greek male Hermes and the female Aphrodite. Greek mythology tells of the gods that produced Hermaphrodites who at age 15 (puberty), fell in love with a nymph and fused his body with hers - Hermaphrodites was a description of a male hermaphrodite who was born over 2,000 years ago!!

In many true hermaphrodites, the testicles and ovaries develop separately but equally on the right and left sides; in some the gonads fuse forming an ovo-testes. Frequently, at least one of the gonads functions, producing sperm or ova as well as the appropriate male and/or female hormones.

Pseudo hermaphrodites have the same two gonads (i.e.- testicles or ovaries) in concert with the male (XY) or the female (XX) chromosome complement.

Male pseudohermaphrodites have testicles and XY chromosomes, yet they also have a vagina and a clitoris and at puberty develop breasts. They do not cycle or menstruate.

Female pseudohermaphrodites have ovaries, XX chromosomes, and sometimes a uterus, but they also have some external genital features of the male.

Because of the wide biological variation in these congenital defects, there is no classification system that describes each and every recorded anatomical intersexual. In 1969, Paul Guinet of the Endocrine Clinic, Lyons, France and Jacques Decount of the Endocrine Clinic, Paris, listed 98 different types of true hermaphrodites, based on the appearances of external genitalia and associated tubes and ducts. In some, the intersexual showed strong female development with seperate openings for the vagina and urethra, a a cleft vulva with both large and small labia (vaginal lips). At puberty they developed breasts and began to cycle and menstruate; however, their oversized and sexually sensitive "clitoris" when aroused looked and functioned as a penis.

A second type of hermaphrodite exhibits breasts and a feminine body, they also menstruate, however, their labia and vulva fuse forming a well defined scrotum, and the phallus (clitoris/penis) can reach almost three inches long. The most frequent type of true hermaphrodite (55 %) described by the French investigation have a masculine body, their urethra runs through or near the phallus which looks physically like a penis.

According to historians, Plato is the only recognised authority to have surmised that there were "three sexes (male, female and hermaphrodite)."

According to Plato, members of the human race were origionally joined in pairs, two men, two women and a man/woman pair. "Zeus cut each pair apart to diminish their power and to teach them to fear the gods. Humans thus spend their time on the Earth searching for their other half, with whom they can merge in love."

"The disposition of these people differed," Plato wrote, "according to original pairing: those whose sex had been mixed were obsessed by coupling and often became adulterers, where as people sprung from single - sex pairs were more fitted for the everyday business of the world. In particular men whose bond was with another man were most suited for government and leadership!" Thus Plato gave the first in-

terpretation of the origin of homosexual behavior.

In ancient times, the penalty for those poor souls with congenital intersex birth defects could be death. In the 1600's, a Scottish hermaphrodite living as a woman was buried alive as a witch after getting "her" bosses daughter pregnant.

In 1937, Hugh H. Young, a urologist at John Hopkins, published "Genital Abnormalities, Hermaphraditism and Related Adrenal Diseases," in which he accumulated many cases of intersexual "accidents of birth." One of the intersexual cases he cited was a hermaphrodite, Emma, a "female" who had a penis-sized clitoris and a vagina which made it possible for this intersexual to have sex with heterosexual men or women!! As a teen, Emma had sex with several females, at 19 she married a heterosexual man but "her" sexual relationship with "her" husband gave little pleasure, so Emma kept several girl friends on the side!!

In 1967, Drs. Christopher J. Dewhurst and Ronald R. Gordon wrote" The Intersexual Disorders," in which they state "intersexual infants are a tragic event which immediately conjurs up visions of someone doomed to live always as sexual freaks in loneliness and frustration."

Veterinarians have a lot of experience with normal animals that have unusual sexual anatomy and also abnormal congenital defects as a result of embryonic nutritional deficiencies. Marsupials, such as kangaroos, wallabies and mouse opposums for example, normally have three vaginas, sperm may ascend any or all of the two lateral or central vaginas and the babies or joeys may be "born" through any one of them. The duck billed platypus, a mammal lays eggs in a nest!!

Many species of animals have multiple baby litters that results in the embryos competing for nutrition - the more limited the nutrition, the greater number of embryos that are affected and the more severe the defects. Every known congenital defect of the sexual organs of man has been recorded in many species of animals (frequently many different defects in the same litter if nutrients are not available).

"Freemartin" is a term given to female animals born as fraternal twins of males (80 % occur in cattle, 5% in sheep and goats); they are infertile and frequently have congenital defects of the genitalia.

The Alfred Kinsey Report in the 40's and 50's listed homosexuals as 4 to 10 % of the American population. More recently, Dr. Richard Pillard, a psychiatrist from Boston University, says 4 % of males and 2 to 3 % of females in the United States are gay. Overseas, the latest reports indicate that in Great Britain the level has possibly reached 25 % in the 90's. The gradual increase in the percentage of gays in America and other industrialized nations of the world parallels the gradual decrease in the mineral content in our farm and range soils and therefore our food supply.

"Gay" behavior also occurs in animals kept through puberty in single sex groups, similar to opportunistic homosexual behavior that takes place in jails.

The current focus on the "gay" phenomena has moved from that of a learned behavior or a "lifestyle choice" to that of a prenatal biological event - in other words a preventable congenital defect caused by a deficiency of minerals and or vitamins in early pregnancy. This 180 degree change in thinking resulted from the finding of a common physical defect in the brains of gay men. This change in thinking actually started in the 70's when German doctors felt that an area of the preoptic area of the hypothalamus in the brain of gay men was abnormal and they tried with surgical procedures to normalize the defect. The Germans were not successful and the study was abandoned.

Pillard looked at 50 straight men and 50 gay men and found that gay men had significantly more gay brothers. He joined forces with Michael J Bailey, a psychologist at Northwestern University, Chicago and they found that only 52 % of the identicle twins of gay men were gay themselves (proving that gay behavior is not genetic, for if it was genetic 100 % of the identicle gay twins would have to be gay!!); 22 % of gay mens fraternal twin brothers and other biological brothers were gay, while less than 10 % of adopted brothers were gay.

"It is a mistake to think there is a gay gene" says Dean Harmer, a geneticist at the National Cancer Institute.

Simon LeVay, head of the Institute of Gay and Lesbian Studies in West Hollywood, California is well known for finding anatomical brain differences between gay and straight men. In autopsy studies, he found that an area in the brain of the preoptic area of the hypothalamus (center of sexual appetite and sex drive) is smaller in gay men than it is in heterosexual men .

In 1990 LeVay compared cells from the medial preoptic region of the hypothalamus (third interstitial nucleus of the anterior hypothalamus) from 19 homosexual men (all of whom had died from AIDS) with those of 16 heterosexual men (of whom 6 had died from AIDS).

A primary concern with LeVay's study was the fact that some of the men died of AIDS which affects and destroys brain cells. However, other cell collections in the brains of gay men in the study were identical in size and character with those of heterosexual men.

Another brain feature that shows a difference between gay and heterosexual men is the size of the anterior commissure, a bundle of nerve fibers that connects the right and left sides of the brain. The anterior commissure is smallest in the heterosexual man and of identical size in gay men and women. The two physical differences in the brains of gay and heterosexual men are most likely the result of a congenital malformation of the physical structure and or a biochemical defect - again resulting from a congenital deficiency of minerals!!!

Roger A. Gorski, UCLA (1978) found the preoptic hypothalamic nuclei in rats that controlled sexual appetite. In addition to size differences in male and female cell groups, Gorski found that male hormones play a key roll in producing the size differences in males and females. Initially males and females have the same size and number of cells in the preoptic area - a surge of testosterone secreted by the male fetus before birth appears to stabilize these cell populations - in females the lack of the testosterone surge allows them to atrophy. Removing testosterone from adult males by castration does not cause a shrinking of the cells!!

Combined with the study of identical twins that failed to show a genetic pattern (the rate of both identical twins being gay would have to be 100 %) the LeVay study is a sure indication that gay behavior is a congenital defect rather than a genetic de-

fect or behavioral choice!!

A parallel study of 147 gay women who had identical twin sisters showed only 48 % who have twins that are gay and 16 % of fraternal twins of gay women are gay while only 6 % of adopted sisters are gay - approximately the same results as in the identicle twin study in gay men.

Simon LeVay's findings agree with the German studies of the 70's.

When viewed in the light of known physical and behavioral sexual defects in animals from multiple embryo litters suffering from congenital mineral and vitamin deficiencies (rats with 14 embryos to "Freemartins" in cattle with fraternal twins) where embryos compete for limited nutrition, the high percentage (but not total) of gay twins in identical and fraternal twins is understandable. Human twins are competing for limited resources to a greater degree than single embryos - therefore, more congenital defects in multiple births.

It is an easy mental jump to perceive that one should be able to prevent the congenital hermaphrodite and the intersexual as well as the gay embryo with complete preconception nutrition with 90 nutrients including minerals (i.e.- zinc, manganese, magnesium, gallium, copper, etc.), vitamins (B-12, folic acid, vitamin A), amino acids and essential fatty acids. This can perhaps best be discribed as insurance against gay embryo's.

"Runts" in multi baby animal litters are the equivalent of low birth weight babies in humans, especially when twins and triplets are involved. When the pregnant womans diet is incomplete in calories, protein, minerals and vitamins she competes with her embryo for nutrition and the baby will be born small, lacking vigor and lacking a robust immune system, which decreases its chances of survival in the first year of life. A low birth weight baby is a heavy price to pay (both in health and in extra days necessary in the hospital) for a shortened delivery time to allow the doctor to "get in and get out!!"

More serious than low birth weight is of course birth defects and incomplete seperation of twins.

The World Health Organization (WHO) ranks Americans as 23rd in live births and first year survivability for our newborns; they rank Americans as 32nd for birth defects when we are compared with the other industrialized nations of the Earth - not a very good record for the nation with the "most advanced" and most expensive medical system (union) in the world!!!

POSTNATAL DEVELOPMENT:

After the human child is born and assuming it is physically and emotionally perfect there is still a "genetic potential" to fullfill - physical development, emotional development, IQ, small muscle dexterity skills, and height and longevity. The development, growth and longevity of the new born is not guaranteed by genetics if optimal nutrition (minerals, vitamins, essential amino acids, essential fatty acids, calories, proteins, etc.) and nurturing are not available. The human child, even though they are perfectly formed physically and chemically at birth, must still jump through nutritional and biochemical "hoops" at every developmental juncture and if any piece of critical nutrition is missing at the wrong moment the childs physical or mental development, sociability, IQ, musical talent , athletic ability, growth and longevity will

be drastically affected.

The average American male is five foot eight inches tall and the average female is five foot four inches tall, even though our human genetic potential for height is is approximately seven feet.

It was not too many years ago that a six foot tall professional basketball player was a wonder to behold; today if the college or professional team does not have a seven foot center and six foot seven guards they can't compete (Table 7-6)!! It was the availability of calories, protein, and enough minerals that allowed men and women to finally reach their genetic potential for height.

Texans were typically over six foot in the 19th century, Americans in general were tall compared to most Europeans and Asians - yet Texans and Americans were not a homogenous genetic group, they in fact were a mixture of every culture from every corner of the Earth - it was the relatively unlimited calories and high quality mineral rich food that allowed us to come nearer to reaching our human genetic potential for height than the European or Asian with limited calories, minerals and proteins.

One of our favorite demonstrations of genetic potential for physical development was an experiment in which 100 identical ducklings with the same mother and father (one keeps stealing eggs from the nest and refrigerating them until you collect 100, then all 100 eggs are incubated at the same time) were divided into four groups of 25 ducklings each and fed four different diets:

1) lettuce
2) hydroponically grown barley
3) Purina duck grower pellets
4) Purina duck grower pellets
   and barley grass

Table 7-6

Sizable 6 are tallest of tall

Six players currently on NBA rosters are 7-2 or taller. Washington's Gheorghe Muresan, at 7-7, is the tallest. Five of the six were born outside the USA, and only Rich King of Seattle isn't a starter. How the Sizable Six are doing:

Player (Ht.), team	Birthplace	Min.	FG%	FT%	Reb	Blk	PPG
Rik Smits (7-4), Ind.	Netherlands	26.6	51	81	5.7	1.1	14.5
Dikembe Mutombo (7-2), Den.	Zaire	34.1	55	53	12.4	3.7	11.7
Shawn Bradley (7-6), Phi.	Germany	28.7	40	61	6.4	3.1	10.3
Luc Longley (7-2), Min.	Australia	19.8	46	70	5.8	1.1	6.5
Gheorghe Muresan (7-7), Was.	Romania	10.6	48	66	3.5	0.5	4.7
Rich King (7-2), Sea.	Lincoln, Neb.	2.6	44	43	0.8	0.0	1.4

The results were spectacular (Fig. 7- 9), after one month groups 1 and 2 showed identical growth and development rates (almost zero); group 3 ducks were three times larger than group 1 and 2; and group 4 was twice as large as group 3 and six times larger than group 1 and 2 - only group 3 and 4 came close to fulfilling their genetic potential for physical growth and development at age one month; only group 3 and 4 were fed supplemented pellets that contained all of the known nutrients required by ducklings. The additional growth and development of group 4 can be attributed to more calorie intake because of the added juice of the barley grass made the pellets more acceptable or palatable and or the living plant enzymes of the barley grass.

A human parallel to the duck experiment is the Japanese immigrants who came to the United States as small wiry people about 4' 11 inches tall and weighing 100 pounds soaking wet - their genetic potential for growth and development was never met by eating the low calorie rice, vegetable and fish diet of their native Japan. The second generation Japanese conceived and born in the United States was a different story - the son was six foot tall, weighed 220 pounds and played tight end for a university football team - their genetic potential was met by having access to unlimited calories, protein, milk and mineral and vitamin supplements.

Physical output is another gauge of development. American youth ranks very poorly with the rest of the world - our average kids could win in a television watching marathon but when it comes to athletics or basic physical strength we fail. Few of our fifth graders can do ten push ups or run/walk a mile in eight minutes - doing aerobics with Arnold Schwarzeneger without mineral supplements will not get the results we are looking for - in fact exercise without vitamin and mineral supplementation is downright dangerous and could be fatal (i.e.- Jim Fix, Reggie Lewis, Hank Gathers, etc.).

Fortunately, it is never too late to start taking in all 90 nutrients required by our bodies. A comparison of two groups of marathon runners (one group received a mineral supplement containing Ca, P, I, Fe, Mg, Cu, K, Zn, Mn, Cr, Se, and a trace mineral rich clay containing a total of 72 minerals) showed an improvement in their average race times after six months of training in relation to supplemental intake. The unsupplemented group showed an improvement of 5:27 minutes following training, while the supplemented group showed an improvement of a whopping 16:57 minutes following training!!!

It is interesting that some groups of people and some individuals reach the pinnacle of intelligence, high SAT scores and high IQ, including math, music and language while others never do better than becoming mental vegetables or work units in our society - some completely drop out, become the "Bad Seeds," the homeless and the unemployable.

The difference between the child prodigy (i.e.-music, art, math, physics, etc.)and the high school dropout is not genetics or income level of the parents but rather the nutritional (and especially the mineral intake) competency of the child during pre and post natal development.

Simply translated, for $300 to $500 worth of minerals and vitamins per pregnancy, to include preconception supplements and monthly supplements during

Fig. 7-9 Identical six week old ducklings fed four different rations (from left). 1) lettuce; 2) hydroponically grown barley; 3) duck pellets; 4) duck pellets and barley grass.

pregnancy and $50 per month for growth, development and longevity, the unnecessary production of millions of low birth weight babies and severely physically and emotionally disabled children would be eliminated - the ability for more people to reach their longevity potential of 120 to 140 years would be realized.

Setting aside the unforgivable human tragedy of emotionally and physically disabled children as well as "Bad Seeds" and all of the unnecessary human suffering, the ultimate savings to the American public over the lifetime of a disabled or jailed child would range from $500,000 to several millions of dollars each, for an annual savings to ourselves, the tax payers, in the trillions of dollars!!!

MAINTENANCE HEALTHFULLNESS:

The WHO ranks Americans as 19th in healthfullness when we are compared with the other industrialized nations. This means that there are 18 other nations whose peoples live longer than Americans do before developing chronic degenerative diseases such as hypertension, heart disease, aneurysms, arthritis, osteoporosis, diabetes, cataracts, gluacoma, cancer, etc.

In translating the WHO ranking it simply says we wear out quicker than other people and cultures do, not because of inferior genetics as the "orthodox" medical doctors would have you believe (if you believe "bad genes" are the cause of all disease from farting to cancer it lets them off the hook of responsibility to solve your problem) but because our soils are depleted of minerals, thus our grains, fruits and vegetables are depleted of minerals, thus we are depleted of minerals.

Additionally, our immune system requires all 90 nutrients (60 minerals, 16 vitamins, 12 essential amino acids and three essential fatty acids) to maintain and repair itself in order to protect us from infectious diseases (i.e.- colds, flu, Strep-throat, "flesh-eating" Streptococcus A, Epstein-Barr virus, HIV, Candida albicans, rhuematoid arthritis, Herpes virus, Hanta virus, Cancer, etc.).

Our immune system is very complex, it defends us from attack on all sides and is

---

Table 7- 7.
Componants of the Human Immune System.

WBC - Lymphocytes - T-cells
B-cells
Natural Killer cells
Neutrophils
Monocytes
Eosinophils
Basophils
Bone marrow
Liver-albumin/globulin
Antibodies
Lymphatic system- thymus
tonsils
appendix
spleen
lymph nodes
Skin
Gastrointestinal tract
Tears
Mucus
Urine

Deaths of Teen-Age Athletes Raise Questions Over Testing

By WILLIAM C. RHODEN

Susie Gary sat in her North Chicago home and recalled how her grandson, Devon Mills, would transform the living room into a basketball arena.

With imaginary fans cheering, Devon would do his own play-by-play as he hit the winning shot on a makeshift goal. Mills told his grandmother that he was going to be a star one day and predicted that television crews and reporters would flock to their home.

As she told the story, Mrs. Gary was torn by the irony of how Devon's predictions had been fulfilled. The home had in fact been swamped by camera crews and reporters, but, she said, "He never thought it would be because of something like this."

Devon, 16, had just finished getting a drink of water when he collapsed and died after playing in a game for the North Chicago High School freshman team on Feb. 12. The cause of death was an undetected heart problem.

"Sometimes I wish I could just wake up and have it not happen," Mrs. Gary said. "You just don't know how badly something like this hurts."

The sudden deaths of young people like Devon Mills do not receive the widespread attention that was paid Hank Gathers, the Loyola Marymount basketball star who died during a game four years ago this month, or Reggie Lewis, the Boston Celtics' captain who collapsed and died last summer.

But for medical professionals and school administrators, the deaths have produced difficult questions: Can more be done to detect hidden and potentially

Continued on Page B9, Column 1

Heart attack blamed in death of Marine, 19

Camp Pendleton

A 19-year-old Marine corporal died Sunday, apparently of a heart attack, while making a telephone call on the base.

Base officials said CPR was administered immediately, but the Marine was pronounced dead at the naval hospital.

The identity of the Marine, a truck driver with the 3rd Battalion, 9th Marines, was withheld. An autopsy was planned and the death is being investigated by military authorities.

OBITUARIES

Autumn (Hawkins) Meadows, 22; Had Rare Defect Of The Heart

Autumn Heather (Hawkins) Meadows, who underwent four open-heart operations as a child and young adult, died Monday (May 30, 1994) after a heart attack at the base hospital at Fort Leonard Wood. She was 22.

Mrs. Meadows grew up in Troy, Ill. She graduated from Triad High School in 1990 and married her high-school sweetheart, Michael W. Meadows, the next year. He is in the Army. They lived in base housing at Fort Leonard Wood, which is in south-central Missouri. She was stricken at home Monday morning and taken by ambulance to the hospital, where she was pronounced dead.

Mrs. Meadows was born with a rare heart defect and underwent her first surgery at Cardinal Glennon Children's Hospital when she was a few months old. Her most recent operation was in 1990.

Mrs. Meadows was a student at the Drury College branch at Fort Leonard Wood.

Among survivors in addition to her husband are her father, Angelo Hawkins of Collinsville; her mother, Maxine Johnson of Collinsville; stepmother, Colleen Hawkins of Collinsville; stepfather, John Johnson of Collinsville; two sisters, Tricia Leverett of Collinsville and Terri Andrews of Fairview Heights; a brother, Scott Hawkins of Collinsville; and three grandparents, Chester and Gloria Hawkins of Collinsville and Grace Landert of Highland.

Visitation will be from 5 p.m. to 8 p.m. Wednesday at Herr Funeral Home in Collinsville. The funeral will be at 10 a.m. Thursday at St. John United Church of Christ in Collinsville with burial at Riggin Cemetery in Troy. Memorials should be made to Cardinal Glennon.

made up of tissues and organs not normally considered part of the immune system (Table 7-7).

Chronic degenerative diseases that affect Americans are totally preventable with mineral, vitamin, amino acid and essential fatty acid supplements (Table 7- 8).

The healthiest and longest lived cultures on the planet consistently consume high levels of 60 to 72 minerals with each meal, generation after generation - their reward is a drug free, crime free, disease free, healthful people who live long productive and joyful lives that have fulfilled their genetic potential for longevity!!!

LONGEVITY:

"Old age" is not a disease - it is a sad fact, however, that everyone who dies of "infirmities" or "natural causes" dies of nutritional deficiency diseases - what a waste!!

In a survey of Americans, most people want to live healthfully to age 100 and are willing to put out a lot of effort to accomplish this reasonable goal. Another survey pointed out that Americans are also going off of the strict cholesterol watch and again

eating red meat and sugar - after five to ten years of national sacrifice and a collective dietary fat and cholesterol paranoia (we spent a whopping $117 billion for cholesterol testing alone in 1993) our American statistics for health and longevity have changed little or none.

Longevity, regardless of each of our genetic potentials for long life, in fact requires a consistent daily intake of the 90 essential nutrients (60 minerals, 16 vitamins, 12 essential amino acids and 3 essential fatty acids) required by humans if we are to fulfill that potential!!!

Remember, the average life span for Americans is 75.5 and the longest lived peoples of the industrialized nations are the Japanese who on the average reach 79.9. Americans rank 17th in longevity (Table 7-) when we are compared with the other industrialized nations - again we Americans fall short, not because of poor genetic make up or the lack of "the right stuff," but rather from the lack of attention to the basics of the flesh. If you want to get the 300,000 miles from your Mercedes that it was engineered for you must put in motor oil, lubricants and coolant - even for a Mercedes!!!

USA TODAY

Life

MONDAY, APRIL 26, 1993

LIFELINE

Malnutrition afflicts 1 in 4 elderly patients

By Mike Snider
USA TODAY

One in 4 elderly patients is malnourished, says a survey of health-care providers who treat patients 65 and older.

The patients aren't getting proper nutrients because of deficiencies, excesses or imbalances in their diets, says the report by the Nutrition Screening Initiative, a project of health-care associations. That weakens the ability to fight off sickness and recover from surgery and illness, say most of the 750 physicians, nurses and administrators answering the survey.

The Nutrition Screening Initiative releases findings today in Washington, D.C., including:

▶ About half the elderly patients in hospitals and 2 of every 5 in a nursing home suffer from malnutrition.

▶ Malnourished patients are more likely to have major complications and more expensive hospitalizations than healthy older patients.

Nutritional assessments for those of all ages should be included in the health benefits package that the White House Task Force on Health Care Reform is now formulating, says U.S. Rep. Ron Wyden, D-Ore.

The findings suggest that many elderly Americans have become "a walking bull's-eye for diseases (like heart disease, diabetes, cancer) that target the malnourished," he says.

Table 7- 8. Common Degenerative Diseases of Humans and Their Cause.

Disease	Deficiemcy
Osteoporosis	Ca, Mg, B, Cu, S
Arthritis (Ankylosing spondylitis)	Ca, Mg. B, Cu, S
Hypertension	Ca, Mg, B
Bone spurs, heel spurs, Ca deposits	Ca, Mg, B
Cancer	Se
Diabetes	Cr, Va, Zn
Aneurysms	Cu
Cardiomyopathy	Se
Cataracts	Se
Deafness	Sn

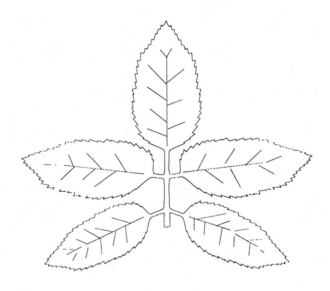

"I want to prove that the boundaries (of age) set up by the gods are not unbreakable"

- Gilgamesh, King of Sumaria
Clay tablets, 5000 BC

Chapter 8

THE AGE BEATERS:

The Fifth Essence

All species have a "genetic potential" or upper limit for longevity - mice 700 days, dogs 23 years, horses 32 years, elephant 45 years, chimpanzee 52 years and man 145 years (Table 8-1): whether or not an individual of that species reaches their genetic potential for longevity depends on two basic concepts:

1) Avoiding the "land mines" or eliminating unnecessary and wasteful death from predators or road accidents, not smoking, not drinking alcohol to excess, avoiding the use of illegal (and prescription) drugs, avoiding chemicals and toxic wastes in our food, air and water and avoid going to the doctor.

2) Do those positive things necessary to make it to 145 including consuming each of the 90 essential nutrients in optimal amounts each day.

Assuming that you avoid the "land mines" of life, longevity then depends on how faithfully one takes in optimal amounts of the 90 essential nutrients necessary for health and longevity each and every day!!! An analogy to our "genetic potential" for longevity is the engine of a Mercedes which is a wonder of German automotive engineering - the engine is designed to run 300,000 miles before it needs a major overhaul or needs to be replaced, yet if you the owner/driver doesn't maintain the Mercedes engine by supplying the essential coolants, lubricants and motor oil that wondrous engine designed to run 300,000 miles won't run 50 miles!!! Without oil or coolant even a Mercedes won't make it to its engineered potential ("genetic potential") of 300,000 miles (120 - 140 years).

The association between maximizing one's longevity and the intake of optimal amounts of essential nutrients is well documented in the laboratory for many species and in isolated third world cultures in far-flung areas of the Earth. While the people of the long-lived third world cultures do not each have a Ph.D. in biochemistry or nutrition they have by serendipity set up their homelands in an idyllic biochemical Garden of Eden; and while these idyllic homelands are superficially quite different it is their similarities or common denominators that give the net result of healthful longevity that we can learn and benefit from.

The oldest known story relating to the

OBITUARIES

OLDEST AMERICAN DIES

ASSOCIATED PRESS

Margaret Skeete, shown here in a 1992 photo, died in her sleep yesterday at her home in Radford, Va. She was 115 and was bedridden since a fall three weeks ago. She had been listed in the Guinness Book of Records as the oldest American.

Wilhelmina Bonk, 104; Was Native Of Chouteau Island

Wilhelmina "Minnie" Bonk, a native of Chouteau Island, died Saturday (March 12, 1994) of infirmities on her birthday at the Hampton Nursing Home in Alhambra. She was 104.

Mrs. Bonk was born on Chouteau Island, near Granite City, and grew up and lived most of her life on a farm near Granite City. She has been a member of the United Church of Christ in Alhambra for over 50 years.

A funeral service will be held at 10 a.m. today at the Dauderman Mortuary, Ltd., 609 East Main Street, in Alhambra. Burial will be in the Salem United Church of Christ cemetery in Madison County.

Among the survivors are her daughter, Dorothy Hertel of Alhambra; a granddaughter; and two great-grandchildren.

Margaret Skeete, 115; Oldest American

RADFORD, Va.—Margaret Skeete, listed in the Guinness Book of World Records as the oldest American, died Saturday at her home. She was 115.

Mrs. Skeete had been bedridden since a fall three weeks ago and died in her sleep, said her daughter, Verne Taylor.

Guinness listed Mrs. Skeete for the first time in its 1993 edition, after verifying her age from an 1880 census that listed her as a 2-year-old, Mrs. Taylor said.

Mrs. Skeete was born Oct. 27, 1878, in Rockport, Tex. When her husband died 41 years ago, she moved from Texas to Virginia to live with Taylor's family.

She outlived two children.

Mrs. Skeete was unimpressed by her longevity. "I guess that's something, but it doesn't buy me anything," she said at her 115th birthday party in October. Her daughter said she maintained a craving for sweets until a few weeks ago.   —*Associated Press*

George Burns 98 year old and 87 year old friend (No exercise, 10 cigars a day!)

LOS ANGELES TIMES

SATURDAY, AUGUST 20, 1994

Two-Time Nobel Winner Linus C. Pauling Dies at 93

■ **Science:** Noted researcher led fight against nuclear weapons and advocated large doses of Vitamin C.

By DAVID FERRELL
TIMES STAFF WRITER

Linus C. Pauling, the only winner of two unshared Nobel Prizes and a prolific, visionary scientist who led the fight against nuclear weapons and became a controversial advocate for the use of Vitamin C to prevent cancer, died Friday at his ranch in Big Sur. He was 93.

Pauling, who had been found to have prostate cancer in December, 1991, was in poor health for several months, according to the Linus Pauling Institute of Science and Medicine in Palo Alto. In one of his last interviews, he was philosophical about contracting the disease that was the target of much of his

Please see PAULING, A24

Associated Press

Linus Pauling in 1992

THE SAN DIEGO UNION-TRIBUNE

Educated, wealthy live healthier, longer lives

By Mike Snider
USA TODAY

Education and income not only make you wiser and wealthier, they also are linked to health and longevity.

People who at least finish high school may live two to five years longer than those who don't, finds one of several studies in today's *New England Journal of Medicine.*

And another study finds the poorest people had 3 to 7 times higher rates of early death than the richest.

In fact, the studies of blacks and whites suggest status is a more important risk factor than race or even smoking, says *NEJ* editor Marcia Angell.

"No one knows quite how" status affects health, she says, but in addition to social and political costs of inequity, "We are now learning that the medical costs are also very high."

More findings from researchers at the National Institute on Aging and National Center for Health Statistics:

▶ Among people ages 25 to 64, those earning less than $9,000 annually have a death rate 3 to 7 times higher than those earning $25,000 or more.

▶ Among people age 65 or older, those who had 12-plus years of education lived 2.4 to 3.9 more healthy years than those with less education.

Education seems to increase how long a person lives actively and independently, says Dr. Jack Guralnik, National Institute on Aging. Luckily, "education level is a risk factor that can be changed," he says.

Margueritte B. Nobles, 100; voice teacher

Margueritte Barkelew Nobles, a retired musician and voice teacher, died Wednesday in her San Diego home, six days short of her 101st birthday.

Mrs. Nobles broke a hip in a fall April 15, after which her health began to deteriorate, said a nephew, Tom Chapman, of Carlsbad.

Mrs. Nobles, a native of Williamstown, Mo., lived in San Diego 76 years. She served for more than 40 years as organist and music director at the former First Congregational Church in San Diego and held the same positions for more than 35 years at Temple Beth Israel.

She belonged for many years to Mission Hills First Congregational Church and the American Organists Guild.

Mrs. Nobles maintained a music studio in her San Diego home, giving private voice lessons. Her husband of 57 years, Orion E. Nobles, was an executive with the Thearle Music Company. He died in 1982.

Survivors include three nephews and a niece. Cremation is planned, and memorial services are pending.

Baour, at 126, chief in Niger

NIAMEY, Niger — The oldest, most famous and most feared animist chief in Niger — a man who people believed could kill with a handshake and send birds to wipe out crops — has died at the age of 126, national radio says.

The radio said the chief, known only as Baoura, died in his native village of Bagagi on Monday and "was still in possession of all his teeth."

It said the spiritual leader, whose widely practiced religion is based on the belief that all natural phenomena have souls, was liked and respected but also feared because of his great powers.

The government-run station said he had been known to send crickets to devastate harvests if people wronged him.

—AP

■ Count Edward Raczynski; Former Polish Diplomat to Great Britain

Count Edward Raczynski, 101, the aristocratic Polish diplomat who was ambassador to Britain at the outbreak of World War II and a member of the wartime Polish government-in-exile. Raczynski witnessed the rise and fall of Communism, and saw his native country pass from German occupation to Soviet control to multi-party democracy. He never returned home after the war. Raczynski was ambassador in London from 1934 to 1945. During the war, he was acting foreign affairs minister in the London-based exiled Polish government and then minister of state in charge of foreign affairs. The British government withdrew its recognition of the government in July, 1945, following the Yalta Conference at which Britain, the United States and Soviet Union agreed to recognize a rival, Soviet-backed government. He felt betrayed, but continued to help settle Polish refugees in Britain. Raczynski began his diplomatic career after World War I and served in Copenhagen, Warsaw, Geneva and London. In London on Friday.

THE SAN DIEGO UNION-TRIBUNE

Man said to be 133 dies from a stroke

REUTERS

DAMASCUS, Syria — A Syrian man who fathered nine children with a wife he married when he was 80 has died at the age of 133, the official news agency SANA said yesterday.

Hamoudi al-Abdullah, whose age if authenticated would have made him the oldest human in modern records, died from a stroke Wednesday. SANA said the man, from the northern town of Qamishli, had married for a fourth time at the age of 80, after which he fathered four boys and five girls.

The Guinness Book of Records lists the world's oldest living person as Jeanne Calment of France, who celebrated her 118th birthday in February. It says the greatest authenticated age to which a human has lived was 120 years 237 days in the case of Shigechiyo Izumi of Japan, who died in 1986.

Life expectancy in 32 countries

Rankings of developed countries, according to the Centers for Disease Control.

Country	Age	Country	Age
Japan	79.1	U.S.	75.0
Switz.	77.6	Denmark	74.9
Iceland	77.4	Finland	74.8
Sweden	77.1	Malta	74.8
Spain	76.6	Belgium	74.3
Canada	76.5	New Zea.	74.2
Greece	76.5	Lux.	74.1
Neth.	76.5	Portugal	74.1
Australia	76.3	Ireland	73.5
Norway	76.3	E. Germ.	73.2
France	75.9	Bulgaria	71.5
W. Germ.	75.8	Czech.	71.0
Italy	75.5	Poland	71.0
Britain	75.3	Yugo.	71.0
Israel	75.2	Romania	69.9
Austria	75.1	U.S.S.R.	69.8

The San Diego Union

U.S. is 17th on life-expectancy list

Average for Americans is 75 years; Japan leads at 79.1

Associated Press

ATLANTA — The United States ranks 17th in average life expectancy on a list of 33 developed nations, while Japan holds the lead, the U.S. Centers for Disease Control reported yesterday.

The average U.S. life expectancy of 75 years trails Japan's life expectancy by 4.1 years, but beats the lowest of the group, Hungary, by more than five years. The average Hungarian lives 69.7 years, the CDC said.

The United States also ranked near the middle of the 33 nations in death rates from all causes; 828.4 deaths are reported in the United States for each 100,000 people each year. Japan was best at 628.8, and Romania was worst at 1,242.

The leading cause of death in the United States, heart disease, hits harder here than in other countries. The U.S. mortality rate from heart disease was 382 per 100,000 per year for men and 214 for women, compared with 339 and 206 in the other 32 developed countries.

Throughout the 33 countries, heart disease accounted for 30 percent of all deaths, with cancer causing 21 percent and stroke causing 14 percent.

The CDC study included countries defined as developed according to a 1963 United Nations standard pegged to reproductive rates: countries where the average woman has fewer than two daughters who, themselves, survive their childbearing years. Such areas include the United States and Canada, the Soviet Union, most of Europe, some Latin American nations, Japan and Australia.

Fourteen percent of all deaths in the 33 countries — about 1.5 million a year — are attributed to smoking, the CDC said. And fewer Americans smoke, compared with the other countries; 31 percent of U.S. males and 26 percent of American females smoke, compared with 41 percent of men and 29 percent of women in the other countries.

"The large number of deaths attributable to cigarette smoking indicates that reduction of this risk factor would substantially increase life expectancy in the developed world," the Atlanta-based CDC said.

Life expectancy hits a record 75.4 years

By Tim Friend
USA TODAY

Life expectancy in the USA continued to climb in the '80s. But a darker picture of more deaths by homicide and infection with HIV, the AIDS virus, is emerging for younger generations, federal statistics show.

New figures out Thursday from the *Advance Report of Final Mortality Statistics, 1990*, show overall life expectancy reached a record high of 75.4 years, up from 75.1 in 1989.

For women, longevity remained higher than for men: 78.8 years vs. 71.8 years. But white men made the strongest gains in the 1980s, while black men lagged far behind.

The average white male life span rose from 70.7 to 72.7 years from 1980 to 1990. For black males, it rose from 63.8 in 1980 to 64.5 in 1981, then stayed the same through 1990.

Sandra Smith, National Center for Health Statistics, says the extra two years are due to declines in heart disease, stroke and accidents.

But for younger age groups, life became more tenuous because of HIV and homicide. Overall, HIV was the 10th leading cause of death in 1990 and provisional data show it moved to ninth place in 1991. Death rates rose 14% from 1989 to 1990. For males of all races, HIV was the eighth leading cause of death.

For people ages 15 to 24, HIV became the sixth leading cause of death; third for those ages 25 to 44, says report author Brenda Gillum.

After accidents, homicide was the second leading cause of death for ages 15 to 24. Among the men, death rates rose 23% from 1989 to 1990.

"Both homicide and HIV infection are continuing to increase in younger age groups," Gillum says. "These trends are very worrisome and should be carefully monitored by public health people."

The New York Times

THURSDAY, DECEMBER 1, 1994

Susie Brunson

Perhaps the Oldest American, 123

WILMINGTON, N.C., Nov. 30 (AP) — Susie Garvin Daniels Brunson, who may have been the oldest American, died on Tuesday at New Hanover Regional Medical Center here.

Her family put her age at 123. She lived with her family in Roosevelt, L.I., until 1987, when they moved to Wilmington.

The family based its claim that she was born on Dec. 25, 1870, in Bamberg, S.C., on an entry in the family Bible. The claim has never been verified.

At a celebration in 1989, she was asked how it felt to grow old. "There's nothing bad about it," she said. "You're alive, aren't you?"

She was married and widowed three times and she had 12 children. Two survive her. She is also survived by seven grandchildren, 27 great-grandchildren, 15 great-great grandchildren and 10 great-great-great grandchildren.

active human search for the secrets of longevity is the 5,000 year old saga of Gilgamesh, the Sumarian King from Uruk who along with Enkidu, a good friend and the general of his armies decided they would live forever. When Enkidu, his friend and general died suddenly of disease in the mid-years of his life, Gilgamesh panicked and decided to put all of his fortune and energies into a do or die search for eternal youth and immortality. Gilgamesh climbed to the tops of the highest mountains, searched in the dense forests and dove deep into the depths of rivers and oceans in his legendary and fanatical search for youth and longevity.

Gilgamesh was originally regarded as a gerontological myth until the discovery of 12 clay tablets that archeologists determined to be 5,000 years old. Pieced together after their discovery in the ancient city of Sumar, the tablets confirmed that Gilgamesh was in fact a king, adventurer and hero of his times who led a great quest for the "key to immortality" - he called for a "revolt against death itself!!"

As the legend goes, Gilgamesh eventually and heroically found a wise old man in the high mountains, who spoke of a fragrant flower that "looked like a buckthorn and prickled like a rose." The wise prophet shared with Gilgamesh that the plant could be found at the floor of the world's deepest sea, and by coming into possesion of this plant and tasting it one could regain his youth - Gilgamesh located the plant, however, before he could eat sufficient quantities to rejuvenate himself, it was stolen from him by a serpent seeking a new skin.

Hyperborean legends of longevity tell of the Island of the Blest, where according to the ancient Greeks Strabo and Pindar and Pliny, the Roman, live "blessed humans" with very healthy and exceedingly long lives.

"Hyperborean" translates to "beyond the north wind" - a wonderous legendary place of health, joy and pleasures of the unknown and a place of great difficulty to reach. Many cultures still have deep be-

(Table 8 -1) Recorded Longevity of Several Species	
Species	**Recorded Longevity**
Bristle Cone Pine	2000 years
Indian Fruit Bat	31 years 5 months
Capuchin Monkey	46 years 11 months
Giant Anteater	25 years 10 months
Chimpanzee	48 years 6 months
Gorilla	47 years 6 months
Orangutan	49 years
Cloud Rat	13 years 7 months
Chinchilla	19 years 6 months
Coyote	21 years 10 months
Grizzly Bear	35 years 11 months
Hyena	32 years
Bobcat	32 years 4 months
Lion	24 years
Elephant	57 years
Indian Rhino	40 years 4 months
Wild Horse	32 years 10 months
Hippo	49 years 6 months
Galapagos Tortoise	200 years

liefs in the ability to attain immortality by masters and still embrace this "Golden age" (i.e.-Hindus, Iranians, Celtics and Chinese).

The Chinese Taoists developed a whole way of life to ensure immortality through training and self-discipline directed at conservation of what limited resources one was given at birth. Translation of Tao gives us "the way," the way to immortality. Through the accomplishment or mastery of the Taoist techniques one would become a "hsien" or an immortal or man/god. If you could master the knowledge of primal substances (alchemy and knowledge of minerals and metals) and quintessences of life and sex and become a hsien, you could control physical reality and be as a master magician, course through the air as a bird, control the weather, take different animal shapes as you wish, become invisible, become immortal and thus in effect ageless.

The three basic truths of Taoism are:
1) Naturalism
2) Empiricism
3) Special skills

According to the Tao everyone begins their life at birth with a fixed or given amount of Qi or life force, which you must conserve as a major factor in attaining immortality. Conservation of Qi requires progressing towards a state of "effortless action," thus gaining optimal benefit in life, health and longevity with a minimal expenditure of energy or Qi.

The Taoist techniques include respiratory, dietary (alchemy, minerals and metals), gymnastic, sexual and meditative - meditation is applied as a basic for mastering all of the Taoist techniques.

To become a "hsien" you must reduce your rate of breathing, on exhalation swallow the breath for nourishment, and while the breath is internal, direct it on a specific course through the body and cause it to ascend to the brain, the main organ to maintain and rejuvenate because it controls all others."

The Taoist dietary practices include avoidance of grains, meat, wine and most vegetables and subsistence on roots and fruit - the master hsien are able to live on "breath for meat and saliva for drink."

The dietary, sexual and breathing techniques are meant to prolong life long enough to allow one sufficient time for making the elixir of immortality - "potable gold" or the mixture of cinnabar (mercuric chloride) and gold.

Kung Fu was designed to be the gymnastics of the hsien or Taoist masters - its function is to eliminate obstructions from within the body to be exhausted through the external circulation of the breath and sexual essences.

In Tao, during sex you reach sexual fervor to the point of orgasm, but you don't ejaculate - you meditate (in fact men lose 420 mcg of Zn per ejaculation)!!

By mastering the Taoist techniques, the successful apprentice alters his physical body into a purer, more esoteric form - "the bones become as gold, the skin as jade, and further transformation takes you toward the state of the transparent diamond body of a hsien." The final words of the Taoist master Chao Pi Ch'en to his apprentice are found in his book, The Secrets of Cultivating Essential Nature and Eternal Life:

"The training should continue no matter how long it takes until the four elements scatter, and space pulverizes, leaving no traces behind; this is the golden immortal stage of the indestructible diamond body. This is the ultimate achievement of the training which now comes to an end."

The 20th century Taoists include the practice of Chinese Chi Gong, Yoga, mind-body duality and the body, mind, spirit practitioners who use crystals, pendulums and dowsing rods.

Roger Bacon in his Opus Magnus wrote:

"The body of Adam did not posses elements in full equality ... but since the elements in him approached equality, there was very little waste in him; and hence he was fit for immortality, which he could have secured if he had eaten always of the tree of life. For this fruit is thought to have elements approaching equality."

Bacon felt he could extend life by 100 years if he could "reduce the elements in some form of food or drink to an equality or nearly so and have taught the means to this end." For talking and writing about a balanced diet and essential elements that could promote health and extend life Bacon was put in jail for his heretical remarks!!

Paracelsus (1493-1541) came to his end in a bar room brawl in the White Horse Inn in Salzburg, Germany - he straddled the end of the middle ages and the beginning of the Renaissance, a university professor, a legendary physician, a social outcast and an insatiable traveler - he brought Chinese alchemy to its appreciation in the western cultures as a ritualized chemistry.

Paracelsus described alchemy as "the ultimate matter of anything, that state in which the substance has reached its highest grade of exaltation and perfection." It was this state that Paracelsus felt could provide health and extended life or immortality.

The German physician, Christopher Hufeland (1796) published the book, Art of Prolonging Human Life (later changed to Makrobiotik) which featured hygiene to maintain health and the dietary and health practices of Makrobiotik to attain longevity.

Benjamin Franklin (1780) wrote a letter to Joseph Priestly -

"Agriculture may diminish its labor and double its produce; all diseases may by some means be prevented or cured, not excepting even that of old age, and our lives lengthened at pleasure even beyond the antediluvian standard."

Aristotle had labeled this state of perfection that would provide immortality the fifth essence:

1. Earth
2. Air
3. Fire
4. Water
5. The fifth essence

Alchemist Basil Valentine wrote in his, The Triumphal Chariot of Antimony, how to formulate the Elixir's of Life and Immortality:

"Take equal parts of this precipitate and of our sweet oil of antimony; put into a well-closed phial; if exposed to a gentle heat, the precipitate will gradually be dissolved and fixed in the oil; for the fire consumes its viscidity, and it becomes a red, dry, fixed, and fluid powder, which does not give out the slightest smoke.

Keep reverent silence: for now the king enters his bridal chamber, where he will delight himself many months with his spouse; and they will only leave the chamber when they have grown together, and produced a son who, if not the king of kings, is at least a king, and delivers his subjects from disease and want. When you have reached this point, my friend, you have the Medicine of Men and of metals, it is pleasant, sweet, and penetrating, and may be used without any risk. Without being a purgative, it expels all impure and morbid matter from the body. It will restore you to health, and relieve you of want in this life; nor can you ever discharge to God your obligation of gratitude for it. I fear that as a monk and a religious man I have transcended the proper bounds of retrance and secrecy, and spoken out too freely; and if after all that has been said you do not discover the secret, it will not be my fault."

Dr. Alexis Carrel (1912) grew fibroblasts (connective tissue cells) from chicken hearts in flasks fed with extracts of blended chicken embryo and the cells kept multiplying and growing for 34 years (2 years after Carrel's own death). Carrel's colleagues got bored with the experiment and threw the fibroblasts out. The experiment resulted in the theory that cells are inherently immortal if fed a perfect diet and kept in a perfect environment. Carrel had won the Nobel Prize for developing the end to end anastomosis of blood vessels with fine suture.

Unfortunately Dr. Leonard Hayflick came along and used artificial media with major mineral deficiencies for human fibroblasts - in his experiment (faulted from the start) human fibroblasts could only divide 50 times before dying out and showing accumulations of lipofuscin (pigments of aging that indicate a selenium deficiency). Hayflick attributed Carrel's success to contamination by embryonic fibroblasts from the chick embryo media, rather than admitting that poor and limited nutrition prematurely ended the life of his human fibroblasts. The 50 replication limit is known as the "Hayflick limit."

James Hilton made Shangri-La famous through his 1934 novel, *Lost Horizon* where people lived healthful, loving, productive and long lives. The novel was made into a classic movie of the same name in 1937 and then remade in the 60's as a color film entitled, Shangri-La. In the original novel and movie the people of Shangri-La attributed their youthfulness, health and longevity to a Spartan diet, peaceful attitude, a work ethic devoted to gardening and farming and a rich Christian faith and lifestyle; the remake film version portrayed an eastern type meditation as the basis of their health and longevity which contributed to the passion for Eastern meditation by the "hippy" movement of the 60's and 70's.

The modern day "Kryologists" have such faith in the technology of science and medicine as a route to immortality that they pay huge sums of money ($45,000 for a head and $120,000 for a whole body) to have themselves quick frozen in liquid nitrogen ("Kryonic Suspension") after they die to be "stored" until a cure is found for their terminal malady.

The immortalists of the Flame Foundation (also known as "CBJ") believe that "if you become cellularly alive, you will not be influenced by the mass program of death." The immortalists, like Gilgamesh are having a revolt against death. "CBJ" is derived from the first initials of its three founders, Charles Paul Brown, Bernadeane Sittser and James Russell Strole. All three are ordained Christian ministers who no longer preach the word of God - they now preach against death.

The immortalists claim an active membership of over 4,000 rabid followers and have celebrated their 26th anniversary as an organization in 1994. The CBJ's believe "we die because we think we must." To "neutralize" the "death program" a strong and equal but opposite action or belief is required - "people reinforcing the idea that you don't have to die; to live as an immortal people need to close off their 'exits,' things like a belief in heaven or hell or reincarnation or even holding onto a family burial plot."

When confronted with the fact that CBJ members have died, the groups leaders say, "they left an opening." Investigative journalists have portrayed the CBJ leaders as the Jim and Tammy Baker of immortality.

There are all kinds of food preservatives, drugs and pharmaceuticals available that are purported to extend life (i.e.- BHT, GH3, Deprinel, etc.), yet there are no living centenarians who have tried these chemical shortcuts to support the theories with truly extended years.

There are all kinds of proponents of exercise as the progenitor of health and longevity. Human history or experience does not bear the exercise theory out.

The great distance runners, Jim Fix and Dr. George Sheehan, believed that exercise was the elixir of health and foundation of longevity and to that end they ran or jogged 10 miles per day, neither took mineral or vitamin supplements.

Jim Fix, who started the whole running shoe craze with his best seller, *Jog Your Way to Health*, died following multiple cardiomyopathy heart attacks (a simple selenium deficiency disease - he refused to supplement with vitamins and minerals in the fervent hope to prove exercise as the one true route to health and longevity) at the age of 48 (when one fails to take mineral supplements, exercise becomes a negative - it's like running the Mercedes without oil!!) - exercise really helped him.!!!!!

Then there was Dr. George Sheehan, medical editor for Runners World Magazine and a "runner's runner," whose only concern with diet and supplements was that, "they didn't interfere with running" - Dr. Sheehan died of widely disseminated prostate cancer at the age of 76, all that running, pain and sweat without supplementation bought him just six months longer than the classic American "couch potato" who averages 75.5 years of age.

The United States government has hired and isolated 350 longevity scientists in an abandoned military facility in Arkansas to study aging and how to slow it down on tens of thousands of mice and rats on calorie restricted/nutrient dense diets.

Clive Mckay's caloric "undernutrition"

(60 % reduction from free choice calories) in the mid-thirties doubled the 50% survival rate and doubled the known life span of laboratory rats. Undernutrition (low calorie intake) without malnutrition (diet contains excess vitamins and minerals above RDA) experiments show great benefit even when the low calorie/high mineral diet is begun in mid adulthood.

Low calorie/nutrient dense diets are not for children as there is a relatively high mortality on the front end of this program.

Children will flourish and do well on optimal calorie/nutrient dense programs.

Biblical patriarchs are notable for having had great longevity (Table 8 -2); as time moved ahead chronologically in the bible from The Creation, the longevity recorded for the patriarchs declined - did this reflect the loss of Rare Earths from their soil and thus their food? If so, how come the Great Flood didn't replenish the soil with silt, reimplant minerals into the soil and thus into the patriarchs food delivering health and longevity? Yes, certain floods will bring life giving mineral rich silt, other floods are devestating in their effect by covering rich farmland with useless sand and clay.

Anthropologists theorize the maximum lifespan of ancient man based on physical traits and cultural skills and assets:

"Missing link" - 43 years maximum
            lifespan ?

Australopithecus - 47 years maximum
            lifespan
            3.4 million years ago

Homo erectus - 72 years maximum
            lifespan
            1.5 million years ago

Homo sapiens 100 - 110 years maximum
            lifespan
            100,000 years ago

The maximum survival rate or longevity for fish has been extended by 300 % in the UCLA laboratory of Roy Walford by maximizing the micronutrients fed to the fish as well as lowering the water temperature by just a few degrees.

Before the "Industrial Revolution" man

Table 8-2. Age of the Biblical Patriarchs at Their Time of Death	
BEFORE THE FLOOD	
Adam	930
Seth	912
Enos	905
Cainan	910
Makalaleel	895
Jared	962
Methuselah	969
Lamech	777
Noah	950
AFTER THE FLOOD	
Shem	600
Arphaxad	436
Salah	433
Eber	464
Peleg	239
Reu	239
Serug	230
Nahor	148
Terah	205
Abram	175
Issac	180
Jacob	147

ST. LOUIS POST-DISPATCH

OBITUARIES

PETER STEPHAN, 50, founder of a private clinic that prescribed lamb placenta as an elixir of youth, died Sunday (March 20, 1994) after a heart attack at his home in London.

A homeopathist, Mr. Stephan injected lamb placenta into patients on the theory that it would replace dying cells. He sold beauty products and wrote books promoting lamb placenta.

Mr. Stephan's former partner, sex therapist Dr. Brian Richards, was convicted 10 years ago of trying to arrange Mr. Stephan's murder so he could inherit the clinic. The police learned of the plot before any attempt was made.

Brian Wayne DeCelle

Brian Wayne DeCelle, 37, formerly of Sarasota, died Dec. 17, 1992, in Raleigh, N.C., of a heart attack.

Born Feb. 7, 1955, in Townshend, Vt., he attended Sarasota High School and was a graduate of the University of South Florida in Tampa. He most recently was a resident of Raleigh, N.C., where he was administrator of Stewart Health Center in the Springmoor Retirement Community and also was a certified dietary manager.

as a species survived the "Age of Pestilence and Famine" - from before written history to the 1700's wars, famine and epidemics of infectious disease combined to kill 30 to 50 % of the human populations of the various continents. As more calories and protein became available, more cultures increased their average age of survival - the wealthy (including royalty, merchants and doctors) always did well as they acquired mineral rich food in great variety and adequate quantities from far flung corners of their spheres of influence.

The organized searches for new land, herbs and spices, and treasure to support the kings adventures always included a search for the "Fountain of Youth."

Ponce de leon was in fact a clerk on one of Columbus' ships that journeyed to the New World with a Royal Charge to find the "Fountain of Youth" if it existed in the New World.

Despite "heroic" efforts by the 20th century "health care" professions the maximum survival to 110 years hasn't changed for urban man since the days of ancient Rome; however, the 50 % survival rate has

Table 8-3.
50 % SURVIVAL RATE FOR URBAN MAN

50 % survival to 22 years ancient Rome

50% survival to 40 years 19th century

50 % survival to 49 years 1900

50 % survival to 67 years 1946

50 % survival to 72 years 1960

50 % survival to 74.9 years 1990

50 % survival to 75.5 years 1994

increased 300%(Table 8-3).

Humans must come to grips with the fact that if we are to reach our "genetic potential" for health and longevity we must become independent of our minerally depleted soil and food and poisoned environment . We must not bet our lives on or depend on the random distribution of essential minerals being in or not in our food or we will surely fail in our quest for health and longevity.

In examining our options for reaching our maximum genetic potential for longevity we have two control groups to evaluate for an optimal and rational approach in humans:

1) Those, who as a group do not take supplements, in fact this group pooh poohs the use of supplements and fully believes one can get all of the essential nutrients they need from "the four food groups" - this homogenious non-supplement control group is made up almost exclusively of allopathic physicians whose average lifespan is 58 years of age (the average American lifespan is 75.5 years of age - therefore for advice on longevity you're better off asking a bus driver than an allopathic physician and statistically you can gain 20 years by not going to medical school!!!);

2) Those, who as a group do not take supplements, yet live to be well over a hundred years of age - this control group includes several ancient cultures which have common denominators that are in fact the long sought after "Fountain of Youth." And while there is some controversy as to whether these people live to 120 or 160, they do in fact do a much better job than

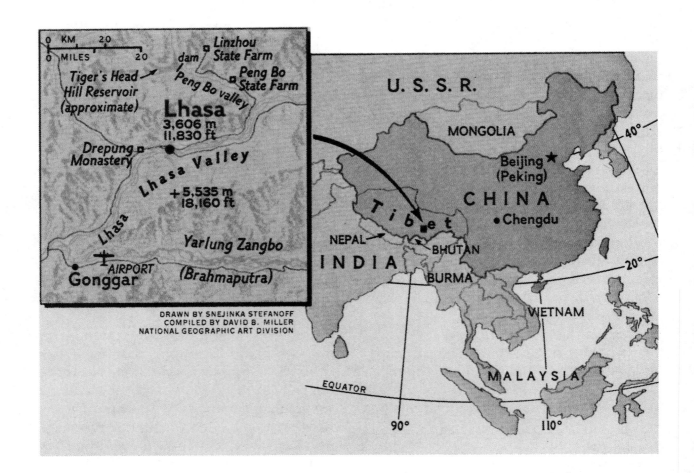

Tiger's Head
Hill Reservoir
(approximate)

Linzhou
State Farm
dam
Peng Bo valley
Peng Bo
State Farm

Lhasa
3,606 m
11,830 ft

Drepung
Monastery

Lhasa Valley

+5,535 m
18,160 ft

Lhasa

Yarlung Zangbo

AIRPORT

Gonggar

(Brahmaputra)

0   KM   20
0   MILES   20

DRAWN BY SNEJINKA STEFANOFF
COMPILED BY DAVID B. MILLER
NATIONAL GEOGRAPHIC ART DIVISION

U. S. S. R.

MONGOLIA

Beijing
(Peking)

CHINA

Tibet

Chengdu

NEPAL

BHUTAN

INDIA

BURMA

VIETNAM

MALAYSIA

EQUATOR

40°

20°

90°

110°

we do in reaching their genetic potential so we will set aside for a time the cynical comments of the nay sayers (usually agitated allopaths who can't conceive of anyone doing well or better without their modern techniques) and get what positives we can.

There are five well-known human cultures whose peoples routinely live to their maximum genetic potential of 120 to 140 years of age - the fact that all five cultures are third world countries is significant (the longest average longevity for an industrialized nation is the 81.1 held by the Japanese).The Tibetans in the northwest of China, the Hunzakut of eastern Pakistan, the Russian Georgians (and their sister cultures of Armania, Azerbaijian and Abkhazia in the Caucasus Mountains) and certain regions of Turkey, the Vilcabamba in the Andes of Ecuador and the Titicaca of the Peruvian Andes are all famous for their large numbers of centinarians.

The common denominators of the five long lived cultures include:

1) The communities are found at elevations ranging from 8,500 feet to 14,000 feet in sheltered mountain valleys.

2) The annual precipitation is less than 2 inches.

3) Their water source for drinking and irrigation comes from glacial melt and is known universally as "Glacial Milk" because the highly mineralized water is opaque and whitish in color like milk.

4) There is no heavy industry to pollute air, water or food.

5) Only natural fertilizer (manure, plant debris and "Glacial Milk") is employed.

6) Western allopathic medicine was not historically available to these cultures (they avoided the "land mines").

THE TIBETANS:
The Tibetans were the inspiration for the Pulitzer Prize winning book by James Hilton, The Lost Horizon. Tibet's old people are found on Chang Tang or the northern plateau, elevation 15,000 feet, which consists of salt lakes fed by glaciers from the eastern slopes of the Himalayan Mountains. This mountain culture has about 500,000 people who are devout Buddists. The Tibetans are a mix of nomadic herdsmen, merchants of salt, farmers and great cavalrymen on camel or horse.

Tibet makes up almost 10 % of China's land mass and was founded in the 7th century by King Songtsan Gambo. The Chinese government took over Tibet in 1950 by sending a large army to establish a military governer. Since 1965 the region has been administered and known as the Tibetan Autonomous Region (T.A.R.) of China.

The herdsmen build their corrals, huts and roads out of salt bricks carefully cut from dried salt lakes on the top of the plateau; they hunt Marco Polo Sheep, antelope, gazelle, wild asses and yak.

The yak which translates to "wealth" provides meat, sausage, milk, cheese, yogurt, butter, wool, skins and animal power for plowing, riding and to carrying freight.

The staple diet consists of "tsampa", a

smelly hand-mixed paste of lightly toasted barley flour, yak butter, salt and black tea. Tsampa is supplemented with turnips, cabbage, potatoes, trout, omelettes and beans.

Tibetans routinely drink 30 to 40 medium sized cups of black or green tea daily because the high elevation is extremely dry requiring a high fluid intake. Each cup of black or green tea is flavored with a chunk of rock salt the size of a concord grape and two pats of yak butter.

The Tibetan capital city of Lhasa (translates to "Place of the Gods") was the inspiration for James Hilton's legendary city of Shangri-La. The city is found at an elevation of 12,000 feet, temperatures can fluctuate as much as 80 to 100 degrees each day.

In the center of old Lhasa is the holiest shrine in Tibet - The Jokhang built in 650 AD. The Jokhang is the "Mecca" to the Tibetan Buddhists - many of the faithful would trek through the mountains for years to come and pray at this holy site.

In the mountains west of Lhasa is Drepung, a gigantic monastery that houses 10,000 monks, 25,000 serfs and assistants working 185 estates and tending over 200 pastures.

The Potala, "high heavenly realm," is a sprawling mountain top palace of the Dalai Lama (translates to "ocean of wisdom" and represents the living prophet of the Buddhist faith and the inspiration for the ancient prophet in James Hilton's, *The Lost Horizon*) built into the mountain 700 feet above Lhasa. The Potala is famous for its 1,000 rooms, 10,000 altars, 200,000 statues of Buddha and the eight gold gilded tombs of past Dalai Lamas.

South of Lhasa are tens of thousands of acres of terraces fed and watered by mineral rich "Glacial Milk" which originates in the Himalayan glaciers and supplies an endless source of minerals from "Glacial Milk" to ensure the Tibetans will reach their genetic potential for longevity.

Li-Ching-Yun lived to the age of 256, he outlived 23 wives! Li of Kaihsien, in the Province of Szechwan, China, was born in 1677 and died in 1933 at the age of 256 years (and was the inspiration for the 200 year old leader of Hilton's Shangri-La). Professor Wu-Chung-Chien, the Dean of the Department of Education, of the Minkuo University claims to have found records showing that Li was in fact born in 1677 (the Chinese have the most accurate of all census records in the history of man), and that on his 150th birthday (1827), he was congratulated by the Chinese Imperial Government. Fifty years later, in 1877, Li was sent another official congratulations on his 200th birthday. Fifty years later, at the age of 250 years, Li lectured to a thousand medical students in Beijing on the art of living a long healthy life.

London Times May 8, 1933

Telegrams in Brief-A telegram from Chungking in the province of Szechwan, China, states that Li-Ching-Yun, reputed to be the oldest man in China and presumably the world, has died at Kiah-Sien, at the alleged age of 256. - Reuters

New York Times May 6, 1933

Li-Ching-Yun-Dead;
Gave his age as 197

"Keep quiet heart, sit like a tortoise, sleep like a dog" His advice for long life.
Inquiry put age at 256

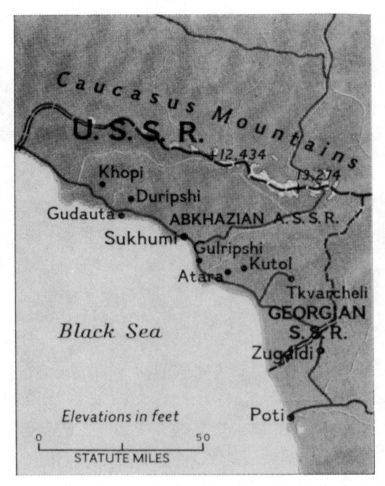

Los Angeles Herald-Examiner, Wednesday, February 12, 1975

Russ Passes 140th Year

MOSCOW (AP) — Mejid Agayev, oldest citizen in an Azerbaijan village that numbers among its inhabitants 54 people over 100, recently celebrated his 140th birthday, Tass reported Tuesday.

The mountainous village of Tikyaband in the southern Soviet republic is described as "a village of centenarians," Tass said. But it is not uncommon for residents of the mountains in Azerbaijan and Georgia to reach 100 years.

The Soviet news agency did not say if Agayev was the oldest man in the village. It said he is alert and continues his favorite occupation, wood carving.

Shirali Mislimov, an Azerbaijani farmer claimed to be the oldest man in the world, died in 1973 at the age of 168, Soviet officials said.

RUSSIAN GARDENS ON 168TH BIRTHDAY

MOSCOW (UPI) — The man the Soviet government calls the oldest in the world, Shirali Mislimov, celebrated his 168th birthday yesterday by working in his garden and taking his daily half-mile walk.

He attributed his longevity at least partly to avoiding smoking, drinking and catnaps. "I never sleep in the daytime," he said.

Mislimov, who lives with his 107-year-old third wife, Hartun, in the village of Bazavu in the Soviet republic of Azerbaijan, was in "fine fettle," according to the newspaper Trud. The Soviet press notes his birthday every year.

The reference to "fine fettle" indicated Mislimov has recovered from a winter bout with pneumonia, the first time in his life he had been sick, according to the newspaper.

Mislimov says he tried smoking cigarettes once about 150 years ago, but got sick after three or four puffs and has not smoked since.

The only time he ever tried whisky, he once said, was in 1831. "I thought I was burning inside," Mislimov said.

This newspaper article commemorated Mislimov's 168th birthday May, 1973.

Reported to have buried 23 wives and had 180 decendents - sold herbs for first 100 years.

THE RUSSIAN GEORGIANS:

The Russian Georgians as well as the Abkhazians, Azerbaijanis and Armanians are found at the timber line of the Caucasus Mountains which have peaks of 12,434 to 13,274 feet above sea level. They live in simple stone houses without electricity, their blood pressure is typically 104/72 at age 100, women continue to have children after age 52, they typically drink an eight ounce glass of vodka with breakfast and have a large glass of wine with lunch and dinner. Almost all of the "old people" are from rural backgrounds or occupations such as farmers, shepards and/or hunters.

This group of centinarians from the Cacasus Mountains are found between the coasts of the Black Sea and the Caspian Sea and mountain villages at or above 4,500 feet above sea level. This region supports over 500,000 people 4,500 to 5,000 of whom are over 100 years of age:

1,844 in Russian Georgia ..... (39/100,000)
2,500 in Azerbaijian .... (84/100,000)
Vilcabamba .... (1/100)
United States........................... (3/100,000)

The oldest known living person from the Caucasus region in 1973 was Shirali Mislimov, at age 167 he still worked in the village tea plantation in the small Azerbaijiani village of Barzavu on the Iranian border. They feel that youth is up to 80 years of age, 80 to 100 years is middle age and 100 to 160 years of age are the seniors. Many married couples were married over 100 years. In studying 15,000 people over the age of 100, only the married individuals attained advanced age and still have an active sex life after age 100.

Mejid Agayev celebrated his 140th birthday in February 12, 1975. Agayev was the oldest living citizen in the Azerbaijian village of Tikyaband that bragged of having 54 people over the age of 100 years!

Work relegated to centinarians included weeding fields, feeding livestock, shepards, picking tea, washing laundry, house work and baby sitting.

Women over 100 years of age usually had between 4 and 15 children during their child bearing years.

The staple diet of the Caucasus region includes chicken, mutton, beef, goat milk, cheese, yogurt and butter, bread, tomatoes, cucumbers, green onions, garlic, fruit, pita bread, boiled corn meal mush (abusta), red pepper, tea and wine and salt. Their total caloric intake per day ranges between 1,800 and 1,900. Their terraced fields have been irrigated with highly mineralized "Glacial Milk" for over 2,500 years.

THE VILCABAMBA:

Ecuador's star shaped "Sacred Valley of Longevity" (Vilcabamba) is actually five valleys that converge and sit between two Andean Mountains at 12,434 feet above sea level. The western skyline of Vilcabamba is dominated by the summit of Mandango, the tallest mountain whose glaciers supply the mineral rich "Glacial Milk" which is used to irrigate the terraced fields. The "Glacial Milk" originating from the high peaks of Podocarpus National Park pours into the Rio Yambala which converges with the Chamba River which is also used for irrigation.

In 1971 a census revealed nine people

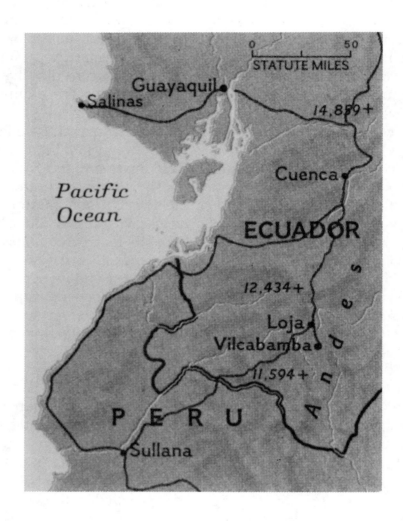

over 100 years of age for every 819 or an astounding one centinarian per 100 people!!! Miguel Carpio at age 123 was the oldest living Vilcabamban found at the census - he still smoked, drank wine and "chased women."

The staple diet of the Vilcabamba Indian includes corn, beans, goat meat, chicken, eggs, milk, cheese and a soup known as repe which is made from bananas, beans, white cheese, salt and lard. Their average total calorie intake is 1,200 to 1,800 calories per day.

THE TITICACA:

Gucilaso de la Vega whose father was Spanish and whose mother was an Inca princess recorded (1609) the legend of the beginnings of the Titicaca peoples:

"Our Father, the Sun, seeing that men lived like wild animals, took pity on them, and sent to earth a son and daughter of his, in order that they might teach man the knowledge of our Father the Sun, and that they might know how to cultivate plants and grains and make use of the fruits of the earth like men and not beasts. With these orders and mandate our Father the Sun placed his son and daughter in Lake Titicaca."

Thus as legend holds, the first Incas came to earth on an island in Lake Titicaca, to start what was to become the most advanced civilization of pre-Columbian America.

Titicaca is found in the Andean highlands of Peru at 12,506 feet above sea level. The main city of Titicaca is Puno (population 32,000); the people of the Altiplano (high plains) are divided into the pure indians and the "mestizos" who are a mix of indian and Spanish. The treeless hills that form the Altiplano surrounding Lake Titicaca are covered with "pata pata", or the stone terraces built by the Incas to provide level farming areas, and as catchments for the mineral rich "Glacial Milk" from the great Andean mountain, Mt. Cardillera Real with which they irrigated their crops.

Because the extreme elevation of the Altiplano, maize or indian corn wouldn't grow in the Lake Titicaca region, instead the Incas grew tubers never before seen by the Spanish, "they supplant the lack of bread with some roots they call "papas" (potatoes) and which produce under the earth," noted Father Acosta. When introduced into Europe by the Spanish the potato became more valuble than all the gold in the world. The Inca also invented a freeze drying technique to save harvested potatoes for the winter, described in 1609 by a Spanish Friar:

"To keep potatoes from rotting, they leave them out for many months to freeze. After they have been repeatedly frozen they tread gently on them, to press out the moisture they contain. When they have been well squeezed, they are placed in the sun until they are thoroughly dry. In this manner the potato keeps for a long time, and it changes its name to chunci."

The original indians of the Lake Titicaca region are the Aymara; the Quechua who still speak the language of the Incas were decendents of Inca slaves after the Inca occupation in the 12th century.

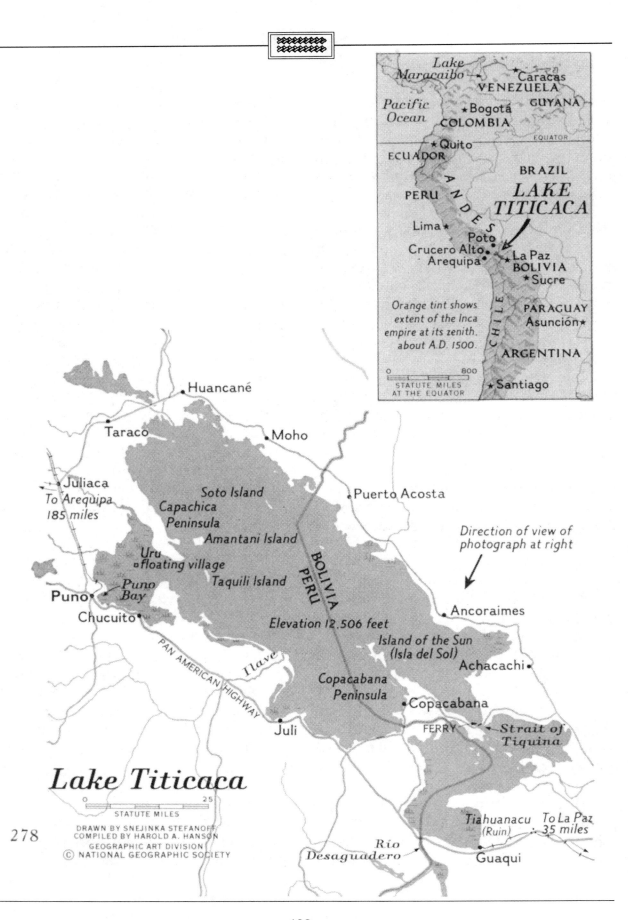

Lake Maracaibo
VENEZUELA
*Caracas
Pacific Ocean
*Bogotá
COLOMBIA
GUYANA
EQUATOR
*Quito
ECUADOR
BRAZIL
PERU
LAKE TITICACA
Lima *
Poto
Crucero Alto
*La Paz
Arequipa *
BOLIVIA
*Sucre
A N D E S
Orange tint shows extent of the Inca empire at its zenith, about A.D. 1500.
PARAGUAY
Asunción *
CHILE
ARGENTINA
0   800
STATUTE MILES AT THE EQUATOR
*Santiago

Huancané
Taraco
Moho
Juliaca
Puerto Acosta
To Arequipa 185 miles
Soto Island
Capachica Peninsula
Amantani Island
Direction of view of photograph at right
Uru floating village
BOLIVIA
PERU
Taquili Island
Puno
Puno Bay
Ancoraimes
Chucuito
Elevation 12,506 feet
Island of the Sun (Isla del Sol)
Achacachi
PAN AMERICAN HIGHWAY
Ilave
Copacabana Peninsula
Copacabana
Juli
FERRY
Strait of Tiquina

Lake Titicaca

0   25
STATUTE MILES

Tiahuanacu (Ruin)
To La Paz 35 miles

278

DRAWN BY SNEJINKA STEFANOFF.
COMPILED BY HAROLD A. HANSON
GEOGRAPHIC ART DIVISION
© NATIONAL GEOGRAPHIC SOCIETY

Río Desaguadero
Guaqui

The melting glaciers of the Cordillera Real, the towering Andean Mountain that reaches over 20,000 feet produces a mineral rich "Glacial Milk" that is used to irrigate the terraced fields that feeds the Titicacas and supplies the water to Lake Titicaca itself.

When Francisco Pizarro arrived in 1532 the Inca Empire was in the midst of a great civil war, making it easy for a small band of Spaniards to conquer a kingdom of over 3,000 miles in length reaching from Ecuador to Chile. In the early days of the Inca culture, Inca referred only to the king and not to a race or nation.

The ancient ancestors of the Titicaca worshipped many gods; today they have settled on a patchwork of ancient gods and Catholicism that was injected by the Spanish.

Lake Titicaca itself is over 3,200 square miles in surface area, 122 miles long and 47 miles wide - when viewed from a plane the outline of the lake looks like a jaguar ready to pounce on a rabbit, thus the name Titicaca translates to "Rock of the Puma (or Jaguar)." The effluent or Rio Desaquadero from Lake Titicaca flows from the "head of the rabbit."

The Incas used irrigation ditches to channel water from the lake itself as well as from the "Glacial milk" to water and remineralize their well manicured terraces.

Like all alpine habitats, the Lake Titicaca area has a very little variety when it comes to wildlife. Father Acosta noted in his early writings that the lake held only two kinds of fish, a large catfish and a minnow. The catfish made up a major source of animal protein for the local Indian tribes. In 1939 trout were released into the lake and to no one's great surprise they flourished. Within two years the Indians began landing lake trout weighing more than 25 pounds - the highly mineralized waters of Lake Titicaca produced a bounty beyond anyone's wildest dreams.

The Isla de Sol, the mythical birthplace of the Incas is located 40 miles into Lake Titicaca. Manco Capac and Mama Ocllo appeared approximately 1,100 AD.

The Incas, much like the Romans were at the same time conquerors and lawmakers, engineers and very firm taskmasters - "their totalitarian state was a benevolent dictatorship." Whenever the Incas conquered a culture they basically left it intact, requiring only a tax in the form of salt and that the conquered people worship the Sun God. No one went hungry or naked but nothing was left to free will.

When the first Aymaras came to Lake Titicaca, they found other Indians, the Urus, already living on floating islands made of Tartara reeds. "Whole villages of Urus were to be found on the lake living on their rafts of Tartara wrote the Jesuit Father Jose' de Acosta in 1590. The Uru still live long healthy lives today and still refuse to give up their Tartara islands.

The quinoa, a grain of Titicaca begins to ripen in late April or May, it is used as Europeans use wheat, barley is also grown. At 15,400 feet the barley never ripens to seed heads so the Indians use it for cattle feed. The Titicaca shepherds live and work at 17,000 feet.

The Inca "cattle" were in fact llamas or New World camels that feed on moss and lichens:

"There is nothing in Peru of greater value and utility than the cattle of the land, which our people call sheep of the Indies, but the Indian in their tongue call llama," wrote

Father Acosta.

The Incas also built 10,000 miles of stone roads to provide rapid communication around Lake Titicaca. Messengers were stationed every 1.5 miles and ran messeges in relay much like a human pony express - these warriors could relay messeges over 150 miles per day. Inca nobles also used the roads to reach the Isla del Sol to worship the Sun god.

THE HUNZA:

"The single most important food as used by the people of Hunza consists of dried apricots and whole ground grain mixed together to form a toddy."

- John H. Tobe
Hunza: Adventure in a
Land of Paradise

The story of the Hunza began 2,300 years ago with Alexander the Great. Alexander was the first born son of King Philip of Masedonia. Legend has said that "the night before the consumation of Philip's marraige with Olympias, she dreamed that a thunderbolt fell upon her body and kindled a great fire whose divided flames dispersed themselves all about and then were extinguished."

"Philip dreamed "that he sealed up his wifes body with a seal whose impression was the figure of a lion." Some of the alchemists and diviners interpreted Philips dream as a warning to "look narrowly to his wife;" however, Aristander of Telnessus assured Philip that the meaning of his dream was "that the queen was with child of a boy, who would one day prove as stout and courageous as a lion."

Alexander was born on the sixth of Hecatombaeon, which is called Lous by the Macedonians - the same day that the Temple of Diana at Ephesus was burned to the ground. The temple caught fire and was destroyed while its priestess was assisting at the birth of Alexander. All of the diviners in Ephesus ran to and fro beating their faces and predicting "that this day had brought forth something that would prove destructive and fatal to all Asia!"

Following Philips military victory and occupation of Potidea, he received three messeges simultaneously:

1) his commander Parmenio had overthrown the Illyrians in a great battle;

2) his race horse had won the course at the olympic games;

3) and his wife Olympia had given birth to a son - Alexander!"

Philip was overjoyed and he was assured by the diviners "that a son whose birth coincided with three such successes could not fail to be invincible."

"Alexander was fair and of light color, passing into ruddiness in his face and upon his breast." From his early childhood Alexander was energetic and eager, he displayed a love of glory and pursued glory with an endless spirit. As a teen ager Alexander was very bold; when he was asked if he would compete in the Olympic games, he replied,"I will if I might have kings to run against!"

While still a boy Alexander entertained

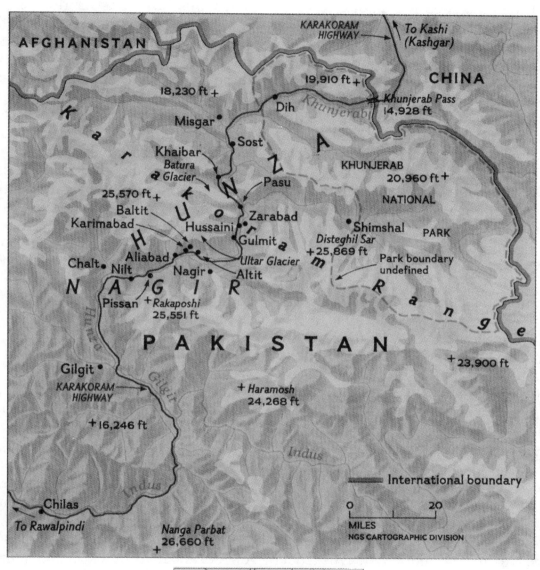

AFGHANISTAN

Karakoram Highway — To Kashi (Kashgar)

CHINA

18,230 ft +

19,910 ft +

Dih

Khunjerab

Khunjerab Pass
14,928 ft

Misgar •

Sost •

KHUNJERAB

Khaibar

Batura Glacier

Pasu

20,960 ft +

NATIONAL

25,570 ft +

Baltit

Zarabad

Shimshal •

PARK

Karimabad

Hussaini

Disteghil Sar
+25,869 ft

Gulmit •

Park boundary
undefined

Aliabad

Ultar Glacier

Chalt •
Nilt

Nagir •

Altit

Pissan • + *Rakaposhi*
25,551 ft

NAGIR

+ 23,900 ft

PAKISTAN

Gilgit •

*KARAKORAM
HIGHWAY* →

+ *Haramosh*
24,268 ft

+ 16,246 ft

Indus

▬▬▬ International boundary

Chilas •

To Rawalpindi

Nanga Parbat
26,660 ft
+

0   20

MILES
NGS CARTOGRAPHIC DIVISION

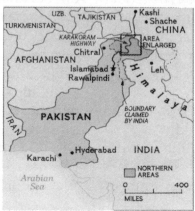

UZB. TAJIKISTAN
• Kashi
• Shache
CHINA

TURKMENISTAN

Karakoram Highway

AREA
ENLARGED

AFGHANISTAN

Chitral •

• Leh

Islamabad +
Rawalpindi •

Himalaya

PAKISTAN

*BOUNDARY
CLAIMED
BY INDIA*

Karachi • • Hyderabad

INDIA

IRAN

NORTHERN
AREAS

*Arabian
Sea*

0   400

MILES

visiting royalty in the stead of his father. The visitors included the ambassadors of the king of Persia. Alexander asked," What is the nature of the road to inner Asia, the character of your king, and how does he carry himself to his enemies? What forces is he able to bring into the field?" His forwardness and lofty purpose appeared early in his life and the visiting royalty "looked upon Philip's famed ability as nothing compared to that of his son Alexander."

Whenever Alexander heard that his father had conquered a town of importance or had won some notable victory , instead of being happy, Alexander would tell his companions, "father would anticipate everything and leave him and them no opportunities of performing illustrious actions."

A Thessalian horse trader brought king Philip a fiery war horse called Bucephalus, offering him at a price of thirteen talents. When Philip and his party went into the field to try him out, they found him so vicious and unmanageable that he reared up when they mounted him and would not so much as endure the voice of any of Philip's grooms. They were just about to lead Bucephalus away as totally useless and intractable, when Alexander said," what an excellent horse do they lose for want of boldness to manage him!" When Alexander repeated this several times Philip said, "Do you reproach those who are older than yourself, as if you knew more and were better able to manage him than they?"

"I could manage this horse," replied Alexander, "better than others do!"

"And if you do not," said Philip, "what will you forfeit for your rashness?"

"I will pay the whole price of the horse" replied Alexander.

At this boy's answer the kings entire company began to roar with laughter. As soon as wagers were settled, Alexander ran to Bucephalus, took hold of the bridle, turned him directly into the sun (Alexander had observed the horse was shying from his own shadow). He let the horse move forward a little, still keeping the reins in hand he stroked him gently; when the horse grew eager and fiery, "he let fall his upper garment softly and with one nimble leap securely mounted him; when he was seated, little by little he drew in the bridle and curbed him without either striking or spurring him. Presently, when he found him free from all rebelliousness and only impatient for the course, he let him go at full speed, inciting him with a commanding voice and urging also with his heel."

King Philip and his court looked on, first in silence then nervousness until, seeing him turn at the end of the course and return rejoicing and waving in triumph - they all burst into cheers and applause. Philip, shedding tears of joy and pride, kissed Alexander as the boy dismounted and said, "Oh my son, look for a kingdom equal to and worthy of thyself, for Macedonia is too little for thee!"

Philip now looked upon the instruction of Alexander to be of greater importance than to be entrusted to ordinary masters of music, poetry and typical school subjects, and to require as Sophocles stated, "The bridle and the rudder, too."

Philip sent for Aristotle, the most learned and most celebrated Greek philosopher and scholar of his time. Philip rewarded Aristotle with "a munificence proportionate with the private tutelage of his son prince Alexander."

Aristotle taught Alexander his doctrine of morals and politics, herbal medicine, alchemy and abstract and profound theories only shared by philosophers amongst themselves. Alexander as a student had a feverish inclination to practice medicine; for whenever his friends were sick, he would "prescribe healing diets and medication (herbs and minerals) proper to their disease."

Alexander loved Aristotle no less than if he were his own father, "as he had received life from one, so the other had taught him to live well."

While in Asia, Alexander heard that Aristotle had publicly published several of the oral treatises normally reserved for communications between great thinkers and he was disturbed enough to write him a letter:

"Alexander to Aristotle, greeting,

You have not done well to publish your books of oral doctrines; for what is there now that we excel in, if those things which we have been particularly instructed in be laid open to all? For my part, I assure you, I had rather excel in the knowledge, of what is excellent, than in the extent of my power and dominion,

Farewell!"

Later, while King Philip was absent on his extended expedition against the Byzantines, he left Alexander, now only 16 years old, "as his lieutenant in Macedonia, committing the charge of his seal to him." Alexander refused to sit idling away the time

so he declared war on the Maedi and reduced them to slaves after conquering their capital city by storm - not too surprising Alexander renamed the conquered city Alexandropolis!

During the battle of Chaeronea, which Philip fought against the Greeks, Alexander was the first man in the charge against the fierce and sacred Thebams guards near the Cephisus River.

Despite king Philip's pride and love for his brave son they soon became enemies. The straw that broke the camel's back was the marriage of King Philip to Cleopatra, the child queen of Egypt. When Cleopatra's uncle Attalus, toasted the marriage and asked the gods for "a lawful successor to the kingdom, Alexander became furious and threw a cup at him shouting, "you villain; what am I then a bastard?" Philip, took to Attalus' defense, rose up from his bride's side and would have run Alexander through with a sword but in his drunken rage he slipped and fell to the floor. Being the young cock, Alexander couldn't resist mocking his father, "see there, the man who makes preparations to pass out of Europe into Asia, overturned in passing from one seat to another." Philip and Alexander were soon reconciled by Demaratus, a family friend.

The marriage between Philip and Cleopatra was not an affair of the heart or the product of lust for a flat chested gangly pre-teenage girl but rather a political treaty between Macedonia and Egypt - the Macedonians wanted and got exclusive rights to the highly mineralized wheat from the Nile flood plains, wheat that was legendary in providing strength and stamina to the armies that ate it - Macedonia needed this Egyptian wheat to support its armies for the coming invasion of Asia! The Egyptians wanted and got a peace treaty from the Macedonians exempting them from participating in the war with Asia and protection by the Macedonians from the Asian hordes. It was a marriage made at the bargain table.

However, the father and son reconciliation was short lived. Pixodorus, viceroy of Caria, sent an emissary to make a match between his oldest daughter and Philip's son Arrhidaeus. Alexander's contemporaries and friends convinced him that Philip by a political marriage and important alliance was going to transfer the Macedonian Kingdom to his brother Arrhidaeus.

Alexander out of alarm sent Thessalus as his own representative into Caria to urge Pixodorus to change his mind and offer his daughter in marriage to Alexander himself, so that Alexander might be his son-in-law. Pixodorus responded that Alexander's offer was much more favorable to him.

Philip, enraged at Alexander's offer, "chastised Alexander bitterly" for being unworthy of the power he was to inherit, as to marry a low Carian, who at best was a slave of a barbarous prince. Philip further wrote to the Corinthians to send Thessalus (Alexander's messenger) to him in chains; he also banished Alexander's closest friends for their part in the intrigue.

Soon after these terrible events, a Macedonian named Pausanias was stripped of his post and properties in Egypt by Cleopatra and her uncle Attalus. Pausanias, unable to get the decision overturned and himself reinstated by Philip, became enraged and assassinated Philip. The guilt for the murder of Philip was laid at the feet of Alexander's mother, Olympias, who was reported to have incited young Pausanias to revenge.

Some accusing fingers also pointed to Alexander, however, these suspicions were dispelled after he captured Pausanias and his conspirators and had them summarily executed. Alexander was now 20 years old.

Alexander inherited a troubled Macedonia, besieged on all sides with restless and dangerous enemies. The barbarians that had been conquered by Philip's armies were anxious to be governed by their own princes. Philip had also been victorious over the Greeks, however, he hadn't had time to consolidate his battlefield gains and win over to Macedonian law and culture all he had conquered before being assassinated.

Alexander's response was to declare war and he immediately invaded the heart of the barbarian territory as far east as the Danube River, conquering and overthrowing Syrmus, the king of the Triballians.

The Thebans revolted and became allies with the Athenians against Alexander. Alexander ordered his armies into a forced march through the pass of Thermopylae; he sent the following message to the Greek Demosthenes," You called me a child when I was in the country of the Tribillians and a youth when I was in Thessaly - I will appear as a man before the walls of Athens."

When Alexander arrived at the walls of Thebes he only demanded the authors of the rebellion -Phoenix and Prothytes and declared a general amnesty to all who would summit to Macedonian Law. The Thebans responded by demanding Philotas Antipater be surrendered to them and invited the Macedonian army to become Greeks. Alexander and his army immediately fell on Athens, sacked the city and burned it to the ground; then to terrify the rest of Greece into submission he publically executed 6,000 of the Theban leaders and sold 30,000 lesser members of the Athenean Court into slavery - only the priests and those who had historically been friends of the Macedonians were spared.

The ambassadors of Greece assembled at the Isthmus and voted to join their armies with Alexanders in his march against the Persians and to prove their allegiance they voted Alexander their general of the allied armies.

Alexander's armies were actually the smaller of the forces in the alliance - he commanded 30,000 foot soldiers and 4,000 cavalry. After gaining a positive, "You will be victorious" from the head priests of Athens, Alexander marched northeast towards Persia (Iran).

Darius, the great warlord king of Persia, had his armies camped on the eastern banks of the Granicus River - the Gateway to Asia. It seemed that Alexander would have to fight at the very entrance to Asia when he reached the western banks of the river in the evening. Parmenio, military advisor to Alexander pleaded with Alexander to wait until morning as dark was but moments away. Alexander, immediately spurred his horse into the river and called his army to him:

"They advanced against whole showers of darts thrown from atop the almost sheer eastern bank. Despite his lack of prudence Alexander prevailed, he and 13 troops of cavalry gained the top of the bank where they engaged in hand to hand combat.

Alexander, easily recognized, was attacked from all sides, his cuirass was pierced by a javelin. Two Persian officers, Rhoesaces and Spithridates set on him at once; he dodged one of them and broke his spear striking at Rhoesaces so that he was forced to defend himself with a dagger; while engaged in this hand-to-hand combat, the other Persian officer Spithridates rode his horse full tilt at Alexander and struck him such a blow on his helmet with his battle axe that it sheared off the plumed crest and the edge of the blade clipped off a large shock of blond hair. As Spithridates raised up in his stirrups to deliver a second and probably fatal blow, Alexander's leutenent - the black Clitus pierced his body through and through with his spear at the same time as Alexander killed Rhoesaces with his dagger."

While the advance cavalry were engaged in the dangerous hand to hand combat the Macedonian foot soldiers crossed the river and forming a great pincher advanced into the battle. When the Persian advance force turned and fled they left 20,000 foot soldiers and 2,500 cavalry of their own dead on the river bank. Alexander had lost only 34, of whom five were foot soldiers and the balance cavalry.

The overwhelming victory at the Granicus River resulted in the surrender of Sardis, the capital of the Persian maritime province as well as hundreds of other small towns and villages, Only the two cities of Halicarniossus and Miletus held out; Alexander destroyed them by force.

While Alexander was deciding what route to take into the heart of Persia, an ancient copper plate was washed up on the flooded banks of a spring near the city of Xanthus in Lycia. The inscription on the plates edge stated, "the time will come when the Persian Empire would be destroyed by the Greecians." Enthused by this finding, Alexander took his armies to destroy Cilicia and Phoenicia and then along the seacoast to Pamphyia; normally this coastline was rugged and pounded by great waves and surf, but an unusually low low tide allowed Alexander and his armies a speedy unhampered passage.

Alexander conquered the Pisidians and the Phrygians at their capital of Gordium, the home of the ancient Midas. Alexander came across the fabled chariot fastened to a pillar by braided cords made from the bark of a cherry tree. The legend stated, "Whosoever should untie this, for him was reserved the empire of the world." Alexander, unable to untie the knot cut it through with his sword. He then advanced to Pophlagornia and Cappadocia, both of which he destroyed.

When Darius, king of Persia heard that Memnon, his finest officer along with thousands of cavalry was killed in the battles he decided to carry on the war with the Macedonians in the upper mountainous provinces of Asia. Darius Marched from Susa very confident, number one because of his superiority of numbers which totaled 600,000 men and number two in a dream he saw the Macedonian army on fire and Alexander waiting for him clad as the child he saw when he visited Philips court ten years earlier.

Darius' confidence grew stronger as Alexander and his armies remained encamped in Cilicia so Alexander could recover from an illness - Darious mistook this delay as a sign of cowardice in Alexander.

A Macedonian general named Amyntas and two other generals married to Persian women were in contact with the Persian king Darius giving him Alexanders proposed battle plans. When Amyntas learned Darious was going to ambush Alexander in the mountain passes he advised the king to keep his larger army in the open plain where his superior numbers could be brought to advantage. Darius, instead of heeding this advice, said he was afraid that Alexander would flee and escape to fight another day; however, Amyntas stated,

"That fear is needless, for assure yourself that far from avoiding you, he will make all the speed he can to meet you, and is now most likely on his march towards you!"

Amyntas' advice to Darious was to no avail, as Darius immediately marched into Cilicia at the same time as Alexander advanced into Syria to confront him. Passing one another in the night, they turned their armies around toward each other; Alexander took up position in the passes using the sea, the mountains and the Pinarus River to force Darius to split his forces. Not to allow himself to be outflanked by such a superior number Alexander strung out his right flank much wider than his left flank and fought there himself in the forward ranks where he was wounded in the thigh by an arrow. After putting the Persian army to flight Alexander counted 110,000 dead of Darius' army - unfortunately Darius was not found amongst the dead.

Learning that Amyntas and his two fellow generals had Persian wives and had most probably given council to Darius regarding this last battle, Alexander sent members of his personal body guard to execute the three generals and their wives. The generals in turn learned of the execution orders and thus forewarned were able to fight their way free and with their wives, fled northeast following the Indus River and eventually crossing through the pass of Babusar and across the 3,000 foot deep chasm of the Hunza River.

The pass into Hunza is 13,700 foot high and is only passable during the three summer months. This was part of the trade route taken by Marco Polo on his return from Cathay in 1326; over the 3,000 foot deep Hunza River Gorge via a suspended bridge made of braided goat hair.

The three generals and their wives formed the nucleus of a warrior tribe that initially flourished by preying on and raiding the trade routes and caravans that flowed from China to India and back again.

The Hunzas were not always known as Hunzas; up until the turn of the 20th century, the valley was known as the Kanjut and the people known as the Kanjuts. When the Indian Girkis tried to invade Kanjut they gave the valley and the people in it the name Hunza, because all of the people in the valley were allied and united as arrows in a quiver. In the Burushaski language (a mix of ancient Masedonian and Persian) the name Hunza translates to "arrow."

The indiginous plant life of the Hunza Valley was rather limited. Ninety-nine percent of the original valley was bare rock. Cultivated plants included barley, millet, wheat, buckwheat, potatoes, turnips, carrots, beans, peas, pumpkins, tomatoes, melons, onions, garlic, cabbage, spinach, cauliflower, apricots, mulberries, walnuts, apples, plums, peaches, cherries and pears. Pomegranate trees are scattered throughout the valley. They consume milk, butter milk, yogurt and butter (which they put in their tea and use as a cooking shortening). Hunza children are breast-fed until two to four years of age.

A large variety of indiginous wildlife (i.e.- ibex or "Markhors", Marco Polo sheep, geese, ducks, pheasants and partridge) provided the early Hunza with meat.

The Hunza does not cook the majority of their food because of a lack of fuel (even the animal manure is added back to their fields).

The Hunza salt supply is mined from hills near the Shimshal and Muztagh Rivers and used in their tea and for cooking in its raw brown state (the color comes from trace minerals included in the salt deposit when the ancient seas dried up).

THE 14 HUNZA PRACTICES

1) Basic diet is grains (whole grain and sprouted), vegetables (raw or steamed), fruits (fruits are dried and reconstituted in water or diced and served in gelatin (goat and mutton tendon and cartilage). Meat at 2 to 4 pounds per week (i.e,- mutton, goat, yak, beef, poultry, brain, kidney, liver, etc) is eaten as available; dairy (i.e.- whole milk, soured milk, yogurt, cheese and butter)is a staple; Grape wine known as Pani is consumed daily.

2) Their farm soils are maintained by organic agricultural practices,"That which is taken from the soil is returned to the soil." Composting, plant debris and animal manure is turned back into the soil.

3) All Hunzas work seven days each week (work never killed anyone) - to them there is no sabbath! They work 12 hours each day.

4) Fat sources include whole milk, butter, ghee, apricot oil and animal fats.

5) Total absence of additives, preservatives or chemicals in their air, food and water.

6) Daily consumption of salt by adding chunks of rock salt to their tea and in cooking vegetables and meat.

7) No agricultural sprays or chemicals of any kind.

8) All children are breast-fed for 2 (girls) to 4 (boys) years (no vaccinations or antibiotics; no birth defects and only two hermaphrodites or "mukhanas" recorded in the 2,300 year Hunza history).

9) All grains, vegetables and fruits dried for storage have been exposed to the sun.

10) Native herbs are used for medicine, seasoning and as food (salads).

11) "Glacial milk" is the exclusive water source used for drinking and irrigation purposes (the fields are flooded, when the water soaks into the soil a thick layer of mineral silt or "rock flour" is left on top of the soil - this silt is plowed into the soil before it is planted).

12) Apricot oil is used for cooking along with ghee (clarified butter) and animal fat (tallow).

13) Whole grains are used exclusively - no processed flours.

14) The Hunza eats a meager fare each day usually around 1,800 to 2,000 calories.

The Hunza remained unvanquished until 1891 when the British Empire conquered and pacified the Hunzas by installing an Ismali ruler known as the Mir.

The average annual precipitation in Hunza is less than two inches and the surrounding mountains, the Karakorum Range is only 300 miles long, the mountains are bare, naked and metallic gray looking. Mount Rakaposhi, 25,550 foot high overlooks the 8,500 foot high Hunza Valley along with more than 60 summits higher than 22,000 feet (Table 8-4)! Mount Rakaposhi is one of the most dificult mountains on Earth to climb - it took 23 attempts to conquer the summit of Rakaposhi. The first 22 attempts failed but a British expedition in 1958 finally succeeded in scaling the nearly sheer face.

Maps refer to this Karakorum Range at the junction of many countries as the Pamirs - the Afghanistan Pamir; the Russian Pamir; the Chinese Pamir, etc. Pamir translated from Persian becomes "Roof of the World." Tibet is often called "the Roof of the World" however, Lhasa is at an elevation of only 13,000 feet and is surrounded by summits only 18,000 feet high or less.

A few miles above the junction of the pearl gray waters of the Hunza River and the Gilgit River ia a village called Secundersbad; it is here that the Hunza Valley begins; the Hunza Valley follows the Hunza River up to its sources beyond

Table 8-4. The 25 Highest Peaks of the Karakorum Range.	
Name	Height Above Sea Level In Feet
Haramash	24,270
Mukorum	23,050
Unnamed	25,868
Kampire Dior	23,434
Unnamed	21,200
Kanjut Sar	25,460
Unnamed	23,440
Unnamed	25,540
Godwen Austin (K-2)	28,250
(2nd tallest mountain on a land mass)	
Masherbrun	25,660
Gasherbrun	26,470
Tera Kangri	24,489
Saltora Kangri	25,400
Unamed	22,400
Saser Kangri	25,170
Unnamed	21,270
Unnamed	22,891
Nanga Parbat	26,660
Unnamed	21,870
Unnamed	22,200
Unnamed	22,120
Rakaposhi	25,550
Bilckhar Doboni	20,126
Unnamed	21,907
Unnamed	23,890

Misgar, almost on the Chinese border where it springs from glacial torrents spewing from under the 5,000 square mile Ultar Glacier.

The Hunza Valley is barely 200 miles long. There were no naturally fertile valleys in Hunza as compared with the Willamette Valley in Oregon. The Hunza Valley was originally bare rock, the soil only being carried basket by basket up the 3,000 foot gorge walls and placed in hand crafted stone terraces. This soil is continuosly replaced by hand from the mineral laden silt dredged by hand from the bed of the Hunza River 3,000 feet below.

Then there was the problem of water in the barren "safe haven," fortunately one of the Masedonian generals was a military engineer. He was able to locate a year round source of water roaring from under the Ultar Glacier 50 miles away; the Ultar Glacier originates on the 25,550 foot high Mount Rakaposhi. He was able to design and construct a gravity propelled aquaduct which carried water for drinking and irrigation.

The aquaduct was a wonder of engineering as it was made from grooved logs attached together to form a 50 mile long trough which was hung from the sheer cliffs by steel nails hammered into the rock walls.

The water originating from under the millions of tons of ice grinding on the parent rock of Mount Rakaposhi was so rich with minerals that it was a bluish white - so white that the original peoples called it "Glacial Milk." For generation after generation, crop after crop and year after year for more than 2,300 years the Hunza people have drunk (Table 8-5) and irrigated their terraced fields with "Glacial Milk," unwittingly assuring their people of an optimal intake of the more than 60 minerals in the "Glacial Milk" of the Ultar Glacier!!!!

Table 8-5

CHEMICAL ANALYSES OF DRINKING WATER FROM KARIMABAD, HUNZA, PAKISTAN (Data expressed as mg/l except for pH, specific conductance and suspended solids.)

	(1)	(2)
SiO_2	4,180	89,000
Fe	380	40,000
Ca	11,500	17,000
Mg	1,260	15,900
Na	760	2,100
K	5,800	-
As	0.3	-
Ba	43	400
Be	<1	<1
Cd	0.3	<1
Co	<3	20
Cu	<1	76
Li	11	675
Mn	8	<1
Mo	<10	1
Pb	<10	10
Se	<1	-
Sr	32	55
V	1	-
Zn	2	85
SO_4	3,200	-
Cl	300	-
F	60	-
HCO_3	8,000	-
pH	6.98	-

Specific conductance

123 micromhos @25°C

Suspended solids, 396 mg/l

Note: (1) Clear liquid after centrifugation
       (2) Aliquot after acidification to 12% HNO_3 at 60°C
           for 1 hr

In recent history, Sir Mohomed Nazim Khan, K.C.I.E. (Knight Commander of the Indian Empire), the late Mir (king) ruled from 1892 to 1938 (a total of 46 years). His successor, Mir Mohammed Jamal Khan ruled from 1945 - it is said his grandfather assended to the throne :

"He there upon had Taighoon, Nematulla, and Misiab killed; Sakhowot Shah and Ssahandor Shah rolled down a precipice below Ghulkin; then their mother put to death and arranged for the murder of Solan Khan in Shimshal, However, he allowed his brother, Nazim Khan to live."

He then sent a letter to the Maharajah of Kashmir to notify him of his assent to the throne as the Mir of Hunza:

"By the will of Allah and a decree of fact, my late father and I fell out. I took the initiative and settled the matter, and have placed myself on the throne of my ancestors."

The Mir of Hunza and various kings of the neighboring countries (Nagir, Punial, Yasin, and Baltistan) supported the revolt from India and joined the government of Pakistan. The reason for the Hunza revolt from India was an unwanted tax by the British Empire.

History shows that the Hunza had a stable and flourishing trade with China through the neighboring Chinese province of Singkiang. For centuries the caravans moved both ways; the Hunza wanting rice and salt paid an annual tribute to the Chinese government at Kashgar.

The ancient Mir of Hunza owned huge acreages in China near the Yarkand River, where he grazed yak, cattle, goats, sheep, camels and horses. However when the British came into Hunza in 1947, enough pressure was exacted on them to cause them to bolt to Pakistan.

"Two years later Colonel Bruce came to Gilgit (capital of Hunza) as temporary British agent and he told me (the Mir) that the government had decided that I might still pay my annual tribute to China. To this, however, I demurred as I pointed out to him that having relations with both was like sitting between two stools. He, however, retorted that if this was the case and one stool broke there was always the other to sit on and that no suspicion would attach to me as long as there were friendly relations between the British government and the Chinese Emperor. He did make one stipulation, though; and that was that I should let the political agent in Gilgit see the letter that accompanied the toll before it was dispatched."

In turn the Chinese sent a contingent of troops each year to Hunza with rich gifts from China to the Mir. The reason for the ancient tribute was clear. The trail through Hunza is the shortest and safest route to Gilgit, Rawalpindi, Pashawor, Kabul, Persia, Kashmir and the Indian interior. The Chinese caravan could only travel in safety at the will of the Mir of Hunza. If the caravan failed to pay the tributes a few men at the order of the Mir would hide in the cliffs and would create landslides forcing the freight-laden animals and the soldiers over the 3,000 foot cliffs to their deaths. There are 200 miles of cliffs making the toll the easiest and most prudent way to assure safety along the trail. The Mir had full control of his tribesmen so it was better to give him half of the value of the caravan than to lose it all!!

Except for the polar glaciers, the Karakorum Range has the largest collection of glaciers in the world. Millions of tons of glacial ice (in some places hundreds or thousands of feet thick) grind four inches of living mountain rock into a fine "rock flour" each year, which is carried in suspension as "Glacial Milk." No rock, no mineral or no metal is resistant enough to be exempt from the grinding forces of these millions of tons of ice.

The "Glacial Milk" ejaculates from under the glaciers in great white water "nullahs." Thousands of glacial nullahs merge and join the Hunza River, very quickly the Hunza River joins the Gilget River; the two great rivers now married join the Indus River.

The Hunza and the Gilget Rivers are purely glacier rivers, almost entirely made up of "Glacial Milk," whereas the Indus River is a conglomerate of hundreds of smaller brooks, streams and rivers that drain the great Indian and Pakistan watersheds.

There are sister mountain ranges paralleling the Karakorums - the Hindukush (translates to "the Hindu Killers") and the Himalayas have most of the worlds tallest peaks; yet their "Glacial Milks' are not as complete or dense with minerals as the "glacial milk" from the Ultar Glacier that feeds the Hunza Valley.

"Glacial milk" is a mixed liquid, a solution of ionically disolved elements and a suspension of the finely ground rock dust ("rock flour") ground from the living parent rock of the mountain by glacial friction. The suspended minerals in "Glacial Milk" are referred to as metallic colloidal minerals. The average particle size of the metallic colloidal minerals are 7,000 times smaller than a human red blood cell - so small they can only be visualized with an electron microscope.

The individual elements in "Glacial Milk" are not found in their seperate pure atomic form, but rather in aggregations or mini-alloys to form suspended solute particles. The presence of these aggregate particles (ranging in size from one hundred thousandth to one ten millionth of a centimeter in diameter) are only detected by chemical analysis or the electron microscope.

The raw rock inorganic colloids cannot pass through semipermeable membranes and therefore produce little or no osmotic pressure, depression of the freezing point of water (unlike a salt solution) or elevation of the boiling point. These molecular mini-alloys or aggregates carry a uniform negative electrical charge.

Plants, wild forms and crops such as grains, vegetables, fruits and nuts take up these inorganic metallic colloids and convert them into intracellular (within the cell) organic plant colloids - these organic plant colloids are the form of minerals found in and used by all living cells of plants, animals and humans. It is the eating of the plants rich in organic colloidal minerals that is the secret of health and longevity of the five cultures we have called the "Agebeaters"!!!!

When these centenarians do die its not

from cancer, diabetes, heart disease, stroke or any other of the miriad of "natural causes," "infirmaties," or degenerative diseases (mineral deficiencies) that plague western cultures; they do not spend their last hours, days, weeks, months or years in clinic waiting rooms, in line at the pharmacy, hospitals, nursing homes or the ICU (intesive care units) hooked up to tubes, wires or devices smelling of death - or even contemplating suicide because of unbearable pain or overwhelming medical bills. When a centenarian does die it is usually in the cold of the winter, which can be quite cold above the 8,500 foot level. Hypothermia is usually the most common cause of death in these long lived cultures -"So Allah wills!"

Organic colloidal minerals derived from plants are 98 % available to humans as compared to 8 to 12 % availability for the metallic minerals. The serendipitous irrigation of their terraced fields with the common denominator of "Glacial Milk" from the mountains containing 60 or more minerals is the secret of the five cultures who live to be 120 to 140 years of age. Their terraced land, their "Glacial Milk" and their organic agriculture are their whole life. Only they have been able to fulfill their genetic potentials for longevity - and they have done it without the "blessings of modern high tech medicine, vaccines, antibiotics, steroids or transplants."

" Those who have lived the longest seem to be those remote from medical practice."

-Ruth Wegg,M.D.,Professor
University of Southern California

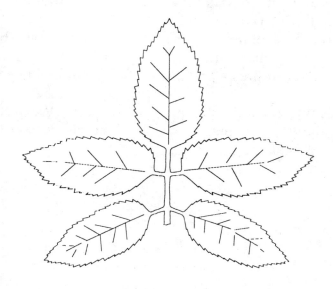

"If you choose to go to a hospital, go into hospitals with your eyes wide open. Medical care, like so many other things, is problematic; its not a sure thing. Patients must understand hospitals are hazardous and medical care is a dangerous enterprise - you must be willing to put a considerable amount of energy into self-protection."

- Lowell Levin, M.D., Professor
Yale School of Medicine
Department of Public Health

Chapter 9

THE KILLING FIELDS:
The Mineral Deficient Health Care System

We are firstly and ultimately responsible for our own safety, health and longevity - we do not contract with anyone to keep us healthy or warranty our bodies for 100 years of age; the responsibility is all ours; we only seek "health care" when we screw up somewhere along the line. Unfortunately, most Americans have given up their rights and their responsibilities to a doctor (or two or three!). They cast aside the simple needs of the flesh (90 essential nutrients) and go innocently to the physician and surgeon as a child goes wide-eyed and hopeful with a stranger offering candy to get into the car for a ride - a ride not of joy or comfort, but of kidnaping, torture and murder.

In 1991 a Harvard University, School of Public Health study revealed that 1.3 million injuries and 198,000 deaths occur in American Hospitals each year as a result of "iatrogenic" or doctor caused mishaps or "adverse events."

Iatrogenic injuries and deaths run from four to five times greater numbers than deaths and injuries on the highways!!! Out of 31 million hospital admissions in 1991 about 1% (that's one out of every 100) ended in disaster - far too high when the Harvard study pointed out that seven out of ten "adverse results" were totally avoidable and that nearly 33.3 % were the result of negligence. "Medical injury is a hidden epidemic," declares Lucien Leepe, M.D., Director of the Harvard study. "Hundreds of mistakes occur every day in a medical lab or hospital, many going unreported, unrecognized, uninvestigated and unknown."

According to Dr. Sydney Wolfe (director of the Ralph Nader-founded watchdog group, Public Citizen Health Research Group, Washington, D.C.) in a January 13, 1993 news release, "300,000 Americans are

TILTING AT PILL MILLS

'Quackbuster' Stephen Barrett takes on the vitamin industry

In his basket of bad eggs ...

What crusader Stephen Barrett has to say about a few trendy treatments:

Acupuncture: 'Utter nonsense, total drivel.'

Vitamins: 'If you eat a proper diet, you don't need vitamins.'

Chiropractic: 'Chiropractic theory is not scientific ... there's a lot of rotten apples in the barrel.'

Homeopathy: 'The ultimate nothing. ... a $250-million-a-year-scam.'

By Marcia Staimer, USA TODAY

USA TODAY · FRIDAY, SEPTEMBER 16, 1994

Doctors urge acting class in med school

By Tim Friend
USA TODAY

Doctors should take acting classes so they can at least pretend they're concerned about their patients' health, say two articles in *The Lancet*.

Not to say doctors are cold, but the stress of medical practice sometimes spoils a compassionate mood. So knowing how to act a bit wouldn't hurt, suggest Drs. Hillel Finestone and David Conter of the University of Western Ontario.

"We do not put forward the idea cynically," they say. Their concern: If a doctor doesn't have the skills "to assess a patient's emotional needs and to display clear and effective responses . . . the job is not done."

They say acting classes should be required in medical school so doctors can learn just when to provide a perfectly timed compassionate look, or a touch on the hand.

But which is better? Classical Laurence Olivier or method acting like Marlon Brando?

The doctors hope "comparative testing in practice" will answer that question.

An accompanying commentary in the British journal by Dr. Chris McManus of St. Mary's Hospital Medical School, London, says acting may ultimately save doctors at risk of professional burnout.

Meanwhile, McManus writes, "the surgeons, those *prime donne* of medicine, hold center stage, acting out tantrums with thrown scalpels and cutting remarks."

2½ prescription-writing errors made daily at N.Y. hospital, researchers say

Associated Press

CHICAGO — Errors in prescription writing averaged 2½ a day in a large New York teaching hospital, and one in five of the mistakes could have caused severe medical problems or death, researchers said.

Doctors wrote 289,411 prescriptions during 1987 at the hospital, and errors occurred in 905 of them, including 182 mistakes that could have caused serious harm or even death if they had gone undetected, the researchers said.

"Medication errors are an all too common occurrence in the provision of modern health care and one of the many 'hazards of hospitalization,'" the researchers wrote in the *Journal of the American Medical Association.*

"Errors of physician prescribing are of particular concern, as such errors have been associated with a higher risk for serious consequences than errors from other sources," said the researchers from Albany Medical Center Hospital, where the study was conducted.

However, "quality assurance procedures operative within our hospital and in most health-care systems ... appear to be quite effective," said Timothy S. Lesar, assistant pharmacy director for clinical services at Albany and the research team's co-leader.

"All these errors were averted. They never put a patient at risk," he said in a telephone interview Monday.

Five years ago, Albany Medical Center was cited by the state Health Department for lacking effective policies to control dangerous drugs. The citation came after two doctors improperly injected a drug into the spine of a pregnant cancer patient, leaving her comatose and near death.

The center acknowledged responsibility and began requiring more quality control procedures in drug administration. Now, for written prescriptions, pharmacists check the orders and enter them into a computer that rechecks them against patient data about drug allergies and other factors, researchers said.

Drugs accounted for 20 percent of the 27,000 injuries to patients caused by treatment in New York state hospitals in 1984, said Dr. Howard H. Hiatt, head of a Harvard Medical School study released last month.

The study, however, did not identify how many of the injuries might have been caused by prescription errors, Hiatt said in a telephone interview Monday.

The Albany study found a prescription error rate of 3.13 per 1,000 orders written. Of the 905 errors, 522, or 57.7 percent, were "significant."

Such mistakes varied from ordering too strong a tranquilizer for the size or age of a patient to prescribing penicillin or a related drug to an allergic patient, said Dr. Henry Pohl, senior associate dean for the academic program at Albany Medical College and co-lead researcher.

Sunday, July 18, 1993

Nation

Update

FBI to probe VA hospital deaths

OMAHA, Neb. — A veterans hospital where one of four patients died after receiving the wrong medication will be investigated by the FBI, Sen. Bob Kerrey said yesterday.

Criminal intent is not believed to have been involved in the incident but all avenues must be investigated, Kerrey, D-Neb., said after meeting with hospital director John J. Phillips. The investigation will begin tomorrow, Kerry said.

A pharmacist, pharmacy technician and three nurses at the Omaha Veterans Administration Medical Center have been transferred to administrative duties pending the outcome of the investigation, Phillips said.

Associated Press

CHICAGO SUN-TIMES, FRIDAY, AUGUST 26, 1994

Medication Errors And Kids: Nation's Other Drug Crisis

News USA

Every year, medicine misuse leads to the hospitalization and even death of thousands of children. In fact, medication mistakes could be seen as America's other drug crisis.

Experts say that of the 200 million prescriptions dispensed for children each year, nearly half are taken incorrectly.

When children don't take enough of their medicine, or stop taking it too soon, they may not control such serious diseases as cancer, kidney failure and epilepsy.

When they take too much of a medication, they may experience such annoying and dangerous side effects as diarrhea or stomach upset, loss of consciousness or fatal breathing problems.

What's a Parent To Do?

It's important for parents to understand their children's medications. Here are some of the things you need to know.

Find out the name of the medicine and what it's supposed to do.

Ask how much medicine the child should take, when it should be taken and for how long.

Find out about possible side effects and what to do if they occur.

Ask if there is written information about the medicine that you can take home.

When talking with your children about medicine, explain the difference between using illegal drugs and taking medicine in order to get well. It's important to get the child involved in the correct treatment.

And be sure baby sitters and relatives who take care of the children understand a child's medication routine. If the child must take medicine at school, be sure to notify teachers and the school nurse.

Also discuss your children's medications with your pharmacist. That way, you can be sure your kids get all the benefits of their medicine.

U.S. Says 349,000 Caesareans Last Year Were Unnecessary

ATLANTA, April 22 (AP) — Doctors performed 349,000 unnecessary Caesareans in this country in 1991 at a cost to the nation of more than $1 billion, the Centers for Disease Control and Prevention said today.

But the number of mothers who delivered vaginally after a previous Caesarean is rising to 108,000 in 1991 — or 24.2 births per 100 deliveries, up from 20.4 in 1990, according to the latest figures from the agency.

"That's the good news," said Dr. Sidney Wolfe of the consumer group Public Citizen in Washington. "Women need to know that the fact they had a C-section once does not mean they have to have C-sections from then on."

Among the 966,000 Caesarean deliveries in 1991, about 35 percent were repeats. The overall Caesarean rate was 23.5 per 100 births, unchanged from 1990. Only Brazil and Puerto Rico reported higher rates.

Federal health officials hope to lower the rate in the United States to 15 Caesareans per 100 births by the turn of the century, a rate the Centers for Disease Control deems medically appropriate. But the goal will probably not be met, said Selma Taffel, a statistician at the agency.

"It's going to be extremely difficult," Ms. Taffel said. "We would have to have a rather large reduction in the primary Caesarean rate, and the primary rate has not changed substantially since 1986."

The American College of Obstetricians and Gynecologists has also said that the Caesarean rate was too high but has opposed setting a national target rate.

Rare at one time, Caesarean sections, the surgery in which an obstetrician cuts open the uterus to deliver the baby, can cause infection and longer hospital stays. But the rate soared, from 10.4 births per 100 in 1975 to 24.7 births for every 100 in 1988.

Consumer groups say many such operations are unnecessary. They accused doctors of choosing the costly procedure to make money and of scheduling deliveries for their own convenience, a view the Government ultimately concurred in.

The Centers for Disease Control noted in its report that Caesareans had been performed most often in profit-making hospitals on women covered by private health insurance.

The average Caesarean costs $7,826, compared with $4,720 for a vaginal delivery, the agency said. The estimate of $1 billion that could have been saved in 1991 represents the cost of the 349,000 operations that the agency says would not have been performed if doctors had performed Caesareans at the target rate of 15 per 100 births, the report said.

The agency encouraged more hospitals to follow the example of Mount Sinai Hospital Medical Center in Chicago. In two years the hospital reduced its Caesarean rate from 22 to 11 births for every 100 by establishing a peer-review system for the procedure and requiring a second opinion for non-emergency Caesarean sections.

Comparing the rate in the United States with 21 other countries or commonwealths that track the operation, the agency found that only Brazil and Puerto Rico had higher C-section rates, 32 and 29 per 100 births, respectively. Japan and the former Czechoslovakia were lowest, both with 7.

In the United States, the rate was highest in the South — 27.6 for every 100 births — compared with 19.8 in the West, 21.8 in the Midwest and 22.6 in the Northeast.

Doctor investigated in cancer scam

HUNTINGTON BEACH — A respected dermatologist, whose recent death is being investigated as a suicide, may have diagnosed skin cancer in hundreds of healthy patients in order to get higher fees, a state investigator said yesterday.

Former employees accused Dr. Orville Stone, 61, of using cancerous skin samples to fabricate diagnoses, said Steve Rhoten, an investigator with the Medical Board of California.

Stone was hit by a truck and killed Friday, a day after investigators searched his Huntington Beach office and questioned him about the allegations.

Associated Press

Doctor overseers stand accused

SACRAMENTO — The state Department of Consumer Affairs has asked the California Highway Patrol to investigate "serious allegations of misconduct" by the staff of the state board that licenses doctors and other health professionals.

The focus of the investigation is the Enforcement Unit of the Medical Board of California, according to internal letters and memorandums.

If substantiated, Consumer Affairs Director James Conrad said in one of the letters, "that misconduct may have jeopardized the health, safety and welfare of hundreds of California citizens."

McClatchy News Service

Doctors' Financial Motives Linked to Testing Habits

Reuter

BOSTON, Nov. 18—Doctors who own radiation treatment facilities, rehabilitation clinics or other health-related businesses tend to order more tests and treatments for patients than doctors who don't have a financial stake in the businesses, two studies released today said.

The studies, published in the New England Journal of Medicine, found that physician entrepreneurs who invest in medical services may help drive up the cost of health care.

The authors of one study, on radiation therapy centers, say doctors should be banned from owning such joint ventures. Under federal law, doctors can't send patients to laboratories they own. But other types of investments are not prohibited.

Last December, the American Medical Association passed a tough rule prohibiting doctors from sending patients to a health care facility "when they have an investment interest in the facility." Six months later, the AMA rescinded the rule.

The new studies suggest the AMA's now-defunct restrictions may have been a good idea because doctors apparently do a poor job of policing themselves when they are in a position to control how lucrative their health-related business will be.

In one new study, a team led by Alex Swedlow of William Mercer Inc. of San Francisco examined worker's compensation claims in California. They found that when physicians owned part of the business:

■ Recommendations for physical therapy doubled.

■ Costs for psychiatric evaluations were 26 percent higher.

■ Thirty-eight percent of MRI scans were unnecessary, compared with 28 percent in cases where the physician had no conflict of interest.

The second study, of radiation centers in Florida, Jean Mitchell of Georgetown University and Jonathan Sunshine of Florida State University found evidence that doctor-owned centers were responsible for a higher incidence of radiation treatments and higher costs.

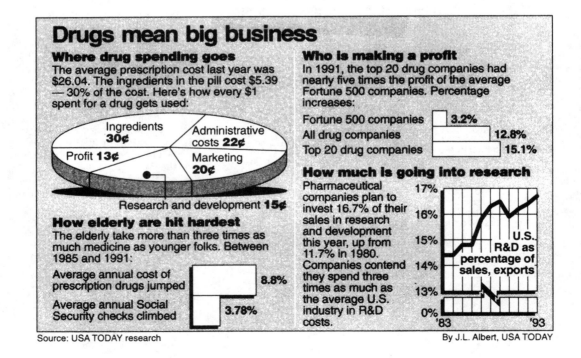

Drugs mean big business

Where drug spending goes
The average prescription cost last year was $26.04. The ingredients in the pill cost $5.39 — 30% of the cost. Here's how every $1 spent for a drug gets used:

- Ingredients 30¢
- Administrative costs 22¢
- Profit 13¢
- Marketing 20¢
- Research and development 15¢

How elderly are hit hardest
The elderly take more than three times as much medicine as younger folks. Between 1985 and 1991:

- Average annual cost of prescription drugs jumped 8.8%
- Average annual Social Security checks climbed 3.78%

Who is making a profit
In 1991, the top 20 drug companies had nearly five times the profit of the average Fortune 500 companies. Percentage increases:

- Fortune 500 companies 3.2%
- All drug companies 12.8%
- Top 20 drug companies 15.1%

How much is going into research
Pharmaceutical companies plan to invest 16.7% of their sales in research and development this year, up from 11.7% in 1980. Companies contend they spend three times as much as the average U.S. industry in R&D costs.

U.S. R&D as percentage of sales, exports

'83 — '93

Source: USA TODAY research

By J.L. Albert, USA TODAY

21-YEAR COVERUP

Suppressed 1971 US report linked diet, disease

A long-suppressed US government report assessing $30 million worth of research found that major health problems are related to diet, the solution to illness may be found in nutrition, and an improved diet's real potential is that it may defer or modify the development of diseases.

Alexander Schauss, executive director of the new Citizens for Health (CFH) organization, which has reprinted the "one copy which mysteriously missed confiscation and recently surfaced," said:

"The government has known for 21 years that such illnesses as heart disease, many types of cancers, and other serious degenerative diseases can be prevented by diet . . . It is inexcusable that they have kept this information from the public all these years.

"Had this information been made available in 1971 we would be ten years ahead of where we are today in our knowledge of the role of nutrition in the prevention and treatment of disease. The loss of lives and suffering of two generations of citizens denied this information should go down in history as one of the greatest tragedies of modern medicine."

The document, a US Department of Agriculture publication called *Human Nutrition, Report No.2, Benefits from Human Nutrition Research*, was issued in 1971. The referenced, 129-page report was the culmination of $30 million worth of federal nutrition research.

But it was suppressed, Schauss told *The Choice*, by then Secretary of Agriculture Earl Butz, presumably at the behest of the food processing industry.

"Because the government destroyed copies of the 1971 report, it wasn't until the *1977 Senate Select Committee on Nutrition and Human Needs, Diet Related to Killer Diseases* report that the public was made aware of the amount of supportive evidence of a role for diet in the prevention of disease," said Schauss.

"Yet due to the destruction of the 1971 report, even the 1977 Senate committee was unaware of the wealth of evidence available from their own government agencies."

CFH has copies of the suppressed report available for $9.95 plus $3 for shipping from Citizens for Health, PO Box 368, Tacoma WA 98401.

1,200 people may need new lab tests

AIDS results could have been botched

By BARBARA WALSH
Staff Writer

About 1,200 Broward residents may have been tested improperly for health problems ranging from AIDS to diabetes.

County health officials say a Hollywood laboratory may have botched as many as one-third of the original test results of patients at three public clinics in the past seven months.

The county's greatest fear is that patients infected with the HIV virus may have received a clean bill of health through inaccurate lab work by Hollywood Diagnostics Center.

"It is [a matter of] life and death," said Carolyn Graham, Broward's human services director. "We are committed to straightening this out."

A lab official said the county's fears are unfounded.

"We're no different from any other lab. Any lab is going to have a little bit of problems," said Pedro Rodriguez of Hollywood Diagnostics.

On Wednesday, the lab canceled its county contract in the middle of a *Sun-Sentinel* investigation of the controversy.

Broward health officials have since contracted with two new labs.

On Monday, health workers will begin reviewing about 1,200 patient files to pinpoint those people with medical problems requiring additional testing.

At least half of the 1,200 patients were tested for the human immunodeficiency virus, the precursor to AIDS, county health officials told the *Sun-Sentinel.*

"I don't want to alarm the residents," Graham said. "But we will be in touch with these patients and ask them to come in for further testing. I will be honest and tell them that we've had some problems with the lab that we have been using."

The testing problems came to a head when a Fort Lauderdale woman found she had been falsely diagnosed as HIV-positive after being tested last July at the Edgar P. Mills Multi-Pur-

ST. LOUIS POST-DISPATCH

SUNDAY, NOVEMBER 7, 1993

Diseased Transplants Turn Recipients' Hope To Despair

© 1993, Los Angeles Times

LOS ANGELES — Ruth Glor's family was devastated, her doctor baffled. Just months after receiving a transplanted kidney that revitalized her life, Glor was dying of metastatic melanoma, a particularly virulent form of skin cancer.

Around the country, other transplant recipients — at first unknown to one another — were making similarly grim and mysterious discoveries: They, too, were dying of metastatic melanoma. Their new organs, all from the donor who provided Glor's kidney, were not life-sustaining; they were lethal.

Glor's transplant and recovery had gone so smoothly that only 11 days after the operation that she was able to leave Kansas University Medical Center, and return home to the small farming community of Buffalo, Mo., about 30 miles north of Springfield.

"She was real happy," said her son, Danny, 35, a dairy maintenance man in Buffalo. "She built flower beds outside. . . . She got a bicycle. . . . She just thought it was a new lease on life."

Then, 15 weeks later, Glor grew weak and felt excruciating pain in her back. Her local doctor sent her to a nearby hospital, which quickly flew her to the university medical center in Kansas City, Kan. On Aug. 17, 1991, five months after the transplant, Glor died. She was 57.

Oncologists and transplant experts say there is no fast, routine way to screen organs and tissues for most cancers, even in living patients.

killed each year in hospitals alone as a result of medical negligence." First of all Wolfes' figures are very conservative because Naders group used the mortality numbers supplied by the medical profession, a neutral outside task force may have found this number to be only 50 % of the real figure, or 600,000!

To appreciate how big a figure 300,000 dead is, we have to compare Wolfes figures of Americans killed by "friendly fire" in American hospitals with our U.S. military losses in Vietnam over the course of the 10 year war where we lost 56,000 for an average loss of 5,600 per year!!! According to these figures, you would have been safer on a Vietnamese battlefield where an enemy had guns and artillery and wanted to kill you than in an American hospital!!!!

In protest to the Vietnam War millions of irate Americans poured out into the streets, students took over universities with weapons and explosives, a president was chased from office and there was political anarchy in America for the last three years of that war. Where are the protests and the protestors for the 300,000 Americans killed each year in hospitals as a result of negligence?

If Sears Automotive centers were to destroy 300,000 personal car engines each year by negligently putting vinegar in the oil pan instead of oil, there would be hundreds of lines to file a class action suit - we would bet our house on that one - yet there are no protests in the streets - not even a crazy street preacher, for no one protests a "free service" even if it kills or maims a few "unlucky ones."

Prescribing for those Americans treated in offices and outpatient facilities is no safer than for those hapless souls taken to hospitals. Inappropriate prescriptions or multiple prescriptions ("Poly-pharmacy") are dangerous to 25 percent or more of Americans over the age of 65 living at home. Many of the drugs are prescribed to counteract the side effects of any originally prescribed drug.

Allopathic doctors (70 % of whom flunked a 1994 survey quiz on prescription drugs and prescribing to seniors!!) are incorrectly prescribing pharmaceuticals to 25 percent of American senior citizens and experts say the revealing study published in a July 1994 issue of The New England Journal of Medicine is "only the tip of the iceberg" of the problem with the lack of prescribing skills of American doctors.

"Twenty five percent of American elderly," according to Dr. David Himmelstein of Harvard Medical School,"are getting drugs that are likely to do them more harm than good. It points out the need for much more and better education of doctors on drug prescribing."

Dr. Sidney Wolfe of Public Citizen Health Research Group, says "Young and old are being given the wrong drugs, the wrong dose and the wrong combinations."

An expert panel found that 20 drugs (Table 9-1) from a list that should never be taken by the elderly are in fact prescribed to more than 6.6 million seniors each year (because of the poly-pharmacy trap, many seniors get several of the no-no drugs at the same time!!).

The Harvard study and others "reflects an abysmal ignorance on the part of doctors," says Wolfe, "this is due to medical schools and residence programs doing a terrible job of educating on drug prescribing practices."

Data from survey's compiled in Public

WEDNESDAY, AUGUST 4, 1993

Martin S. Ackerman Dies at 61; Executive and Magazine Publisher

By BRUCE LAMBERT

Martin S. Ackerman, a flamboyant businessman who specialized in financially troubled companies and closed The Saturday Evening Post amid protests against his dealings, died on Monday at Mount Sinai Hospital in Manhattan. He was 61 and lived in Manhattan, Sharon, Conn., and Paris.

The cause was acute sepsis after an operation, his family said.

Mr. Ackerman, the chairman of Company at his death, was a lawyer and businessman whose career was in mergers, acquisitions, financial workouts and banking. Business Week magazine described him as "a razzle-dazzle financial operator."

In 1968 he became president of Curtis Publishing by lending $5 million through the Perfect Film and Chemical Corporation, a conglomerate that he had built. His introduction to the Curtis staff was: "Good evening. I am Marty Ackerman. I am 36 years old, and I am very rich. I hope to make the Curtis Publishing Company rich, again."

1969

Martin S. Ackerman

THE SAN DIEGO UNION-TRIBUNE   **Tuesday, May 10, 1994**

State probing surgeon after car hit 2 officers

**By KELLY THORNTON
and REX DALTON**
Staff Writers

The state agency that licenses and disciplines doctors began investigating a prominent San Diego physician yesterday who was arrested on suspicion of drunken driving after a late-night crash that cost a police officer his right leg.

If the Medical Board of California finds evidence that spinal surgery specialist Dr. Roger Philip Thorne has a substance-abuse problem, it could move to have his physician's license suspended immediately, said board spokeswoman Candis Cohen.

While police and medical authorities pressed on with their inquiries yesterday, friends of San Diego Police Officer Nate Hom said the 28-year-old sports enthusiast remembers nothing of the accident that amputated his leg.

"The whole incident is complete-

Dr. Roger Philip Thorne:
Accused in late-night crash.

Citizen's, Worst Pills Best Pills II, the older adult guide to avoiding death or illness, shows:

1) People over age 60 make up one-sixth of the U.S. population yet use 40 percent of the prescription drugs and are given an average of 15.4 prescriptions per year.

2) 659,000 people a year are hospitalized for adverse drug reactions - 66.6 % are the direct result of poor presribing practices.

3) 16,000 car crashes a year are due to adverse drug reactions (we think doctors should be held accountable just as the bartender who serves too many drinks to the drunk driver!!).

4) 61,000 people suffer drug-induced Parkinson's symptoms - when the drug is withdrawn the symptoms frequently go away.

5) 41,000 are hospitalized each year for ulcers caused by prescribed pharmaceuticals (usually non-steroidal anti-inflammatory drugs used for arthritis pain and inflammation).

The expert panel determined that the poor prescribing practices are due to the $10 billion dollar a year spent by the pharmaceutical industry to get doctors to use their drugs - an amount far greater than the drug companies spend on research and development! "In short, doctors' main source of information about prescribing drugs is the drug industry," says Ray Woosley, professor and chairman of pharmacology at Georgetown University Medical Center - "and should be enough to make patients, young and old, terrified when being given a prescription drug." "They ought to be paranoid. It's horrible, and one of the biggest problems in our country today, medically speaking," says Woosley.

Woosley and other experts say poor prescribing practices cause more medical problems than illicit drug use. According to Himmelstein,"The quickest and easiest route to get the patient out of the office (and the next one in) is to write a prescription; and in the day of the seven-minute office visit, that's what (allopathic) doctors resort to. I'd like to see every American saying, "Do I really need to be on all these pills?"

Seven tips on how to avoid and recover from "poly-pharmacy" :

1) Have a "brown bag" session with an alternative health care giver (ND, DC, DO, MD, DDS, DVM, etc.).

2) Look in the PDR (Physicians Desk Reference) and personally look up side effects and adverse reactions to any drug a doctor wants to give you.

3) Assume any new symptoms you develop after visiting a doctor are due to the treatment or medication.

4) Ask for (look up for yourself, too) safe nutritional alternatives to pharmaceuticals your doctor wants to prescribe.

5) If you are going to use a pharmaceutical, start out with a dose less than the recommended adult dose to avoid severe reactions.

Washington Post Editorial
November 2, 1992

Lining docs' pockets

On another topic, USA TODAY believes that doctors should swear off owning treatment centers.

If you go to a doctor, you want him to think of you as a patient, not a cash cow.

But two studies in this month's *New England Journal of Medicine* show that some doctors are out to milk you dry.

They do it by sending patients to get unnecessary tests and treatment at clinics in which they have a financial stake.

An analysis of 6,581 workers' compensation cases in California, for example, found that:

▶ Doctors with money in physical therapy centers were twice as likely as other doctors to order patients to get physical therapy.

▶ While doctors generally order psychological tests of patients who complain of job stress, the bills for treatment averaged $672 more if doctors had investments in such clinics.

▶ Doctors using imaging centers they invested in ordered unnecessary MRI scans more often than other doctors.

A similar study of doctor-owned treatment centers in Florida found much the same thing.

What it all adds up to is billions of dollars and millions of hours of waste.

A new federal law this year protects taxpayers by barring the practice of physician referral of Medicare and Medicaid patients to labs that the doctor owns.

Private patients and their insurers need similar protection.

At a minimum, the American Medical Association should renew an ethics statement condemning such conflict of interest that it withdrew last year.

Better yet, the Clinton administration should embrace President Bush's proposal to bar this as a form of medical malpractice.

Doctors should see their patients as people, not dollar signs.

Doctors Fined for Fight in Operating Room

WORCESTER, Mass., Nov. 27 (AP) — A state medical board has fined a surgeon and an anesthesiologist $10,000 each for brawling in an operating room while their patient slept under general anesthesia.

After their fight, the anesthesiologist, Dr. Kwok Wei Chan, and the surgeon, Dr. Mohan Korgaonkar, successfully operated on the elderly female patient.

In addition to imposing the fines, the state Board of Registration in Medicine last week ordered the doctors to undergo joint psychotherapy. It also directed officials at the Medical Center of Central Massachusetts, who had already put the doctors on five years' probation, to monitor Drs. Chan and Korgaonkar for five years.

The medical board said that on Oct. 24, 1991, Dr. Korgaonkar was about to begin surgery when he and Dr. Chan began to argue. Hospital officials would not provide the nature of their disagreement.

Dr. Chan swore at Dr. Korgaonkar, who threw a cotton-tipped prep stick at Dr. Chan, the board said. The two then raised their fists and scuffled briefly, at one point wrestling on the floor. A nurse monitored the anesthetized patient as the doctors fought.

Afterward, the doctors resumed the operation.

L.A. surgeon allegedly left saw running on his break

ASSOCIATED PRESS

LOS ANGELES — An orthopedic surgeon allegedly left an operation room to make a phone call and go to the bathroom without turning off a cutting tool running in a patient's back, state medical officials charged.

Dr. Fereydoune Shirazi also operated on patients' knees while improperly using an instrument that enables the physician to monitor the surgery on a TV screen, the Medical Board of California said.

Shirazi, 55, said in an interview with the *Los Angeles Times* that he had done nothing improper.

The surgeon could lose his physician's license if an administrative judge upholds the board's charges of gross negligence, incompetence and repeated negligent acts.

Les Williams, an investigator for the medical board, said no patients were seriously injured by Shirazi, but "the potential was there for some very serious . . . harm."

According to the board, Shirazi left the operating room for 11 minutes, to make a phone call and use the bathroom, in the midst of surgery on a man's back in 1990.

Shirazi was using a cutting tool called a nucleotome, activated by a foot pedal. When he left the room, he placed a sandbag on the pedal, which kept the blades of the device rotating in the man's spinal column, the board said.

Shirazi told the *Times* he did forget to turn the tool off but he said the patient was not at risk because the device is designed only to cut away degenerated spinal disk tissue and cannot cut healthy tissue.

The nucleotome was shut off by an anesthesiologist, Shirazi said.

Shirazi blamed his problems with the medical board on Dr. H. William Frank, a former chief of surgery at Simi Valley Hospital.

"Dr. Frank, personally, he is against me," Shirazi said. "What he's saying is exaggerated and his opinion."

Frank said Shirazi's alleged ineptness prompted the hospital to suspend his surgical privileges.

Table 9-1. Drugs Regarded as not Suitable for Older Patients.

Pharmaceutical	Mineral Replacement
Tranquilizers & Sleeping Aids: **Diazepam** (Valium) - Tranquilizer. Addictive and too long-acting, causing drowsiness, confusion and falls.	Ca, Mg, Li, Cr, Va (avoid sugar, natural and processed and caffeine).
Chlordiazepoxide (Librium) - Tranquilizer. Too long-acting causes falls.	Same as above
Flurazepam (Dalmane), a sleeping aid. Too long-acting, causes falls.	Same as above
Meprobamate (Miltown, Deprol, Equagesic, Equanil) - Tranquilizer, sometimes combined with an anti-depressant or pain reliever. Addictive, too long-acting, causes falls.	Same as above
Pentobarbital (Nembutol)- Sedative. Addictive, long-acting, can cause falls.	Same as above
Secobarbitol (Seconal). Addictive, long acting, causes falls.	Same as above
Antidepressants: **Amitriptyline** (Elavil, Endep, Etrafon, Limbitrol, Triavil). Stops the ability to urinate, causes dizziness and drowsiness, causes falls.	Same as above
Arthritis Drugs: **Indomethacin** (Indocin). Can cause confusion and headaches.	Ca, Mg, B, Cu, Se, Li , chondroitin sulfate (Knox gelatin).
Phenylbutazone (Butazolidin) - risk of bone marrow toxicity.	Same as above
Diabetes Drugs: **Chlorpropramide** (Diabinase) Can cause dangerous fluid retention is excreted slowly - overdose requires long intensive treatment period.	Cr, Va, Zn (No sugar - Natural or processed)

Table 9-1. Drugs Regarded as not Suitable for Older Patients. (Continued...)

Pharmaceutical	Mineral Replacement
Pain Relievers:	
Propoxyphene (Darvon Compound, Darvocet, Wygesic). Addictive, no more effective than aspirin, has more side effects than morphine, causes seizures and heart complications.	Ca, Mg, Cu, Se
Pentazocine (Talwin). Addictive, no more effective than aspirin, has more side effects than morphine, causes seizures and heart complications.	Same as above
Dementia Treatments:	
Cyclandelate -Not effective	Ga, Ge,Se, Ca, O_2, Cr, Va, Li, B-1, B-3 no sugar. no caffeine.
Isoxsuprine - Not effective	Same as above
Blood Thinners:	
Dipyridamole (Persantine). Except in patients with artificial heart valves, not shown to be effective.	Se, Mn, Mg, Vit E Omega 3 Oils
Muscle Relaxants, Spasm Relievers:	
Cyclobenzaprine (Flexeril) - Causes dizziness, drowsiness, fainting, falls.	Ca, Mg, B, Li
Orphenidrine (Norflex, Norgesic) - Causes dizziness, drowsiness, fainting, falls.	Same as above
Methocarbamol (Roboxin) - Causes dizziness, drowsiness, falls.	Same as above
Carisoprodol (Soma) - Potential for nervous system toxicity is greater than potential benefit.	Same as above

Table 9-1. Drugs Regarded as not Suitable for Older Patients. (Continued...)	
Pharmaceutical	Mineral Replacement
Anti-Nausea Drugs, Anti-Vomiting Drugs: **Trimethobenzamide** (Tigan). Not very effective. Causes drowsiness, dizziness and falls.	Bi, Ca, Li
Antihypertensive : **Propranolol** (Inderal). Feeling slowed mentally and physically.	Ca, Mg, Omega 3, B_6
Methyldopa (Aldoril, Aldomet). Feeling mentally and physically slowed.	Same as above
Reserpine (Regroton, Hydropres). Depression	Same as above

6) Ask an alternative doctor to coordinate your overall health care program.

7) Prescription "drugs" are seldom necessary - the fewer you take, the safer you are.

After the collapse of the Soviet Union, there was a mad rush to down size the military and take the dollar difference as a "piece dividend." There was to be a $100 Billion "piece dividend" as a result of base closings and military trimming in 1994.

There are those who argue, "We are the healthiest and longest lived people in the world, it costs a few bucks for high tech medicine, but what the heck, we're Americans and we deserve it!" When one looks at who gets the $1.2 trillion "health care" dollars lets see if were still pleased - do we get the money as a health allotment -"take your $20,000 and get healthy." We all know the answer, the dollars go to the allopathic M.D.s and hospitals (most private hospitals, hospital management corporations, HMO's, PPO's, etc.) are owned by M.D.s.

The medical profession (doctors, visiting nurses, nurse practitioners, physicians assistants, and hospitals) is the only private service industry that is paid

Year	$ Spent for "Health Care"	$ Spent for Defense
1991	750 Billion	293 Billion
1992	936 Billion	280 Billion
1993	1.2 Trillion	180 Billion

with tax dollars ($1.2 trillion) the government takes from us (and then they pay us back by killing 300,000 of us each year)!!!

The next thing that needs to be examined is the record of the medical profession in America for the living - the World Health Organization (WHO) ranks Americans longevity against the longevity of other industrialized nations:

AMERICAN RANKING COMPARED TO
INDUSTRIALIZED NATIONS
17th in longevity
19th in healthfulness
23rd for first year survivability and
       live births of our babies
32nd for birth defects

The WHO rankings compare us to the industrialized nations of the world - the bottom line is we are not getting our dollars worth from a "health care system" that is the highest paid in the world!!! There are 16 industrialized nations whose citizens live longer than we do; there are 18 countries whose people live longer than we do before they develope degenerative, debilitating and life threatening diseases; there are 22 countries that have a better record of live births and first year survivability of their babies - and God help us there are 31 industrialized countries that have fewer babies born with low birth weights or congenital defects than we do!!!

If you take a rough average and say there are 20 industrialized countries whose peoples are healthier than us and compare us to them, their total combined population is greater than that of the U.S. and if you add up their total combined financial outlay for health care it is approximately 50 % of our health costs!!!!

If any other industry in America were to perform the way our "health care" system does the American People would rebel, there would be senate investigations, there would be class action suits. Remember in the 80's when the Cadillac divison of GM ran out of finished Cadillac engines and they inserted Oldsmobile engines into Cadillacs so as not to slow production, there was a major class action suit, senate investigations - GM had done America wrong!!!!

The only time in history that American hospital deaths dropped were during doctor strikes (Fig. 9 - 1), when the doctors returned to the hospitals the death rates rose again (the rise in death rates upon their return was at first higher than normally expended for the first weeks - doctors had a lot of back Mercedes and mortgage payments to make up).

Our health problems seem to have begun in the late 1700's and early 1800's when Americans were setting up homesteads on the prairies and great plains of our young nation. Sod houses were built, babies were born, gardens and small farms established. In five to 10 years some of the children died, the milk cows dried up, eventually the corn didn't grow any higher than two feet tall and didn't produce ears and ma or pa developed consumption.

To survive, the devastated family knew it had to move on - so they went west to get their share of free virgin land - whatever life giving stuff (minerals) that had been in the prairie was used up and the farm "played out,"

The only families who flourished in those days were those who owned bottom land - these bottom land farms flooded every year or so and each time the land was about to be depleted, floods brought min-

1976 LOS ANGELES DOCTORS STRIKE:
DEATHS PER 100,000 HEAD OF POPULATION

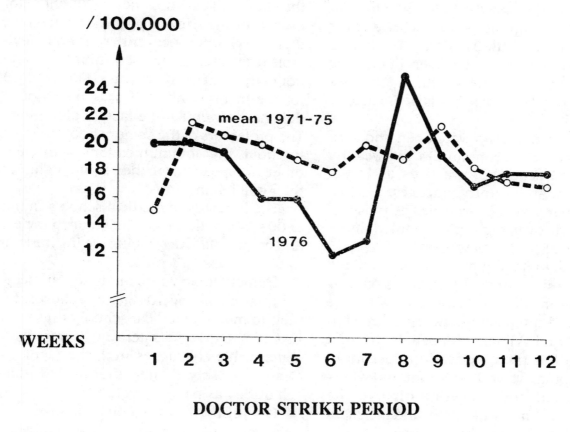

Fig. 9-1

In 1976 doctors in Los Angeles went on strike for 6 weeks to protest increased malpractice insurance premiums. The death rate in the L.A. hospitals dropped precipitously until the 7th week when the strike ended - initially the death rate rose sharply surpassing the years average until the 9-10th week when the death rate dropped again to its yearly average.

eral rich silt from hundreds or thousands of miles away. Bottom land was fought over, bottom land farmers were the well-to-do farmers, they had slaves, 10 healthy children, real glass windows and maybe even a piano in the living room - best of all they could afford to send their oldest son to Europe to become a doctor!!

Nothing devastated the American level of health and longevity more than the bitter feuds and divisions that beset doctors through the late 1800's. Partly, the hatred were personal battles between monstrous egos, partly they were sectarian rivalries between the different schools of practice or philosophy.

Medical civil wars were open and acrimonious, and as common in the wealthy urban and academic practices as in the more mundane country practices. Doctors fought over practice territories as prospectors fought over high grade gold claims - the medical gold rush was on!!

Philadelphia, the political center of the budding American medical profession, was a maelstrom of professional ill will. The hatred and animosity between John Morgan, MD and William Shippen, Jr. MD, the first two full time medical professors in Philadelphia, was notorious far and wide - their hatred and bickering divided the country's first medical school and then split the Medical Corps of the Continental Army, during the Revolutionary War, as the two doctors conspired against each other for political control.

During the great Philadelphia yellow fever epidemic in 1793, medical rivals took to the press to denounce each others therapies; the public mud slinging became so outrageous that Benjamin Rush, MD was moved to say, " a Mohammedan and a Jew might as well attempt to worship the same supreme being in the same temple and through the medium of the same ceremonies, as two physicians of opposite principles and practice, attempt to confer about the life of the same patient."

Medical schools were particularly notorious sources of fraternal "bile and hatred." Since a professional appointment to the staff of the school had the potential for increasing the size of a physician's practice, there was highly vocal criticisms and inevitable resentment by those doctors who were not in the "in crowd." It was commonplace for the faculty and staff of one school to defame and rebuke the faculty of another. The professors of the same schools refused to "hold any communications with each other except to meet the requirements of their official positions."

The histories of medical schools in the 1800's is a "tale of schisms, conspiracies, and coups, often destroying the institutions in the process."

Daniel Drake wrote an essay on medical quarrels listing 10 different causes, he then founded a medical school of his own in Ohio. During his tenure he removed some of his colleagues from the faculty - Drake was shortly thereafter ousted himself during a "palace revolt."

One of the most exciting "imbroglios" between medical factions occurred in 1856 at the Eclectic Medical Institute of Cincinnati, where the faculty and student allies divided into two factions over the financial management of the school and the introductions of the new "concentrated" pharmaceuticals". One of the two groups seized control of the school building and locked out its opponents, who then collected as an angry mob outside the school doors. "This was the declaration of war," writes the school historian. "Knives, pistols, chisels, bludgeons, blunderbusses, etc. were freely displayed." A truce was called when the excluded group of faculty and students rolled a six-pound cannon up to the front door of the school!

Of all the arguments that tore at the political and professional core of the medical profession, sectarianism was the most vile and most virulent. Medical "sects" flourished in the mid-1800's because of the overwhelming shortcomings of 19th century medicine, particularly the "disasterous errors of heroic therapy," which featured bleeding (this proceedure killed George Washington), heavy doses of mercury, and other modes of treatment ranging from the "ineffective to the lethal."

A sect, religious or medical, is a dissident group that seperates itself from the "established institution; their constituancy often see themselves as neglected and scorned apostles of the truth." Sects classically find their beginnings in the charismatic leadership of a new thought or philosophy and have a voluntary following. One can join a sect, usually one is born into a church (or graduated from an accredited medical school into the medical profession).

Medical and religious sects are similar in their adherence to certain definite ideas as prerequisites for membership. Religious sects classically pontificate a complete way of life; medical sects tend (not always) to limit their concerns to worship of treatment modalities or tests.

The mormons followed Thomisonian medicine (herbal) and the Millerites hydropathy (hydrotherapy), the Swedenborgians supported homeopathic medicine, the Christian Scientists originated from the joint concerns of medicine and religion.

Religious groups that still follow healings through their "word" or health philosophies are constantly under attack by the medical profession or the government at the behest of the medical profession (look what happened to the harmless "Branch Davidians"). Medical sectarianism intensified not only because the American political system was open, but because it was closed! The cliquishness of medical schools of practice drove excluded "heretical" practitioners to create counter revolutions to justify their philosophies and professional positions. For the "less educated" medical doctors or the highly educated immigrant doctors denied access to hospital and medical school appointments, medical sects offered status and prestige.

In the second half of the 1800's, the principal American medical sects were the Eclectics and the homeopaths. The Eclectics, who absorbed most of the failed earlier movements were primarily herbal doctors, although they tended to take what were the best therapies from all medical schools of of practice. The Eclectics neither denied the value of "scientific training" nor did they hesitate to found their own medical schools - they also destroyed the medical schools by political warring.

The Eclectics accepted and taught "orthodox" medical knowledge of the day, but they lobbied vigorously against excessive use of "poly-pharmacy" and bleeding that were favored by the "allopathic" doctors.

The Eclectics were the third largest group of medical practitioners in America, after the "regulars" and homeopaths. The Eclectics were characterized by their stand against the harsh medical procedures of the "regulars," their efforts to be reformers, their empiricism, and their home grown American roots.

The homeopaths of thre 1800's were different animals from the Eclectics, they had a highly developed doctrine, attracted most of their followers from German immigrant physicians and they appealed primarily to the wealthy upper class.

The field of homeopathy was founded by Samuel Hanneman (1755-1843), a disenchanted German physician who cringed at the terrible torture inflicted on patients by the "regulars."

Hanneman developed three basic principals for homeopathy:

1) Diseases could be cured by "drugs' (i.e.-herbs, minerals, animal tissues, etc.) which produced the symptoms of the disease being treated when given to a normal healthy person (this is known as a "proving") - this is the "law of similars" or "like cure like."

2) The effects of the homeopathic "drugs" could be increased by using them in dilutions or greater reduced doses; the more dilute the dose, the more dramatic the effect.

3) Almost all disease is the result of a "Psora" or suppressed dermatitis.

At this point in American medical history, the Eclectics and homeopaths, the main opponents to the "regulars," had the basic medical training almost identical with that given at "regular "medical schools. The Eclectics and the homeopaths of 1852 attracted heavy opposition from the "regulars" because they actively preached to the lay public of the wonderful and safe results of their modalities.

A written report to the Connecticut Medical Society in 1852 stated, " very different would have been the professions attitude towards homeopathy if it had aimed, like other doctrines advanced by physicians, to gain a foothold among medical men alone, or chiefly, instead of making its appeal to the popular favor and against the profession." Homeopaths did not secede, the "regulars" tossed them out and created strict rules of conduct to prevent "regulars" from consorting with Eclectics and homeopaths. The "regulars" self-righteously refused hospital privileges to Eclectics and homeopaths, keeping them off large city hospital boards for more than 30 years.

During the Civil War, the "regulars" dominated the military medical boards, and the homeopaths even with broad congressional support were not able to get approved for military service as a physician.

Between 1835 and 1860 the Eclectics and homeopaths represented ten percent of the total numbers of doctors in America, by 1871 they grew to 13 percent (6,000 alternative doctors to 39,000 regulars).

In 1880, "regulars" operated 76 medical colleges, the homeopaths 14 and the Eclectics eight - ten years later the totals were 106, 16 and nine. The numbers of medical schools do not necessarily indicate quality, because a medical school diploma had been introduced as a recquesit for state licensing - many mail order schools were established by the "regulars" to pump up their numbers.

During most of this medical "civil war" period the media, the courts and state legislatures were "agnostics." They didn't believe or disbelieve any medical group and made extraordinary efforts to stay out of the fray - whenever the "regulars" attacked the Eclectics and the homeopaths, the media called for restraint and joined forces with the oppressed alternatives.

When the Massachusets State Medical Board expelled the homeopaths the New York Times stated,"That while the medical society had ment to disgrace the heretical physician...we have little doubt that in the minds of intelligent persons, they have only suceeded in bringing disgrace upon themselves."

Most of the general American public saw the diversity in the types of health practitioners available to them as analogous to religious choices. When the "regulars" made a concerted effort to control all of the medical practice, the general public rebelled - "one could no more have boards of orthodox doctors passing on homeopaths than Protestant boards ruling on the acceptability of Catholic priests.

Ultimately the "regulars" were forced to accept the fact that they had been fought to a "Mexican Stand-off." High levels of public resistance to the "regulars" daring to seek exclusivity brought compromise and concessions.

In Michigan, the state legislature required the incorporation of homeopathy into the University of Michigan School of Medicine. The "regulars" were aghast but reluctantly submitted in 1875; acting through the state legislature, the general public forced the availability of alternative medicine.

The state of Missouri exemplifies the gradual extension of licensing control. The state passed an initial licensing law in 1874; however, it only required a doctor to register a degree from a legally chartered school with the county clerk. The statute had the effect of attracting more "regular" doctors to Missouri since incorporation laws allowed anyone to start a school by simply applying for a charter; Missouri very quickly had more "regular" medical schools than anyone could keep track of - most were diploma mills!!

In 1882 more than 5,000 doctors practiced in the state of Missouri and less than half had graduated fully acredited schools.

In 1894 the Missouri State Department of Health tried to enact a pre-med school requirement for students before they could be eligible to enter medical school. Most of the medical schools responded by printing certificates to give to any new student who could pay for them.

The board announced that graduate medical students would have to take and pass state board exams to demonstrate their proficiency in basic medical education. The "regular" medical schools sought relief from the courts and the Supreme Court of Missouri ruled that in raising the issue of pre-medical requirements the board of health had in fact exceeded their authority.

It was not until 1901 that a medical practice act was passed in Missouri empowering the board of health to act as a board of medical examiners - they had been able to enlist the support of the Presbyterian and Methodist churches, which were paranoid at the time because of the growing popularity of Christian Science and Weltmerism(a local Missouri "mind-cure cult").

Social Darwinist in1898, followed the English social and medical theorist Herbert Spencer, who said,"Very many of the poorer classes are injured by druggist's prescriptions and quack medicines; but there is nothing wrong with that; it was the penalty nature attached to ignorance. If the poor died of their own foolishness, the species would improve."

In 1888 in the case of Dent vs. West Virginia, Frank Dent, an Eclectic physician in practice in West Virginia for six years had been convicted and fined for not graduating from a reputable medical school and refused to accept his degrees from the American Medical College of Cincinati. In delivering the unanimous decision, Justice Stephen Field noted," Few professions require more careful preparation than that of medicine; it has to deal with all those subtle and mysterious influences upon which health and life depend; and required knowledge not only of vegetable and mineral substances, but of the human body in all its complicated parts, and their relation to each other, as well as their influence upon the mind."

The Eclectics and homeopaths were absorbed into the state association of the "regulars" - they became part of the "good ole boy club" and their zeal to fight the "regulars" dissipated with their new found privilege. Actually, the old sects gave way to the newly arrived sects; the 1890's had seen the appearance of two new sects with diametrically opposed views.

The first of the new sects, osteopathy, was founded by a Missouri engineer, Andrew Still, who believed that the human body when sick had to be repaired by placing its parts back in alignment and proper relationship, additionally, vitamins, minerals and basic nutrition and general health practices (exercise, hygene, etc.) were major features in this profession.

"Quite your pills and learn from osteopathy the principle that governs you," Still proclaimed. "Learn that you are a machine, your heart an engine, your lungs a fanning machine and a sieve, your brain with its two lobes an electric battery." In 1891, Still opened a school of Osteopathy in Kirksville, Missouri which he got chartered by the state of Missouri in 1892. In 1897, Osteopathy won legal protection from the Missouri State Legeslature.

Christian Science, the second of the new sects was conceived in the eastern United States near Boston by Mary Baker Eddy. Her teachings point out that disease is primarily a function of mind and spirit.

The basic practice of Christian Science embraces nutrition (including vitamin and mineral supplements) and excluding dangerous habits such as smoking, alcohol, the use of drugs and using the services of "orthodox" physicians.

The basic clean living habits of Christian Scientists work so well in preventing disease that as a group their average life span is 80.5 (five years longer than the average American; as a result of their good health records they enjoy lower health insurance rates and they spend little or no money on health care.

A new gold rush is upon us in America in the 1990's; everyone is rushing to cash in on the new "health" programs - when all is said and done it will be the "orthodox" physicians and surgeons who will benefit most from the "Mother Load" and yet our rankings amongst the industrialized nations for longevity, healthfullness, live births and birth defects will not improve but will in fact get worse. The doctor of today is like a starved junkyard dog protecting a bone - if anyone tries to snatch it away they get vicious - how will they make their Mercedes payment? How will they pay for their 1.2 million dollar mortgage? How will they pay for the tuition to send their children to medical school at Harvard or law school at Yale? How will they pay the alimony to their five ex-wives? You guessed it - they send out those little notices that say ,"It's time for your annual physical, please call and make an appointment."

An example of their reactions to anyone taking from their largest is their huge and cry over the activities of Dr. Jack Kavorkian, the Michigan physician known as "Dr. Death." In our favorite old time cowboy and World War II movies it was the greatest act of love for a fellow comrade in arms to end their life with a merciful bullet when they had been mortally wounded (gut shot) and in intractable pain -"They shoot horses don't they?"

After 3 years and some 19 assisted suicides "Dr. Death" did his thing unimpeded; however, once the Michigan M.D.s realized that every assisted suicide cost them $250,000 to $500,000 by eliminating three to 12 months of terminal, critical and ICU care monies that they would normally siphon out of insurance or milk out of Medicare they went berserk and charged "Dr. Death" with murder to keep any other would be "good Samaritan" physician from cutting off their otherwise bottomless larder.

Who are these people who have been placed in a position of trust and have violated that trust? - they are worse than the priests who fondle choir boys or young girls in the choir; they are worse because our government pays them (with our money) so they feel its okay to test and treat us to death because "we're getting a free service."

They drive us with fear into hospitals for tests and therapies under the guise of "defensive medicine." The September 1993 issue of Reader's Digest pointed out that doctors get a $421 kickback for every patient sent in for a CAT scan or an MRI - that is not a stick - it's a golden carrot!!! If you believe that doctors do all the extra tests to avoid a malpractice suit we have some ocean front property in Montana to sell you!!

On June 29, 1994 National Medical Enterprises Inc., one of the nations largest hospital chains agreed to plead guilty to charges of paying more than $40 million dollars in referral kickbacks to physicians between 1985 and 1990 and then attempted to get Medicare reimbursement for the kickbacks. They also agreed to pay $362.7 million dollars in fines; their CEO and top executives each faced up to 10 years in prison for Medicare fraud and $500,000 in fines - the R.I.C.O. laws should have been brought into play here and all of the assets of the hospital chain confiscated.

Prosecutors said the case,"provided the best window yet on misconduct now endemic to medicine that will ultimately prove more costly to the American public than the corruption that ravaged the savings and loan institutions."

"In the medical world," said Paul E. Coggins, the United States Attorney in Dallas, "practices that are illegal have been accepted and tolerated - very much akin to the climate that pervaded the savings and loans."

Federal officials have estimated that fraud gulps approximately ten percent of America's health care expenses to the tune of $100 billion per year.

Today, a physician and surgeon makes an average of $170,000 per year (thats almost 100% profit folks, because we pay for all of the tests, Q-Tips, rubber gloves, surgery rooms, anesthetics, nursing care, recovery rooms, etc.); the higher priced specialties of anesthesiology, orthopedic surgery and neurosurgery make over $225,000 per year (that's up from $88,000 in 1983).

The very highest monthly premiums for malpractice insurance is $1,400 per month - thats only $16,800 per year, which sounds like a lot of money to you and me, but when you're making $225,000 per year it's just the cost of doing business.

In November of 1992, two articles appeared in the New England Journal of Medicine which stated that "doctors are out to milk us dry." We spent $3.4 billion for unnecessary cataract surgery in nursing home patients with Alzheimer's disease, we spent $117 billion for cholesterol testing in 1992, we have over 400,000 unnecessary hysterectomies per year and a ceasarian rate of over 34 % each year and doctors double their fees if they know you have insurance.

We get charged $750,000 for a heart transplant, the medical treatment of choice for cardiomyopathy - the surgeon's real cost is about $500.00 - they get the heart free from a donor, they get the blood for the surgery from the recipients relatives and they use $12.00 in suture material and rubber gloves. After the L.A. earthquake in 1994, people were put in jail for price gouging for selling gallons of water to earth quake victims for $4.00. We are supposed to accept the $750,000 fee for the heart transplant without challenge because its "high-tech medicine." In fact one trace mineral (selenium) at the rate of $0.10 per day will prevent cardiomyopathy and in the initial phases of the disease clinically cure it!!!

Medical costs have risen more than 50 % between 1983 and 1991 and the cost of pharmaceuticals has risen by more than 150 %, yet the average American income has risen only 5% during the same time period. These unchecked and skyrocketing costs in the health care field are the result of government programs and insurance medical commitees that are inhabited only by allopathic doctors - if we had to pay the bills ourselves we would demand better results at a cheaper cost or we would refuse the service (we would get safer and more effective treatment from vitamins and minerals).

There are a lot of excellent automotive detail services available, but most of us choose to wash and wax our own car to save money - if insurance companies paid for the wax job on our cars we would all use the detail service - the detail services would spring up everywhere, unfortunately many of them would be backyard types more interested in the insurance money than in the condition of your car's paint job so they would use inferior waxes and electric buffers (scratching your paint) to run more cars through the mill.

We would like to think that "someone is watching" over us, someone is regulating these doctors; however, they have been allowed to watch themselves.

There are an average of four innocent citizens killed each year in each major city by policemen making the wrong split second decision on the street - there are citizens committees and Grand Jury investigations, there are police internal affairs investigations and armies of average people out there with video cameras just waiting for a cop to screw up - who are the doctors' overseers, who gets judged and punished for the 300,000 people who are killed each year by doctors involved in malpractice?

In 1993 the California State Board of

Medical Examiners was investigated by the California State Police at the request of the California Department of Consumer Affairs because they had shredded all of the patient complaints against California doctors without investigating them to get them off of their books for a particular fiscal year - so much for self policing!

A great letter appeared in an Ann Landers column - it was entitled "Losing patience with the doctor."

"Dear Ann Landers: I'm on the side of the woman in Serasota who complained about the cardiologist who always arrived in his office an hour late. I'm especially angry because you slapped her down and made excuses for the doctor.

I work for a surgeon and you would not believe what goes on in this mans office. "Dr. D" sits at his desk, feet up, talking to his broker, his kids, his mother or a golf buddy for an hour while patients are waiting to see him. If anyone complains about waiting we've been instructed to say, "Dr. D" is consulting with another doctor.

Sometimes between patients "Dr. D" goes to his desk and counts checks and money while people are waiting to see him. When he strolls in late because he overslept (or got frisky), we are told to say he was delayed in surgery.

-Just Plain Fed Up"

Medical specialists have "tunnel vision," especially if their livelihood is affected - that's why doctors count the till four or five times each day - they need to know how many patients to put in the hospital and how much to milk the last ten patients that comes into his office each day to meet his office and personal overhead!!!!

If an allopathic physician and surgeon refers you to a specialist to have your feet amputated because of diabetic gangrene, the surgeon is not going to tell you about chromium and vanadium or hyperbaric oxygen tanks that might save your foot - why should he, he's a surgeon and he has a Mercedes payment coming up. The crime and horror of all this is that he will sleep well and play happily with his girlfriend believing he did you a favor and a service.

Medical specialists also have a grave personality defect, they believe that they are more clever than you and I, so they can do whatever they like. As a result it is well documented that "22,000 to 33,600 are alcoholics, recovering alcoholics or soon to be alcoholics. Alcoholism is a primary disease to which physicians as a group seem highly susceptible and often goes hand in hand with drug abuse," says Stephen C. Scheiber, M.D. in, The Impaired Physician.

A recent Harvard study revealed that "59 % of physicians and 78 % of medical students use psychoactive drugs (usually marijuana and cocaine) and that 40% of "orthodox" doctors get high with friends on a regular basis; lastly the United States loses the equivalant of seven medical school classes each year to drug addiction, alcoholism and suicide" In the book, Medicine on Trial, they calculate that patient visits to these ticking "Drug Head" time bombs exceed 45 to 100 million each year!!!!

Dispite their code of professional ethics one in 10 doctors has had sex with their patients, and as many as 25 % say patients

Doctor accused of billing state for 'therapy' of sex-for-drugs

ASSOCIATED PRESS

OAKLAND — A psychiatrist accused of trading drugs for sex and billing the state for the swap under the guise of therapy is expected to surrender tomorrow, according to state officials.

"The state was paying for these little trysts," said Deputy Attorney General Christiana Tiedemann. "Not only was he doing it, but we were paying for it."

Bail of $37,400 has been set for Paul Lowinger, 68, who has offices in Oakland and San Francisco. He was charged Thursday with inappropriate sexual activity with patients, prescribing controlled substances without legitimate medical purposes, filing false medical claims and 16 counts of grand theft.

Lowinger, who allegedly had sex with five female patients between 1982 and 1991, attempted to seduce a female undercover investigator in February, according to Alameda County Municipal Court documents. Court records describe the patients as drug addicts and prostitutes.

If convicted of all charges, Lowinger faces six years in prison and $173,000 in fines plus resti-

> "The state was paying for these little trysts. Not only was he doing it, but we were paying for it."
>
> **CHRISTIANA TIEDEMANN**
> *Deputy attorney general*

tution, according to Tiedemann.

Lowinger was chief of psychiatry at Contra Costa County Hospital in Martinez in 1982-83 and director of psychiatric residents at Highland General Hospital in Oakland in 1976-78. From 1958 to 1971, he was psychiatric chief at Detroit Memorial Hospital.

He served as national chairman of the Medical Committee on Human Rights in 1969-70 and president of the Michigan Association of Neuropsychiatric Physicians in 1969-70.

The case is the first brought by the state attorney general's office under a law criminalizing sex between psychotherapists and their patients.

In April, Yuba City psychiatrist Valentino Andres was sentenced to 45 days in jail and fined $2,020 for having sex with a patient. That case was prosecuted by county officials, however.

The sexual misconduct law makes a first conviction for sex with patients a misdemeanor and a second a felony.

A spokesman for the state Medical Board, Janie Cordray, said the panel will seek a temporary restraining order.

1 in 10 doctors has had sex with patient, survey finds

REUTERS

SAN FRANCISCO — Despite professional ethics, nearly one in 10 U.S. physicians has had sex with a patient and almost 25 percent say patients have reported sexual contact with other doctors, according to a survey published yesterday.

Nearly 90 percent of the contacts were between a male doctor and a female patient, 6 percent were between female doctors and male patients, and 5 percent were homosexual, according to the study by researchers at the University of California in San Francisco.

"I'm very disturbed by the prevalence and very concerned about the potential harm to the patients," San Francisco psychiatrist Nanette Gartrell, who led the study, told Reuters yesterday.

The survey was published in the San Francisco-based *Western Journal of Medicine*. It is the first large-scale sex study of physicians other than psychiatrists.

"I think we're basically talking about an abuse of power — very vulnerable patients and physicians who have a lot of power," she said.

She said the findings mirror relationships in society at large. "It's typical of sexual assault throughout our culture," she said. "Sexual assault is usually perpetrated by adult males.

The Hippocratic Oath, which is 2,400 years old, prohibits sex between doctors and patients. The American Medical Association also considers sex with patients unethical and sex even with former patients unethical in many cases.

Questionnaires were mailed in May 1990 to more than 10,000 doctors nationwide, all members of the American Medical Association. Mental health practitioners were excluded.

Slightly fewer than 1,900 responded, and Gartrell attributed the rate of return to fear of self-incrimination, even though the results were anonymous. Astonishingly, nearly two-thirds of all doctors surveyed — and 38 percent of those who admitted having sex with their patients — acknowledged that the experience hurt the patient.

THE SAN DIEGO UNION-TRIBUNE

Death may be manslaughter, but it wasn't murder, insists attorney

By VALERIE ALVORD
Staff Writer

VISTA — A doctor accused of killing a woman with an overdose of chloroform could be guilty of involuntary manslaughter, but certainly did not commit murder, his attorney told a jury here yesterday.

The unusual concession, based on a legal theory involving negligence, came at the end of the monthlong trial in which Dr. Sam Dubria has insisted he did nothing to cause the death of Jennifer Klapper in a Carlsbad motel room two years ago.

In two days of testimony Dubria told the jury he never studied chloroform or used it and that he did not have access to the highly volatile 19th century anesthetic.

But in closing arguments yesterday, his attorney, Barry Bernstein, said the 29-year-old medical resident could have used the drug with Klapper for recreational purposes and then refused to admit it because it would have meant the end of his medical career.

Dubria is charged with using chloroform to knock out the 20-year-old Cincinnati woman so he could rape her. In the process, he killed her, the prosecution alleges. If convicted of rape and murder, Dubria could face life in prison without possibility of parole.

Bernstein did not elaborate on his suggestion that chloroform may have been used as a recreational drug or in some other recreational way. As an alternative theory, he suggested to the jury that Klapper, who was found dead at the All Star Inn on Interstate 5 on Aug. 16, 1991, might have used chloroform to numb her severe headaches. The attorney did not say whether chloroform was an accepted medical remedy for a headache.

Prosecutor Tim Casserly, meanwhile, told the jury that Dubria is "a piece of garbage" and "the biggest liar you will ever see."

He suggested that Dubria might be the unluckiest man to ever have sex with a woman.

"The very first time he's alone with this girl and has sexual intercourse with her, she dies! And from an overdose of chloroform! And here he is — a doctor. How unlucky can you get?" the prosecutor asked.

Klapper, who met Dubria at the Cincinnati hospital where they both worked, was on a sightseeing trip with Dubria when she died. She had told numerous friends that she did not consider Dubria attractive, and that she had no intention of letting their relationship become sexual.

The morning after her death, Dubria told police that he and Klapper were casual friends who had sex for the first time the night she died. The doctor said Klapper simply fell to the floor unconscious for no apparent reason and that his attempts to resuscitate her were unsuccessful.

He told the jury that he and Klapper were intimate friends who had "made love without intercourse" for a number of months, but first had sex the night she died.

Casserly yesterday told the jury that Dubria had to lie about what happened because he couldn't bring himself to admit to his parents that after all their hard work and sacrifice to put him through medical school, he had thrown his life away on an uncontrollable desire for a woman.

The jury was to begin deliberations on the case this morning.

have had sex with other doctors. Nearly 90 % of these contacts were between male doctors and their patients, six per cent were attributed to female doctors and five percent attributed to homosexual doctors according to Dr. Nanette Gantrell, Psychologist at the University of California, San Francisco. The Hippocratic Oath which is 2,400 years old prohibits sex between doctors and patients.

Doctors have gone to the extent of billing cities, counties, states and medicare for sexual liaisons with their patients - talk about having your cake and eating it too!!!

"The state was paying for these little trysts. Not only was he doing it, but we were paying for it," said Deputy Attorney General Christiana Tiedemann of Oakland California when referring to psychiatrist Dr. Paul Lowinger, who allegedly had sex with five female patients between 1982 and 1991 and was only found out when he attempted to seduce a female undercover investigator. Lowinger who was chief of psychiatry at Contra Costa County Hospital in Monterey, California, 1982 to 1983 he was the Director of psychiatric residents at Highland General Hospital in Oakland, California 1976 to 1978; from 1958 to 1971 he was psychiatric chief at Detroit Memorial Hospital. He served as national chairman of the Medical committee on Human Rights in 1969 and 1970 and served as president of the Michigan Association of Neuropsychiatric physicians in 1969 to 1970. We would venture a wager that Dr. Lowinger was an opponent of Dr. Kavorkian!!!

Doctors go still further, they have killed unwilling patients with anesthetics trying to subdue them for sex. One doctor, a respected California dermatologist was accused of diagnosing cancer in hundreds of patients by sending known cancerous specimens to a lab for diagnosis with their name on it - Medicare and MediCal pay considerably more for removing a cancer than a mole!!!

In May of 1994, Jackie Kennedy entered the hospital on a Friday for chemotherapy for a type of cancer that will only kill you in 10 to 15 years without treatment (there was no death watch for Jackie - she was not a terminal cancer patient), three days later she was dead (most likely from the effects of the chemotherapy or even an error in the calculation of the dosage!!) - if they can kill Jackie Kennedy and get away with it, what chance do we as average Americans have?

It should be obvious to even the most skeptical reader that there is reason to take control of your own health, get information before you make health decisions and avoid going to the "orthodox" doctor as much as possible. Make sure you take in your 90 essential nutrients each day , it's cheap insurance and you will probably live longer!!

"For all the talk about good medicine, though, the current battle over access to patients is a sobering reminder that at bookkeeping time, patients are just a source of cash."

-Janice Castro
Time, July 18,1994

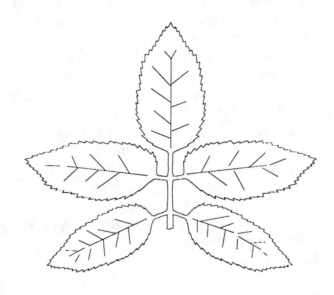

> *"Our most optimistic expectations are no less than the realization of an old dream: What will fertilizing with stone dust accomplish? It will turn stones into bread... make barren regions (fruitful) (and) feed the hungry."*
>
> *- Julius Hensel*
> *Bread From Stones, 1894*

Chapter 10

"GLACIAL MILK":
Plant derived colloidal minerals

The human pursuit of health and longevity has been long and tortuous, the answers seemingly just beyond reach and comprehension. Doctors, scientists, alchemists, priests, and kings have been frustrated in their pursuit of the "philosophers stone," the "fountain of youth," the "fruit of life" and pharmaceuticals - ironically the answer was just underfoot wherever they went - the minerals in the soil!!

Georges Buffon, an 18th century naturalist put to paper the "truth" of his time (unfortunately a "truth" is limited by the number of facts available):

"If we consider the European, the Negro, the Chinese, the American, the highly civilized man, the savage, the rich, the poor, the inhabitant of the city, the dwellers in the country, so different from one another in every respect, agree on this one point, and have the same duration, the same interval of time to run through

'twixt the cradle and the grave, that the difference of race, climate, of food, of comforts, makes no difference in the duration of life, it will be seen at once that the duration of life depends neither upon habits, nor custom, nor the quality of food, that nothing can change the fixed laws which regulate the number of our years."

Unfortunately, Buffon did not know about the 90 essential nutrients (60 minerals, 16 vitamins, 12 essential amino acids and 3 essential fatty acids) that are required daily by humans - his observations and writings essentially doomed 18th, 19th and 20th century man to pharmaceuticals and the surgeon's knife and wiped his scientific and medical contemporaries' slates clean from any notion that essential nutrients and Rare Earths are required to attain and fulfill one's genetic potential for health and longevity.

We already know the common denominators of the long-lived cultures, they are few, simple and very clear. Their basic truth for health and longevity boils down to the routine daily availability of a highly usable source of 90 essential nutrients of which the most critical are the plant derived colloidal minerals - simple, yes, but it works and works and works!!!

Plant derived colloidal minerals start in the parent rock and frigid heights of great mountain ranges, the Caucasus, the Karakorums, the Himalayas, the Andes, etc. Ageless glaciers scrape, grind and pulverize from two to six inches of parent rock from the mountain surface each year into a fine dust or rock "flour" that is carried from under the glaciers by water melted from the glacial ice by the frictional heat of the moving glacier.

The great glaciers of the Pleistocene age began retreating 14,000 years ago - yet many thousands of glaciers still lie heavy on the surface of the Earth. The state of Alaska, alone has 30,000 square miles of glacial ice. Glaciers basically are slow motion rivers of ice, flowing down the slopes and precipices of the worlds highest mountains and are conceived from the weight of millions of tons of accumulating snow.

The glacial ice flows continuously like a "conveyor belt" pulled by gravity and pushed by the ever-accumulating snow in a region called the "accumulation zone;" in the leading regions of the advancing glacier, or "ablation zone" the glacier gives up ice through melting, evaporation and loss of great chunks of ice known as icebergs; the "equilibrium line" separates the two distinct zones of the glacier - if the formation and loss of ice is equal the glacier is stable with no advance or retreat; if the production or loss of ice changes, advance or retreat occurs.

Advancing glacial ice grinds, scrapes and shears bedrock, boulders and gravel alike under millions of tons of ice pushing ahead of itself a "terminal moraine" or a ridge of mud and gravel.

Glacial melt water flows under the glacier through eroded channels and tunnels, lubricating the glacial flow and springing from under the glacier's face as a highly mineralized opaque water - "Glacial Milk."

The mineral composition of "Glacial Milk" is highly variable from one glacier to the next depending on the mineral content of the parent rock of the mountain it came from - the great common denominator of the "Glacial Milk" that nourishes the long-lived cultures is that they contain 60 to 72 minerals; there are thousands of glaciers in the world that produce vast quantities of "Glacial Milk," however, they may only have three to 20 minerals in them - not the number required to fulfill the human genetic potential for longevity!!!

The color of "Glacial Milk" is highly variable, ranging from pearl gray, silvery gray, to white, to bluish white to a brownish gray, again depending upon the mineral combinations of the parent rock.

Strictly speaking, "Glacial Milk" is both a suspension of finely ground rock dust of the particle size of clay ("rock flour") and a solution of soluble minerals from the portions of rock that is initially soluble, plus those minerals rendered soluble during the hydrolysis of pulverized rock.

The parent rocks of the "Glacial Milks" found in the long-lived cultures are essentially all metamorphic; they range from light colored, granitic-type gneiss through garnet-mica schist (including gem quality garnets - of interest here is the fact that Ayruvadic medicine uses gem stones including garnets as therapeutic medicines) to dark banded metamorphics rich in dark mafic minerals including hornblende and biotite mica.

A mineral analysis of the suspended rock flour from the Giltar Glacier of Hunza gives an indirect look into the rock type being pulverized by the glacier (Table 10- 1).

Suspended solids in "Glacial Milk" ranges in quantity from 3.2 ppm to 7100 ppm (Table 10 - 2) depending on the type of parent rock under the glacier, the softer the rock the more "rock flour" is produced; the soft metamorphic rocks from the Caucasus, Himalayan, Karakarum and Andes mountains lend themselves perfectly to the production of vast quantities of suspended "rock flour" which are found in their "Glacial Milk's."

Table 10 - 1 . X -Ray Powder Diffraction of "Glacial Milk" Rock Flour
Biotite mica (Fe, Mg, Al silicate) 70 - 80 %
Plagioclase feldspar (Ca, Na, Al silicate) 10 - 20 %
Vermiculite mica (elements as in biotite) up to 5 %
Hornblende (Ca, Mg, Fe, Al silicate) 3 % +/-
Serpentine (Mg, Fe silicate) 2 % +/- K - feldspar (K, Al silicate) trace
Muscovite mica (K, Al silicate) trace
Quartz (SiO_2) trace

There is an upper limit to the amount of dissolved minerals that can be acquired by drinking water whether it is "Glacial Milk" or just a mineral water from California (Geyser water) or France (Evian), so it is the suspended solids or "rock flour" that makes the difference for the centenarians.

The long lived centenarians drink the heavily mineralized water containing large quantities of "rock flour" known as "Glacial Milk" to be sure; however, they are only able to absorb and biologically utilize from five to 12 per cent of these suspended metallic colloids (ground up rocks).

The bottom line for the centenarians to reach their genetic potentials of 120 to 140 years of age is in fact their utilization of the "Glacial Milk" as irrigation water. They take great pain to flood and uniformly cover each terrace with "Glacial Milk" so that each millimeter of soil and each crop plant has access to the "rock flour" which forms a white powder layer on the fields surface after the water is absorbed - the rock "flour" is then plowed into the soil. Plants are then able to efficiently convert these metallic minerals from the "Glacial Milk" into highly usable organic plant derived colloidal minerals.

For 2,500 to 5,000 years, depending upon the culture, they have built stone terraces, filled them by hand, basket by basket with the highly mineralized muck and silt dredged by hand from the bottoms of the glacial rivers and have irrigated with "Glacial Milk," day by day, month by month, year by year, generation to generation since their beginings. For their reward they have been blessed with optimal health without hypertension, heart disease, stroke, aneurysms, arthritis, osteoporosis, dental disease, cataracts, diabetes, cancer, lupus,

Table 10-2

No.	Locality	Dissolved major ions, ppm							Total	Suspended solids ppm	pH
		Si	Al	Ca	Mg	K	Na	P			
1-milk	Emmons Glacier	8.00	.011	2.1	.4	.85	1.51	3.05	12.87	7100	7.5
-susp.*	Mt. Rainier, Wash.	7.50	1.07	9.22	1.95	9.4	14.0	..	43.14	..	9.2
-ratio†		.93	10	4.3	4.9	11	9.3	..	3.3	..	..
2-milk	Nisqually Glacier	4.28	.007	2.07	.74	.57	1.54	1.89	9.81	2900	7.4
-susp.	Mt. Rainier, Wash.	8.8	1.49	7.9	1.68	6.2	23.0	..	49.07	..	9.1
-ratio		2.1	200	3.8	2.3	11	14	..	5.1	..	..
3-milk	Zermatt, Switz.	1.18	.001	10.6	1.11	.74	.40	.49	14.03	173	6.7
-susp.		7.42 ·	.040	7.24	8.60	9.0	7.8	..	40.1	..	9.8
-ratio		6.3	40	1.5	7.7	12	20	..	2.9	..	..
4-milk	Les Diablerets,	1.35	.001	26.6	3.83	.18	1.30	.60	33.26	5	7.5
-susp.	Switz.	5.20	.044	34.38	7.80	3.90	7.0	..	58.32	..	8.9
-ratio		3.9	44	1.29	2.0	21.7	5.4	..	1.75	..	..
5-milk	Grinnell Glacier	.55	.001	8.5	1.42	.10	.22	.27	10.79	6	7.05
-susp.	Glacier Nat'l.	7.42	1.12	8.44	2.88	24.1	5.0	..	48.96	..	8.2
-ratio	Park, Montana	13.4	112	1.0	2	240	23	..	4.5	..	..
6-milk	Stechelberg,	.61	.026	19.4	1.51	.26	.44	.36	22.25	87	7.5
-susp.	Switz.	3.4	.344	16.68	2.04	20.6	8.5	..	51.56	..	8.8
-ratio		5.6	132	.87	1.4	7.9	19	..	2.3	..	..
7-milk	Grindelwald,	.66	.001	17.5	.525	.62	.22	.33	19.53	34	6.8
-susp.	Switz.	4.24	.1	20.38	1.86	12.1	7.6	..	46.24	..	9.0
-ratio		6.4	100	1.2	3.5	19.5	34.5	..	2.4	..	..
8-milk	Trient, Switz.	1.49	.001	10.6	7.62	1.05	.46	.59	21.22	5	6.9
-susp.		9.9	.586	.94	.22	17.6	18.9	..	48.15	..	9.3
-ratio		6.6	586	.09	.03	17	41	..	2.3	..	..
9-milk	Rhone Glacier	1.14	.001	4.1	2.56	.95	.34	.49	9.09	109	6.6
-susp.	Gletsch, Switz.	5.3	.202	11.58	.79	11.6	18.2	..	47.67	..	9.2
-ratio		4.6	200	2.8	.31	12	53	..	5.3	..	..
10-milk	Bossons Glacier	.45	..	7.0	.14	1.72	.21	.16	9.52	5	6.7
-susp.	Chamonix, France	6.4	.6	1.04	2.44	11.6	12.6	..	34.68	..	9.2
-ratio		14.2	..	.14	17	6.7	6.	..	3.6	..	..
11-milk	Teton Glacier	.62	.003	.82	.24	.53	.31	.22	2.52	38	6.4
-susp.	Teton Nat'l. Pk.	6.4	.74	tr.	.1	9.0	7.0	..	23.24	..	8.8
-ratio	Wyoming	10	246	..	2.4	17	..	..	9.2	..	..
12-milk	Dinwoody Glacier	.68	.003	4.5	2.2	.59	.65	n.d.	8.62	5	6.85
-susp.	Wind River Mts.,	8.7	1.1	9.3	1.3	14.6	13.0	..	48.00	..	8.7
-ratio	Wyoming	12.7	366	2.1	.6	24.7	20	..	5.6	..	..
13-milk	Nigards Glacier	.42	.001	.585	.04	.13	.24	.16	1.58	3.2	4.1
-susp.	Gaupne, Norway	7.0	.44	1.54	.72	9.8	11.5	..	31.00	..	..
-ratio		16	440	2.6	18	75	48	..	19.6	..	..
14-milk	Fanarak Glacier	1.06	.38	1.25	.08	.41	.24	.49	3.42	5	4.2
-susp.	Lom, Norway	5.66	.174	10.2	1.41	12.5	23.4	..	53.34	..	9.4
-ratio		5.3	.46	8	18	30	10	..	16	..	..
15-milk	Bover Glacier	.48	..	.70	.08	.38	.16	.25	1.80	32	4.5
-susp.	Lom-Skjolden,	5.24	.634	5.2	1.52	13.1	15.6	..	41.23	..	9.2
-ratio	Norway	11	..	7.4	19	34	10	..	23	..	..
16-melt-water	Taylor Glacier West end of Lake Bonney, Antarctic	.2	.09	17.9	.94	1.14	6.9	..	27.17	..	7.4
17-melt-water	Wright Glacier Wright tongue of Wilson Piedmont Glacier	.2	.03	..	.09	.4	2.14	..	2.86	..	7.2

*"Susp." refers to the suspension produced by grinding rock from the moraine by standardized procedure.
†"Ratio" refers to the weight of dissolved ion(s) in suspension divided by weight of ion(s) in glacial milk.

Repetitive Motion Syndrome, obesity, birth defects, hyperactive children, learning disabilities, ADD, depression, drug problems, "Bad Seeds" or crime.

The centenarians return everything that came from the soil back to the soil in their terraces to keep the organic material level high. Plant debris, after their harvest is not burned, but composted. Animal manure (children walk the roads with baskets looking for animal droppings to put in their fields) from stalls and barns is faithfully put into the fields. This organic material feeds the soil organisms (bacteria and fungi) which are able to further break down and hydrolize the "rock flour" into usable forms for assimilation by the crop plants.

The crops of the centenarians, the wheat, millet, buckwheat, barley, potatoes, cabbage, tomatoes, spinach, turnips, apples, apricots, grapes, nuts, etc. are able to absorb the converted metallic minerals from the land and process them into organic plant derived colloidal minerals.

Plant derived colloidal minerals are 98 % available for absorption and biological use by animals and people. The plant derived colloidals are in fact the form in which animals and humans store, utilize and transport minerals in their bodies.

Like almost all great discoveries, the use of "Glacial Milk" for irrigation was an accident; the centenarians did not seek these places for longevity like kings of old, they rather picked them as secure havens from outside marauders and for year round sources of water.

The standard farm in the world has veins of minerals coursing through them like ribbons of chocholate through chocolate ripple ice cream, thus one field blessed with a "high mineral content" can produce wheat with some mineral content and some wheat with little or none. The lack of uniformity and disparity in mineral content of our fields has produced spotty areas of heavy crops interspersed with areas of limited growth. American farmers are aware of this problem so they installed satilite navigation systems or lorans to accurately relocate these sparse areas of their fields so they can apply more fertilizer (NPK), which does result in more uniform crop production (tons and bushels) but the mineral value of these groups is nearly zero.

Many people are aware today that they need nutrient supplementation to augment their daily diets to assure their intake of the 90 essential nutrients but are frustrated in the results they get from the huge variety of multiple vitamin/mineral programs available.

Vitamins are pretty much the same, there are fat soluble and water soluble vitamins and they are about equally available in just about any multiple tablet; minerals, however, are a different story - there are three basic types of minerals:

1. METALLIC MINERALS

Metallic minerals include egg shell, oyster shell, calcium carbonate, lime stone, dolamite, mineral salt, sea water and Great Salt Lake Water, mineral oxides (i.e. - iron oxide, copper oxide, etc.), vortex waters, sea bed minerals, "soils"(which are usually clay), sea bed clays and clays, "rock flours" and various antacids such as Rollaids and Tums.

Typically metallic minerals are found in tablets and powders as gluconate (calcium gluconate, zinc gluconate, etc.), lactate, sulphates, carbonates and oxides (iron oxide = rust!!!).

Metallic minerals despite wild claims to the contrary are only eight to 12 % biologically available to animals and humans; after attaining the age of 35 to 40 years the availability of metallic minerals to humans drops to three to five percent.

We know of a man with a "Porta Potty" business in Grand Rapids, Michigan who finds literally thousands of multiple vitamin/mineral tablets in the bottom screens when the "Porta Potty" is pressure cleaned after a public event. We asked, "how do you know they are multiple vitamin/mineral tablets?" and he replied, "because the names are still on the coatings (i.e.- One-A-Day, Theragram M, Centrum, etc.)!! Over the years he has accumulated a literal mountain of these tablets!!!

A typical metallic mineral supplement either alone or as part of a multiple is calcium lactate. Calcium lactate can be obtained in 1,000 mg tablets which breaks down to 140 mg of metallic calcium and 860 mg of milk sugar or lactose. Two 1000 mg calcium lactate tablets do not give you 2,000 mg of calcium they only give you 280 mg of metallic calcium - at a 10 % bioavailability rate, you get 28 mg of biologically available calcium, therefore to get enough calcium from these tablets to meet your needs, you would have to take 30 tablets with each meal or 90 tablets a day and you have 59 more minerals to go (Table 10 - 3)!!

2. CHELATED MINERALS

Chelated (Key-late) minerals were created by the livestock industry in the 1960's to ensure maximum availability of dietary minerals to animals being fed and fattened for market. The original chelating agent used was calcium EDTA, a man made amino acid that was invented by the Germans just prior to WW II to antidote arsenic and lead exposure in chemical warfare attacks (calcium EDTA is used today for intraveinous chelation therapy to clean out arterial obstructions).

The term chelated literally means "claw," but is used to describe the process by which an amino acid, protein or enzyme (enzymes are proteins that do work) is wrapped around the mineral molecule which enhances the bioavailablility of the metallic mineral.

Chelated minerals are approximately 40 % bioavailable, a significant improvement over the original metallic minerals - your septic tank in the back yard gets the other 60 % (Table 10 - 4).

Chelated minerals are easily recognized on the label of a multiple vitamin/mineral supplement by the amino acid suffix such as selenium aspartate, chromium picolinate, or sometimes as an "amino acid chelate."

Table 10 - 3. Amounts of Metallic Calcium in a 1000 mg Tablet	
Calcium gluconate	90 mg
Calcium carbonate	400 mg
Calcium acetate	230 mg
Calcium citrate	210 mg
calcium lactate	140 mg
Cows milk (1000 mg fluid)	10 mg

3. COLLOIDAL MINERALS

Colloidal (Kol-oid) chemistry is not new, but it is not widely known about or understood by the general public. Simply said, a colloid refers to a substance that exists as ultra-fine particles that are suspended in a medium of different matter. The colloidal state is the state of a solute (mineral or other substance such as a paint pigment) in a solution when its molecules do not seperate into atoms as with a true solution (sodium chloride or salt seperates into seperate sodium and chloride atoms while in solution), but rather they remain grouped together to form solute particles.

The presence of these inorganic colloidal particles, which are approximately one hundred-thousandth to one ten-millionth of a centimeter in diameter (about 400 thousandths to four millionths of an inch), can often be detected by means of an electron microscope. As a result of the grouping of the molecules, a solute in the colloidal state cannot pass through a suitable semipermiable membrane and gives rise to negligible osmotic pressure (they will pass through filter paper), depression of freezing point and elevation of boiling point effects.

These ultra-fine particles of the colloid are just barely larger than most molecules and so small they can't be seen with the naked eye - about one billion of these colloid particles would fit into a cubic 0.01 of an inch (Fig.10- 1).

The "solution" part of a colloid provides a solid, gas or liquid medium in which the colloid particles are suspended. The suspended particles in a colloid can also be a solid, a gas or a liquid.

Solutions were classified by H. Freundlich (1925) into three catagories:

1) True solutions
2) Colloidal solutions
3) Emulsions and suspensions.

The four part method of classifying solutions is as follows:

1) Identify particle size.
2) Determine presence of Brownian movement (random movement of particles suspended in liquids or gasses resulting from the impact of molecules of the fluid sur-

Table 10 - 4. Absorption Comparison of Chelated and Metallic Minerals.			
	Amino Acid Chelate vs. Carbonates	Amino Acid Chelate vs. Sulphates	Amino Acid Chelate vs. Oxides
Copper	5.8 : 1	4.1 : 1	3.0 : 1
Magnesium	1.8 : 1	2.6 : 1	–
Iron	3.6 : 1	3.8 : 1	4.9 : 1
Zinc	–	2.3 : 1	3.9 : 1

Fig. 10-1A

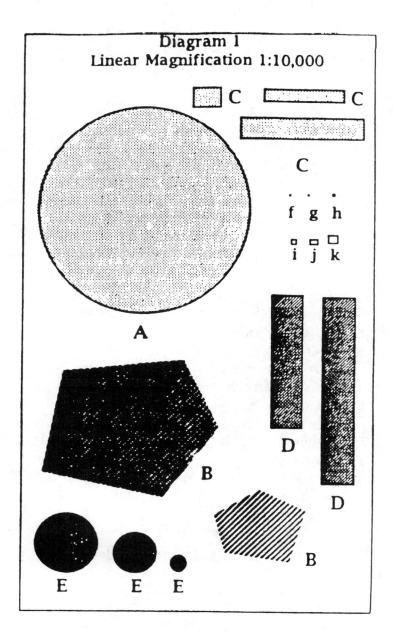

Diagram 1
Linear Magnification 1:10,000

A. Human redblood cell (7.5u)
B. Starch granual
C. Kaolin rock dust crystals
D. Anthrax bacilli
E. Cocci bacteria
f. g. h. colloidal mineral

Fig. 10-1B Veins of humic shale.

rounding the particles).
3) Ability to pass through filter paper
4) Level of solubility

In 1975, S. S. Voyutsky (a Russian) wrote the classic text on colloidal chemistry. Voyutsky referred to solutions as "molecular dispersion systems" and "heterogeneous highly dispersed colloidal systems."

The exact point between the molecular and colloidal degrees of dispersion cannot be established because the transition from molecularly dispersed systems to coarsely dispersed systems is a continuous range.

A colloidal system must have three basic characteristics:

1) It must be heterogeneous (consists of dissimilar ingredients or constituents).

2) The system must be multi-phasic (i.e.-solid/liquid, gas/liquid, etc.).

3) The particles must be insoluble (do not dissolve in the solution).

Each one of these classifications interacts with the others to give colloids their unique qualities. The interesting thing about colloids is that they remain heterogeneous, multi-phasic and insoluble at different concentrations as long as a larger number if not all of the particles are within the range of sizes of colloids (1n to 100n). The molecular groups or particles of the colloid solute carry a resultant electrical charge, generally of the same sign (negative) for all of the particles. A small percentage of these inorganic colloids will pass through the intestine of a living animal or human because a natural chelating process takes place in the gut in the presence of protein-containing food.

Inorganic colloidal material which readily passes through filter paper may be separated from dissolved substances, such as starch, sugar or salt, by placing the mixture of mineral colloid and noncolloid in a parchment shell surrounded by distilled water. The inorganic colloids are "too large" to pass through the membrane, but the molecules of salt, starch and sugar or any other dissolved substance pass readily through the semipermeable membrane (they separate into individual atoms or very small molecules). This kind of separation process is called dialysis.

In the process of digestion the inorganic minerals in food or supplements soon become inorganic colloids and as an inorganic colloid they cannot penetrate the intestinal wall to enter the blood stream. In the presence of amino acids a small percentage of the inorganic colloids form chelated minerals and organic colloids which are able to be dialyzed through the mucus membranes of the intestinal walls into the blood stream - this form of bioavailable mineral state is known as a "crystalloid."

Crystalloids or organic colloids readily pass through cell walls, while inorganic colloids are "too large." Additionally we must remember that in the living organism there are other physiological forces at work which interfere with or modify the expected osmotic phenomenon.

Colloidal mineral supplements and commercial colloids are found in four different forms:

A. Unprotected colloids are made of bare "rock flour," this is the form of inorganic metallic colloid found in sea bed minerals, clays, "soils," and "Glacial Milk." This form of inorganic colloid is in fact a metallic mineral and is only available to plants when there is a healthy soil population of bacteria and fungi.

B. The second type of mineral colloid is found in the living systems of bacteria, fungi, green plants (food crops), animals and humans and is coated by a water loving (hydrophilic) substance such as gelatin, albumin, albuminoids, or collogen. This coating protects the now "organic mineral colloid" and allows it to be a crystalloid for absorption, storage and physiological uses and thus maximizing its bioavailability to 98 %.

C. The third type of organic mineral colloid has a protective coating of carbon with a molecular chain length of 10 to 12 carbon atoms. This type of colloid is also found in bacteria, fungi, plants (including some forms of petrified wood), animals and humans and is thought to be the most stable form of natural organic mineral colloid.

D. The fourth type of mineral colloid is not found in nature, but rather is manufactured industrially by coating the metallic colloid with sulfated castor oil (lipophillic or fat or oil loving) to form commercial detergents.

Bee pollen, blue green algae (the Aztecs tried this one and had to turn to cannibalism to meet their mineral needs), kelp (the Japanese who consume the most kelp world wide only live to be 79.9) and "green drinks" contain some plant derived colloidal minerals, however, the number of minerals is highly variable depending on what is and what is not in the soil or lakes they came

from and lastly, the concentrations of the colloidal minerals are so small that you would have to eat more than 400 pounds a day to meet your essential daily needs.

Juicing has been a popular method of obtaining maximum nutrition from fresh fruits and vegetables and in fact there is no better way to get vitamins from fresh fruits and vegetables than to juice. When one talks about minerals from juicing, the level of confidence drops precipitously - remember U.S. Senate Document 264 says there are few if any nutritional minerals left in our farm and range soils and therefore there are few if any nutritional minerals left in our grains, fruits and vegetables. Even when you juice you should supplement your dietary program with minerals to include all of the major minerals, trace minerals and Rare Earths.

"Humic shale" is a unique source of plant derived colloidal minerals (Fig. 10-1). Humic shale originated from plants some 75 million years ago, those lush tropical plants took up the 60 plus metallic minerals available to them from a fertile soil that had as many as 84 minerals. The ancient soil was so rich with minerals that trees grew as much as 25 feet per year and the great brontosaurus or "thunder lizard" attained a body weight of 140,000 pounds (70,000 tons) with a mouth no larger than that of a horse - the ability of the brontosaurus to attain such a bulk with so little a mouth meant he was consuming plants rich with concentrated mineral nutrients.

A volcanic eruption covered these mineral rich forests with a thin layer of mud and ash, thick enough to create an air-tight "vault" and dried or desiccated the plants into a deep accumulation of "hay," but not

Table 10-5

SPARK SOURCE MASS SPECTROGRAPHIC ANALYSIS OF HUMIC SHALE
Suspended Solids 38 gm/L.   Concentration in PPM (unless otherwise specified)
Humic Shale is a plant derived colloidal nutritional supplement produced under Consent Decree by the US Department of Human Services.

Mineral	Conc.	Mineral	Conc.	Mineral	Conc.	Mineral	Conc.
Tantalum	0.6	Lutetium	0.05	Ytterbium	0.2	Thulium	0.02
Erbium	0.1	Holmium	0.1	Dysrosium	0.5	Terbium	0.1
Gadolinium	0.1	Eropium	0.1	Samarium	0.8	Neodymium	0.8
Praseodymium	0.4	Cerium	4.0	Lanthanum	2.0	Barium	0.3
Cesium	0.1	Iodine	0.1	Tin	0.03	Cadmium	0.1
Silver	0.2	Molybdenum	0.04	Niobium	0.02	Zirconium	0.2
Yurium	4.0	Strontium	14.0	Rubidium	0.8	Bromine	0.2
Selenium	0.9	Germanium	< 0.01	Gallium	0.1	Zinc	47.0
Copper	2.0	Nickel	30.0	Cobalt	9.0	Iron	43.0
Manganese	36.0	Chromium	0.4	Vanadium	0.1	Titanium	1.0
Scandium	0.1	Calcium	1gm/L	Potassium	1gm/L	Chlorine	8.0
Sulfur	1gm/L	Phosphorus	12.0	Silicon	1gm/L	Magnesium	1gm/L
Sodium	1gm/L	Flourine	5.0	Boron	0.2	Beryllium	0.1
Lithium	10.0						

* WAL INC, Golden, Colorado 80403   (4/87)

deep enough or heavy enough to pressurize the dried plant material into coal or oil.

The entombed humic shale never fossilized or petrified, in other words they never became rocks - just compressed, dried, prehistoric "hay" that contains large amounts of plant derived colloidal minerals (Table 10 - 5). Humic shale can be used as an excellent soil conditioner for organic gardens, farms and ranches as it supplies a rich source of humus and no less than 60 plant derived colloidal minerals.

Humic shale can also be ground into a fine plant flour and soaked for three to four weeks in filtered spring water until it reaches a specific gravity of 3.0, it then provides a high quality plant derived colloidal mineral supplement that contains 38 grams of plant derived colloidal minerals per liter.

It takes 78 pounds of humic shale to reach the concentration of 38 grams of colloidal minerals per liter; the 78 pounds of humic shale represents approximately 1034 pounds of lush prehistoric green mineral rich plants. The fluid extract of high grade humic shale contains no less than 60 plant derived colloidal minerals and is 98 % available for animals and humans.

If we are to flourish and fullfill our genetic potential for health and longevity we must supplement with all ninety essential nutrients including 60 minerals. Anything less is to tragically throw away ones life.

"Live long and prosper."
-Spock
  Star Trek

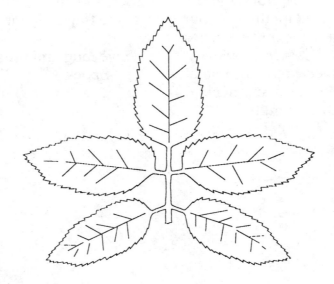

"You don't need insurance to be able to afford them! You don't need a doctor's permission to get them! You don't have to be a genius to use them! You never have to worry about dangerous side effects! And you'll be amazed at how superior they are to what your taking now! At best, drugs are pale imitations of these natural medicines. They repair hidden damage to your cells, organs and arteries - something no man-made drug could ever do!"

- Julian M. Whitaker, MD
Health & Wellness Today

Chapter 11

RARE EARTHS:
Their secrets of health and longevity

Wide scientific interest in trace elements roles in animal physiology began more than 100 years ago with the discovery that metals were associated with biologically significant processes and tissues. Turacin, a red porphyrin pigment in the feathers of certain birds contained no less than 7 % copper; hemocyanin, another copper compound was found in the blood of snails; sycotypin, a zinc containing blood pigment in mullussca and a vanadium respiratory compound in the blood of sea squirts.

Initially, the discoveries of trace minerals in animal tissues were treated as curiosities and created little or no interest in the broader implications of metals in the basic physiological process.

Zinc was initially recognized as an essential element in the bread mold *Aspergillus niger*. The recognition that low soil iodine content was associated with endemic goiter was a major discovery. In the first quarter of the 20th century Kenall isolated an iodine-amino acid (tyrosine) crystalline complex (65 % iodine) that he called thyroxin (thyroid hormone).

The production of emission spectrography technology early in the 20th century allowed the identification of more than 20 trace elements in animal tissue.

In the second quarter of the 20th century spectacular knowledge in trace mineral nutrition and physiology were gained by the animal and livestock industry.

In the 1920's, Bertrand of France and McHargue of the United States pioneered the purified diet approach to animal nutritional studies and trace mineral nutrition. The origional theory for the use of purified rations was great but the early laboratory diets were a disaster because the diets were so deficient in other nutrients (i.e. - vitamins and amino acids) that animals showed a veritable kaleidoscope of deficiency diseases simultaneously.

The University of Wisconsin, led by

E.B.Hart (1928), brought in a new era when he demonstrated the need for supplementary copper as well as iron for growth and hemoglobin formation in rats fed a pure milk diet; within a few years, Hart's studies also showed that manganese and zinc were essential nutrients for mice and rats. These findings were quickly extended to other laboratory and agricultural species.

Almost 20 years passed before the purified diet technique again identified the essentiality of additional trace elements (i.e. - Mo -1953; Se -1957; Cr -1959).

During the 1930's, a diverse range of nutritional disorders of humans and farm animals were related to deficiencies and excesses of trace elements and toxic metals.

In 1931, mottled tooth enamel was found to result from an intake of excessive flouride in drinking water; copper deficiency was identified in Florida and Holland; two years latter "Alkali Disease" and "Blind Staggers" of livestock was related to acute or chronic excessive selenium intake in certain areas of the American Great Plains.

In 1935, cobalt deficiency was identified and related to the cause of wasting diseases of range cattle in the south and west of Australia.

In 1936, a dietary deficiency of manganese was identified as the cause of perosis or "slipped tendon" or "angel wing" and nutritional chondrodystrophy in poultry (this is the same disease as "Repetitive Motion Syndrome," "TMJ" and "carpal tunnel" in humans).

In 1937, enzootic neonatal ataxia in lambs (cerebral palsy) was found to be the result of copper deficiency in ewes during early pregnancy that were grazing on copper deficient soils in Australia.

It soon became evident that other, milder health and disease problems involving trace mineral deficiencies could exist and be identified.

The criteria for essentiality of a trace mineral or Rare Earth Are:

1. Present in all healthy tissues of living organisms.

2. Concentration in tissue is relatively constant from one species to the next.

3. Withdrawal from the body induces reproducable physiological and structural abnormalties in several species.

4. Its replacement reverses (this one is not always true - i.e.- deficiencies in the embryo during developement that result in congenital defects cannot be corrected in later in life) or prevents the disease or abnormalty.

5. The abnormalties of the trace mineral deficiency always have a biochemical change.

6. The biochemical changes of the deficiency disease can be prevented or cured when the deficiency is corrected.

The deficiency or toxicity effects of trace minerals were often found to be affected by other elements, nutrients that were or were not present in the soil, food or water - while studying copper poisoning in sheep in Australia, Dick (1950's) found that a three way interaction exists between copper, molybdenum and inorganic sulfate and that the ability of Mo to limit Cu retention in ani-

Table 11-1

Elements in mammalian blood, plasma and red cells

Element	mg l^{-1} blood	mg l^{-1} plasma	mg l^{-1} red cells	atoms/red cell
Ag	0·024 G	0·004 G	(0·051)	23000
Al	0·32 G	0·44 G	(0·16)	270000
As	0·49	0·040	(1·1)	700000
Au	0·00004	<0·0025 L	(0·00004?)	10
B	0·13 A	0·17	(0·077)	340000
Ba	0·069 G	0·079 E, G	(0·056)	19000
Be	<0·0001	<0·004 L	(<0·0001)	<500
Bi	<0·01	<0·0006 L	(<0·0006)	<150
Br	4·6	3·9	(5·6)	$3·3 \times 10^6$
C	94200	40500	166000	$6·6 \times 10^{11}$
Ca	62 G	99	6·3? H, I, J	$7·5 \times 10^6$
Cd	0·0074 A	<0·09	(0·015)	6300
Ce		<0·002 L	(<0·002?)	<700
Cl	2900	3950	1890	$2·5 \times 10^9$
Co	0·00033	0·00038 K	0·00015	120
Cr	0·026? A, O	0·024	0·020	18000
Cs	0·0028	0·0031	(0·0028)	1000
Cu	1·07	1·12	0·98	730000
Dy		<0·002 L	(<0·002?)	<600
Er		<0·006 L	(<0·006?)	<1700
Eu		<0·004 L	(<0·004?)	<1200
F	0·36	0·28?	0·43?	$1·1 \times 10^6$
Fe	475	1·14	1110	$9·5 \times 10^9$
Ga	0·00052	<0·006 L	(0·0005?)	340
Gd		<0·002 L	(<0·002?)	<600
Ge		<0·03 L	(<0·06)	<40000
H	98000	106000	87000	$4·1 \times 10^{12}$
Hf		<0·002 L	(<0·002?)	<500
Hg	0·0065	0·0030	0·0067	1600
Ho		<0·002 L	(<0·002?)	<600
I	0·063 D	0·077	(0·044)	16000
In		<0·004 L	(<0·004?)	<1600
Ir		<0·0025 L	(<0·0025?)	<600
K	1690	170	3690	$4·5 \times 10^9$
La		<0·006 L	(<0·006?)	<2000
Li		<0·005 E	(<0·005?)	<30000
Lu		<0·0006 L	(<0·0006?)	<160
Mg	41	22	61	$1·2 \times 10^8$
Mn	0·026	0·0029	0·022	19000
Mo	0·0041 F		(<0·008)	<5000
N	33000	12000	51000	$1·7 \times 10^{11}$
Na	1990	3280	260	$5·4 \times 10^8$
Nb		<0·01 L	(<0·01?)	<5000
Nd		<0·002 L	(<0·002?)	<700
Ni	0·038 A	0·042	0·049	40000
O	775000	848000	698000	$2·1 \times 10^{12}$
Os		<0·0025 L	(<0·0025?)	<500
P	370	132	620	$9·5 \times 10^7$

Element	mg l⁻¹ blood	mg l⁻¹ plasma	mg l⁻¹ red cells	atoms/red cell
Pb	0·27	0·043	0·34	78000
Pd		< 0·01 L	(< 0·01?)	< 4500
Pr		< 0·05 L	(< 0·05?)	< 10000
Pt		< 0·04 L	(< 0·04?)	< 10000
Ra		< 2 × 10⁻¹³?	(< 2 × 10⁻¹³?)	≪ 1
Rb	2·7?	1·2?	5·3?	3 × 10⁶
Re		< 0·002 L	(< 0·002?)	< 500
Rh		< 0·004 L	(< 0·004?)	< 2000
Ru		< 0·004 L	(< 0·004?)	< 2000
S	2040	1220	3600	5·4 × 10⁹
Sb	0·0047	0·054? L	(0·005?)	2000
Sc	0·075?	< 0·03 L	(< 0·14)	< 150000
Se	0·27 F, N	0·11	0·26?	160000
Si	4·0	2·5 C, M	4·1?	7 × 10⁶
Sm		< 0·002 L	(< 0·002?)	< 600
Sn	0·13?	0·033?	0·25?	100000
Sr	0·039? G	0·038? L	(0·040?)	22000
Ta		< 0·006 L	(< 0·006?)	< 1500
Tb		< 0·0006 L	(< 0·0006?)	< 180
Te		< 0·03 L	(< 0·03?)	< 11000
Th		0·04?	(0·04?)	8000
Ti	0·026	< 0·04 L	(< 0·056)	< 55000
Tl	< 0·02	< 0·0025 L	(< 0·02)	< 5000
Tm		< 0·0006 L	(< 0·0006?)	< 180
U	0·00055 B	< 0·001 L	(< 0·0011?)	< 220
V	0·017?	0·010? P	(0·026?)	25000
W	0·001		(< 0·002)	< 500
Y		< 0·01 L	(< 0·01?)	< 5000
Yb		< 0·002 L	(< 0·002?)	< 600
Zn	6·5	1·6	12·3	8·9 × 10⁶
Zr		< 0·006 L	(< 0·006?)	< 3000

Red cell concentrations were mostly calculated from blood and plasma concentrations, assuming that 1 litre blood = 572 ml plasma + 428 ml red cells; calculated values are enclosed in brackets.

Atoms/red cell were calculated assuming there are $1·26 \times 10^{13}$ red cells per l of packed cells; hence

$$\text{atoms/red cell} = 4·75 \times 10^7 \times m/A$$

where there are m mg l⁻¹ red cells, and the atomic weight is A.

Most values are taken from the compilation by Bowen (1963) with the following additions:

A—Imbus et al., 1963
B—Boirie et al., 1962
C—Aumonier and Quilichini, 1962
D—Perkin and Lahey, 1940
E—Niedermayer et al., 1962
F—Bruno et al., 1964
G—Butt et al., 1964
H—Keitel et al., 1955

I—Wallach et al., 1962
J—Hunter, 1960
K—Parr and Taylor, 1964
L—Wolstenholme, 1964
M—Ivanov and Rozenberg, 1962
N—Bowen and Cawse, 1963
O—Bowen, 1964
P—Gofmann et al., 1962

mals can only occur in the presence of adequate sulfate.

The third quarter of the 20th century has produced many notable advances in trace element nutrition and physiology - principally by the animal industry, Atomic absorption, neutron activation and microelectron probe techniques have been particularly valuble.

Radioactive isotopes increased our knowledge of the concentration kenetics of trace elements in specific organs. Numerous metallo-proteins (enzymes) and identification of their diverse symptoms of deficiency or toxicity, including the identification of the role of copper in elastin biosynthesis and its relationships to the cardiovascular disorders (aneurysms) of animals.

At the end of the third quarter and the begining of the fourth quarter of the 20th century, the identification in mice of "new" trace element essentiality for lithium, fluorine, silica, vanadium, nickel, arsenic, cadmium, tin, and lead exploded. Progress in this field of study was facilitated by the plastic isolator technique developed by Smith and Schwarz at the University of Wisconsin - in this animal holding system there is no metal, glass or rubber; the unit has an air lock to eliminate contamination by dust and has a filter to remove dust at a particle size of 0.35 microns.

The most significant development in the trace element field during the last 25 years of the 20th century has been the recognition that trace elements have a fundamental role in health maintenance and that optimal intakes from food sources can no longer be taken for granted.

The essential role of trace elements in the support and maintainance of the immune system against bacteria, viruses, fungi and cancer, degenerative diseases and birth defects are well documented. The mode of action and the tissue concentrations varies considerably. The only common denominator of trace minerals is that they are all found in exceedingly low amounts in the healthy tissue. They are usually found in parts per million (ppm); micrograms/gram (u/g); or with some even parts per billion (ppb) or nanograms per gram (ng/g).

The concentration of trace elements in tissue or requirement levels does not represent their relative importance in nutrition. The concentrations of trace elements and their functional concentration must be maintained within narrow physiological limits if the functional and structural fabric of the tissues and organs of the animal and human body are to be maintained for optimal fertility, development, growth, health and longevity.

Higher species such as birds, mammals and humans have a "homeostatic" mechanism that maintains tissue concentrations of trace minerals at optimal levels at their physiological sites.

Almost all trace elements function as catalysts for a cellular or subcellular enzyme system. Enzymes are simply proteins that do work and in their role as catalysts their function ranges from that of a weak ionic (ph affects) modulator to highly specific metalloenzyme ("metal finger") functions for RNA.

In metalloenzymes the metal atom cannot be substituted by any other trace element. Although Vallee has demonstrated that Co and Cd can replace Zn in certain enzymes with some changes in substrate specificity but the enzyme is not deactivated.

Because of the frequently wide disparity between the absolute and dietary requirements (results from different intestinal absorption efficiencies for individual elements) the most efficient form of trace mineral supplement, such as plant derived colloidal minerals should be consumed.

For the metallic form of iodine the ratio is almost 1:1; for iron it's 1:10 and for chromium it's 1:100.

The RDA and other dietary recommendations for trace minerals are conceived by the National Science Foundation to meet the needs of "practically all healthy people" - they are not applicable to people with "health challenges" or full blown disease states.

Mineral analysis of 3,000 year old bones of Japanese temple monks showed that they contained a greater spectrum of minerals and greater amount of each mineral than the bones of modern day Japanese.

Dr. Wilhelm Heinrich Schuessler (1821-1898), a physician from Oldenburg, Germany realized that minerals, "tissue salts" or "cell salts," as he called them were the basics of the flesh and even of life itself. Schuessler, who studied medicine and kindred sciences at the finest schools of Paris, Berlin, Geissen and Prague, is known as the founder of biochemistry.

Schuessler was heavily influenced by the noted German chemist Liebig, who postulated that the human body is composed of "cells" which are complex building blocks made up of organic material, water and "salts" or minerals. Schuessler burned the corpses of indigent humans dying in German hospitals and analyzed the resultant ash - with the analytical methods available in his day he was only able to identify 12 "cell salts." Given the amount of information he had available to him, and given the fact that some of his mineral deficiency to disease relationships were incorrect, Schuessler showed great insight for realiz-

ing the connection between mineral deficiencies and imbalances and the relationship to chronic degenerative disease (Table 11 - 1). Schuessler also tried to use his "cell salts" as a homeopathic remedy rather than as food supplements which severely limited the effectiveness of his results.

INITIAL DEPLETION PHASE:

Initial depletion of trace elements in animals and humans is characterized by changes only in the metabolism of the element itself in response to a suboptimal intake, the individual target tissue compensating so that no disturbance of biological structure or function are detectable by means of a test. Increased intestinal absorption efficiency and/or reduction of excretion and gradual diminishment of body reserves takes place. This phase of trace mineral deficiency returns to normal very quickly with a return of normal intake.

COMPENSATED METABOLIC PHASE:

The compensated metabolic phase is characterized by a reduction of certain specific biochemical functions, such as trace mineral dependent enzyme reactions or receptor sites. The "homeostatic" mechanism becomes ineffective in maintaining the normal trace element concentrations at receptor sites causing a reduction in biochemical function (i.e. low blood sugar, irregular heart beat, white hair, hair loss, etc.).

DECOMPENSATED METABOLIC PHASE:

The decompensated phase of trace element deficiency is characterized by the

Table 11 - 1. Schuesslers 12 Cell Salts

Calcarea Fluor (Fluoride of lime) - is found in the surface of the bones, in the enamel of the teeth and in the elastic fibers of the skin, muscular tissue and blood vessels. A deficiency results in a relaxed condition of the tissues and is a predisposing cause in a number of diseases. It is indicated in ailments which can be traced to a relaxed condition of elastic fibers, including dilation of the blood vessels, haemorrhoids, enlarged varicose veins, hardened glands, cracks in the skin, etc.

Calcarea Phos (Phosphate of lime) - is a constituent of the bones, teeth, connective tissue, blood corpuscles and the gastric juice. It unites with the organic substance albumin, giving solidity to the bones, building teeth and entering into all the important secretions of the body.

Calcarea Sulph (Sulphate of Lime) - is found in the epithelial cells in the blood. It acts as a preventitive of cell disintegration and suppuration. A deficiency allows suppuration to continue too long; therefore, wounds that are too slow to heal (i.e.- catarrhs, boils, carbuncles, ulcers, abscesses, pimples and pustules of the face) need this remedy.

Ferrum Phos (Phosphate of Iron) - is the remedy for inflammation and feverish conditions. This tissue salt is found in the blood, where it colors the corpuscle red and carries oxygen to all parts of the body. It is indicated in cases of relaxed conditions of the muscular tissue, and in abnormal conditions of the corpuscles of the blood themselves.

Kali Mur (Chloride of potash) - unites with albumin, forming fibrin, which is found in every tissue of the body with the exception of the bones. A deficiency of this tissue salt, with a consequent release of albumin, causes a discharge or exudation of a thick white, sticky character from the mucus membrane, and a white or gray coating of the tongue.

Kali Phos (Phosphate of potash) - is a constituent of all the tissues and the fluids of the body, notably of the brain and nerve cells. It is the great nerve nutrient. It also has an antiseptic action and hinders decay of the tissues. A deficiency of Kali Phos produces brain-fag, mental depression, irritability, fearfullness, timidity, lack of nerve power.

Kali Sulph (Sulphate of potash) - is a carrier of oxygen to the cells of the skin. The oxygen in the lungs is taken up by the iron in the blood and carried to every cell in the organism by the reciprocal action of Kali Sulph and Ferrum Phos. It is a remedy for the skin.

Natrum Mur (Chloride of soda or Sodium chloride) - this tissue salt is a constituent of every liquid and solid part of the body. It regulates the degree of moisture within the cells by virtue of its property of attracting and distributing water. The human body is composed of about 70 % of water, which in the absence of Natrum Nur, would be inert and useless. Any deficiency of this tissue salt causes an imbalance of water in the human organism. The patient then shows a watery, bloated appearance; is languid, drowsy and inclined to watery exudations; and sometimes there is the opposite condition of excessive dryness.

Magnesia Phos (Phosphate of Magnesia) - the biochemical action of Magnesia Phos is anti-spasmodic. Its work is chiefly confined to the delicate white nerve fibers of the nerves and muscles. A deficiency of this tissue salt in the fibers allows it to contract, hence it produces spasms, cramps, etc.

Natrum Phos (Phosphate of soda) - this tissue salt is present in the blood, muscles, nerve and brain cells, as well as in the intercellular fluids. It splits up lactic acid into carbonic acid and water and is the remedy where there is an excess of acid in the system. An acid state gives rise to rheumatic troubles, digestive upsets, intestinal disorders, and has an adverse effect upon assimilation.

Natrum Sulph (Sulphate of soda) - this tissue salt is found only in the intercellular fluids and its principal function is to regulate the quantity of water in the tissues, blood and fluids of the body. It has an affinity for water and eliminates only excess from the blood and blood serum. It also works with the bile and keeps it in normal consistency.

Silicea (Silica) - this substance is found abundantly throughout the vegetable Kingdom, especially in grasses, grains, palms, etc. It is also found but less commonly, in the animal world. Silicea is present in the blood, bile, skin, hair and nails. It is also a constituent of connective tissue, bones, nerve sheaths and mucus membranes.

appearence of symptoms or defects in the metabolic (prediabetes), cognative (learning disabilities, ADD, ADHD), emotional (DR. Jykell/Mr.Hyde, "Bad Seeds"), developmental (dyslexia, gay behavior), structural (dystrophy of muscles), work-stamina and longevity of a species.

CLINICAL PHASE:

The clinical phase of trace mineral deficiency is characterized by the onset of full blown disease states and even death (i.e. - cardiomyopathy, diabetes, cancer, aneurysms, etc.). For most trace mineral deficiencies in the clinical phase diagnosis by the "orthodox" physician is almost non-existent, the cure, however, is simply a matter of replacement of the trace element (a correct diagnosis can lead to a remarkably rapid positive clinical response ranging from 48 hours to 30 days for recognizable results); others do not reach full return to normal after permanant biochemical, chromosomal or gross physical damage has occured.

HAIR ANALYSIS

The best way to evaluate ones mineral status is through the use of a hair analysis. Blood and urine tests are not universally useful or infalable in monitoring the bodies mineral status - either for nutritional evaluation or for determining toxic levels of heavy metals as our bodies do everything possible ("homeostatic" mechanism) to keep blood levels of minerals in the normal range even though we have raging mineral deficiencies.

Studies by Dr. Bryan Pate, Simon Fraser University, have indicated that the levels of minerals in hair can show changes in an hourly fashion which is related to the growth rate of the hair. Hair is also biologically stable and can be stored for long periods of time for reanalysis; hair is also easily obtained by a non-invasive technique from the nape of the neck, the axilla (under arm) or pubic hair.

The growth of some hair (i.e.-pubic, axillary, beard and mustache) is hormone dependent, while other hair (i.e.- eye lashes, eye brows and head hair) growth is less dependent on hormone output.

The normal human scalp has about 100,000 individual hairs, a few more for blonds and a lesser amount for red hair; about 10 to 11 per cent (10,000) are in a resting non-growth phase contributing to a normal daily loss of about 100 hairs. The average human hair grows at a rate of 0.4 to 0.5 mm each day or about one half inch per month. The healthy hair follicle producing hair is richly supplied with blood that contains essential minerals as well as toxic minerals which are laid into the growing hair protein as a function of the rate of growth of the hair and its sulphydral groups (sulfur to sulfur bonds).

Hormonal or other chemical influences on the follicle affect the incorporation of specific minerals and the level of the mineral in the blood affects the amount deposited in the hair. It is well documented that the rate of hair growth is influenced by such factors as age, race, sex, season, nutrition status as well as hormonal status.

The energy for the metabolism and growth of the hair follicle is provided by blood glucose; therefore variations in blood glucose (hypoglycemia or diabetes and thus levels of Cr and Va) levels can affect the energy cycle of the hair follicle. Adrenal insufficiency is known to result in a reduction of the amount of pubic hair and axillary hair, appears to be related to direct hormone involvement and the effects of the glucocorticoids have upon glucose levels in the blood and glucose metabolism.

Hair is predominantly protein, therefore changes in protein nutritive status of the host can alter the make up and composition of the hair, its growth rate and the rate and level of trace element accumulation. Changes in hair structure can result from changes of protein metabolism, protein malnutrition which affects the hair diameter, growth rate and tensile strength.

Crounse and Van Scott have demonstrated that hair root protein is a more sensitive indicator of protein metabolism and malnutrition than serum albumin.

Hair is composed of epithelial cells arranged in three layers:

1) Cuticle
2) Cortex
3) Medulla

The cortex forms the bulk of the hair mass; it is a column of epithelial cells that is formed into a rigid homogeneous material. In new hair, the cortex is comprised of irregularly shaped cells that perculate tissue fluid. As the hair grows, the hair shaft dries out and the cavities lose the fluid.

The chemical structure of hair protein in the cortex layer (keratin) is similar to the protein of dental enamel and finger and toe nails. When human hair is treated with cold waving solutions, bleaches, synthetic organic hair dyes or depilatories, a significant decrease in the cystine (sulfur amino acid) levels occur; this changes the physical characteristics of the hair and its ability to bind trace minerals.

The pigment in the hair is produced in the cells of the hair bulb and continues to form in the cells of the cortex. Hair pigment is a type of melanin which is formed in the presence of the enzyme tyrosinase and its effects on the essential amino acid tyrosine (copper is required as a cofactor for this reaction - therefore a copper deficiency results in white, silver or gray hair). The pigment in red hair (tricosiverin) is an iron-containing pigment resulting in relatively high iron content in red hair.

Some 72 elements have been identified in human hair in concentrations ranging from 0.1 to 100 micrograms per gram (ppm); the vast majority of these trace minerals in human metabolism function chiefly as key components of enzyme systems (metallo enzymes or RNA or DNA replications (metal fingers). These trace minerals and Rare Earths serve as facilitators for enzymes and when deficient or absent the enzymes, RNA and DNA are either unable or have a reduced capacity to perform their specific function.

Human head hair is considered a "recording filament" that records metabollic changes of trace elements and Rare Earths over a long period of time and therefore like the growth rings in a tree are recordings of past nutritional events. Dr. Gordus, University of Michigan, tested the head hair of naval midshipmen, Anapolis and army cadets from West Point - when the incoming freshman cadets arrive at their respective academies, they have widely different levels of trace minerals in their hair, reflecting the variation in their local nutritional intakes - as they accumulate time at the academies their hair trace mineral patterns became more and more alike showing very clearly that the nutritional intake, not individual genetics, is the primary factor determining hair levels of trace minerals and Rare Earths.

Blood and urine are relatively free of toxic minerals during the chronic stages of exposure, even though large harmful levels may be in the brain, liver, kidneys and bones. Adequate blood levels of calcium and other essential minerals are maintained at normal levels in blood even during a raging deficiency state by drawing on ever deminishing body reserves from the bones, liver, kidneys, muscles and heart.

Hair analysis are performed on nonperishable samples of body tissue minerals and are a recording of the bodies mineral status over a period of several months - additionally hair concentration of trace minerals and Rare Earths are 200 times greater than those found in blood.

Detection of lead, arsenic, mercury and cadmium in hair samples are used as forensic evidence in every court in the land. Hair analysis was first used by forensic investigators to detect murder by chronic arsenic poisoning. It is well known that Napoleon's hair, which was analyzed in 1961, contained at least 100 times the normal average values for arsenic - two possibilities exist:

1) Napoleon was murdered by chronic arsenical poisoning over a long period of time.

2) Napoleon was impotent and was using arsenic as an aphrodesiac or to satisfy deep cravings (pica) like James Maybrick ("Jack the Ripper") - both uses of supplementary arsenic were common during their times.

SAMPLE COLLECTION:

Samples of hair should be taken from the first inch of hair from the nape of the neck to reduce the environmental effects on the mineral values of the hair (the excess length over one inch should be clipped off and discarded). In the event insufficient head hair is available, body, axillary or pubic hair may be used (identify the source of hair with the sample). The hair sample should be collected with a stainless steel scissors or a plastic scissors to prevent metal contamination from soft steel scissors. Sample size should be a heaping tablespoon, which should be placed in a new unused # 10 business sized envelope and sealed, the sample containing envelope is then placed in a mailing envelope.

Hair anaysis results and a computerized evaluation are available for $100. Hair samples and checks made to Dr. Joel Wallach should be mailed to :

Dr. Joel D. Wallach
P.O. Box 1222
Bonita, CA 91908

Please enclose your name, address, telephone number, age, sex and source of hair with the sample.

The hair sample is washed in a detergent and solvent to remove all surface contaminants. The cleaned hair is weighed and converted to a liquid by digestion in a strong acid. The liquified hair is analyzed in an atomic absorption spectrometer. Hair analysis and mineral evaluation can indicate and identify many nutritional deficiencies and give early risk warnings, but alone are usually insufficient for a diagnosis of disease. Hair analysis can identify toxic metal exposure and monitor progress towards recovery.

Haphazard collection and handling of the hair sample can affect the results. The laboratories washing methods of the samples vary resulting in varying results between labs. Tints, shampoos and bleaches affect the levels of calcium, magnesium, zinc, copper, selenium and many of the Rare Earths.

Results of hair analysis are reported in ppm or micrograms/ gram.

INTERPRETATION OF THE HAIR ANALYSIS:

Various patterns of mineral deficiencies and their associations with disease are well documented in the literature:

Schizophrenia - high Ca; low Iron; high Copper.
Sociopath/violent (Dr.Jykel/Mr. Hyde rages) - low in copper, zinc, sodium, chromium, vanadium and lithium.
Arthritis - (osteoporosis/ hyperparathyroidism) - high Lead, Calcium and Phosphorus; low Iron and Copper.
Anemia - low Iron, Copper, Selenium, Cobalt.
Diabetes (prediabetes/hypoglycemia) - low Chromium, Vanadium, sodium, potassium, manganese, Zinc.

If all of the mineral levels in the hair analysis are universally low it indicates maldigestion (hypochlorhydria - low stomach acid) and/or malabsorption (celiac disease - wheat gluten or cows milk albumen allergy).

In some cases "elevated" hair level values represent actual depletion or shedding of minerals from body stores, i.e.- elevated calcium and magnesium levels reveal very active osteoporosis and associated arthritis, periodontitis and prediliction for kidney stones.

Elevated hair levels of sodium, potassium and chloride indicate deficiencies of essential fatty acids, with resultant malfunctions of the skin glands which loose electrolytes instead of conserving them. These false "elevations" return to normal following the proper mineral and essential fatty acid supplementation.

The ratios of trace minerals and Rare Earths in hair are of interest in the interpretation of a hair analysis as they are good barometers of what is happening in specific organ systems or tissues (Table 11 - 2).

Table 11 - 2. Ideal Hair Mineral Ratios

Ratio	Ideal	Affected Systems
Zn/Cu	8:1	Cardiovascular, liver function female reproductive system
Zn/Mn	150:1	Musculoskeletal, collagen, cholesterol biosynthesis
Zn/Ca	3:1	Cardiovascular, osteodynamics, kidney function
Na/P	2:1	Adrenal function, general endocrine function
Ca/Mg	8:1	Cardiovascular, osteodynamics, dietary imbalances
Fe/Cu	2.5:1	Hematology, energy production, cellular respiration

TOXIC METAL ELIMINATION
BY MINERAL SUBSTITUTION:

It is very well known among nutritional chemists that minerals can neutralize or reverse the toxic effects of other minerals (i.e.- Se is a specific antidote for Hg poisoning, Ca for Pb, etc.) therefore, we are making available the results of an interesting clinical study carried out and published by Gary Price Todd, MD.

Lead is considered one of the more universally dangerous toxic minerals because of its wide distribution in nature as well as being a major feature and toxic waste of modern industry. The magnitude of the lead problem is illustrated by the statistic that more than 400,000 tons of industrial lead is pumped into the American bios annually resulting in the incidious poisoning of over 38 million Americans each year!!

For almost 75 years, tetraethyl lead was added to gasoline motor fuel during production to reduce the cost; drivers unwittingly distributed the lead in the form of an ultra-fine dust over the roads and thoroughfares of the world contaminating the fields and thus the crops we consumed. Until the mid-fifties, lead was widely used in the paint and pigment industry because of the broad range of brilliant colors that can be obtained with lead compounds.

Lead paint became and is still a serious potential problem to urban children, especially those living in older homes as the oxidized lead paint chips and dust are tempting to little children suffering from pica or mineral deficiency induced cravings. Another source of dietary lead comes in the beautiful ceramic glazes used in decorative pottery from third world countries mistakenly used for food containers. Lead from paint and fuel also gets into the soils of urban gardens.

Another source of lead in our food chain is the sealant materials used to close the seams in steel or tin canned foods. One study showed that canned tuna has nearly double the level of lead as fresh tuna.

Cadmium is widely distributed as a result of its use in the rubber and metal fabricating industries. Cadmium plating is used on many metals to prevent rust and cadmium is added to the rubber in automobile tires to enhance the quality of the rubber and as a result of this wide industrial use is rapidly becoming a major health challenge in America.

Tobacco contains 23 micrograms of cadmium per pack of cigarettes. The major portion of the cadmium in tobacco is volatilized when the tobacco is burned and is inhaled and the residue not absorbed is passed out in the exhaled smoke as a major feature of "second hand" smoke.

Cadmium interferes with the biological function of several metalloenzymes, especially those containing zinc (deficiency lowers the effectiveness of the human immune system as well as producing a wide variety of preventable birth defects in pregnant woman who smoke), copper (deficiency increases loss of elastic fibers. therefore smokers have more skin wrinkles and aneurysms), calcium (deficiency results in hypertension, osteoporosis and arthritis) and selenium (deficiency increases the individuals risk of cataracts, cancer and cardiomyopathy heart disease). Kidney damage, liver disease and treatment resistant glaucoma have been attributed to elevated tissue cadmium levels.

Mercury is widely distributed in nature and is used as a manufacturing inhancer as well as an antifungicidal agent to protect seed grain from molding in the ground;

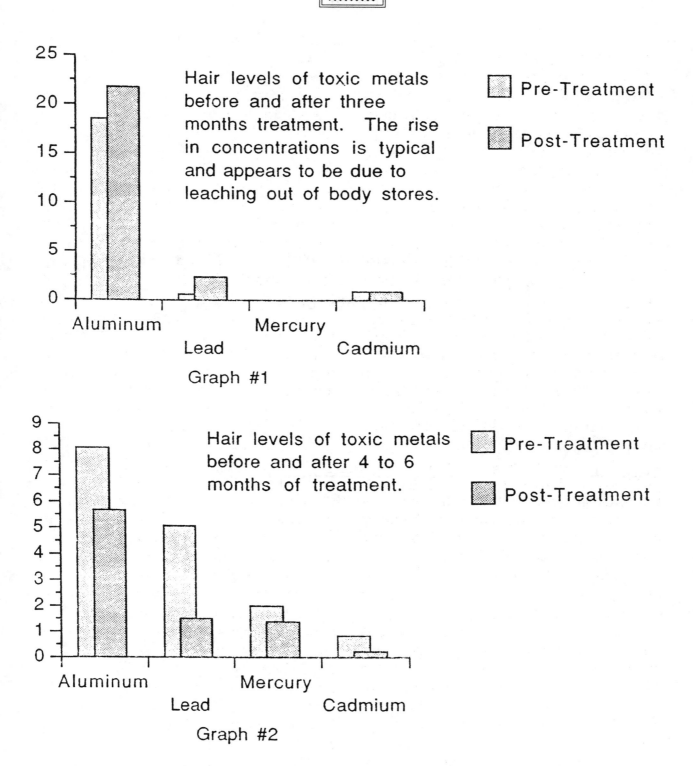

Graph #1: Hair levels of toxic metals before and after three months treatment. The rise in concentrations is typical and appears to be due to leaching out of body stores.

Graph #2: Hair levels of toxic metals before and after 4 to 6 months of treatment.

Table 11-4 Elevated toxic metals in subject hair at the beginning of Dr. Todd's study.

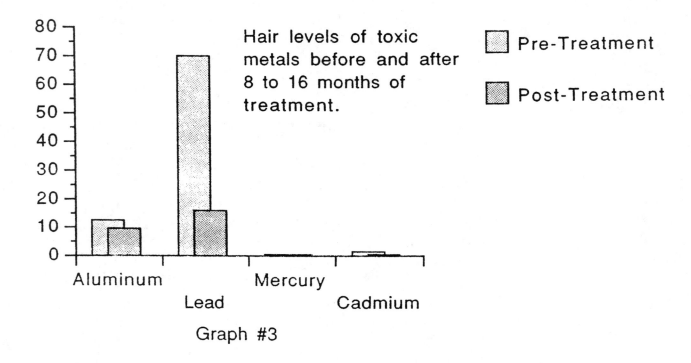

Hair levels of toxic metals before and after 8 to 16 months of treatment.

Pre-Treatment

Post-Treatment

Graph #3

Table 11-5 Reduced toxic metal levels in hair analysis from Dr. Todd's patients 8-16 months after the start of the study.

mercury is also in common use as a dental amalgam to fill in dental caries and as a result is a common toxic waste of a variety of dental, agricultural and industrial processes.

Although the American Dental Association argues that the mercury used in dental amalgams is permanently trapped in the fillings, the reality is that 50 % or more of the mercury in dental amalgams is slowly volatilized over a decade. The mercury of dental amalgams is sufficiently dangerous to prompt the EPA to class the left over scrapings from newly applied dental amalgams as a toxic waste and the ADA to warn dentists, "Handling amalgams requires extreme caution and a no touch technique should be employed." Mercury toxicity from dental amalgam is associated with the cause of multiple sclerosis (MS), Lou Gehrig's Disease (ALS) and Parkinson's Disease.

Dr. Todd took patients with elevated hair levels of lead, mercury or cadmium for his studies on mineral substitution. Blood tests were performed to determine blood levels of the toxic metals. The participating patients were given three ounces of liquid plant derived colloidal minerals daily and the hair analysis was repeated at three month intervals.

The results of Todd's study was very revealing. Initially, many participants of the study showed low levels of the toxic minerals in their hair. In fact, the three-month repeat hair analysis showed that in the majority of patients with measurable levels of lead, cadmium and mercury in their hair at the onset of the experiment there was an increase in hair levels of the toxic minerals (Table 11-3). Since the levels of toxic minerals are increased in the hair during the first few months, use of Todd's protocol may

be an effective method of unmasking latent (hidden) body stores of lead, cadmium or mercury.

In the subsequent three month hair analysis there was a significant drop in the hair levels of lead, cadmium and mercury. Todd translated his findings to mean that there is a mobilization of tissue stores of the toxic minerals by the plant derived colloidal minerals that resulted in the initial hair analysis increase at the three month test repeat. Repeated hair analysis at six to 16 months demonstrated that the rate and degree of toxic mineral reduction in the hair appears to be time and dose related (Table 11- 4).

THE PERIODIC TABLE OF: METALS, MINERALS, TRACE MINERALS & RARE EARTHS

Some 79 minerals have been detected in animal and human tissue (i.e.-blood, liver, muscle, brain,etc.(Table 11 - 5)) fullfilling part of the requirements for essentiality, numerous, literally thousands of animal studies on pregnant, suckling, weanling and mature laboratory mice , rats, rabbits, dogs, cats, pigs, sheep, cattle, chickens, turkeys, ducks, etc. have documented additional support for the essentiality of at least 60 minerals (i.e.- act as mineral cofactors for DNA, RNA or enzyme systems or vitamin utilization).

The periodic table (Table 11 - 6) represents the Earth's elements in an organized format that is the basis for the systematics of chemistry. Initially, the table listed the elements in order of increasing atomic weight (combined mass of protons, electrons and neutrons). The usefullness of the periodic table increased enormously in terms of it's predictive value when the ele-

Table 11-6

The Periodic Table

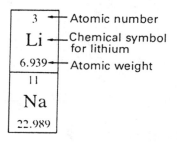

3	Atomic number
Li	Chemical symbol for lithium
6.939	Atomic weight
11	
Na	
22.989	

Periodic Table of the Elements

1 H 1.0																	2 He 4.0
3 Li 6.9	4 Be 9.0											5 B 10.8	6 C 12.0	7 N 14.0	8 O 16.0	9 F 19.0	10 Ne 20.2
11 Na 23.0	12 Mg 24.3											13 A1 27.0	14 Si 28.1	15 P 31.0	16 S 32.1	17 C1 35.5	18 Ar 39.9
19 K 39.1	20 Ca 40.1	21 Sc 45.0	22 Ti 47.9	23 V 50.9	24 Cr 52.0	25 Mn 54.9	26 Fe 55.8	27 Co 58.9	28 Ni 58.7	29 Cu 63.5	30 Zn 65.4	31 Ga 69.7	32 Ge 72.6	33 As 74.9	34 Se 79.0	35 Br 79.9	36 Kr 83.8
37 Rb 85.5	38 Sr 87.6	39 Y 88.9	40 Zr 91.2	41 Nb 92.9	42 Mo 95.9	43 Tc (97)	44 Ru 101.1	45 Rh 102.9	46 Pd 106.4	47 Ag 107.9	48 Cd 112.4	49 In 114.8	50 Sn 118.7	51 Sb 121.8	52 Te 127.6	53 I 126.9	54 Xe 131.3
55 Cs 132.9	56 Ba 137.3	see below 57-71	72 Hf 178.5	73 Ta 180.9	74 W 183.9	75 Re 186.2	76 Os 190.2	77 Ir 192.2	78 Pt 195.1	79 Au 197.0	80 Hg 200.6	81 Tl 204.4	82 Pb 207.2	83 Bi 209.0	84 Po 210	85 At (210)	86 Rn (222)
87 Fr (223)	88 Ra (226)	see below 89-103															

57 La 138.9	58 Ce 140.1	59 Pr 140.9	60 Nd 144.2	61 Pm (145)	62 Sm 150.4	63 Eu 152.0	64 Gd 157.3	65 Tb 158.9	66 Dy 162.5	67 Ho 164.9	68 Er 167.3	69 Tm 168.9	70 Yb 173.0	71 Lu 175.0

89 Ac (227)	90 Th 232.0	91 Pa (231)	92 U 238.0	93 Np (237)	94 Pu (244)	95 Am (243)	96 Cm (247)	97 Bk (247)	98 Cf (251)	99 Es (254)	100 Fm (257)	101 Md (256)	102 No (254)	103 Lw (257)

ments were reorganized according to atomic number (number of protons in the nucleus and the number of electrons that an atom of the element contains).

Minerals associated with human physiology (positive and negative) and disease (deficiency and toxicity) are presented in alphabetical order by chemical symbol for convenient access.

Ac - Actinium originates from igneous rocks; usually found at an extremely low concentration of 5.5 x 10⁻¹⁶ ppm. Actinium is readily absorbed by plant roots; however, very little is transported to the stem, leaves and shoots of the plant. Actinium accumulates and presumably has metabolic functions in the bones and liver.

Ag - Silver originates from igneous rocks and sedimentary rocks and is found at the rate of 0.07ppm in rocks and in soils at the rate of 0.1ppm; fresh water at 0.00013 ppm; sea water at 0.0003 ppm; marine algae at 0.25 ppm; land plants from 0.06 ppm to 1.4 ppm in accumulator plants growing near silver ore. *Epiogonum ovalifolium* is a silver indicator plant. Silver is found at 3.0 to 11.0 ppm in marine animals; in land mammals generally 0.05 to 0.7 ppm; muscle at 0.16 to 0.8 PPM and tortoise shell at 0.05 to 0.7ppm.

Silver has been employed in human health care and in the search for immortality since the days of the Chinese alchemist 8,000 years ago. Many feel that silver is in fact an essential element, not because it is required for an enzyme system, but rather as a systemic disinfectant and immune system support.

Sir Malcom Morris reported in the British Medical Journal (May 12,1917) that

colloidal silver is "free from the drawbacks of other preperations of silver, viz-pain caused and discoloration of the skin; indeed, instead of producing irritation it has a distinctly soothing effect. It rapidly subdues inflammation and promotes healing of the lesions, it can be used with remarkable results in enlarged prostate with irritation of the bladder, in pruritis ani and perineal eczema, and in haemorrhoids."

J.Mark Hovell reported in the British Medical Journal (December 15, 1917) that, "colloidal silver has been found to be beneficial for permanently restoring the patency of the eustachian tubes and for reducing nasopharyngeal catarrh. Colloidal silver has also been used sucessfully in septic conditions of the mouth (including pyorrhea alveolysis - Rigg's disease), throat (including tonsilitis and quincies), ear (including Menier's symptoms and closure to Valsalva's inflation), and in generalized septicemia, leucorrhea, cystitis, whooping-cough and shingles."

Taken internally, the particles of colloidal silver are resistant to the action of dilute acids and alkalies of the stomach and intestine, and consequently continue their catalytic action and pass into the intestine unchanged.

T.H. Anderson Wells reported in Lancet (February 16, 1918) that a preperation of colloidal silver was "used intraveinously in a case of peurpural septicemia without any irritation of the kidneys and with no pigmentation of the skin."

Silver sulfadiazine (Silvadene, Marion Laboratories) is used in 70 percent of the burn centers in America; discovered by Dr. Charles Fox, Columbia, University , sulfadiazine has been used successfully to treat syphilis, cholera and malaria; it also stops the herpes virus responsible for "cold sores" and "fever blisters."

Silver is an anti-bacterial, anti-viral, anti-fungal anti-metabolite that disables specific enzymes that micro-organisms use for respiration. Silver is such an efficient anti-bacteriacidal that our "Great-grand mothers put silver dollars in fresh milk to keep it from spoiling at room temperature."

Humans can consume 400 mg of silver per day. A silver "deficiency" results in an impaired immune system. In, The Body Electric, Dr. Robert Becker identified a relationship between low levels of tissue and dietary silver and the rate of illness (i.e.- flu, colds,etc.); he stated, "silver deficiency was responsible for the improper functioning of the immune system, and silver does more than just kill disease causing organisms; it was also causing major growth stimulation (another criteria for essentiality) of injured tissue." Human fibroblast cells were able to multiply at a great rate, producing large numbers of primitive, embryonic cells in wounds that are able to differentiate into whatever cell types that are necessary to heal the wound.

Dr. Bjorn Nordstrom, of the Karolinska Institute, Sweden, has used silver in his alternative cancer therapy programs.

According to Science Digest (Silver: Our Mightiest Germ Fighter. March,1978) silver is an antibiotic, silver kills over 650 disease causing organisms; resistant strains fail to develop; silver is absolutely non-toxic to humans at standard rates of consumption.

Al - Aluminum is found in igneous rocks at 5,000 ppm, shales at 82,000 ppm, sandstone at 25,000ppm, limestone at 4,200ppm and clay at 71,000 ppm. Aluminum represents 12% of the Earths crust(most common metal in the Earth's crust) and is found in high concentrations in all plants grown in the soil (Table 11 -7) including food crops. Acid soils yield highest amounts of soil aluminum to plants. It is found in marine plants at 60 ppm and is especially high in plankton and red algae; land plants at (0.5 to 4,000 ppm) an average of 500 ppm; marine mammals at19 to 50 ppm and is found in the highest levels in the hair and lungs. Known biological function is to activate the enzyme succinic dehydrogenase, increases survival rate of newborn and according to professor Gerhardt Schrauzer, head of the department of chemistry at UCSD, is probably an essential mineral for human nutrition.

European chemists realized a lightweight metal was associated with clay in the early 1700's. A particularly rich aluminum clay was found in Las Baux, France - giving aluminum rich clay (Bauxite) its name.

Aluminum does not appear as a free metal in nature, but is found only in tight combination with oxygen forming a hard oxide known as alumina. When contaminated with traces of other elements alumina becomes a gem such as rubies or sapphires (used in Ayruvedic medicine).

Sir Humphrey Davy, a prominent English chemist of the 16th century named the "metal of clay" aluminum.

The Danish physicist, Hans Christian Oerstad (1825) "discovered" electromagnetics and first isolated aluminum by treating alumina containing clay with carbon, chlorine amalgam of potassium to get a mixture of volital mercury and aluminum; he boiled the mercury away as a vapor which left a powdery metal that "in color and luster somewhat resembles tin."

Napoleon III, realizing the potential military value of aluminum, personally sponsored aluminum smelting research and although production costs fell, aluminum remained a semiprecious metal.

In 1884, an American metallurgist produced a pyramid of pure aluminum to fit the top of the 555 foot Washington Monument in Washington, DC. The pyramid at 100 ounces was the largest lump of aluminum ever produced; before the monuments crowning ceremony, the aluminum pyramid was displayed at Tiffany's in New York City to the amazement of viewers (at that time aluminum was more valuable than silver and they used eight platinum lightening rods to protect it).

In the College of Oberlin, Ohio Charles Hall, a minister's son used a cast iron skillet, a gasoline stove and a crude homemade crucible to smelt aluminum. Hall used an electrolysis process to isolate aluminum; this technique had not been successfully employed by Sir Humphrey Davy 80 years earlier, however, Hall added a step to the procedure.

Prior to sending the electricity through the Bauxite clay, Hall dissolved the alumina in a molten superheated cryolite solvent. Then in February 23, 1886 at the age of 22 Hall pulsed battery electricity through the molten mixture - when the mix cooled, he broke open the mass with a hammer to find " a clutch of silvery pellets."

A similar process was discovered in Gentilly, France by 22 year old Paul L. T. Heroult. Almost all of today's metallic aluminum is produced by the Hall-Heroult smelting process: Hall's young company (Alcoa) was the first company to use the hydroelectricity generated by Niagara Falls in 1895.

Kaolin, another fine particle clay used medicinally to control diarrhea (kaopectate) is a clay with a high alumina content (35 %!!!). Alunite and anorthosite are aluminum containing rocks that are found in Wyoming, Utah and other western states. Laterite, a low yield bauxite has been discovered in large quantities in Oregon, Washington and Hawaii. Metallic aluminum is also found in oil shale and fly ash from coal furnaces (the metallic aluminum from these industrial pollutants contaminate our air, water and food supply).

Aluminum makes up 12 % of Earth's crust and is therefore the Earth's most abundant metallic element. Aluminum is found in large biological quantities in every plant

Table 11- 7. Organic Colloidal Aluminum in Food Crops.

Food	Aluminum in ppm
Asparagus	20 - 200
Beans	20 - 250
Brussel sprouts	20 - 150
Celery	20 - 300
Cucumbers	20 - 200
Cabbage/lettuce	20 - 200
Spinach/mustard greens	50 - 150
Melons	20 - 150
Peas	10 - 80
Peppers	50 - 200
Potatoes	50 - 250
Turnips/carrots	20 - 300
Tomatoes	20 - 200
Alfalfa	40 - 300
Canola	90 - 150
Corn	20 - 300
Wheat	20 - 300
Soybeans	50 - 200
Mint	20 - 300
Peanut	50 - 200
Sunflower seeds	50 - 100

grown in soil (Table 11- 7), animal and human. You can't eat any grain, vegetable, fruit or nut or drink any natural water source or juice without taking in large quantities of aluminum!!!

The aluminum found in plants is organically bound colloidal aluminum and appears not to have any negative affect and in fact appears to be an essential element in human nutrition.

Many studies have linked chronic exposure to metallic aluminum to Alzheimer's Disease, a relatively new disease that results in a loss of reasoning, memory and speach. Alzheimer's Disease strikes 4 million Americans annually and is the fourth leading cause of death in adults after cancer, heart disease and stroke.

In a study that appeared November 5, 1992 in the science journal, Nature, Frank Watt, et al (University of Oxford) used a highly accurate laboratory techniques to quantify the levels of aluminum in the brains of Alzheimer's patients. To their great surprise, they found the same levels of aluminum in the brains of the non-Alzheimer's controls as they did in their Alzheimer's patients!!! Watts believes that aluminum contaminated stains gave faulty results in the early studies that high lighted aluminum. A 1994 study "implicated" zinc as a causitive factor in the genesis of Alzheimer's disease (if you believe this one, we have some ocean-front property in Montana to sell you.

A July 1992 study released by UCSD stated that vitamin E would relieve memory loss in Alzheimer's patients - this result is not too surprising in light of the history of "star-gazing" in poultry, where encephalomalacia or brain wasting (Alzheimer's Disease) was prevented and in the early stages cured by high doses of vitamin E and selenium.

A study reported in the Medical Journal of Australia, that it was a fact that drinks in aluminum cans contained more aluminum than water from the local water supply. In 106 aluminum cans and bottles representing 52 different beverages, all had higher aluminum content than the local water supply which was 1.8 umol/L. Non cola softdrinks averaged 33.4 umol/L from cans and 5.6 umol/L from bottles (Table 11-); cola drinks averaged 24.0 umol/L from aluminum cans and 8.9 umol/L from bottles; beer in cans and bottles averaged 6.0 umol/ L thus adding another source of metallic aluminum to the human food chain.

Am - All isotopes of Americum are radioactive and have a 7,950 year half life. Americum accumulates in mammalian bone.

Ar - Argon is found in Igneous rocks at 3.0 to 5.0 ppm and can be used to date

Table 11- 8. Metallic Aluminum Contamination of Drinks in pbb.			
EPA Limit	Norfolk, Va Water supply	Blue Sky Natural Soda	Coca Cola Classic
50	40 - 70	620	6,160

ancient rocks using the potassium/argon dating system; fresh water and sea water at 0.06 ppm and mammalian blood at 0.75 ppm.

As - Arsenic is found in igneous rock at 1.0 to 8.0 ppm; shale at 13.0 ppm; sandstone and limestone at 1.0 ppm; fresh water at 0.0004 ppm; sea water at 0.003ppm; soils at 6.0 ppm (Argentina and New Zealand have toxic high arsenic soils in some regions); marine plants 30.0ppm; land plants 0.2 ppm; marine animals 0.005 to 0.3ppm (accumulated by coelenterates, mollusca and crustaceans; land animals < 0.2 ppm (concentrates in hair and nails); essential for survivability of newborn and neonatal growth.

Arsenic metabolism is affected by tissue and blood levels of zinc, selenium, arginine, choline, methionine, taurine and guaniacetic acid, all of which affect methyl-group metabolism and polyamine synthesis which is the site of arsenic function in human physiology.

Arsenic promotes the growth rate of chicks at 90 to 120 ppm. The rate of growth and metamorphosis of tadpoles is enhanced by the presence of arsenic.

Arsenic was first identified in dead human bodies in 1834 by the French Academy. Arsenic normally appears in female human blood at 0.64 ppm, it rises to 0.93 ppm during menstruation and 2.20 ppm during months five and six of pregnancy.

All marine life is richer in tissue arsenic levels than in terrestrial animals:

Sea Fish (vertebrates)
0.1 to 3.0 ug/Kg
Prawns and clams
3.0 to 174 ug/Kg

Shrimp (October)
152 to 172 ug/Kg
Shrimp(May/June)
21 to 51 ug/Kg

Eighteen percent of dietary As_2O_3 was stored in rat liver whereas only 0.7 percent of shrimp tissue arsenic was stored in rat livers (65 times greater toxicity potential from metalic arsenic than from organically bound arsenic).

Arsenic in combination with choline prevents 100 percent of perosis ("slipped tendon") in chickens and poultry. Perosis in birds results in a "carpal tunnel," "TMJ" and "repetitive motion" type degeneration (Fig. 11 - 1).

At - All isotopes of Astatine are radioactive; they have an extremely short half life of 7.2 to 8 hours. It is accumulated by the mammalian and human thyroid after ingestion but is rapidly excreted.

Au - Gold is found in igneous and sedimentary rocks at 0.004 ppm; fresh water at 0.00006 ppm; sea water at 0.000011 ppm; marine plants at 0.012 ppm; land plants 0.0005 to 0.002 ppm (gold concentrates in the horse tail plant); marine animals 0.0003 to 0.008 ppm; land animals 0.00023 ppm and in mammalian liver forms a colloid.

Gold compounds (gold sodium thiomalate, gold thioglucose also known as aurothioglucose) are frequently given by allopathic physicians as an add on therapy with salicylates (aspirin) for arthritis when added pain relief is required. Gold has been reported only to be effective against active joint inflammation and is not usually helpful for advanced destructive rheumatoid

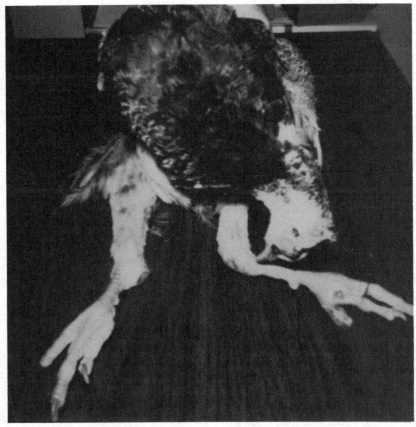

Fig. 11-1 "Perosis" or "slipped-tendon" in a young peafowl. Note unusual angle of left leg resulting from an arsenic, manganese and or choline deficiency.

arthritis.

Gold is not analgesic but may have anti-inflammatory effects. Standard doses are given IM at weekly intervals: 10 mg initially, 25 mg second week and 50 mg per week until a total of 1 G has been administered then the maintenance dose is reduced to 50 mg every two to four weeks. Relapse is expected three to four months after withdrawl of the gold treatments.

Gold compounds are not to be used in patients with liver or kidney disease, blood diseases or SLE.

Toxic reactions to gold therapies include pruritus (itching), dermatitis, stomatitis, GI discomfort, increase in urine albumin, blood in the urine, aplastic anemia, reduced WBC, hepatitis and pneumonitis.

B - Boron is found in igneous rocks at 10 ppm; shale 100 ppm; sandstones at 35 ppm; limestone at 20 ppm; fresh water at 0.013 ppm; sea water at 4.0 to 6.0 ppm; soil 2.0 to 100 ppm (highest in saline and alkaline soils); in California certain deserts have toxic levels; marine plants 120 ppm (highest in brown algae); land plants at 50 ppm; Chenopodiaceae and Plumboginaceae are indicator plant families; marine animals at 20 to 50 ppm; land animals 0.5 ppm; boron is essential for bone metabolism including efficient use of calcium and magnesium and proper function of endocrine glands (i.e.- ovaries, testes and adrenals).

Pure boron is hard and grey and melts at over 4,000 degrees F. Boron, a non metallic mineral, occurs as a combination in nature, i.e.- borax, boric acid (sassolite), ulexite, colemanite, boracite and tourmaline.

Large deposits of borax or "diamond boron" were discovered in Death Valley in 1881. The Death Valley deposits were made famous by the 20 mule team wagons that hauled out the mined borax. The rear wheels were 7 foot high, each wagon bed was 16 foot long and could carry 24,000 pounds (12 tons) of borax. Each 20 mule team pulled two wagons plus a 1,200 gallon water wagon (36.5 tons in each load!!), the total length of the team and equipment was 120 foot long. The rail head in Mojave was 165 miles from the Death Valley mine site.

Prior to 1981, boron was not considered an essential nutrient; boron was first shown to be an essential mineral for growing chicks. It was not until 1990 that boron was accepted as an essential nutrient for humans.

Boron is required for the maintenance of bone and normal blood levels of estrogen and testosterone; within eight days of supplementing boron women lost 40 percent less calcium , 33 percent less magnesium and less phosphorus through their urine.

Women getting boron supplementation had blood levels of estradiol 17B doubled to "levels found in women on estrogen replacement therapy," the levels of testosterone almost doubles.

Ba - Barium is found in igneous rocks at 425 ppm; shales at 580 ppm; sandstone at 50 ppm; limestone at 120 ppm; fresh water at 0.054 ppm; sea water at 0.03 ppm; soil at 500 ppm (can be "fixed" or tightly bound by clay minerals); marine plants at 30 ppm (highest in brown algae); land plants 14 ppm (the fruit of *Bertholletia excelea* can have up to 4,000 ppm) marine animals 0.2 to 3.0 ppm (highest in hard tissues such as bone and shell); land animals 0.0 to 75 ppm (highest in bone, lung and eyes) - thought to be essential to mammals (Rygh,O. : Bull Soc Chem Biol.31. 1052 & 1403.1949).

Be - Beryllium is found in igneous rocks at 2 to 8 ppm; shale at 3 ppm; sandstone and limestone < 1.0 ppm; fresh water 0.001 ppm; sea water at 0.0000006 ppm; soil at 0.1 to 40 ppm; marine plants at 0.001ppm (highest in brown algae); land plants at < 0.1 ppm (highest in volcanic soils); land animals at 0.0003 to 0.002 ppm in soft tissue.

Bi - Bismuth is found in igneous rocks at 0.17 ppm; shale at 1.0ppm; sea water at 0.000017 ppm; land plants at 0.06 ppm; marine animals at 0.09 to 0.3 ppm; land animals at 0.004 ppm.

Stress has historically been blamed as the boogy-man causing stomach and peptic ulcers of the stomach and duodenum. Human studies have in fact demonstrated that the true cause of peptic ulcers is a gastric infection with a bacterium known as *Helicobacter pylori*.

Australian gastroenterologist Barry Marshall, M.D. and pathologist J. Robbin Warren proposed their theory for the bacterial cause of peptic ulcers in 1983 (the bacterial cause of gastric ulcers in pigs was known in 1952).

Marshall, now on the staff of Virginia Health Sciences Center in Charlottesville, said, "we were going against medical dogma."

During a study of recurrent duodenal ulcers by eight Australian researchers, our group of patients received antibiotics, the others a placebo for 12 days. For six to ten weeks both groups received the standard Zantac, one of the commonly prescribed drugs used to block the production of stomach acid.

After six weeks the ulcers of 92 percent of the patients on antibiotics had healed, whereas only 75 percent of the placebo group had healed. One year later only four of the 50 people treated with antibiotics had a recurrence of their ulcers, whereas 42 of the 49 given the placebo had a return of their ulcers.

A study by Dr. David Graham, Chief of Digestive Diseases at the Veterans Administration Medical Center, Houston confirmed that *H. pylori* is the cause of most gastric and duodenal peptic ulcers -"the proof is there," according to Graham.

The treatment of choice for ulcers is ten days to four weeks on tetracycline antibiotics, anti-ulcer medication and bismuth subsalicylate - (the active ingrediant in Pepto Bismol).

Br - Bromine is a "halogen" related to iodine and is found in igneous rocks at 3.0 to 5.0 ppm; shale at 4.0 ppm; sandstone 1.0ppm; limestone 0.2 ppm; fresh water 0.2 ppm; sea water 65 ppm; soil 5 ppm; marine plants 740 ppm (highest in brown algae); land plants 15 ppm; marine animals 60 to 1000 ppm; land animals 6.0 ppm; functions by brominated amino acids, strong evidence for essentiality for mammals.

C - Carbon is found in igneous rocks at 200 ppm; shales at 15,300 ppm; sandstones at 13,800 ppm; limestones at 113,500 ppm; fresh water at11ppm; sea water at 28 ppm; soils at 20,000 ppm; (up to 90 % of carbon in soil is bound in the hu-

VIA SATELLITE

USA TODAY

Life

THURSDAY, FEBRUARY 10, 1994

ULCER CAUSE: The National Institutes of Health has confirmed that peptic ulcers can be caused by a bacterium and drug therapy can prevent a recurrence in 90% of cases. An NIH panel stated Wednesday that *Helicobacter pylori* plays a significant role in causing peptic ulcer, which can be cured with a combination of bismuth, tetracycline and metronidazole. The panel also said that *H. pylori* is linked to gastric cancer but found no data to show preventing or treating infection reduces the cancer risk.

mus); marine plants at 345,000 ppm; land plants at 454,000 ppm; marine animals at 400,000 ppm; land animals 465,000 ppm (280,000 ppm in bone).

Carbon functions as an essential structural atom for all organic molecules(i.e.-carbohydrates, fats, amino acids, enzymes, vitamins, etc.) including stored, transported and functioning organic colloidal minerals.

Carbohydrates normally furnish most of the energy required to move, perform work and for the basic biochemical functions of life itself. The chief sources of carbohydrates include grains, vegetables, fruits and sugars. In their simplest form the formula for carbohydrates is CH_2O - the hydrogen and oxygen being present in the same ratio that is found in water H_2O and there is one carbon for each molecule of water.

Plants are able to manufacture carbohydrates (sugar and starch), vitamins, amino acids and fatty acids. The plant leaves take CO_2 from the air and in the presence of chlorophyll (Mg carbon ring structure) and with the energy from sunlight (process known as photosynthesis) manufacture carbohydrate and release O_2 as a by product of the reaction.

Carbohydrates are classified as monosaccharides (glucose or "grape sugar", fructose), disaccharides (sucrose = glucose and fructode; maltose = glucose and glucose; lactose = glucose and galactose) , oligosaccharides and polysaccharides (starch, dextrin, fiber, cellulose and glycogen or "animal starch" are all complexes of glucose units).

Lipids or fats like carbohydrates are composed of carbon, hydrogen and oxygen. Fats have the common property of being insoluble in water, soluble in organic solvents such as ether and chloroform and utilizable as energy by living organisms. Fats as a group of carbon compounds includes ordinary fats, oils, waxes and related compounds. The primary food sources of lipids are butter, flax seed oil, olive oil, animal fat (i.e - pork, chicken, fish, beef, lamb, etc.), nuts, seeds, whole grains, olives, avocados, egg yolks, dairy products, etc. Fats serve as a source of energy (9 calories per gram compared with 4.5 calories per gram for carbohydrates) both immediate and stored (body fat).

Triglycerides (the primary componant of fats and oils) are composed of carbon, hydrogen and oxygen. Structurally, they are esters of a trihydric alcohol (glycerol) and fatty acids. The fatty acids can have from four to 30 carbon atoms and constitute the bulk of the triglyceride mass. One hundred grams of fat or oil will contain 95 grams of fatty acids.

A fatty acid or hydrocarbon chain is described with regard to three characteristics: chain length, degree of "saturation" with hydrogen and location of the first "double bond." The length is a reference to the number of carbon atoms in the chain (i.e.- C_{16} has 16 carbons in the chain). The term "short" (less than 6 carbons), "medium" (7 to 11 carbons) and "long" (12 or more carbons) are used to describe the chains of fatty acids in the structure of triglycerides.

The degree of hydrogen "saturation" in fatty acids is defined by the number of double bonds between carbon atoms in the fatty acid chains. A chain can contain all the hydrogen it can hold and have no double bonds, in which case it is referred to as a saturated fatty acid. It can contain one double bond (monounsaturated fatty acid) or it may contain several double bonds (polyunsaturated fatty acids).

The locations of the first double bond as counted from the "tail" or methyl end of the fatty acid is referred to as the "omega" number (i.e.- omega 3, omega 6, etc.).

Three polyunsaturated fatty acids (linoleic, linolenic and arachidonic acids) are known as essential fatty acids (EFA). However, only two (linoleic and linolenic) are designated as EFA as arachidonic acid can be synthesized by the human from lenoleic acid. EFA have essential roles in fat transport and metabolism, and in maintaining the function and integrity of cell walls (bi-lipid layer membranes). They are also part of the fatty acids of cholesterol esters and phospholipids in plasma lipoproteins and mitochondrial lipoproteins. Serum cholesterol can be lowered by the consumption of EFA. (Fig. 11-2)

EFA are also the raw material for the human body to manufacture prostaglandins that help regulate blood pressure, heart rate, vascular dilation, blood clotting, bronchial dilation, and central nervous system (brain and spinal cord) function.

EFA deficiency in human infants results in a poor growth rate, eczema, lowered resistance to infectious diseases.

Cholesterol is a member of a large group of fats known as sterols. They all have a complex carbon ring structure. Cholesterol is only found in animal tissue, but similar sterols are found in plants. Cholesterol is an essential part of the structure of cell walls, brain and spinal cord, and is the raw material for the human body to manufacture vitamin D, bile acids, adrenocortical hormones, estrogens (a cholesterol deficiency makes going through menapause a living hell so eat two eggs every morning to slip through menopause almost symptom free), progesterone and testosterone (a cholesterol deficiency turns hubby into a TV watching steer who is totally disinterested in sex).

Ergosterol, a yeast sterol, is converted to vitamin D_2 on exposure to sunlight or ultrviolet light. Beta-sitosterol, another plant sterol, is usually absorbed in small amounts by during high levels of consumption will actually raise the blood cholesterol level.

Proteins are the fundamental structural components of the living cell (cytoplasm), they are essential parts of the cell nucleus and protoplasm. Proteins are the most abundant of all of the carbon containing organic compounds in the human body. The greatest mass of body protein is found in the skeletal muscle, the remainder is found in other organs (liver, kidney, stomach, etc.), bones, teeth, blood and other body fluids (lymph). Hormones and enzymes are proteins that do work.

Proteins like carbohydrates and fats contain carbon, hydrogen and oxygen , and in addition they also contain 16 % nitrogen (the amine group) sometimes along with sulfur and other elements such as phosphorus, iron, sulfur and cobalt. The basic structural unit of a protein is the amino acid, they are united by peptide bonds into long chains of various geometric structures to form specific proteins. Digestion of proteins breaks the peptide bonds to release individual amino acids. Use of protein for energy provides 4.5 calories per gram.

Classically there are nine essential amino acids that are required in the daily diet as they can't be manufactured by the human body. Forty three percent of protein for infants must be the essential amino acids, 36 % for the growing child and only 19 % essential amino acids are required for adult maintenance (to this classic list of essential amino acids we would add three

Fig. 11-2

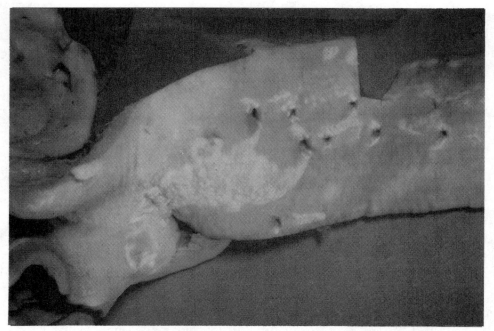

A) Athrosclerosis (cholesterol) in the aorta of a sheep with essential fatty acid deficiencies.

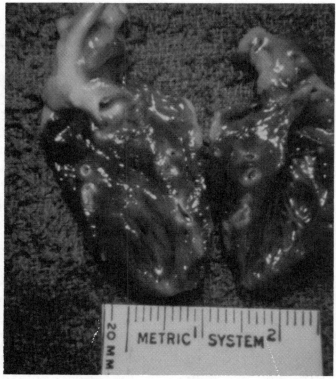

B) Athrosclerosis in the coronary arteries of a pheasant with essential fatty acid deficiencies.

additional essential amino acids as over the long haul they prevent certain diseases from cancer {arginine}, macular degeneration {taurine} to goiter (tyrosine}).

The classic essential amino acids are:

Amino acid   Function
Valine -
lysine
threonine
leucine
isoleucine
tryptophan ....precursor of the vitamin
                        B$_3$ or niacin and serotonin.
phenylalanine ....precursor for thyroxin
                        and epinephrine.
methionine - .... involved in the formation
                of choline and creatine phosphate.
histidine - ..... required for formation of histamine.

An individual consuming protein at even 300 gm per day (almost 3/4 of a pound of meat a day) have no adverse effects as long as they do not have kidney or liver disease.

Vitamins are a major carbon group of unrelated organic carbon compounds needed by the human body in minute quantities each day - they are essential for specific metabolic reactions of the cell and are required for normal growth, developement, maintenance, health, longevity and life itself. Vitamins work as coenzymes or activating side groups for essential subcellular enzyme systems. Vitamins regulate metabolism, facilitate the conversion of fat and carbohydrate to energy and are required for the formation and repair of tissues in embryos, childrin, teens, adults and seniors.

Many of the solutions to preventing birth defects (Fig. 11-3), reduced effectiveness during our daily lives, debilitating de-generative diseases and fatal diseases are simply to ensure an optimal intake of the essential vitamins (Table 11- 9).

Ca - Calcium is found in igneous rocks at 41,500 ppm; shales at 22,100 ppm; sandstone at 39,100ppm; limestone at 302,000 ppm; fresh water at 15 ppm; sea water at 400ppm; soils at 7,000 to 500,000ppm (lowest in acid soils and highest in limestone or alkaline soils); marine plants 10,000 to at 300,000 ppm (highest in calcareous tissues - red, blue-green and green algae and diatoms); land plants 18,000 ppm; marine animals 1,500 to 20,000 ppm; 350,000 ppm in calcarious tissue(sponges, coral, molluscs, echinoderms); land animals at 200 to 85,000 ppm; 260,000 ppm in mammalian bone, 200 to 500 ppm in soft tissue and < 5 ppm in RBC. Functions include essentiality for all organisms; cell walls of plants; all calcareous tissues and mammalian bones; electrochemical functions in cells and activates several enzymes.

Calcium is the fifth most abundant mineral element in the crust of the Earth and the biosphere and is essential to all Earth life forms. There is evidence that clearly shows humans are designed to consume and use high calcium diets. The late Paleolithic Period of 35,000 to 10,000 years ago was the most recent time that our human forebearers lived in the bios for which they had been biochemically designed. The agricultural revolution occured 10,000 years ago and it reduced the wide variety of wild foods in the human food chain and increased food energy. These changes universally and forever decreased man's dietary intake of minerals, trace minerals and Rare Earths.

The uncultivated food plants and wild

Fig. 11-3

A)Hydroencephlocoel in a newly hatched duckiling from folic acid deficient eggs.

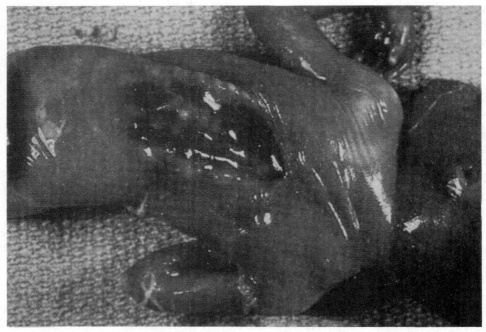

B) Human embryo with spinal bifida resulting from folic acid or zinc deficiency.

Table 11- 9. Vitamins and the common result of their deficiencies.

Vitamin	Deficiency Disease
FAT SOLUBLE	
A (Retinol) - 1913	Night blindness (Nyctalopia), conjunctivitis, xerophthalmia, keratomalacia (corneal ulcers), infertility, birth defects, depressed immune system, bone disease, poor growth, acne, dermatitis, hyperkeratosis ("goose flesh"), ichthyosis, increased cancer risk.
D -	Rickets, rachitic rosary, bow-legs, knock-knees, osteomalacia, osteoporosis, arthritis, pigeon chest, profuse sweating, restless leg syndrome, enlarged wrists, delayed or poor tooth development.
E (Tocopherol) - 1922	Infertility, lowered immune system, age spots (liver spots, lipid peroxidation, free radicals), ischemic heart disease, fibrocystic breast disease, muscle weakness, myalgia, muscular dystrophy, anemia (hemolysis), increased risk of cancer, Alzheimer's syndrome.
K (Menaquinone) - 1939	Extended clotting time, hemorrhage, osteoporosis (osteocalcin deficiency).
WATER SOLUBLE	
B$_1$(Thiamine) - 1897, 1911	Congestive heart failure (Beriberi), loss of memory (Wernicke-Korsakoff syndrome), mental confusion, depression, lethargy, muscular weakness, paralysis, emotional instability, loss of appetite.
B$_2$ (Riboflavin) - 1879,1932 . . .	Soreness and burning of lips,mouth and tongue, erosions and swelling of tongue ("geographic" tongue), magenta tongue, photophobia, lacrimation (tearing), chelosis, angular stomatitis, seborrheic dermatitis of the nasal folds, capillary "injection" of cornea, anemia, neuropathy.
B$_3$ (Niacin) -1900	Pellagra (dermatitis, diarrhea, dementia and retardatiion), muscular weakness, anorexia, sore "beef tongue," darkened skin pigmentation, scaly dermatitis.
B$_5$ (Pantothenic acid) - 1940 . .	Dermatitis, burning of feet, loss of appetite, quarrelsome, sullen, depressed, tachycardia, fainting, indigestion.
B$_6$ (Pyridoxine)	Depression, nausea, vomiting, seborrheic dermatitis, mucus membrane lesions and peripheral neuritis, ataxia (instability), hyperirritability, head tic (Tourette's syndrome), convulsions.
B$_{12}$ (Cobalamin, see Co) - 1948	Spinal cord demyelination, progressive neuropathy, pernicious anemia.

Table 11- 9. Vitamins and the common result of their deficiencies. (continued)

Vitamin	Deficiency Disease
Folic acid (Folacin) -1946	Anemia, poor growth , birth defects (spina bifida).
Biotin - 1936	Eczema, alopecia (baldness), depression, hyperesthesia, paraesthesia, blepharitis, gray or white hair.
Vitamin C (Ascorbic acid)	Scurvy, bleeing gums, anemia, poor appetite, poor growth, high risk for infection, high risk for cancer, loosened teeth, skin hemorrhages, swollen wrist and ankle joints, rib/cartilage fractures.
Choline	Fatty liver, kidney hemorrhage, Alzheimer's disease, tardive dyskinesia, Huntington's disease (treatment requires 20 G per day).
Inositol	Fat metabolism problems
Bioflavonoids -1936	capillary hemorrhage, reduced immune function.

game commonly available to Stone Age humans would supply 1600 mg at basal energy intakes and between 2,000 and 3,000 mg of calcium at the energy levels required to support hunting and work.

During the 20th century, American adults have a calcium intake of only one-fifth to one-third as much as did Stone Age humans. The National Health & Nutrition Examination Survey II reported a median calcium intake for American women of between 300 and 508 mg per day and only 680 mg for men.

Other nutrients that are rich in the American diet aggravate the national calcium deficiency. Diets rich in salt and protein (phosphates) result in an increased calcium "cost", that in effect, increases the requirements for calcium. Urinary calcium increased from 96 mg per day to 148 mg per day when food was heavily salted. As protein (phosphate) intake is doubled the output in urinary calcium increases 50 %.

There are no less than 147 deficiency diseases that can be attributed to calcium deficiency or imbalances. The most recent clinical research clearly points out that the entire scope of American diets are critically deficient in calcium and that the only practical way to get enough calcium is through supplementation (the allopaths doing the study failed again by recommending five cups of brocolli a day as a valuble sourch of calcium - try to get a kid or president to eat that!).

The more common calcium deficiency diseases (Table 11-10) are easy to recognize and run from poor clotting time of the blood when you nick yourself shaving (calcium is a co-factor in the clotting mechanism), arthritis (which the allopaths treat with pain killers), to the well known osteoporosis.

Famous people who have suffered

Table 11-10. Common Calcium Deficiency Diseases.

Disease	Complicating factors
Osteoporosis (kyphosis, Dowagers Hump, lordosis, Legg-Perthe's, spontaneous fractures)	Deficiencies of: Mg, B, Cu, S, Se, St, Ac, Fl; Excess of: Fl, P, Cd, fat.
Receeding gums (osteoporosis of facial bones and jaw bone)	Same as osteoporosis
Osteomalacia (failure to mineralize the protein bone matrix)	Same as osteoporosis (in children)
Arthritis (Degenerative, osteo, spondylitis)	Same as osteoporosis
Hypertension (High blood pressure)	Same as osteoporosis
Insomnia (inability to get restfull sleep)	Same as osteoporosis
Kidney stones	Same as osteoporosis
Bone spurs (heel spurs or anywhere tendons or ligaments attach to the bone)	Same as osteoporosis
Calcium deposits (anywhere tendons or ligaments attach to the bone)	Same as osteoporosis
Cramps and twitches (foot, calf, eye lids, hamstring muscles, etc.)	Same as osteoporosis
PMS (emotional and physical symptoms)	Same as osteoporosis
Low back (sciatica, muscle spasm, disc problems)	Same as osteoporosis
Bell's Palsy (drooping facial muscle because of strangulated facial nerve)	Same as osteoporosis
NSH (nutritional secondary hyperparathyroidism)	Same as osteoporosis Excess of Vit. D and P
Osteofibrosis (enlargement of bones with fibrous scar tissue)	Same as NSH
Tetany (convulsions, usually in infants fed undiluted cows milk which contains more phosphorus than calcium)	Same as NSH, excess P
Panic attacks (hyperirritability)	Same as osteoporosis

from calcium deficiency include Pope John Paul II (fractured hip/osteoporosis); Elizabeth Taylor (osteoporosis/ hip replacement surgery; "Bo"Jackson (fractured hip/ osteoporosis); Bill Walton, a vegan of basketball fame (knee, foot and bone spur problems), Ted Williams of baseball fame (osteoporosis and arthritis), etc.

Calcium is the most abundant mineral in the human body, the average male has 1,200 grams and the average female has 1,000 grams, makes up one to two percent of the body weight (water makes up 65 to 75 %) and up to 39 percent of the total mineral reserves of the body (ash); 99% is found in the bones and teeth, the other one percent is found in the blood, extracellular fluids, and within cells where it is a cofactor and activator for numerous enzymes.

Calcium in bones is in the form of hydroxyapatite salts composed of calcium phosphate and calcium carbonate in a classic crystal structure bound to a protein framework (put a chicken "drumstick" bone in vinegar for 10 days and the calcium will be leached leaving a protein matrix). Similar types of hydroxyapatite are found in the enamel and dentin of teeth, however, little is available from teeth to contribute to rapidly available Ca to maintain blood levels.

In addition to being a major structural mineral, Ca is also required for the release of energy from ATP for muscular contraction, blood clotting (ionized Ca stimulates the release of thromboplastin from the platelets, converts prothrombin to thrombin - thrombin helps to convert fibrinogen to fibrin - fibrin is the protein web that traps RBC's to make blood clots); Ca mediates the transport function of cell and organelle membranes; Ca effects the release of neurotransmitters at synaptic junctions; Ca mediates the synthesis, secretion and metabolic effects of hormones and enzymes; Ca helps to regulate the heart beat, muscle tone and muscle receptiveness to nerve stimulation.

Calcium is mainly absorbed in the duodenum, where the environment is still acid. Once the food in the intestine becomes alkaline, absorption drops. Calcium is absorbed from the small intestine by active cellular transport and by simple difussion. Metallic calcium absorption may be limited to 10 percent or less and is affected by many substances in the gut. Calcium may be absorbed in the organically bound plant derived colloidals and water soluble chelates.

Lack of vitamin D results in calcium deficiency, as well as deficiency of stomach acid (hypochlorhydria results from a restricted NaCl intake); lactose intolerance, celiac disease, high fat diet and low protein intake and high phytate consumption (phytic acid is a phosphorus containing acid compound found in the bran of grains and seeds as well as in the stems of many plants, especially oatmeal and whole wheat which combine to form calcium phytate which is insoluble and unavailable to humans) all result in calcium deficiency; oxalic acid in rhubarb, spinach, chard and greens combines with Ca to form an insoluble calcium oxalate which is not absorbed; fiber itself, besides the phytate content, prevents calcium absorption; alkaline intestine, gut mobility (too rapid-too much fiber, too much fruit, etc.), pharmaceuticals (antiseizure drugs, diuretics,etc.) result in decreased absorption and retention; excess of caffeine from coffee, tea, colas, etc. will leach calcium from the bones.

Parathormone secreted by the parathyroid gland and calcitonin secreted by the thyroid gland maintain a serum calcium of

8.5 to10.5 by drawing on calcium reserves from the bones. The parathormone can also affect the kidney so that it retains more calcium and the gut to be more efficient in absorption; when the blood calcium begins to rise from too much parathyroid activity, calcitonin reduces availability of calcium from the bones.

In 1980, McCarron, et al, theorized that chronic calcium deficiency probably led to hypertension. More than 30 subsequent studies supported the original theory of calcium deficiency as the cause of hypertention, additionally recent studies have shown that serum ionized calcium is consistently lower in humans with untreated hypertension. In a recent review article, Sowers, et al, noted that the association of calcium intake and blood pressure is most clear in people with daily calcium intakes of less than 500 mg a day.

The phenomenon of salt sensitivity consists of a rise in blood pressure and sustained increased in urinary loss of calcium in response to salt consumption. Among black and elderly whites with essential hypertension, restricted intakes of calcium and potassium, rather than elevated salt consumption is responsible for salt sensitivity. In a four year study of 58,218 nurses, hypertension was more likely to develop in females who took in less than 800 mg of calcium per day.

In a 19 year observational study of 1,954 men, 49 cases of colorectal cancer were identified. Analysis of the results showed very clearly that the incidence of colorectal cancer increased 300 % as the calcium intake decreased from 160 mg/100kcal to 24,9 mg/100 kcal of diet.

Up to 75% of consumed Ca is lost in the feces, two percent is lost in the urine and sweat (15 mg per day is lost in normal sweating - this can double or triple in active athletes); in cases of excess urine loss of calcium (osteoporosis, NSH, excess P, etc.) kidney stones (Fig. 11-4), bone spurs (Fig. 11-5) and calcium deposits will develop.

Bone spurs and heel spurs and calcium deposits always develope at the sites of insertions of tendons and ligaments during a

Table 11- 11. The Ca:P Ratio of Various Food Items.

Food/Item	Ca	P
Ideal Ca:P Ratio	2	1
beef	1	17
liver/kidney	1	44
poultry	1	17
Alfalfa	8	1
Whole animal (mouse)	2	1
Apple	1	1
Grape	1	1
Sardines	1	6
Mackeral	1	34
wheat	1	8
Millet	1	6
Milo	1	14
corn	1	37
Oats	1	8
Sunflower seeds	1	7
buckwheat	1	8
rice	1	8
Peanut	1	7
Beer	1	6
milk(Cow)	1.3	1
cottage cheese	1	4
Yogurt	1	1
Minute Maid OJ with Ca	1.3	1
Colas	1	20

Fig. 11-4

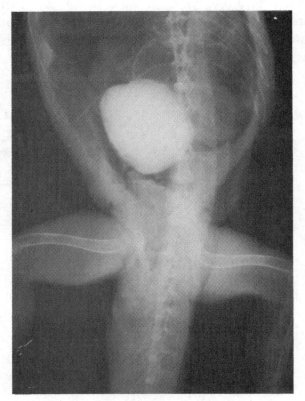

A) Urinary calculi (stone) in an unsupplemented iguana
fed only calcium poor fruit diet.

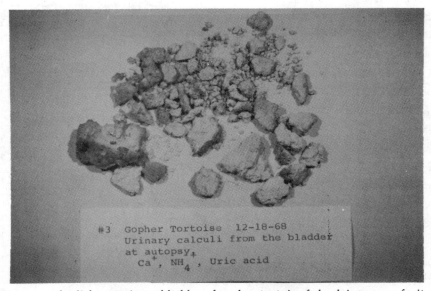

B) Urinary calculi from urinary bladder of gopher tortoise fed calcium poor fruit diet

Fig. 11-5

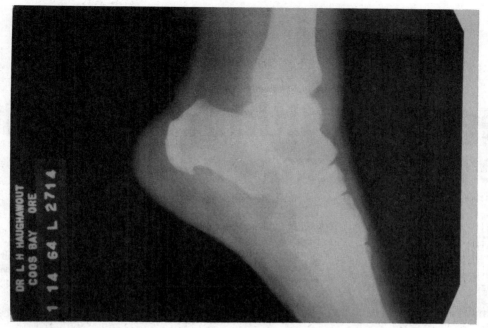

Heel spurs in osteoporetic humans (note tendon attachments at spur site.)

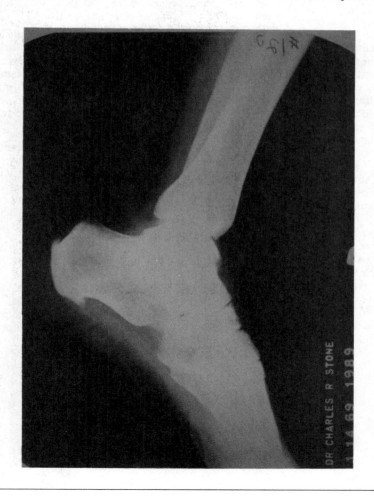

Plague of brittle bones: Adults are not getting enough calcium

ASSOCIATED PRESS

BETHESDA, Md. — Half of America's adults are not getting enough calcium, and that's contributing to a plague of brittle bones and fractures that costs the health care system $10 billion a year, a federal committee said yesterday.

A committee of experts assembled by the National Institutes of Health said the current recommended daily allowance for calcium is too low, leading to weakened bones for children, adults and, especially, for elderly women.

"Calcium is an essential nutrient for developing and maintaining strong bones," the committee said.

And, yet, said Dr. John P. Bilezikian, a professor of medicine at Columbia University and chairman of the committee, most Americans are calcium-poor.

"Recent nutrition surveys have shown that the average diet of Americans has a calcium intake considerably below the recommended daily allowance," said Bilezikian at a news conference.

Without proper levels of calcium, the panel said, children enter adulthood with weakened skeletons, increasing their risk later for osteoporosis, the brittle bone disease. Inadequate calcium in later years aggravates the problem.

Osteoporosis affects more than 25 million Americans, causing an estimated 1.5 million fractures and leading to medical costs of about $10 billion, Bilezikian said.

New studies, the committee found, show that recommended levels of calcium now carried on most food labels is far below what nature requires for strong bones.

In its report, the panel recommended these levels of calcium, with the currently recommended daily allowance in parenthesis:

Children and young adults, 11 through 24: 1,200 to 1,500 milligrams (1,200 mg).

Women 25 to 50: 1,000 mg. (800 mg).

Men 25 and older: 1,000 mg. (800 mg).

Postmenopausal women: 1,000 to 1,500 mg. (800 mg).

Women over 65: 1,500 mg. (800 mg).

For very young children, the committee endorsed the current recommended levels of 400 mg daily for the first half year of life, 600 mg from age 6 months to 1 year, and 800 mg to age 10.

Bone absorption occurs in women for up to eight years after menopause because levels of the hormone estrogen drop, the panel said. Increased calcium does little to re-

duce this bone loss, but it can be controlled with hormone therapy. A boost in calcium levels to 1,500 mg after age 65, however, "may reduce the rates of bone loss in selected areas of the skeleton, such as the . . . neck."

The panel said that during the adolescent growth spurt, calcium can accumulate in bones at the rate of 400 to 500 mg a day.

"Peak adult bone mass . . . is largely achieved by age 20 years, although important additional bone mass may accumulate through the third decade," the study said. As a result, "optimal calcium intake in childhood and young adulthood is critical to achieving peak adult bone mass."

The committee said that foods, principally dairy products and green leafy vegetables, are the best sources of calcium, but that most Americans may need to supplement their diet with calcium pills or processed foods enriched with calcium.

This is particularly true for older women requiring higher doses, said Bilezikian.

"It is a task to get up to 1,500 milligrams," he said. "Therefore, calcium supplements have been a viable option to get the needed levels."

THURSDAY, JUNE 16, 1994 • USA TODAY

Hip surgery done with, Liz steps out

LOS ANGELES — In her first public appearance since March hip replacement surgery, **Elizabeth Taylor** made arriving in an unadorned wheelchair seem as grand as an entrance in a gilded carriage.

"No pictures till she's out of her chair," photographers were warned at Tuesday night's opening of the **Carole** and **Barry Kaye** Museum of Miniatures, which benefited the Elizabeth Taylor AIDS Foundation. But as soon as she took her place at the dais, bulbs began popping like a frenzied Fourth of July.

Dressed in a gold gown and perfectly coifed, Taylor — escorted by husband **Larry Fortensky** and longtime friend **Roddy McDowall** — stood to speak without help. Flanked by

By Fred Prouser, Reuters

TAYLOR: Stands on her own at benefit museum opening.

the late Malcolm Forbes' son **Kip,** whose *Forbes* magazine underwrote the event, and museum co-creator Barry Kaye, the star said it was great to be out again.

What about the strain that a recuperating spouse can sometimes put on a marriage? "My husband has been very supportive," she said, "and I know it hasn't been easy."

Taylor posed for photos with Fortensky, and when she turned to get back in her wheelchair, held onto his hand for support.

Asked what message she wanted to send, she said: "Just send all my love and admiration to all the heroes in the AIDS war."

The museum contains a collection of miniature houses and dioramas. Carol Kaye builds and collects miniatures; her financier husband Barry is the author of books such as *Die Rich and Tax Free.*

— Susan Bullington Katz

raging osteoporosis. Bone spurs, heel spurs and calcium deposits can be reversed and eliminated by supplementing with significant amounts of chelated and colloidal calcium sources.

Not only are our soils and food deficient in calcium, additionally the American diet is rich in P, which is found in just about everything we eat (NPK fertilizer and food additives).

Ideally, the Ca:P ratio in our daily diet should be 2:1 (Table 11-11); however, this ideallic ratio is not possible (you would have to eat 25 pounds of broccoli every time you ate a 16 oz steak!!). The only possible way to approach the 2:1 ideal is to avoid as much as possible the high P containing items (we hate to call colas, processed "cheese", etc. foods) and supplement with plant derived colloidal and chelated calcium.

Cd - Cadmium is found in igneous rocks 0.2 ppm; shale 0.3 ppm; sandstone 0.05ppm; limestone 0.035 ppm; fresh water 0.08 ppm; sea water 0.00011ppm; soils 0.06 ppm; marine plants 0.4 ppm; land plants 0.6 ppm; marine animals 0.15 to 3.0 ppm; land animals 0.5 ppm (accumulates in kidney). Functions by stimulating the hatching of nematode cysts (worms). Cadmium bound proteins have been isolated from molluscs and the horse kidney.

Ce - Cerium, a Rare Earth, is found in igneous rocks 60 ppm; shale 59 ppm; sandstones 92 ppm; limestones 12 ppm; sea water 0.0004 ppm; soil 50 ppm; land plants accumulates to 320 ppm by *Corya spp.*; land animals 0.003 ppm (accumulates in bone). Cerium nitrate is used as a topical disinfectant for severe burn victims.

Cl - Chlorine is found in igneous rocks 130 ppm; shales 180 ppm; sandstones 10 ppm; limestone 150 ppm; fresh water 7 to 8 ppm; sea water 19,000 ppm; soil 100 ppm (higher in alkaline soils, near the sea and in deserts- a major exchangeable anion in many soils); marine plants 4,700 ppm; land plants 2,000 ppm; marine animals 5,000 to 90,000 ppm (highest in soft coelenterates); land animals 2,800 ppm (highest in mammalian hair and skin.

Essential for all living species - electrochemical and catalytic functions, activates numerous enzymes and is the basic raw material for our stomachs to make stomach acid (HCl) for protein digestion (pepsin), B_{12} absorption (intrinsic factor) and absorption of metallic minerals.

Sodium chloride or salt is the universal source of chloride ions.

Cm - Curium is found in igneous rocks at 0.0001 ppm. All isotopes are radioactive with a 2.5×10^8 years half life; exists in some molybdenites; this radioactive mineral will accumulate in mammalian bone.

Co - Cobalt is found in igneous rocks at about 25 ppm; shales at 19 ppm; sandstones at 0.3 ppm; limestone at 0.1 ppm; fresh water at 0.0009 ppm; sea water at 0.00027 ppm; soils at 8 ppm (higher in soils derived from basalt or serpentine. Vast areas of the Earth are known to be absolutely devoid of cobalt.

Marine plants contain cobalt at 0.7 ppm; land plants at 0.5 ppm (accumulator plants include *Nyssa sylvatica* and *Clethra barbinrvis*).

Marine animals contain cobalt at 0.5 to

5.0 ppm; land animals 0.03 ppm with greatest concentrations in the bone and liver.

Essential for blue green algae, some bacteria and fungi, some plants, insects, birds, reptiles, amphibians and mammals including man. Cobalt functions as a cofactor and activator for enzymes, fixes nitrogen during amino acid production; a single cobalt atom is the central metal componant of vitamin B_{12} which itself is a cofactor and activator (cobamide coenzymes) for several essential enzymes.

B_{12} cobalt is chelated in a large terapyrrole ring similar to the phorphyrin ring found in hemoglobin and chlorophil. The original B_{12} molecule isolated in the laboratory contained a cyanide group, thus the name cyanocobalamine; there are several different cobalamine compounds that have vitamin B_{12} activity, with cyanocobalamine and hydroxycobalamine the most active.

Vitamin B_{12} is a red crystalline substance that is water soluble; the red color is due to the cobalt in the molecule. Vitamin B_{12} is slowly deactivated by acid, alkalai, light and oxidizing or reducing substances; about 30 percent of B_{12} activity is lost during cooking (electric, gas or microwave).

In 1948, B_{12} was isolated from liver extract and demonstrated anti pernicious anemia activity.

The essentiality of cobalt is unusual in that the requirement is for a cobalt complex known as cyanocobalamine or vitamin B_{12}. A pure cobalt requirement is only found in some bacteria and algae and the need for B_{12} cobalt is thought by some to represent a symbiotic relationship between microbes which generate and manufacture B_{12} from elemental cobalt and vertebrates that require B_{12}.

Rumenants (i.e.-cows, sheep, goats, deer, antelopes, giraffe, etc.) can use elemental cobalt, however, the microbes fermenting and digesting plant material in their first stomach (rumen) convert elemental cobalt into vitamin B_{12}, which the animal can use.

Carnivores can get their B_{12} from the rumenant by consuming stomach contents, liver, bone and muscle from their kills.

Poultry, lagomorphs (rabbits and hares), and rodents actively eat feces during the night (coprophagy) and in the process obtain B_{12} manufactured by intestinal microorganisms.

Metallic cobalt itself, is absorbed at the rate of 20 to 26.2 percent in mice and and humans if intrinsic factor is present in the stomach and the stomach ph is 2.0 or less. Intrinsic factor is a mucoprotein enzyme known as Castle's intrinsic factor and is part of normal stomach secretions.

If a person has hypochlorhydria (low stomach acid - usually a NaCl deficiency) the intrinsic factor will not work and B_{12} cobalt is not absorbed - this is why doctors frequently give B_{12} shots to older people on salt restricted diets. Sublingual (under the tongue) and oral spray B_{12} is available; plant derived cobalt is very bioavailable, however, because of low salt diets and cobalt depleted soils vegetarians frequently have B_{12} deficiency.

The B_{12} intrinsic factor complex is primarily absorbed in the terminal small intestine or ileum; calcium is required for the B_{12} to cross from the intestine into the bloodstream as well as an active participation by intestinal cells. Simple difussion can account for one to three percent of the vitamins absorption.

There is an enterohepatic (intestine direct to the liver) circulation of B_{12} that recycles B_{12} from bile and other intestinal secretions which explains why B_{12} deficieny in vegans may not appear for five to ten years.

The maximum storage level of B_{12} is 2 mg, which is slowly released to the bone marrow as needed. Excess intake of B_{12} is shed in the urine (expensive urine).

Vitamin B_{12}/cobalt joins with folic acid, choline and the amino acid methionine to transfer single carbon groups (methyl groups) in the synthesis of the raw materials to make RNA and the synthesis of DNA from RNA (directly involved in gene function - remember preconception nutrition to prevent birth defects!!). Growth, myelin formation (converts cholesterol to the insulating material myelin found around nerves in the brain and large nerve trunks) and RBC synthesis are dependant on B_{12}.

The discovery of the essentiality of cobalt came from observing a fatal disease ("bush sickness") in cattle and sheep from Australia and New Zealand; it was observed that "bush sickness" could be succesfully treated and prevented by cobalt supplements.

Bush sickness was characterized by emaciation (unsupplemented vegans), dull stare, listless, starved look, pale mucus membranes, anorexia (loss of appetite), anemia (microcytic/hypochromic) and general unthriftiness.

In humans, a failure to absorb B_{12}/cobalt results in deficiency disease. This can result from a surgical removal of parts of the stomach (eliminates areas of intrinsic factor production), or surgical removal of the ileum portion of the small bowel, small intestinal diverticula, parasites (tape worm), celiac disease (allergies to wheat gluten and cows milk albumen) and other malabsorption diseases. Pernicious anemia and demyelination of the spinal cord and large nerve trunks are classic for B_{12}/cobalt deficiency.

Less than 0.07 ppm Co in the soil results in cobalt deficiency in animals and people who eat crops grown from those soils; 0.11 ppm Co in the soil prevents and cures Co deficiency.

The RDA for B_{12}/cobalt is 3 to 4 mcg per day, we prefer expensive urine and like 250 to 400 mcg per day, especially while preparing for a pregnancy and nursing (remember a baby being nursed by a deficient mother has their deficiency extended over a long period of time and may result in serious permanant nerve damage.

Cobalt excess in man (20 to 30 mg/day) may create erythropoiesis (RBC production) with increased production of the hormone erythropoieten from the kidney. Cobalt is also a necessary cofactor for the production of thyroid hormone.

Cr - Chromium is found in igneous rocks at 100 ppm; shales at 90 ppm; sandstones 35 ppm and limestone at 11 ppm; fresh water at 0.00018 ppm; sea water 0.00005 ppm; soils at 5 to 3,000 ppm (highest in soils derived from basalt and serpentine); marine plants 1 ppm; land plants 0.23 ppm; marine animals 0.2-1.0 ppm; land animals 0.075 ppm; accumulated by RNA and insulin.

Chromium activates phosphoglucosonetase and other enzymes and is tightly associated with GTF (glucose tolerance factor - a combination of chromium

III, dinicotinic acid and glutithione).The reported plasma levels of chromium in humans over the past 20 years has ranged from 0.075 to 13 ng/ml. Concentrations of chromium in human hair is ten times greater than in blood making hair analysis a much more accurate view of chromium stores and function in the human (there is 1.5mg in the human body).

Very little inorganic chromium is stored in the body, once inorganic chromium is absorbed, it is almost entirely excreted in the urine (therefore urine chromium levels can be used to estimate dietary chromium status). Dietary sugar loads (i.e.- colas, apple juice, grape juice, honey, candy, sugar, fructose, etc.) increase the natural rate of urinary Cr loss by 300 % for 12 hours.

The average intake of 50 to 100 ug of inorganic chromium from food and water supplies only 0.25 to 0.5 ug of usable chromium, by contrast 25 % of chelated chromium is absorbed. The chromium RDA for humans is a range of 50 to 200 ug per day for adults.

The concentration of chromium is higher in newborn animals and humans than it is in later life. In fact, the chromium levels of unsupplemented human tissue steadily decreases throughout life - of even more concern has been the steady decline in the average American serum chromium since 1948:

Mean Cr blood levels (u/l)	Year
28 - 1000	1948
13	1971
10	1972
4.7 - 5.1	1973
0.73 - 1.6	1974
0.16	1978
0.43	1980
0.13	1985

The fasting chromium plasma level of pregnant women is lower than that of non-pregnant women. Increasing impairment of glucose tolerance in "normal" pregnancy is well documented and reflects a chromium deficiency oftentimes resulting in pregnancy onset diabetes. One study demonstrated abnormal glucose tolerance in 77 percent of clinically "normal" adults over the age of 70. According to Richard Anderson , USDA, "90 percent of Americans are deficient in chromium."

Table 11-12. Diseases and Symptoms of Chromium Deficiency.

- Low blood sugar
- Prediabetes
- Diabetes (ulcers/gangrene) (Fig. 11-6)
- Hyperinsulinemia
- Hyperactivity
- Learning disabilities
- ADD/ADHD
- Hyperirratability
- Depression
- Manic depression
- "Bi-polar" disesase
- Dr. Jykell/Mr. Hyde rages ("Bad Seeds")
- Impaired growth
- Peripheral neuropathy
- Negative nitrogen balance(protein loss)
- Elevated blood triglycerides
- Elevated blood cholesterol
- Coronary blood vessel disease
- Aortic cholesterol plaque
- Infertility and decreased sperm count
- Shortened life span

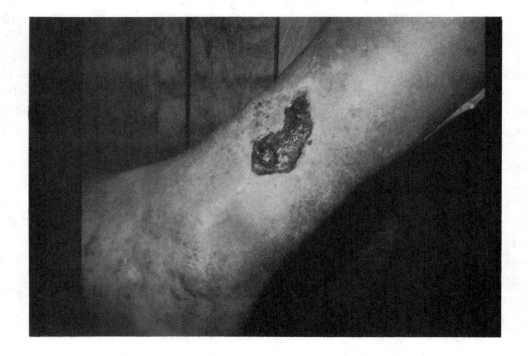

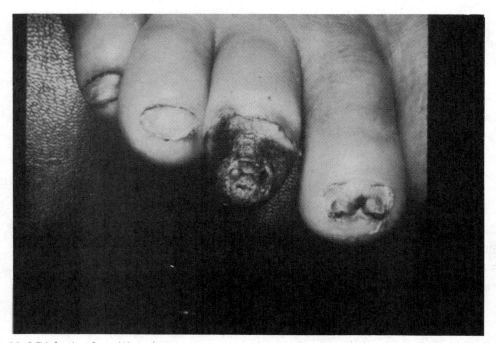

Fig. 11-6 Diabetic ulcer (A) and gangrene on toe. (B) resulting from chronic Cr and V deficiency.

Hispanics are at higher risk for diabetes

By Anita Manning
USA TODAY

Hispanics are twice as likely to have diabetes as non-Hispanic whites, says a new report from the American Diabetes Association.

Based on data from the Centers for Disease Control and Prevention and other sources, the report shows:

▶ One in 10 Hispanics has diabetes, compared with 1 in 20 non-Hispanic whites.

▶ Only about half are aware of their illness.

▶ Among those age 45-74, 25% of Mexican-Americans and Puerto Rican-Americans, and 16% of Cuban-Americans have diabetes vs. 12%-13% of non-Hispanic whites.

An effort to raise awareness among Hispanics was launched this week at a summit in Washington, D.C. A survey released there found that in Hispanic communities, poor access to health care and language problems often are barriers to diagnosis and treatment.

This can delay medical care until advanced stages of the disease, when complications such as blindness and vascular problems are more likely.

Why some ethnic groups are at greater risk is "not totally understood," says the ADA's Jerry Franz. Risk factors include family history of diabetes and being 30 pounds or more overweight.

Likelihood of developing diabetes, compared with non-Hispanic whites:

▶ Native Americans, 2.7 times as likely.

▶ Puerto Rican-Americans, 2.2.

▶ Mexican-Americans, 2.1.

▶ African-Americans, 1.6.

▶ Cuban-Americans, 1.5.

CAPE COD TIMES, SATURDAY, NOVEMBER 27, 1993

Former Yarmouth officer Thomas Minckler dies at 42

By MARK MERCHANT
STAFF WRITER

HARWICH — A former Yarmouth police officer who was instrumental in developing police dog programs across Cape Cod died Wednesday at his home.

An illness caused by diabetes claimed the life of Thomas E. Minckler, 42.

Mr. Minckler had been working with police dogs since he joined the Yarmouth police department in 1973. He developed dog programs for many towns and at the county level and continued training dogs after a traffic accident forced his retirement from the department in 1986.

Collegues reacted with sadness to his death. Yarmouth Police Chief Robert Chapman said Mr. Minckler had been ill for some time, but the death took everyone by surprise.

Others said Mr. Minckler's loss would be felt in K-9 units across the Cape.

"He was so devoted to the dogs and his work," said David Yoo, the Dennis police department's K-9 officer. "If it wasn't for Tom, you wouldn't see a K-9 program on the Cape, he was that important."

Born in Worcester and raised in Leicester, Mr. Minckler had been in law enforcement since graduating from Quinsigamond Community College in Worcester in 1971. He worked for the Leicester police department for a short time before joining the Chatham police in 1972. After a year, he moved to the Yarmouth police where he started their police dog program.

■ **Thomas E. Minckler with one of his K-9 partners, Luke.**

OBITUARIES

Moses Gunn, 64; stage, screen actor

N.Y. TIMES NEWS SERVICE

Moses Gunn, an actor whose career of more than three decades included roles ranging from Othello to Booker T. Washington, died Friday at his home in Guilford, Conn. He was 64. The cause was complications of asthma, said his wife, Gwendolyn. He had been ill since May, she said.

Moses Gunn

Once hailed by critics as one of the country's finest actors, Mr. Gunn continued to work until his final illness, ending his career as he began it: playing provocative roles on stage and screen.

He made a guest appearance last year on the television series "Homicide" and most recently co-starred in productions of "Blood Knot" and "My Children, My Africa," both by the South African playwright Athol Fugard.

Mr. Gunn, a co-founder of the Negro Ensemble Company, played myriad roles. He received an Image Award from the National Association for the Advancement of Colored People for his performance as Booker T. Washington in the 1981 film "Ragtime," and an Emmy nomination for his role in the television mini-series "Roots" as Kintango, the leader of a secret society in Africa that preserved and performed the rites of manhood.

His numerous stage appearances included "Othello" and the original New York production of "The Blacks," by Jean Genet, in 1962.

He also appeared in several feature films, including "The Great White Hope" and "Shaft," and television series like "Little House on the Prairie" and "Good Times." He was featured in a television production of "Of Mice and Men."

Mr. Gunn is survived by his wife, a son and daughter.

Compiled by Harry Levins
Of the Post-Dispatch Staff

A sad note: Complications from diabetes have cost jazz singer **ELLA FITZGERALD** her legs. Doctors amputated both limbs below the knee in separate operations last year, her spokeswoman says.

The spokeswoman couldn't explain why the news had been withheld for so long but added, "She's fine, and she's at home. She is in really good shape and good spirits."

Fitzgerald, 75, underwent heart-bypass surgery in 1986; the next year, surgeons removed bone particles in her right foot.

WEDNESDAY, JULY 6, 1994

ST. LOUIS POST-DISPATCH

Ex-Champ Said To Be In A Coma

Douglas' Condition Upgraded To Stable

COLUMBUS, Ohio (AP) — Former heavyweight champion James "Buster" Douglas was reported to be hospitalized Tuesday in a diabetic coma.

WBNS-TV, citing no sources, said Douglas, 34, was upgraded from poor to stable condition at Grant Medical Center on Tuesday afternoon.

Douglas

The hospital refused to comment, and hospital spokeswoman Karen Waldbillig said the family asked that no information be released.

Other relatives told the station that Douglas was taken to the hospital Monday and had slipped in and out of a coma since then. They said Tuesday afternoon that his condition was improving.

It was not known whether Douglas previously had been diagnosed as a diabetic or which form of the disease he might have. In some cases, if diabetes goes untreated, the victim may go into a diabetic coma, which can lead to death.

Douglas' father, Bill Douglas, could not be reached for comment.

Douglas, a native of Columbus, was the heavyweight champion for only eight months.

Gary Evans, Bemidji State University, Minnesota, very clearly showed an increased life span in laboratory animals by 33.3 per cent when they were supplemented with chromium. Prior to this study gerontologists, led by Roy Walford, felt a severe restriction of calories was the only way to extend life past the expected average.

Deficiencies of chromium in humans are characterized by a wide variety of clinical diseases as well as a shortened life expectancy (Table 11-12). The clinical diseases of chromium deficiency are aggravated by vanadium deficiency.

Cs - Cesium is found in igneous rocks at 1 ppm; shales at 5 ppm; sandstones and limestones at 0.5 ppm; fresh water at 0.0002 ppm; sea water at 0.00005 ppm; soils at 0.3 to 25 ppm; marine plants at 0.07 ppm; land plants at 0.2 ppm; and land animals at 0.064 ppm (highest concentrations in the muscle).

As an alkaline mineral, cesium behaves similarly to sodium, potassium and rubidium chemically. Cesium and potassium enter into a solute complex which participates in ion antagonism, osmosis, permiability regulation and maintenance of the colloidal state in the living cell. The increase in supplemental potassium increases the rate of excretion or loss of cesium.

Cesium chloride is used as part of alternative cancer therapy. Cesium provides "high ph therapy for cancer "by entering the cancer cell and producing an alkaline environment. It has been recommended for all types of cancers including sarcomas, bronchiogenic carcinoma and colon cancer.

Cu -Copper is found in igneous rocks at 55 ppm; shale at 45 ppm; sandstone at 5 ppm; limestone 4 ppm; fresh water at 0.01 ppm; sea water at 0.003 ppm; soils at 2 to 100 ppm (copper is strongly absorbed by humus; there are known areas of the world with extreme copper deficiency); marine plants 11 ppm; land plants 14 ppm; ma-

---

Table 11 - 12. Symptoms Associated with Copper Dificiency.

- White hair
- Gray hair
- Dry brittle hair ("steely wool" in sheep)
- Ptosis (sagging tissue - eye lids, skin, breasts, stomach, etc.)
- Hernias (Congenital and acquired)
- Varicose veins
- Aneurysms (large artery blowouts, cerebral artery blowouts)
- Kawasaki Disease (congenital aneurysms with Streptococcal infection)
- Anemia (especially in vegan and high milk diets)
- Hypo and hyper thyroid
- Arthritis (especially where growth plate is involved)
- Ruptured vertebral disc
- Liver cirrhosis
- Violent behavior, blind rage, explosive outbursts, criminal behavior
- Learning disabilities
- Cerebral palsy and hypoplasia of the cerebellum (congenital ataxia)
- High blood cholesterol
- Iron storage disease (abnormal iron accumulation in liver)
- Reduced glucose tolerance (low blood sugar)
- Neutropenia

rine animals 4 to 50 ppm (accumulates in thge blood of annelids (worms), crustaceans and molluscs, especially cephlopods; land animals at 2 to 4 ppm with highest levels in the liver.

Copper is essential to all living organisms and is a universally important cofactor for many hundreds of metalloenzynes. Copper deficiency is widespread and appears in many forms (Table 11 -13). Copper is required in many physiological functions (i.e.- RNA, DNA, lysil oxidase cofactor, melanin (Fig. 11-7) production (hair and skin pigment), electron transfer of oxygen subcellular respiration, tensile strength of elastic fibers in blood vessels, skin, vertibral discs, etc.).

Neonatal enzootic ataxia (sway back, lamkruis) was recognized as a clinical entity in 1937 as a copper deficiency in pregnant sheep. Copper supplements prevented the syndrome which was characterized by demyelination of the cerebellum (Fig. 11-8) and spinal cord. Cavitation or gelatinous lesions of the cerebral white matter, chromatolysis, nerve cell death and myelin aplasia (failure to form). These are all changes identical with human cerebral palsy.

Famous people affected or dying of an obvious copper deficiency include Albert Enstein (ruptured cerebral aneurysms), Paavo Aerola (ruptured cerebral aneurysms), Conway Twitty (ruptured abdominal aorta aneurysm), George and Barbara Bush (thyroid disease, white hair) - four to six of every 100 Americans autopsied have died of a ruptured aneurysm, an additional 40 percent have aneurysms that had not yet ruptured.

The average well-nourished adult human body contains between 80 and 120 mg of copper. Concentrations are higher in the brain, liver, heart and kidneys. Bone and muscle have lower percentages of copper but contain 50 percent of the body total copper reserves because of their mass. It is of interest that the greatest concentration of copper is found in the newborn and their daily requirement is 0.08 mg/kg, toddlers require 0.04 mg/kg and adults only 0.03 mg/kg.

The average plasma copper for women ranges from 87 to 153 mg/dl and for men it ranges from 89 to 137 mg/dl; about 90 percent of the plasma copper is found in ceruloplasmin.

Copper functions as a co-factor and activator of numerous cuproenzymes that are involved in the development (deficiency of Cu in the pregnant female results in congenital defects of the heart,i.e.-Kawasaki Disease and brain - i.e.- cerebral palsy and hypoplasia of the cerebellum) and maintenance of the cardiovascular system (deficiency results in reduced lysyl oxidase activity causing a reduction in conversion of pro elastin to elastin causing a decrease in tinsel strength of arterial walls and ruptured aneurysms (Figs. 11-9,11-10 and 11-11)) and skeletal integrety (deficiency results in a specific type of arthritis of the young in the form of spurs in the bones growth plate); deficiency can result in myelin defects; deficiency results in anemia; and poor hair keratinization and loss of hair color. Neutropenia (reduced numbers of neutophillic WBC) and leukopenia (reduced total WBC) are the earliest indicators of copper deficiency in infants; infants whose diets are primarily cows milk frequently develop anemia; iron storage disease can result from chronic copper deficiency.

Menkes' Kinky Hair Syndrome is

Fig. 11-7 A) Gray hair associated with copper deficient diet. B) Normal color returned six months after supplementing with colloidal copper.

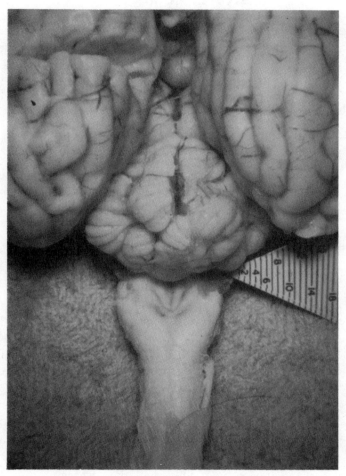

Fig. 11-8 Hypoplasia (failure to form) of the cerebellum and cerebral myelin typical of cerebral palsy resulting from a congenital copper deficiency.

KRISTOFFER HOOD

PALM BAY — Kristoffer Woodside Hood, who was 5, died Thursday, May 6, at Holmes Regional Medical Center in Melbourne.

Kristoffer was born in Mount Kisco, N.Y. He came to Brevard County in 1988 from Bedford Hills, N.Y.

Kristoffer loved all sports. He like to bowl and he participated in the Palm Bay Youth Softball League. He was a member of Christ United Methodist Church in Palm Bay.

Survivors include his parents, Clifford and Tracey Hood of Palm Bay; sister, Heather Hood of Palm Bay; grandmother, Carmine Brown of Palm Bay; grandfather, William Brown of Millerton, N.Y.; and grandparents, William and Agnes Brown of Vero Beach and Carmine and Marguerite Mazza of Newfield, Maine.

Calling hours will be from 6 to 9 p.m. Sunday at Palm Bay Funeral Home. Services will be at 10 a.m. Monday at Chapel of Peace in Fountainhead Memorial Park in Palm Bay.

Donations may be made to United Cerebral Palsy of Central Florida, 930 S. Orange Ave., Orlando, FL 32806 or to Serenity House for AIDS Babies, P.O. Box 680338, Orlando, FL 32868.

Fig. 11-9

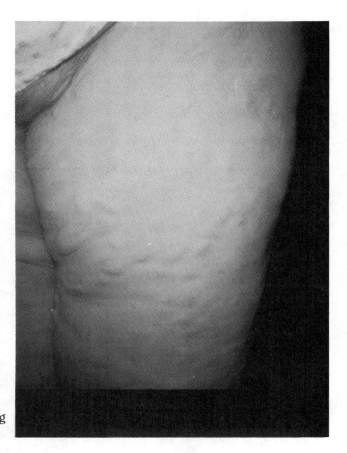

A) Varicous veins resulting from copper deficiency.

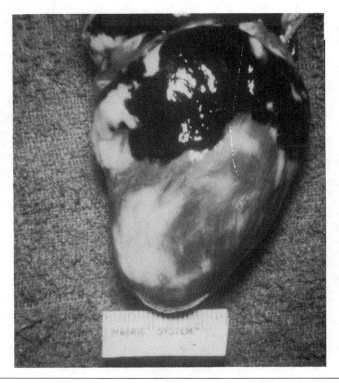

B) Ruptured coronary aneurysm (kawasaki disease)in a pheasant resulting from a copper deficient diet.

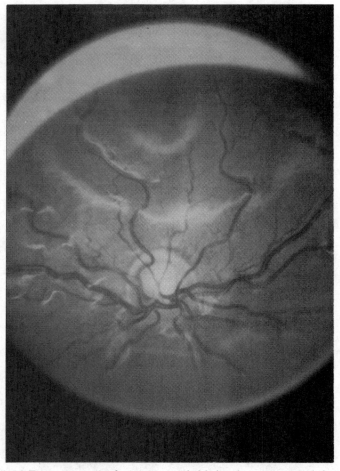

Fig. 11-10 Tortuous retinal arteries in child that has a copper deficiency.

Fig. 11-11

A
Normal configuration of elastic fibers in
aorta

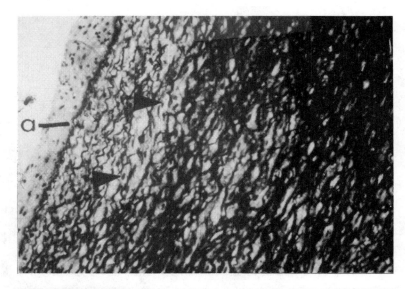

B
Aortic elastic fibers disrupted by "dissecting" aneurysm

C
Ruptured aortic aneurysm in a copper
deficient squirrel monkey.

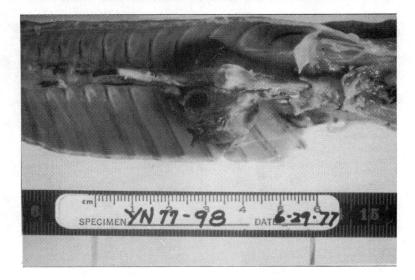

THE BOSTON SUNDAY GLOBE • JANUARY 9, 1994

'Northern Exposure' moose dies

ASSOCIATED PRESS

PULLMAN, Wash. - Morty, the moose that ambles through the opening credits of television's "Northern Exposure," died last week of an illness linked to a mineral deficiency.

The 1,000-pound moose, brought five years ago from Alaska as an orphan yearling, was a subject of behavior and nutrition studies- headed by Charles Robbins, a Washington State University professor.

Researchers found that a cobalt and copper deficiency in the diets of Morty and Minnie, another research moose, led to their deaths. The problem was discovered after Minnie's death more than a week ago, but by then it was too late to save Morty, who died Thursday, Robbins said.

"He rallied and we thought we had him on the way back, but it was just too late." Robbins said. "I lost a friend."

One goal of the research was to learn why captive moose rarely live past the age of 6 or 7, while in the wild they live as long as 16 years, Robbins said.

Sunday, January 24, 1993   *THE SAN DIEGO UNION-TRIBUNE*

OBITUARIES

Stewart Cartwright, 38; family practice physician

Stewart Mark Cartwright, 38, a family practice physician formerly with Kaiser Permanente in La Mesa, died suddenly Wednesday at his Tierrasanta home.

Dr. Cartwright practiced at the La Mesa Kaiser Permanente Outpatient Clinic for the last 2½ years and was in the process of joining a local medical group.

He died of a cardiac aneurysm, his family said.

As the son of an Air Force officer, Cartwright lived all over the world. He settled in San Diego after completing his residency in Philadelphia.

"He wanted to help people," said Dr. Cartwright's girlfriend, Diane Gallo. "He wasn't in it for the money. He spent his lunch hour calling patients to see how they were doing or calling patients' families to tell them what was happening."

Aside from his dedication to his job, Dr. Cartwright was an avid athlete who played softball, tennis and basketball, his family recalled.

"He was a home-run hitter from Little League to (the age of) 38," said his mother, Mary Frances Cartwright of Houston. His father, Lt. Col. Bruce Cartwright, died last year.

In addition to Gallo and his mother, Dr. Cartwright is survived by a sister, Jacquelyn Cartwright; brother, Scott Cart-

Union-Tribune
Stewart Mark Cartwright, M.D.: *Specialized in family practice.*

wright; aunts, Janet Cartwright and Harriet Marx, and cousins, Bruce and Keith Cartwright and Gene and Jimmy Marx.

There will be a visitation from 4 to 8 p.m. tomorrow and a memorial service at 7 p.m. Tuesday at El Camino Mortuary on Carrol Canyon Road. The family asks that donations be sent to the American Heart Association or any cardiac charity.

Ellen Joyce Alter
Detroit Lawyer, 44

Ellen Joyce Alter, a Detroit civic leader and bankruptcy lawyer, died on Saturday at St. Joseph Mercy Hospital in Pontiac, Mich. She was 44.

Her family said the cause was a cerebral aneurysm.

Born in Cambridge, Mass., Mrs. Alter graduated from Brandeis University and the University of Michigan law school. She was an adjunct professor of law at the University of Detroit and a member of the Anti-Defamation League and the Jewish Welfare Federation of Metropolitan Detroit.

She was a partner in the law firm of Jaffe, Raitt, Heuer & Weiss, and specialized in the rights of creditors and debtors.

She is survived by her husband, Peter; a son, Daniel; a daughter, Jessica, and her parents.

SUNDAY, JUNE 6, 1993

ST. LOUIS POST-DISPATCH

Country Music Star Conway Twitty Dies

compiled From News Services

SPRINGFIELD, Mo. — Conway Twitty, who started as a teen rock idol in the 1950s and crossed over to country to become a star, died Saturday at age 59.

His wife, Dee Henry, and some of his band members were with him at Cox Medical Center-South when he died of complications from surgery after a blood vessel ruptured in his stomach.

Mr. Twitty collapsed on his tour bus during a rest stop in southwestern Missouri on the way home to Hendersonville, Tenn., from a performance Friday night in Branson, Mo.

Mr. Twitty was born Sept. 1, 1933, as Harold Lloyd Jenkins. He changed his name in 1957 by borrowing from Conway, Ark., and Twitty, Texas.

Twitty

After spending many years as a song-writer, his performing career took off with the name change. He recorded more than 40 No. 1 hits, including "Hello Darlin'," "Tight-Fittin' Jeans" and "Linda On My Mind."

"Everyone will remember Conway Twitty, industry and fans alike, as the consummate singer and performer, who has been this wonderful and dynamic presence in our business for over 30 years," said Bruce Hinton, chairman of MCA Records in Nashville.

Mel Tillis, who said Mr. Twitty and his wife were at Tillis' Branson theater Thursday night, called Twitty a great singer. "He didn't do a lot of talking on stage; he said he let his music do his talking," Tillis said. "He was a song's best friend, because he could really sing."

Mr. Twitty and Loretta Lynn won the Country Music Association's Vocal Duo of the Year award in 1972, 1973, 1974, and 1975. They won a Grammy for their 1971 duet, "After The Fire Is Gone."

Mr. Twitty got his break as a rockabilly artist in the 1950s, writing songs for the Sun Records' stable of singers that included Elvis Presley and Jerry Lee Lewis.

His first hit was "It's Only Make Believe," which soared to No. 1 on the pop charts in 1958.

Despite the advice of managers, booking agents and record company people, Mr. Twitty made the switch to country and turned out a string of No. 1 hits.

In 1982, Mr. Twitty opened Twitty City, a nine-acre tourist complex in Hendersonville, a suburb of Nashville.

As a boy in Friars Point, Miss., Mr. Twitty learned his first guitar chords from his father, a riverboat captain on the Mississippi.

"My Dad told me when I was a kid: 'When the cotton is out there, you get it. When it's not out there, you can rest,' " Mr. Twitty said in an interview in 1990. "I've been fortunate. It has been out there for me for a long time."

Besides his wife, among survivors are his four children.

OBITUARIES

David Houston; Star At Grand Ole Opry

Houston

NASHVILLE, Tenn. (AP) — David Houston, the Grand Ole Opry star who won a Grammy for the country music classic "Almost Persuaded," died Tuesday (Nov. 30, 1993) at the age of 57.

Mr. Houston suffered a ruptured brain aneurism Thanksgiving Day and never regained consciousness, said Paul Hockett, a spokesman for Bossier Medical Center in Bossier City, La., where Mr. Houston died.

"Almost Persuaded," a million-seller hit in 1966, chronicled a honky-tonk flirtation in which a married man considered cheating on his wife.

He was one of the most successful country singers in the mid-1960s and had performed at the Grand Ole Opry since 1972.

Among his other hits were "Already It's Heaven," "You Mean the World to Me," "Can't You Feel It," "The Twelfth of Never," "I Love You, I Love You" and "With One Exception."

Mr. Houston and Barbara Mandrell were duet partners in the early 1970s. He also recorded "My Elusive Dreams" with Tammy Wynette in 1967.

Mr. Houston, who lived in Kenner, La., last appeared on the Opry on Nov. 6. He had not been an active recording artist for the past 10 years.

thought to be a sex-linked recessive defect of copper absorption. The affected infants exibit retarded growth, defective keratin formation and loss of hair pigment, low body temperature, degeneration and fracture of aortic elastin (aneurysms), arthritis in the growth plate of long bones, and a progressive mental deterioration (brain tissue is totally free of the essential enzyme cytochrome c oxidase). Because of absorption problems of metallic copper, injections of copper are usefull.

Serum and plasma copper increase 100 % in pregnant women and women using oral contraceptives. Serum copper levels are also elevated during acute infections, liver disease and pellegra (niacin deficiency).

Accumulations of copper in the cornea form Kayser-Fleischer rings.

Dy - Dysprosium, a RareEarth, is found in igneous rocks at 3 ppm; in shale at 4 to 6 ppm; sandstone at 7.2 ppm and limestone at 0.9 ppm. Concentrations in terrestrial animals (0.01 ppm) are highest in the bones.

Er - Erbium, a RareEarth, is found in igneous rock at 2.8 ppm; shale at 1.9 ppm; sandstone at 1 ppm; limestone at 0.36 ppm; land plants up to 46 ppm in Carya spp.; marine animals at 0.02 to 0.04 ppm and land animals primarily in bone.

Eu - Europium is a "light" Rare Earth found in igneous rocks at 1 to 2 ppm; shales at 1.1 ppm; sandstone at 0.55 ppm; limestone at 0.2 ppm; land plants at 0.021 ppm(accumulate up to 16 ppm in Carya spp.); marine animals 0.01 to 0.06 ppm; land animals 0.00012 ppm in soft tissue and 0.2 ppm in bone.

Europium has extended the life of laboratory species over their normal expected lifespan by 100 percent. Europium is found in higher concentration in breast milk from women in third world countries than in American women.

1.*Tang, R-H., et al.*: Stimulation of Proliferation of *Tetrahymena pyriformis* by Trace Rare Earths. Biol. Trace Ele. Research.7:95.1985.

F - Flourine is found in igneous rocks at 625 ppm; in shale at 740 ppm; sandstone at 270 ppm; limestone at 330 ppm; fresh water at 0.09 ppm; sea water at 1.3 ppm; soils at 200 ppm (flouride can be "fixed " or tightly bonded in several types of clays. Certain F rich soils in Madras, Spain and South America are toxic to grazing livestock.

Flourine is found in marine plants at 4.5 ppm; land plants at 0,5 to 40.0 ppm(accumulated by *Dichapetolum cymosum*); marine animals at 2.0 ppm (accumulates in fish bone); land animals at 150 to 500 ppm in mammalian soft tissues and 1,500 ppm in bone and teeth.

Prior to 1972, flouride was considered essential in animals because of its apparent benefit for tooth enamel in warding off dental caries ("cavities"). In 1972, Schwarz proved that flouride was in fact an essential mineral.

The skeletal reserves of flouride in an adult man reach 2.6 grams; the average daily intake by Americans is 4.4 mg from combined sources of food and water.

Flouridation of drinking water is still highly controversial - some studies show that flouridated water helps reduce fractures from osteoporosis while other studies showed an increase in hip fractures.

Friday, April 15, 1994

THE SAN DIEGO UNION-TRIBUNE

Calcium, fluoride supplements deter osteoporosis, study finds

NEW YORK TIMES NEWS SERVICE

WASHINGTON — A study released yesterday supports the idea that a careful regimen of fluoride and calcium supplements appears to prevent new spinal fractures in patients with a major form of osteoporosis while helping to rebuild bone loss.

Experts on osteoporosis, the debilitating bone-thinning condition that afflicts millions of elderly Americans, said that if the findings stood up, the treatment would be the first to restore bone mass lost to the disease.

The interim results of the study were reported by researchers at the University of Texas.

Dr. Charles Y.C. Pak and his colleagues said their controlled study of 99 post-menopausal women who were diagnosed with osteoporosis showed that fracturing in the spinal vertebrae could be greatly reduced with low doses of fluoride given in slow-release form along with a readily absorbed type of calcium not commonly used.

Half the group had an increase of about 5 percent per year in the bone mass of their vertebrae, and their spinal fractures decreased by more than 50 percent.

The findings, reported in *The Annals of Internal Medicine*, should renew interest in the treatment, pioneered at the university's Southwestern Medical Center at Dallas.

The results of the new Texas study are being hailed as solid indications that the right combination of fluoride and calcium, given on a particular schedule, may have a major impact on the bone disease.

"This study suggests that at the lower doses of fluoride that they used, using their different formulations of the drugs and using their schedule of treatment, that fluoride may be helpful," said Dr. B. Lawrence Riggs of the Mayo Clinic in Rochester, Minn., a researcher who led a study published in 1990 that raised doubts about the fluoride treatment.

"This is good, solid work, and it should encourage others to do more research on fluoride and osteoporosis."

Dr. Judith L. Vaitukaitis, the director of the National Center for Research Resources, a unit of the National Institutes of Health that sponsors the Texas work, said the few therapies for osteoporosis slow bone loss but do not stop it. The Texas study shows that fluoride can rebuild weakened bones, she said.

More than 25 million older Americans — 90 percent of them women — have osteoporosis, which is responsible for 1.5 million fractures of the hip, spine and wrist each year, according to the National Osteoporosis Foundation.

With the spinal form of the disease, fractures occur in the vertebrae, causing them to compress and the back to curve, a condition sometimes called dowager's hump.

Pak said his group had been successful because lower doses of sodium fluoride stimulated the production of bone cells while reducing the toxicity the drug, which can cause severe nausea, vomiting and other problems.

The researchers also use a time-release form of sodium fluoride, developed by Mission Pharmacal Co. of San Antonio, that puts the drug in a porous wax capsule that passes through the stomach, the primary site of complications.

Clinical toxicity is observed as dental flourosis at flouride concentrations of 2 to7 ppm and osteosclerosis at 8 to 20 ppm; chronic systemic toxicity appears when the flouride levels reach 20 to 80 mg per day for years.

Approximately 10,000 American towns and cities serving 100 million people have added flouride to their drinking water at the rate of 1 mg /L which has reportedly reduced dental caries by 60 to 70 percent. In certain western states in the United States, there is an excess of flouride, reaching levels of 10 to 45 ppm with resultant mottling of teeth in children.

As a result of epidemiological studies by Yiamouyiannis and Burk in 1977, full scale congressional hearings were held to examine the charge that 10,000 excess cancer deaths were caused by flouridation of certain public water systems. As a result of those hearings, the committee mandated that the U.S. Public Health Service conduct animal studies to confirm or refute the theory that flouridated water increased cancer deaths. The studies were carried out by the National Toxicology Program under the supervision of the U.S. National Public Health Service with special focus on oral, liver and bone cancers.

In 1990, the results of the flouride study showed an increase in rat precancerous in oral mucus membrane cells; there was an increase in cancers of the oral mucus membranes (squamous cell carcinoma); a rare form of osteosarcoma appeared at double the rate in males as females; and there was an increase in thyroid follicular cell tumors and liver cancer (hepatocholangiocarcinoma).

Fe - Iron is found in igneous rocks at 56,300 ppm; shale at 47,200 ppm; sandstone at 9,800 ppm and limestone at 3,800 ppm; fresh water at 0.67 ppm; sea water at 0.01 ppm; soils at 38,000 ppm (iron content is responsable for most soil color); iron is most available in acid soil and availability is greatly determined by bacterial activity in the soil; marine plants at 700 ppm (very high in plankton); land plants at 140 ppm; marine animals at 400 ppm (high in the blood of annelids (worms), echinoderms, fish and in eggs of cephalad molluscs); essential to all land animals.

Boussingault in the 1860's was the first to regard iron as an essential nutrient for animals. During the 1920's an animal model for iron deficiency research was created by feeding rats on an exclusive milk diet.

In a healthy adult human there is 3 to 5 gms of iron. The newborn infant has nearly double the amount of iron per kg than adults. Sixty to 70 percent of tissue iron is classed as essential or functional iron, and 30 to 40 percent as storage iron. The essential iron is found as an integral part of hemoglobin, myoglobin (muscle oxygen storing pigments - particularly rich in deep diving animals such as whales, walrus, seals, etc.) and respiratory enzymes involved with intracellular oxidation-reduction processes.

Functions of iron include cofactor and activator of enzymes and metallo enzymes; respiratory pigments (hemoglobin - iron is to hemoglobin what Mg is to chlorophyll) and electron transfer for utilization of oxygen.

Iron is stored in bone marrow and liver (i.e.- hemosiderin and ferritin). Heme iron from meat is 10 percent available for absorption while iron from fresh plant sources are only one percent available because of phytates. Absorption takes place primarily in the duodenum where the intestinal environment is still acid.

Experimental evidence shows very clearly that "pica" is a specific sign of iron deficiency. Pica can drive children and adults to eat ice (pagophagia), dirt (geophagia) or lead paint.

Iron deficiency results from pregnancy, menstruation, chronic infections, hypochlorhydria (low stomach acid from salt restricted diets), chronic diarrhea, chronic bleeding (i.e.- cancer, ulcers, parasites, etc.) and impaired absorption (i.e.- high fat diets, celiac disease, etc.).

Symptoms of iron deficiency include listlessness, fatigue, heart palpitations on exertion, reduced cognation, memory deficits, sore tongue, angular stomatitis, dysphagia, hypochromic microcytic anemia.

Stomach hydrochloric acid is required for optimal absorption of iron, ascorbic acid increases absorption of iron, clays and phytates decrease absorption of iron. The RDA of 18 mg per day as metallic iron is very low if one is a vegan eating high fiber, high phytate plant material.

Iron can cause cirrhosis of the liver, fibrosis of the pancreas, diabetes and heart failure - these diseases are not direct affects of iron per se, but rather the increased iron causes increased needs for selenium, copper, zinc, etc.

Fr - Francium is found only as radioactive isotopes; the longest lived has a half life of 22 minutes.

Ga - Gallium is found in igneous rocks at 15 ppm; shales as 19 ppm; sandstones at 12 ppm; limestones 4 ppm; fresh water at 0.001 ppm; sea water at 0.00003 ppm;

soils at 0.4 to 6.0 ppm to 30.0 ppm; marine plants at 0.5 ppm; land plants at 0.06 ppm; marine animals at 0.5 ppm; land animals at 0.006 ppm.

Gallium was claimed to be essential in 1938 and again in 1958. Gallium has specific areas of metalloenzyme activity in the human brain and has been reported to specifically reduce the rate of brain cancer in laboratory animals.

British research shows that supplemented diets of pregnant women reduces the rate of brain cancer in children.

1.*Spezioli, M., et al.*: Gallium Distribution in Human Brain Areas. Biol. Trace Ele. Research. 22:9.1989.

Gd - Gadolium, a RareEarth, is found in igneous rocks at 5.4 ppm; shales at 4.3 ppm; sandstones at 2.6 ppm; limestones at 0.7 ppm; land plants at up to 70 ppm by Carya spp.; marine animals at 0.06 ppm; land animals accumulate gadolium in bone and liver very quickly after absorption.

Ge - Germanium is found in igneous rocks at 5.4 ppm; shales at 1.6 ppm; sandstones at 0.8 ppm; limestones at 0.2 ppm; sea water at 0.00007 ppm; soil at 1 ppm in humus, especially in alkaline soils; marine animals at 0.3 ppm.

The existence of the element germanium had been predicted by Mendeleev in his periodic table, but it was not until 1886, that a German scientist, Clemens Winkler isolated this element and named it germanium. Radio do-it-yourself kits from the 40's and 50's utilized the germanium diode crystal to attract the radio signal to your radio. The germanium atom is structured so it accepts and transmits electrons, thus acting as a semiconductor - it is therefore not

SUNDAY, AUGUST 1, 1993

THE NEW YORK TIMES

Representative Paul B. Henry, 51, Dies After Battling Brain Cancer

GRAND RAPIDS, Mich., July 31 (AP) — Representative Paul B. Henry, whose hard work and moderate views made him a rising star in the national Republican Party, died Saturday at his home here. He was 51.

Mr. Henry died of brain cancer, which was diagnosed in October after he complained of headaches while campaigning for his fifth term, according to a statement released by his office.

On Oct. 21, doctors removed most of a 3-inch malignant tumor from the right frontal lobe of Mr. Henry's brain. Despite the surgery and prognosis, he easily won re-election two weeks later. Thousands of letters of support flooded his home and offices.

While Mr. Henry's doctors initially expressed optimism, cancer experts said patients with his type of cancer, glioblastoma multiforme, survived an average of about a year, and fewer than 5 percent survived five years.

Associated Press, 1993

Paul B. Henry

Increasing Margins of Victory

In the months after the surgery, Mr. Henry, his family and staff members tried to remain upbeat and did not address the possibility of his resignation. But by late spring, he was mostly bedridden, and by midsummer, his staff said that he could no longer communicate and that they were not sure if he recognized friends.

First elected to Congress in 1984, Mr. Henry earned increasing margins of victory in each election.

In 1990, he was named one of the 11 "rising stars" by the National Journal. He was said to be a strong contender for the 1994 race against Senator Donald W. Riegle Jr., a Democrat.

The district Mr. Henry represented is in western lower Michigan and included Grand Rapids.

Taught Political Science

A Chicago native, Mr. Henry graduated from Wheaton College in Illinois and then served with the Peace Corps in Ethiopia and Liberia for two years before earning a master's degree and doctorate from Duke University.

He taught political science at Duke in 1969 and at Calvin College from 1970 to 1978 before being elected to the Michigan Legislature in 1979. He served in the state House from 1979 to 1982, and in the state Senate in 1983 and 1984.

He was elected to Congress in 1984, to the seat once held by former President Gerald R. Ford.

Mr. Henry served on the House Committees on Education and Labor and Science, Space and Technology, as well as the Select Committee on Aging. Shortly after the cancer was diagnosed, he failed in an effort to win a seat on the House Ways and Means Committee.

He is survived by his wife, Karen, and his three children, Kara, Jordan and Megan.

OBITUARIES

THE SAN DIEGO UNION-TRIBUNE

Dr. Helen F. Cserr, 57; brain researcher

NEW YORK TIMES NEWS SERVICE

Helen F. Cserr, a professor of physiology at Brown University in Providence, R.I., whose research focused on the anatomy and mechanism of the human brain, died Aug. 11 at her home in North Dighton, Mass. She was 57.

She died of a brain tumor, said her daughter, Ruth, of Princeton, N.J.

Dr. Cserr joined the Brown faculty in 1970 after serving as a researcher at Harvard University, where she received a Ph.D. in physiology.

NEW YORK TIMES NEWS SERVICE

ST. LOUIS POST-DISPATCH

WEDNESDAY, SEPTEMBER 1, 1993

RICHARD JORDAN, 56, an award-winning actor and director whose career spanned movies, television and the stage, died of a brain tumor Monday (Aug. 30, 1993) in Los Angeles.

Mr. Jordan won a Golden Globe as best actor in the mid-1970s television miniseries ''Captains and Kings,'' playing a poor immigrant who rose to prominence in Taylor Caldwell's tale of an Irish dynasty in America.

He made his movie debut in ''Lawman'' in 1970. He went on to do such movies as Woody Allen's ''Interiors,'' ''Rooster Cogburn,'' ''Raise the Titanic,'' ''A Flash of Green,'' ''Dune,'' ''The Mean Season,'' ''Romero,'' ''The Hunt for Red October,''

Jordan

''Shout'' and ''Posse.''

His television productions include ''The Bunker,'' ''Les Miserables,'' ''The Murder of Mary Phagan,'' ''Breakdown,'' ''The Equalizer'' and ''Killer Angels.'' His latest project, which he helped to write, was the television epic ''Gettysburg,'' scheduled to be shown on TNT next month.

On stage, Mr. Jordan appeared in more than 100 plays on and off Broadway and spent eight years with the New York Shakespeare Festival.

Los Angeles Times

SUNDAY, NOVEMBER 13, 1994
COPYRIGHT 1994 / THE TIMES MIRROR COMPANY / CC†/ 676 PAGES

Olympic Legend Wilma Rudolph Dies

HULTON DEUTSCH / Allsport

Rudolph races to 100-meter gold in '60 Olympics.

■ **Sports:** Triple gold medalist who inspired a generation of women's track stars loses battle with brain cancer at 54.

By RANDY HARVEY
TIMES STAFF WRITER

NASHVILLE, Tenn.—Wilma Rudolph, who as a child walked with the aid of a leg brace but ran to three Olympic gold medals and inspired a generation of future champions, died at her home Saturday of brain cancer. She was 54.

Rudolph overcame childhood battles with pneumonia, scarlet fever and polio to become the first U.S. female track and field athlete to win three gold medals in the same Olympics, finishing first in the 100 meters and 200 meters and running the anchor leg for the victorious 400-meter relay team in 1960 at Rome.

"She's a legend in track and field, like Jesse Owens," said Ollan Cassell, executive director of USA Track & Field. "After Jesse died, she became the icon, a symbol of what the Olympics mean to this country and this sport. This is really a sad day."

Cassell and other sports officials are in Nashville for the U.S. Olympic Congress, which opened Thursday

Please see RUDOLPH, A34

too surprising that germanium is closely related to silica and carbon.

Biologically, germanium is a highly efficient electrical impulse initiator intracellularly and acts as a metallic cofactor for oxygen utilization.

In 1950, Dr. Kazuhiko Asai, a Japanese chemist, found traces of germanium in fossilized plant life. Russian researchers quickly attributed anti-cancer activity to germanium. Dr. Asai was able to connect the healing properties of certain herbs to relatively high levels of germanium - many of these herbs are accumulator plants for germanium. Germanium is known to enhance the immune system by stimulating production of natural killer cells, lymphokines such as IFN(Y), interferon, macrophages and T-suppressor cells.

Asai synthesized GE-132, carboxyethyl germanium sesquioxide in 1967 by a hydrolysis method. This organic germanium structure forms a cubic structure with three negative oxygen ions at the base of a cubic triangle.

As an organic or chelate form of germanium GE-132 is absorbed at the rate of 30 percent efficiency and the total intake is excreted in one week.

Food plants and animals contain small amounts of germanium (i.e.- beans-4.67 ppm; tuna-2.3 ppm). Healing herbs such as garlic, aloe, comfrey, chlorella, ginseng, watercress, Shiitake mushroom, pearl barley, sanzukon, sushi, waternut, boxthorn seed and wisteria knob contain germanium in amounts ranging from 100 to 2,000 ppm.

The "holy waters" at Lourdes, known world wide for their healing properties contains large amounts of germanium.

Deficiencies of germanium are typified by severely reduced immune status, arthritis, osteoporosis, low energy and cancer.

Twenty to 30 mg per day is the recommended maintenace dose for germanium; 50 to 100 mg per day are commonly used when an individual has a serious illness that requires an increased oxygen level in the body.

1.*Goodman,S.*: Therapeutic Effects of Germanium. Med.Hypoth.26:207.1988.

2.*Suzuki,F.*, et al.: Ability of Sera From Mice Treated With Ge-132, an Organic Germanium Compound, to Inhibit Experimental Murine Ascites Tumours. Br.J.Cancer.52:757.1985.

H - Hydrogen is found in igneous rocks at 1,000 ppm; shale at 5,600 ppm; sandstone at 1,800 ppm; limestone at 860 ppm; fresh water at 111,000 ppm; sea water at 108, ppm; soil at 600 to 24,000 ppm (in very acid soils it can become the major exchangeable cation); marine plants at 41,000 ppm; land plants at 55,000 ppm; marine animals 52,000 ppm; land animals 70,000 ppm; additionally hydrogen makes up a small portion of the gaseous atmosphere.

Functions as a major constituant of water (70 % of the human body is water) and all organic molecules. The regulation of the acid-base balance in the human body is in fact the regulation of the hydrogen ion (H+) levels of cellular and extracellular fluids.

The acidity of the body is critically regulated within a very narrow range by numerous and complex homeostatic mechanisms. The pH of healthy blood ranges from 7.36 to 7.44; when the pH falls below 7.30, the patient has acidosis and when the pH rises above 7.44, the person has alkalosis.

Blood pH below 6.8 and above 7.8 are rapidly fatal. Intracellular pH ranges between 6.0 and 7.4; rapid metabolism (hyperthyroid) or decreased blood flow (heart attack) increases the carbon dioxide levels and therefore decreases pH or acidifies the blood.

In contrast to the internal body, the pH of secretions and excretions can be more variable and range from 1.0 in stomach acid to 8.2 in pancreatic juice and alkaline urine of vegans.

Hydrogen ions circulate in the body in two forms, volatile and non-volatile (metabolic hydrogen ions). Volatile hydrogen ions are found as a weak acid (carbonic acid), which must continuously be excreted from the lungs as carbon dioxide and water.

Non-volatile (metabolic) hydrogen ions are produced by the normal metabolic processes of the body or are consumed as part of food. The largest amounts of hydrogen ions are produced by normal and abnormal metabolism. Large amounts of hydrogen ions may be generated and/or retained as part of a disease activity (i.e.- emphysema, diabetes, anxiety or loss of chloride ions (NaCl deficiency, cystic fibrosis, Addison's Diseases, etc.).

Hydrogen ion concentration (pH) is controlled by the body by means of dilution, buffering, respiratory control of volatile hydrogen ion concentrations and kidney control of non-volatile hydrogen ions. Buffer systems react to hydrogen ion concentra-

tions in fractions of seconds, respiratory controls react in minutes and the kidneys may require as much as an hour to several days to respond.

Metabolic hydrogen ions must be excreted by the kidney in one of three forms:

1) 60 % as ammomium ions
2) 40% as weak acids
3) trace amounts as free hydrogen ions

It is the amount of free hydrogen ions in the urine that determines the urine's pH. Bladder infections (cystitis) can often times be controlled by acidifying the urine with unsweatened cranberry juice.

He - Helium is found in igneous rocks at 0.008 and sea water at 0.0000069 ppm.

Hf - Hafnium is found in igneous rocks at 3 ppm; shale at 2.8 ppm; sandstone at 3.4 ppm; limestone at 0.3 ppm; sea water at 0.000008 ppm; soil at 3.0 ppm; marine plants at 0.4 ppm; land plants at 0.01 ppm; land animals at 0.04 ppm.

Hg - Mercury is found in igneous rocks at 0.08 ppm; shale at 0.4 ppm; sandstone at 0.03 ppm; limestone at 0.04 ppm; fresh water at 0.00008 ppm; sea water at

Table 11-14:Mercury Mine Workers (Cinnabar Miners) Tissue Mercury Levels (ppm)					
	Thyroid	Pituitary	Kidney	Liver	Brain
Miners	35.2	27.1	8.4	0.26	0.70
Controls	0.03	0.04	0.14	0.3	0.0042

0.00003 ppm; soil at 0.03 to 0.8 ppm(lowest in the surface layers of the soil because it is leached and also it is volatilized); marine plants at 0.03 ppm; land plants at 0.015 ppm (*Arenaria setacea* is an accumulator plant); land animals at 0.046 ppm (accumulates in the brain, kidney, liver and bone); marine animals at 0.0009 to 0.09 ppm.

Mercury occurs universally in the bios and has long been known as a toxic element (although the early Chinese alchemist insisted that the regular consumption of mercury or potable gold was the path to immortality) concentrated by industry, mining operations, agriculture, dental repairs (amalgams) and microorganisms that "methylate" mercury in the sediments at the bottoms of fresh water or salt water rivers, lakes, oceans and seas.

Mercury has been detected in all tissues of accident victims, with no known mercury exposure except dental mercury amalgam fillings.

Mercury in fish is present as methyl mercury. People who rarely eat fish have very low levels of mercury (2-5 ug/kg); moderate fish consumers have 10 ug/kg; high fish consumers (especially if they eat shark, tuna or swordfish) have higher values of 400 ug/kg.

Mercury mine workers accumulate mercury which can reach levels that produce disease (Table 11- 14).

The biological half time of methyl mercury in humans is 70 days and four days for inorganic mercury. The placenta acts as a barrier against the passage of inorganic mercury but not methyl mercury; methyl mercury transfers very easily to the fetus ("congenital" Minamata disease in infants).

The main industrial source of mercury is the chloralkali industry; additional major sources include the manufacture of electrical appliances, paint, dental amalgams, pharmaceuticals, slimicides and algicides (paper and pulp industry), seed treatments as agricultural fungicides - especially dangerous as methyl mercury; burning of fossil fuels.

The metabolic antagonism between mercury and selenium results in the protection from selenium poisoning by mercury and the protection against mercury poisoning by selenium. A mutual antagonism between Hg and Se exists; Se protects the human kidney from necrosis (tissue death) by mercury poisoning and the placental transfer of mercury.

Mercury vapor from dental amalgam has been shown to increase the percent of antibiotic resistant bacteria in the gut from 9 percent to 70 percent in monkeys given dental mercury fillings; the drug resistant bacterial population dropped to 12 percent when the fillings were removed.

Mercury poisoning from inhalation of mercury vapors was reported during the Victorian Age in "hatters" who used mercuric nitrate paste to prevent mold from growing on felt hats ("mad as a hatter" - from Alice in Wonderland), goldsmiths and mirror workers; in modern times dentists have developed mental disease from chronic exposure to mercury vapors (they have the highest rate of suicide amongst all the health professionals); dental patients have developed several disease syndromes including multiple sclerosis (Fig. 11-12), ALS (Lou Gehrig's Disease) and Parkinson's Disease depending on what part of the brain was most severely affected.

Annette Funichello contracted multiple sclerosis which is known to be caused by vapours from dental mercury amalgams.

The manifestations of direct Hg poison-

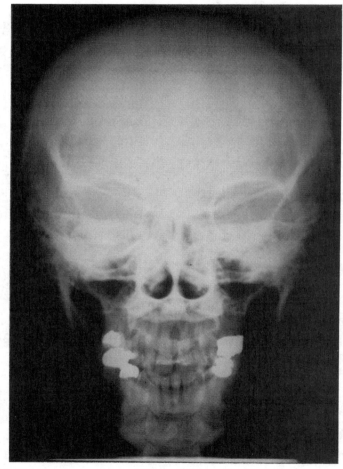

Fig. 11-12 Mercury amalgam "fillings" in a patient with multiple sclerosis

OBITUARIES

Dr. Samuel L. Gilberg; Dentist, Playwright And Businessman

Dr. Samuel L. Gilberg — a dentist, a businessman and a playwright — died Monday (Aug. 9, 1993) at his home in Glencoe after a 10-year struggle with amyotrophic lateral sclerosis, or Lou Gehrig's Disease. He was 73.

Dr. Gilberg gave up his dental practice in St. Louis County in 1983, when doctors told him he had the disease. To fill the time, he turned to writing plays.

He was already an accomplished businessman. In 1963, he founded the Missouri School for Doctors' Assistants. The school, in Warson Woods, trains medical and dental assistants and medical and dental office workers. Today, the school is run by Dr. Gilberg's daughter, Laurel Vander Velde, and her husband, Michael, of Des Peres.

Dr. Gilberg also founded the Dental West Laboratory, which closed with his practice, and was first president of the Missouri Association of Private Career Schools, an organization he helped to found.

In the last decade, he became a prolific writer, turning out 20 plays, dozens of short stories and many articles. One of his plays, "The Lash," has been staged by the City Players and the Jewish Community Centers Association. It was inspired by the life of Uriah Phillips Levy, the first Jew to achieve high rank in the Navy and a 19th-century crusader against the tradition of flogging errant sailors.

Dr. Gilberg had his own Naval background, serving as a Navy dentist in World War II. After the war, he practiced in University City, Warson Woods, Clayton and Creve Coeur; his family said he was a pioneer in such techniques as dental implants and cantilever bridges. In his spare time, he enjoyed inventing novelty items.

Among survivors, in addition to his daughter, are his wife of 49 years, Muriel Gilberg; another daughter, Candace Stuckenschneider of Pacific; two sons, Kenneth Gilberg and Douglas Gilberg, both of Glencoe; a brother, David Gilberg of Mount Vernon, N.Y.; four sisters, Lillian Chasen of Altadena, Calif., Esther Knox of Mount Vernon, Betty Silberman of Mission Viejo, Calif., and Roslyn Brock of Fort Lee, N.J.; six grandchildren; and one great-grandchild.

Visitation will be from noon until 1 p.m. Wednesday at the Berger Memorial Chapel, 4715 McPherson Avenue. The funeral service will be held there at 1 p.m., with burial at United Hebrew Cemetery. The family will sit shiva at Dr. Gilberg's home, 2900 Ossenfort Road in Glencoe, until Friday afternoon.

OBITUARIES

Dr. Edward A. Kemler; activist in S. Bay service organizations

By JACK WILLIAMS, Staff Writer

Dr. Edward A. Kemler, a retired orthodontist whose commitment to South Bay area service organizations spanned parts of five decades, died Friday of Lou Gehrig's disease at his Bonita home. He was 67.

Dr. Kemler was diagnosed with amyotrophic lateral sclerosis in January of last year and had been participating in an experimental drug study program for ALS patients. The disease, characterized by a deterioration of nerve cells and loss of muscle control, is named after the legendary Hall of Fame first basemen.

Dr. Edward A. Kemler

Dr. Kemler remained active until early this year with the Chula Vista Rotary Club and the Community Congregational Church of Chula Vista. He was on the board of trustees of the Chula Vista City School District from 1968 to 1976 and served as president in 1971-72, overseeing an extensive expansion program.

At various times from the '50s through the early '90s, Dr. Kemler served as president and director of the Chula Vista Community Chest, volunteered for the Salvation Army and the Sharp-Chula Vista Community Hospital Auxiliary and served as a Boy Scouts leader.

Family and friends say Dr. Kemler adhered to the credo "service before self," suggesting ways to help survivors of the Jan. 17 Northridge earthquake even while bedridden with his disease.

Dr. Kemler opened his private orthodontics practice when he and his wife, June, came to Chula Vista in 1956 from his native Chicago. He taught orthodontics at Loma Linda University in 1961-65.

Dr. Kemler received his dentistry and orthodontics degrees from Northwestern University. He served in the U.S. Navy during World War II and the Korean War.

An active outdoorsman, Dr. Kemler built two of his family's pleasure boats and enjoyed fishing, camping and restoring and showing Chevrolet Corvairs. He often drove his Corvairs in parades, escorting VIPs.

In addition to his wife of 41 years, Dr. Kemler is survived by two daughters, Susan Walker, of Bellflower, and Carol Budden, of Englewood, Colo.; two sons, David, of Santee, and Richard, of Chula Vista; and a sister, Constance Kent, of Monterey.

A memorial service is scheduled at 11 a.m. Saturday at Community Congregational Church of Chula Vista, where a reception will follow.

The family suggests contributions to a remembrance fund at Community Congregational Church of Chula Vista, the Chula Vista Rotary Foundation or the MDA Center for ALS.

ing are primarily neurological (i.e.- tremers, vertigo, irritability, moodiness (suicidal), depression, salivation, inflammation of the mouth {stomatitis} and diarrhea).

In poisoning with inorganic mercury, the liver and kidney's are the target organs primarily affected; poisoning with the more toxic alkyl mercury results in progressive incoordination, loss of vision, heart palpitations, loss of hearing and mental deterioration caused by a toxic neuro-encephalopathy in which the neuronal cells of the cerebral and cerebellar cortex are selectively affected.

In 1962, Minamata, Japan, mercury contaminated factory effluent (waste water) was dumped into the bay, which in turn contaminated aquatic plant material which was eaten by fish; the contaminated fish were eaten by the bay residents with disasterous results.

The Minamata disaster was characterized by a high incidence of "congenital" damage to the newborn (i.e.- mental retardation, cerebral palsy, and high infant mortality).

In Iran, large scale methyl mercury poisoning was reported when large numbers of people were fed bread made with mercurial fungicide treated seed grain and meat (liver and kidneys) from animals fed the treated grain.

The result of consuming the mercury contaminated grains was thousands of babies born retarded, a high incidence of congenital brain defects including cerebral palsy.

Ho - Holmium, a RareEarth, is found in igneous rocks at 1.2 ppm; in shale at 0.6 ppm; sandstone at 0.51 ppm; limestone at 0.17 ppm; land plants at 16 ppm in *Carya*

spp.; marine animals at 0.005 to 0.01 ppm; and land animals at 0.5 ppm in bone.

I - Iodine is found in igneous rocks at 0.5 ppm; in shale at 2.3 ppm; sandstone at 1.7 ppm; limestone at 1.2 ppm; fresh water at 0.002 ppm; sea water at 0.06 ppm; soil at 5 ppm (strongly bound in humus- large areas of Earth known to be devoid of I); marine plants at 30 to 1,500 ppm; land plants at 0.42 ppm; marine animals at 1.0 to 150 ppm; land animals at 0.43 ppm (concentration in the thyroid gland and hair).

Known to be essential to red and brown algae and all vertebrates.

Iodine in combination with the amino acid tyrosine is manufactured into the thyroid hormone thyroxin. Iodine intake is usually low to begin with, but since Americans have begun restricting their salt intake at the advice of their "allopath" goiter (Fig. 11-13) and hypothyroidism has become epidemic.

The average American takes in 170-250 mcg/day of I; humans lose considerable amounts of I in their sweat (up to 146mcg/day with only moderate exercise).

Metallic iodine is not toxic up to 2,000 mcg/day.

Goiter develops in Japanese living along the sea coast despite high daily iodine consumption. Japanese subjects were fed Chinese cabbage, turnips, buckwheat, noodles. 2.0 mcg I, soybean or seaweed - goiter developed in all groups except the seaweed group.

Northern parts of the Adictis Islands had more clinical goiter than the southern areas while the southwest was goiter-free(46% of the population of Pisila; 40% of the population of Polje and only 3% of the population of Milahnici); there is identical

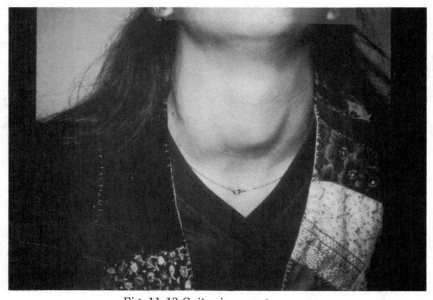

Fig. 11-13 Goiter in young women

iodine content of the soil in all three locations; however, there is a severe copper deficiency in the soils of the north and the south (copper is required to utilize iodine).

Some 11 million Americans have either a hypothyroid (low, underactive) or a hyperthyroid (overactive) condition. Thyroid hormones control and regulate digestion, heart rate, body temperature, sweat gland activity, nervous and reproductive system, general metabolism and body weight.

SYMPTOMS of HYPOTHYROISM
(Hashimoto's Disease)
Fatigue
Cold intolerance
Muscle aches & pains
Heavy or more frequent periods
Low sex drive
Brittle nails
Weight gain
Hair loss
Muscle cramps
Depression
Constipation
Elevated blood cholesterol
Puffy face
Dry skin and hair
Inability to concentrate
Poor memory
Goiter

SYMPTOMS of HYPERTHYROISM
(Grave's Disease)
Insomnia
Heat Intolerance
Excessive sweating
Lighter/less frequent periods
Hand Tremors
Rapid pulse
Exophthalmos ("bug-eyes")
Weight loss
Increased appetite
Muscle weakness
Frequent bowel movements
Irritability
Nervousness
Goiter

Many foods and food aditives are known as "goitrogens" because they interfere with the thyroids metabolism and produce goiter when consumed in inordinate amounts(i.e.- nitrates, broccoli, cabbage, brusselsprouts, etc.).

In - Indium is found in igneous rocks at 0.05 to 1.0 ppm; shale at o.1 ppm; sandstone and limestone at 0.05 ppm; land animals at 0.016 ppm.

Ir - Iridium is found in igneous rocks at 0.001 ppm; Land plants at 0.62 ppm and land animals at 0.00002 ppm.

K - Potassium is found in igneous rocks at 20,000 ppm; shale at 26,000 ppm; sandstone at 10,700 ppm; limestone at 2,700 ppm; fresh water at 2.3 ppm; sea water at 380 ppm; soil at 14,000 ppm (a major exchangeable cation in all, but the most alkaline soils); marine plants at 52,000; land plants at 14,000 ppm; marine animals at 5,000 to 30,000 ppm; land animals at 7,400 ppm (highest levels in soft tissues).

Potassium is essential to all organisms and is the major cation in cell cytoplasm with wide variety of electrochemical and catalytic functions for enzyme systems. Potassium constitutes five percent of the total mineral content of the body; it is the major cation of the intracellular fluid and there is a small amount in the extracellular fluid. With sodium, the other "electrolyte," K participates in the maintenance of normal water balance, osmotic equilibrium and acid-base balance. Potassium participates with Ca in the regulation of neuromuscular activity.

Potassium is easily absorbed, 90 % of ingested K is excreted through the urine, there is essentially no storage of K in the human body requiring significant daily intake of 5,000 mg.

Muscular weakness and mental apathy are features of K deficiency, hypokalemic cardiac failure is the most serious K deficiency event. Diuretics, both natural and prescribed and sweating from colds and flu or exercise, vomiting and diarrhea increase the rate of loss of all minerals, including K,compared with normal expected excretion.

Kr - Krypton is found in igneous rocks at 0.0001 ppm; sea water at 0.0025 ppm. Krypton is legendary for having debilitating effects on "Superman" but in fact is totally harmless for humans and may in fact be an essential element.

La - Lanthanum is a "light" Rare Earth and is found in igneous rocks at 30 ppm; shale at 20 ppm; sandstone at 7.5 ppm; limestone at 6.2 ppm; sea water at 0.000012 ppm; soil at 30 ppm; marine plants at 10 ppm; land plants at 0.085 ppm (accumulated by *Carya spp.* and by the yeast *Candida albicans* up to 370 ppm /day - this may be how Candida causes a debilitating energy sapping "chronic fatigue-like" disease by "stealing" Lanthanum from the patient); marine mammals at 0.1 ppm; land animals at 0.0001 ppm in soft tissue and 0.27 ppm in bone.

The growth of the protozoa *Blepherisma* and *Tetrahymena pyriform*is is stimulated and life span doubled by the presence of the Rare Earth Lanthanum at concentrations of 0.32 ppm.

Li - Lithium is found in igneous rocks at 20 ppm; shale at 66 ppm; sandstone 15 ppm; limestone 5 ppm; fresh water at 0.0011 ppm; sea water at 0.18 ppm; soil at 30 ppm (Li^+ is freely mobile in the soil); marine plants at 5 ppm; land plants at 0.1 ppm; marine animals at 1 ppm; land animals at 0.02 ppm.

Since 1915, the risk of clinical depression nearly doubles with each succeeding generation. Myrna M. Weissman, a psychiatrist at Columbia University, New York City, says that, " Depression is a world wide phenomenon happening at younger and younger ages."

In 1935, the age of early onset of depression was during the late 20's; in 1955 onset dropped to between 15 and 20. One in four women and one in ten men will develop depression. While the professional psychiatrist verbally says that depression and manic depression are due to "feelings that we are out of control of our lives, negative thinking, self recrimination ("I'm a loser") are the root cause of depression," they treat depression successfully with the trace mineral lithium - depression and manic depression with all that implies are simply a lithium deficiency aggravated by high sugar consumption.

344

DEPRESSION COSTS PUT AT $43 BILLION

Study Says Impact of Illness Ranks It Second Behind Heart Disease in U.S.

By DANIEL GOLEMAN

The annual cost of depression in America is $43.7 billion, on a par with heart disease, according to a study made public yesterday.

About 11 million people suffer from depression in a given year, and for nearly two-thirds it goes undiagnosed and untreated, said the study, which was published in The Journal of Clinical Psychiatry.

"What's striking is that the costs of depression are comparable to those for other major diseases," said the leader of the study, Paul Greenberg, a health economist at the Analysis Group, a business consulting concern in Cambridge, Mass. "In allocating resources as a society, we should consider depression as an important health problem, too."

Dr. Frederick Goodwin, director of the National Institute of Mental Health, said that among major diseases, clinical depression ranks second only to advanced coronary heart disease in the total number of days patients spend in the hospital or disabled at home. "Major depression is far more disabling than many medical disorders, including chronic lung disease, arthritis and diabetes," he said.

Tipper Gore's Comment

The study shows that health insurance for mental illness is not a luxury or a frill, said Tipper Gore, the Vice President's wife, who advises President Clinton on the issue.

The greatest source of economic burden, accounting for more than half the total, comes from depression's impact on work performance, especially among those who receive no treatment. The cost of days lost from work is about $11.7 billion, and impairment from the symptoms while people continue on the job costs $12.1 billion more.

The impairments include poor concentration and memory, indecisiveness, fatigue, apathy and a lack of self-confidence — and, in those with mania, a grandiose, unrealistic overconfidence. All these symptoms reduce people's capacity to work; on average, for those who are well enough to work, the report estimates that depression reduces a worker's output by 20 percent.

"Depression tends to strike people in the most productive phase of life, and the most productive people," Dr. Goodwin said.

When someone is depressed on the job it can also hamper co-workers, although the report did not include the costs of this effect in the estimates.

Burden on Employers Cited

The costs of depression were calculated for 1990, the most recent year for which complete data are available. In that year 290 million working days were lost because employees' depression was so severe that they could not work at all, the report estimates.

"Because depression strikes early in life and is so often ongoing, depression imposes an especially large burden on employers," said Mr. Greenberg, the health economist.

Depression costs businesses an average of $3,000 for each depressed worker, the report said. A lot of money could be saved if there were more aggressive diagnosis and treatment of depression; treating depression shortens an episode by an average of one-third, the report estimates.

Suicides are another source of costs, because of the loss of lifetime earnings. In 1990 about 15,000 men and 3,400 women in the Untied States committed suicide because of depression, at a cost of about $7.5 billion, the report says.

Psychiatric care, including hospitalization, psychotherapy and medications, totaled $12.4 billion.

Hidden Costs Not Counted

Dr. Goodwin said the report did not consider such hidden costs from depression as the cost of treatment for substance abuse or other problems deriving from the depression, or the cost of unnecessary medical tests ordered by doctors who mistake depression for other diseases.

"Most depressed people present their symptoms to a nonpsychiatrist, and only one in four of these physicians accurately diagnose the problem," Dr. Goodwin said. He suggested that workplace programs "focus as much on depression as they do now on substance abuse."

The report was prepared by a team led by Mr. Greenberg and Laura Stiglin of the Analysis Group, Dr. Stan Finkelstein of the Sloan School of Management and Ernst Berndt of the National Bureau of Economic Research.

The study was based on 1990 figures for the prevalence of three kinds of depression: major, minor and manic. Symptoms of major depression are severe enough to be debilitating. In addition to sadness, the symptoms include thoughts of worthlessness or self-blame, feelings of hopelessness, confusion and indecision, loss of appetite and insomnia, agitation or lethargy.

Symptoms of mild depression include a dour mood that lasts for months or years, a loss of interest in pleasures and any of the symptoms of major depression, though not at such an incapacitating level.

Manic depression, or bipolar disorder, is marked by periods of grandiosity and elation and bad judgment and agitation alternating with periods of deep depression; at its extreme, symptoms include brief psychosis.

Of the nearly 11 million Americans who suffered from depression in 1990, more than 5 million had major depression, about 1.8 million had bipolar disorder and about 4.1 million had mild depression, the report said.

Herve Villechaize, Actor, 50, Commits Suicide at His Home

LOS ANGELES, Sept. 4 (AP) — Herve Villechaize, the diminutive actor whose shout, "The plane! The plane!" greeted arriving guests on the television show "Fantasy Island," died Saturday at his home in Los Angeles. He was 50.

Mr. Villechaize, who left a note and a tape recording saying he was despondent over longtime health problems, died of a self-inflicted gunshot wound, his publicist David Brokaw said. Mr. Brokaw said Mr. Villechaize's companion, Kathy Self, found the actor's body at their home shortly after the shooting.

Associated Press, 1978

Herve Villechaize

Mr. Villechaize, who was 3 feet 11 inches tall, played Tattoo, the comical sidekick to Ricardo Montalban's Mr. Rourke on "Fantasy Island," which ran on ABC from 1978 through 1984.

He had a history of medical problems stemming from his undersized lungs and nearly died of pneumonia last year. He also suffered from ulcers.

Began as Painter

Mr. Villechaize, a native of Paris, appeared on "Fantasy Island" from 1978 to 1983, leaving after a salary dispute.

In France, he had studied to be a painter, but turned to acting after moving to New York. He was a supporting player on stage and in films in the 1960's and 1970's before obtaining a role in a "Fantasy Island" television movie in 1977.

He was troubled by legal problems in recent years and did not find much work after leaving "Fantasy Island."

"It was kind of limited," said another publicist, Sandy Brokaw. "Every time I got something for him I was elated and kind of surprised because there wasn't a lot of demand for his services."

In 1985, he was sentenced to a year's probation and fined $425 for illegally carrying a loaded weapon.

He had appeared recently in commercials for Dunkin' Donuts and Coors beer, as well as in an episode of the "Larry Sanders Show."

"We were trying to do a remake of Fantasy Island and we weren't able to put it together," Mr. Brokaw said.

Table 11-15

Mean Arrest Rates (from 1981–1986[a]) in 27 Texas Counties for Possession of Opium, Cocaine, and Their Derivatives (Morphine, Heroin, and Codeine), Possession of Marijuana, Driving Under the Influence of Alcohol, and for Drunkenness, in Relation to Drinking Water Lithium Levels

Category	Group A, High Lithium (70–160 μg Li/L)	Group B, Medium Lithium (13–60 μg Li/L)	Group C, Low Lithium (0–12 μg Li/L), all counties	Group D, Low Lithium (0–10 μg Li/L), low pop. counties
Possession of opium, cocaine, and so on	18.4 ± 6.0	28.1 ± 13.9	53.7 ± 24.7	61.8 ± 22.4
Possession of marijuana and so on	180.0 ± 27	147.8 ± 27.3	201 ± 24	197.0 ± 31
Driving under the influence of alcohol	758 ± 153	875 ± 136	635 ± 100	837 ± 114
Drunkenness	1661 ± 68	2535 ± 500	1580 ± 241	1678 ± 143

t-Values and Levels of Statistical Significance[b]

Category	A–B	A–C	A–D	B–C	B–D	C–D	Remarks
Possession of opium and so on	2.25*	4.18**	6.14***	5.14***	4.92***		***$p < 0.005$.
Possession of marijuana and so on	NS	NS	NS	2.75*	2.39*	NS	**$p < 0.01$.
Driving under the influence	NS	NS	NS	i	NS	2.63*	*$p < 0.05$.
Drunkenness	5.23***	NS	NS	i	i	NS	i = opposite trend. NS = Not significant.

[a]Per 100,000 pop.
[b]Calculated by paired *t* test.

Table 11-16

Homicide Rates[a] in 27 Counties of Texas, Classified in Four Categories, According to the Lithium Content in the Municipal Drinking Water Supplies

Year	Group A, High Li (70–160 µg/L)	Group B, Medium Li (13-60 µg/L)	Group C, Low Li (0–12 µg/L), all counties	Group D, Low Li (0–10 µg Li/L), low pop. counties
1978	5.8	12.0	19.3	18.5
1979	5.5	8.2	17.9	12.9
1980	10.6	14.7	18.8	13.1
1981	7.9	21.4	18.9	12.0
1982	8.3	17.2	18.3	13.5
1983	7.9	14.6	17.0	13.7
1984	5.6	12.7	15.8	11.8
1985	6.4	12.3	14.3	9.9
1986	8.2	12.4	15.6	11.2
1987	6.3	8.8	13.4	10.2
$\bar{x} \pm$ SD	7.5 ± 1.8	13.4 ± 3.7	16.9 ± 2.1	12.7 ± 2.4

[a] Per 100,000 population.

Table 11-17

Mean Crime and Suicide Rates in 27 Texas Counties from 1978–1987" in Relation to Drinking Water Lithium Levels

Category	Group A, High Lithium (70–160 µg Li/L)	Group B, Medium Lithium (13–60 µg Li/L)	Group C, Low Lithium (0–12 µg Li/L), all counties	Group D, Low Lithium (0–10 µg Li/L), low pop. counties
Homicide	7.5 ± 1.8	13.4 ± 3.7	16.9 ± 2.1	12.7 ± 2.4
Suicide	8.7 ± 0.85	14.8 ± 2.9	14.2 ± 1.3	13.9 ± 1.2
Rape	28.3 ± 5.3	47.6 ± 6.4	58.8 ± 6.6	50.9 ± 6.4
Robbery	110.3 ± 9.5	123.3 ± 21.9	264.6 ± 39.9	150.5 ± 16.6
Burglary	1537 ± 194	1970 ± 243	2135 ± 216	1847 ± 220
Theft	3076 ± 447	3986 ± 582	4033 ± 577	3827 ± 511
MV Theft	435 ± 36	427 ± 83	668 ± 114	365 ± 32
Assault	357 ± 104	270 ± 69	298 ± 38	283 ± 31
Total crime	5533 ± 763	6838 ± 790	8097 ± 1022	6805 ± 838

t-Values and Levels of Statistical Significance

Category	A–B	A–C	A–D	B–C	B–D	C–D	Remarks
Homicide	5.07*	8.07***	4.47**	3.01*	NS	3.61*	
Suicide	7.84***	7.14**	6.70**	NS	NS	NS	***$p < 0.005$.
Rape	5.13*	8.11***	6.00**	3.94*	NS	NS	
Robbery	NS	13.98***	3.64*	12.80***	NS	10.34***	**$p < 0.01$.
Burglary	4.42*	6.10***	3.16*	NS	NS	2.94*	*$p < 0.05$.
Theft	3.82*	4.02*	3.16*	NS	NS	NS	NS = Not Significant
MV Theft	NS	6.99**	NS	7.23**	NS	9.09***	
Assault	NS	NS	NS	NS	NS	NS	
Total crime	3.39*	6.67**	3.31*	3.28*	NS	3.36*	

"Standard deviations, statistical significance of differences, as calculated by Students *t*-test; *p* values with Bonferroni correction for multiple comparisons. Degrees of freedom: between groups, 3; within groups, 36. Numbers based on per 100,000 population.

Prozac, America's "leading" antidepressant pharmaceutical was introduced in 1987, sales soared to $350 million in 1989, more than was spent on all antidepressants just two years earlier - projections estimate Prozac sales to top $1 billion in sales by 1995 as a result of allopathic doctors generating 650,000 prescriptions per month!

Animal studies show that a deficiency of lithium results in reproductive failure, infertility, reduced growth rate, shortened life expectancy and behavioral problems. In humans, manic depression, depression, "Bi-polar" disease, rages, Dr. Jekyll/Mr. Hyde behavior, hyperactivity, ADD, "Bad Seeds" are hallmarks of Li deficiency.

Chelated Li supplemented at 1,000 to 2,000 ug/d causes a dose-dependent increase in hair Li levels; hair Li levels increased after four weeks of supplementation and leveled off and became stationary after three months; when the Li supplementation was stopped, hair Li levels dropped to presupplement values in two months. This picture does not extend to lithium carbonate (metallic).

A comparison of 2,648 subjects showed that 65 % had hair Li values ranging between 0.04 to 0.14 ug/G; 16 % contained more than 0.14 ug/G and 18.4 % had less than 0.04 ug/G. The highest levels of Li were found in university students from Tijuana, Mexico and the lowest levels were found in Munich, Germany.

Normal controls showed almost 400 times more hair Li than do the violent criminal (Table 11-15, 11-16, 11-17) from California, Florida, Texas and Oregon.

The estimated daily intake of Li by the EPA ranges from 650 to 3,100 ug/d; however, much of this Li is metallic and not biologically available. Lithium supplementation increases the hair concentrations of V, Al, Pb, As and Co. Short term supplementation of Li elevates serum B_{12} levels; with long term supplementation serum B_{12} drops.

1.*Schrauzer,G.N., et al.*: Lithium in Scalp Hair of Adults, Students, and Violent Criminals. Biol.TraceEle.Research.34:161.1992.

2.*Schrauzer,G.N., et al.*: Lithium in Drinking Water and the Incidences of Crimes, Suicides, and Arrests Related to Drug Addictions. Biol. Trace Ele. Research.25:105.1990.

Lu - Lutecium, a Rare Earth, is found in igneous rocks at 0.5 ppm; shale at 0.33 ppm; sandstone at 0.096 ppm; limestone at 0.067 ppm; land plants at up to 4.5 ppm by *Carya spp.*; marine animals at 0.003 ppm; land animals at 0.00012 ppm in soft tissue and 0.08 ppm in bone.

Mg -Magnesium is found in igneous rocks at 23,300 ppm; in shale at 15,000 ppm; sandstone 10,700 ppm; limestone at 2,700 ppm; fresh water at 4.1 ppm; sea water at 1,350 ppm; soil at 5,000 ppm (highest in soil derived from basalt, serpentine or dolamite) - Mg is the second most common exchangeable cation in most soils; marine plants at 5,200 ppm; land plants at 3,200 ppm; marine animals at 5,000 ppm; land animals at 1,000 ppm (accumulates in mammalian bone).

Magnesium is essential to all living organisms and has electrochemical, catalytic and structural functions, activates numerous enzymes and is a constituent of all chlorophylls.

The adult human contains 20 to 28 grams of total body magnesium. Approximately 60 % is found in bone, 26 % is associated with skeletal muscle and the balance is distributed between various organs and body fluids. Serum levels of Mg range from 1.5 to 2.1 mEq/L; it is second to K as an intracellular cation - half of the Mg, including most that is bound in the bone is not exchangeable.

Magnesium is required for the production and transfer of energy for protein synthesis, for contractility of muscle and excitability of nerves , and as a cofactor in myriads of enzyme systems. AN EXCESS OF MG WILL INHIBIT BONE CALCIFICATION. Calcium and Mg have antagonistic roles in normal muscle contraction, calcium acting as the stimulator and Mg as the relaxer. An excessive amount of Ca can induce signs of Mg deficiency.

The rate of absorption of Mg ranges from 24 to 85 %. The lesser absorption rate is for metallic sources of Mg, the higher levels are associated with plant derived colloidal sources. Vitamin D has no effect on Mg absorption,; the presence of fat, phytates and calcium reduces the efficiency of absorption . High performance athletes lose a considerable amount of Mg in sweat.

The RDA for Mg is 350mg/day for adult males, 300mg/day for adult females and 450 mg/day for pregnant and lactating females. If kidneys are healthy there is no evidence of toxicity at up to 6,000 mg per day.

Deficiencies of Mg result in a wide variety of deficiency diseases and symptoms (Table 11- 18).

Mn - Manganese is found in igneous rocks at 950 ppm; shale at 850 ppm; sandstone at 50 ppm; limestone at 1,100 ppm; fresh water at 0.012 ppm; sea water at 0.002 ppm; soil at 850 ppm (can be a major exchangable cation in very acid soil); marine plants at 1 to 60 ppm (lowest in fish); land animals at 0.2ppm (highest concentrations in mammalian liver and kidney); the total body content of Mn in humans is only 10 to 20 mg.

Manganese is essential to all known living organisms; it activates numerous enzyme systems including those involved with glucose metabolism, energy production and superoxide dismutase; it is a major constituent of several metalloenzymes, hormones, and proteins of humans. Manganese is part of the developemental process and the structure of the fragile ear bones and joint cartilage. Excessive levels of Mn found in certain community water supplies and in some industrial processes can produce a Parkinsonian syndrome or a psychiatric disorder (locura manganica) resembling schizophrenia.

Table 11- 18. Deficiency Diseases of Magnesium.

- Asthma
- Anorexia
- Menstrual migraines
- Growth failure
- ECG changes
- Neuromuscular problems
- Tetany (Convulsions)
- Depression
- Muscular weakness
- Muscle "Ties"
- Tremors
- Vertigo
- Calcification of small arteries
- "Malignant" calcification of soft tissue

Deficiency diseases of Mn are very striking ranging from severe birth defects (Congenital ataxia, deafness, Chondrodystrophy),asthma, convulsions, retarded growth, skeletal defects, disruption of fat and carbohydrate metabolism to joint problems in children and adults (TMJ, Repetitive Motion Syndrome, Carpal Tunnel Syndrome)(Table 11-19).

Repetitive Stress Injury or Repetitive Motion Syndrome now costs corporate America $20 billion dollars per year and accounts for 56% of the 331,600 gradual onset work related illnesses. In 1991 orthopedic surgeons performed 100,000 Carpal Tunnel operations (at $4,000 per surgery) with a lost work, wages and medical cost of over $29,000 per case.

Table 11-19. Deficiency Diseases of Manganese.

- Congenital ataxia
- deafness (malformation of otolithes)
- Asthma
- Chondromalacia
- Chondrodystrophy
- "Slipped Tendon"
- Defects of chondroitin sulfate metabolism (poor cartilage formation)
- TMJ
- Repetitive Motion Syndrome
- Carpal Tunnel Syndrome
- Convulsions
- Infertility (failure to ovulate; testicular atrophy)
- Still births or spontaneous abortions (miscarriges)
- Loss of libido in males and females
- Retarded growth rate
- Shortened long bones

At risk for The Repetitive Motion Syndromes are those working in the fields of computers (journalism, airline reservations, directory assistance, law, data entry, graphic design and securities brokerage. Chief among the blue collar victims are the auto assembly workers, chicken pluckers, meat cutters, postal employees, dock workers, etc. Repetitive Motion Syndrome was observed three centuries ago in monks who were scribes and was described in 1717 by Bernardo Ramazzini , an Italian physician (considered the father of occupational medicine).

Repetitive Motion Syndrome victims have reached such numbers that federal legislation has been passed in the form of OSHA and Americans with Disabilities Act (ADA) to ensure work place safety. Large numbers of ergonomically correct keyboards and devices have been developed, we see literally millions of people at work with Velcro wrist, neck, elbow, finger, knee, back and hip supports - all for manganese deficiencies!!! The allopathic medical profession would still prefer to spend your money than to admit that the human flesh needs Mn.

Mo - Molybdenum is found in igneous rocks at 1.5 ppm; shale at 2.6 ppm; sandstone at 0.02 ppm; limestone 0.4 ppm; fresh water at 0.00035 ppm; sea water at 0.01 ppm; soil at 2 ppm (strongly concentrated by humus, especially in alkaline soils; a few soils worldwide are rich enough in molybdenum to cause Mo poisoning in animals consuming the plants; numerous soils are known for Mo deficiency); marine plants at 0.45 ppm; land plants at 0.9 ppm; marine animals at 0.6 to 2.5 ppm; land animals at 0.2 ppm (highest levels in the liver

Table 11-20. Nitrogen/Protein Utilization Values of Common Foods

N Source (Protein)	Chemical Score	Rats
Whole egg	100	94
Human milk	100	87
Cow's milk	95	82
Soya bean	74	65
Sesame	50	54
Peanut	65	47
Cotton seed	81	59
Maize	49	52
Millet	63	44
Rice	67	59
Wheat	53	48

and kidney).

Molybdenum is essential to all organisms as a constituant of numerous metalloenzymes. Molybdenum is known to be an integral part of no less than three essential enzymes:

1- Xanthine ozidase
2- Aldehyde oxidase
3- Sulfite oxidase

The average American daily intake in food ranges from 76 to 109 mcg per day - the RDA for Mo is 250 mcg per day.

Toxicity occurs at 10 mg per day as a gout-like disease and interference with copper metabolism.

N - Nitrogen is found in igneous rocks at 20 ppm; fresh water at 0.23 ppm; sea water 0.5 ppm; soils 1,000 ppm (99 % present as non-basic N bound in humus); marine plants at 15,000 ppm; land plants at 30,000 ppm; marine animals at 75,000 ppm; land animals at 100,000 ppm.

Nitrogen functions as a structural atom in protein, nucleic acids (RNA, DNA) and a wide variety of organic molecules. Dietary N (as protein) furnish the amino acids for synthesis of tissue protein and other special metabolic functions:

1) Proteins are used to repair worn-out body tissue (anabolic process)

2) Proteins are used to build new tissue (muscle, infant growth, childhood, teenagers, pregnancy)

3) Proteins can be an emergency source of heat and energy (albeit more expensive in biological terms than fat or carbohydrate)

Sunday, July 11, 1993

Heat toll up to 21 in East

12 die in one day in Philadelphia

By The Associated Press

Twelve people died of heat-related causes in the Philadelphia area alone yesterday as a record-setting heat wave gripped the East Coast.

The heat has now killed 21 people along the Eastern seaboard during the past week.

The latest victims included a 4-year-old boy who had climbed into his aunt's parked station wagon while visiting relatives outside Philadelphia, police said. It was not known how long he'd been in the car, police said.

Meanwhile, triple-digit heat fried New York City for a third straight day yesterday, tying a record dating to 1948. No relief was expected until Tuesday, when a frontal system from the West was forecast to arrive.

Philadelphia also tied its record for consecutive days of above 100-degree temperatures. The last time its temperatures reached triple digits for three days in a row was in 1966.

In Massachusetts, 20,000 chickens died in the heat after lightning struck a henhouse ventilation system.

By noon yesterday, temperatures in Atlantic City had reached 97, breaking the old record for the date set in 1880. And those teeming to the New Jersey shore had to cross a scorching strip of sand before reaching the cool Atlantic.

"The sand is dangerous," said Lt. Jack Schellenger of the Cape May Beach Patrol. "It'll take the skin right off your feet. We see a lot of people jumping around."

4) Proteins make up essential body secretions and fluids (i.e.- enzymes, hormones, mucus, milk, semen, etc.)

5) Blood plasma proteins maintain osmotic fluid balance (hypoproteinemia results in edema)

6) Proteins maintain acid-base balance of blood and tissues

7) Proteins aid in transport of other essential substances (i.e. - minerals, fats, vitamins, etc.)

8) Proteins make up basic immunoglobulins (antibodies)

9) Proteins provide a N pool for the synthesis of amino acids and new proteins

Classic protein deficiency results in infertility, poor growth, lowered immune status, edema and Kwashiorkor (potbellied, thin children of third world countries). The availability and usability of N from various foods is quite different and must be considered when choosing N sources (Table 11- 20).

Na - Sodium is found in igneous rocks at 23,600 ppm; shale at 9,600 ppm; sandstone at 3,300ppm; limestone at 400 ppm; fresh water at 6.3 ppm; sea water at 10,500 ppm; soil at 6,300 ppm (is a major exchangeable cation in soil especially alkaline soil; marine plants at 33,000 ppm;land plants at 1,200 ppm; marine animals at 4,000 to 48,000 ppm; and land animals at 4,000 ppm.

"Salt hunger" dates back to the very beginning of animals and man and is one of the very basic cravings of living organisms. Carnivores (man or beast) do not show the great craving for salt because meat contains relatively large amounts of NaCl, but herbivores and human vegetarians demand large amounts of NaCl because there is little or no natural NaCl in grains, vegetables and fruits. The average sodium dietary intake per day in western cultures is five to 12 G/day while the Japanese who on the average out live Americans by four years consume an average of 28 G/day!!

Sodium, Cl and K are three indispensable "electrolytes" so intimately associated in the body that they can be presented together. Sodium makes up two percent , K five percent and Cl three percent of the total mineral content of the human body. All three are widely distributed throughout the body tissues and fluids , however, Na and Cl are primarily extracellular (outside the cell) minerals while K is an intracellular (inside the cell) mineral. Sodium, K and Cl are involved in at least four important physiological functions in the body:

1) Maintenance of normal water balance and distribution

2) Maintenance of normal osmotic equilibrium

3) Maintenance of normal acid-base balance

4) Maintenance of normal muscular irritability

Hormonal control of Na, K and Cl balance is regulated by the adrenal cortex hormones as well as by the anterior pituitary gland. Addison's Disease, a loss of function of the adrenal cortex, results in the loss of Na and K retention with clinical signs of general weakness, muscle cramps, weight loss and a marked "salt hunger." The symptoms can be relieved with the supplementation of NaCl or by administering adrenal cortical hormones.

Deficiencies of NaCl occur primarily in hot weather (the heat wave of July 1993) or heavy work in a hot climate when large volumes of sweat are required for body cooling. "Water intoxication" occurred in infants fed low Na formulas because of the allopathic doctors paranoia with Na - their brains swelled causing death from a simple Na deficiency.

The treatment for Na deficiency is water and salt either orally or IV (saline 0.9 %).

Nb - Niobium is found in igneous rocks at 20 ppm; shale at 11 ppm; sandstone at 0.05 ppm; limestone 0.3 ppm; sea water 0.00001 ppm; land plants 0.3 ppm and marine animals 0.001 ppm.

Nd - Neodymium, a RareEarth, is found in igneous rocks at 28 ppm; shale at 16 ppm; sandstone 11 ppm; limestone 4.3 ppm; marine plants at 5 ppm; land plants accumulates up to 460 ppm in *Carya spp.*; marine animals at 0.5 ppm; accumulates in the liver and bone of land animals.

Neodymium is a "light" Rare Earth proven to enhance normal cell growth and double life spans of laboratory species.

Ne - Neon is found in igneous rocks at 0.005 ppm and sea water at 0.00014 ppm.

Ni - Nickel is found in igneous rocks

at 75 ppm; shale at 68 ppm; sandstone at 2 ppm; limestone at 20 ppm; fresh water at 0.01 ppm; sea water at 0.0054 ppm; soils at 40 ppm (higher in soils derived from serpentine); marine plants at 3 ppm; land plants at 3 ppm (accumulated by *Alyssum bertalonii*); marine animals at 0.4-25ppm and land animals at 0.8 ppm (accumulates in RNA).

Table 11-21. Symptoms of Nickel Deficiency in the rat.
• Poor growth
• Lower hematocrit (anemia)
• Depressed oxidative ability of the liver
• High newborn mortality
• Rough/dry hair coat
• Dermatitis
• Delayed puberty
• Poor zinc absorption

Less than 10 % of ingested metallic nickel is absorbed. Nickel deficiency was first reported in 1970 (Table 11- 21).

Nickel functions as a cofactor for metalloenzymes and facillitates gastrointestinal absorption of iron and zinc. Optimal tissue levels of B_{12} is necessary for the optimal biological function of nickel - B_{12} deficiency results in an increased need for nickel by animals and man.

Np - All isotopes of neptunium are radioactive. the half life of Np is 2.2×10^6. Np accumulates in mammalian bone after ingestion; Np has been found in fresh water organisms in the Hanford River (USA).

Did the dinosaurs suffocate?

By Tim Friend
USA TODAY

The end of the dinosaur era was marked by a rapid decline in atmospheric oxygen — creating an environment in which wheezing giants roamed, too tired to compete, a new theory says.

"If you're chasing down dinner and pass out before you get to eat, that would not enhance survivability," says Gary Landis, U.S. Geological Survey in Boulder, Colo.

Researchers analyzed ancient gas bubbles trapped in amber. Results, reported Wednesday at the Geological Society of America meeting, shows oxygen levels declined rapidly before the dinosaurs disappeared.

Why did the decline occur so fast? Landis and his colleagues say the air was rich with oxygen because volcanic activity pumped out carbon dioxide, which was converted to oxygen by plants.

When the volcanic "super plumes" shut down, carbon levels fell, plant life declined and oxygen levels dropped.

That seems to have happened over 6 million years about 65 million years ago.

The main competing dinosaur theory: They died after an asteroid hit the Earth and dust clouds blocked the sun.

O - Oxygen is found in igneous rock at 464,000 ppm; shale at 483,000 ppm; sandstone at 492,000 ppm; limestone at 497,000 ppm; fresh water at 889,000 ppm; sea water at 857,000 ppm; soils at 490,000 ppm; marine plants at 470,000 ppm; land plants at 410,000 (except anaerobic organisms); marine animals at 400,000 ppm; land animals at 186,000 ppm.

Terrestrial O consists of 99.76 % ^{16}O with a half life of less than two minutes.

Oxygen is a structural atom of water (in and out of living systems) and of all organic compounds of biological interest; O_2 is required for "respiration" by all organisms (except for anaerobic organisms). We can live for 30 days without food, 3 to 7 days without water under ideal circumstances, but only four minutes without gaseous oxygen - oxygen is the most critical of all elemental factors for the maintenance of human life.

According to the 1980's U.S Geological Survey, our Earth's atmosphere had 50 % oxygen 75 million years ago when dinosaurs flourished (these oxygen level estimates were arrived at by inserting microneedles into trapped air bubbles in polar ice and determining the oxygen level in ancient ice) - some paleontologists claim that the simultaneous and universal demise of the dinosaurs followed the widespread quieting of the Earth's volcanoes which reduced the levels of atmospheric CO_2, which in turn reduced the oxygen levels to 38 %. It is theorized that the 12 % drop in the Earth's oxygen levels was sufficient to cause the apocalyptic end of the dinosaurs.

The Geological Survey also reported that the Earth's atmosphere still contained 38 % oxygen as late as 100 years ago. During the 1950's the percentage of oxygen in

Table 11- 22. Anaerobic Diseases of Humans.	
Disease	**Year of Appearance**
VIRAL	
Mycoplasma (rheumatoid arthritis - virus-like organism)	?
Herpes II (sexually transmitted herpes)	1978
HIV (AIDs virus)	1982
EBV, CMV (chronic fatigue syndrome)	1982
Hanta Virus ("Four Corners Disease")	1993
BACTERIA	
Staphylococcus (Toxic Shock Syndrome)	1982
E. coli (Toxic Shock Syndrome)	1993
Type A *Streptococcus* ("flesh-eating" Strep)	1994
YEAST/FUNGUS	
Candida albicans ("Candida")	1982
Coccidioidomycosis ("Valley Fever")	1900 35/yr
	1992 - 1,450/yr
Cancer (all types)	1900 1/10
	1994 3/4

our atmosphere dropped to 21 % and today only 19 % of our gaseous atmosphere is oxygen! The continued drop in oxygen levels reflects an increase in oxygen consuming species (including the runaway human population) and fossil fuel burning machines (i.e. - vehicles, electric and power generating plants, etc.) and less oxygen producers (i.e.- decreasing acreages of rain forests and aquatic algae). The net result of

Child Dies From Bacteria; Parents Had Voiced an Appeal to Clinton

From Reuters

SEATTLE—A child whose parents appeared on President Clinton's electronic town meeting earlier this month became the third person to die from an outbreak of food poisoning, doctors said.

The boy, 17-month-old Riley Detwiler, died Saturday at Seattle Children's Hospital from respiratory failure brought on by an infection with the *E. coli* bacteria, they said.

His parents, Darin and Vicki Detwiler, appeared on Clinton's Feb. 11 electronic town meeting to ask him to move quickly on health reform and to improve the U.S. system of meat inspection.

The death is the third linked to an outbreak of food poisoning caused by *E. coli* that began in early January and has caused more than 450 people in Washington state to become ill.

According to the state health department, 94% of the cases have been tied to Jack in the Box restaurants.

The Detwilers contend that their son was infected by the bacteria at his day care center from another child who had eaten at Jack in the Box.

During the town meeting, Vicki Detwiler told the President the family faced a staggering health bill because her husband lost his job—and the family's medical insurance—just two days before their son fell ill.

According to state health officials, frozen hamburger patties taken from the Jack in the Box restaurants were found to be heavily contaminated with *E. coli* bacteria.

THE NATION

Tainted meat traced to California herd

SEATTLE — Tainted fast-food hamburger meat blamed for the death of at least one child and the illnesses of more than 300 people is thought to have come from cows in California, a health official said on Friday.

Dr. John Kobayashi, the state's chief epidemiologist, said federal health and agricultural investigators had not pinpointed a specific herd or slaughterhouse.

"It appears most of the cattle for the implicated lot of hamburger meat we're looking at comes from the Central Valley in California," he said.

The raw beef was supplied to The Vons Cos. of Arcadia, Calif.

GEORGIA

Mass vaccination begun in meningitis outbreak

CARROLLTON — Residents of the western county of Carroll lined up for bacterial meningitis vaccinations Friday amid an outbreak of the disease blamed for one death.

Health officials in Carroll County hope to vaccinate more than 20,000 people between ages 2 and 29 by Sunday. By Friday afternoon, 2,745 people had received shots, said Jeanne Mathews of Tanner Medical Center.

The disease has killed one girl, and six residents have become ill since November.

IN WASHINGTON

From Herald Wire Services

AIDS EPIDEMIC

Panel urges Clinton to mobilize response

The National Commission on AIDS has urged President Clinton to address the American public about the epidemic, boost research spending and lift immigration restrictions on people with the virus.

The 15-member commission on Thursday released a letter it has sent the president on ways to "mobilize America's response to AIDS."

It urged him to make good on a campaign promise to appoint an AIDS coordinator at the White House.

The commission, which was often at loggerheads with former President Bush, urged Clinton to "discuss the AIDS crisis with the American people" early and often.

A Second Child Dies in Bacterial Outbreak

SEATTLE, Jan. 28 (Reuters) — A second Washington State child died today of E. coli infection, an outbreak that has been traced to tainted hamburgers sold by Jack in the Box fast-food restaurants in the Pacific Northwest.

Doctors said the child's case had not been linked to the tainted meat, and it is unclear whether she was infected through contact with someone who had eaten the contaminated hamburgers or fell victim to the bacterial outbreak in some other way.

"As far as we know, this child and her family had no contact with Jack in the Box," Dr. Ed Marcuse told reporters at the Children's Hospital Medical Center here. "She was a previously well 2½-year-old girl who developed some fever and diarrhea over the weekend."

The girl, who was not identified, suffered a seizure while traveling to the hospital by car for treatment and could not be resuscitated in the emergency room, the doctors said. An autopsy is planned.

The infection is caused by a virulent strain of a common bacterium, E. coli O157:H7, which produces potent toxins that cause bloody diarrhea and other ailments. Children are especially vulnerable to life-threatening complications.

The current outbreak has caused illness in more than 250 people since it was detected early this month. One of the victims, a 2-year-old Tacoma boy who had eaten at Jack in the Box, died last week.

Nation Update

Boy's death blamed on bacteria in food

LANSING, Mich. — The death of a 3-year-old boy who apparently was infected with deadly bacteria from food prepared at home prompted health officials yesterday to warn campers and picnickers to cook meat thoroughly.

Two Florida children remained hospitalized in Chicago after becoming infected with a deadly strain of E. coli near Ludington, the same Lake Michigan resort area where the boy was poisoned.

Last week, a 6-year-old Chicago boy and a 7-month-old boy from Merrillville, Ind., died from E. coli infections apparently contracted near their homes.

Associated Press

AMERICAN LUNG ASSOCIATION

Drug resistent tuberculosis reapperars to hound humans in low oxygen atmosphere

this continued drop in oxygen levels is a relative "anaerobic state" compared with the 38 % of just 100 years ago and a very marked "anaerobic state" compared with the 50 % oxygen levels 75 million years ago. Most pathogenic organisms (disease producing) are by themselves anaerobic and are "happier," flourish and reproduce with more vigor in the absence of oxygen (i.e.- gangrene organisms, type A Streptococcus, etc.) or are able to survive and grow in living cells weakened by low oxygen environments (i.e.- viruses, yeast, fungus, cancer, etc.).

The question is why have anaerobic diseases "suddenly appeared" in the 80's and 90's - the last quarter of the 20th century, diseases with which we have little or no human history or experience? Regardless of the name, tuberculosis or consumption or scrufula can be found in 5,000 year old mummies from Egypt and China, 1,000 year old corpses from Peru and ancient writings from the Greeks and Romans. The "new" modern day anaerobic diseases have no history with humans, nor will you find them in biblical or ancient writtings describbing HIV, EBV, CMV, Herpes II, Hanta Virus, Candida, Toxic shock from E. coli or "flesh-eating" Type A Streptococcus.

The most plausable theory is that the anaerobic disease causing organisms laid around in dormant states (for 100's, 1,000's or even millions of years) as long as relatively high levels of oxygen (i.e.- 50, 38 or even 21%) were present in our atmosphere to inhibit their activity and growth - with the precipitous dip in atmospheric oxygen we are having an "oxygen counter revolution" with a return to an anaerobic bios (Table 11- 22)!!

Dr. Otto Warburg, of the Max Plank Institute, Germany, was the recipiant of two Nobel Prizes (Linus Pauling was the only other individual to be awarded two Nobel Prizes) - one for discovering the amino acid and describing the basic composition of proteins and the other for determining that the metabolism of the cancer cell is fermentative and anaerobic while the normal non-cancerous cell is aerobic. During the 1950's, Warburg was able to demonstrate clearly that cancer cell's ferment sugar under anaerobic conditions and die in the presence of oxygen.

Neutrophils, a type of white blood cell that help defend us by identifying, engulfing and destroying invading micro-organisms (i.e.- virus, bacteria, yeast, fungus, etc.), parasites and cancer cells, use hydrogen peroxide as their "lethal weapon." Neutrophils are packed with small organelles (microscopic organs) called peroxisomes, whose sole function is to produce hydrogen peroxide and eject it onto the captured pathogen or cancer cell for the specific purpose of destroying it. Neutrophils tend to be very sloppy, dribbling their over-production of hydrogen peroxide freely into the blood stream.

The potential danger of hydrogen peroxide free in the blood stream could be a loose cannon, but fortunately we humans are blessed with an enzyme called catalase in amounts that literally covers our red blood cells and coats the inside walls of our blood vessels. The function of catalase is to rapidly facilitate the decomposition of hydrogen peroxide down to water (H_2O) and singlet oxygen (O).

There are concerns by the uninitiated regarding the "free radical" status of "singlet" oxygen (O) which has a free electron when either ozone (O_3), hydrogen peroxide (H_2O_2), magnesium peroxide (MgO_2) or chlorine dioxide (ClO_2) decompose into

Wednesday, February 16, 1994

RICKY J. SEBOLT
Jockey and trainer, 35

Ricky J. Sebolt, a jockey and trainer who worked at the Del Mar Racetrack and at tracks around the country, died Feb. 7 at the Veterans Administration Hospital of complications from AIDS. He was 35.

Mr. Sebolt was born in Florida. Until 1989, he was licensed in Florida and California as a jockey, trainer and exercise rider, according to state officials.

"He was a person who would take in practically anyone off the street who gave him a hard-luck story," said Janet Manley, an in-home health-care worker who assisted him during his illness.

Mr. Sebolt, who lived in Hillcrest, was active in substance-abuse programs and volunteered for the AIDS Foundation.

He is survived by his mother and father, who live in Florida, and two sisters, Sherry Martz of Miramar, Fla., and Christina Peightal of Las Vegas.

Remains were cremated and ashes were scattered at the Del Mar Racetrack, Manley said. Donations to the Shoemaker Foundation at the Del Mar Thoroughbred Club were suggested.

Kim Foltz
Reporter and Columnist, 44

Kim Foltz, a reporter and columnist for The New York Times, died Thursday at New York Hospital. He was 44.

Mr. Foltz, a resident of Manhattan, died of AIDS. After he learned he had the virus that causes AIDS, he wrote about his experiences as a man infected with H.I.V. in an article for The Times Magazine on Jan. 5, 1992.

A journalism graduate of the University of Utah, Mr. Foltz started his career as an associate editor and writer at Gentlemen's Quarterly. In 1980 he joined Newsweek magazine, where he worked as a business writer before moving to Adweek five years later, advancing to national editor in 1987.

Mr. Foltz joined the staff of The Times in October 1989 as a reporter for the media department. He later wrote a daily advertising column and feature articles on advertising.

He is survived by his companion, James N. Baker; his parents, Mr. and Mrs. J. G. Foltz of Midville, Utah; a sister, Karen St. Clair, and a brother, Craig Foltz, both of Salt Lake City.

Dr. Jay Brown, 50, A Medical Professor And a Cardiologist

By WOLFGANG SAXON

Dr. Jay Brown, the chief of cardiology at Harlem Hospital Center and an associate professor of medicine at the College of Physicians and Surgeons of Columbia University, died on Monday in Los Angeles. He was 50 and lived in Manhattan until recently.

The cause was AIDS, said his companion, Jeffrey Tennyson, at whose home he died.

Dr. Brown was credited with rebuilding Harlem Hospital's acute coronary-care unit for the treatment of cardiovascular disease. He was also project director for the Heart of Harlem Healthy Heart Program and developed new approaches to preventing cardiovascular disease in inner-city areas. These included church-based health programs, education via cable television and promoting healthful foods in groceries and restaurants.

He was a member of the Cardiac Advisory Committee of the New York State Department of Health and of the Emergency Cardiac Care Committee of the American Heart Association. He helped to set cardiac-care standards and policies statewide.

A past president of the Association of Black Cardiologists, he enhanced that organization's scientific program and helped to define the needs of blacks and other minority groups.

At Columbia, with which Harlem Hospital is affiliated, he helped to train a generation of students and medical residents in cardiology. His research, described in many articles and papers, led to insights into the effects of sickle-cell anemia and hypertension on cardiac functions, among other things.

A native of Atlantic City, Dr. Brown graduated from Rutgers University and New York University Medical School. His association with Harlem Hospital dated to 1968, when he began his internship there. He became chief of cardiology in 1977. He joined the Columbia faculty in 1973.

Besides Mr. Tennyson, Dr. Brown is survived by seven brothers, Lawrence, Ronald, Cortez and Aaron, all residents of New Jersey; Frederick of New York City, and Alan and Walter, residents of North Carolina.

Tice Alexander
Interior Designer, 35

Tice Alexander, an interior designer in New York who was known for the elegance of his rooms, died on Monday at New York Hospital. He was 35.

His companion, Glenn Albin, said the cause was AIDS.

Mr. Alexander worked with Parish-Hadley Associates from 1980 to 1986 and then formed his own design concern, Tice Alexander Inc. at 260 West 72d Street in Manhattan. His first name was Matthew, but he had been known since childhood as Tice.

He was a contributing editor for Connoisseur magazine, for which he wrote a monthly column called Connoisseur's Choice. The magazine is no longer published.

Mr. Alexander was born in Kansas City and attended the University of Kansas and the Kansas City Art Institute before graduating from the Fashion Institute of Technology in Manhattan in 1980.

He is survived by his companion; his mother, Lorna Burge of Kansas City; his father and stepmother, Bill J. and Jinny Alexander of Kansas City, and a brother, Britton, of Chicago.

John B. Manning Jr.
Executive, 43

John B. Manning Jr., an executive with Merrill Lynch & Company in New York, died on Wednesday at his home in Manhattan. He was 43.

Mr. Manning died of AIDS, said Gregory Manning, a brother.

John Manning, who was known as Jay, served at Merrill Lynch as first vice president general counsel-trading. Before joining Merrill Lynch in 1983, he had for nine years been a lawyer for the Securities and Exchange Commission in Washington. He graduated from Fairfield University and the University of Connecticut Law School.

He is survived by his parents, Marie and John B. Manning Sr. of Belle Air Bluffs, Fla.; three brothers, Christopher, of West Haven, Conn., Gregory, of Cypress, Calif., and Joseph, of Madison, N.J., and two sisters, Elise Marvelle of Norton, Mass., and Lea Manning of Guilford, Conn.

THE NEW YORK TIMES

FRIDAY, AUGUST 6, 1993

Stephen R. Endean, 44, Founder Of Largest Gay Political Group

By BRUCE LAMBERT

Stephen R. Endean, who was the nation's first professional lobbyist for gay men and lesbians and the founder of the nation's largest gay political organization, died at home on Wednesday. He was 44 and lived in Washington.

He died of AIDS, said a spokesman for the Human Rights Campaign Fund, the organization he created.

Drawn to politics as a youth in Minnesota, Mr. Endean volunteered as an aide for local and state political candidates starting at the age of 18.

The gay rights movement, which arose after homosexuals clashed with the police at the Stonewall gay bar in Greenwich Village in 1969, inspired him at 22 to become open about his homosexuality. Feeling that his declaration precluded a career as a politician, he decided to use his skills to promote gay rights through the political process.

His initial efforts drew critics ranging from homosexuals uncomfortable with a public campaign to the strident foes of homosexuality.

Success, After Many Years

Mr. Endean's first major project was in the early 1970's, campaigning for a Minnesota bill to bar discrimination against homosexuals. He lobbied during the day on a $300 monthly salary paid by supporters of the bill, supplementing that salary by working nights as a coat checker at a gay bar. He recalled that one enraged legislator yelled a slur and threw a book at his head.

The bill was finally passed this spring. Although weakened by his illness, he returned to lobby for its enactment.

That original campaign drew national attention, and in 1978 he became the first executive director and the lobbyist for the Gay Rights National Lobby in Washington. When he took charge, the struggling group had a single desk in another organization's office, a disconnected telephone and a pile of unpaid bills. Within two years the group had a new building with a staff of 10 and an annual budget of more than $300,000.

In 1982 he created the Human Rights Fund Campaign as a political action committee; the gay rights lobby group eventually merged with the campaign fund. The fund, which claims 75,000 members, raised $5 million last year for lobbying and organizing.

Survivors include his parents, Robert Endean and Marilyn Endean Lowe, and a sister, Mary Ellen Barna, all of Minneapolis.

368

Clues sought on illness killing young Navajos

From Chicago Tribune wires

SANTA FE—A small army of medical investigators swarmed over a sprawling Navajo reservation Monday, seeking clues to the cause of a mysterious epidemic that has killed 11 young people.

Three more victims were hospitalized during the weekend with adult respiratory distress syndrome (ARDS), a flu-like illness that strikes suddenly and can kill in a day. The first case dates to March 8, although doctors didn't connect the illnesses until two people from the same New Mexico family died in mid-May.

The sickness is striking relatively young, healthy people who lived on or near the nation's largest Navajo reservation, which straddles northwestern New Mexico and northeastern Arizona.

Ron Wood of the federal Indian Health Service said the Navajos are scared.

"There's a lot of fear. . . . There's a lot of hysteria, there's a lot of concern. They want to know what is going on," Wood said.

Medical investigators are checking 18 cases, 14 in New Mexico and four in Arizona. A dozen cases have occurred among Indians, five in whites and one in a Hispanic. Eight of the Indians, two of the Anglos and the Hispanic died.

"We've excluded the usual bacterial, fungal and parasitic infections. It's not anthrax, it's not the plague, it's not Legionnaires," and it's not related to the virus that causes AIDS, said Dr. Ron Voorhees, deputy state epidemiologist.

Five other cases may have been caused by the disease, while four others are "questionably related," Voorhees said.

A few people appear to have recovered from the illness, but doctors said they don't know whether treatment — primarily antibiotics — was responsible.

Dr. Frederick Koster, who treated several of the patients at University Hospital in Albuquerque, said some had few or no symptoms before collapsing, while others were ill for days before developing respiratory failure.

The youngest and most recent victim was a 13-year-old girl who collapsed at a party Friday and died the next day. Of the previous 10 victims, the oldest was 31.

Investigators are searching for an infectious substance, a toxic chemical or some other cause, but have come up with nothing. The illness may be contagious, but not highly contagious because most relatives and others who were in contact with victims haven't developed it.

"The early symptoms are extremely non-specific. They're your basic cold and flu symptoms," said Dr. Jim Cheek of the Indian Health Service.

Deer mice carrying fatal virus in Southwest, preliminary report says

Associated Press

SANTA FE, N.M. — Government scientists say they have evidence that the virus suspected of killing 16 people in the Southwest is carried by a species of deer mouse common in much of North America.

A preliminary report by the Centers for Disease Control said 42 rodents of different types were tested, and 12 deer mice were found to have antibodies indicating exposure to a hantavirus.

Scientists have said for weeks that they suspect the flulike illness is caused by a hantavirus, a member of family of viruses carried by rodents. They have been trapping rodents in an effort to identify which species carries the virus.

The CDC report was obtained by the Albuquerque Journal. The CDC did not return several calls seeking comment.

Researchers have not yet determined whether the virus to which the mice were exposed is the same strain that infected the victims of the disease. Genetic material from a hantavirus has been found in at least two of the dead.

The deer mouse is found from Alaska to South America. The virus is in their urine and becomes airborne, health officials said.

The disease is suspected of killing at least 16 people, according to a CDC count.

Diphtheria Sweeps Russia and Ukraine At Quickening Pace

A Diphtheria Epidemic Sweeps Across Russia

By CELESTINE BOHLEN
Special to The New York Times

MOSCOW, Jan. 28 — Diphtheria, an acutely infectious disease that has been practically eliminated in the West through regular immunization, is now spreading rapidly through Russia, reaching what the World Health Organization calls epidemic proportions.

In the last two years, the number of people stricken by the disease has risen from 1,000 to 4,000 at the end of 1992, according to estimates, with the numbers of new cases doubling from July to December. It is also rising dangerously in Ukraine, where more than 1,300 cases were reported in the first 10 months of last year, and cases are being reported in other former republics of the Soviet Union.

First reported mostly in Russia's largest cities, Moscow and St. Petersburg, which have more than 650 registered cases each, the disease is now showing up in the more distant regions, where doctors are even less likely to give a prompt and effective diagnosis,

Continued From Page A1

experts say.

"From our point of view, it is an epidemic," said Dr. George Oblapenko, acting regional adviser for communicable diseases at the W.H.O. offices in Denmark. "If you have 1,000 cases where you previously had 100, then it is clearly another level of transmission. It will take time to control it now, in a huge country like Russia, to bring levels down to zero."

Failings in Program

Diphtheria is a highly contagious disease, transmitted by airborne bacteria, that may be spread in particles and produces a toxin that causes an inflammation of the heart and nervous system. Untreated, it progresses rapidly and can be fatal in a short period of time. Doctors say the initial symptoms are commonly confused with angina, or inflammation of the throat and chest.

Most experts attribute the increase in diphtheria to failings in the Russian immunization program, which allows a high number of infants to be turned down for the normal schedule of inoculations for medical reasons, while not keeping many adults, particularly those from age 20 to 50, up to date on their immunizations.

But doctors also say the situation has been worsened by the social and economic upheavals that have sent thousands of people migrating across the former Soviet Union and slowed down the response of the health authorities to an increasing crisis.

"People are on the move, mostly from the areas where the conflicts are," said the City of Moscow's chief epidemiologist, Igor A. Andreyev. "There is more mixing of the populations, and more carriers — drifters, people who live in the subway tunnels. It is part of the social problems created by the country's collapse, by the lack of social and political stability."

The number of diphtheria cases is also increasing in Ukraine, which in the first 10 months of 1992 reported 1,344 cases. The last official number for Russia is 3,278 as of November 1992, but with the number of new cases rising at more than 500 a month, it was expected to pass 4,000 at year's end.

water and singlet oxygen, magnesium and singlet oxygen or chlorine and singlet oxygen. When singlet or atomic oxygen come into direct contact with tissue cells outside of the circulatory system (i.e.- cell culture, test tube, wound, etc.) the cells will die; however, in the whole animal or human other factors come into play to prevent the "free radical" damage.

When ingested in proper dilution on an empty stomach or administered IV under proper conditions, food grade hydrogen peroxide is readily absorbed through the stomach and duodenal walls directly into the blood stream where it is immediately broken down into water and singlet oxygen. The free electron of the singlet oxygen either combines with a free electron of a carcinogenic free electron (carcinogenic chemicals) or with the free electron of another singlet oxygen, becoming O_2. Carcinogenic free electrons frequently remain free electrons under many circumstances, actually "quite happy" with their free electron status - on the other hand the free electron of the singlet oxygen does not like to be a singlet electron and if it doesn't locate another free electron to attach to it will in nanoseconds grab onto another singlet oxygen and become an O_2 - the required stuff of respiration!!

$$Ozone \ (O_3) \ -> H_2O_2 + O -$$
$$catalase \ -> H_2O + O_2$$

Oxygen in the form of hydrogen peroxide has been used topically, intravenously and orally since the Civil War, it has been used widely in Europe for over 50 years for alternative cancer therapies, circulatory disease, arteriosclerosis, emphysema, asthma, gangrene and more recently as a therapy for long time stroke victims (stroke victims have inactive but living cells surrounding the stroke site known as "sleeping beauty" cells that can be reactivated or jump started when they are exposed to several atmospheres of oxygen in hyperbaric chambers).

In Dr. Renate Vicbahn's book, *The Use of Ozone in Medicine*, cited 22 referred medical journal articles that illustrate the therapeutic effect of ozone against cancer cells. There does appear to be a bell shaped curve or "therapeutic window" for the optimal dosage of ozone (20 to 100 u/ml of blood); anything less is ineffective - anything more can be damaging to normal cells.

According to Ed McCabe, a medical investigative reporter and world reknowned expert on oxygen therapies, "The reason that ozone in very rare instances might seem to aggravate some conditions temporarily is explained by the mineral deficient diets that most people have. Their minerally deficient bodies simply do not have the functioning antioxidant enzymes systems to use the oxygen correctly."

Os - Osmium is found in igneous rocks at 0.0015 ppm. It oxidizes organic matter as OsO_4 and is reduced to Os.

P- Phosphorus is found in igneous rocks at 1,050 ppm; shale at 700 ppm; sandstone at 170 ppm; limestone at 400 ppm; fresh water at 0.005 ppm; sea water at 0.07 ppm; soil at 650 ppm ("fixed" by hydrous oxides of Al and Fe in acid soil). Great and vast reaches of Earth are deficient in P; marine plants at 3,500 ppm; land plants at 2,300 ppm; marine animals at 4,000 to 18,000 ppm; land animals at 17,000 to 44,000 ppm.

Phosphorus is an extremely important

essential mineral, however, it gets little or no attention from nutritionists because it is widely available in all foods. Phosphorus is a major structural mineral for bones and teeth, it has more functions in the human than any other mineral including its role as a vital constituent of nucleic acids, activates enzymes, for several steps of the ATP energy cycle; RBC metabolism (a complete discussion of P would require a discussion of every metabolic function in the body). Second in abundance only to calcium in the human body, it comprises 22 percent of the bodies total mineral content. The human body contains about 800 grams of P (just short of two pounds) of which 700 grams is found in bones and teeth as insoluble calcium phosphate (apatite crystals). The balance of P in the human body is found as biologically active intra and extracellular colloidal P in combination with carbohydrates, lipids, protein and a wide variety of other biologically active organic compounds including the bloods's major buffering system. B-complex vitamins function as coenzymes to intracellular metabolic functions only when combined with P.

Phosphorus is part of most proteins and as such becomes problematic (elevated P intake increases Ca requirements) when "high protein diets" are consumed by aggravating osteoporosis, arthritis, high blood pressure, loose teeth, etc. Phosphorus is present as phytates in cereals and grain flours, therefore, if bread is made from unleavened flours, the phytic acid will complex with Ca, Fe, Zn and other minerals further lowering their absorption rate.

The average adult human dietary intake of P is 1,000 to 1,500 mg/day. In adults and older children, the absorption of metallic P is limited to about three to five percent and as high as eight to 12 percent in infants. Mixed dietary sources of P (chelated forms) may be absorbed at the rate of 40 to 50 %. Optimal absorption of metallic and chelated P occurs when the Ca:P ratio is 1:1. Colloidal P is absorbed up to 98 %.

Deficiencies of P have long been recognised in livestock but only recently have been deemed important in humans. The widespread, universal and ultimately fatal results of P deficiency are the result of its widespread biological functions, significantly as the result of a decrease in ATP synthesis (complete metabolic energy failure) with associated neuromuscular, skeletal, blood and kidney disease.

Clinical P depletion and resultant low blood P (hypophosphatemia) result from IV administration of glucose or TPN (Total Parenteral Nutrition) without P supplementation, excessive use of antacids, hyperparathyroidism (low calcium/ high phosphate diets are the cause of this one), improper treatment of diabetic acidosis, use of diuretics, sweating during exercise and alcoholism with and without liver disease.

Vegetarians and vegans who do not supplement with minerals rarely have P deficiency, however, because of their high phytic acid intake they always have other mineral deficiencies icluding Ca, Cu, Cr, V. Li and Zn.

Pa - Protoactinium is found in igneous rocks at 1.4×10^{-6} ppm and sea water at 2.4×10^{-31} ppm. All isotopes are radioactive with a half life of 32,000 years. Protoactinium accumulates in mammalian bone after ingestion.

Pb - Lead is found in igneous rocks at

Lead tests for all kids under 3 urged

By Marilyn Elias
USA TODAY

All U.S. children should be screened for lead poisoning before they're 3 years old, the American Academy of Pediatrics advised Tuesday in a new policy.

The group's earlier code had left the decision on lead tests up to individual doctors. But mounting evidence suggests that routine checks are the only way to avoid serious intellectual and physical damage to youngsters, says Dr. J. Routt Reigart of the academy.

A $20 finger-stick blood test "can help us prevent permanent loss of IQ and behavior abnormalities," he says. At toxic levels, lead damages multiple organs, hinders physical and mental growth and produces symptoms of hyperactivity.

The academy recommends screening first at 9 months, when blood levels start rising in exposed youngsters, then again at 18 to 24 months, when lead usually reaches its peak.

"We know that the younger you're exposed, the more you're likely to suffer harmful effects," Reigart adds.

Lead paint in older, inner-city housing is the main source of childhood lead poisoning. About 2 million poor children in large cities are most at risk; one federal estimate is that 55% of low-income black kids may have above-normal levels.

Newer studies, though, point to hazards for middle-class youngsters, too. "With gentrification going on in our urban centers, more and more middle-class children are turning up with high lead levels," says David Bellinger of Harvard Medical School, Boston.

The basic safety standard, set by the Centers for Disease Control and Prevention, is under 10 micrograms of lead per deciliter of blood.

To bring down lead levels, homes must be cleaned of lead paint and dust, which can be ingested or inhaled. Kids with very high levels may be treated with lead-removing drugs.

12.5 ppm; shale at 20 ppm; sandstone at 7 ppm; limestone at 9 ppm; soil at 10 ppm (higher in limestone soils and humus); fresh water at 0.005 ppm; sea water at 0.00008 ppm; marine plants at 8.4 ppm; land plants at 2.7 ppm (many plant species are adapted to Pb-rich soils and accumulate Pb including *Amorpha canescens*); marine animals at 0.5 ppm (highest in fish bones); land animals at 2.0 ppm (highest levels found in bone, liver and kidney).

Children with cravings (pica) for non-food items (i.e.- paint, sand, dirt, etc.) are very susceptible to lead poisoning (plumbism). Infants and children with pica will chew on their toys, cribs, window sills, furniture and paint - a chip of lead paint the size of a penny can contain as much as 50 to 100 ug of lead (consuming this amount daily over three months will result in lead poisoning).

The "normal" blood lead level is below 40 ug/dl - children with blood lead above 60 to 80 ug/dl have symptoms of vomiting, irritability, weight loss, muscular weakness, headache, abdominal pain, insomnia and anorexia. Children with blood levels of lead above 80 ug/dl show anemia, kidney damage (Fanconi syndrome - increased urinary loss of amino acids, glucose and phosphorus), peripheral neuritis, ataxia and muscular incoordination, joint pain and encephalopathy (brain damage, learning disabilities, etc.) with eventual death.

The approach to treating lead poisoning includes supplementing with 60 colloidal minerals (especially Ca and Fe to eliminate pica and further ingestion of Pb), restoring fluid and electrolyte balance (especially P) and the use of IV or IM chelation using CaEDTA (ethylenediaminetetraacetic acid) and BAL (British Anti-Lewisite) for a minimum of five days. It is not unusual for as many as 25 % of Pb poisoned individuals to have residual loss of IQ, loss of coordination, hyperactivity, learning disabilities and impulsiveness.

Pd - Palladium is found in igneous rock at 0.01 ppm and land animals at 0.002 ppm. Palladium accumulates in mammalian liver and kidney after ingestion.

Pm - Promethium isotopes are all radioactive with a half life of 2.6 years. Promethium is an important fission product that has entered the biosphere (prior to man-made nuclear explosions Pm did not exist in nature) - Pm accumulates in mammalian bone and liver after ingestion.

Po - Polonium is found in igneous rocks at 2×10^{-10} ppm.

Pr - Praseodymium is a "light" Rare Earth found in igneous rocks at 8.2 ppm; shale at 6 ppm; sandstone at 2.8 ppm; limestone at 1.4 ppm; marine plants at 5 ppm; land plants accumulates up to 46 ppm (*Carya spp.*); marine animals at 0.5 ppm; land animals at 1.5 ppm (accumulates in mammalian bone and liver).

Enhances proliferation of normal cell growth and doubling of the life spans in laboratory species.

Pt - Platinum is found in igneous rocks at 0.005 ppm and land animals at 0.002 ppm.

Pu - All plutonium isotopes are radioactive with a half life of 24,000 years. Plutonium was released into the Earth's atmosphere by nuclear explosions. Marine plants concentrate Pu up to 4,000 times above the background level of sea water. Land plants record 0.4 to 2.2 disintegrations/sec/kg; land animals record 0.07 to 6.8 disintegrations/sec/kg (Pu accumulates in bone after contact or ingestion).

Ra

Ra - Radium is found in igneous rocks at 9×10^{-7} ppm; shale at 11×10^{-7} ppm; sandstone at 7×10^{-7} ppm; limestone at 4×10^{-7} ppm; fresh water at 3.9×10^{-10} ppm; sea water at 6×10^{-11} ppm; soils at 8×10^{-7} ppm; marine plants at 9×10^{-8} ppm; Land plants at 10^{-9} ppm; marine animals at $0.7 - 15 \times 10^{-9}$ ppm; land animals at 7×10^{-9} ppm (highest concentrations in mammalian bone); all isotopes of Ra are radioactive.

Rb

Rb - Rubidium is found in igneous rocks at 90 ppm; shale at 140 ppm; sandstone at 60 ppm; limestone at 3 ppm; freshwater at 0.0015 ppm; sea water at 0.12 ppm; soil at 100 ppm (fixed by clay soils); marine plants at 7.4 ppm; land plants at 20 ppm; marine animals at 20 ppm; land animals at 17 ppm (highest levels in liver and muscle - lowest levels in bone).

Rubidium can replace the electrolyte function of K in many species including bacteria, algae, fungi and certain invertebrates (echinoderms -starfish).

Re

Re - Rhenium is found in igneous rocks at 0.005 ppm; marine plants at 0.014 ppm; marine animals at 0.0005 to 0.006 ppm; land animals accumulate Re in the thyroid tissue.

Rh

Rh - Rhodium is found in igneous rocks at 0.001 ppm.

Rn

Rn - Radon is found in igneous rocks at 4×10^{-13} ppm; fresh water at 1.7×10^{-15} ppm; sea water at 6×10^{-16} ppm; all isotopes of Rn are radioactive with a half life of 54 seconds to 3.8 days; Rn is carcinogenic and highly toxic when inhaled. Radon is a common household hazard, it is odorless and colorless; detection requires the use of a kit which are generally available.

Ru

Ru - Ruthenium is found in igneous rocks at 0.001 ppm; land plants at 0.005 ppm; land animals at 0.002 ppm (RuO_4 is highly toxic to animals).

S

S - Sulfur is found in igneous rocks at 260 ppm; shale at 2,400 ppm; sandstone at 240 ppm, limestone 1,200 ppm; fresh water at 3.7 ppm; sea water at 885 ppm; soils at 700 ppm (up to 90 % of soil S is bound tightly in humus; SO_4 is a major exchange anion in many soils; occurs in soils near volcanoes liberating SO_2 and SO_3) ; marine plants at 12,000 ppm (accumulates in red algae, *Desmarestia spp.*); Land plants at 3,400 ppm (lower in most bryophytes and gymnosperms); marine animals at 5,000 to 19,000 ppm (highest in coelenterates and molluscs); land animals at 5,000 ppm (highest in cartilage, tendons, keratin, skin, nails and hair - lowest in bones).

Sulfur is an important structural atom in most proteins as sulfur amino acids (cystine, cysteine and methionone)and small organic molecules. Glutathione, a tripeptide containing cysteine, is essential to cellular reactions involving sulfur amino acids in protein. Sulfur is found in a reduced form (-SH) in cysteine and in an oxidized

Muscle, Sickle Cell Problems Cited In Death During Fire Test

By Bill Bryan
Of the Post-Dispatch Staff

Excessive exertion and undetected medical problems caused the death of a man who collapsed while taking a physical test for firefighter applicants, the St. Louis medical examiner said Wednesday.

Ricky Brison, 28, collapsed Nov. 24 while taking the St. Louis Fire Academy's fitness exam, known as the Phoenix Performance Test. He died the next day at Cochran Veterans Administration Hospital.

"His death was related to the breakdown of muscle, known as Rhabdomyolysis, and Sickle Cell Trait," said Dr. Michael Graham, the city's medical examiner.

"Excessive exertion by someone not adequately prepared can cause death.

"The muscle breakdown is very, very unusual but is well-recognized [in medical circles], and the Sickle Cell Trait is also well known.

"Both have been documented for causing deaths during military basic training."

Brison's wife, Lynetta Brison, said she had not been informed of Graham's ruling and had no comment. Brison's mother, Orlie Middleton, said:

"I can't understand this. It seems they're covering up. My son was in the service. He was a security guard. He was a healthy person."

Graham said the reason his ruling on Brison's death took so long was that numerous microscopic tests had to be conducted.

The St. Louis Fire Academy's test simulates necessary firefighting maneuvers that include raising and lowering a ladder, running while fully extending a 200-foot hose, hitting a spring-loaded metal pad 50 times with a sledgehammer and dragging a 140-pound dummy.

form (-S-S-) as the double molecule, cystine. This "sulfhydryl group" is important for the specific configuration of some structural proteins and for the biological activities of somes enzymes (proteins that do work).

Sulfur containing proteins work in indirect ways to maintain life:

- Hemoglobin
- Hormones (Insulin, adrenal cortical hormones)
- Enzymes
- Antibodies

Sulfur also occurs in carbohydrates such as heparin, an anticoagulant that is concentrated in the liver and other tissues, and chondroitin sulfate (cartilage, Knox gelatin). The vitamins thiamine (B_1) and biotin have S bound in their molecule. The toxic propertie's of arsenic are the result of it's ability to combine with sulfhydryl groups.

Deficiency of sulfur results in degenerative types of arthritis involving degeneration of cartilage, ligaments, tendons, Systemic Lupus Erythematosis, Sicklecell anemia and various "collagen diseases."

Sb - Antimony is found in igneous rock at 0.2 ppm; shales at 1.5 ppm; sandstones at 0.05 pp; limestone at 0.2 ppm; sea water at 0.00033 ppm; soil at 2 to 10 ppm; land plants at 0.06 ppm; land animals at 0.006 ppm (concentrates in mammalian heart muscle).

Antimony potassium tartrate (tartar emetic) is still used today as the preferred treatment for blood flukes (schistosomiasis or Bilharziasis).

Sc - Scandium is found in igneous rock at 22 ppm; shales 13 ppm; sandstone and limestone at 1 ppm; sea water at 0.000004 ppm; soils at 7 ppm; lant plants at 0.008 ppm; land animals at 0.00006 ppm (concentrates in mammalian heart and bone).

Se - Selenium is found in igneous rocks at 0.05 ppm; shale at 0.6 ppm; sandstone at 0.05 ppm; limestone at 0.08 ppm; fresh water at 0.02 ppm; sea water at 0.00009 ppm; soils at 0.2 ppm (not universally distributed, vast areas of Earth are deficient or even totally devoid of Se {Fig. 11-14}; Se is found in the humus of alkaline soils when present); marine plants at 0.8 ppm; land plants at 0.2 ppm; land animals at 1.7 ppm (highest concentrations found in liver, kidney, heart, and skeletal muscle).

Selenium is the most efficient antioxident (anti-peroxident) and is found at the subcellular level in the glutathione peroxidase enzyme system and metallo amino acids (selenomethionine, etc.). Selenium prevents cellular and subcellular lipids and fats from being peroxidized which literally means it prevents body fats from going rancid (seen externally as "age spots" or "liver spots" - this brown gold peroxidized lipid is known as ceroid lipofucsin).

Selenium also functions to protect cellular and organelle bi-lipid layer membranes from oxidative damage - the cover illustration is an electron photomicrograph of a selenium deficient rhesus monkey liver mitochondria magnified 126,000 times. The inner membrane of the mitochondria (made up of enzymes and RNA) has precipitated out of the normal structure to become a nonfunctioning organic crystalloid. This type of damage seen through the standard light microscope is called "age pigment". High intakes of vegetable oils including salad dressing, margarine and cooking oils

Table 11- 23. Selenium Deficiency Diseases.

Disease

- HIV (AIDS)
- Anemia (RBC fragility)
- "Age Spots" & "Liver Spots"
- Fatigue
- Muscular weakness
- Myalgia (muscle pain and soreness)
- Scoliosis
- Muscular Dystrophy (MD, White Muscle Disease, Stiff Lamb Disease)
- Cystic Fibrosis (congenital)
- Cardiomyopathy (Keshan Disease, "Mulberry heart" Disease)
- Multiple Sclerosis (MS) - associated with Hg poisoning
- Heart palpitations
- Irregular heart beat
- Liver cirrhosis
- Pancreatitis
- Pancreatic atrophy
- Lou Gehrig's Disease (ALS) - associated with Hg poisoning
- Parkinson's Disease - associated with Hg poisoning
- Alzheimer's Disease - associated with high vegetable oil consumption
- Adrenoleucodystrophy (ALD -"Lorenzo's Oil" Syndrome)
- Infertility
- Low birth weight
- High infant mortality
- Sudden Infant Death Syndrome (SIDS)
- Cancer - associated with carcinogen contact as well as high vegetable oil intake
- Clinical AIDS (HIV infection)
- Sickle cell anemia

concurrent with a selenium deficiency is the quickest route to a heart attack and cancer. The polyunsaturated configuration of the oils when heated or treated with hydrogen ("trans fatty acids") literally causes the rancidity ("free radical" damage) of cellular fat.

The clinical diseases associated with selenium deficiency are diverse and to the uninformed (allopathic physicians) shrouded in mystery (table 11-23). Selenium deficiency is one of the more costly mineral deficiency complexes affecting embryos, the newborn, toddlers, teens and

Selenium Levels in the U.S.

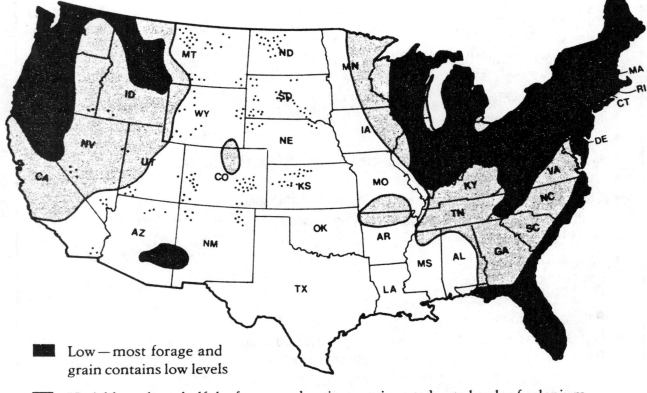

■ Low — most forage and grain contains low levels

▦ Variable — about half the forage and grain contains moderate levels of selenium

☐ Adequate — most forage and grain contains ample selenium

∵ Local areas where selenium accumulator plants contain unusually high amounts of selenium

Parts of the Northwest, southern coastal plains and most of the Northeast are low-selenium areas, as reflected in plant concentrations.

SOURCE: Adapted from *Micronutrients in Agriculture*, 1972, p. 542, by permission of the Soil Science Society of America, Inc., 677 S. Segoe Rd., Madison, WI 53711.

Fig. 11-14 1972 map of the continental United States showing areas of Se depletion.

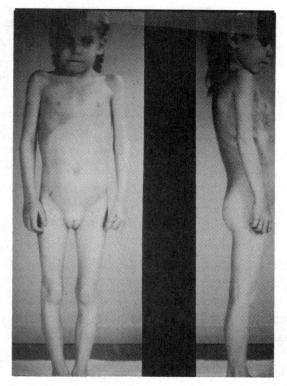

Cystic fibrosis patient untreated with colloidal Se

Fig. 11-CF Cystic fibrosis patient (left) after four years of colloidal Se

adults alike.

Selenium deficiency can result in infertility in both men and women. Congenital selenium deficiency during pregnancy can result in a wide variety of problems ranging from miscarriage, low birth weight, high infant mortality, cystic fibrosis (Fig. 11-CF), muscular dystrophy and liver cirrhosis.

Selenium deficiency in growing children can result in crib death or SIDS (Sudden Infant Death Syndrome) slow growth, small size (failure to reach genetic potential for size and mass), muscular dystrophy, scoliosis (Fig. 11-15), cardiomyopathy (muscular dystrophy of the heart muscle or Keshan Disease), anemia, liver cirrhosis (Fig. 11-16), muscular weakness, lowered immune capacity and neuromuscular diseases such as ALD (Adrenoleucodystrophy or "Lorenzo's Oil" type syndromes).

In young adults, selenium deficiency appears as anemia, chronic fatigue, muscular weakness, myalgia, muscle tenderness, pancreatitis, infertility, muscular dystrophy (Fig. 11-17, 18 & 19), scoliosis, cardiomyopathy (this is especially common in young athletes such as basketball players and football players at the high school, college, university and professional levels), part of the anorexia nervosa complex, multiple sclerosis (adequate Se protects against Hg poisoning), Lou Gehrig's Disease (ALS) and liver cirrhosis.

Selenium deficiency in adults appears as reduced immune capacity, anemia, infertility, "age spots" or "liver spots (Fig. 11-20 & 11-21)," myalgia, muscle weakness multiple sclerosis, ALS, Parkinson's Disease, Alzheimer's Disease, palpitaions or irregular heart beat, cardiomyopathy, hypertrophy or thickening of the cardiac muscle, liver cirrhosis, cataracts and cancer.

In a review of the anti-cancer effects of selenium Dr. Gerhard N. Schrauzer, head of the Department of Chemistry, UCSD states:

Selenium is increasingly recognized as a versatile anticarcinogenic agent. Its protective functions cannot be solely attributed to the action of glutathione peroxidase. Instead, selenium appears to operate by several mechanisms, depending on dosage and chemical form of selenium and the nature of the carcinogenic stress. In a major protective function, selenium is proposed to prevent the malignant transformatioin of cells by acting as a "redox switch" in the activation-inactivation of cellular growth factors and other functional proteins throught the catalysis of oxidation-reduction reactions of critical -SH groups or -S-S- bonds. The growth-modulatory effects of selenium are dependent on the levels of intracellular glutathione peroxidase and the oxygen supply. In general, growth inhibition is achieved by the Se-mediated stimulation of cellular respiration (more oxygen less cancer). Selenium appears to inhibit the replication of tumor viruses and the activation of oncogenes by similar mechanisms. However, it may also alter carcinogen metabolism and protect DNA against carcinogen-induced damage. In additional functions of relevance to its anticarcinogenic activity, selenium acts as an acceptor of biogenic methyl groups, and is involved in detoxification of metals and certain xenobiotics. Selenium also has immunopotentiating properties. It is

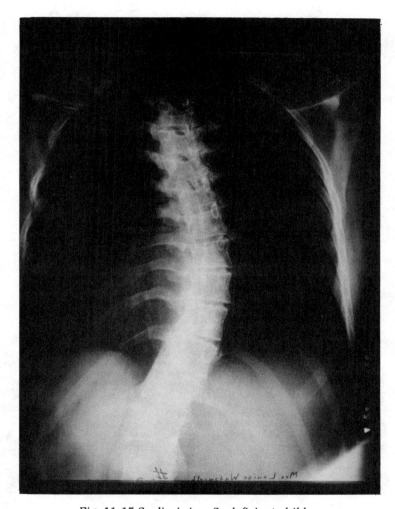

Fig. 11-15 Scoliosis in a Se deficient child

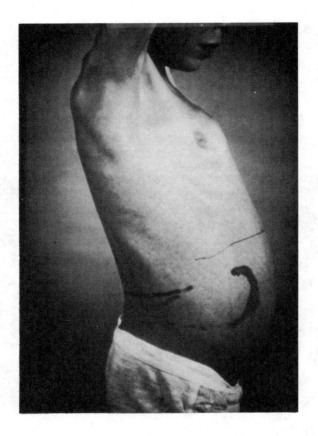

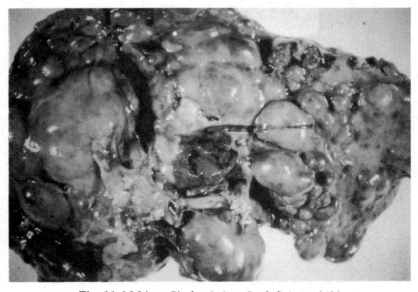

Fig. 11-16 Liver Cirrhosis in a Se deficient child

Fig. 11-17

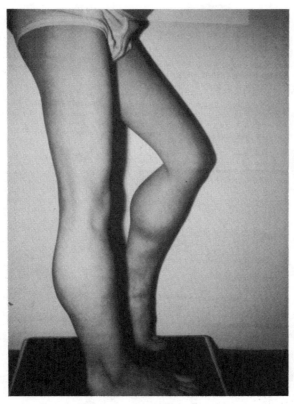

A) Muscular dystrophy (note enlarged calves).

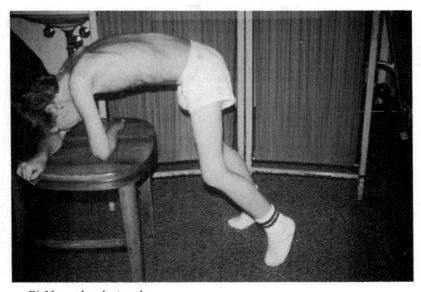

B) Muscular dystrophy

SATURDAY, OCTOBER 23, 1993

ST. LOUIS POST-DISPATCH

Robert Hapka-Tracy; Paraquad Specialist

Robert S. Hapka-Tracy, a specialist in independent living for Paraquad, died Friday (Oct. 22, 1993) at St. Mary's Health Center in Richmond Heights after suffering from muscular dystrophy. He was 35 and lived in St. Louis.

Mr. Hapka-Tracy was born in Sheboygan, Wis. He was diagnosed with muscular dystrophy when he was a child and had used a wheelchair since he was 16. He earned a bachelor's degree in safety education from the University of Wisconsin at Whitewater and a master's degree in social work from the University of Wisconsin at Madison.

He began working at Paraquad in 1986.

A funeral service will be at 5:30 p.m. Sunday at Mayer Funeral Home, 4356 Lindell Boulevard. Visitation will be from noon to 5 p.m. Sunday at the funeral home. His body will be cremated.

Among the survivors are his wife, Joan Hapka-Tracy; his parents, Raburn and Theresa Tracy of Plymouth, Wis.; a sister, Tammy Reich of Sheboygan; and two brothers, Randy Tracy of Plymouth and Tony Tracy of Cascade, Wis.

Fig. 11-18

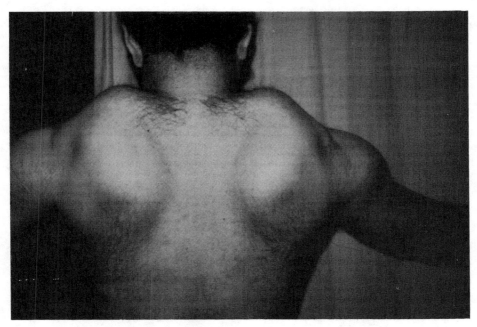

A) Muscular Dystrophy in an adult

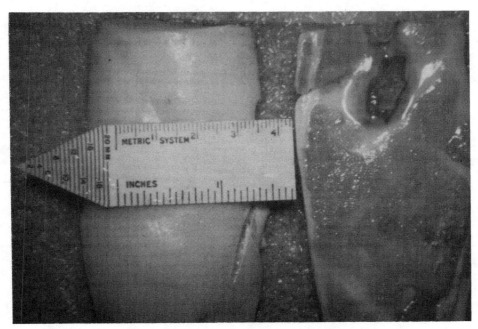

B) Ceroid lipofucion (pigment of aging) accumulated in body fat (right) as a result
   of Se deficiency, normal fat on left.

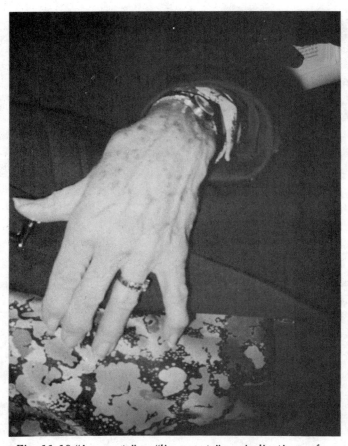

Fig. 11-19 "Age spots" or "liver spots" are indications of a
high vegetable oil, low selenium diet.

required for optimal macrophage and natural killer cell functions.

The school of pharmacy from the University of Georgia released a report in August of 1994 that concludes a human selenium deficiency is related to the onset of full blown AIDS in chronically infected HIV patients. According to their report, HIV requires large amounts of selenium for replication and in selenium deficient patients, the virus competes with the patient for limited amounts of the essential mineral. The HIV patient actually dies of selenium deficiency encephalopathy, liver cirrhosis or cardiomyopathy. Long term HIV patients (20 years or more) that never developed full blown AIDS had supplemented with relatively large amounts of selenium.

1. *Bostedt, H. and Schramel, P.*: The importance of Selenium in the Prenatal And Postnatal Development of Calves and Lambs. Biol.Trace Ele. Research. The Humana Press,Inc. 24:163.1990.

2. *Brizzee, K.R. and Ordy,J.M.*: Age Pigments, Cell Loss and Hippocampal Function. Mechanisms of Ageing and Development. 9:143.1979.

3. *Chan, F.I., et al.*: Selenium Deficiency and Keshan Disease, Chinese J.Med. June 1979.

4. *Hintz, H.F., et al.*: Effect of Selenium, Sulfur and Sulfur Amino Acids on Nutritional Muscular Dystrophy in the Lamb. April 1964. J.Nutr.pp495-498.

5. *Hoekstra, W.O.*: Biochemical Functions of Selenium and its Relationship to Vitamin E. Federation Proceedings.34:2083.1975.

6. *Kulczycki, L.L. and Schauf, V.*: Cystic Fibrosis in Blacks in Washington, D,C, Am. J. Dis. Child. 127:64.1974.

7. *Maron, B.J., et al.*: Sudden Death in Hypertrophic Cardiomyopathy: A Profile of 78 Patients. Circulation.65:1388.1982.

8. *Maron, B.J., et al.*: Sudden Death in Young Athletes. Circulation. 62:218.1979.

9. *Muth,O.H., et al.*: White Muscle Disease (Myopathy) in Lambs and Calves VII. Etiology and Prophylaxis. Am.J.Vet. Res.22:466.1961.

10. *Olmsted, L., Schrauzer, G.N., et al.*: Selenium Supplementation of Symptomatic Human Immunodeficiency Virus Infected Patients. Biol. Trace Ele. Research. Humana Press,Inc. 20:59.1989.

11. *Oppenheimer, E.H. and Esterly, J.R.*: Pathology of Cystic Fibrosis. Review of the Literature and Comparison with 146 Autopsied Cases. In: Perspectives in Pediatric Pathology. Vol.2. Yearbook Medical Pub., Inc. Chicago.1975.pp241-278.

12. *Proctor, J.F., et al.*: Selenium, Vitamin E and Linseed Oil Meal as Preventatives of Muscular Dystrophy in Lambs. J.Animal Sci. 17:1183.1958.

13. *Revis, N.W., et al.*: Metabolism of Selenium in Skeletal Muscle and Liver of Mice with "Genetic" Muscular Dystrophy. Proc. Soc. Exper. Biol. Med. 160:139.1979.

14. *Schrauzer, G.N. *: Selenium in Nutritional Cancer Prophylaxis: An Update. Vitamins, Nutrition and Cancer, Karger. Basel. pp240-250.1984.

15. *Schrauzer, G.N.: Selenium*: Mechanistic Aspects of Anticarcinogenic Action. Biol. Trace. Ele. Research. The Humana Press,Inc. 33:51.1992.

16. *Schrauzer, G.N., et al.*: Effect of Simulated American, Bulgarian, and Japanese Human Diets and of Selenium Supplementation on the Incidence of Virally Induced Mammary Tumors in Female Mice. Biol.Trace Ele. Research. The Humana Press, Inc. 20:169.1989.

![Decorative header ornament]

THE DENVER POST

Voice of the Rocky Mountain Empire

Final Edition /
35 cents in Designated

Wednesday, September 15, 1993

Anti-cancer diet found?

Tests in China link beta carotene, vitamin E, selenium

By Jeff Nesmith
Cox News Service

WASHINGTON — Daily doses of beta carotene, vitamin E and selenium dramatically reduced the risk of dying from cancer among thousands of residents in a rural area of China.

The experiment, sponsored by the National Cancer Institute, is the first hard evidence that some antioxidant substances can provide a "protective" effect against cancer, scientists said yesterday.

Other dietary supplements — vitamin C, retinol, zinc, riboflavin, molybdenum and niacin — had no statistically significant effect on cancer deaths after five years, the scientists said.

However, in a group of middle-aged adults who took the combination of beta carotene, vitamin E and selenium for five years, the results were striking: 13 percent fewer deaths from all cancers, 21 percent reduction in deaths from stomach cancer and a 9 percent decrease in deaths from all causes.

In presenting their results at a press conference, the government scientists cautioned that partici-

Health

pants in the experiment have some of the worst cancer rates — and worst diets — in the world.

That could mean that the results may not apply to people whose basic diets provide more of the critical nutrients.

"This is a hopeful sign that vitamins and minerals may help prevent the onset of cancer in healthy individuals," said Dr. William J. Blot of the institute's biostatistics branch, "but the results don't automatically translate to Western populations."

The experiment was conducted among residents of Linxian, a rural county in Henan Province of north-central China. The rates of esophageal cancer and cancer of the gastric cardia, the point where the esophagus attaches to the stomach, among the people of Linxian are among the highest in the world, said Dr. Blot.

Epidemiologists have investigated pickled vegetables, mycotoxins in food and a tendency to gulp down scalding hot tea as possible causes. The diet of residents of the area is low in fruits and meats and other animal products and persistently deficient in a number of vitamins and minerals.

After selecting about 29,000 people between 40 and 69 years old, the scientists arranged daily pill-taking schemes in which various participants received different combinations of supplements: retinol and zinc, riboflavin and niacin, vitamin C and molybdenum, beta carotene, selenium and vitamin E, and a placebo pill that contained none of the nutrients.

Participants received from one to two times the U.S. recommended daily allowances. Daily doses of beta carotene, for which no RDA has been established, was 15,000 micrograms — or about the amount found in a carrot.

Beta carotene is common in carrots, leafy vegetables and some fruits. Vitamin E is plentiful in margarine, vegetable oil, meats, nuts and leafy greens.

TUESDAY, JUNE 8, 1993

ST. LOUIS POST-DISPATCH

Dr. Sol F. Cantor; Osteopathic Physician

Dr. Sol F. Cantor, an osteopathic physician in south St. Louis County, died Friday (June 4, 1993) of cancer at Jewish Hospital. He was 56 and lived in Chesterfield.

Dr. Cantor had lived in the St. Louis area since about 1973, and until about six years ago practiced emergency medicine at hospitals in Missouri and Illinois.

About 1987, he opened the Sunset Hills Family Medical Practice. Through this office, Dr. Cantor sponsored many community education courses, ranging from health prevention to earthquake preparedness.

He was most recently on the staffs of Missouri Baptist, Incarnate Word and Deaconess hospitals.

Dr. Cantor was a native of Richmond, Va., and earned his undergraduate degree about 1956 from the University of Richmond. He received his osteopathic medicine degree from the Kirksville (Mo.) College of Osteopathic Medicine in the early 1960s and operated a private practice for 10 years in Columbus, Ohio.

In the St. Louis area, Dr. Cantor was on the board of the Southwest County unit of the American Cancer Society and was active in the St. Louis and the Missouri medical societies, and the American Academy of Physicians.

A funeral service will be held at 11 a.m. Thursday at Berger Memorial, 4715 McPherson Avenue, St. Louis. Burial will be at Chesed Shel Emeth Cemetery in Chesterfield.

Among the survivors are his wife, Phyllis Cantor of Chesterfield; a daughter, Lauren Fasbinder of Lenexa, Kan.; four sons, Chuck Cantor of Leawood, Kan., Dr. Michael Cantor of Boston, Bruce Cantor of Urbana, Ill., and Daniel Cantor of Phoenix; and four grandchildren.

Joy Garrett, starred in 'Days of Our Lives'

ASSOCIATED PRESS

LOS ANGELES — Actress Joy Garrett, best known as the mother figure Jo Johnson on television's "Days of Our Lives," has died of liver failure. She was 47.

Garrett died Thursday at the University of California, Los Angeles, Medical Center, said hospital spokesman Rich Elbaum.

Her acting career spanned film, stage and television, but it was in daytime soap operas that Garrett found her greatest success.

During the seven years she portrayed Jo Johnson, Garrett was named best supporting actress by *Soap Opera People Magazine* and *Soap Opera Digest.*

Earlier, she appeared for one year on another daytime soap, "The Young and the Restless."

A native of Fort Worth, Texas, she was educated at Texas Wesleyan University and the American Academy of Dramatic Arts in New York.

Terry Langer, Doctor And Heart Expert, 52

Dr. Terry Langer, director of clinical cardiology at Presbyterian Medical Center in Philadelphia since 1985, died Tuesday at the Hospital of the University of Pennsylvania. A resident of Cherry Hill, N.J., he was 52.

The cause of death was liver failure, his family said.

A native of the Bronx, Dr. Langer was a summa cum laude graduate of New York University and graduated magna cum laude from Harvard Medical School. In the late 1960's, he did research at the Heart Institute of the National Institutes of Health and became recognized as an expert on lipid metabolism and lipid diseases.

After a stint at Columbia-Presbyterian Medical Center in New York, he moved to the Hospital of the University of Pennsylvania. There he was director of clinical cardiology from 1972 to 1985 as well as an associate professor of medicine at the university.

Dr. Langer is survived by his wife of 30 years, the former Joan Gordon; three sons, Dr. David Langer of Philadelphia, Robert of Manhattan, and Jonathan of Chicago; his mother, Francine Langer of Atlantic Beach, L.I., and his sister, Marlene Edelstein, also of Atlantic Beach.

Myers infant

Nicholas S. Myers, infant son of Michael and Lucy Myers of 17214 Roosevelt Ave., Falls Church, Va., died Monday in Wolf Trap, Va.

Surviving in addition to his parents are a sister, Jessica M., at home; his paternal grandparents, Margaret Myers and Charles Myers; and his maternal grandmother, Theresa Kistler, all of Harrisburg.

Funeral Liturgy for a Child will be celebrated at 11 a.m. Friday in Holy Family Catholic Church, Harrisburg. Burial will be in Resurrection Cemetery, West Hanover Twp.

Viewing will be from 9:30 to 10:30 a.m. Friday at Hetrick Funeral Home, Susquehanna Twp.

Memorial contributions may be made to the National SIDS Foundation, P.O. Box 344, Oakton, Va. 22124.

SPORTS

• WEDNESDAY, JULY 28, 1993

Celtics Star, 27, Collapses, Dies
Conflicting Medical Opinions Confused Lewis

c.1993 N.Y. Times News Service

NEW YORK — Reggie Lewis, the Boston Celtics star who collapsed with a heart ailment during a playoff game last April, died Tuesday night after collapsing while shooting baskets at the team's training center at Brandeis University in Waltham, Mass.

Lewis, 27, was pronounced dead at Waltham-Weston Hospital after being taken there at 5:41 p.m.

Soon after he arrived, hospital officials said Lewis was unconscious and being treated for a "cardiac event," but shortly thereafter, citing instructions from Lewis' wife, Donna Harris, the officials refused to give any further information on his condition even as announcements were made on Boston radio and television stations that Lewis had died.

It was not until after 10 p.m. that doctors confirmed the death.

Lewis, who had been hospitalized for 11 days after he collapsed during a playoff game against the Charlotte Hornets on April 29, had received conflicting medical advice since then about the nature and severity of the ailment that led to the collapse.

A team of 11 cardiologists initially told him that he suffered from a severe form of heart disease that would pose a danger to his life if he resumed his basketball career.

Later, after Lewis abruptly switched hospitals, moving from New England Baptist to Brigham and Women's Hospital in Boston for a week of further tests, Dr. Gilbert Mudge announced that the player suffered from a comparatively benign neural condition, neurocardiogenic syncope, in which

See LEWIS, Page 6

Thursday, September 16, 1993

THE DENVER POST

Grad collapses, dies at CU center

Boulderite was shooting baskets at gym

By Mary George
Denver Post Staff Writer

A 22-year-old graduate of the University of Colorado collapsed and died on the basketball court at the Boulder campus recreation center Monday night.

Darren Mallot of Boulder, who graduated from CU-Boulder in May with a degree in international relations, was shooting baskets and waiting to get into a pick-up basketball game about 10:30 p.m. Monday.

Following a lay-up, the 6-foot 5-inch, 170-pound athlete fell to the gym floor. Mallot was pronounced dead at Boulder Community Hospital at 11:01 p.m.

"He was in excellent health, he was an excellent athlete," said Mallot's father, Jerry Mallot, in Boulder from Tampa, Fla., for funeral arrangements. "The coroner said he found nothing associated

BOULDER with the heart or brain or blood that would explain his death. Just nothing."

The cause of death won't be known until the results of further laboratory tests are available, said Tom Faure, chief medical investigator at the Boulder County coroner's office. Results should be available next week.

Gary Chadwick, the recreation center director, said Mallot was shooting baskets and waiting to get a game going when he collapsed. "There wasn't any contact between him and anyone else. It was completely unexpected. A real tragedy," Chadwick said.

Mallot grew up in Wichita and started his studies four years ago at CU.

He had just started work at a sports clothing store in Boulder, his father said.

Boston star Lewis collapses, dies at 27

By Jack Carey
USA TODAY

Boston Celtics captain Reggie Lewis, 27, who passed out during an NBA playoff game in April, died Tuesday night after collapsing while shooting baskets.

"It's a time of incredible grief," said Celtics executive Dave Gavitt late Tuesday.

After Lewis' April collapse, team doctor Arnold Scheller said he had a life-threatening heart ailment like the one that killed college basketball star Hank Gathers in *Loyola Marymount*

1990, and probably would not play again.

"You can die from this," Scheller said he told Lewis, a 1987 first-round draft pick.

But Lewis, against team wishes, sought a second opinion and was told he had a nerve condition that could be controlled.

Lewis arrived at Brandeis University at about 4 p.m. ET Tuesday and was shooting baskets, said Brandeis' Jack Molloy.

Witnesses said Lewis fell to the court about 5 p.m., was limp and shaking, stopped breathing and had no pulse.

Lewis "wasn't doing anything too strenu-

ous," said Amir Weiss, who was at the gym.

Local paramedics said they found Lewis in complete cardiac arrest; he was pronounced dead at 7:30 p.m. ET at Waltham-Weston Hospital.

Celtics' president Red Auerbach, who is recovering from heart bypass surgery, called Lewis "a warm, kind, gentle and generous man."

He is survived by his wife, Donna Harris, and a son, Reggie Jr.

▶ **'Hearts are very heavy,' 1,9C**

REGGIE LEWIS   USA TODAY

THE NEW YORK TIMES **SPORTS** *TUESDAY, JANUARY 4, 1994*

Death of Basketball Player Still a Mystery

Before returning to classes yesterday after the holiday break, the 90-member student body at the Hudson Vocational Technical High School in North Bergen, N.J., held a memorial service for Jackson Muamba, the 17-year-old junior who collapsed last Friday during a basketball game against Bayonne, and later died.

"Jackson's friends are very distraught," said Frank Gargiulo, the school's superintendent. "This is a small, close-knit school."

According to Gargiulo, Muamba collapsed during the early minutes of the second half against Bayonne. Gargiulo said players from both teams were lining up for a foul shot by a player from Bayonne.

Just before the first free-throw attempt, Muamba, a 5-foot-10-inch forward, walked over to Coach Tom Killeen and asked to be taken out of the game, saying he felt tired. While Killeen was making the substitution, Muamba collapsed. He never regained consciousness.

"There was a nurse at the game, and she rushed onto the court to give Jackson mouth-to-mouth resuscitation," said Gargiulo. "An ambulance got here very quickly and took him to Bayonne Hospital, but it appeared that Jackson was already gone."

With no history of medical problems, Muamba's death remains a mystery to his family, friends and Hudson school officials. An autopsy

North Bergen student had no history of medical problems.

report from a medical examiner's office in Jersey City is still to be completed.

"We don't have any medical answer or any reason for it to happen," said Muamba's brother, Constantine, speaking yesterday on the New Jersey News Network. "The only thing we could think was that it was his time, his purpose in life was filled. We don't have any explanation for that."

Gargiulo said that Muamba had passed a preseason physical examination before joining the team, and had never complained about feeling sick or injured.

"This school opened up just three years ago," said Gargiulo, who brought in crisis counselors to help faculty members and students try to deal with the tragedy. "And what's really sad is that Jackson was one of the kids who lobbied for a basketball team. He was a real popular kid, and we're really going to miss him."

Constantine Muamba said that his brother was "a very strong person who lived every day of his life to the fullest."

"Everybody is trying to stick together and keep up the strength," Constantine added. "That's what Jackson would have wanted."

Drysdale dies of heart attack

ASSOCIATED PRESS
and ORANGE COUNTY REGISTER

MONTREAL — Hall of Fame pitcher Don Drysdale, who teamed with Sandy Koufax to form baseball's best 1-2 pitching punch for the Dodgers of the 1960s, was found dead of a heart attack yesterday in his hotel room.

Drysdale, who had a history of heart trouble, would have been 57 in three weeks. He spent the past 23 years as a baseball broadcaster, the past six on Dodgers games.

Drysdale is the second Dodgers Hall of Famer to die in the past week. Former catcher Roy Campanella died of heart attack eight days ago at age 71.

"I was just with him at Campy's

■ Phil Collier remembers an intense competitor—**C-3**

funeral," former Dodgers reliever Clem Labine said from Vero Beach, Fla. "Holy Toledo! Of all the things to happen. It's just hard to believe. My God, one on top of the other."

Drysdale had accompanied the Dodgers to Montreal to start an 11-day Eastern road trip. He announced Friday night's game with no problems. When Drysdale was not at Olympic Stadium about a half-hour before the start of yesterday's game at 7:35 p.m. EDT, his colleagues at KTLA-TV and KABC-AM radio tried to call him at the Le Centre Sheraton.

They discovered a short time later that Drysdale had died in his room.

Dodgers manager Tommy Lasorda recalled Drysdale as "a good man, a great man. It's going to be a severe loss. He loved the Dodgers very, very much. He loved his family very much. What a guy. I'll tell you something, he was something as a baseball player. He was something as a man, a real man."

Drysdale won the 1962 Cy Young Award as the National League's best pitcher.

Drysdale, who was 6-foot-5, was known as "Big D" during a 14-year pitching career with the Brooklyn and Los Angeles Dodgers in which he was a National League All-Star

10 times. He pitched on World Series championship teams in 1959, 1963 and 1965 and had a career record of 259-167 with a 2.95 ERA.

Drysdale was known for never backing down to hitters, constantly challenging them with inside fastballs.

Most of his pitches were thrown with a sneer.

"Once, the manager came out to the mound," Drysdale once said, "and instructed me to walk a batter. I wound up hitting him instead. Why waste four pitches when one will do? Sooner or later you have to say

See **Drysdale** on Page C-3

News-Leader

Monday, July 11, 1994

James L. Gentry Jr., M.D.

Dr. James L. Gentry Jr., 37, Springfield, died at 9:32 p.m. Saturday, July 9 1994, in St. John's Regional Health Center following an apparent heart attack suffered earlier in the day on Table Rock Lake.

Dr. Gentry was born in St. Louis and moved to Springfield at age 8 where he attended St. Agnes Catholic School. He attended the University of Missouri-Columbia for his undergraduate work and was a 1982 graduate of the University of Missouri School of Medicine. He served his three-year internship and residency at Franklin Square Hospital, Baltimore, Md. He had practiced in Springfield since 1985 with Smith-Glynn-Callaway Clinic and served as a member of the Executive Board. At the time of his death, he was a family practitioner in the Sunshine office of the Clinic. He was board certified by the American Board of Family Practice and was a member of Greene County Medical Society, Missouri State Medical Association, American Academy of Family Practice and Missouri Academy of Family Practice. He was a member of Immaculate Conception Catholic Church.

He is survived by his wife, Marty; ten-year-old twins, James L. Gentry III and Sarah Jane Gentry, all of the home; his parents, James L. Sr. and

ST. LOUIS POST-DISPATCH

THURSDAY, JULY 29, 1993

Dr. Gail L. Clark, 47; Was Cardiologist

Dr. Gail L. Clark, a cardiologist and head of the cardiac rehabilitation program at St. Luke's Hospital in west St. Louis County, died Monday (July 26, 1993) at St. Mary's Health Center in Richmond Heights after suffering a heart attack. She was 47.

Dr. Clark lived in University City.

She was a native of Rochester, N.Y. She began her medical career as a nurse in the coronary care unit at Barnes Hospital, which opened in 1969. She then enrolled at St. Louis University Medical School and graduated in 1974.

"She was highly respected as a cardiologist and a leader in the field of stress medicine as it relates to heart disease," said Dr. Robert Paine, cardiologist and clinical professor at Washington University School of Medicine.

Dr. Clark was a member of the St. Louis Society of Internal Medicine.

Clark

A funeral Mass will be held at 10 a.m. Friday at Our Lady of Lourdes Church, 7148 Forsyth Boulevard. Burial will follow at Resurrection Cemetery in Affton. No visitation will be held.

Among survivors are her husband, Kenneth W. Clark, two daughters, Sara E. Clark and Emily J. Clark, and two sons, Scott W. Clark and Christopher R. Clark, all of University City; her mother, Elizabeth D. Bommele of Rochester; two sisters, Ethel McCormack of Norfolk, Va., and Connie Campisi of Rochester; and two brothers, Gary Lergner of Southern Pines, N.C., and Robert Bommele of Rochester.

U.S. Refuses to Finance Prison Heart Transplant

By GINA KOLATA

If DeWayne Murphy were not in Federal prison, he would be on a waiting list for a heart transplant or might even have had one by now.

But the Federal Bureau of Prisons, which is responsible for his medical costs, does not pay for organ transplants, so the 33-year-old Mr. Murphy is living in a medical ward at the Rochester Federal Medical Center in Minnesota, agonizing over his case. One prisoners' rights advocate argues that by not financing a heart transplant for Mr. Murphy, the Bureau of Prisons has converted his four-year sentence to a death sentence.

Mr. Murphy says his health is rapidly deteriorating as his heart fails. He says he is weak and short of breath, and that he must sleep sitting up, with an oxygen mask over his face. His mother, Pat Murphy of Liberty, Mo., says her son is afraid to fall asleep at night.

Mr. Murphy's case, ethicists and lawyers say, raises troubling questions about access to health care for those in the criminal justice system.

A Host of Questions

Should the nation provide expensive care and scarce organs to convicted felons? Can it justify a system in which an estimated one in four employed Americans cannot have a transplant because they are uninsured or underinsured, yet ask the Bureau of Prisons to provide them for prisoners?

If the Bureau will not pay for a transplant, should it pay for a quadruple bypass? Or, looking at it another way, should a nonviolent criminal like Mr. Murphy get a heart, but a murderer or rapist not? What about someone convicted of a white-collar crime, like tax fraud? Where, if at all, should society draw the line?

According to Esther Benenson, a spokeswoman for the United Network for Organ Sharing, the national group that allocates organs for transplant, 2,856 Americans were waiting for heart transplants on Jan. 26. She said that about half the people on heart-transplant lists eventually receive organs.

Mr. Murphy was arrested in March 1991 for possession, with intent to sell, of about a pound of methamphetamine. It was his first Federal offense and he pleaded guilty. He was already desperately ill with cardiomyopathy, a progressive weakening of the heart muscle.

THE SAN DIEGO UNION-TRIBUNE

April 20, 1994

OBITUARIES

William A. Kennedy; introduced readers to 'Abby' and 'Heathcliff'

By JACK WILLIAMS
Staff Writer

William Kennedy

William Alvey Kennedy, a features-syndicate executive who helped introduce the wisdom of "Dear Abby" and the whimsy of "Heathcliff" the cat to newspaper readers nationwide, died April 12 of a heart attack while vacationing in Dublin, Ireland.

Mr. Kennedy, 68, had suffered from a deterioration of the heart muscle known as cardiomyopathy, said his wife, Joyce Lain Kennedy, of Encinitas. One of his last wishes before he died was to visit the Auld Sod, where his family's roots are firmly planted.

He was executive vice president of the McNaught Syndicate in New York City in the mid-1960s to the early '70s, during which time he helped launch George Gately's "Heathcliff" comic strip. He also was instrumental in expanding the nationwide network of newspapers carrying the popular advice column, "Dear Abby," which debuted in 1956 in the *San Francisco Chronicle.*

Mr. Kennedy later founded his own syndication firm, Sun Features Inc., in Rockville, Md., and moved it in 1977 to Encinitas, where he lived for the last 17 years. Sun Features distributes features to daily newspapers nationwide.

In 1954, before beginning his career in publishing, Mr. Kennedy became a partner in Box Cards Inc., which grew into one of the the world's largest manufacturers of black-and-white studio greeting cards. The long, slim cards were known for their provocative drawings and the one-liners they contained inside.

Mr. Kennedy also sang professionally and recorded songs with big-band leader Les Baxter. "Suddenly" was his best-known song, said his wife.

During the height of the Cold War, Mr. Kennedy was dispatched on a goodwill tour of the Soviet Union by television personality Art Linkletter to represent "the typical American man."

A native of Vincennes, Ind., Mr. Kennedy grew up in St. Louis and Chicago, where he attended Loyola University.

In addition to his wife, he is survived by sons, William Kennedy, of Windsor, Calif., and James "Skip" Kennedy, of DeKalb, Ill.; and daughter, Kandis Kennedy, of San Diego.

Family and friends celebrated Mr. Kennedy's life last Saturday at his Encinitas home with a traditional Irish wake.

The family suggests contributions to North County Meals-on-Wheels, 890 Balour Dr., Encinitas, CA 92024, or Rancho Coastal Humane Society, 389 Requeza St., also in Encinitas.

Obituaries

Dr. Stephen Boros

Stephen Boros dies; doctor was a leader in treating infants

By Anne O'Connor
Staff Writer

Dr. Stephen Boros helped develop the technology to save the lives of babies with lung problems. He worked with critically ill newborns and their families. He published and presented work that is used worldwide to help save infants' lives.

But no matter how well-recognized he was, one friend said, he never lost his humor or his human touch.

"He had a great zest for life," said Dr. Michael Coleman. "He taught you not to take yourself so seriously."

Boros, 53, director of neonatal medicine at St. Paul Children's Hospital, died of cancer Saturday in his Minneapolis home.

He was born in Aurora, Ill., and educated at the University of Illinois. He interned in Chicago and served in the Navy during the Vietnam War.

ST. LOUIS POST-DISPATCH

TUESDAY, MAY 31, 1994

DR. HIROSHI HATANAKA, 62, a Japanese neurosurgeon who persevered with research on a new treatment for brain tumors when most of his peers had given up on it, died of a stroke May 14 in Tokyo.

Dr. Hatanaka was internationally recognized for advancing the treatment known as the boron neutron capture therapy. The therapy combines the use of a boron-containing drug with neutron irradiation of the brain. Hatanaka succeeded in curing some patients and prolonging the lives of others. As a result, there is a growing belief that the treatment has "great potential."

In 1980 British actor Peter Sellers died of a heart attack at the age 54.

Dr. Stanley B. Lyss, 57; Clayton pediatrician

Dr. Stanley B. Lyss

Dr. Stanley B. Lyss, a pediatrician and community leader, died Friday, Sept. 17, 1993, at St. Mary's Health Center in Richmond Heights after a heart attack. He was 57.

Dr. Lyss, of Clayton, was in private practice and on the staff of St. Louis Children's Hospital for the past 26 years. From 1981-83, he was president of the medical staff at the hospital. He was also on the staffs at Barnes and Jewish hospitals and St. John's Mercy Medical Center.

He served on many community boards and committees, including the Clayton School Board's Future Planning Committee, the Clayton Task Force on Drug Abuse and the Good Shepard School for Children.

He was also a consultant and adviser to several community groups and a member of many national, state and local professional groups.

He was vice president of Shaare Emeth Congregation and a past chairman of several committees there.

He got the Jewish Federation of St. Louis Leadership Award in 1974 and was selected with the Best Doctors in America in 1975 and in 1980.

Dr. Lyss was born in Clayton and graduated from Clayton High School He earned his bachelor's degree from Harvard University and his medical degree from Washington University School of Medicine, where he was an assistant professor of clinical pediatrics.

Among the survivors are his wife of 32 years, Esther Bryan Lyss; three daughters, Sheryl Lyss, Julie Lyss and Pamela Lyss, all of Clayton; and two brothers, Ronald Lyss of Creve Coeur and Dr. Carl Lyss of Clayton.

Instead of flowers, memorial contributions may be made to the Stanley B. Lyss Adult Education Fund in care of Shaare Emeth Congregation, 11645 Ladue Rd., St. Louis, Mo., 63141 or to St. Louis Children's Hospital.

THE WASHINGTON POST

FRIDAY, JUNE 5, 1992

OBITUARIES

SANDRA LOUTREECE EZELL
Physician

Sandra Loutreece Ezell, 40, a physician who since 1985 had been director of the trauma service at D.C. General Hospital, died of cancer May 26 at her home in Sawyerville, Ala.

Dr. Ezell was born in Sawyerville and graduated from Tuskeegee Institute. She received her medical degree from Howard University and did her internship and residency in general surgery at Howard University Hospital. She joined the staff of the emergency care center at D.C. General Hospital in 1982.

In addition to her duties at D.C. General Hospital, Dr. Ezell had been an assistant professor at Howard University Medical School, clinical instructor for the American College of Surgeons Advanced Trauma Life Support Course at Georgetown University and course director for the Advanced Trauma Life Support Course at the Maryland Institute for Emergency Medical Services Systems.

A former resident of Silver Spring, she returned to Sawyerville two days before her death.

Her mariage to Curtis Toliaferro ended in divorce.

Survivors include her parents, Ulysses and Sarah Ezell of Sawyerville; and two brothers, the Rev. Torenzo Dawson Ezell of Huntsville, Ala., and Frederick Ulysses Ezell of Sawyerville.

SUNDAY, APRIL 11, 1993

ST. LOUIS POST-DISPATCH

Donald Lingle, 49; Was Chiropractor

Dr. Donald L. Lingle, a longtime chiropractor in St. Louis, died Thursday (April 8, 1993) at St. Anthony's Medical Center in south St. Louis County after a heart attack. He was 49.

Dr. Lingle, of Arnold, was in private practice in St. Louis for 28 years. He was born in De Soto, Ill., and reared in Murphysboro, Ill. He earned his chiropractic degree from Missouri College of Chiropractic (now Logan College of Chiropractic).

A funeral Mass will be celebrated at 10 a.m. Monday at St. David's Catholic Church, 2334 Tenbrook Road in Arnold. Burial will be in Shepherd Hill Cemetery in Barnhart, Mo. Visitation will be from 5 p.m. to 8 p.m. Sunday at Lang-Fendler Funeral Home, 630 Jeffco Boulevard, Arnold.

Among the survivors are his wife of 28 years, Susan Lingle of Arnold; two sons, David M. Lingle of Philadelphia and Joseph T. Lingle of Fenton; a sister, Sandra DeRosette of Mantino, Ill.; and two brothers, Paul W. Lingle of Paducah, Ky., and Terry L. Lingle of Shelbyville, Ky.

In lieu of flowers, memorial contributions may be made to a charity of the donor's choice.

St. Louis Jewish Light   April 20, 1994

Dr. Kenneth Hirsch Solomon; was geriatric psychiatrist

Dr. Kenneth Hirsch Solomon, a geriatric psychiatrist, author and musician, died Tuesday (April 23, 1994) at St. Luke's Hospital in west St. Louis County after a brief illness.

He was 46 and lived in Creve Coeur.

Dr. Solomon was an associate professor of psychiatry in geriatric psychiatry at St. Louis University School of Medicine since 1989. He was also an associate professor in the school's department of internal medicine since last year.

He wrote three books, including one of poetry. Dr. Solomon also was the author or co-author of nearly 80 professional papers and articles.

He gave more than 500 lectures in the United States, Canada and Brazil.

He was an accomplished jazz and classical pianist. He performed with noted jazz musician Jack DeJohnette and played backup for Natalie Cole and for the Ink Spots.

Dr. Solomon was born in Brooklyn, N.Y. He earned a bachelor's degree in history in 1967 from New York University and his medical degree in 1971 from the State University of New York at Buffalo.

Among survivors are his wife, Dr. Barbara W. Brown; a daughter, Lori Funderburk of Vanceboro, N.C.; a son, David Karl Solomon of Columbia, Mo.; his parents, Estelle Reitman of Patchogue, N.Y., and Solomon Solomon Solomon of Fort Lauderdale, Fla.; and a sister, Susanne Policano of Middleton, Wis.

Memorial contributions may be made to the Traditional Congregation of Creve Coeur, 12437 Ladue Rd., St. Louis, Mo. 63141. ■

Boris G. Moishezon, Columbia Professor Of Math, Dies at 55

By WOLFGANG SAXON

Boris G. Moishezon, a mathematics professor at Columbia University who defected from the Soviet Union in 1972 and came to the United States five years later, died Wednesday. He was 55 and lived in Leonia, N.J.

Dr. Moishezon had a heart attack while jogging and was pronounced dead in Holy Name Hospital in Teaneck, N.J., said his wife, Natalia.

Dr. Moishezon was among the foremost experts in algebraic geometry. He began his career 30 years ago in Moscow, tutored by the Soviet mathematician Igor Shafarevich at the Steklov Institute of Mathematics. But he made his international reputation at Tel Aviv University and at Columbia.

Born in Odessa, Ukraine, he received a doctorate in physical and mathematical sciences from Moscow State University and became a senior scientist at the Central Institute of Mathematical Economics in Moscow.

The New York Times, 1983

Boris G. Moishezon

Émigré Driven by Frustration

Dr. Moishezon belonged to a growing contingent of young intellectuals who felt their Jewishness barred them from the top echelons, especially in mathematics and physics. He and nine peers signed a public statement in 1972 decrying the high fees for exit visas imposed on holders of doctoral degrees. The fees, as much as $25,000, were intended by the Soviet Government as repayment for the émigrés' education.

By then the 10 were in the midst of the complicated process of seeking passage to Israel during the Soviet drain brain of the 1970's. Dr. Moishezon got his exit visa in 1972 and took the post of professor of mathematics at Tel Aviv University. He came to the United States as a visiting professor at the University of Utah in 1977, the year he was appointed a professor of mathematics at Columbia.

Besides his wife, Dr. Moishezon leaves a daughter, Hanna, of Tel Aviv; a son, Tsvi, of Leonia; and a half-brother, Friedrich, of Yalta, Ukraine.

Boris B. Yegorov, 57, First Physician in Space

By WILLIAM DICKE

Boris B. Yegorov, the first physician to fly in space, died in his apartment in Moscow on Monday night, Russian news agencies reported yesterday. He was 57.

The cause was a heart attack, the Itar-Tass news agency said.

Dr. Yegorov and two colleagues were launched aboard the Voskhod (Sunrise) 1 spacecraft from the Baikonur space center in Kazakhstan on Oct. 12, 1964, on the seventh manned Soviet space flight. The three astronauts were crammed aboard a spacecraft designed for one. The flight was the first with more than one astronaut, the first in which trained scientists were sent into space and the first in which Russian astronauts flew without space suits, perhaps because there was too little room.

During the 24-hour, 16-orbit flight, Dr. Yegorov, a 27-year-old lieutenant in the Soviet Army's medical corps, observed the astronauts' reactions to microgravity and drew blood samples. He also experimented with fruit flies and plants.

One other crew member, Konstantin P. Feoktistov, was an engineer and scientist. The third was the mission commander, Col. Vladimir M. Komarov of the Soviet Air Force.

Upon their return to Moscow, the astronauts were given a triumphal reception and honored in ceremonies at Red Square. An editorial in The New York Times said: "Space is no longer the exclusive preserve of the astronaut; now many sciences will look forward to preparing some of their practitioners to use their knowledge and skills outside this planet and to bring back new knowledge for the benefit of mankind."

Dr. Yegorov was born in Moscow on Nov. 26, 1937, the son of Boris G. Yegorov, one of the Soviet Union's leading brain surgeons. The younger Yegorov decided at an early age to go into medical research and entered the First Moscow Medical Institute, where he chose aviation and space medicine as a specialty.

He worked in several medical research institutes before being trained for space flight. After his flight aboard Voskhod 1, he earned the equivalent of a Ph.D. from Humboldt University in East Berlin. Later in his career he was the head of a number of medical research institutions in Russia. From 1984 to 1982, he was the director of the Scientific-Industrial Center for Medical Biotechnology under the Soviet Health Ministry.

Dr. Yegorov was awarded some of his nation's highest decorations, including the gold star of the Hero of the Soviet Union and the Order of Lenin.

He and his wife, Eleonora, also a physician, had a son, Boris.

17. *Schrauzer, G.N., et al.*: Cancer Mortality Correlation Studies-III: Statistical Associations with Dietary Selenium Intakes. Bioinorganic Chemistry.7:23.1977.

18. *Schrauzer, G.N., et al.*: Selenium in the Blood of Japanese and American Women With and Without Breast Cancer and Fibrocystic Disease. Jpn. J. Cancer Res. 76:374. May, 1985.

19. *Schwarz, K. and Foltz, C.M.*: Selenium as an Integral Part of Factor 3 Against Dietary necrotic Liver Degeneration. J.Am.Chem.Soc.19:3292.1959.

19. *Shu-Yu Yu, et al,*: A Preliminary Report on the Intervention Trials of Primary Liver Cancer in High-Risk Populations with Nutritional Supplementation of Selenium in China. Biol. Trace Ele. Research. 29:289.1991.

20. *Shu-Yu Yu, et al.*: Chemoprevention Trial of Human Hepatitis with Selenium Supplementation in China. Biol. Trace Ele. Research. The Humana Press, Inc. 20:15. 1989.

21. *Shwachman, H., et al.*: The Heterogenicity of Cystic Fibrosis. Birth Defects. 8:102. 1972.

22. *Tus,H. st al.*: Keshan Disease as it Relates to Selenium Status. Chinese J.Med.1979. Selenium in the Heart of China. Lancet. 27 Oct,1979. p899.

23. *Van Vleet, F.J. and Ferrans, V.J.*: Ultrastructure of Hyaline Microthrombi in Myocardial Capillaries of Pigs with Spotaneous Mulberry Heart Disease. Am. J.Vet. Res. 38:2077.1977.

24. *Van Vleet, E. J., et al.*: Hepatos Dietetia and Mulberry Heart Disease Associated with Selenium Deficiency in Indiana Swine. J.Am.Vet Med. Assoc. 157:1208.1970.

25. *Wallach, J.D. and Garmaise, B.*: Cystic Fibrosis: A Perinatal Manifestation of Selenium Deficiency. 13th Annual Conference on Trace Substances in Environmental Health. June 4-7,1979. University of Missouri, Columbia, Mo.

26. *Wallach, J.D.*: Cystic Fibrosis: A proposal of Etiology and Pathogenesis. Workshop on Model Systems for the Study of Cystic Fibrosis. May 25-26, 1978. N.I.H., Bethesda, Md.

27. *Wallach, J.D., Ma Lan, Wei Han Yu, Bo-Qi Gu, Feng Teng Yu and Goddard, R.F.*: Common Denominators in the Etiology and Pathology of Visceral Lesions of Cystic Fibrosis and Keshan Disease. Biol. Trace Ele. Research. Humana Press,Inc. 24:189.1990.

Si - Silica is found in igneous rocks at 281,500 ppm; shale at 73,000 ppm; sandstone at 368,000 ppm; limestone at 24,000 ppm; fresh water at 6.5 ppm; sea water at 3 ppm; soils at 330,000 ppm (found as SiO_2, the most abundant form of Si in nature, in silicates and clays); marine plants at 1,500 to 20,000 ppm; accumulated by diatoms, horsetail, ferns, Cyoeraceae, Graineae and Juncaceae and by the flowers of Pappophorum silicosum; marine animals at 70,000 ppm; land animals at 120 to 6,000 ppm (highest levels in hair, lungs and bone).

Silicon supplementation increases the collagen in growing bone by 100 %. Tissue levels of Si decrease with aging in unsupplemented humans and laboratory species. Silica deficiency is characterized by dry brittle hair, brittle finger and toe nails, poor skin quality, poor calcium utilization and arterial disease. High fiber diets contain lots of Si which leads many investigators to think that Si helps to lower cholesterol.. The recommended intake of Si ranges from 200 to 500 mg/day.

1. *Carlisle, E.M.:* In Vivo Requirements for Silicon in Articular Cartilage and Connective Tissue Formation in the Chick. J.Nutr.106:478. 1976

2. *Kaufmann, K.: Silica:* The Amazing Gel. Burnaby, B.C., Canada. Alive Books. 1992.

Sm - Samarium is a "light" Rare Earth found in igneous rocks at 6 ppm; shale at 5.6 ppm; sandstones at 2.7 ppm; limestone at 0.8 ppm; land plants at 0.0055 ppm (accumulates up to 23 ppm); marine animals at 0.04 to 0.08 ppm; land animals at 0.01 ppm in heart muscle and 0.0009 in mammalian bone and liver..

Samarium enhances normal cell proliforation and doubles the life span of laboratory species.

Sn - Tin is found in igneous rocks at 2 ppm; shale at 6 ppm; sandstone and limestone at 0.5 ppm; fresh water at 0.00004 ppm; sea water at 0.003 ppm; soils at 2 to 200 ppm (strongly absorbed by humus); marine plants at 1 ppm; landplants at 0.3 ppm (highest in bryophytes and lichens); marine animals at 0.2 to 20 ppm; land animals at 0.15 ppm (highest levels are found in the lungs and intestines).

Originally the presence of tin in tissue was attributed to environmental contamination; however, careful and detailed studies by Schwarz demonstrated that tin produced an acceleration of growth in rats and further met the standards for an essential trace element. As a member of the fourth main chemical group of elements, tin has many chemical and physical properties similar to those of carbon, silica, germanium and lead.

Rats fed tin at 17.0 ng/gm show poor growth, reduced feeding efficiency, hearing loss, and bilateral (male pattern) hair loss, while rats fed 1.99 ug/gm were physiologically and anatomically normal; tin was demonstrated to be an essential element by Schwarz in 1970. Tin has been shown to exert a strong induction effect on the enzyme heme oxygenase, enhancing heme breakdown in the kidney. There is also evidence for tin having cancer prevention properties.

A federal study released in November of 1991 showed that men in recent generations have poorer hearing at any given age than in men in earlier generations. Men over age 30 lose their hearing more than twice as fast as woman of the same age.

1. *Cardarelli, N.F.:* Tin as a vital Nutrient: Implications in Cancer Prophylaxis and other Physiological Processes. CRC-Press, Boca Raton, Florida.1986.

2. *Katsuhiko, Yokoi, et al.:* Effect of Dietary Tin Deficiency on Growth and Mineral Status in Rats. Biol. Trace Ele. Research. The Humana Press,Inc. 24:223.1990.

Sr - Strontium is found in igneous rocks at 375 ppm; shale at 300 ppm; sandstone at 20 ppm; limestone at 610 ppm; fresh water at 0.08 ppm; sea water at 8.1 ppm; soils at 300 ppm; marine plants at 260 to 1,400 ppm; land plants at 26 ppm; marine animals at 20 to 500 ppm; land animals at 14 ppm (highest in mammalian bone).

Strontium can replace calcium in many organisms (including man) - there is considerable evidence for essentiality in mammals including man.

Deficiencies of Sr are associated with

certain types of Ca and B resistant osteoporosis and arthritis.

Strontium 90, the man made product of fission atomic explosions and the greatest biohazard fear during the cold war, does not occur in nature.

Ta - Tantalum is found in igneous rocks at 2 ppm; shale at 0.8 ppm; sandstone and limestone at 0.05 ppm; sea water at 0.0000025 ppm; marine animals accumulated up to 410 ppm.

Tb - Terbium is found in igneous rock at 0.9 ppm; shale at 0.58 ppm; sandstone at 0.41 ppm; limestone at 0.071 ppm; land plants at 0.0015 ppm; marine animals at 0.006 to 0.01 ppm; land animals at 0.0004 ppm (accumulates in mammalian bone).

Tc - All isotopes of technetium are radioactive and not known to occur in nature. Technetium is poorly absorbed by mammals.

Te - Tellurium is found in igneous rocks at 0.001 ppm; land plants at 2 to 25 ppm and land animals at 0.02 ppm.

Th - Thorium is found in igneous rocks at 9-6 ppm; shale at 12 ppm; sandstone and limestone at 1-7 ppm; soils at 5 ppm; marine animals at 0.003-0.03 ppm and land animals at 0.003-0.1 ppm.

Ti - Titanium is found in igneous rocks at 5,700 ppm; shale at 4,600 ppm; sandstone at 1,500 ppm; sea water at 0.001 ppm; soils at 5,000 ppm; marine plants at 12-80 ppm (accumulates in plankton); land plants

at 1 ppm; marine animals at 0.2 to 20 ppm and land animals at 0.2ppm.

Tl - Thallium is found in igneous rocks at 0.45 ppm; shale at 1.4 ppm; sandstone at 0.82 ppm; limestone at 0.05 ppm; sea water at 0.00001 ppm; soils at 0.1 ppm; land animals at 0.4 ppm (accumulates in the mammalian kidney and is highly toxic to mammals including man).

Tm - Thulium is a "heavy" Rare Earth and is found in igneous rocks at 0.48 ppm; shales at 0.28 ppm; sandstone at 0.3 ppm; limestone at 0.065 ppm; land plants at 0.0015 ppm and land animals at 0.00004 ppm.

Thulium supplementation enhances the growth of normal cells and has doubled the life spans of laboratory species.

U - Uranium is found in igneous rocks at 2,7 ppm; shale at 3.7 ppm; sandstone 0.95 ppm; limestone at 2.2 ppm; fresh water at 0.001 ppm; sea water at 0.003 ppm; soil at 1 ppm (absorbed by humus, especially in alkaline soils); land plants at 0.038 ppm (Astragalus spp. is an accumulator plant); marine animals at 0.004 to 3.2 ppm; land animals atr 0.013 ppm; all natural isotopes are alpha emiters and may also decay by fission. Uranium is accumulated by mammalian kidney and bone after ingestion.

V - Vanadium is found in igneous rocks at 135 ppm; shale at 130 ppm; sandstone at 20 ppm; limestone at 20 ppm; fresh water at 0.001 ppm; sea water at 0.002 ppm; soils at 100 ppm (V is absorbed by humus, especially in alkaline soils); marine plants at 2 ppm; land plants at 1.6 ppm (accumulated by the fungus *Arnanita muscaria*); marine animals at 0.14 to 2 ppm; land animals at 0.15 ppm.

Metallic vanadium (vanadyl sulfate) is absorbed from the intestinal tract very poorly at only 0.1 to 1.0 %; vanadium chelates at 40 % and plant derived colloidals at up to 98 %.

Vanadium was proven to be an essential trace mineral in 1971. Vanadium stimulates glucose (blood sugar) oxidation and transport in fat cells and glycogen (animal starch) synthesis in liver and muscle, and inhibits liver gluconeogenisis (production of glucose from fat) and absorption of glucose from the gut. Vanadium enhances the stimulating effect of insulin on DNA synthesis. Despite low serum insulin, the blood glucose levels of diabetic rats fed vanadium was the same as normal controls.

Vanadium appears to function like insulin by altering cell membrane function for ion transport processes, therefore vanadium has a very beneficial effect for humans with glucose tolerance problems (i.e. - hypoglycemia, hyperinsulinemia and diabetes) by making the cell membrane insulin receptors more sensitive to insulin. Several cultures including American Indians, Hispanics and Hawaiians have an increased rate of diabetes when they cease to eat their ethnic foods and consume canned, processed and fast foods. Vanadium supplementation can have a major positive economic impact by reducing or even eliminating most cases of adult onset diabetes - diabetes alone costs American taxpayers a minimum of $105 billion each year.

Vanadium inhibits cholesterol synthesis in animals and humans; this is followed by decreased plasma levels of cholesterol and reduced aortic cholesterol.

Vanadium initiates an increase in the contractile force of heart muscle known as the "inotropic effect."

Vanadium has known anticarcinogenic properties. Induction of mouse mammary tumor growth was blocked by feeding 25 ug of vanadium per gram of diet. The vanadium supplement reduced tumor incidence, average tumor count per animal and prolonged median cancer free time without inhibiting overall growth or health of the animals (sure beats chemotherapy and radiation!).

Clinical diseases associated with Vanadium deficiency include:

Slow growth
Increased infant mortality
Infertility
Elevated cholesterol
Elevated triglycerides
Hypoglycemia
Hyperinsulinemia
Diabetes
Cardiovascular disease
Obesity

1. *McNeill, J.H.:* Biological Effects of Vanadium.The University of British Columbia, Vancouver, B.C. June 16,1993.

2. *Nielsen, F.H.:* Vanadium. in Trace Elements in Human and Animal Nutrition. Vol.1.5th ed(Mertz,W. ed).1987.

W - Tungsten is found in igneous rocks at 1.5 ppm; shale at 1.8 ppm; sandstone at 1.6 ppm; limestone at 0.6 ppm; sea water at 0.0001; soils at 1 ppm; marine plants at 0.035 ppm; marine animals at 0.0005 to 0.05 ppm; land animals at 0.005 ppm (accumulates in heart muscle and teeth at 0.00025 ppm).

Xe - Xenon is found in igneous rocks at 0.00003 ppm; sea water at 0.000052 ppm.

Xenon binds to mammalian hemoglobin and myoglobin producing an anesthetic affect.

Y - Yttrium is a "heavy" Rare Earth found in igneous rocks at 33 ppm; shale at 18 ppm; sandstone at 9.1 ppm; limestone at 4.3 ppm; sea water at 0.0003 ppm; soils at 50 ppm; land plants at 0.6 ppm (accumulates in ferns); marine mammals at 0.1 to 0.2 ppm; land animals at 0.04 ppm (found in mammalian bone, teeth and liver).

Yttrium enhances normal cell growth and doubles the life span of laboratory species. Exposure of pregnant mice to yttrium leads to rapid placental transfer, 14% of ingested Y can be detected in newborn mice.

1. *Zhang,W.E. et al* : Effects of Traces of Rare Earth Elements on the Protozoan Blepherisma and on Mice.Biological Trace Element Resesarch. 17:81-90.1988

2. *Tang, R-H, et al.*: Stimulation of Proliferation of Tetrahymena pyriformis by Trace Rare Earths. Biol. Trace Ele. Res. 7:95. 1985.

Yb - Ytterbium is a Rare Earth found in igneous rocks at 3 ppm; shale at 1.8 ppm; sandstone at 1.3 ppm; limeston at 0.43 ppm; land plants at 0.0015 ppm; marine animals at 0.02 ppm; land animals at 0.00012 ppm (accumulates up to 1.3 ppm in bone, teeth and liver). Exposure of preg-

nant mice leads to rapid placental transfer, 14% of ingested Yb can be detected in newborn mice.

Zn - Zinc is found in igneous rocks at 70 ppm; shale at 95 ppm; sandstone at 16 ppm; limestone at 20 ppm; fresh water at 0.01 ppm; sea water at 0.01 ppm; soils at 50 ppm; marine plants at 150 ppm; land plants at 100 ppm; marine animals at 6 to 1,500 ppm; land animals at 160 ppm (ac-

---

Table 11-24. Congenital Birth defects associated with Zinc Deficiency.

- Down's Syndrome
- Cleft lip
- Cleft palate
- Brain defects (dorsal herniation, hydroencephaloceol
- Micro- or anopthalmia (small or absent eyes)
- Micro- or agnathia
- Spina bifida
- clubbed limbs
- Syndactyly (webbed toes and fingers)
- Diaphragmatic hernias (hiatal hernia)
- Umbilical; hernias
- Heart defects
- lung defects
- Urogenital

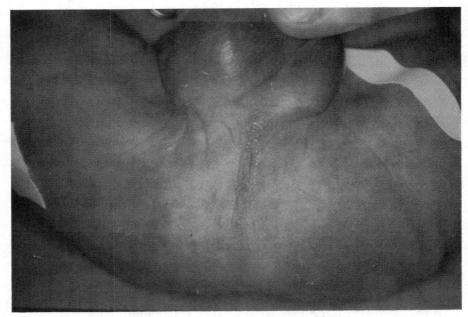

Fig. 11-22 Atresia ani (child born with no anal opening).

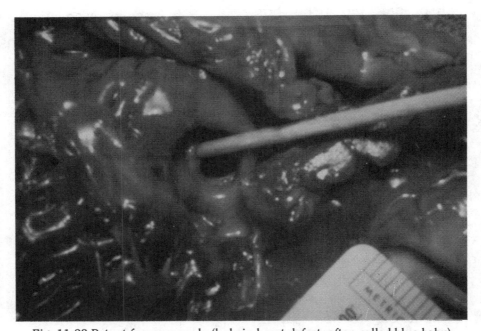

Fig. 11-23 Patent foramen ovale (hole in heart defect, often called blue baby)

Fig. 11-24 Polydactyly (multiple feet on cat)

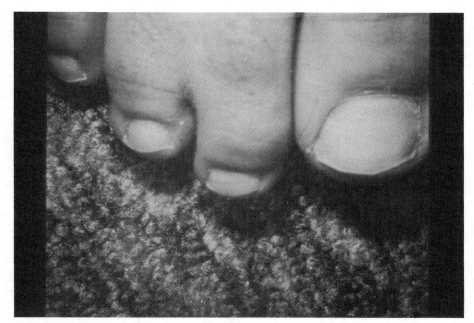

Fig. 11-25 "Webbed toes"

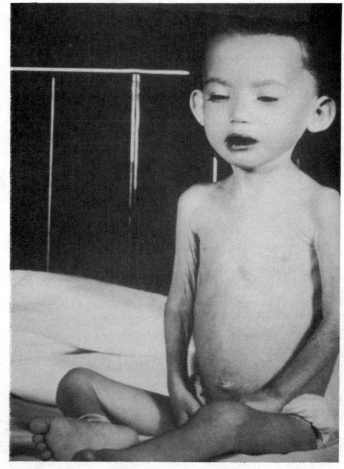

Fig. 11-26 Child with Celiac disease and secondary zinc deficiency

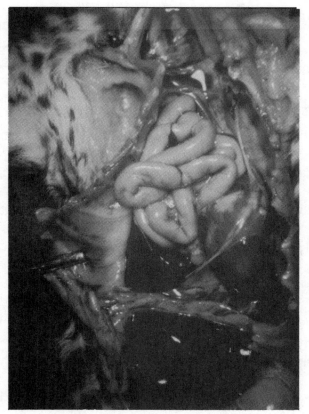

Fig. 11-27 Fatal hiatal hernia in newborn leopard

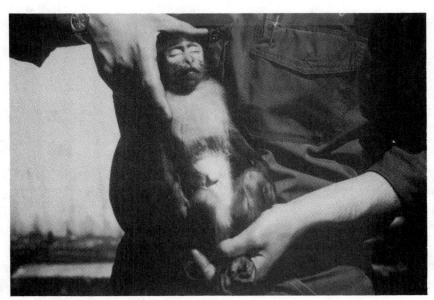

Fig. 11-28 umbilical hernia in a monkey

Table 11-25. Symptoms and Diseases of Zinc Deficiency

- Pica (geophagia, wool eating, hair eating,etc.)
- Loss of sense of smell
- Loss of sense of taste
- Infertility
- Failure of wounds and ulcers to heal
- Immune status failure
- Poor growth (short stature)
- High infant mortality
- Hypogonadism (small poorly functioning ovaries and testes)
- Remains in a prepuberty state
- Anemia
- Alopecia (hair loss)
- Acrodermatitis enteropathica (Parakeratosis in pigs and calves)
- "Frizzy" hair
- Diarrhea
- Depression
- Paranoia
- Oral and perioral dermatitis
- Weight loss (anorexia nervosa)
- Benign prostatic hypertrophy (prostate enlargement)
- Severe body odor ("smelly tennis shoe" syndrome)
- Anorexia & Bullemia

cumulates in mammalian kidney, prostate and eye).

Zinc was known to be essential for bread mold 100 years ago, essential for rats 50 years ago and for humans only 20 years ago. Zinc deficiency produces a wide range of diseases including birth defects (Table 11-24) and degenerative diseases of all age groups (Table 11-25).

There is 1.4 to 2.3 grams of Zn in the adult human. The liver, pancreas, kidney, bone and skeletal muscles have the greatest reserves of Zn, lesser amounts are found in the eye, prostate gland, semen, skin, hair, fingernails and toenails.

There are no less than 70 metalloenzymes that require Zn to function, these include carbonic anhydrase, alkaline phosphatase, lactic dehydrogenase and carboxypeptidase. Zinc helps to bind enzymes to substrates by maintaining spacial and configurational relationships. Some enzymes bind Zn so tightly that even during severe Zn depletion they can still function. Zinc participates in the metabolism of nucleic acids and the synthesis of proteins; Zinc is also an integral part of the RNA molecule itself (Zinc "metal fingers") and participates in cell division and synthesis of DNA - the DNA-dependent RNA polymerase is a zinc-dependent enzyme, as is thymidine kinase.

Excesses of copper and iron and high phytate diets (vegans) will reduce availability of dietary zinc. Heavy losses of Zn occurs in sweat, therefore unsupplemented athletes are particularly at risk for Zn deficiency (i.e.- anorexia nervosa, muscle weakness, pica, etc.).

1. *Beardsley, D.W. and Farbes,R.M.:* Growth and Chemical Studies of Zinc Deficiency in the Baby Pig. J.An.Science. 1957.p.1038.

2. *Edwards,H.M., et al.:* Studies on Zinc in Poultry Nutrition.1: The Effect of feed, water and Environment on Zinc Deficiency in Chicks. Poultry Sci.37:1094.1958.

3. *Erten, J., et al.:* Hair Zinc in Healthy and Malnourished Children. Am.J.Clin. Nutr. 32:570.1979.

4. *Herkovits, J. and Perez-Coll,C.:* Zinc Protection Against Delayed Development Produced by Cadmium. Biol.Trace Ele.Research. The Humana Press,

Anorexia, bulimia rise in athletics

By ALAN BAVLEY
Medical Writer

Anorexia nervosa and bulimia, the eating disorders that claimed the life of world-class gymnast Christy Henrich Tuesday, are an increasingly recognized hazard among female athletes, experts say.

Driven to succeed and to maintain what coaches and judges consider an ideal weight or body shape, many female athletes are falling prey to a triad of potentially deadly conditions: disordered eating, loss of menstruation and osteoporosis.

"Christy Henrich is an example of how serious it can be," said Aurelia Nattiv, a Santa Monica, Calif., physician who treats many female athletes for eating disorders. "It can really be a downward spiral to death."

Henrich, an Independence resident who came close to qualifying for the U.S. Olympic team in 1988, died after battling eating disorders for several years. She was 22.

Though Nattiv emphasized that Hen-

The Associated Press

rich's case was an extreme, numerous studies of female athletes reveal striking evidence that they are driving themselves to unhealthy degrees:

■ As many as 62 percent of female college gymnasts suffer from disordered eating patterns, one study found.

These eating patterns include anorexia, the severe self-denial of food that can lead to malnutrition and even starvation; bu-

See **EATING, A-11,** Col. 1

Christy Henrich competed at the 1988 Olympic trials and missed qualifying by 0.118 of a point. The gymnast died Tuesday of complications arising from eating disorders. Coaches' and gymnasts' remembrances of her are on **Page D-1.**

Inc.24:217.1990.

5. *Hove,E.,et al:* Further Studies of Zinc Deficiency in Rats. Am.J.Physiol.124:750.1938.

6. *Kienholz,E.W., et al.:* Effects of Zinc Deficiency in the Diets of Hens. J.Nutr.75:211.October, 1961.

7. *Klug,A. and Rhodes,D.:* Zinc Fingers: A Novel Protein Motif for Nucleic Acid Recognition. in Trends in Biochemical Sciences.12:464.Dec.1987.

8. *Legg, S.P. and Sears,L.:* Zinc Sulphate Treatment of Parakeratosis in Cattle. Nature.186:1061.1960.

9. *Miller, J.K. and Miller,W.J.:* Experimental Zinc Deficiency and Recovery of Calves. J.Nutr.76:467.April,1962.

10. *Morrison, A.B. and Sarett,H.P.:* Studies on Zinc Deficiency in the Chick. J.Nutr.June,1958.p267-280.

11. *Ott, E.A., et al.:* Zinc Deficiency Syndrome in the Young Lamb. J.Nutr. 82:41.Jan.1964.

12. *Rhodes,D. andKlug,A.:* Zinc Fingers.Scientific American.February 1993.p.56.

13. *Tucker, H.F. and Salman, W.D.:* Parakeratosis or Zinc Deficiency Disease in the Pig. Proc. Soc.Exp.Biol.Med. 88:613.1955.

14. *Vohra, P. and Kratzer,F.H.:* Influence of Various Chelating Agents on the Availability of Zinc. J.Nutr.82:248.1964.

Zr - Zirconium is found in igneous rocks at 165 ppm; shales at 160 ppm; sandstone at 220 ppm; limestone at 19 ppm; fresh watre at 0.0026; sea water at 0.000022 ppm; soils at 300 ppm; marine plants at 20 ppm; land plants at 0.64 ppm; marine animals at 0.1 to 1 ppm; and land animals at 0.3 ppm.

" (Roger) Bacon deduced that, if, after the Fall, men (Methuselah and the other antediluvian patriarchs) still were able to live almost a thousand years, then the short life span of his own times might be the result not of the will of God but of the ignorance of man."

-Gerald W. Gruman
A History of Ideas About the Prolongation of Life, 1966

Chapter 12

Dr. WALLACH'S "SEE-FOOD DIET":

A day without a hamburger is a day without sunshine!

We are what's in (or isn't in) the food we eat, therefore it matters not whether one follows the concepts of the Beverly Hills Diet, Dr. Atkin's Diet, the Fit for Life Diet, the Mediterranean Diet, Dr. Berger's Immune Power Diet, The Pritikin Diet, the Macrobiotic Diet, Pearson's and Shaw's Life Extension Diet, The 120 Year Diet, become a vegan or a carnivore and eat blubber like an Eskimo or eat dozens of burgers each day like Wimpy (the original "junk food junky" from Popeye cartoons) - if you don't supplement daily with optimal amounts of each of the 90 essential nutrients your throwing from 50 to 75% of your life away as sure as if you had jumped in front of a speeding commuter train.

In contrast to the methodical, science based approach to formulating animal rations, humans have unfortunately relied on "the wisdom of the body" theory recommending the "four food groups" and "variety" as the way to "ensure" a "healthy" diet.

The "wisdom of the body" theory was first proposed by Clara Davis, a pediatrician, in 1928 when she published the results of a "feeding experiment" in newly weaned seven to nine month old human babies - the babies were offered a great variety of simple natural foods and they chose the healthier combinations of food without prompting. Davis was sure that this experiment proved that our bodies "know best."

Curt P. Richter, a highly respected psychologist gave Davis' work his seal of approval in the 1940's, after which, the "wisdom of the body" theory rapidly found it's way into the annals of human nutrition texts, medical curriculum, medical belief and finally medical dogma.

Richter published one of his own cases in 1940 in which a 3 1/2 year old boy demonstrated a "morbid craving for salt." The child had begun licking salt off of soda crackers at age one, then ate salt from the shaker at 18 months. At 3 1/2 years of age, the boy was hospitalized to restrict his salt intake - 48 hours after being denied salt the boy died (another great victory for psychology) - his autopsy revealed that he had had Addison's Disease (adrenal cortical insufficiency). The boys salt cravings (pica) were correct and had kept the boy alive - when the hospital restricted salt the boy died.

Pregnancy associated cravings (pica) support the "wisdom of the body" theory - the increased demand for minerals by the developing embryo/fetus further deprive a mineral deficient mother to be with limited mineral reserves, thus accentuating her cravings. In fact fat and salt cravings increase with advancing pregnancy - pregnant women do require a net increase in salt and protein consumption to keep water from leaving the blood vessels and seeping into the body tissue (i.e.- edema, "swelling", etc.); therefore, a craving for salty food (i.e.- pickles, chips, crackers, etc.) makes sense. Pregnant women also crave fat (i.e.- ice cream, chocolate, fatty meats, etc.) and sweets (i.e.- candy, sugar, soft drinks, pastry, etc.) in their first trimester of pregnancy - these pica type cravings represent a misinterpreted craving for minerals.

Chocolate appears to be the number one sweet craving in premenopausal women (39%) as opposed to 14% in men. Women as a group tend to be more depleted of minerals than men because of their additional mineral losses as a result of their cyclic menstrual periods, pregnancy and lactations.

In general human diets are "formulated" by cultural, ethnic and religious tradition which was originally dictated by the length of local growing seasons, altitude of the fields, temperature during the growing season, soil types, average rainfall, etc. (Table 12-1). As a result of the environmental, social, ethnic and religious limits, human nutrition is bogged down with catch phrases such as "wisdom of the body," "the Mediterranean diet," "the four food groups," "variety,"and religious restrictions of various kinds.

All human societies have integrated strict dietary rules into their religions and religious practices, devised taboos on certain food plants or animals that were either venerated (totemism) or feared (witchcraft), incorporated fasts and detailed rituals for animal sacrifices prior to feasts. There are societal or religious laws against overindulgence of strong alcoholic drinks and gluttony ("The seven deadly sins").

Religious vegetarianism is as old as Hinduism and Jainism and as new as Seventh-day Adventism and the New Age beliefs. Today only the untouchables of India eat red meat, while devote high-caste Hindus restrict their diets to grains, vegetables, fruits and dairy products - high-caste Hindus feel towards eating beef as an American feels about eating the family cat or dog, and yet there was the time when beef was commonly eaten throughout India just as McDonald's burgers are eaten throughout America. In 2500 B.C., the first large villages appeared along the banks of the Indus River - these

Table 12 - 1 .Subsistence Patterns of Earth's Peoples.		
People	**Environment**	**Subsistence Pattern** (Plant:Animal)
Mediterranean	Temperate	70:30
Europe	Temperate	60:40
Oriental	Temperate/Tropical	70:30
North America	Temperate	60:40
Age-Beaters	High Desert	70:30
Hadza	Tanzania/Semitropical	80:20
Kung San	Botswana/Desert	65:35
Aborigines	Australia/ Extreme Desert Sea Coast	90:10 25:75
Ache'	Paraguay:Rainforest	50:50
Agta	Philippines/Tropical	40:60
Eskimo	North American Arctic	10:90

early Indians raised and ate with relish cattle, sheep and goats along with wheat, millet and barley. Vegetarianism was far from anyone's mind!! Among the archaeological kitchen debris of the ancient Indian cities of Harappa and Mohenjo-Daro burned bones of cattle, sheep, goats, pigs, water buffalo, poultry, camels and elephants were common.

The great cities of Harappa and Mohenjo-Daro were precipitously deserted shortly after 2000 B.C. as a result of ecological disasters (rivers changed their channels). As a result of the societal breakdown and anarchy, barbarians (Aryans) speaking Vedic (the mother-tongue of Sanskrit) swept into the Punjab and took over the Ganges Valley. The way of life of the bronze-age Vedics were similar to those of the pre-Homeric

Greeks, Teutons and Celtics. The holy writings of the Vedic peoples up to 1000 B.C. showed very clearly they were allowed to eat animal flesh including beef (and apparently they did with frequent feasts and "with great gusto.") Archaeological studies of Hastinapur show that cattle, buffalo, sheep and goats were among the meat species most commonly eaten.

Om Prakash, in his authoritative work, Food and Drinks in Ancient India, summarized the eating habits of the Vedic period of India:

Fire is called the eater of ox and barren cows. The ritual offering of flesh implied that the priests would eat it. A goat is also offered to fire to be carried to forefathers. A barren cow was also killed at the time of marriage obviously for food (and the wedding feast). A slaughter house is also mentioned. The flesh of horses, rams, barren cows and buffaloes was cooked. Probably flesh of birds was also eaten.

In the later Vedic period, it was customary to kill a big ox or a big goat to feed a distinguished guest. Sometimes a cow was also killed. Atithigva also implies that cows were slain for guests. Many animals - cows, sheep, goats and horses continue to be killed at sacrifices and the flesh of those sacrificial animals was eaten by the participants.

The late Vedic-early Hindu kingdoms of the Ganges Valley had priestly-castes (Brahmans) similar to the Levites of the Hebrews and the Druids of the Celtics; the duties of the Brahmans are laid out in the Sanskrit holy writings known as the Brahmanas and sutras. The sutras state that animals should not be killed except as offerings to the gods and in extending "hospitality to guests" and that "making gifts and receiving gifts" were the sole responsibility of the Brahmans (a religious labor union) - what the sutras reveal is that the Brahmans were originally a caste of priests who directed the rituals of redistributive feasts sponsored by "open-handed" Aryan chiefs and warlords.

Like priests and rulers throughout the world, the Brahmans were not able to keep up with the public demand for animal protein, as a result the eating of beef and other flesh became the privilege of the nobles, high-caste Aryans and Brahmans, while the lowly peasant, lacking the authority or force of arms to tax or confiscate another individuals animals, had little choice but to conserve their own livestock for traction /plowing power, milk and manure production for the fields.

Long after the ordinary peasant in northern India had become vegetarians, the Hindu nobles and upper castes (eventually to become the most zealous of the vegetarians) continued to consume beef and other types of animal flesh with great gusto. Mohandes Gandhi summed it up when he said," The Hindus worshiped the cow, not because she gave milk, but because she made agriculture possible (by providing draft energy for plowing and manure for soil conditioning). On this same theme, Mao Tsetung made the following statement when he addressed the masses in Hunan," Draught-oxen are a treasure to the peasants. As it is practically a religious tenet that "Those who slaughter cattle in this life will themselves become cattle in the next," draught oxen must never be killed. Before coming to power, the peasants had no way of stopping the slaughter of cattle except religious taboo."

Toward 500 B.C., a number of new religions challenged the sole right of the Brahman caste to slaughter and consume animal flesh and preside over rituals, of these new religions, the most successful were the Buddhists and the Jainists. Founded in the sixth century B.C. by "charismatic holy men," both Buddhism and Jainism outlawed caste distinctions and hereditary priesthoods, made poverty a precondition for spirituality, and advocated personal communion with the "spiritual essence of the universe" through meditation rather than through the sacrifice of animals - in their condemnation of violence, war and cruelty, and their compassion for animal and human suffering, both of these movements preceded these basic elements of Christianity.

There are strict dietary rules of Judaism and the evolution of those rules which became part of Mohammedanism. There are the religious rules of diet that segregate people from people and caste from caste.

Christianity features feast days and days of fasting (abstinence and self-denial) and the Sacrament of the Lord's Supper - very specifically there is Christ's specific direction to his disciples to mention bread in their daily prayers.

Across the mural of human history is the awareness that man is dependent on nature, the Earth and therefore God or various pagan gods for the very food of life:

In fact, it is not too fanciful to say that in the beginning God created diet!! " and the Lord God Commanded the man, saying, of every tree of the garden thou mayest freely eat;

"But of the tree of the knowledge of good and evil (hallucinatory plants), thou shalt not eat of it; for in the day that thou eatest thereof thou shall surely die."

"We are part of the Earth and it is a part of us ... for all things are connected."
-Chief Seattle

The "forbidden fruit," as the tree of knowledge of good and evil" was called in modern translations of the bible is generally thought to be sexual in nature. However, early biblical translations contend that the "forbidden fruit" was just what the bible says it was - a food that was unfit for man (a hallucinatory plant).

It was, therefore, via dietary laws and cultural food taboos that man in fact gained "culture" and a knowledge of good and evil, the consequences of wrong action and literally "cause and effect." Such literal translations of the Book of Genesis has been the core of Christian culture for centuries and is thought to be the root of the ancient German proverb "Man ist was man isst" (man is what man eats) - the belief that certain foods are "unclean" and pollute the body, thus making the body an unfit sanctuary for the spirit has long been part of most religious dogma.

The taboo on scavengers (hyenas, vultures, shellfish, catfish, etc.), carnivores (lions. dogs, hawks,etc.) and garbage eaters (pigs, bears, etc.) appears across the board in most faiths as does the recommendations for the use of "cleansing foods" such as fruits, grains (bread) and blood (Christianity, Judaism, Aztec Sun worshipers, etc.).

"Manna" was a food from God - a food

that became the mainstay of the Israelite diet as they wandered the Sinai Desert for 40 years. There were two reported types of "manna," one that "rained" from heaven (pollen, locusts, etc.) and one that sprang from the ground - the latter is believed to have been a common desert lichen of the genus *Lecanora spp.* which in fact tastes like honey on a wheat cracker. The lichen growing on the rock would have been very rich in minerals as lichens have enzymes that are capable of extracting minerals from parent rock (this Earthly lichen is still eaten in great quantities by animals and humans).

There is anthropological evidence that shows that many ancient dietary rules came into being as a result of a crude awareness of ecological limits (i.e.- the taboos on meat consumption in India), grain producing farm land was much more valuable than rangeland as many people could flourish on the amount of grain required to feed one bull - there were times in India when crops failed or when cattle became too numerous and the meat-taboo was temporarily lifted!!

Usually religious or cultural taboos on food were designed to separate one caste from another, as the priestly Brahman caste was set apart from the "untouchables" in India. Even in modern Japan, the dietary limits of Shinto and the strong influence of Buddhism, which forbids killing for meat, reinforce the ideas of caste, and the slaughterer and the butcher are considered lower castes.

Fertility rites and folklore having to do with the Earth's bounty were an essential part of the religion and mythology of ancient Sumer and the epic of Gilgamesh. So even before the written story of the "Creation" was recorded in Genesis, the abundance of the Earth was part of human culture, legend and intercoursed with human worship - food and directives of diet as part of religious practice is in the holy records ever since.

There are interesting parallels between the Gilgamesh Epic and Genesis:
1) There is a man who builds a house boat to save his family from a vast flood (equivalent of Noah).
2) There is an Eden-like paradise and a magic food to impart immortality.
3) There is a demon in the form of a serpent that steals the magic food from Gilgamesh making him vulnerable to disease, decay (degenerative disease) and death. In a parallel with the mythology of ancient Greece, Gilgamesh bears a distinct resemblance to the Greek hero Hercules.

FASTING

Along with human gratitude for abundance, there is the ever present need for appeasement for mans "sins" in his relationship with God. The practice of fasting or severely restricting ones diet in order to control the "desires of the flesh" and purify and strengthen the spirit is as old as religion itself. There were ancient sects amongst the Jews who made abstinence part of their basic doctrine - the Essenes.

Prior to starting his ministry, Christ retired to the desert wilderness, fasted and prayed for 40 days and then with new found strength was able to deny the temptations of the devil.

Paul, in his first epistle to the Corinthians, compares the athlete's life and the Christian's life. The word "ascetic" is derived from the Greek word for exercise and was intended to convey the concept of the strict regimen and careful diet of the athlete. Asceticism has ever since been thought to be the major tool in the war against the "Seven Deadly Sins":

1. Gluttony
2. Envy
3. Pride
4. Sloth
5. Covetousness
6. Anger
7. Lust

The Anchorite Christians chose to wander the deserts of the Middle East and Africa, eating only what could be found in the desert. Present day Catholics, for example have rules of abstinence for Lent, even though they have given up the the taboo on meat consumption on Fridays. The Mormons fast the first Sunday of each month and give the price of two skipped meals to the poor.

Eastern faiths use fasting and diet to reinforce the belief of the unity of all things and in the eternal war against the longings of the flesh and ego.

Qi and Vital Energy

In the Tao of China, diet has an essential role, with specific food items and herbs supplying the vital energy for certain organs, which are intimately involved with the "the vital life force" or Qi: (See Table)

In Confucianism, dietary rules were usually connected with ancestor worship - when a man was about to pray and make

ORGAN	LIFEFORCE	FOODS
Heart	Fire	Poultry, Fish & Vegetables
Lungs	Metal	Poultry, Fish & Vegetables
Kidneys	Water	Poultry, Fish & Vegetables

a sacrifice to the family spirits, he took exceptional care to see that his diet was ritually correct and proper.

The Hindus and Jainists of India forbade the consumption of meat on the concept of transmigration of souls (reincarnation). No living creature could be killed for meat as the soul inhabiting the flesh and blood body could have been or might be in the future the soul of a man. The Jainists were so strict regarding this taboo that they would ritualistically inspect fruits, vegetables and nuts before they ate them to assure themselves that no bugs or worms were present.

Buddhism, which, has its origins in India and then spread throughout all of Asia, has strict taboos forbidding the killing of animals - not about eating them! Often the Buddhists dietary rules were and still today are influenced by the culture or country that adapted the religion. Usually the only time meat-eating per-se is strictly forbidden is during rituals and vegetarian feasts.

In their early writings of the "Promised Land," the Israelites had the striking imagery of a "land flowing with milk and honey" (plenitude, efficient ecology and dietary thought). Milk is the universal symbol of abundant animal production and it is near being a perfect food (except for those who are allergic to it). Honey conjures up a picture of lush and/or ripe fields and blooming orchards as well as being a form of pure food energy.

The Hebrew restrictions of Leviticus and Deuteronomy are simple and straight forward:

1) No meat of predators (Eagles, lions, cats, dogs, etc.).
2) No meat from animals that do not have cloven hooves or do not chew a "cud."
3) No meat from fish or invertebrates that do not have fins and scales.
4) No meat from reptiles
5) No blood
6) No meat from flying things with four legs (i.e.- bats, flying squirrels, etc.)

Later came the Jewish Talmud and the "Hedge about the law" which was the most strict and complex dietary laws in religious history and were created to keep the Jews identity while they were in captivity in Egypt and later during the great trek through the desert. The Talmudic dietary laws are still observed by many Jews - to a lesser degree, it has been with all religions throughout human history. Not only in primitive tribal cultures, but also in the great religions of Asia and the Middle East.

Also with Christianity - even after it separated from Judaism and, in the book of Mark, declared "all food good for man."

HINDUS

In 1857, the British Empire brought the new Enfield rifle to British-trained native troops in Bengal, India. Among those troops were Hindus known as Sepoys. The Hindu troops soon learned that the Enfield cartridge was coated with animal fat for water-proofing and that the end had to be bitten off before it was chambered into the rifle. The Hindu Sepoys put down their rifles and refused to use them.

The British military tried to correct their religious offense to the Hindus, but it was too late the Sepoys, inflamed and agitated by the local princes and nobles, that had had their power eroded by the British bureaucrats, mutinied. When the mutiny was finally crushed a year later, hundreds of people had been killed including Sepoys, British soldiers and British women and children.

A year before the Enfield uprising in India, the first United States ambassador to Japan had arrived on the other coast of the Asian continent.

Ambassador Townsend Harris, set up his official embassy in the Japanese fishing village of Shimoda, just south of Tokyo in the Izu Peninsula. After being in Japan for a few months Harris had a craving for beef steak so he ordered a cow slaughtered and butchered - today there is a memorial to that sacred cow in Shimoda.

These two events of religious transgression by a foreign power, although separated by an enormous stretch of the Asian Continent as well as by vast differences in Asian cultures, reveal the importance and weight of religious diet codes - they also reveal the complex and strange melding of the different religions of the East.

Obituaries

Rita Gara, 55; taught meditation, yoga

By Kenan Heise
TRIBUNE STAFF WRITER

Rita Sieben Gara, 55, a psychiatric nurse, was director of the Himalayan Institute in Schaumburg, where she taught meditation, yoga and stress management.

A resident of Elk Grove Village, she died Monday in her home.

"She was always learning something new and always helping people," her husband, John, said. "She did things her way. Rita worked for some time with people burned out of their homes and for low-income housing. She went to India four or five times to help on establishing a hospital there and was going to go and work there for some months after it would open. She helped raise funds here to build the hospital."

After her fifth child was born, Mrs. Gara went to Northern Illinois University, where she received a bachelor's degree in nursing. She helped establish a mental health program at Westlake Community Hospital in Melrose Park, served as an assistant supervisor in the mental

Rita Sieben Gara (center) leading a meditation class at the Himalyan Institute in Schaumburg, where she also taught yoga.

health unit at Elmhurst Memorial Hospital and was working part-time as an out-patient therapist at Alexian Brothers Hospital's Samaritan House.

She studied and taught yoga and meditation for many years. The hospital project in India was connected to the Himalayan Institute of Glenview.

"You can't change the stress in your life, so we teach people to handle it," she said of the institute's courses in a Tribune interview in April.

Survivors, in addition to her husband, include three sons, Kevin, John and James; two daughters, Julie and Mary Nehlsen; three grandchildren; and two sisters. A memorial mass will be said at 10 a.m. Saturday in St. Raymond Catholic Church, 311 S. I-Oka Ave., Mt. Prospect.

HINDU DIETARY RULES
From the Maitri Upanishad
(Hindu) Chapter 6

11- This, verily, is the highest form of the soul, namely food; for truly this life consists of food. For thus it has been said: If one does not eat, he becomes a non-thinker, a non-hearer, a non-toucher, a non-seer, a non-speaker, a non-smeller, non-taster and he lets go his vital breath. (but) If, indeed one eats, he becomes well supplied with life; he becomes a thinker; he becomes a hearer; he becomes a toucher; he becomes a speaker; he becomes a taster; he becomes a smeller; he becomes a seer, for thus it has been said:

From food, verily, creatures are produced, whatsoever dwell on the Earth. Moreover by food, in truth they live. Moreover into it also they freely pass.

There is considerable controversy on the origin of the Hindu taboo against the eating of meat, however, the exclusion of meat from the diet appears to have begun with the ancient agricultural cultures which flourished about 2500 to 3000 B.C. in the rich flood plains of the Indus River - the origin of the names of India and the Hindu faith. Anthropological and archaeological evidence show that the early people of India, the Dravidians, revered the cow and prohibited its slaughter. It is believed that the protection of the cow by ancient peoples arose from the simple fact that "one cows milk could feed more people than one cow's meat!"

When famine struck because of a burgeoning population or natural disaster that severely damaged crops, then the "believers" ate the cow's food and the cow. Rather than having a deep understanding of ecology, the limited ability of the land to support ever growing populations and feed efficiency, the ancient peoples of the Indus Valley knew from horrible experience that they were helpless before the untamed forces of the flooding of rivers and the Earth's answer to overpopulation (real or relative-then, now and forever) is famine and starvation!!! The religious peoples of India, therefore, prohibited the consumption of meat in times of plenty and returned to consumption of meat during famine.

The ancient scriptures of the Hindus were the Vedas - the Vedas indicated that the Hindu masses liked and ate food of all kinds - in fact the Vedic god Indra was famous for his consumption of beef. The word for guest in Sanskrit translates to, "one for whom a cow is killed." In subsequent scriptures called Upanishads, it is written that, "through food comes the end of all ignorance and bondage."

FROM THE VISHNU SUTRA (Hindu) Chapter 51

72 - Reflecting upon the origin of flesh and upon hunting or confining of animated creatures, he must abstain from animal food of any kind.

72 - He who transgresses not the law and eats not flesh is beloved by men and remains free from disease.

74 - He who gives his consent to the killing of an animal, he who cuts it up, he who kills it, the purchaser and the seller, he who prepares it, he who serves it up, and he who eats it, all these are denominated slaughterers of an animal.

75 - There is no greater sinner than he, who, without giving their share to the manes and the gods, wants to increase his own flesh with the flesh of another creature.

76 - Those two, he who performs a horse-sacrifice annually for a hundred years and he who does not eat meat, shall both obtain the same recompense for their virtue.

77 - By eating sacred fruits or roots, and by living upon such grains as are the food of hermits, a man does not reap so high a reward as by avoiding meat.

Hinduism as it evolved from 1500 B.C. became extremely complex, with untold numbers of gods and hundreds if not thousands of sects - it became the very soul of the devote; to the Hindu, all things in the great cycle of creation and death have deep significance. Some Hindu sects (Dravidians) were vegetarians and forbade the consumption of meat, other Hindu sects ate beef when it was available, some ate asses, dogs and vultures, others ate snakes, lizards and scorpions - some Hindu sects were in fact cannibals!!

According to the ancient Ayruvedic medical writings there were therapeutic foods - flesh being for a persons flesh, bone the raw material for bone, blood for blood and brains for brains, and aphrodisiac foods - rhinoceros flesh and horn being the ultimate therapy for the impotent.

A modern day incorporation of Ayurvedic dietary law is the weight control program of Dr. Deepak Chopra. According to Ayruvedic dietary rules, your personal body type is the best guide to how and what you should eat, exercise programs and even decision making. Ayruvedic dietary law has organized this information into a system of psychophysiological body types ("prakiti" from Sanskrit, a term that translates to "essential nature").

Chopra employs the three "doshas" (mind-body principles that govern the flow of intelligence through your body) - Vata, Pitta and Kapha, each is tied to elements in nature (minerals) as a ecosystem. Find out your body type and you will know which dosha is the most dominant feature of your own physiology. Nature needs all three doshas (90 nutrients) to build and maintain the human flesh, however, each individual contained different levels of each dosha. Only rare individuals are classed as pure Vata, Pitta or Kapha types (able to be a vegan or pure carnivore). Frequently two doshas blend to characterize a person's physiology, and on rare occasion all three are found in equal amounts in one individual.

Doshas are the Ayruvedic version of genetic potential for health and longevity - they are a "kind of fate," however, only in the positive sense. The correct identification and appreciation of your mind-body type gives you access to your genuine nature and to your healthy, beautiful, perfectly balanced self.

According to Chopra diets that impose stress on your dosha or physiology by cutting off its natural inclinations invite rebellion - deep hunger, slowed metabolism and even disease. Instead, by understanding and heeding the needs of your body type, you can know what your real hunger level is, when to eat, and which foods are best. People who are overweight frequently have an imbalance of Kapha, perhaps accompanied by imbalances in the other doshas (for instance, an imbalance in Vatta or Pitta can lead to nervous or compulsive eating). Those foods that are light, dry, warm, or spicy, bitter and astringent (plant derived colloidal minerals) reduce Kapha.

As a rule of thumb eat hot cooked foods, especially vegetables and grains, rather than cold foods:

DAIRY- boil low fat milk, drink warm.

FRUIT- apples, pomegranates and cranberries.

SWEETENERS- Cold honey.

BEANS- all beans are good.

GRAINS- (give up wheat) use barley, corn, millet, buckwheat and rye.

SPICES- all spices are good.

VEGETABLES-all vegetables and sprouts are good.

MEAT AND FISH-try to keep two days a week meatless.

FATS-Deep fried foods are out.

DRINKS-water and juices, no carbonated drinks. Herbal tea and decaffeinated coffee.

SOUPS- eat liquefied diet one day each week.

DRINK HOT WATER- frequently throughout the day.

BUDDHISM

Buddha (Siddartha Gautama), the Enlightened One came during the sixth century - Hinduism and all greater and lesser religions in all of Asia would never be the same. The evolution in India was based on the doctrine of non-injury to any living creature - this doctrine was supported and reinforced during the sixth century by a prophet called Nataputta (Mahavira -the Great One) or Jina (the Conquerer) by his followers - the Jainists.

Buddhism flourished in the south of India and Jainism flourished in the north. The Jainists were regarded as zealots of the doctrine of non-injury - they would ceremoniously examine everything they ate to ensure that they were not inadvertently swallowing any worms or insects, they would strain their water before drinking it or cooking with it - both Jainists and Buddhist monks carried strainers along with their begging bowls.

The ultra devote Jainists wore masks over their face and nose to ensure that they would not inhale tiny creatures and thereby injuring them - the devote of the devote would not eat particular root vegetables because they were identified as having "two senses" and therefore were a "higher form of life." Such belief dove-tailed perfectly with the Hindu doctrine of the transmigration of souls (reincarnation) - every living soul could eventually be or could have been a human soul.

The Hindus originally believed they were helpless in the great scheme of things and if they killed it was their

"Karma" - it was their destiny; however, the non-injury doctrine, more specifically Buddhism modified the fatalistic acceptance of "Karma." Buddhism affected all of the religions of Asia as sure as all religions of Asia modified Buddhism. This spiritual and dietary doctrine was to sweep through Asia - an epic in mans dietary rules.

The concept of caste enforced by the Brahman priests in India and reinforced by the restrictions of diet was tolerated

---

DOSHA NAME: VATA

WHAT IT DOES
Related to air. Controls all movement in the body, including vocal cords as you speak, the movement of thought, the movement of blood through your heart. Qualities of Vata are dry, cold, light and, above all, changeable. In balance , maintains energy, motion, respiration. Out of balance, brings about dehydration, coldness and emotional instability.

WHAT IT LOOKS/FEELS LIKE
Vata-type people have a light, thin build. They perform activities quickly but tire easily. They may have irregular hunger and digestion, and their sleep is often light and interrupted. Usually enthusiastic, vivacious and imaginative, their emotions can change quickly, and under stress may be transformed into anxiety. In general, Vata people are unpredictable. Since Vata goes out of balance more easily than the other doshas, it's important to create stability and regularity in habits. Impulsive eating is especially evident when under stress. In extreme cases, when Vata becomes seriously unbalanced, any calories taken in are used up by nervous energy and chaotic activity, and nothing gets stored as fat. This may seem appealing to a person who's over weight, but it's definitely not a healthy state of affairs. In deep stages of imbalance, muscle tissue may even begin to waste away.

BEST DIET
Take meals on a regular schedule and be sure to select a balanced variety of foods. Avoid cold food and drink, which will immediately unbalance the dosha; emphasize heavy, hearty foods like stews, breads and warm desserts that have a settling and comforting effect. Thoroughly cook almost everything so that it is easier to digest; raw fruits and vegetables should make up only a small part of a Vata-balancing diet.

DOSHA NAME: PITTA

WHAT IT DOES
Related to fire. Controls metabolism and digestion. In balance, Pitta accurately regulates hunger, thirst, heat and the acuity of intelligence. Aggravated, Pitta can bring on sensations of anger, frustration and extreme hunger.

WHAT IT LOOKS/FEELS LIKE
Pitta people are usually of medium build, with average levels of strength and endurance. They are fair in appearance, with ruddy, often freckled skin. Hunger and thirst are felt very

sharply. They have strong digestions and hate to skip meals. The basic theme of the Pitta type is intensity. Characteristics include sharp-witted, outspoken, bold, argumentative or jealous; when in balance , pittas are warm and ardent in their emotions. It is very Pitta to feel ravenously hungry if dinner is half an hour late, to live by the watch, to walk with a determined stride. Convinced their robust digestion can handle anything, Pitta types tend to overeat, causing their dosha to go out of balance and spurring stomach and intestinal pain, heartburn and even ulcers. The self-discipline of a Pitta can make losing a few pounds or sticking to an exercise regimen extremely easy. But if Pittas become unbalanced, the compulsion to self-destruct can become powerful; there can be alcohol abuse or chronic overeating, as well as clinical eating disorders, which can develop if Pitta anger turns inward in the form of guilt.

BEST DIET
Eat moderately. Avoid eating when angry or emotional, and try·to take meals in relaxed settings that will create the proper mood. Eating outdoors amid the beauty of nature is especially good. Pittas benefit from cold drinks and salads. Avoid spicy or very hot food and keep meat a relatively minor part of the diet. Pittas are well suited to a vegetarian diet, and they can thrive on fresh, unprocessed foods.

DOSHA NAME: KAPHA

WHAT IT DOES
Derives from water and earth. Controls the structure of the body, even down to the cellular level. Maintains strength and physical form through the bones, muscles and tendons. Out of balance, it can cause congestive illnesses such as colds and flu, and is principally responsible for conditions of overweight.

WHAT IT LOOKS/FEELS LIKE
Kapha people are of solid build, with great physical endurance and strength. They move slowly and gracefully. Their skin is cool, smooth and pale. Their digestion is slow and hunger mild. Kapha tend to be tranquil personalities. Their sleep is heavy and prolonged, and they tend toward obesity. Usually affectionate, tolerant and forgiving, under stress they can become possessive and complacent. The basic Kapha theme is relaxed. As a rule, Kaphas enjoy sound health. But they seek emotional comfort sometimes from eating and many Kaphas have been struggling with their weight throughout their lives. Face the fact that a Kapha body does not conform to the media's ideal of a hyper-thin build, yet this in no way implies a lack of beauty or any inferiority. Kapha's digestion and metabolism are inherently slow, and Kaphas tend to lose weight more rapidly. But Ayurveda teaches that a balanced body is never overweight; once Kapha types stabilize, they will naturally return to their ideal weight.

BEST DIET
Avoid ice cream, butter, milk, desserts and other high-fat and very sweet foods, including anything fried or oily. Choose light, warm food instead. Most important, eat only when you're hungry, not just because it's mealtime or food is available. In fact, most Kaphas can benefit from fasting one day a week, during which they take only fruit juices or skim milk. This will result in greater energy and alertness .

A TEST TO DETERMINE YOUR AYRUVEDIC BODY TYPE (from CHOPRA)

Mark 0 to 6 for each question or statement according to how it rates with you.
(0 - does not apply; 3 - applies sometimes; 6 - bulls-eye).

SECTION 1: VATA

1. I am not good at memorizing things and remembering them later. _____
2. I have a thin physique and don't gain weight very easily. _____
3. My characteristic gait while walking is light and quick. _____
4. I tend to have difficulty making decisions. _____
5. I tend to develop gas and become constipated easily. _____
6. I tend to have cold hands and feet. _____
7. I become anxious or worried frequently. _____
8. I speak quickly and my friends think I'm talkative. _____
9. My moods change easily and I am somewhat emotional by nature. _____
10. I often have difficulty falling asleep or getting a good night's sleep. _____
11. My skin tends to be very dry, especially in winter. _____
12. My movements are quick and active; my energy tends to come in bursts. _____
13. I am easily excitable. _____
14. I tend to be irregular in my eating and sleeping habits. _____
15. I learn quickly, but I also forget quickly. _____

VATA SCORE _____

SECTION 2: PITTA

1. In my activities, I tend to be extremely precise and orderly. _____.
2. I am strong-minded and have a somewhat forceful manner. _____
3. I tend to perspire easily. _____
4. If I skip a meal or a meal is delayed, I become uncomfortable. _____
5. One or more of the following characteristics describes my hair: early graying or balding; thin, fine, straight; blonde, red or sandy-colored. _____
6. I have a strong appetite; if I want to, I can eat quite a large quantity. _____
7. I am very regular in my bowel habits—it would be more common for me to have loose stools than to be constipated. _____
8. I become impatient very easily. _____
9. I get angry quite easily, but then I quickly forget about it. _____
10. I am very fond of cold foods, such as ice cream, and also ice-cold drinks. _____
11. I am more likely to feel that a room is too hot than too cold. _____
12. I don't tolerate foods that are very hot and spicy. _____
13. I am not as tolerant of disagreement as I should be. _____
14. I enjoy challenges; and when I want something, I am very determined in my efforts to get it. _____
15. I tend to be quite critical of others and also of myself. _____

PITTA SCORE _____

SECTION 3: KAPHA

1. My natural tendency is to do things in a slow and relaxed fashion. _____
2. I gain weight more easily than most people and lose it more slowly. _____
3. I can skip meals easily without any significant discomfort. _____
4. I have a tendency toward excess mucus or phlegm, chronic congestion, asthma or sinus problems. _____
5. I must get at least eight hours of sleep in order to be comfortable the next day. _____
6. I sleep very deeply. _____
7. I am calm by nature and not easily angered. _____
8. I don't learn as quickly as some people, but I have excellent retention and a long memory. _____
9. Weather that is cool and damp bothers me. _____
10. My hair is thick, dark and wavy. _____
11. I have smooth, soft skin with a somewhat pale complexion. _____
12. I have a large, solid body build. _____
13. I have very good stamina and physical endurance as well as a steady level of energy. _____
14. I generally walk with a slow, measured gait. _____
15. I am a slow eater and am slow and methodical in my actions. _____

KAPHA SCORE _____

Now you can determine your body type. Although there are only three doshas, Ayurveda combines them in ten ways to arrive at ten body types.

• **If one score is much higher than the others, you are probably a single-dosha type, i.e., either Vata, Pitta or Kapha.**

You are definitely a single-dosha type if one score is twice as high as another dosha score, but a smaller margin also applies. In single-dosha types, the characteristics of Vata, Pitta or Kapha are very evident. Your next-highest dosha will still show up in your natural tendencies, but it will be much less distinct.

• **If no single dosha dominates, you are a two dosha type, i.e., Vata-Pitta or Pitta-Vata; Pitta-Kapha or Kapha-Pitta; or Vata-Kapha or Kapha-Vata.**

If you are a two-dosha type, the traits of your two leading doshas will predominate. The higher one comes first in your body type, but both count. A Pitta-Vata type, for example, might have a score like this: Vata=55, Pitta=65, Kapha=15.

• **If your three scores are nearly equal, you may be a three dosha type, i.e., Vata-Pitta-Kapha.**

This type is rare. Check your answers, or have a friend go over them with you.

by Buddhism - Buddhism did not teach the concept of reincarnation but did teach the concept of "Karma." It also teaches that the journey to the "perfect state" of non-being includes a cycle of death and rebirth taking into account different levels or castes of human development. In Hinduism, an individuals level of development or caste was ultimately due to his "Karma" - fate controlled his life and his acts. The early Brahmans did not view the killing of animals for food as sinful - they in fact abhorred vegetarianism as it was practiced by the "less civilized" natives of southern India. The irresistible force of Buddhism over 1,000 years changed the liberal laws for the consumption of meat - Hindu scriptures made it a canon law - anyone who eats flesh or causes a cow to be slaughtered will "rot in hell for as many years as there are hairs on the cow."

FROM THE DHAMMAPADA (a canonical Buddhist text)

Destroying living beings, killing, cutting, binding, stealing, speaking falsehood, fraud and deception, worthless reading, intercourse with another man's wife - this is Amagandha (what defiles a person), but not the eating of flesh.

Those persons who in this world are unrestrained in sensual pleasures, greedy of sweet things (pica), associated with what is impure, skeptics, unjust, difficult to follow - this is Amagangha, but not the eating of flesh.

Those who are rough, harsh, backbiting, treacherous, merciless, arrogant, and do not give anything to anyone - this is Amagandha, but not the eating of flesh.

Anger, intoxication, obstinacy, bigotry, deceit, envy, grandiloquence, pride and conceit, intimacy with the unjust - this is Amagandha, but not the eating of flesh.

Those who in this world are wicked, and such as do not pay their debts, are slanderers, false in their dealings, counterfeiters, those who in this world being the lowest of men commit sin - this is Amagandha, but not the eating of flesh.

Food could not be prepared or served or touched by members of the lower castes. If even the shadow of an untouchable, a member of the lowest caste, crossed over food, it was polluted and uneatable. There were dietary laws that had the direct effect of stopping disease:

1) Food left sitting overnight was a taboo.

2) Food touched by the foot or skirt hem was forbidden.

3) Food sniffed by an animal or another human was forbidden.

4) Food contaminated by hair, insects or mouse droppings was forbidden.

CHINESE RELIGIONS:

China is another example of an Asian country where Buddhism had a deep influence on the dietary practices over a long period of time and then faded away. The Chinese ate anything (and still do) that could be made to taste good or please the eye including dogs and rats ("household deer"). Pork is the meat of China - the Chinese word for pork and

5,300-year-old 'Ice Man' had modern-day ailments

The Associated Press

CHICAGO — The 5,300-year-old "Ice Man," whose well-preserved body was discovered in a glacier three years ago, had the same kind of aches and pains as we do, researchers reported Wednesday.

Arthritis. Hardening of the arteries. Broken ribs.

"It's really not much different from modern man," said William Murphy Jr., who reported on the medical miseries of the mummy at the annual meeting of the Radiological Society of North America. "There are just very impressive similarities."

Researchers believe the gap-toothed ice man — dubbed "Otzi" because he was found in

Italy's Otzval Valley — was 25 to 40 when he died.

But he already had developed osteoarthritis in his neck, lower back and one hip.

And calcium deposits were discovered in the blood vessels of Otzi's chest, pelvis and neck, indicating heart disease stalked the Stone Age man despite a rigorous existence.

He also had fractured ribs.

"It's the kind of thing that . . . certainly would have sent modern man to the emergency room," Murphy said.

Murphy is part of a team at the University of Innsbruck, Austria, examining the mummy with X-ray technology.

Otzi is the best-preserved European from an age 4,000 to 6,000 years ago. The body is

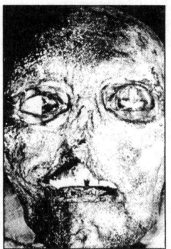
University of Texas via AP
'OTZI': Ice man had arthritis, hardening of the arteries

stored in a freezer in Innsbruck, and researchers are allowed to work on it only 30 minutes at a time to prevent deterioration.

ST. LOUIS POST-DISPATCH

TUESDAY, AUGUST 31, 1993

Buddhists Enshrine Panchen Lama's Body, 4 Years After Death

BEIJING (AP) — The body of the second-highest leader of Tibetan Buddhism was enshrined Monday more than four years after he died.

The Panchen Lama died Jan. 28, 1989, after a heart attack at age 50. His body had been stored in Xigaze, southwest of the Tibetan capital of Lhasa, while a shrine was built.

In a ceremony Monday, the Panchen Lama's body, wrapped in yellow satin, was taken by car to the newly completed structure, the Xinhua News Agency reported.

A more elaborate ceremony is planned next month to mark the for-

mal inauguration of the three-story shrine and memorial palace, which together cost $11 million to build, the report said.

The Panchen Lama was the high-

est-ranking Tibetan Buddhist leader in China. The Dalai Lama, the faith's top leader, has lived in exile since a failed Tibetan revolt in 1959 against Chinese rule.

the Chinese word for meat are almost the same. Milk and dairy are totally omitted from the Chinese dietary habit (many Chinese lack the enzyme lactase needed to digest milk sugar after they are two years of age).

Buddhism infiltrated China during the Han dynasty (206-220 A.D.) - when it arrived the Buddhist monks found that Confucianism and Taoism were already well established in China; the Great Wall had already been built to prevent grain raids in the northern plains of China by the Mongolians; government was totalitarian and bureaucratic and directed by the semi-official religion (Confucianism); the emperor was supreme under heaven and the family was the basis of social rules and personal ethics.

When the Chinese of the Han dynasty worshiped it was to their ancestral family that they prayed and their dietary rules were limited to those times of prayer (i.e.- food that made the "breath obnoxious" to the ancestors was looked down upon - pork for example: flossing would help here).

Initially Buddhism had a hard time in China because it was considered barbaric, "otherworldly" and "unfilial." Buddhism also had an affinity for Taoism, which was "otherworldly" in the extreme. Tao was the highly metaphysical "way" of the mythical teacher Lao-tzu. He was said to have been born about the same time as as Buddha; there were enough similarities between the two prophets that Buddha according to the Chinese was Lao-Tzu reincarnate!!

The Taoist "way" to the "ecstatic union with the eternal course of nature and the attainment of bodily immortality" involved mental and physical disciplines - including the use of the "right kinds of foods."

FROM "DIRECTORY FOR A DAY": (a Taoist text from Zah Yung King)

Upon partaking of the mysterious Taoist elixirs: The true powers of the five elements (Fire, Water, Air, Earth and Wood) unite and form the boat-like cup of jade. The body seems to be full of delicious harmony. This spreads like the unguent of the chrismal rite on the head. Walking, resting, sitting, sleeping, the man feels his body flexible as the wind, and his belly a sound like that of thunder. His ears hear the songs of the immortals, that needs no aid from any instrument; vocal without words, and resounding without the drum. The spirit and the breath effect a union and the bloom of childhood returns.

The Taoist had special diets and foods that nourished vital organs of the body, and those vital organs were in turn related to the vital elements of the universe - the body was an ecosystem whose parts were the equivalent of the parts of the universe and the body was inhabited by the same gods that inhabit the universe (additionally, when the proper spiritual and physical perfection and balance had been achieved, the individual could "ascend into heaven in broad daylight.").

The complicated dietary programs and the use of herbs, exercise, breathing techniques and meditation are found in an ancient Taoist text that could have been influenced by Hindu Yoga. Taoist alchemists believed that immortality could be attained by consuming an elixir of "potable" gold (gold mixed with cinnabar or "quick silver"). Taoist herbalists assembled the first written collection of mineral and herbal "pharmaceuticals."

Resisted by the Confucianists and Buddhists, Taoism modified the stiffness of Confucianism and injected an element of metaphysics into Buddhism. Taoism helped develop the Buddhist monastic life in China, Tibet, Korea and Japan; and it directly influenced the Chinese Buddhist sect of Ch'an, which evolved into the Zen of Japan.

Following the collapse and the fragmentation of the Han dynasty into several small territories ruled by warlords, Buddhism enjoyed its greatest popularity in China; however, even with its moderate approach to life and dietary laws as suggested by the Buddhist Middle View, China never accepted Buddhism as the one path of diet or religion.

The Buddhist approach to meat eating is a dichotomy - meat is not actually forbidden (their approach to diet was similar to that of the early Christians: it was not so much what a man ate, but what he does and what he is that makes him good or evil) - yet there was a law against killing animals for meat. Buddhism's dietary quirks left their mark on the Chinese culture, just as it did throughout Asia.

There were vegetarian feasts that still were celebrated in China up to 1947 when Mao's Communists took over power. The vegetarian feasts were celebrations of various events in the small village communities such as birthdays, weddings, completion of a temple, etc. Many of the Buddhists vegetarian feasts were huge affairs with hundreds or thousands of guests - one emperor reportedly held a vegetarian feast for 1,000 monks who "had interceded with the gods and brought rain to parched fields," another held a vegetarian feast for 10,000.

JAPAN -SHINTO & ZEN

Buddhism arrived in Japan in the sixth century A.D. with very good timing - just before the Japanese court and nobles deliberately imported Chinese cultural refinements of music, spices, recipes and sport. Classical Chinese was adopted for the language of the academic, warrior and upper classes along with Confucianism and Taoism.

The original religion of Japan, Shinto, was the worship of nature, with each family or clan praying to "their deity," much like the patron saints of of the Catholics. About the same time the Japanese emperor was elevated to a descendant of the Sun Goddess and Shinto became interlocked with the political state of Japan. For the society at large, Shinto, and it's relationship to the state reinforced the concept of caste with the Samari warrior class and the ruling nobles on the highest rungs of society. The Buddhism that was imported from China was blended with Shinto and this mixture persists today.

In Shinto, the mysterious essence of the universe, the originator of all creation, is referred to as Kami - both physical and spiritual purification is mandatory. During festivals of thanksgiving at Shinto shrines in the Spring and Fall, special food offerings are made (i.e.- rice, rice cakes, sake, fish, vegetables and birds of various types).

In ancient Shinto festivals, the people offering the food ate the food in order to be in communion with Kami - no animal was offered because of the laws against shedding of blood on the sacred grounds of the shrine. The concept followed in Shinto that the butchers task of killing, letting blood and butchering changed his very soul and that his tarnished nature was indeed inherited by his children and was even considered a communicable sin - as this Shinto belief became rooted amongst the nobles of Japan they began to exclusively eat fish as their source of animal protein.

The tea ceremony originated with Zen - wherever practiced, the highly ritualized tea ceremony has religious connections. The tea room is usually built so that a person has to enter on his knees and this posture of piety contributes to the event - only recently has the tea ceremony become a ritualized social event.

One of the priests who brought Zen to Japan wrote a book, "Rules for Improving One's Health Through Tea Drinking." In Zen monasteries great emphasis is directed toward eating fully ripened seasonal foods that the monks produced themselves and local foods such as buds, flowers, leaves and wild sprouts. Rice, soy beans and sesame seeds are part of the staple diet of the Zen monasteries - fish and meat are taboo. Monks living near the coasts eat more sea vegetables and kelp than anyone in the world yet live little longer than someone consuming a Western diet.

A modern Japanese nutritionist who analyzed the monastic diets of Shinto and Zen monks reported that " I was most surprised by the (high) amount of natural salts (minerals) ...I discovered."

JUDAISM
"a diet for the Chosen People"

Ancient Judaic law looked upon dietary transgressions as the highest of sins. It is a written fact that many of the conquerors of the Holyland (i.e.- Babylonians, Syrians, the Greeks and Alexander the Great, the Romans, the Turks and the British) attempted to force the Jews to abandon their ancient religion and eat forbidden and "unclean" foods. Jews accepted torture and were even killed rather than break the food laws.

Josephus recorded that during the time of the Romans, the Essenes, a rebellious sect of the Jews were put to every form of torture:

"They were racked and twisted, burned and broken and made to pass through every instrument of torture in order to induce them to blaspheme their lawgivers and to eat some forbidden thing. Yet they refused to yield to either demand, not even once did they cringe to the persecutor or shed a tear.

Smiling in their agonies, mildly deriding their tormentors, they cheerfully resigned their souls, confident that they would receive them back."

FROM THE OLD TESTAMENT
Leviticus Chapter 7

22 - And the Lord spoke unto Moses, Saying: Speak unto all the children of Israel, saying:

Ye shall eat no fat of ox or sheep or goat. And the fat of that which is torn by beasts, may be used for any other service;

Lubavitch legend dies at age 92

By Keith Greenberg
Special for USA TODAY

By Mike Albans, AP

SCHNEERSON: Believed by some followers to be the Messiah, many of whom insist his resurrection is near.

BROOKLYN, N.Y. — Thousands of followers of Rabbi Menachem Mendel Schneerson honored the legendary leader of Judaism's ultra-Orthodox Lubavitch sect following his Sunday death.

Followers thought Schneerson, 92, was the Messiah, and many celebrated immediately after word of his death by eating fruit and drinking beer in the streets, firm in their belief that a resurrected *rebbe* would lead them to Israel.

After a frenetic day, followers interred Schneerson's pine coffin in a small granite mausoleum in a Queens cemetery.

His death came three months after a massive stroke confined him to a hospital bed. As the faithful gathered in front óf Lubavitch headquarters in Crown Heights, many could not accept the news.

"He didn't die," insists 8-year-old Yehuda Moskowitz, who came here with his parents from New Haven, Conn. "He will come back to us."

About 12 bearded men in black danced in agreement.

"Our books teach us that there will come a time when the soul of our *Moshiach* (Messiah) goes into the heavenly realms," says an overjoyed Daniel Karsai, 17. "That time is now. Soon the soul will re-enter the body of our *Moshiach*."

Others were less optimistic.

"As much as we believe the Messiah is coming soon, this just makes it harder now," says rabbinical student Eliezer Sehach, 21. "We didn't think he would pass away."

but ye shall in no wise eat of it. For whosoever eateth the fat of the beast, of which men present an offering made by fire unto the Lord, even the soul that eateth it shall be cut off from his people. and ye shall eat no manner of blood, whether it be of fowl or of beasts, in any of your dwellings, whosoever it be that eateth any blood, that soul shall be cut off from his people.

The basic dietary laws found in the Old Testament book of Genesis, Leviticus and Deuteronomy are simple and straight forward:

All fruits and vegetables are for the use of man. Animals (used for food) must be herbivorous (plant eaters - not meat eaters) and they must have cloven hooves and chew a "cud." (i.e.- cows, buffalo, goats, sheep, oxen, deer and antelope) - this does not include pigs, which have cloven hooves but do not chew their "cud" or camels which chew their "cud" but do not have cloven hooves.

FROM THE OLD TESTAMENT
Leviticus Chapter 11

1 - And the Lord spoke unto Moses and Aaron, saying unto them: Speak unto the children of Israel, saying:

These are the living things which ye may eat among all the beasts that are on the Earth. Whatever parteth the hoof, and is wholly cloven-footed, and cheweth the cud, among the beasts, that may ye eat. Nevertheless these shall ye not eat of them that only chew the cud, or them that only part the hoof: the camel because he cheweth the cud but parteth not the hoof, he is unclean to you.

And the rock-badger, because he cheweth the cud but parteth not the hoof, he is unclean to you. And the hare, because she cheweth the cud but parteth not the hoof, she is unclean to you. And the swine, because he parteth the hoof and is cloven-footed, but cheweth not the cud, he is unclean to you. Of their flesh ye shall not eat, and their carcasses ye shall not touch; they are unclean to you.

9 - These may ye eat of all that are in the waters: whatsoever hath fins and scales in the waters, in the seas, and in the rivers, them may ye eat.

All predators, animals, or birds were prohibited as food; birds not predators (fowl) were fit to eat. All reptiles, amphibians and all aquatic species that did not have both scales or fins were taboo. Some locusts and crickets were allowed for food but all other swarming animals (bats) were taboo.

The Pentateuch (the first five books of the Old Testament which made up the Torah) expressly forbade the consumption of blood and the cooking of a kid or lamb by boiling it alive in it's mothers milk.

The "fence" or "hedge" devised by the rabbis evolved around the dietary law after the "children of Israel" had arrived at the "promised land" under the stewardship of Moses; lived there for almost five centuries; had split into two kingdoms (Israel in the north and Judah in the south); and had again been conquered and carried off in chains into bondage - the Israelites by the Syrians and the Jews of Judah by the Babylonians.

The "hedge" was made up of a series of oral codes called the Misnah and eventually rabbinical editorials on the teachings called the Gemara - these oral laws or the "hedge" became dogma, then eventually gained the status of law and made up the Jewish Talmud.

"Unclean meat" was forbidden, so was clean meat if not properly killed and prepared (Kosher). The rules, law and ritual of the slaughter and preparation were so strict that they had to be carried out by a licensed expert - he must assure all of the blood has been drained from the carcass, that there are no defects or disease in any organ:

1) No missing organs
2) No punctured organ walls
3) No missing limbs
4) No injuries related to the animal's death
5) No infections
6) No fertile eggs
7) No blood-spot eggs

The Koshering of meat includes salting (preservation in the desert) or roasting, this includes the type of salt (assured trace minerals from certain types of salt). On the eve of the Sabbath, the meat may be soaked in salt brine for 30 minutes instead of one hour. Cooking meat and milk together is forbidden; even separate sets of cooking and eating utensils for meat and milk are required.

FROM THE OLD TESTAMENT
Leviticus Chapter 11

20 - All winged swarming things that go about on all fours (bats) are a detestable thing unto you. Yet these may ye eat of all winged swarming things that go upon all fours, which have jointed legs above their feet (locusts), wherewith to leap upon the earth; even these of them ye may eat; locusts after its kinds, and the cricket after its kinds, and the grasshopper after its kinds.

23 - But all winged swarming things, which have four feet (bats), are a detestable thing unto you.

27 - And whatsoever goeth upon its paws (dogs, cats, lions, etc.), amongst all beasts that go on all fours, they are unclean unto you; who so toucheth their carcass shall be unclean until even. And he that beareth the carcass of them shall wash his clothes, and be unclean until the even; and they are unclean unto you.

The great numbers of modern day Jews are from one or another of two groups that split and went different directions during the Diaspora (dispersal). The Ashkenazic Jews who went to Eastern Europe and then spread to all of Europe and to North and South America - these are the "Yiddish" speaking Jews.

Secondly, there were the Jews who associated with the Arabs of the Middle East and spread to Asia, Africa and Southern Europe. The Jews who were associated with the spread of Islam into Southern Europe are called Sephardic (Spanish) Jews. They created the Ladino language which like "yiddish" is written in Hebrew characters. There are dozens of sub-groups or sects of Jews, whose dietary habits relate to their geographical origins (i.e.- Russian Jews, Lithuanian Jews, Balkan Jews, European Jews, American Jews, Arab Jews, etc.) and on their level of adherence to ancient Hebrew dietary law (Orthodox, Conservative, Reform, Traditionalists and non-religious).

Sephardic diets use spices, olive oil, rice and lamb, while the Ashkenazic diets

Grand Ayatollah Ali Araki, Senior Shiite Cleric, Is Dead

By YOUSSEF M. IBRAHIM
Special to The New York Times

PARIS, Nov. 30 — Grand Ayatollah Ali Araki, who was considered to be the world's most eminent Shiite Muslim cleric, died Tuesday in Teheran, plunging the religious and political establishment into a debate over the choice of a successor.

The holder of his title of supreme guide and Marjaa Taqlid, which means source of emulation, is in a position to challenge the Iranian Government on religious as well as policy matters.

Ayatollah Araki was widely viewed among Shiites as the supreme authority on theological affairs only. He stayed out of politics, leaving that function to Ayatollah Ali Khamenei, who holds the title of the supreme leader of the Iranian revolution and who served for eight years as President of Iran.

Iranian Government radio said Ayatollah Araki "bade farewell to the living world after a long illness despite the efforts of doctors." He was admitted to the intensive care unit in Teheran Hospital three weeks ago.

Ayatollah Araki's exact age is unknown but he was believed to be 106 years old. Teheran announced today that the nation would begin a week-long period of mourning.

The choice of a successor is complicated by the fact that some clerics eligible for consideration are in Iraq and Lebanon, and Iran believes that the central leadership in religious matters should remain in Qum, the Iranian religious city that is the home of several Shiite universities and institutes.

A leader has traditionally been chosen by consensus among the learned of the Shiite religious establishment largely inside Iran but also in Iraq and Lebanon. Ayatollah Araki had held the position for only a year.

Since the Iranian Islamic revolution led by Ayatollah Ruhollah Khomeini in 1979 overthrew the Persian monarchy, Iranian religious leaders have worked to galvanize Shiite communities, enhancing Iran's leading role in Shiism.

Ayatollah Araki was the third successor to the title after Ayatollah Khomeini. While Ayatollah Khomeini combined his political role as the leader of the Iranian revolt with his theological prominence to exercise his influence among Shiites worldwide, his successors have not.

Iran has been anxious about preserving both qualities in its supreme religious leader, but many of the senior Shiite figures in Iran, Iraq and Lebanon hold different political views from the militant clerics of Teheran.

Some Shiite voices in Iraq and Lebanon have argued for some time for a return to the seperation of religion from politics practiced by most Shiite communities for much of this century. And Iran's inability to find a religious figure who possesses the charisma and appeal of Ayatollah Khomeini has diminished its theological domination of the Shiite branch of Islam.

The responsibilities of grand ayatollahs include lecturing, conducting studies, writing and publishing essays and collecting a religious following, hence the reference to emulation in the titles of religious leaders.

There are at least five grand ayatollahs in Qum who may qualify for

Associated Press

Grand Ayatollah Ali Araki

the marjaa position and three in Iraq and Lebanon. But Iran has made it clear that it plans to select the successor and has already denounced any attempt to depoliticize the position.

"We understand the clerics outside Iran believe religion should be separate from politics," said the speaker of Iran's Islamic Consultative Assembly, Ali Nateq Nuri, himself a militant cleric. But he added that "someone who believes in the separation of religion and politics is not fit to be a marjaa."

Actually, tradition within the Shiite religious establishment has strongly favored the choice of a person who is extremely learned in theocracy with a record of scholarly achievement. Ayatollah Khomeini had published seven books and numerous essays on religion and society by the time he went into the politics of opposition.

have a preference for beef, boiled vegetables, fats, sugar and onions. Both sects use wheat, rye, dates, nuts olives, grapes, figs,pomegranates, lentils, beans and peas, squash, cucumbers, melons, leeks, onions and garlic. Many modern day Jews ignore the dietary laws (Kashrut), while others such as the Yemini Jews follow exactly the ancient dietary laws of the Talmud.

ISLAM

The parallel between the basic dietary laws of the Moslems and the Jews are not surprising for they as peoples are half-brothers! The Jews descended from Abraham and his wife Sarah; the Moslems or the Nation of Islam descended from Abraham and Sarah's hand-maiden, Hagar, who gave birth to a son named Ishmael. Both Jews and Moslems are semetic people descended from Shem, one of the three sons of Noah.

Hagar was driven from Abraham's house by Sarah and she traveled south into the Arabian Desert; when Hagar arrived in the general area of Mecca she was thirsty and searched frantically for water. She laid her son Ishmael in the sand while she searched for water - while she searched the child cried and kicked the sand, water filled the depression he had made and a well came into being.

For centuries, prior to the Prophet Mohammed founding Islam, the Semetic peoples of the Arabian Peninsula made pilgrimages to this well and to a sacred rock that "fell from heaven in the days of Adam." Abraham himself built the Ka'bah, a cubical shrine that surrounds this rock - it is now considered the most sacred spot in the world of Islam. Moslem pilgrims reaching Mecca walk back and forth between the well and the rock seven times in ritualistic observance of Hagar's frantic search for water.

Ishmael, the son of Abraham and half-brother of Isaac is credited with the founding of Mecca, one of the Holiest cities of the Moslem world. Isaac was the father of Jacob, who was called Israel.

The Koran, the holy book of Islam, which contains the teachings of the Prophet Mohammed and his revelations from Allah, traces the matter of proper food clear back to Adam, as does the Old Testament:

"And God said, 'O Adam, dwell thou and thy wife in paradise and eat therefrom amply as you wish; but do not draw near this tree'."

Mohammed was born in 570 A.D. and the Arabs had been in a close cultural mix with the Jews for some centuries, and in some trade and wars with the Christians for 500 years. Mecca and Medina to the north were on caravan routes to the southern tip of the peninsula - there were large populations of Jews in both cities and Christianity had already spread into the cities.

**From the Koran
Chapter 5, Section 1**

In the name of Allah, the Beneficent, the Merciful.

1- O you who believe, fulfill the obligations (food laws). The cattle quadrupeds are allowed to you accept that which is recited to you, not violating the prohibition against game (hunting) when you are on the pilgrimage (to Mecca). Surely Allah orders what He pleases.

Islam contains the basic teachings of Mohammed - they are simple laws of the faith. The primary one of these tenets is repeated daily by 500,000,000 Moslems each day : "There is no God but Allah and Mohammed is his prophet." People who are Moslems believe that the Koran as revealed to Mohammed, is the undeniable word of God:

"O ye who believe! Eat of the good things with which we have supplied you, and give give God thanks if ye are His worshipers. Only that which dieth of itself and blood and swine's flesh, and that over which any other name than that of God has been invoked (food sacrificed to a heathen idol), hath God forbidden you."

The Koran goes on, that if a person is forced to eat forbidden food to keep from starving that is no sin.

The diet of the nomadic Bedouins was made up of dates and milk from camels and sheep, they ate meat from camels and sheep and grain but few vegetables. It is the duty before God for a Moslem to remain alive and healthy, food, except for pork (which is considered "filth") and blood and meat found dead, "is one of the greatest blessings from God" and is to be consumed with humility and full awareness of that fact. The Koran denounces men who would deprive people of food by setting forth arbitrary food taboos.

Meat is favored, but as with the Jewish law, meat animals must be slaughtered properly - the throat , the windpipe, the carotid arteries and the gullet must be severed with a single stroke and the man doing the killing must repeat, " In the name of God; God is great." When a hunter kills a bird or animal with a gun or arrow he must repeat the same words,

then the animal is clean and fit to eat - a Moslem may even eat animals killed by Jews or Christians if the animal has been slaughtered in a proper manner.

Fruits and vegetables of all kinds are good, and with the spread of Islam into the Fertile Crescent around the confluence of the Tigris and the Euphrates Rivers, the Arabs became familiar with a greater variety and "more abundant blessings from God."

Fish were considered good food; grain was good food, especially rice brought to Arabia through the trade routes from India; rice was a grain of the nobles and the wealthy, wheat is looked upon as food for the commoners. Sugar was first brought to the Arabs from India and is mixed with vinegar for sweet-and-sour dishes. Figs are most favored as they are specifically mentioned by God in the Koran.

Doctors and nutritionists in the Moslem world (influenced by the Greeks) prescribed specific foods for specific diseases and injuries. Fresh ripe dates were used for stomach pain; a sheep's heart, liver and kidneys gave strength to the heart, liver and kidneys of whoever ate them. Moslem boys just circumcised are fed soup made of sheep testicles to help them heal and to attain strength. The sheep's brain is not eaten because it is thought to be a stupid animal and to eat a sheep brain would make the eater stupid.

Honey is used to ease mental suffering and is commonly used in pastries eaten at funerals. Many Moslems refuse to consume food that is not grown in their own country. Some holy men of the Middle East claim that potatoes are the "food of Satan" and that tomatoes are made of human blood.

Moslems in China will eat pork because it is the only meat available in some provinces. Meat that a predator (cheetah, falcon, etc.) has grabbed in its claws or talons is unclean. Meat even sniffed by a dog is forbidden. Even the method of eating by a Moslem is prescribed in a supplemental scripture to the Koran called the Traditions:

1 - Repeat the name of God, otherwise the devil has power over the food.

2 - Eat only with the first three fingers of the right hand.

3 - When finishing a dish, lick the fingers before washing them.

4 - Lick the dish afterward (so the devils can't) and the dish will intercede with God.

5 - Do not eat with shoes on.

FROM THE KORAN
Chapter 5, Section 1

4- they ask thee to what is allowed to them (the people). Say: The good things are allowed to you, and what you have taught the beasts and the birds of prey, training them to hunt - you teach (the people) of what Allah has taught you; so eat of that which they catch for you and mention the name of Allah over it; and keep your duty to Allah. Surely Allah is swift and reckoning.

5 - This day good things are made lawful for you. And the food of those who have been given the Book is lawful for you, and your food is lawful for them.

Fasts are part of the Moslem tradition and ritual, in particular during the holy month of Ramadan. In the Traditions, Mohammed is quoted, "Every good act a man does shall receive from 10 to 700 rewards, but the rewards of fasting are beyond bounds, for fasting is for God alone and He will give it's rewards."

Fasting is one of the "Five Pillars" of the Moslem religion:

1 - Fasting
2 - Repetition of "There is no God but Allah and Mohammed is His prophet."
3 - Prayer five times each day.
4 - Alms-giving (charity)
5 - Pilgrimage to Mecca at least once in one's lifetime.

As a result of their being traders in the commercial crossroads of the world it is generally accepted that the Moslems have contributed more to the food and eating habits of the world than any other faith.

CHRISTIANITY

Christ separated himself and his followers from the traditional Jews and their laws in many ways including their dietary laws.:

"There is nothing from without a man, that entering into him can defile him; but the things which come out of him (hygiene - avoid urine and feces), those are they that can defile the man." Mark 7:15

When Christ's own disciples questioned him on the subject of diet restrictions in various places they were doing missionary work he told them it was not what goes into a mans belly that defiles him, but rather the evil that comes out of him.

"And into whatever city ye enter, and they receive you, eat such things as are set before you." Luke 10:8

While Christ taught "reverence for the "body, more than once referring to the body as "the temple of God," he also attended feasts and banquets and was

THE BOSTON HERALD, THURSDAY, APRIL 28, 1994

Rev. Richard Mazziotta of North Easton, at 44

The Rev. Richard Mazziotta of North Easton, an associate professor of religious studies at Stonehill College and a member of the Congregation of Holy Cross, died Monday at Massachusetts General Hospital of complications resulting from a brain aneurysm. He was 44.

Born and raised in Queens, N.Y., he received a bachelor's degree from Stonehill in 1972, a master's degree in theology from Notre Dame in 1975 and a doctorate in ministry from Boston University in 1983. He was ordained in 1976.

Before becoming a tenured member of the Stonehill Department of Religious Studies, Rev. Mazziotta taught in the college's writing program, coached the women's cross country team and served as campus minister. He also taught at Holy Cross High School in Flushing, N.Y.

Rev. Mazziotta was the local superior of the religious community at Stonehill College and a member of the Provincial Council of the Eastern Province of the Congregation of Holy Cross. In addition, he assisted at Our Lady of Sorrows Parish in Sharon. From 1980-87, he assisted at Our Lady of Lourdes Parish in Brockton. He also served as an assistant pastor at Christ the King Parish in South Bend, Ind.

A computer buff, he also enjoyed racquetball, cooking and gardening.

Rev. Mazziotta served as a chaplain with the 26th Infantry Division of the Massachusetts National Guard and rose to the rank of major.

He is survived by his mother, Concetta (Frascinella) of Williston Park, N.Y.; two sisters, Maryann McDermott of Mineola, N.Y., and Barbara Robinson of Westbury, N.Y.; one brother, Joseph of English Town, N.J.; and several nieces and nephews.

A funeral Mass will be celebrated at 10:30 a.m. tomorrow at St. Mary's Chapel, Stonehill College.

Burial will be in Holy Cross Cemetery, Easton.

Arrangements are by Robert J. Kane Funeral Home, South Easton.

known to have associated with the drinkers of wine ("bibbers"- in fact Christ followed the See-Food diet!).

There were Christian converts from the Jews who refused to shed the old dietary laws, and they formed a Jewish-Christian sect called the Nazarenes or Ebionites.

FROM THE KING JAMES BIBLE
Matthew 4

4 - But he answered and said, it is written, man shall not live by bread alone, but by every word that proceedeth out of the mouth of God.

Matthew 15:

20 - these are the things that defile a man: but to eat with unwashed hands defileth not a man.

1 Corinthians 3:

17 - If any man defile the temple of God, him shall God destroy; for the temple of God is holy, which temple ye are.

1 Corinthians 6

19 - What? Know ye not that your body is the temple of the Holy Ghost which is in you, which ye have of God, and ye are not your own?

20 - For ye are bought with a price; therefore glorify God in your own body, and in your spirit, which are God's.

The apostle Paul insisted that "Christian love" was the fulfilling of the law and that there was no need for food taboos and no need to be concerned about "clean" and "unclean" things when dealing with the rules of diet. As a compromise it was agreed that it was only necessary to refrain from eating the meat of animals that had been sacrificed to heathen idols, meat from animals that had been strangled and blood - these vestiges of Jewish dietary laws were retained by the Christian church for several centuries.

After public services were over, Christians would assemble for a feast of "brotherly love" and thanksgiving; they commemorated Christ's sacrifice of His body and blood by eating bread and wine (communion) - non-Christians were excluded from these feasts causing Roman bureaucrats to murmur that the assemblages were secret, that the "love feast" was an orgy and that the sacrament was in fact "cannibalism." The Greek word for the "love feast" was "Eucharist," translated to "give thanks," and the Eucharist developed into the Roman Catholic Mass.

There were no food taboos in the original Catholic church and there are none today - there are fasts, abstinence, and sobriety. Thomas Aquinas, in his Summa Theologica, stated that it is not that abstaining from food (fasting) is good in itself, for if that were so, the eating of food would be by very reason would be bad.

There were early Christian sects, such as the Anchorites, who were ascetics - some wandered in the deserts and subsisted on insects; there were hermits who lived in caves to whom people threw food; some Christians lived in trees; and then came monastic orders including the Benedictines, who lived quiet humble lives whose feature was prayer, work and a "simple diet."

Pope, Citing Health, Calls Off Visit to New York

Abrupt Postponement Renews Speculation on His Condition

By ALAN COWELL
Special to The New York Times

ROME, Sept. 22 — In another sign of the Pope's physical frailty, the Vatican announced today that John Paul II was postponing a visit to the New York City area and Baltimore, planned for next month, because he had not fully recuperated from a fall in April in which he broke his leg.

The unexpected announcement renewed speculation about the 74-year-old Pope's broader state of health, particularly because he planned an important speech at the United Nations on the family in which he was expected to discuss the Vatican's views of the recent population conference in Cairo.

The Pope had planned to leave Oct. 20 on a four-day visit to New York City, Yonkers, Newark and Baltimore. Among other events, he had been scheduled to celebrate masses at Yonkers Raceway, Giants Stadium, the Cathedral of the Sacred Heart in Newark, and Camden Yards in Baltimore and to lead prayer services at St. Patrick's Cathedral, Shea Stadium.

The Vatican's chief spokesman, Joaquín Navarro-Valls, said in a statement that the visit was being postponed until November 1995 because the Pope had been "advised not to intensify his activities in this period following orthopedic surgery." Doctors inserted metal alloy replacements for parts of a broken right femur, or thighbone, after the Pope's fall in April.

Speaking to reporters later today, Mr. Navarro-Valls denied that the Pope was suffering from any undisclosed illness. "The only reason, the exclusive reason, for this postponement is what is written in that statement," he said.

Associated Press

Pope John Paul II climbed a step toward his chair on Wednesday after arriving for his weekly audience at Nervi's Hall at the Vatican.

It was in fact the Benedictine sect at the monastery of Monte Cassino at Selerno that gave support to the early "science" of dietetics.

The first medical school in Europe was started in Selerno, it was a secular school with close associations to the Benedictine monastery. The school was limited by the early Christian taboo on dissection of the human body, however, it was very productive in elucidating the role of diet in maintaining and restoring health.

The Benedictine effort in the area of diet was written in verse. The monks and doctors of Selerno, using the dietary teachings of the Greek physicians Hippocrates and Galen (who took them from Ayruvedic medicine and Chinese alchemy) invested the human body with four basic substances or "humors":

1. Blood
2. Yellow bile
3. Phlegm
4. Black bile

A healthy body did not suffer from an excess of any one of the four humors - therefore a "balanced diet was essential."

For a patient suffering from an excess of yellow bile, cool and moist foods (i.e.- fruits) were prescribed. An excess of phlegm required hot (cayenne pepper) highly seasoned food as a cure.

From the King James Bible Romans 14

2. For one believeth that he may eat all things: another, who is weak eateth herbs.

3. Let not him that eateth despise him that eateth not; and let not him which eateth not judge him that eateth; for God hath received him.

1 Corinthians 10

27. If any of them that believe not bid you to a feast, and ye be disposed to go; whatsoever is set before you, eat, asking no questions for conscience sake.

31 - Whether therefore you eat, or drink, or whatsoever ye do, do all to the Glory of God.

It is noteworthy that the concept of "humors" or concepts similar to them (i.e.- the basic substances of the body) were common in all early religions. The Hindus and the Taoists believed in basic elements of the body were parallel to the basic elements of the universe:

1. Air
2. Fire
3. Earth
4. Water

It is not known whether or not these concepts of the basic substances arose independently in each culture and faith or if they spread from one culture and faith by the efforts of missionaries or by the teachings of traveling "healers." The humoral theory of health and diet was spread through medieval Europe by monks of the Roman Catholic church. Rome in the 12th century forbade monks and canons of the Catholic church from practicing medicine for material gains (the medical lobby and union already was at work).

The concept of "humors" survived many centuries - phlegm from the brain (drippy nose, upper respiratory problems), wet and cold similar to the basic element of water; blood from the heart, wet and hot like air; yellow bile (choler) from the liver, hot and dry like fire; black bile from the spleen, dry and cold like the Earth.

An excess of yellow bile caused irritability and anger - thus the word "choleric." An excess of black bile brought on gloominess and depression ("melancholic"). An excess of phlegm produced sluggishness and apathy ("phlegmatic").

The Selerno Regimen for health were used by all and should still be used today:

"Use three physicians still:
First doctor quiet,
Next doctor merryman,
and then doctor Diet."

The New Testament noted that Paul fasted regularly, and that other ministers fasted just before they were ordained into the priesthood - fasts were usually entered into just before feats - to "temper the mind and spirit so the feasting would not become too barbaric." It would be three centuries before fasts of Easter were made official part of the Catholic church and several more centuries before the fasts of Lent and Easter Holy Week became the rule.

Then came the concept of personal fasting employed by the friars and nuns to "help cleanse the body, sharpen the mind and purify the spirit."

When Martin Luther separated from the Catholic church he reasoned there was no need to change the Christian tenets of diet - all food and drink in moderation and with thanksgiving, is good for humans.

Later Protestant faiths - the Anabaptists (Mennonites), the Puritons (Quakers) - featured simple diets (many forbade alcohol) with the basic concept that God made all things for the good of man.

Meat historically was forbidden to Catholics on Friday as that was the day that Christ was crucified, meat is still forbidden on Ash Wednesday and Good Friday and suggested abstinence during Lent.

Seventh-day Adventists, while meat is not actually forbidden, they are supposed to avoid it. Mormons (Latter-day Saints) are counseled to eat meat sparingly. Jehovah's Witnesses won't eat meat unless the blood has been drained.

Alcohol is forbidden to Adventists, Mormons, Jehovah's Witnesses and Christian Scientists. Drunkenness is forbidden in all Christian faiths.

Mary Baker Eddy, the founder of Christian Science, called drugs (i.e.- coffee, tea, opium, tobacco and alcohol) the "depraved appetite" (she hit the mark as it is the "depraved appetite" or pica, which leads people to addictions are the result of mineral deficiencies!!) and it was the "depraved appetite" or pica that ultimately destroyed the person.

No religious movement, ancient or modern placed more emphasis on diet and nutrition than the Seventh-day Adventist church. Ellen G. White, a missionary for the Adventist church instructed Adventists on the basic concepts of healthful living. She denounced the use of alcohol, addictive

Tues., Jan. 17, 1995   Rocky Mountain News

Obituaries

Local, national and international

Iran reports death of woman at 161

Rocky Mountain News wire services

Masoomeh Dousti, who was believed to be the world's oldest woman, died at her home in the Iranian village of Kalatenbala in Khorasan province.

The Iranian News Agency reported Monday that she was 161.

She is survived by six children between 120 and 128, the news agency said, plus 120 grandchildren and great-grandchildren.

Gholam, her eldest son, said his mother had never visited a doctor nor taken chemical medicines, except for herbal remedies.

drugs and smoking. She preached more than 90 years ago that tobacco is a "slow, insidious, but most malignant poison." she also lectured on a well-balanced diet, before the phrase was even invented; she emphasized fresh natural foods without preservatives, she rejected refined white flour and sugar before nutritional science even suspected the existence of the 90 essential nutrients - she was in fact a natural food enthusiast.

From the writings of Ellen G. White.
"Grains, fruit, nuts and vegetables constitute the diet chosen for us by our creator. These foods, prepared in as simple and natural a manner as possible, are the most healthful and nourishing. They impart a strength, a power of endurance, and a vigor of intellect, that are not afforded by a more complex and stimulating diet (1905).

In grains, fruit, vegetables and nuts are to be found all the food elements (90 nutrients) that we need, If we will come to the Lord in simplicity of mind, He will teach us how to prepare wholesome food free from the taint of flesh meat."

Today, Adventists follow the dietary instructions in Leviticus concerning clean and unclean food - pork is forbidden, as is shell fish and predators, they abstain from the use of alcohol, tobacco, coffee, tea and drugs (prescription and street drugs).

Ellen White became highly suspicious of doctors and their "careless and widespread use of poisonous drugs" (and for this we dearly love her!!).

At the Adventist Battle Creek Sanitarium the "true remedies" were pure air, sunlight, abstenciousness, rest,

exercise, proper diet, pure water and faith in the healing power of God. By 1903, when the church headquarters moved to Washington, D.C. the sanitarium was the largest and most completely equipped health facility in the world. It's medical director was Dr. John Harvey Kellogg, and it was he and his brother W.K. Kellogg, who gave the world prepared cereals - corn flakes!!!

The Seventh-day Adventist church has long been involved in the health-food industry and today the church operates no less than 15 health-food companies, the largest being Loma Linda Foods from Arlington, California.

The Adventist church operates 345 hospitals, sanitariums, clinics and dispensaries around the world - most offer nutrition classes that are open to the public. In 1905, when Ellen White was 78, she personally chose the site for Loma Linda University. This University was for years called the college of medical evangelists and includes one of the worlds leading medical schools, including schools of dentistry nursing, nutrition and allied health fields.

For their health efforts, the Adventists have been rewarded with some of the healthiest individuals in America - 77 years on the average for men and 80 years on the average for women (an average of 78.5 years compared to 75.5 for all Americans). The Adventist average age is similar to that of the Japanese but still only about 50% of the genetic potential for the human - 120 to 140 years.

MORMON

It is of interest that Utah which is 70

% Mormon, is the healthiest state in the Union. According to the CDC, Utah has the lowest death rate from all of the chronic degenerative diseases.

The Mormons have a simple law of diet and health called the Word of Wisdom. This law forbids the use of tobacco, alcohol, coffee and tea; and it advises that meat be consumed sparingly, it also gives instruction about what foods are best for man: fruits, vegetables and grains of all kinds.

In the U.S., approximately 130 people out of 100,000 die each year from cancer, in Utah only 95 per 100,000 die of cancer - 28% lower than the national rate.

According to the book of Mormon, Adam understood the basic truth that every man was free to make his own decision - he understood the consequences when he ate the fruit of the tree of knowledge of good and evil - "it was a food unfit for the perfect physical body God had formed as the temple of Adam's young spirit, and when he and Eve ate it, their bodies degenerated and eventually died."

In 1820, near the town of Manchester in New York state, Joseph Smith (a 14 year old boy) prayed asking God for guidance in choosing a religious faith and "God the Father and Jesus Christ appeared to him and told him not to become involved with any religion."

Joseph waited three years for the rest of the message, when finally the messenger appeared in the form of a man called Moroni. Moroni shared with Joseph the story of a historical record that had been accumulated and hidden by his father (a man called Mormon) before being killed by Indians.

Moroni told Joseph Smith where the record was hidden and how it could be translated. Today, the book of Mormon along with the Bible, is the basic set of scriptures for the Mormons.

Smith was killed by a mob in 1844, jut before the Mormons fled the city of Navoo, however, he had already compiled a book of his visions and revelations and this book was to be the Doctrine and Covenant of Mormon; and it is in the 89th Section of this book. The Word of Wisdom, that gives Mormons their basic rules on diet and health.

The complete Word of Wisdom was revealed on February 27, 1877, however, the question of meat-eating had come up in 1831 when a new member of the church, a vegetarian, started preaching his own views - Joseph Smith prayed to the Lord and was given the answer that, "Any man who forbids the use of meat is not ordained of God."

"For, behold, the beasts of the field and the fowls of the air, and that which cometh of the Earth, is ordained for the use of man for food and for rainment, and that he might have in abundance."

Doctrine and Covenants 49:18,19

Mormon dietary Taboos are for non-foods such as tobacco, alcohol and "hot drinks," translated to mean drinks containing harmful drugs, such as tea and coffee and, to some Mormons today, even cola drinks and chocolate. The rest is a positive statement about nutrition and the sensible use of foods in lean times:

"Every herb in its season and every fruit in its season to be used with prudence and thanksgiving.

Flesh of beasts and fowl to be used sparingly, and it is pleasing to me that they should not be used, only in times of winter, or cold, or famine. All grain is good for man and all plant food, whether in the ground or above the ground. Wheat for man, corn for the ox, oats for the horse, rye for fowls and swine, and barley for all useful animals and for mild drinks."

Doctrine and Covenants
Section 89

12. Yea, flesh also of beasts and of fowls of the air, I, the Lord, have ordained for the use of man with thanksgiving; nevertheless, they are to be used sparingly;

13. And it is pleasing unto me that they should not be used, only in times of winter, or of cold, or famine.

14. All grain is ordained for the use of man and of beasts, to be the staff of life, not only for man but for the beasts of the field, and the fowls of heaven, and all wild animals that run or creep on the earth:

15. And these hath God made for the use of man only in times of famine and excess of hunger.

16. All grain is good for the food of man; as also the fruit of the vine; that which yieldeth fruit, whether in the ground or above the ground.

17. Nevertheless, Wheat for man, and corn for the ox, and oats for the horse, and rye for the fowls and for swine, and for all beasts of the field, and barley for all useful animals, and for mild drinks, as all other grain.

American orthodox "health experts" are hopelessly out of touch with reality and pontificate in the news media how you can get everything you need from your diet and "taking vitamins and minerals just give you expensive urine" and that they themselves rely on their food and brag that they do not take supplements - as a result America is not calorie deficient but we are malnourished because of a lack of the 90 essential micro-nutrients.

America's great interest in food, fast food, fad foods, snack foods, fun foods, finger foods, desserts, caffeine, alcohol, drugs and cigarettes is a direct result of mineral malnutrition. The casual review of the longevities of the proponents of various dietary beliefs and health beliefs throughout the world brings a reality check!

If you look to the American medical system and or your allopathic physician for help with your personal nutrition program (diet) you are putting yourself in grave danger as their interests and expertise stops at the "four food groups," cholesterol testing and the martini at their high priced health club. We believe "the proof is in the pudding" and therefore it seems fair to examine how well orthodox doctors do themselves when it comes to avoiding nutritional diseases and deaths from preventable nutritional diseases. If they are doing all of the right nutritional things they should all live to be over 120!!

The first task in checking out the orthodox doctors was to look at their average age at death when compared to the general U.S. population (75.5) - an examination of the monthly obituaries listed in the Journal of the American Medical Association (JAMA) January of

Merits of a Mediterranean diet

Studying the nutritional and health benefits of regional cuisine

BOSTON — What's the best diet for good health? That subject sparks hot debates among nutrition experts.

But one cuisine that's worth considering is the traditional Mediterranean diet. The diet, which varied between regions, has lost some of its healthful advantages in recent years, but traditionally it included lots of fruits and vegetables, beans, bread, pasta, rice, grains. Olive oil was the main fat, and lean red meat was eaten only a few times a month. Fish and poultry, cheese and yogurt were also consumed in moderation.

Ditto for wine. To explore the nuances of the Mediterranean diet, more than 60 food and nutrition experts from around the world gathered here for a conference sponsored by the Harvard School of Public Health and the Oldways Preservation & Exchange Trust. Next year, experts will discuss the diets of Asia; in 1995, the diets of the Americas. USA TODAY talked to some of the key speakers about their diets.

Stories by Nanci Hellmich

Olive oil and exercise

Name: Dr. Walter Willett
Title: Chairman of the Department of Nutrition, Harvard School of Public Health. Heads the Nurses Health Study, an ongoing study of 121,700 female nurses.
Age: 47
What he eats: "I borrow on quite a few different cultures. I borrow on the Mediterranean the most. In our house we use nothing but olive oil at the table and in cooking. For breakfast, fresh fruits are hard to beat. Like

many people, I sometimes have bread or toast and cold breakfast cereal, which is an American tradition. For lunch, I pack a sandwich — lettuce, tomato with olive oil. Fruit. (He doesn't eat meat.)

"Like a lot of Americans, I try to cut down on calories because I sit at my desk most of the day. Actually, I like a really good Italian or Greek salad with bread and perhaps a little wine for dinner. Last night, I had roasted potatoes and red peppers in olive oil. And a little soup."

By Sue Owrutsky
WILLETT: Olive oil is the only fat he cooks with.

Exercise: "I ride my bike to work every day — 20 minutes each way. And I do the NordicTrack for 20 minutes a day."

Vitamin supplements: Vitamin E.

Nutrition insights: "We need a full re-examination of the options presented by many dietary patterns. The Mediterranean diet deserves serious consideration because people who live in that part of the world have low rates of virtually every disease (that people in this country die from). There is not a single one healthy type of diet. We might adapt aspects of the French diet, Mediterranean diet, Middle Eastern, Latin American diets. We ought to look seriously at all of them to find out what is healthy and to find an interesting, varied diet."

Wine in moderation

Name: Dr. Dimitrios Trichopoulos (who is from Greece)
Title: Chairman of the Department of Epidemiology, Harvard School of Public Health
Age: 54.
What he eats: "I try to eat vegetables, potatoes, bread, beans. I don't like meat much. I don't think anybody in public health can like meat anymore. We know so much about it. We reserve it for special occasions. Of course, I drink wine, plenty of it."

Exercise: "Personally, I don't exercise. But among the important things people can do easily is exercise and drink moderate quantities of wine when they're not driving."

Vitamin supplements: "I take them because I'm sure they can't harm, and I'm not sure my diet is adequate because I'm living alone. I take vitamin E and a multivitamin. But I wouldn't want to say that it's an established protective effect."

By Barbara Steiner
TRICHOPOULOS: He takes vitamins to be sure.

Nutrition insights: "The traditional Greek diet was heavily based on bread and grains and legumes (beans). More than 40% of the Greek diet comes from fat, which is mostly olive oil. Fat is so tasty. If you are going to have it, you'd better have olive oil. It has plenty of vitamin E in it, which many people believe has an important effect against cardiovascular disease.

"Wine drinking has been traditionally integrated with Greek diet. They'd drink wine during the meals, even during lunch time. They would not use strong spirits except rarely. They have a siesta after that. They have a relaxed attitude. One of the problems we have is we know that the Mediterranean diet is good but we don't know which component is the dominant one or if it's the whole pattern."

Fruits and vegetables help cut the fat

Name: Marion Nestle

Title: Chairman, Department of Nutrition, Food and Hotel Management, New York University

Age: 56

What she eats: "In general, I try to practice what I preach. It's not a vegetarian diet, but I try to eat most of my calories from fruits, vegetables and grains. I eat more than the recommended five (servings) a day of fruits and vegetables.

"On the other hand, I eat out a lot. There are often situations where it's very difficult to apply principles. A large part of my work and social life is going out to dinner. I will order vegetable plates. I will order pasta. I rarely order meat. And I'm rarely in a situation where I can't find something that I'm happy eating."

Exercise: "I have a mini-exercise program. I run around Washington Square Park every morning. It's probably a half

NESTLE: 'I eat huge amounts of vegetables.'

mile. It takes about 10 to 15 minutes. I live in New York, and I walk a lot. I'm blessed with genetics that I don't have a weight problem."

Vitamin supplements. "I don't take any vitamins. I eat huge amounts of vegetables."

Nutrition insights: "The basic dietary advice hasn't changed at all since we started on chronic disease prevention in the early 1970s. ... There are no changes in the core recommendations, which are that a greater part of calories should come from fruits, vegetables and grains. Meat and dairy products should be eaten in smaller amounts.

"The major source of fat (in people's diets) is from meat, dairy products and added fat. That means if you are going to cut down the amount of fat, you have to cut down on meat, dairy products and added fat. But that's a big change for a lot of people."

Conservative quantities of lean meat

Name: Ancel Keys

Title: Professor emeritus, University of Minnesota School of Public Health and author of *Seven Countries: A Multivariate Analysis of Death and Coronary Heart Disease*

Age: 88

What he eats: "After eating around the world (he and his wife, Margaret, have worked in 20 different countries) we've settled down to the Mediterranean diet. We eat meat not more than once a week. When we do, we have very lean meat and small quantities.

"When we buy meats we actually prefer veal, which is terribly expensive, chicken and fish. Fish is our favorite.

"We eat a lot of vegetables and, of course, pasta and rice. We have a green salad at lunch. At dinner, we have mostly cooked vegetables. When we get back to Italy next month (he lives there half the year), it will

KEYS: He eats meat 'not more than once a week.'

be the beginning of artichoke season. We eat peppers. We have wine for dinner."

Exercise: "Not very much now. I use a cane. I used to exercise quite a bit. The main thing I did was farming work, gardening, swimming, hiking."

Vitamin supplements: "No. This is the biggest racket you ever heard of. With the kind of diet I'm talking about, you don't need vitamins except for rare" cases.

Nutrition insights: "This cholesterol business isn't quite as important as we thought it was. The recommended levels of cholesterol in the blood depends somewhat on age — but the 180 to 230 range is perfectly OK. (Current guidelines say anything between 200 to 239 is borderline high.) We find that in every country, by far the greatest hazard to shortened life is cigarette smoking and high blood pressure."

All stories by Nanci Hellmich

Dr. Kenneth Cooper

▶ **Title:** Father of the aerobics movement, president and founder of Cooper Aerobics Center, Dallas

▶ **Vitamins:** Takes 1,000 milligrams of vitamin C; 400 international units of vitamin E; 25,000 I.U. (15 milligrams) of beta carotene; 1,000 milligrams of potassium-magnesium aspartate daily.

▶ **Comments:** ''I take vitamin E because research suggests it may keep LDL cholesterol from oxidizing and depositing on artery walls. Vitamin C enhances the beneficial effects of vitamin E. And there are no long-term side effects of taking these vitamins at these doses. As for other antioxidants like chromium and selenium, I don't think we have enough research about them yet to make recommendations.

"In my new book *(The Antioxidant Revolution,* out in late August from Thomas Nelson Publishers) I'm only concentrating on the three antioxidants that we have studied extensively — that is, vitamin C, vitamin E and beta carotene. We are getting a lot of new data about the value of antioxidants because of advanced technology.

"But just because you take supplements doesn't mean you can eliminate fruits and vegetables. There are many other beneficial substances in fruits and vegetables like fiber.

By David Sams

COOPER: He takes supplements because it's hard to eat all the vitamins you need.

But it's pretty hard to get all the vitamin C you need unless you eat nine servings of fruits and vegetables a day. You can probably get the beta carotene you need from three carrots a day. But it's hard to get the vitamin E. You'd have to eat so much food that you'd gain weight because vitamin E comes from foods that are high in fat (nuts, vegetable oils, wheat germ).

"I do take 1,000 milligrams potassium-magnesium aspartate daily but that's unique for me. I'm not recommending it for everyone. We did a study of marathon runners a few years ago and found a substantial reduction in the magnesium levels after completing a 26.2-mile run, probably due to excess sweating. I sweat profusely — living in Texas and running a lot — so I need to replace the magnesium and potassium, which also is lost through sweat. These supplemental minerals help to reduce muscle cramping."

About getting this level of vitamins in a healthy diet: "I think it's hard. I know yesterday I had two meals on an airplane. There is reduced food value in those TV-type dinners. They are overprocessed and overcooked. I'm not criticizing the airlines — they do the best they can. But you don't get optimum nutrition existing on food prepared in this manner. That is why I take supplements."

Jeffrey Blumberg

▶ **Title:** Chief of antioxidants research lab at the U.S. Department of Agriculture Human Research Center on Aging at Tufts University, Boston

▶ **Vitamins:** Takes a daily multivitamin/mineral supplement formulated with about 100% of the RDAs; plus 500 milligrams of vitamin C, 400 I.U. of vitamin E, 15 milligrams of beta carotene.

▶ **Comments:** "I take them for their potential preventive properties — to reduce the risk of chronic diseases like cancer and heart disease as I grow older. People shouldn't expect these things to give them more pep or grow hair on bald heads.

"In many respects it's naive of us to attribute a whole lot to individual nutrients. They work together in very complex interrelationship. They don't substitute well for each other. You can't say, 'I take a whole lot of vitamin E and so I

Atlantic Photo Service, Inc.
BLUMBERG: Takes vitamins to lower risk of chronic diseases later

don't have to take the others.'

"Nutrient supplements shouldn't be considered nutrient *substitutes*. You must still eat healthfully. And I do. I strive to eat at least five serv-

ings of fruits and vegetables a day. I've cut back on the amount of fat I eat, particularly red meat. I also drink a glass of wine every day.

"If you select your diet quite carefully and pick vitamin C-rich and beta carotene-rich foods, you can obtain levels defined for optimal health. But you can't do that with vitamin E. You'd have to consume the equivalent of two cups of vegetable oil a day.

"In fruits and vegetables, there are lots of carotenoids and other substances in plants that appear to have health-promoting, disease-fighting effects, and we don't know as much about them yet.

"The things I'm doing today may change in another five years as we get even more information. I may change the dosages. I may add some additional nutrients. I may change my diet further. What I do today is based on what I know today. I'm looking forward to the next generation of research information."

Dr. Robert Heaney

▶ **Title:** Calcium researcher at Creighton University, Omaha

▶ **Vitamins and comments:** "I do take vitamins. I take those that I calculate I can't get enough of in my diet. I don't normally get outdoors very much, and I don't get any vitamin D, which comes from sunlight. For that reason, I judged it prudent to be sure I get vitamin D. The only way to do that is take a multivitamin tablet. I probably don't need some of the things in it except that vitamin D.

"I'm naturally concerned with the antioxidants as well. I think the evidence there is fairly impressive, and for that reason I take 1,000 milligrams of vitamin C a day, and 800 I.U. of vitamin E a week.

"I don't take any calcium supplements, because I have a high calcium diet. I think it's always better to get your nutrients from food if you possibly can.

"One of things we've noted in our research subjects — several hundred of them — is women who are low on calcium are often low on other nutrients as well — an average of four other nutrients. It's not possible to fix that with a calcium pill. Women ought to have a high calcium diet. My own view is it would be better to have calcium-fortified foods."

HEANEY: Takes vitamin D to compensate for lack of sun

By David Scarbrough, AP
FOREYT: Takes no vitamins because he's 'not convinced that there's a need' with proper diet.

John Foreyt

▶ **Title:** Director of the nutrition research clinic, Baylor College of Medicine, Houston

▶ **Vitamins:** None.

▶ **Comments:** "My goal is to eat sensibly and exercise regularly. Beyond that I don't see any need for any supplementation. I've read all the (research) articles about supplements, and in my mind, I'm not convinced that there's a need for any of this stuff if you're a person who is leading a healthy lifestyle.

"They are expensive, and I think they are simply not necessary."

Dr. Joycelyn Elders

▶ **Title:** Surgeon General
▶ **Vitamins:** "I don't take vitamins."
▶ **Comments:** "I feel I don't need them. I feel most of our foods are well-fortified with vitamins.

"I try to eat a balanced diet, so I do not feel the need to take additional vitamins."

By Matt Mendelsohn, USA TODAY
ELDERS: Doesn't feel she needs additional vitamins

Sonja L. Connor

▶ **Title:** Co-author of *The New American Diet System* (Simon & Schuster, $14), and a research associate professor at Oregon Health Sciences University, Portland
▶ **Vitamins:** "I don't take vitamins."
▶ **Comments:** "I get the vitamins I need from what I eat. I've worked on changing my diet to lower fat and higher complex car-

CONNOR: Gets all the vitamins, nutrients she needs from her diet

bohydrates, and keeping the sugar down so that I'm getting a good supply of vitamins and minerals and particularly the antioxidants. And I don't smoke.

"I eat a huge variety in the vegetable arena. We eat spinach regularly, and sweet potatoes and squash that are loaded with antioxidants. The dark green and orange vegetables are more concentrated in the beta carotene and C. All the foods in the vegetable kingdom include some. By eating a big variety, you'll naturally get mixtures of them."

Dr. James H. Moller

▶ **Title:** President of the American Heart Association
▶ **Vitamins:** "I take 500 milligrams of vitamin C and 400 I.U. of vitamin E."
▶ **Comments:** "Last time I was in to have a checkup, I asked my doctor (an internist) if he was taking vitamins. He said he took them. But he didn't have a strong recommendation.

"From what I've read I've gotten the impression that it may be a benefit, and it seemed like there was not a lot of risk or complications from doing so.

"As far as the heart association is concerned, we haven't said anything about vitamins. It's something we need to study and to look at what the benefit is. I think we need more information before the American Heart Association would make a recommendation.

"Also, we (he and his wife) eat a pretty healthy diet — fresh fruits, vegetables and salad. And I think that is important."

MOLLER: He eats well but still takes supplements daily because 'it may be a benefit' with little risk.

Jane Fonda

▶ **Title:** Star of 18 fitness videos, author of several books

▶ **Vitamins:** Takes a multivitamin with antioxidants, 1,500 milligrams of calcium, 2,000 milligrams of vitamin C. Takes a maximum of 4,000 milligrams of vitamin C when she feels a cold coming on.

▶ **Comments:** From her book: *Jane Fonda's New Workout & Weight-Loss Program* (Simon & Schuster, $13): "Like many others, I've long advocated daily nutritional supplements as an insurance policy for obtaining at least 100% of the RDAs. Ideally, having a well-balanced diet is all most of us would ever need to ensure our getting the full range of vitamins and minerals. In fact, the food you eat is always the place to start. Food, your natural vitamin pill, should come first. No supplement can make up for poor or inadequate food choices. ...

FONDA: Has long advocated the use of daily nutritional supplements

"There is one nutrient in particular, however, which most women will find they need to supplement separately: the mineral calcium. Diets low in calcium are commonplace, I've learned. The average women consumes far less than the recommended daily allowance. In fact, the average calcium deficiency is associated with significant bone loss and is believe to be one of the major causes of bones thinning to the breaking point — the disease known as osteoporosis, the most common and greatest health threat to women in their later years."

1993 showed an astounding average life span of only 58 years (you can gain 20 years statistically by just not going to medical school!) when you look at all causes. Many people will quickly come to their doctors defense and say, "yes, they die early because of a high-stress profession."

According to one study by King, doctors and lawyers both have shorter life spans than teachers and clergymen of various faiths. Another study showed that there was a higher death rate amongst medical than for surgical specialists within the first 25 years after graduation. The excess of doctor death is ascribed to heart disease, stroke, diabetes and suicide.

Looking at the specific causes of death we find that doctors die of a disproportionately high rate of preventable nutritional deficiency diseases (Table 12-2). As a whole medical doctors refuse to take supplements of the essential 90 nutrients so the medical profession makes a great control group

Table 12-2. Causes of Death In American Allopathic Physicians.	
Cause of Death	**Nutritional Deficiency**
Cardiomyopathy	Selenium, Vitamin E, essential fatty acids
Coronary disease (including aneurysms & stroke)	Selenium, Vitamin E, vitamin C magnesium, copper, essential fatty acids
Cerebrovascular disease (including aneurysms & stroke)	Same as above
Aneurysms	Copper
Diabetes	Chromium, Vanadium, Zinc
Liver cirrhosis	Selenium, Copper, Sulfur
Cancer	Selenium, Tin, Zinc, Gallium, Vitamin E (all types), beta carotene, Germanium, Vitamin C
Suicide	Llithium, Chromium, Vanadium
Alzheimer's disease	Vitamin E, Selenium, Thiamine

1.   Clever,L. H. and Arsham, G. M.: Physicians' Own Health - Some Advice for the Advisors. In: Personal Health Maintenance (special issue). West. J. Med. 141:846.1984.

2.   Ullman,D. et al.: Cause-Specific Mortality Among Physicians With Differing Life-Styles. JAMA. 265:2352. May 8,1991.

for those of us who do supplement. The exceptions were the lactovegetarian Adventist physicians graduating from Loma Linda University who lived longer than other physicians and reaching the U.S. average of only 75.5 - this is because they do not drink alcohol or do drugs (Adventists did have a higher death rate from small plane and fast car accidents - wealthy California doctors can afford fast cars and their own planes).

In addition to examining learned material and great academic surveys published in medical journals we also began a hobby of collecting obituaries of doctors that appear in daily news papers to get a random street view of what is going on with individual flesh and blood doctors - this may sound morbid to some or even cruel, however, if they are going to pontificate on health and nutrition they put themselves under our scrutiny.

Clarence Darrow, the lawyer of the famous "Scopes Monkey trial" said it best when he stated,"I do not like to see anyone die, but there are some obituaries I have enjoyed reading." Darrow's feelings are identical to our own, and while we do not cry out for physician deaths, their published obituaries are public information and it would be such a shame to to let their failings go unannounced.

According to the Register General of England physicians had a higher death rate from intestinal disease than any other profession or trade (Table 12-3). Nutritional deficiencies that result in intestinal disease include niacin, thiamine, selenium, vitamin E, beta carotene, zinc, vitamin C, etc.

It is therefore obvious that we must depend on ourselves and the information we gather to prevent and treat nutritional diseases. We contract with no doctor or technician to keep us healthy and we only use our "health insurance benefits" when we screw up and believe we must go to a doctor of some kind (usually the best specialist money can buy if we have "good" insurance).

There are many sects of vegetarianism, usually they are very zealous in their beliefs and their efforts to convert meat-eaters to their way of life (There are few confrontations more energetic than a vegan trying to convert a meat-eater into "seeing the light.").

There are books by and about famous vegetarians (i.e.- Isaac Bashevis Singer, Cloris Leachman, Dick Gregory, Dr. Gordon Lotto, Swami Satchidananda, Dr. Alan Long, Marty Feldman, Muriel, the Lady Dowding, Dennis Weaver, Brigid Brophy, Malcolm Muggeridge, Susan

Table 12-3. Deaths From Intestinal Diseases By Profession or Trade	
Profession/Trade	Percent of Deaths
Physicians and Surgeons	50
Inn keepers	45
Lawyers	44
Merchant seamen	43
Clergymen	34
Butchers	30
Common carriers	28
Farmers	25
Gardeners	22
Railway guards and porters	20
Agricultural laborers	19

Obituary Listing

AKBARI, Asadolah, 49; Las Cruces, NM; *Pahlavi Medical School, University of Teheran,* Tehran, Iran, 1968; certified by the American Board of Radiology; died June 26, 1992.

ARMENTROUT, John Patrick, 45; Olympia, Wash; *University of Utah School of Medicine,* 1975; certified by the American Board of Family Practice; died May 19, 1992

BALLANTINE, Jerome J., 60, ⊛ St Cloud, Minn; *Indiana University School of Medicine,* 1956; certified by the American Board of Internal Medicine; died May 9, 1992.

BARAK, Stuart, 62; Southfield, Mich; *Wayne State University School of Medicine,* 1954; certified by the American Board of Surgery; died May 5, 1992.

BARWICK, William James, 47, ⊛ Durham, NC; *University of Tennessee College of Medicine,* 1971; certified by the American Board of Surgery and the American Board of Plastic Surgery; died May 30, 1992.

BRENTJENS, Jan R., 55; Buffalo, NY; *Faculteit der Geneeskunde, Rijksuniversiteit te Leiden,* the Netherlands, 1964; died August 8, 1992.

BRONSON, William E., Jr, 55; Columbus, Ohio; *Ohio State University College of Medicine,* 1962; died June 21, 1992.

BUCHBINDER, Mandel, 60; Woodland Hills, Calif; *University of Illinois College of Medicine,* 1958; certified by the American Board of Internal Medicine; died August 20, 1992.

CARANGI, Robert Lawrence, 54; Woodland Hills, Calif; *State University of New York at Syracuse School of Medicine,* 1967; certified by the American Board of Radiology; died August 21, 1992.

CARSON, John Douglas, 64; Longmont, Colo; *University of Nebraska College of Medicine,* 1952; certified by the American Board of Obstetrics and Gynecology; died November 7, 1991.

EDWARDS, David L., Sr, 85, ⊛ Tulsa, Okla; *Northwestern University Medical School,* 1932; certified by the American Board of Ophthalmology; died June 23, 1992.

FAUST, Howard Macy, 60; Anderson, Ind; *Indiana University School of Medicine,* 1957; died August 14, 1992.

⊛ Indicates member of the American Medical Association.
Obituary listing compiled by the Department of Physician Biographic Records.

FIDUCIA, Joseph Paul, 55; Middlefield, Conn; *Faculty of Medicine, The Queen's University of Belfast,* Ireland, 1965; certified by the American Board of Obstetrics and Gynecology; died August 10, 1992.

FRANK, Sumner, 63; Boston, Mass; *University of Louisville School of Medicine,* 1958; died January 28, 1992.

FRANKLIN, David Allan, 33, ⊛ Houston, Tex; *Baylor College of Medicine,* 1985; died August 6, 1992.

GALLAGHER, Philip George, 62; Chestnut Hill, Mass; *Tufts University School of Medicine,* 1955; certified by the American Board of Surgery; died April 7, 1992.

HAYWOOD, John Gerry, 63; Noblesville, Ind; *Indiana University School of Medicine,* 1954; died August 16, 1992.

HITZELBERGER, Anton L., 64, ⊛ Columbus, Ga; *Medizinische Fakultät, Albert-Ludwigs-Universität Freiburgim Breisgau,* Badem-Wurttemberg, Germany, 1953; died May 19, 1992.

HYLAND, Joseph Michael, 47, ⊛ Topeka, Kan; *National University of Ireland,* Dublin, 1968; certified by the American Board of Psychiatry and Neurology; died September 13, 1992.

KEARNS, Edward Eugene, 64; Houston, Tex; *Baylor College of Medicine,* 1953; died June 12, 1992.

KEITH, Thomas Arbuthnot, 64, ⊛ Cincinnati, Ohio; *University of Cincinnati College of Medicine,* 1955; certified by the American Board of Internal Medicine; died May 24, 1992.

KELLAM, Donald Swift, 60, ⊛ Charlotte, NC; *George Washington University School of Medicine and Health Sciences,* 1955; certified by the American Board of Orthopaedic Surgery; died May 15, 1992.

KOCH, Leonard Irving, 60, ⊛ Lubbock, Tex; *University of Texas Medical Branch at Galveston,* 1956; certified by the American Board of Plastic Surgery; died June 25, 1992.

KRUPKA, Miles Albert, 43; Berwyn, Ill; *University of Illinois College of Medicine,* 1975; died January 28, 1992.

LEVENSTEIN, Pamela C., 41; Boca Raton, Fla; *Tulane University School of Medicine,* 1977; died June 4, 1992.

LOTT, John Drew, 57; Roseburg, Ore; *Loma Linda University School of Medicine,* 1959; died October 24, 1991.

MAISEL, Stanley D., 35; Hallandale, Fla; *University of Health Sciences, College of Osteopathic Medicine,* 1982; certified by the American Board of Family Practice; died February 21, 1990.

MANTEL, Fred, 52; Bloomfield, Conn; *New York University School of Medicine,* 1964; certified by the American Board of Surgery and the American Board of Colon and Rectal Surgery; died January 2, 1992.

McDONALD, George, 65; New York, NY; *New York Medical College,* 1955; certified by the American Board of Ophthalmology; died July 24, 1992.

McKEE Thomas Preston, 84, ⊛ Johnson City, Tenn; *University of Virginia School of Medicine,* 1931; certified by the American Board of Ophthalmology and the American Board of Otolaryngology; died June 22, 1992.

MIRZAI, Mahmood, 62, ⊛ Wailuku, Hawaii; *Pahlavi Medical School, University of Teheran,* Tehran, Iran, 1955; died December 2, 1991.

NANNI, Gregg Scott, 38; Bradenton, Fla; *University of Virginia School of Medicine,* 1980; certified by the American Board of Radiology; died March 18, 1992.

PATEL, Babu S., 56; W Long Branch, NJ; *B.J. Medical College, Gujarat University,* Ahmedabad, India, 1961; certified by the American Board of Anesthesiology; died April 4, 1992.

PLEWES, John Lawrence, 45, ⊛ Oklahoma City, Okla; *Queens University, Faculty of Medicine,* Kingston, Ontario, 1970; certified by the American Board of Anesthesiology; died June 21, 1992.

POGGI, Joseph Thomas, Jr, 55, ⊛ Scottsdale, Ariz; *University of Illinois College of Medicine,* 1961; certified by the American Board of Obstetrics and Gynecology; died July 3, 1992.

PRINE, John Milton, 64; Arlington, Tex; *University of Texas Medical Branch at Galveston,* 1952; died May 5, 1992.

PRITCHETT, John H., Jr, 72, ⊛ Bremen, Ga; *Vanderbilt University School of Medicine,* 1943; died May 26, 1992.

SCHISGALL, Richard M., 59; Potomac, Md; *New York University School of Medicine,* 1957; certified by the American Board of Surgery; died April 20, 1991.

SEAGLE, Lee Marcus, 59, ⊛ Hickory, NC; *Duke University School of Medicine,* 1957; died May 22, 1992.

SMITH, Betty Lou McGinnis, 55; Ellenboro, NC; *Tulane University School of Medicine,* 1973; died May 7, 1992.

Dr. Theodore Paletta; Creve Coeur Cardiologist

Dr. Theodore L. Paletta, a cardiologist here, died Saturday (Sept. 18, 1993) at Missouri Baptist Hospital of a cerebral hemorrhage. He was 56.

Dr. Paletta, of Creve Coeur, was born in Arnold, Pa. He graduated from the University of Pittsburgh and got his medical degree from the University of Cincinnati Medical School.

While serving in the Army as chief of medicine and cardiology at an Army hospital in Vietnam, he was the first physician to implant a pacemaker there and the first to organize a cardiac intensive care unit. He was honored by the Chinese and Vietnamese governments for his efforts.

He was in private practice in the St. Louis area since the early 1970s. He was on staff at Missouri Baptist Hospital, St. Louis University Hospital, St. Joseph's Hospital of Kirkwood, St. Mary's Health Center and DePaul Health Center. He was a clinical instructor of cardiology at St. Louis University.

He was a member of numerous medical organizations and a past vice president and counselor of both the

Paletta

Missouri State Medical Association and the St. Louis Metropolitan Medical Society.

He was the recipient of the Physician's Recognition Award from the American Medical Association in 1988 and in 1991.

A funeral Mass will be celebrated at 11 a.m. Tuesday at St. Monica Catholic Church, 12136 Olive Boulevard, Creve Coeur. Visitation will be from 3 to 9 p.m. Monday at Kreigshauser Mortuary-West, 9450 Olive Boulevard, Olivette. The body will be entombed in Calvary Mausoelum.

Among the survivors are his mother, Josephine Cappone Paletta of Creve Coeur; a sister, Mary Ann L. Paletta of Creve Coeur; and two brothers, Drs. Frank L. Paletta and Victor L. Paletta, both of Creve Coeur.

Memorial contributions may be made to the American Heart Association.

Dr. Stanley B. Lyss, 57; Clayton Pediatrician

Dr. Stanley B. Lyss, a pediatrician and community leader, died Friday (Sept. 17, 1993) at St. Mary's Health Center in Richmond Heights after a heart attack. He was 57.

Dr. Lyss, of Clayton, was in private practice and on the staff of St. Louis Children's Hospital for the last 26 years. From 1981 to 1983, he was president of the medical staff at the hospital. He also was also on the staffs at Barnes and Jewish hospitals and St. John's Mercy Medical Center.

He served on many community boards and committees, including the Clayton School Board, the Clayton Task Force on Drug Abuse and the Good Shepard School for Children.

He was also a consultant and adviser to several community groups and a member of many national, state and local professional groups.

He was vice president of the Shaare Emeth Congregation and a past chairman of several committees there.

He got the Jewish Federation of St. Louis Leadership Award in 1974 and was selected with the Best Doctors in America in 1975 and in 1980.

Lyss

Dr. Lyss was born in Clayton and graduated from Clayton High School. He earned his bachelor's degree from Harvard University and his medical degree from Washington University School of Medicine, where he was an assistant professor of clinical pediatrics.

A funeral service will be at 2:30 p.m. Sunday at Shaare Emeth Temple, 11645 Ladue Road, Creve Coeur. Burial will be in Beth Hamedrosh Hagodol Cemetery.

Among the survivors are his wife of 32 years, Esther Bryan Lyss; three daughters, Sherly Lyss, Julie Lyss and Pamela Lyss, all of Clayton; and two brothers, Ronald Lyss of Creve Coeur and Dr. Carl Lyss of Clayton.

Instead of flowers, memorial contributions may be made to the Stanley B. Lyss Adult Education Fund in care of Shaare Emeth Congregation, 11645 Ladue Road, St. Louis, Mo., 63141 or to the St. Louis Children's Hospital.

Sister Ann Manganaro, 46; Pediatrician

Sister Ann Manganaro, a nun and pediatrician from Webster Groves who worked in El Salvador, died Sunday (June 6, 1993) at her mother's home in Webster Groves after suffering from breast cancer. She was 46.

Sister Manganaro began working with Jesuit Relief Services in January 1988 in El Salvador. She served in the neighboring villages of Guarjila and Los Ranchos, in the northern province of Chalatenango.

While in El Salvador, Sister Manganaro operated a clinic in Guarjila and started a program that trained health-care workers.

She joined the Sisters of Loretto in 1964 and took her final vows in December 1976.

Sister Manganaro was a graduate of Nerinx Hall High School and Webster College, now Webster University. She graduated with honors from St. Louis University School of Medicine. She worked in the emergency room at Cardinal Glennon Children's Hospital for several years before going to El Salvador. Sister Manganaro also taught at St. Louis University for a short time.

While still in St. Louis, Sister Manganaro founded The Neighborhood School in the Skinker-DeBaliviere area, and in 1977, was among the founders of the St. Louis Catholic

Manganaro

Workers Community.

She also taught at the old Rock Community School here and at New City School in the Central West End.

A funeral Mass will be celebrated at 1 p.m. Wednesday at Holy Redeemer Catholic Church, 17 Joy Avenue in Webster Groves. Visitation will be from 3 p.m. to 9 p.m. Tuesday at the Loretto Center on the Nerinx Hall campus, 590 East Lockwood Avenue in Webster Groves. She donated her body to science.

Among survivors are her mother, Mildred Manganaro of Webster Groves; five sisters, Mary Manganaro of St. Louis, Kathy Richey and Teresa Norman, both of Webster Groves, Eileen George of Chicago, and Lisa Manganaro of Clayton; and three brothers, John Manganaro of St. Louis, Frank Manganaro of Webster Groves, and Bill Manganaro of Evergreen, Colo.

Memorial contributions may be made to the Sisters of Loretto El Salvador Fund, 590 East Lockwood Avenue, Webster Groves, Mo., 63119-3279.

ST. LOUIS POST-DISPATCH

OBITUARIES

Dr. Kenneth Hirsch Solomon; Psychiatrist, Author, Musician

Dr. Kenneth Hirsch Solomon, a geriatric psychiatrist, author and musician, died Tuesday (April 12, 1994) at St. Luke's Hospital in west St. Louis County after a brief illness.

He was 46 and lived in Creve Coeur.

Dr. Solomon was an associate professor of psychiatry in geriatric psychiatry at St. Louis University School of Medicine since 1989. He was also an associate professor in the school's department of internal medicine since last year.

He wrote three books, including one of poetry. Dr. Solomon also was the author or co-author of nearly 80 professional papers and articles.

He gave more than 500 lectures in the United States, Canada and Brazil.

He was an accomplished jazz and classical pianist. He performed with noted jazz musician Jack DeJohnette and played backup for Natalie Cole and for the Ink Spots.

Dr. Solomon was born in Brooklyn, N.Y. He earned a bachelor's degree in history in 1967 from New York University and his medical degree in 1971 from the State University of New York at Buffalo.

A funeral service was held Thursday at Berger Memorial, 4715 McPherson Avenue. Another funeral service will be held at 11 a.m. today at Levison Brothers Funeral Home in Baltimore. Burial will be in Baltimore.

Among survivors are his wife, Dr. Barbara W. Brown; a daughter, Lori Funderburk of Vanceboro, N.C.; a son, David Karl Solomon of Columbia, Mo.; his parents, Estelle Reitman of Patchogue, N.Y., and Solomon Solomon of Fort Lauderdale, Fla.; and a sister, Susanne Policano of Middleton, Wis.

Memorial contributions may be made to the Traditional Congregation of Creve Coeur, 12437 Ladue Road, St. Louis, Mo., 63141.

Robert L. Krigel, 44, Physician; Led Hospital Residents' Protest

By WOLFGANG SAXON

Dr. Robert Lowell Krigel, a cancer specialist who led a 1979 campaign in New York City to relieve the grinding work schedules of hospital interns and residents, died on Sunday at his home in Elkins Park, Pa. He was 44.

The cause was angiosarcoma of the liver, a rare cancerous tumor, the Fox Chase Cancer Center in Philadelphia reported. Dr. Krigel (pronounced KREE-ghel) was director of hematology at Fox Chase from 1984 until last year.

He specialized in cancers of the blood and immune system. At his death, he was chief of hematology and oncology as well as director of the cancer program at Lankenau Hospital in suburban Wynnewood, Pa., while continuing to work as a researcher and consultant for Fox Chase.

A native of Kansas City, Mo., Dr. Krigel was a high school wrestling star and graduated from the University of Pennsylvania in 1971. He received his medical degree from Mount Sinai School of Medicine in New York and trained in internal medicine at the State University of New York Downstate Medical Center in Brooklyn, where he served as chief resident, and at Kings County Medical Center.

It was at Kings County, in January 1979, that he doffed his white coat and stethoscope, put on a blue parka and, armed with a bullhorn, led some 100 interns and residents in a one-day protest outside. The protest, which received widespread attention, was staged to criticize a cut in financing and to seek a reduced work week, which often reached 80 to 96 hours.

The protesters returned to the hospital as needed, but their picketing had no immediate effect. Only through legislative action a few years ago were the work schedules lightened because of evidence that the wearying hours could affect a young doctor's judgment.

Dr. Krigel went on to train in hematology and oncology at the New York University Medical Center, where he played a role in the clinical management of AIDS and AIDS-related cancers. He was among the first doctors to treat AIDS patients with chemo-

The New York Times, 1979

Dr. Robert Lowell Krigel

therapy and biological agents known as interferons.

Dr. Krigel is survived by his wife, Dr. D. Bonnie Perlmutter; their children, Jonathan, 11, and Anna, 7; his parents, Melvin and Selvi, of Kansas City, and two brothers, Michael, of Sunnyvale, Calif., and Barry, of Shawnee Mission, Kan.

THURSDAY, JULY 29, 1993

Dr. Gail L. Clark, 47; Was Cardiologist

Dr. Gail L. Clark, a cardiologist and head of the cardiac rehabilitation program at St. Luke's Hospital in west St. Louis County, died Monday (July 26, 1993) at St. Mary's Health Center in Richmond Heights after suffering a heart attack. She was 47.

Dr. Clark lived in University City.

She was a native of Rochester, N.Y. She began her medical career as a nurse in the coronary care unit at Barnes Hospital, which opened in 1969. She then enrolled at St. Louis University Medical School and graduated in 1974.

"She was highly respected as a cardiologist and a leader in the field of stress medicine as it relates to heart disease," said Dr. Robert Paine, cardiologist and clinical professor at Washington University School of Medicine.

Dr. Clark was a member of the St. Louis Society of Internal Medicine.

Clark

A funeral Mass will be held at 10 a.m. Friday at Our Lady of Lourdes Church, 7148 Forsyth Boulevard. Burial will follow at Resurrection Cemetery in Affton. No visitation will be held.

Among survivors are her husband, Kenneth W. Clark, two daughters, Sara E. Clark and Emily J. Clark, and two sons, Scott W. Clark and Christopher R. Clark, all of University City; her mother, Elizabeth D. Bommele of Rochester; two sisters, Ethel McCormack of Norfolk, Va., and Connie Campisi of Rochester; and two brothers, Gary Lergner of Southern Pines, N.C., and Robert Bommele of Rochester.

THE DENVER POST

OBITUARIES

■ **AUTHOR Dr. Stuart Berger,** a writer of best-selling diet and health books, died Feb. 23 at his New York City home. He was 40.

The New York City medical examiner's office said the cause of death had not been determined.

Berger wrote several books in which he advocated healing and dieting techniques based on nutrition and improving the strength of the body's immune system. He contended that his programs would result in increased longevity and promised a long life to patients who followed his advice.

"Dr. Berger's Immune Power Diet," a No. 1 best-seller in the advice category, described how Berger, who was 6 feet, 7½ inches tall, reduced his weight to 210 pounds from 420. At the time of his death, his weight was 365 pounds, a preliminary autopsy report said.

Berger, who was known for the Southampton Diet, also wrote "Forever Young — 20 Years Younger in 20 Weeks" and "How to be Your Own Nutritionist."

THE NEW YORK TIMES **OBITUARIES**

Dr. Steven R. Kohn
Professor, 51

Dr. Steven R. Kohn, professor of dermatology at the Yale University School of Medicine, died on March 23 at his home in Guilford, Conn. He was 51.

The cause was cardiac arrest, said a brother, Donald.

Dr. Kohn joined the Yale faculty four years ago after serving on the staffs of the Columbia University College of Physicians and Surgeons and the Hackensack Medical Center. He was a graduate of Rutgers University and the Boston University School of Medicine.

He is survived by his mother, Adele Kohn of Fort Lee, N.J., and two brothers, Dr. Donald Kohn and James Kohn, both of Guilford.

Saint-James, Helen and Scott Nearing, Frances Moore Lappe, and Ellen Buchman Ewald) which do an extremely good job of cataloging emotional, pollution (i.e.- antibiotics and hormones), and geopolitical (i.e.-population vs. food efficiency) reasons for being an "enlightened vegan," they do an excellent job of instructing apprentice vegans and various sects of vegetarianism on how to mix colors ("generally, don't eat anything brown or white and only eat foods that are colorful: purple, red, orange, yellow, green - a vibrant artists palette, so that they picture for you and your own palette something mouth watering. The only exceptions would be brown rice, grains, potatoes with the skins on." - Cloris Leachman); how to mix grains and how to mix grain and bean recipes properly to assure the proper intake of a complete protein (essential amino acids); however, when one looks in the index for a discussion of vitamins and minerals the program begins to acquire holes.

One can theoretically (if you eat 15 to 25 separate grains, vegetables, fruits and nuts each day) get all of the calories, essential amino acids, vitamins, essential fatty acids they require from a well thought out vegetarian diet, that is if the proper amino acids are eaten together in the right proportions. There is no need to fear that vegetable protein might be inferior. Protein is protein and amino acids are amino acids whether they occur in roast beef or mung beens. It is important for the vegetarian to include foods from the four main food categories for "complete" protein: grains, legumes, seeds and dairy products." - Ellen Buchman Ewald) using vegetables, whole grains, legumes, nuts and fruit; however,

in these terrible days of pollution and stress I would not risk my life on what I can theoretically get from my food any more than I would put dirt from the Texas "oil patch" in my car's oil pan and "hope" there is oil in it-we supplement with several times the American RDA of each of the vitamins, if we are going to do stressful things either physically or emotionally or if we are going to eat a high carbohydrate diet on a particular day we may take in 100 times the RDA of B-complex vitamins. Minerals are another story and one cannot depend on getting minerals from grains, vegetables, fruits and nuts - one must without fail supplement with all 60 minerals - plants cannot manufacture minerals, the soils are depleted of minerals; we cannot be healthy, be creative and productive or fulfill our genetic potential for longevity without minerals!!!.

The various versions of the "vegetarian" diet (Table 12-4) and macrobiotic diets are impractical as a life long dietary program for 95% of Americans because of the time required to do a good job of re-education, food procurement and preparation. Additionally, the American farm and range soils are so depleted of minerals (U.S. Senate Document 264 and the 1992 Earth Summit Report) that these diets must be heavily supplemented with plant derived colloidal minerals to prevent serious mineral deficiencies and their resultant symptoms, debilitating diseases and even death - even an updated macrobiotic diet contains fish for extended participation such as practiced by cancer patients.

Juicing is one of the greatest ways I know of to get fresh and natural sources

Table 12-4. Basic Types of Human Dietary Philosophies.	
Diet	**Description**
Vegan	100% maintenance on grains, vege- tables, fruits and nuts.
Ovovegetarian	add eggs to vegan diet
Lactovegetarian	add dairy to vegan diet
Ovolactovegetarian	add eggs & dairy to vegan diet
"Vegetarian"	add poultry, fish eggs and dairy to (in fact an omnivore diet) vegan diet
Omnivore	consumes all known food types
Carnivore	Consumes primarily animal products (i.e.- meat, organ meats, eggs, dairy,etc.)

of beta carotene, vitamin C, folic acid and some of the B-complex vitamins (not B_{12}), however, juicing will not provide a warrantied spectrum of all 60 essential minerals or sufficient amounts of each mineral. After seven years of being associated with Mexican cancer hospitals we can say with great accuracy that almost all patients (other than the Amish) were on some form of vegetarian and or juicing program long before they contracted cancer.

Vegans are people who consume absolutely no animal products; unsupplemented vegans are in a life threatening danger zone as they are totally dependent on plants for their sources of minerals, vitamins, protein, carbohydrates and essential fatty acids. Plants as a group can take CO_2 from the air and manufacture vitamins, proteins, essential fatty acids and carbohydrates as these food essentials are basically carbon chains (molecules of carbons strung together in various configurations to form specific essential compounds). Unfortunately plants can't manufacture minerals and this is where vegans enter the life threatening zone of mineral deficiencies (i.e. cancer, cardiomyopathy, aneurysms, Alzheimer's Disease, etc.).

The ovovegetarian, lactovegetarian and ovolactovegetarian diets are more complete than the vegan diet from the standpoint of access to more usable and complete forms of protein and more minerals as animal products contain much higher levels of major minerals, trace minerals and Rare Earths than do plants.

The omnivore diet covers all kinds of mixed diet types and ethnic diets that include various combinations of fish, poultry, lean red meat, as well as grains, vegetables, nuts and fruit; these broad spectrum ethnic diets are the most practical from the standpoint of time and accessibility as well as the most likely human dietary practices that contain the maximum levels of nutrition from non-supplemented food combinations.

The diets consumed by the "Age-beaters" (i.e.- Tibetans, Hunzas, Russian Georgians, Armenians, Azerbaijanies, Abkhazians, Turks, Vilcabambas and Titicacas) are in fact omnivore diets heavily supplemented with colloidal minerals from "Glacial Milk" (drinking and irrigation thus into their crops). The omnivore diet is the most complete universal survival program that nature can provide; however, even un-supplemented omnivore diets fall far short for providing optimal amounts of essential nutrients required for all of the basic processes of life and for the 90 essential nutrients needed to reach the age of 100 because of soil depletion - no minerals in the soil therefore no minerals in our grains, vegetables, nuts and fruits.

Carnivore diets consumed by the traditional Eskimo societies above the Arctic Circle are adequate sources of most nutrients as the animals they eat "harvest" the basic nutrients from the sea or the tundra. Although the Eskimo diet is comprised 90% of meat (i.e.- whale meat, whale blubber, walrus meat, walrus blubber, reindeer meat, fish, etc.) and bone, they do not have heart disease, cholesterol problems or strokes. The salmon and other cold water fish in their diet provide rich sources of the essential fatty acids required by the liver to properly process cholesterol and prevent platelet clumping.

Eating organ meats such as liver and kidney can significantly increase the availability of selenium, sulfur, cobalt, molybdenum and zinc, but again an exclusive meat diet excludes suitable levels of calcium, magnesium and manganese, etc. resulting in typical disease pictures for pure carnivores (i.e.- short stature, arthritis, osteoporosis, tooth loss, "Repetitive Motion Syndrome," aneurysms, skin wrinkles, etc.).

After 30 years of frustrating crusades trying to get vegans to eat fish and eggs and carnivores to eat more vegetables, we came to the realization that we could not change significant numbers of zealots from any dietary or nutritional camp or philosophy to the middle ground so we decided to find a universal concept that would be acceptable to all and at the same time accomplish the purpose of optimal individual nutrition that would get maximal numbers of people through the hoops necessary to fulfill their genetic potential for longevity (120 to 140 years).

At first, we tried to formulate and calculate dietary programs for each nutritional cult, sect, fad and concept, but quickly realized that by it's very nature trying to provide optimal nutrition through unsupplemented diets to any and all groups was faulty and reckless. We realized we couldn't change truck drivers and farmers from steaks and chops to organically grown broccoli any more than we could convert cats to vegetarianism, and by the same token we couldn't change yuppies from bran muffins, yogurt and expresso to eggs soft scrambled in butter and hot cakes for breakfast any more than we could convert horses to eating red meat. And lastly try to get Americans to go on a 1,200 to 1,800 calorie a day "under-nutrition" program - that's as difficult as trying to get Americans to join the Russian army!!!

Even if we had been successful in putting together a collection of such diets the wide spread education and marketing challenges of such programs necessary to get them to the "guy on the street" was an economic horror and an energy sink far beyond our capabilities - after all the American government's "best efforts" with unlimited resources (our resources) was an abysmal failure (for $7 million they came up with the 6 food group pyramid!!!).

It quickly became apparent that the only hope for being universally successful in our goal to help the average American to surpass the current longevity average of 75.5 and live to be over 100 was to employ the financially successful and result orientated methods used by the veterinary and agricultural industries - preventive herd health programs. The plan was coming together!!

No matter who they were, we wanted people to be able to see food and eat it with out having to count calories, consider RDA's, become a sociopath and "food combine" (the Diamond's Fit for Life Diets) or to spend their lives shopping for special foods - so we decided to let people eat whatever they wanted - what a concept! See food and eat it ("Chicken in a fish place! I love this country!!")! The See-Food Diet was born!!!

The first task was to focus our culinary effort towards eliminating the negative aspects of human eating habits without tampering with anyone's religious or conceptual choices of dietary needs or goals or their perception of just plain fun foods (i.e.- pizza, tacos, hot dogs, burgers -especially burgers - they're Dr. Wallach's favorite!!!). So we decided to first eliminate free radicals.

To accomplish the universal elimination of free radicals we came up with a simple short list:

- No deep fried food (heated poly-unsaturated oils are killers - they have killed more Americans than all of our military losses from all of our past wars)
- No vegetable oils (no, not even extra virgin olive oil or frozen desserts!)
- No salad dressings (use lemon juice & spices or vinegar & spices)
- No margarine (use butter, ghee, mutton fat or water for cooking)

It may take awhile to wean off of salad dressing so use an old trick to help yourself - put salad dressing in a side cup and dip your fork into it before getting a forkful of salad - not only will you cut calories but you will have started eliminating free radicals (trans fatty acids).

The next step in the See-Food Diet program is to eliminate sugar, natural and processed (sugar loads increase the normal rate of mineral loss in sweat and urine by 300 % for 12 hours - so if you have honey on your English muffin for breakfast, ice cream for dessert at lunch and a pastry for dinner dessert, no amount of mineral supplementation or no diet will ever allow you to keep up with or make up for your mineral losses).

Not only will you shed unwanted pounds by giving up sugar, but your thinking will be clearer, you will be less irritable and if you have hypoglycemia you will be half way home towards fixing your problem! :

- No apple juice (the raw fruit is alright)
- No grape juice
- No honey
- No molasses

- No table sugar (its better to use the "blue stuff" or learn to like the taste of herbal teas and decaffeinated coffees black)
- No corn syrup
- No fructose
- No candy (yep - no chocolate!!)
- No colas or soft drinks (water, herbal tea, decaf coffee and juice)
- No ice cream
- No pastries
- No boxed or bagged cereals

If during the process of giving up sugar you get the "munchies" or feel the need to go on the classic "chocoholic" binge take 1oz. of plant derived colloidal minerals per 100 pounds of body weight in 4 to 6 oz. of Calcium Enriched Minute Maid orange juice - even if it's ten times a day at the start (remember - cravings or pica are the sure sign of mineral deficiencies!!).

Lastly the unifying aspect of the See-Food Diet is to supplement with all 90 nutrients (Table 12-5 to 12-8) to warranty your optimal daily intake - don't depend on food to be your source of micro-nutrients - don't throw away significant healthful years (up to 140) like you would junk mail - think of the investment you already have in your physical body:

- You can be a member of any religion and supplement with the 90 essential nutrients.
- You can be a vegan and supplement with the 90 essential nutrients.
- You can be a meat-eater and supplement with the 90 essential nutrients.
- You can juice and supplement with the 90 essential nutrients.
- You can follow just about any dietary program you want if you supplement with the 90 essential nutrients and give up vegetable oils and sugar. To be sure there are certain adjustments you must make (i.e.- if your going to eat a 72 oz. steak you need to take in additional Ca, if your a vegan you need to be aware of phytates and take your minerals in between meals to maximize their absorption, double check B_{12} sources, etc.).

You can even "cheat" on the See-Food Diet once or twice a month or on special occasions (i.e.- holidays, birthdays, weddings, etc.) because your reserves of protective minerals will be filled to capacity and protect you from your occasional dietary sins!!

"At best, the RDAs are only a recommended allowance at antediluvian levels designed to prevent some terrible disease. At worst, they are based on conflicts of interest and self-serving views of certain positions of the food industry. Almost never are they provided at levels for optimum health and nutrition."

- Senator Wm. Proxmire
Let's Live, 1974

1. Eaton, S.B. et al.: The Paleolithic Prescription: A Program of Diet & Exercise and A Design For Living. Harper & Row, Publishers. New York. Cam-bridge. 1988.

2. Galdston, I. (ed): Human Nutrition: Historic and Scientific. The New York Academy of Medicine. International Universities Press, Inc. New York. 1960.

3. Cook, J.: Diet and Your Religion. Woodbridge Press Publishing Company. Santa Barbara, CA. 1976.

4. Harris, M.: Cannibals and Kings. Vintage Books. New York. 1977.

Table 12-5. The 60 Essential Elements, Metals and Minerals

Aluminum	Gold	Rhenium
Arsenic	Hafnium	Rubidium
Barium	Holmium	Samarium
Beryllium	Hydrogen	Scandium
Boron	Iodine	Selenium
Bromine	Iron	Silica
Calcium	Lanthanum	Silver
Carbon	Lithium	Sodium
Cerium	Lutecium	Strontium
Cesium	Magnesium	Sulphur
Chloride	Manganese	Tantalum
Chromium	Molybdenum	Terbium
Cobalt	Neodymium	Thulium
Copper	Nickle	Tin
Dysprosium	Niobium	Titanium
Erbium	Nitrogen	Vanadium
Europium	Oxygen	Ytterbium
Gadolinium	Phosphorus	Ytrium
Gallium	Potassium	Zinc
Germanium	Praseodymium	Zirconium

Table 12-6. Essential Vitamins for Human Health

Vitamin A
Vitamin B_1 (Thiamine)
Vitamin B_2 (Riboflavine)
Vitamin B_3 (Niacin)
Vitamin B_5 (Pantothenic acid)
Viatmin B_6 (Pyridoxine)
Vitamin B_{12} (Cobalamin)
Vitamin C
Vitamin D
Vitamin E
Vitamin K
Biotin
Choline
Flavinoids and bioflavinoids
Folic Acid
Inositol

Table 12-7. The Essential Amino Acids

Valine
Lysine
Threonine
Leucine
Isoleucine
Tryptophane
Phenylalanine
Methionine
Histadine
Arginine*
Taurine*
Tyrosine*

* While not considered classic essential amino acids, their deficiency does result in disease states.

Table 12-8. Essential Fatty Acids

Linoleic

Linolenic

Arachidonic

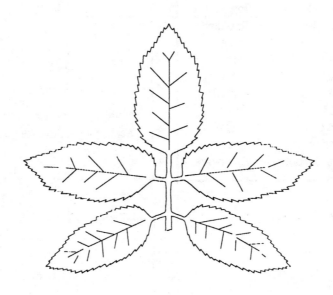

REFERENCES

Abrams, A., et al.: The Effects of a European Procaine Preperation in an Aged Population. J. Gerontology. 20:139.1965.

Adam, W.R. and Dowborn, J.K.: Effect of Potassium Depletion on Mineral Appetite in the Rat. J. Comp. Physical Psychol. 78:51.1972.

Aetios of Amida: The Gynaecology and Obstetrics of the VI th Century A.D. (Translated from the Latin edition of Cosonariores,1542, by J.V. Ricci).

Ahrens, L.H.: Distribution of the Elements in Our Planet. McGraw-Hill. New York. 1965.

Amstey, M.S.: Congenital Absence of the Vagina in the Rabbit. JAVMA.151:862.October,1967.

Anon: Basic Guide to Canine Nutrition. White Plains, New York. Gaines Dog Research Center. 1965.

Anon: Daily Nutrient Requirements of Pigs. Pub.1192. Nat.Acad.Sci. Nat. Res. Council.1964. pp 12 - 14.

Anon: Nutrient Requirements of Beef Cattle. Nat. Acad. Sci. NRC. Pub.1137.1963.

Anon: Nutrient Requirements of Horses. In Nutrient Requirements of Domestic Animals. 2nd ed. Nat. Acad. Sci. Nat. Res. Council. Pub. 1401.1966.

Anon: Selenium in the Heart of China. Lancet.October,1979.pp 899.

Arnold, S.A., et al.: Nutritional Secondary Hyperparathyroidism in the Parakeet. Cornell Vet. 64:37-46. 1974.

Aslan, A. et al: Long-term Treatment with Procaine (Gerovital H3) in Albino Rats. J. Gerontology 20:1.1965.

Atkins, R.C.: Dr. Atkin's Diet Revolution. New York. Bantam Books.1973.

Banik, A.E.: Hunza Land. Whitehorn Publishing Company. Long Beach, Ca. 1961.

Barinaga, M.: How Long Is The Human Life Span? Science.254:936-938.

Barnes, R.H.: Nutritional Implications of Coprophagy. Nutr. Rev. 20:89. 1962.

Barnes, R.H., et al.: Decreased Growth Rate Resulting From Prevention of Corophagy. Fed. Proc. 22:25.1963.

Barney, G.H., et al.: Parakeratosis of the tongue - a unique histopathologic lesion in the zinc-deficient Squirrel Monkey. J. Nutr. 93:511 - 517. 1967.

Barret, M.W. and Chalmers, G.A.: Congenital Anomalies in Neonatal White-tailed Deer in Alberta. J. Wildl. Dis. 11: October, 1975.

Barrows,Jr., C.H. and Kokkman,G.C.: Diet and Life Extension in Animal Model Systems. Age.1:31.1978.

Barten, S.L.: Cardiopathy in a Kingsnake (*Lampropeltis calligaster rhombomaculata*).VM/SAC.75:125 - 129.1980.

Bazzarre, T.L., et al.: Chronic Disease Risk Factors in Vitamin/Mineral Supplement Users and Non-users in a Farm Population. J. Am. Coll.Nutr. 10:3.1991. pp 247 - 257.

Bear, F.E.: Chemistry of the Soil. 2nd ed. Chapman and Hill. London. 1964.

Beardsley, D. W. and Forbes, R.M.: Growth and Chemical Studies of Zinc Deficiency in the Baby Pig. J.Ani.Sci.1957.pp1038.

Becker, R.: The Body Electric. Quill.William Morrow. 1985.

Becker, R.: Cross Currents.Jeremy P. Tarcher,Inc. Los Angeles.1990.

Bengoa, J. and Wood, R. : Magnesium. in Absorption and Malabsorption of Mineral Nutrients. Alan R. Liss, Inc. 1984.pp 69-88.

Berg,B.N.: Nutrition and Longevity in the Rat.I. Food Intake in Relation to Size, Health and Fertility. July,1960. J.Nutr.(71).242 - 254.

Berg, B.N. and Simms,H.S. : Nutrition and Longevity in the Rat.II. Longevity and Onset of Disease with Different Levels of Food Intake. J.Nutrition.71:255 - 263.July, 1960.

Berry, R.: The Vegetarians. Autumn Press. Brookline, Massachusetts. 1978.

Blake, W.D. and Jurf, A.N.: Increased Voluntary Sodium Intake in Potassium Deprived Rats. Comm. Behav. Biol.1968.

Bland, J. Diagnostic Usefulness of Trace Elements in Human Hair. Northwest Diagnostic Services. Bellvue,Wa. 1981.

Bland, J.: Hair Tissue Mineral Analysis: An Emergent Diagnostic Technique. Bellevue-Redmond Medical Laboratories. , Wa. 1979.

Boas, R. and Blundell, N.: The World's Most Infamous Murders. Berkley Books. New York.1983.

Boezo, M.H.: De Pica. Sm.Leipsig.1638.

Bone, W.J.: Pansteatitis in a Lion (*Felis leo*). JAVMA.153:791 - 792. October,1968.

Bostedt, H. and Schramel, P.: The Importance of Selenium in the Prenatal Development of Calves and Lambs. Bio. Trace Ele. Res. 24: 163 - 171. 1990.

Brady, P.S. and Ullrey, D.: White Muscle Disease in Wild Animals. Ann. Proc. Am. Asoc. Zoo. Vet. St. Louis, Missouri. October, 1976.

Brown, T. McP., et al.: Natural Ocurrance of Rheumatoid Arthritis in Great Apes - A New Clinical Model. Pro. Zool. Soc. of Philadelphia. Centennial Symposium on Science and Research. November, 1974. pp 43 - 79.

Carlander,O.: Aetiology of Pica. Lancet. 277:569.1959.

Carlson, A.H. and Hallzel, F.: Apparent Prolongation of the Life Span of Rats by Intermittent Fasting. J. Nutr. 31:363.1946.

Carpenter, J.W. and Novilla, M.N.: Diabetes

Mellitus in a Black-footed Ferret. JAVMA. 171:890 - 893. November, 1977.

Caskey,C.D., et al.: A Chronic Congenital Ataxia in Chicks due to Manganese Deficiency in the Maternal Diet. Poultry Science. 23:516. 1944.

Cole, J.: Saving the Soil. Sky. October, 1994. pp 28 - 33.

Collins, D.: Quantities of Calcium Carbonate Needed to Balance Calcium/ Phosphorus Ratios of Various Meats. J. Zoo Ani.Med. 2:25. April,1971.

Combs,G.f.,et al.:Influence of Arsanilic Acid on Dietary Requirements
of Chicks for Certain Unidentified Growth Factors. August,1954.J Nutr. 511 - 522.

Comfort, A.: The Longevity and Mortality of Thoroughbred Stallions. J. Gerontology.14:9.1959.

Comfort, A.: Studies in the Longevity and Mortality of English Thoroughbred Horses. Ciba Foundation. Colloquia on Aging.5:35.1959.

Conradi, P.: The Red Ripper. Dell Publishing.New York.1992.

Cooper,M.: Pica: A Survey of the Historical Literature as Well as Reports from the Fields of Veterinary Medicine and Anthropology, the Present Study of Pica in Young Children, and a Discussion of it's Paediatric and Physiological Implications. Charles Thomas.Springfield,Ill.1957.

Copper, B.: The Vampire in Legend and Fact. Citadel Press Book. New York.1993.

Coulson, E.J.: Metabolism in the Rat of Naturally Ocurring Arsenic of Shrimp as Compared with Arsenic Trioxide. September,1935.J Nutr.255 - 270.

Crabb, C.:The Nutrients are Blowing in the Wind. U.S. News & World Report.October, 1991. p 66

Cross,J.D. , et al.: Methylmercury in Blood of Dentists. Lancet. Aug.5,1978.p312.

Currents, J. and White, P.D.: Half a Century of Running: Clinical Physiologic and Autopsy Findings in the Case of Clarence DeMar (Mr. Marathon). New Eng J Med. 265:988.1961.

Dahl, L.K.: Salt in Processed Foods. Am. J. Clin. Nutr. 21:787.1968.

Decker, R.A. and McDermid, A.M.: Nutritional Myopathy in a Young Camel (*Camelus dromedarius*) J.Zoo.An. Med. 8:20 -21.June,1977.

Deeming, S. and Weber, C.: Hair Analysis of Trace Elements in Human Subjects as Influenced by Age, Sex and Contraceptive Drugs. Am. J. Clin. Nutr. 31:1175.1978.

Degens, E.T.: Geochemistry of Sediments. Prentice-Hall. New Jersey.1965.

Denton,D.: The Hunger for Salt: An Anthropological, Physiological and Medical Analysis. Springer-Verlag.Berlin. Heidelberg.New York.1982.

Diaz, F. et al.: Comparative Performances of Baby Pigs Fed Infant and Baby Pig Diets. J.Nutr. May,1959. pp 131 - 140.

Dieterich, R.A.: Medial Arterial Sclerosis in Captive Beavers, *Castor canadensis*, Kuhl. Bull.Wildl.Dis. Assoc.4:18-20. January,1968.

Draper, H.H.: Physiological Aspects of Aging V. Calcium and Magnesium Metabolism in Senescent Mice. J.Nut.83:65.1964.

Easton, J.: Human Longevity: Recording the Name, Age, Place of Residence and Year of the Decease of 1712 Persons Who Attained a Century and Upwards from AD 66 to 1799, Comprising a Period of 1733 years with Anecdotes of the most Remarkable. London.1799.

Edwards,C.H. et al.: Odd Dietary Practices of Women.J.Am.Diet Assoc. 30:976.1954.

Edwards,C.H., et al: Clay and Corn Starch Eating Women. J.Am.Diet. Assoc. 35:810.1959.

Edwards,C.H., et al.: Effects of Clay and Corn Starch Intake on women and Their Infants. J.Am.Diet.Assoc. 44:109.1964.

Edwards, H.M., et al.: Studies on Zinc in Poultry Nutrition.1: The Effect of Feed Water and Environment on Zinc Deficiency in Chicks. Poultry Sci.37:1094.1958.

Eliot, J.L.: Glaciers on the Move. Nat. Geo. 171:1. January, 1987. pp 107 - 119.

Emiliani, C., et al.: Isotopic and Cosmic Chemistry. H. Craig, et al. Ed. North-Holland Publishing Co. 1964.

Ewing, C.P.: Kids Who Kill, Avon Books. New York.1992.

Faelten, S., et al.: The Complete Book of Minerals for Health. Rodale Press. Emmous, Pa.1981.

Fernie, W.T.: Precious Stones:For Curative Wear; and Other Remedial Uses:Likewisw the Nobler Metals.Bristol, England.1907.

Feruson,J.H. and Keaton,A.G.: Studies of Diets of Pregnant Women in Mississippi:Ingestion of Clay and Laundry Starch. New Orleans Med.Surg.J. 102:460.1950.

Filer, L.J.: Salt in Infant Foods. Nutr.Rev.29:27.1971.

Fisher,L.E.: Lead Poisoning in a Gorilla. JAVMA.125:478 - 479.1954.

Fitch, C.D. and Dinniy, J.S.: Vitamin E Deficiency in the Monkey. J.Nutr. 81:69. January, 1963.

Flanagan, P. and Flanagan, G.C.: Elixir of the Ageless. Vortex Press. Flagstaff, Az. 1986.

Flynn, A., et al.: Indications of Copper Deficiency in a Subpopulation of Alskan Moose. J.Nutr.107:1182 - 1189. July,1977.

Ford, D.F.: Bilateral Cerebellar, Cortical Sclerosis in a Monkey. Am.J.Vet Res. 27:1489 - 1494. September, 1966.

French, M.H.: Geophagia in Animals. East Afr.Med.J. 22:103.1945.

Gandal, C.P.: White Muscle Disease in a Breeding Herd of Nyala Antelope (*Tragolaphus angasi*) at New

York Zoo. Int. Zoo Yearbook. London Zool.Soc. 6: 277 - 278.1968.

Gaume,J.G.: Nutrition in Space Operations.Food Technol.12:433 1958.

Geargakas, D.: The Methuselah Factors. Simon and Schuster. New York.1980.

Gelford, M.: Geophagy and it's Relation to Hookworm Disease. East Afr.Med J. 22:98.1945.

Generoso, W.M. et al.: Genetic Lesions Induced by Chemicals in Spermatozoa and Spermatids of Mice are Repaired in the Egg. Proc. Nat. Acad. Sci,USA.75:435.1979.

Geraci, J.R.: Thiamine Deficiency in Seals and Recommendations for its Prevention. JAVMA. 185:801-803.1974.

Gershoff, S.N. and Norkin, S.A.: Vitamin E Deficiency in Cats. J. Nutr. 77:303 - 308. 1962.

Gershoff, S., et al.: Trace Minerals in Human and Rat Hair. Am. J. Clin. Nutr. 30:868.1977.

Giroud, A.: Nutrition of the Embryo. Fed.Proc.27:163 - 184.1968.

Goldstein, M. and Beall, C.: The Remote World of Tibet's Nomads. Nat. Geo.175:6.June,1989. pp 752 - 781.

Gordon, J.G., et al.: The Feeding Behavior of Phosphorus Deficient Cattle and Sheep. An.Behav.2:72.1954.

Goss, L.J.: Muscle Dystrophy in Tree Kangaroos Associated with Feeding Cod Liver Oil and it's Response to Alpha-Tocopherol. Zoologica. New York Zool. Soc.25:523 - 524.December,1940.

Green, H.H.: Perverted Appetites. Physiol.Rev.5:336.1925.

Grenoble, P.B.: Pritikin People. Berkley Books. New York.1986.

Gries, C.L. and Scott, M.L.: Pathology of Selenium Deficiency in the Chick. J. Nutr. 102:1282 -

1296.1972.

Gutelius, M.F., et al.: Nutritional Studies of Children with Pica.II.Treatment of Pica with Iron Given Intramuscularly. Paediatrics.29:1018.1962.

Hambidge, K.M. and Rodgerson, D.O.: Comparison of Hair Chromium Levels of Multiparous and Parous Women. Am.J. Obstet, Gynec. 103:320.1969.

Harman,D.: Free Radical Theory of Aging: Nutritional Implications. Age. 1:145.1978.

Harman, D.: Free Radical Theory of Aging:Origin of Life, Evolution and Aging. Age.3:100.1980.

Harman, D. and Eddy,D.E.: Free Radical Theory of Aging:Effect of Adding Antioxidants to Maternal Mouse Diets on the Lifespan of the Offspring. Age. 1:162.1978.

Harrington, A.: The Immortalists. Random House. New York.1969.

Harris, M.: Cannibals and Kings: The Origins of Cultures.Vintage Books. New York.1977.

Hayflick, L.: The Cellular Basis for Biological Aging. in Handbook of the Biology of Aging. (ed C.E. Finch and L.Hayflick.). Van Nostrand Reinhold. 1977.

Heaney, R.P.and Barger-Lux, J.: Low Calcium Intake: The Culprit in Many Human Diseases. Feedstuffs. July,1994.pp 14 - 17.

Hendrikson, P., Krook, L. and Larsen, B.: Mechanism of Bone Resorption in a Case of Human Periodontal Disease. Svensk. Tandl. Tidskn. 62:323. 1969.

Herbert, V.: Nutrition Cultism. George F. Stickley Company. Philadelphia, Pa.1980.

Herkovits, J. et al.: Protective Effects of Zinc Against Spontaneous malformations and Leathality in Bufo arenarum Embryos. Bio Trace Ele Res. 22:247 - 250.1989.

Hill, R.M. and Holtkamp, D.E.: Storage of Dietary Manganese and Thiamine in the Rat. J Nutr. May,1954. 73 - 82.

Hisanaga, A., et al.: Variation of Trace Metals in Ancient and Contemporary Japanese Bones. Bio. Trace Ele.Res. 22:221 - 231.1989.

Hoekstra, W.O.: Biochemical Function of Selenium and It's Relation to Vitamin E. Fed. Proc. 34:2083.1975.

Hove, E.,et al.: Further Studies on Zinc Deficiency in Rats. Am.J. Physiol. 124:750.1938.

Howard, Sir Albert.: The Soil and Health: A Study of Organic Agriculture. Schocken Books. New York.1972.

Hunt,C.D.: Dietary Boron Modified Effects of Magnesium and Molybdenum on Mineral Metabolism in the Cholecalciferol-Deficient Chick. Biol.Trace Ele.Res.22:.201 - 270.1989.

Hunt, R.D., et al.: A Comparison of Vitamins D_2 and D_3 in New World Primates.I. Production and Regression of Osteodystrophica Fibrosa. Lab Ani.Care.17:222 - 234.1967.

Hurley,L.S.,et al.: Manganese Deficiency in Rats: Congenital Nature of Ataxia. J.Nutr.November,1958. pp 309 - 319.

Hurley, L.S., et al.: Anomalous Development of Ossification in the Inner Ear of Offspring of Manganese-Deficient Rats. J Nutr.1960,pp 15 - 19.

Hurley, L.S. and Keen, C.L.: Manganese. in Trace Elements in Human and Animal Nutrition.5th ed (Mertz,W.ed). Academic Press,Inc. New York.1987.

Hurwitz, S. and Cummings,P.: The Response of Plasma Alkaline Phosphatase, Parathyroids and Blood and Bone Minerals to Calcium Intake in the Fowl. J.Nutr.73:179 -190.1961.

Jacob,R. et al.: Hair as a Biopsy Material:Index of Hepatic Copper. Am. J. Clin. Nutr. 31:477.1978.

James,W.P.T., et al.: Calcium Binding by Dietary Fibre. Lancet.1:638.1978.

Johnson, C.E.: The Wild World of Compost. Nat.Geo.158:2. August, 1980. pp.272 - 284.

Johnson,O.S.: A Study of Chinese Alchemy.Commercial Press. Shanghai. 1928.

Jubb, K.V.F., et al.: Thiamine Deficiency Encephalopathy in Cats. J.Comp.Path.66:217 - 227.1956.

Jukes, T.H.: Effect of Choline and Other Supplements on Perosis. November,1940. J Nutr.445 - 458.1940.

Kahlenberg,L. and Class,J.O.: The Presence of Aluminum in Animal and Plant Tissues.J.Biol.Chem.83:261.1929.

Karstad, L.: Fluorosis in Deer (*Odocoileus virginianus*). Bull. Wildl. Dis. Assoc. 3:42 - 46. April,1967.

Kehoe,R.A., et al.: Manganese, Lead, Tin, Aluminum, Copper and Silver in Normal Biological Material.J.Nutr.July,1940.pp 85 - 98.

Kempter, E., et al.: The Utilization of the Calcium of DI-Calcium Phosphate by Children. J.Nutr. :279.Sept,1940.

Kennington, G.S.: Soluble and Fixed Elements in Mammalian Hair. Science.155:588.1971.

Kern, F.: Normal Plasma Cholesterol in an 88 Year Old Man Who Eats 25 Eggs a Day. New Eng.J.Med. March, 1991. pp 896 - 899.

Kienholz, E.W., et al.: Effects of Zinc Deficiency in the Diets of Hens. J Nutr.75:211-221.October,1961.

Kitchen, H., et al.: Hemoglobin Polymorpism: Its Relation to Sickling of Erythrocytes in White-tailed Deer. Science.144:1237 - 1239. June, 1964.

Klevay, L.: Hair as a Biopsy Material. Arch. Intern. Med.138:1127.1978.

Krishnamachair, K.A.V.R.:Flourine.in Trace Elements in Human and Animal Nutrition.Vol 1.5th ed.(Mertz,W.ed.) 1987.

Lane, B. and Gregg,W.: The Encyclopedia of Serial Killers. Diamond Books. London.1992.

Lanzkowsky, P.: Investigation into the Aetiology and Treatment of Pica. Arch.Dis.Child.34:140.1959.

Leaf, A.: Every Day is a Gift When You Are Over 100. Nat. Geo.143:1. January,1973.pp 92 - 119..

Lease, J.G., et al.: The Biological Unavailability to the Chick of Zinc in a Sesame Meal Ration.J Nutr. 72:66-70. September,1960.

LeConte, J.: Observations on Geophagia. South.Med.Surg.J.1:417.1846.

Legg, S.P. and Sears, L.: Zinc Sulphate Treatment of Parakeratosis in Cattle.Nature.186:1061.1960.

LeVay, S. and Hamer, D.H.: Evidence for a Biological Influence in Male Homosexuality. Scientific American.May,1994. pp 44 - 56.

Lewis, P.K. et al.: The Effect of Certain Nutritional Factors Including Calcium, Phosphorus and Zinc on Parakeratosis in Swine.J An.Sci.15:741. 1956

Likuski, H.J.A. and Farbes, R.M.: Mineral Utilization in the Rat IV. Effects of Calcium and Phytic Acid on the Utilization of Dietary Zinc. J.Nut. 85:230.1965.

Liu, R.K. and Walford, R.L.: The Effect of Lowered Body Temperature on Lifespan and Immune and Non-Immune Processes. Gerontologica. 18:363.1972.

Lofgreen, G.P.: The Availability of the Phosphorus in Di-calcium Phosphate, Bone Meal, Soft Phosphate and Calcium Phytate for Mature Wethers. J.Nutr. 70:58.1960.

Long,V.M.,et al.: Manganese Metabolism in College Men Consuming Vegetarian Diets. J. Nutr.85:132 - 138. March,1965.

Loosli, J.K.: Primary Signs of Nutritional Deficiencies of Laboratory Animals.JAVMA.142:1001 - 1004. May, 1963.

Macopinlec, M.P., et al.: Production of Zinc Deficiency in the Squirrel Monkey (*Saimiri sciureus*). J.Nutr.93:499 - 510.1967.

Manselsberg, R.G..(ed): Killer Teens. Pinnacle Books. New York.1981.

Manselsberg, R.G.(ed.): Mass Murderers. Pinnacle Books. New York.1983.

Marden,L.: Titicaca: Abode of the Sun.Nat.Geo.139:2. February,1971. p 272 -291.

Mascetti, M.D. : Vampire: The Complete Guide to the World of the Undead. Mohndruck GmbH, Gutersloh, Germany. 1992.

Maugh, T.: Hair: A Diagnostic Tool to Compliment Blood, Serum and Urine. Science.202.1271.1978.

Maybrick, J. (narrative by Shirley Harrison): The Diary of Jack the Ripper. Hyperion. New York.1993.

McCarry, J.: High Road to Hunza. Nat.Geo March,1994.pp 114 - 134.

McDonald, G.: Arsenic in Napoleon's Hair. Nature.4798:103.1961.

McDonald, R.: The Handling of an Epidemic: Repetitive Stress Injury. Working Women. February, 1993.pp 60 - 65.

McDonald, R. and Marshole, S.R.: Value of Iron Therapy in Pica. Paediatrics.84:558.1964.

McIntyre, L.:The Lost Empire of the Incas. Nat.Geo. December, 1973. 144:6.pp729 - 781.

McKay, C.M. et al.: The Effect of Retarded Growth Upon the Length of Life Span and Upon the Ultimate Body Size. July,1935.J Nutr.63 - 79.

McKenzie-Parnell, J.M. and Guthrie, B.E.: The Phytate and Mineral Content of Some Cereals, Cereal Products, Legumes, Legume Products, Snack Bars, and Nuts Available in New Zealand. Bio.Trace Ele. Res. 10:107 - 121.1986.

Mergiletus, A.F.: Pica: Doctoral Thesis in Medicine.Submitted to Academia Patria.1701.

Mertz,W.(ed.):Trace Elements in Human and Animal Nutrition. Academic Press,Inc. New York.1987.

Meyer, J.H.: Interactions Between a High Concentration of Dietary Sodium Chloride and Various Levels of Protein When Fed to The Growing Rat. J.Nutr.January,1954. pp 137 - 154.

Michaud, S. and Michaud, R.: Trek to Lofty Hunza - and Beyond. Nat. Geo. November,1975.148:5.pp. 644 - 669.

Michel, R.L., et al.: Dietary Hepatic Necrosis Associated with Selenium-Vitamin E Deficiencies in Swine. JAVMA.155:50 -59.1969.

Milne, D.B., et al.: Effect of Ascorbic Acid on Copper and Cholesterol in Adult Cynomologus Monkeys Fed a Diet Marginal in Copper. Am.J.Clinical Nutr. 34:2389.1981.

Miller,J.K. and Miller, W.J.: Experimental Zinc Deficiency and Recovery of Calves. J. Nutr.76:467-474.April,1962.

Miller,R.M.: Nutritional Secondary Hyperparathyroidism in Monkeys. in Kirk, R.:Current Vet. Therapy.4th ed. Philadelphia, Pa.W.B. Saunders Company.1971. pp402 - 408.

Mills,C.F. and Davis,G.K.: Molybdenum. in Trace Elements in Human and Animal Nutrition. Vol.1.5th ed.(Mertz,W.ed.).Academic Press,Inc. New York.1987.

Morgan, D.G.: Dissecting Aneurysm of the Aorta in a Gorilla. Vet Rec. 86:502 - 505. April, 1970.

Morrison, A.B. and Sarett,H.P.: Studies on Zinc Deficiency in the Chick. June, 1958. J.Nutr. pp 267 - 280.

Mortimer, J.: The Oxford Book of Villains. Oxford University Press. Oxford & New York. 1992.

Mraz, F.R., et al.: Metabolism of Cesium and Potassium in Swine as Indicated by Cesium 134 and Potssium 42. J Nutr. 64:541.1958.

Mraz, F.R.: Influence of Dietary Potassium and Sodiumon Cesium 134 and Potassium 42 Excretion in Sheep.Aug,1959.J Nutr.655-662.

Nesbit, E.M.: The Reaction of a Group of Rothschild's Giraffe to a New Environment. East Afr.Wildl.J. 8:53.1970.

Nicoloides, N. and Woodall, A.N.: Impaired Pigmentation in Chinook Salmon Fed Diets Deficient in Essential Fatty Acids. J.Nutr.78:431 - 437. 1962.

Nielson, F.H.: Vanadium.in Trace Elements in Human and Animal Nutrition.Vol.1.5th ed.(Mertz,W.ed.).1987.

Nielson,F.H.: New Essential Trace Elements for the Life Sciences.Biol.Trace.Ele Res.1990.pp 599 - 611.

Norris, L.C. and Caskey, C.D.: A Chronic Congenital Ataxia and Osteodystrophy in Chicks due to Manganese Deficiency.J. Nutr. 17:16.1939.

Norris, L.C. and Scott, M/L/: Proteins, Carbohydrates, Fats, Fiber, Minerals and Water in Poultry Feeding. in Hofstad,M.,et al(ed): Infectious Diseases of Poultry.5th ed. Ames,Iowa. The Iowa State University Press.1965. pp144 - 180.

Norris, T.: Jeffrey Dahmer. Pinnacle Books. New York.1992.

O'Dell, B.L., Newberne, P.M. and Savage,: Significance of Dietary Zinc for the Growing Chicken. J.Nutr. August,1958. pp 503 - 518.

Olmstead, L., Schrauzer, G.N., Flores-Arce, M. and Dowd, J.: Selenium Supplementation of Symptomatic Human Immunodeficiency Virus Infected Patients. Bio.Trace Ele.Res. 20:59 - 65.1989.

Olshansky,S.J., et al.: In Search of Methuselah: Estimating the Upper Limits to Human Longevity.Science.250:634 - 640. November,1990.

Oparin, A.I.: The Origin of Life on Earth. 3rd ed. Oliver and Boyd. Edinburgh.1957.

Oppenheimer, E.H. and Esterly, J.R.: Pathology of Cystic Fibrosis: Review of the Literature and Comparisons with 146 Autopsied Cases. in Rosenberg,H.S. and Balonde, R.P.: Perspectives in Pediatric Pathology. Chicago Yearbook. Vol.2.1975.pp 241 - 278.

Orr, J.B.: Minerals in Pastures. Lewis.London.1929.

Ott, ED.A., et al.: Zinc Deficiency Syndrome in the Young Lamb. J. Nutr. 82:41-50.January,1964.

Parr,J.G. Man, Metals and Modern Magic.Iowa State University Press. Ames,Iowa.1958.

Parr, R.M., et al.: Minor and Trace Elements in Human Milk from Guatemala, Hungary, Nigeria, Phillipines, Sweden, and Zaire. Bio.Trace Ele.Res.29:51 - 75.1991.

Pierson, R.E.: Zinc Deficiency in Young Lambs. JAVMA.149:1279 - 1282. November, 1966.

Pihl, R.O. and Parkes, M.: Hair Element Content in Learning-disabled Children. Science.198:204.1977.

Plutarch's Lives: Alexander. First Century AD.

Powell, R.C., et al.: Algae Feeding in Humans.J. Nutr. Sept,1961.pp 7 - 12.

Pritikin, N. and McGrady,Jr., P.M.: The Pritikin Program for Diets and Exercise. Grosset and Dunlap.1979.

Rabb, G.B., et al.: Spontaneous Diabetes Mellitus in Tree Shrews, *Urogale everetti*. J.Am.Diabetes Assoc. 15:327 -330. May,1966.

Rahman, M.M.,et al.: Selenium and Exudative Diathesis in Chicks and Poults. J.Nutr.72:71. September, 1960.

Reid,I.R. et al.: Effect of Calcium Supplementation on Bone Loss in Postmenopausal Women. New Eng.J.Med. February,1993.pp 460 - 464.

Revis, N.W., et al.: Metabolism of Selenium in Skeletal Muscle and Liver of Mice with 'Genetic' Muscular Dystrophy.Proc. Soc. Exper .Biol. Med. 160:139.1979.

Reynolds, R.D., et al: Pagophagia and Iron Deficiency Anemia. Ann.Inter. Med. 69:435.1968.

Rhodes,D. and Klug, A.: Zinc Fingers. Sci.Am.February,1993.pp 56 - 64.

Rice, D.A., et al.: Sequential Changes in Plasma Methylonic Acid and Vitamin B_{12} in Sheep Eating Cobalt Deficient Grass. Bio.Trace Ele.Res.22:153 - 164.1989.

Rigdon, R.H. and Drager,G.A.: Thiamine Deficiency in Sea Lions (*Otaria californiana*) Fed Only Frozen Fish. JAVMA.127:453 - 455. 1955.

Robbins, J.D., et al.: Influence of Varying Levels of Dietary Minerals on the Development of Urolithiasis, Hair Growth, and Weight Gains in Rats. 85:355.1965.

Rogers,B.A.: The Nature of Metals. Iowa State University Press. Ames,Iowa.2nd ed.1964.

Rosenfeld, A. :Prolongevity II. Alfred A. Knoph. New York. 1985.

Ross, M.H.: Length of Life and Nutrition in the Rat.. J.Nutr.5: 197 - 210.1961

Russell, W.C.: Hypothyroidism in a Grizzly Bear. JAVMA.157:656 - 662.September, 1970.

Rutten,M.G.: The Geological Aspects of the Origin of Life on Earth. Elsevier. Amsterdam.1962.

Sanday, P.R.: Divine Hunger: Cannibalism as a Cultural System. Cambridge University Press. New York.1986

Sandberg, A-S, et al.: The Effect of Wheat Bran on the Absorption of Minerals in the Small Intestine .Br. J. Nutr. 48:185.1982.

Schmidt, H.: Transiant Loss of Smell and Taste During Pregnancy. Clinschwassenschift.1925.p4.

Schroeder, H.A., et al.: Chromium, Lead, Cadmium, Nickel and Titanium in Mice:Effect on Mortality, Tumor and Tissue Levels.J. Nutr.83:239 - 250. 1994.

Schwarz,K.: Essentiality and Metabolic Functions of Selenium.Med.Clin.North Am. 60:745 - 758. July,1976.

Schwarz, K. and Foltz, C.M.: Selenium as an Integril Part of Factor 3 Against Dietary Necrotic Liver

Degeneration. J. Am.Chem Soc. 79:3292. 1957.

Senturia, B.D.:Results of Treatment of Chronic Arthritis and Rhuematoid Conditions with Colloidal Sulphur. J.Bone Joint Surg.16:119-125.1934.

Shaw, J. C. L.: Evidence for Defective Skeletal Mineralization in Low-birthweight Infants: The Absorption of Calcium and Fat. Pediatrica. 57:16. 1976.

Sinet, P., et al.: Trisomy 21 (Down's Syndrome) , Glutathione Peroxidase, Hexose Momophosphate Shunt and I.Q. Science.24:29.1979.

Slusher, R., et al.: Nutritional Secondary Hyperparathyroidism in a Tiger. JAVMA. 147:1109 - 1115. November, 1965.

Smith, R.M.: Cobalt. in Trace Elements in Human and Animal Nutrition.5th ed(Mertz,W.ed.).Academic Press,Inc.New York.1987.

Snowdon,C.T. and Sanderson,B.A.: Lead Pica Produced in Rats. Science. 183:92.1974.

Sokolov, R.:Pyramid Power.Natural History.January,1994.pp72 - 75.

Sonneborn, J.: DNA Repair and Longevity Assurance in *Paramecium tetraurelia*.Science.203:1115.1979.

Spallholz, J.E. and Stewart,J.R.: Advances in the Role of Minerals in Immunobiology. Bio.Trace Ele.Res.19:129-151.1989.

Spector, W.S.: Handbook of Biological Data. W.B.Saunders. Philadelphia.1956.

Spoehr,H.A. and Milner, H.W.: The Chemical Composition of Chlorella: Effect of Environmental Conditions.Plant Physiol.24:120.1949.

Starr, P.: The Social Transformation of American Medicine.1984.

Stiles,W.: Trace Elements in Plants and Animals. 2nd ed. Cambridge University Press. Cambridge.1951.

Sunde, R.A. and Hoekstra, W.G.: Structure, Synthesis and Function of Glutathione Peroxidase. Nutr. Rev. 38:265.1980.

Sutcliffe, A.J.: Similarity of Bones and Antlers Gnawed by Deer to Human Artifacts. Nature.24:428.1973.

Sutcliffe, A.J.: Further Notes on Bones and Antlers Chewed by Deer and Other Ungulates. Deer.4:73.1977.

Szent-Gyorgi,A.: Bioenergetics. Academic Press. New York and London.1957.

Taggart, N.: Food Habits in Pregnancy. Proc.Nutr. Soc. 20:35.1961.

Tarnower, H. and Baker, S.S.: The Complete Scarsdale Medical Diet. New York. Rawson, Wade.1978.

Taylor, R. :Hunza Health Secrets. PrenticeHall, Inc. New Jersey. 1966.

Thomas, W.J.: The Longevity of Man, It's Facts and It's Fiction. London. J.Murray.1873.

Thompson, C.J.S. : The Mystery and Romance of Alchemy and Pharmacy. Scientific Press.London.1897.

Tobe, J. Hunza: Adventures in a Land of Paradise. George J. McLeod. Ltd. Ontario.1960.

Tompkins, P. and Bird, C. : Secrets of the Soil. Harper & Row, Publishers. New York.1989.

Tompkins, P. and Bird, C. : The Secret Life of Plants. Harper & Row, Publishers. New York. 1989.

Trapp, A.L., et al.: Vitamin E-Selenium Deficiency in Swine: Differential Diagnosis and Nature of Field Problems. JAVMA. 157:289 - 300. August, 1970.

Trease,G.E.: Pharmacy in History. Bailliere, Tindall and Cox. London.1964.

Trethowen, W.H., et al.: Cravings, Aversions and Pica of Pregnancy. in Howells,J.G.,ed.Modern Perspectives in Psycho-Obstetrics. Oliver and Boyd.

Edinburgh.1972.

Ueckermann, Z.: Comparative Intake of Salt Licks. Jagdiwiss.14:107 - 118.1968.

Underwood, E.J.: Trace Elements in Human and Animal Nutrition. Academic Press. New York and London. 1962.

Van Reen, R., et al.: Urolithiasis in the Rat.II Studies on the Effect of Diet on the Excretion of Calcium, Citric Acid and Phosphate. J.Nut.69:397.1959.

Van Reen, R., et al.: Urolithiasis in the Rat.1 The Influence of Diet on the Formation and Prevention of Calcium Citrate Calculi. J.Nut. 69:392.1959.

Van Vleet, F.J., et al.: Hepatosis Dietetica and Mulberry Heart Disease Associated with Selenium Deficiency in Indiana Swine.JAVMA.157:1208 - 1219.1970.

Van Vleet, F.J., et al.: Ultrastructure of Hyaline Microthrombi in Myocardial Capillaries of Pigs with Spontaneous Mulberry Heart Disease. Am.J.Vet.Res. 38:2077 - 2080.1977.

Vohra, P. and Kratzer, F.H.: Influence of Various Chelating Agents on the Availability of Zinc. J. Nutr. 82:249-256., February,1964.

Walford, R.L.: The Immunological Theory of Aging. Munkagaard. Copenhagen.1969

Walford, R.L.: Maximum Lifespan. W.W.Norton & Company.New York. London.1983.

Walford, R.L.: The 120 Year Diet. Simon and Schuster.New York.1986.

Wallach, J.D.: Goitrogenic Hypothyroidism in Feeder Lambs. VM/SAC. 60:1051 - 1053. 1965.

Wallach, J.D.: Degenerative Arthritis in A Black Rhino. JAVMA.151:887 - 889.1967.

Wallach, J.D.: Nutritional Diseases of Exotic Animals.JAVMA.157:583 - 599. September, 1970.

Wallach, J.D.: Exotic Diets are Not For Exotic Pets.

Gaines Small Animal Nutrition Workshop. University of Illinois.March,1971.

Wallach, J.D.: Nutritional Problems in Zoos. Proc. Cornell Nutr. Conference for Feed Manufacturers. Buffalo, New York. November,1971. pp 10 - 19.

Wallach,J.D.: The Nutrition and Feeding of Captive Ruminants in Zoos. in Church,D.C.:Digestive Physiology and Nutrition of Ruminants. Corvallis. Oregon State University Press. Vol.3.1972.pp 292 - 307.

Wallach, J.D.: The Mechanics of Nutrition For Exotic Pets. Vet. Clin.North Am. 9:405 - 414.1979.

Wallach,J.D. and Boever,W.J.: Diseases of Exotic Animals. W.B. Saunders Co. Philadelphia.1983.

Wallach, J. D. and Flieg, G.M.: Nutritional Secondary Hyperparathyroidism in Captive Birds. JAVMA.155:1046.1969.

Wallach, J.D. and Flieg, G.M.: Nutritional Secondary Hyperparathyroidism in Captive Psittacine Birds. JAVMA.151:880.1967.

Wallach, J.D. and Flieg, G.M.: Cramps and Fits in Carnivorous Birds. Int.Zoo Yearbook. London Zool. Soc.10:3 - 4.1970.

Wallach, J.D. and Hoessle, C.: Hypervitaminosis D in Green Iguanas. JAVMA.149:912 - 914.1966.

Wallach,J.D. and Hoessle, C.: Fibrous Osteodystrophy in Green Iguanas. JAVMA.153:863 - 865. 1968.

Wallach, J.D. and Hoessle,C.: Steatitis in Captive Crocodilians. JAVMA. 153:845 - 847.1968.

Wallach, J.D., Hoessle,C. and Bennet, J.: Hypoglycemic Shock in Captive Alligators. JAVMA.151:893 - 896. 1967.

Wallach, J.D. and Middleton, C.C.: Naturally Occuring Atherosclerosis in Aoudads (*Amotragus lervia* ,Pallas). Acta Zool. Pathol.Antverpiensia. 50:45 - 54.1970.

Wallach, J.D., Williamson, W.M. and LaGarde, K.:

Normal Blood Values of Siberian Ibex. J.Zoo.Ani. Med. 2:22 - 23. June,1971.

Waller, H.: The Last Journals of David Livingstone in Central Africa from 1865 to His Death. John Murray.London.Vol2.1874.

Ward, F.P.: Thiamine Deficiency in a Peregrine Falcon. JAVMA.159: 599 - 601.1971.

Ward,F.: In Long-Forbidden Tibet.. Nat. Geo.157:2. February,1980. pp218 - 259.

Watson, G.L.: Spina Bifida in A Moose. JAVMA. 153:815. October, 1968.

Weil, A.: WARNING: 11 Medical Practices to Avoid. Natural Health. Sept./Oct.1992. 59-63.

Weisner, M.M.: Calcium. in Absorption and Malabsorption of Mineral Nutrients. (Solomons, N.W. and Rosenberg,I.H., ed.). Alan R. Liss,Inc. New York.1984.15-68.

Werbach, M.R.: Nutritional Influences on Illness. Third Line Press. Tarzana, CA. 1987.

Werbach, M.R.: Nutritional Influences on Mental Illness. Third Line Press,Inc. Tarzana,CA.1991.

Western, D.: Giraffe Chewing a Grant's Gazelle Carcass. East Afr. Wildl. J.9:156.1971.

Whooten,A.C.: Chronicles of Pharmacy; 2 Vols. MacMillan Press. Shanghai.1928.

Williams, R.J.: Nutrition Against Disease. Pitman.

New York.1971.

Williamson, W.M., et al.: Fibrous Dysplasia in a Monkey and a Kudu. JAVMA.147:1017 - 1034. November, 1965.

Willius, F.A. and Smith,H.L.: Further Observations on the Heart in Old Age. A Post Mortem Study of 381 Patients Aged 70 Years or More. Am. Heart Jour. 8:170.1932.

Wilson, J.G. and Gavan, J.A.: Congenital Malformations in Non-Human Primates:Spontaneously and Experimentally Induced. Anat.Rec. 158:99 - 110. May,1962.

Woods, S.E. and Weisinger, R.S.: Pagophagia in The Albino Rat. Science.169:1334.1970.

Wurtman, R.J.: Behavioral Effects of Nutrients. The Lancet.May,1983.pp 1145 - 1147.

Wyatt, J.R.: Osteophagia in Masi Giraffe. East Afr.Wildl.J. 9:157.1971.

Yokoi, K., et al.: Effect of Dietary Tin Deficiency on Growth and Mineral Status in Rats. Biol.Trace Ele.Res.(24)1990. 223 - 231.

York, D.: The Earliest History of the Earth.Sci.Am. January,1993. pp 90 - 96.

Yu, K.K.: Taoist Yoga. New York. Weisner.1970.

Yu, S.Y., et al.: Selenium Chemoprevention of Liver Cancer in Animals and Possible Human Applications. Bio.Trace Ele.Res.15:1988.pp 231 - 241.

INDEX

D

E